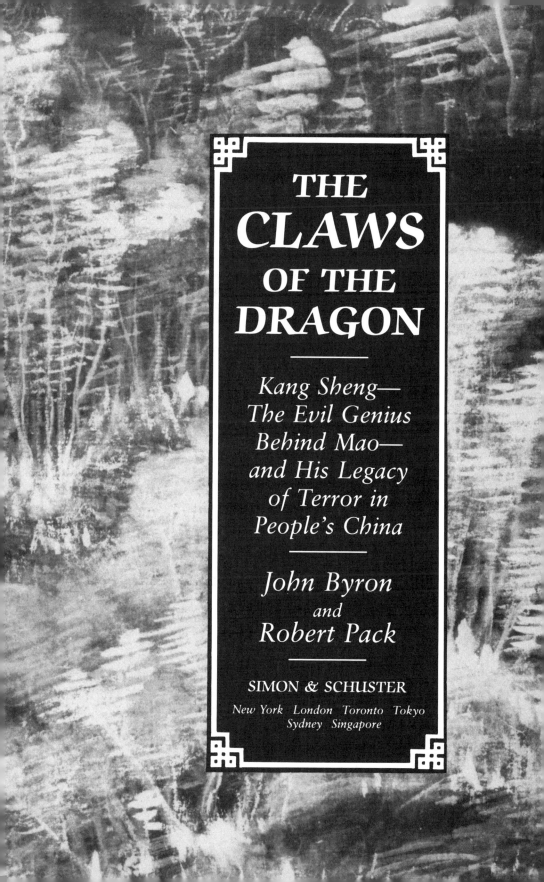

THE
CLAWS
OF THE
DRAGON

Kang Sheng—
The Evil Genius
Behind Mao—
and His Legacy
of Terror in
People's China

John Byron
and
Robert Pack

SIMON & SCHUSTER

New York London Toronto Tokyo
Sydney Singapore

SIMON & SCHUSTER
Simon & Schuster Building
Rockefeller Center
1230 Avenue of the Americas
New York, New York 10020

Designed by Laurie Jewell
Manufactured in the United States of America

1   3   5   7   9   10   8   6   4   2

Library of Congress Cataloging-in-Publication data

Byron, John.
The claws of the dragon : the evil genius behind Mao : Kang Sheng
and his legacy of terror in People's China / John Byron and Robert Pack.
        p.   cm.
Includes bibliographical references (p.   ) and index.
1. Kang, Sheng, 1898-1975. 2. Statesmen—China—Biography.
3. China—Politics and government—1949-1976. I. Pack, Robert,
            date– . II. Title.
        DS778.K29B97   1992
        951.05′092—dc20
        [B]   91-32369
                CIP

ISBN: 0-671-69537-1

ACKNOWLEDGMENTS

THIS BOOK could not have been written without the generous cooperation of scores of citizens of the People's Republic of China, including Foreign Ministry officials, members of Chinese research and media organizations, and the relatives of senior leaders. These people have contributed in many ways, providing documents and articles about Kang and his associates, clarifying details of the Party bureaucracy, and reporting specific episodes in Kang's life. They have invariably asked that we not reveal their names, so despite the magnitude of our debt to them, they must remain anonymous.

Our thanks to the following, who have provided us with information or helped in other respects: David Aikman of *Time* magazine, Geremie Barmé, Judy Bonavia, Ellen Butts of Simon & Schuster, Ku Chow, Vincent Demma, Robert Dunn and H. C. Jen, the staff of the Chinese Section of the Library of Congress, Hans van Ess, Simon Friedman, Culver Gleysteen, Andrew Gosling, Harry Harding of the Brookings Institution, Danny Kane, Peter Kolk, Lo Hui-min, Thomas Keng Lu of *Pai Shing* magazine, the late Van S. Lung, Betty McIntosh, H. Lyman Miller, Frank Mills, Ramon H. Myers of the Hoover Institution, Douglas H. Paal, Jonathan D. Pollack of the Rand Corporation, Richard Rigby, Sidney Rittenberg, Pierre Ryckmans, Mary Ann Seawall, Carlton Swift, Mark W. Tam of the Hoover Institution, Frank Tan, Dick Victory, Wang Ling-ling of the Institute of International Relations in Taipei, Wang Wen-hsing of Taiwan University, Michael Weisskopf of *The Washington Post*, John Wilhelm, and Xue Rui and to several people at the National Archives, including Ed Barnes, Rich Boylan, and Kathie Nicastro.

Several Soviet sinologists provided valuable information about Kang's years in the Soviet Union and his dealings with the Russians. We particularly want to express our gratitude to Mikhail L. Titarenko, Director of the USSR's Institute of Far Eastern Studies, President of the Soviet Association of Chinese Studies, and First Deputy Chairman of the Board of the Soviet-Chinese Friendship Society, and to Tamara A. Karganova, Senior Consultant and Translator at the Institute. Other Soviet experts who helped us include Vladimir I. Antonov of the Institute of Far Eastern Studies; E. Keitaev, Deputy Director of the Institute of Marxism-Leninism; Lev P. Delyusin of the Institute of Oriental Studies; Fyodor Burlatsky, editor of Literaturnaya Gazeta; and Anastasia I. Kartounova of the Institute of Marxism-Leninism.

Bill Reinckens of the U.S. Information Agency, Professor R. Millar of George Washington University, Martin Walker of *The Guardian* newspaper, and Nick Daniloff helped put us in touch with knowledgeable Russians.

Our special appreciation goes to two superb editors, Marie Arana-Ward of Simon & Schuster and copyeditor Douglas Woodyard; to John E. Taylor of the National Archives, a remarkable man with an extraordinary memory and knowledge of documents that pertain to military and intelligence matters; to Arthur Waldron of the U.S. Naval War College in Newport and formerly of Princeton University, who read the unedited manuscript and offered many helpful comments; to Timothy Dickinson, whose encyclopedic grasp of history and literature helped set Kang's story in perspective; and to our agents at William Morris, Robert Gottlieb and Mel Berger.

To David Bonavia,
writer, linguist, and friend,
who has sailed into his rest.

NOTE ON ROMANIZATION

We have used the pinyin system of romanization, with a few exceptions: we have retained the traditional spelling of a number of place names—Peking, Nanking, Swatow, Hankow, Whampoa, Mukden, Louza, and Canton—and the names of two rivers, the Yangtze and the Pearl. For the sake of simplicity, we have used the name Peking for the period from 1928 until 1949 when the capital was successively located in Nanking, Hankow, and Chongqing, and Chinese of all political persuasions called it Peip'ing. We have also adhered to the universally recognized "Chiang Kai-shek" instead of the pinyin rendering of his name, "Jiang Jieshi." Similarly, we have stuck with the well-established forms of Kuomintang, Chiang Ching-kuo, and Sun Yat-sen. We have, of course, employed other systems of romanization when these appeared in quotations, where we have followed whatever form was used in the original.

The Chinese passages quoted in the text have all been translated by John Byron.

CONTENTS

There are three kinds of despots. There is the despot who tyrannises over the body. There is the despot who tyrannises over the soul. There is the despot who tyrannises over the soul and body alike. The first is called the Prince. The second is called the Pope. The third is called the People.

—OSCAR WILDE
The Soul of Man Under Socialism

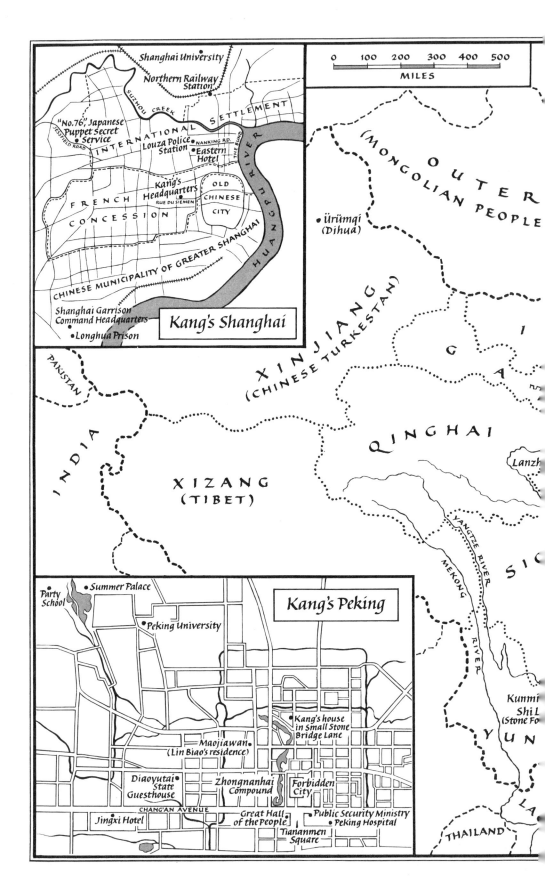

Kang's Shanghai

Shanghai University

Northern Railway Station

SUZHOU CREEK

INTERNATIONAL SETTLEMENT

"No. 76" Japanese Puppet Secret Service

JESSFIELD ROAD

Louza Police Station

NANKING RD.

Eastern Hotel

THE BUND

HUANGPU RIVER

Kang's Headquarters

RUE DU SIEMEN

OLD CHINESE CITY

FRENCH CONCESSION

CHINESE MUNICIPALITY OF GREATER SHANGHAI

Shanghai Garrison Command Headquarters

Longhua Prison

MILES
0   100   200   300   400   500

O U T E R (MONGOLIAN PEOPLE

Ürümqi (Dihua)

X I N J I A N G (CHINESE TURKESTAN)

PAKISTAN

G
A

I

N

INDIA

QINGHAI

Lanzh

XIZANG (TIBET)

YANGTZE RIVER

MEKONG

SIC

Kang's Peking

Party School

Summer Palace

Peking University

Kang's house in Small Stone Bridge Lane

Maojiawan (Lin Biao's residence)

Diaoyutai State Guesthouse

Zhongnanhai Compound

Forbidden City

CHANG'AN AVENUE

Jingxi Hotel

Great Hall of the People

Public Security Ministry

Peking Hospital

Tiananmen Square

RIVER

Kunmi Shi L (Stone Fo

Y U N

LA

THAILAND

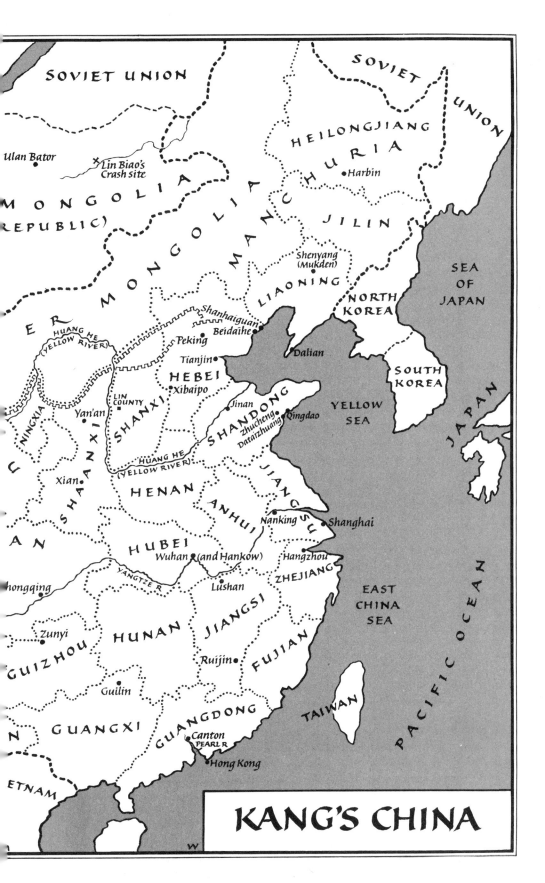

KANG'S CHINA

THE UNSEEN HAND

CHINA WATCHERS have been fascinated for decades by Mao Zedong, the remarkable man who created modern China. Comparing him with other modern despots like Hitler and Stalin, they have noted that Mao never consigned millions upon millions of his own people to the gas chambers or firing squads. He did not purposely starve huge numbers of his countrymen to death when he restructured his nation's economy, replacing an obsolete feudal mode with a modern socialist system. Although he brutally reasserted China's authority over Tibet, he did not invade land after land, gobble up each one, and attempt to rule the world.

True, the people of mainland China suffered under Mao: the savage land reform and "counterrevolutionary" campaigns at the outset of the 1950s, the ruinous Great Leap Forward at the end of that decade, and the demented Cultural Revolution of the 1960s and 1970s were simply his more notorious excesses. Mao may have resorted to drastic measures, the argument goes, but he had no choice: his were drastic measures for drastic circumstances in drastic times. Mao had fought a long, debilitating civil war against an apparently superior force, the United States–backed Kuomintang (KMT); and once he had won that war and driven the KMT to Taiwan in 1949, he was confronted with the task of ruling a war-ravaged nation of almost 600 million people, the overwhelming majority of them backward, illiterate, and impoverished. Many foreign experts have concluded that Mao was one of the great revolutionaries of the twentieth century, and that for a dictator, he was relatively benevolent.*

Very few outsiders, however, have made the connection between Mao and the sinister figure he employed to do his dirty work. To outsiders, Mao might seem like the rough-hewn "good cop" of the Chinese Revolution, but the oppressive regime he imposed upon the People's Republic was profoundly influenced by his wily "bad cop"—that Eastern Machiavelli, largely unknown to the West, Comrade Kang Sheng.

Who was Kang Sheng? A shadowy, enigmatic commissar, Kang was a man of many parts, combining the roles of Mao's matchmaker, expert on international relations, aesthete-in-residence, and adviser on Marxist theory. Above all, though, Kang's fearful eminence derived from his many years as chief of Communist China's secret police. He created a system that exterminated hundreds of thousands of his fellow Chinese, and enslaved and tortured millions more.

The subtlety of Kang's politics, the refinement of his tastes, and his power to control—even mesmerize—Mao make him one of the most influential forces in modern China. Indeed, next to Kang, Mao himself seems to shrink in importance and interest. Mao, for all his magnetism, appears merely two-dimensional in comparison; Kang Sheng was a cold, self-possessed manipulator who fused refinement and intellectual sensibilities with the criminal delight of a Renaissance princeling in the arts of inflicting agony and destruction. Kang's malevolence eventually earned him a fittingly mythic title that might have amused and flattered him had anyone dared utter it to his face: "the King of Hell."

When the students of Peking demonstrated in Tiananmen Square in the spring of 1989, sparking a popular revolt that culminated in the June 4 massacre of about two thousand civilians, their protests began with memorial ceremonies for Hu Yaobang. Hu, the most enlightened leader of the Chinese Communist Party (CCP), had died that April, two years after he was ousted from power for trying to inject a breath

---

* Chinese Communist officials themselves entertained a more realistic opinion. "Mao Zedong, usually pictured by certain foreign experts . . . as a shrewd but kindly philosopher of the peasant class, is, in reality, the main support of the hard, Stalinist wing of the party," observed Chen Qiren, an intelligence officer under Kang who served as an informant for American authorities during the late 1940s. For a complete discussion of Chen and the information he provided, see the Bibliography.

of freedom into the system. In the course of a secret 1978 speech condemning Kang Sheng, Hu Yaobang had compared Kang to Feliks Dzerzhinski* and to the callous murderer who followed in Dzerzhinski's footsteps, Lavrenti Beria. It was an assessment shared by a majority of informed Chinese.

Kang himself enjoyed the Dzerzhinski comparison, and even adopted it, but the more apt parallel was Beria. Kang spent much of his life as head of the CCP's secret police, euphemistically known in its first decade of existence as the Social Protection Department. In fact, his involvement in security work lasted three times as long as Beria's, who, for all the legends that have grown up around him, presided over the Soviet secret police for a mere nine years. But Kang and Beria had much in common beyond being bureaucrats of terror. Beria was a provincial administrator, a captain of industry, a man of notoriously perverted sexual tastes, and one of Stalin's very few intimates. At Politburo meetings, Stalin and Beria would terrify others by lapsing into Georgian, a language no other Soviet leader understood. Like Beria, Kang played many other parts.

He was first and foremost the man Mao trusted more than any other, even though Kang was the last to join the Chairman's inner circle. The rest of Mao's cronies dated back to the 1920s or early 1930s; most had cemented their ties to Mao during the heroic Long March of the mid-1930s, while Kang was stationed in Moscow. Kang did not meet Mao until his return to China in 1937, but he quickly learned how to work his way into Mao's confidence and make himself Mao's intellectual soulmate. Scion of a rich landowning family, Kang was among the more cultivated of the Communist leaders, but his affluent origins did not hamper his dealings with the peasant-born Mao. On the contrary, Kang exploited Mao's resentment against intellectuals who considered themselves superior to the Chairman. Kang and Mao spent countless days together, first in Yan'an, then in Peking, and in later years on tours of the country, discussing politics, Chinese history, and culture. Kang even helped polish Mao's poetry and refine his ideological essays.

Mao repaid Kang by giving him immense influence. Kang was

---

* Dzerzhinski was the Polish revolutionary who headed the Cheka, the ruthless secret police that helped Lenin fasten his grip after the Revolution of 1917. He is perhaps best remembered in the West as the nemesis of the British master-spy Sidney Reilly in the television series *Reilly: Ace of Spies.*

appointed to many important posts and protected from criticism, whatever his crimes against the Chinese people. In 1947, while in charge of land reform in Lin County in Shanxi Province, Kang earned the hatred of many CCP cadres by physically liquidating almost every landlord and well-to-do peasant. A number of CCP leaders were outraged, but Mao saw fit to single out Kang's work and praise it as a triumph over "right deviations." In due course, Kang, as Mao's representative at international Communist functions, would simply distort the record at will, reporting what he thought the Chairman wanted to hear and reflecting the credit on himself. No other Chinese leader who attended those meetings dared challenge Kang's version, and Mao was satisfied that if he heard something from Kang Sheng, it was true.

Kang was also a close friend and—according to plausible evidence—a former lover of Jiang Qing, the beautiful and voluptuous actress who became Mao's fourth wife. Kang and Jiang Qing met in 1924 in the ancient walled town of Zhucheng in Shandong Province; at the time, Kang was twenty-six and Jiang was fourteen, and he may well have been the first of her many sexual partners. Thirteen years later, when Jiang Qing caught Mao's eye at the Communist head-quarters in Yan'an, Kang eagerly handed her over to his patron. Mao's other colleagues suspected that Jiang Qing was a KMT spy, but Kang vouched for her, making it possible for Mao to marry her and earning Kang the lifelong gratitude of both husband and wife.

Kang was the ideological entrepreneur who imported the Stalin-ist armory of repression and control into the Chinese Communist movement. After witnessing Stalin's Great Purge during four years in Moscow as deputy leader of the Chinese delegation to the Comintern, Kang brought back to China a clear understanding of secret-police work: of how show trials, with their manufactured evidence and forced confessions, could achieve total domination over a society. Kang put these powers at Mao's disposal, and in 1942 the two men orchestrated the notorious Rectification Movement. This campaign of thought reform set a pattern for totalitarian control that endured for more than forty years, until the mid-1980s.

Kang used Stalin's methods to destroy traitors to the Communist cause; occasionally, he caught actual KMT spies. But more often, his victims were personal enemies and others whose forced confessions could serve his own dark purposes. Like Joseph McCarthy, the Wis-consin senator who rode high during part of the time Kang was in power, Kang had his lists of imaginary traitors—his "Sixty-one Renegade Clique," for example.* Unlike McCarthy, however, he was not restrained by a legal system that required criminal charges to be proved beyond a reasonable doubt. Kang never had to worry that mere truth would derail a politically useful persecution.

Kang was the creator of China's gulag. He established and presided over a system in which millions of Chinese were imprisoned, tortured, and executed during a half-century of operation in Shanghai, Moscow, Yan'an, and Peking. Kang employed an elite corps of "depraved inquisitors" and gave them carte blanche to administer the cruelest tortures and methods of cross-examination. After years of working as Kang's interrogators and torturers, his men became indifferent to the suffering of their victims. Among their more inventive methods: tying a prisoner to the tail of a horse, then whipping the horse so that it dragged the victim to death; refining the ancient Chinese water torture by forcing vinegar down a victim's throat; and thrusting a hair from a horse's tail into the victim's penis.

When Kang was unsatisfied with the efforts of his corps of sadists, he would intervene personally, supervising tortures and helping to invent new ways of loosening tongues and tormenting the unfortunate. He threatened to throw poisonous snakes into prisoners' cells to expedite "confessions." When a theatrical display of terror was called for, he gleefully chained prisoners by their noses and led them through the streets like cattle.

Kang was a Marxist ideologue whose reputation as an expert on the Soviet Union enabled him to exploit China's clash with Moscow during the late 1950s and early 1960s as a means of expanding his personal influence. Playing on Mao's jealousy and suspicion of Soviet power, Kang falsely attributed disparaging remarks about the Chairman to Soviet leaders and artfully maneuvered his patron into a total break with Moscow. As a result, the balance of world power shifted and the Soviet Union found itself confronted by China as well as the West. The reverberations of Kang's work are still being felt today, as

---

* "The Sixty-one Renegades" were a group of Communist veterans who had been held by the KMT in Peking's Caolanzi Prison during the 1930s. To secure their release before the Japanese occupied Peking in 1937, the CCP leaders authorized them to pretend conversion to the KMT cause. During the Cultural Revolution, Kang revived this incident, claiming that the sixty-one prisoners had in fact thrown in their lot with the KMT and had been moles inside the CCP ever since. They were cruelly persecuted as a result.

the ideological tensions between China and the new regimes emerging on the Soviet land mass grow ever larger.

Kang was the godfather of the Cultural Revolution and, as much as any individual, one of its main instigators. Somewhat in the tradition of Rasputin and Iago, Kang poisoned Mao's mind with the notion that Chinese society must be purified of all reactionary and revisionist elements. Hundreds of thousands were killed, and millions of lives were shattered forever. A single campaign Kang initiated against "foreign agents" claimed 940,000 victims, most of them innocent. Their fates ranged from interrogation to imprisonment to execution.

Once he had helped set the Cultural Revolution in motion, Kang advised Jiang Qing and the other members of "the Gang of Four"— the clique of radicals who ruled China during the late 1960s and early 1970s—on how best to twist it to their own ends. In Hu Yaobang's words, Kang was the "black advisor and decapitator for the Gang of Four. . . . Without the backing of Kang Sheng, whose black hand extended to every part and field of the country, the Gang of Four, merely four clowns, could not [have made] attempts at power-seizure, unless all good party members had died."

Jiang Qing remained in detention—incarcerated in a villa that had been specially built for her in the compound of Qincheng Prison— until she committed suicide, reportedly by hanging, in May 1991.* Kang Sheng, her mentor, might have stood trial with her had he not died in December 1975, before he could be called to account. Even Kang's death, ten months before the arrest of the Gang of Four in October 1976, amounted to a timely exit. Then again, Kang's conspiratorial skills, instinct for survival, and Party seniority might have saved him and his radical allies—had Kang not died, Hu Yaobang speculated, the Gang of Four might never have fallen.

Kang was an unscrupulous conspirator and infighter. He double-crossed virtually every senior leader with whom he came into close contact, save Mao; the gallery of his victims is a hall of fame of the Chinese Revolution. At the end of his life, Kang effected a masterpiece of treachery, leveling charges of treason against his most intimate asso-

---

* News reports uniformly ascribe Jiang Qing's death to suicide, but rumors in Peking claim that she was killed on the orders of Deng Xiaoping. Deng feared, or so these stories go, that she might have become a symbol for the increasing number of Chinese who, in the aftermath of the Tiananmen crackdown, are nostalgic for the days of Mao Zedong.

ciate, Jiang Qing. But his last triumph came from beyond the grave: two months before he died, Kang met with Chairman Mao for the last time and warned him that Deng Xiaoping (formerly an ally and partner of Kang's) would reverse the Cultural Revolution and should be purged—advice that Mao followed, even if after Kang's death.

The final proof of Kang's cunning is that he outlived virtually all his victims. Affecting the image of an intellectual whose interests lay in the realms of ideology and culture, he was able to disarm suspicion and conceal most of his crimes from the public. At seventy-seven, although widely hated, Kang died in his own bed—not at his enemies' hands but from cancer.

Thus ended a long life of hedonism. Kang had become the black sheep of his family, reputedly by seducing his father's concubine. In an attempt to curb Kang's youthful promiscuity and rebellion, his father arranged a match with a local girl, but Kang walked away from that marriage to wed a fellow-Communist named Cao Yi'ou. Never bothering with the formalities of a divorce from his first wife, Kang shared his bed with both his wife and her sister, Su Mei.

Sex with his sister-in-law was not Kang's only indulgence. He was also a habitual opium smoker, as one of the sources of this book discovered one day in the early 1950s when she visited Kang, then a patient at Peking Hospital. She found him there with his personal set of opium implements—pipe, lamp, and the thin needles and small spoons used in boiling the drug over a flame. Taking advantage of his position, Kang maintained a drug habit even as the Communists were pitilessly executing anyone who trafficked in narcotics.

Some of Kang's pleasures were downright trivial, vices only in the absurd context of a People's Republic in which a high-ranking official who kept flowers in her office was accused of bourgeois wastefulness. Kang doted on his pet Pekinese terriers—dogs formerly reserved for occupants of the Imperial Palace—even though the Communist regime prohibited its citizens from owning pets. In the eyes of the government, pets consumed scarce food supplies and recalled China's bourgeois past. Usually, what few dogs there were wound up in the cooking pots of the ravenous populace. Kang's dogs were not his only link with the palace; he also employed a chef who had cooked for Henry Pu Yi, the last Qing emperor, who was deposed in 1911. Kang subscribed to all the puritanical taboos of the Communist Party—as long as they did not apply to him. In his own mind, he was above the law that governed the masses.

Kang was also a painter and calligrapher, famous for his exceedingly rare ability to wield the writing brush with equal skill in right and left hand alike. And as a collector and patron of the arts, he amassed a priceless hoard of paintings, porcelain, bronzes, inkstones, and ancient manuscripts—a treasury of the world he had helped to destroy. Like the American spymaster James J. Angleton, who was renowned for his interest in orchids and poetry, Kang had his aesthetic side. But Kang's artistic pursuits exuded a malevolent air: many of the works of art he "owned" had been obtained by fraud or stolen for him by Red Guards during the Cultural Revolution. Nor did Kang simply want to possess art: at the height of his power, he ruthlessly persecuted artists who had previously aroused his envy, much as his protégé Jiang Qing sought to destroy the producers and actors who had hampered her film career in Shanghai back in the 1930s.

Many of Kang's crimes remained hidden for decades, but to politically conscious Chinese, he was evil incarnate. In the rich body of legend that accumulated around him, he became the all-powerful demon of the shadows. At least two books have reported that during his six-year absence from public view after the Communist triumph in 1949, Kang was orchestrating a plot to steal and develop nuclear weapons for China. In fact, Kang spent those years in a hospital, apparently suffering from some form of nervous collapse. After convalescing for years, Kang was able to return to public life and work his way back to the summit of the Party, displaying his extraordinary skills at political survival and his seemingly endless credit with Chairman Mao.

But in the whispered worlds of myth and gossip, Kang was China's bogeyman, blamed for any sinister or mysterious event. When his archrival, the KMT secret-police chief Dai Li, died in a March 1946 plane crash, many saw Kang as the perpetrator; he was not. When an American military plane carrying a dozen Chinese Communists—including a former security chief reputed to be Kang's rival—crashed into a mountain in Shanxi Province in April 1946, killing all aboard, Kang again was said to have sabotaged the aircraft; he had not. When Lin Biao, fleeing after his abortive attempt to overthrow Mao, was killed in 1971 in yet another air crash, it was again Kang whom some suspected; they were wrong.

Kang was also blamed for the deaths in the 1960s of Shanghai

CCP chief Ke Qingshi and former KMT general Li Zongren, who had defected from the Nationalist cause and thrown in his lot with the Communists. Again, Kang was innocent; Ke suffered heart failure after a peppery Sichuanese dinner, and Li died of old age.

Kang's reputation was such that whenever an unexplainable tragedy occurred in China, he would become the main suspect—just as if one American were held responsible for the mysterious assassinations of John F. Kennedy, Robert F. Kennedy, and Martin Luther King, Jr.* The stories about Kang's alleged crimes and supposed secret achievements say much about his power to capture the imaginations of Chinese and foreigners alike. In his single person, Kang possessed the diabolic mystique that Western conspiracymongers ascribe to such organizations as the Mafia and the CIA.

By the time the Cultural Revolution had burned itself out in the early 1970s, Kang's bogeyman status overshadowed all reality, and he was made one of the main scapegoats for the national self-mutilation of the previous ten years. When Hu Yaobang gave China a glimpse of Kang's record as a political criminal, he was not simply seeking justice for all who had suffered at Kang's hands; by singling out Kang as the source of so much evil and malice, Hu was also protecting the Communist system and its radiant sponsor, Chairman Mao.

In his anxiety to keep Mao from being tainted by Kang's crimes, Hu even insinuated that Kang had plotted against the Great Helmsman, bugging Mao's office in 1972 and then murdering the technicians responsible. But there was no way Kang could have orchestrated these actions; he was too ill that year to even make an appearance on May Day. Moreover, Kang was so close to the Chairman that he had little need for eavesdropping.

Perhaps without the authoritarian tendencies of communism and Mao's profound complicity, Kang would have spent his life as an art teacher or petty functionary. That he rose to be a purveyor of terror to the largest nation in history was possible only because of the conditions he lived in and the people he worked with. Among his fellow CCP rulers, Kang was the most callous and unrestrained in abusing the opportunities presented by China's totalitarianism. To this day,

---

* In outlandish tribute to the long reach of Kang's black hand, an author of spy fiction, Robert Edward Eckels, has hypothesized in his short story "The K'ang Sheng Memorandum," that Kang was involved in the assassination of President Kennedy.

he remains a symbol of the inherent corruption of a system that treats dissent as enmity, criticism as treason, and its own subjects as interchangeable, dispensable automatons.

One sweltering night in the summer of 1983, John Byron, a Western diplomat, swung his air-conditioned Toyota from Peking's Chang'an Avenue into Dahua Road, a narrow side street that leads to the remnants of the old Legation Quarter. He slowed to a crawl as he headed into the shadows beneath a clump of overhanging trees. A tall, lean Chinese youth in his twenties, with hair that was stylishly long by Western standards but showed a measure of defiance for his Communist overlords, stepped quickly away from a gray brick building and reached out to open the door of Byron's car. In one hand the youth carried a parcel about the size of a book.

The search for Kang Sheng had brought Byron to this surreptitious and risky encounter. Byron, an expert on China, had been stationed in Peking for several years, occasionally coming across fragments of information about Kang Sheng; with each one, he had grown more eager to learn everything he could about China's elusive secret-police chief. Now he was face to face with—or, to be more exact, sitting beside, and hardly able to see in the dim light—someone who promised to unlock many of the mysteries of Kang Sheng's past.

As Byron accelerated past Peking Hospital, the modern medical institution reserved for senior members of the Communist elite, his passenger settled low in his seat, reducing his profile without actually seeming to hide. It is unusual for a Chinese to be riding around the city in a foreigner's car. Traditionally, the Chinese have avoided prying into one another's affairs, but in the People's Republic, a police state, you never could tell who might be sitting by the road, seeking relief from the heat in the evening breeze and keeping an eye open for useful information. An off-duty security official or a representative of a street committee might note down a license plate number and set off an alarm in hopes of receiving some reward.

When Byron turned into Minjiao East Lane, a leafy avenue once lined with embassies, hotels, and even a cathedral, his passenger relaxed a little, lit a cigarette, and began to speak, barely above a whisper.

"Remember I mentioned a book about Kang Sheng?" the Chinese youth asked with a note of both amusement and victory. A week or two earlier, he had told Byron about a rare copy of a biography of Kang. "Well, here it is. I borrowed it from a friend's place. He doesn't know I've taken it. I've got to return it tomorrow. You will have to copy it tonight."

When Byron pointed out that it might take him more than one night to reproduce the entire text, since photocopiers are much less available in the People's Republic than in the West, his passenger was insistent:

"This is strong stuff. It's a *neibu* [internal] document for Chinese eyes only. It's already been suppressed, although it only came out less than a year ago. Some of the big shots are outraged by it. They say it reveals too many state secrets. That's their way of saying that it exposes too much of the corruption at the heart of the system. The good life of the top dogs. To get a copy now, you have to register with Red Flag, the company that published it. And only high-level cadres can get away with that."

Byron's rider stopped long enough to light another cigarette. "It's a very interesting book. Kang Sheng was a very interesting man. He wasn't just a secret-police chief. He was an expert on all sorts of cultural matters, including erotic literature."

As Byron's contact had promised, the 437-page book, *Kang Sheng Pingzhuan—A Critical Biography of Kang Sheng*, presented an extraordinary and thus far untold account of Kang's life. Byron soon realized that the author's name, "Zhongkan," was a pseudonym. A week later, Byron's informant told him that there were actually two authors but that he could identify only one of them: Ma Zhongyang, deputy editor of *Red Flag*, the Communist Party's main theoretical journal. It took Byron many months to work out that Ma's collaborator was Li Kan, a senior Party historian who had written several essays deflating Mao's reputation. "Zhong" from Ma Zhongyang plus "Kan" from Li Kan equaled "Zhongkan."

That biography of Kang Sheng had many irritating omissions. When it was frank, it was very frank; but it had been written in China, so it had to skirt, or only hint at, forbidden topics. Byron recognized not only that the book was studiously incomplete but also that "Zhongkan" had compensated for the deliberate omissions by liberally scattering clues and innuendos through the text. Frustrating as the portrait of Kang was, it was also an irresistible invitation to pursue every lead until all the deeply hidden parts of Kang's life would be revealed. "Zhongkan" provided the skeleton of the book you are reading, which has been fleshed out from hundreds of other sources.*

As Byron read of Kang Sheng evolving from a secret-police man into a complex individual who had influenced art, drama, politics, ideology, and foreign policy, he hunted for further bits of Kang's extraordinary story. But that was not easy. The lives of China's leaders have long been shielded from public view. Mao gave a surprisingly frank account of his early years to a sympathetic American reporter, Edgar Snow, in 1936, but as the years passed, the Communist leaders spoke less and less about themselves. Some, like Premier Zhou Enlai and Foreign Minster Chen Yi, made shows of openness by granting occasional interviews to foreign journalists, but these were exceptions to the rule and were intended to reveal as little as possible to the critical and the inquisitive.

Kang, a man with a great deal to hide, had taken elaborate steps to conceal his past. During the Cultural Revolution, he destroyed dozens of reports from decades-old police files in Shanghai about his activities there. As China regained a measure of stability in 1970, Kang went even further, removing all the papers from his personal CCP file and replacing them with a brief but glowing biography he had written himself. Kang created a wealth of legends designed to beguile, intimidate, or terrify the curious. Whenever possible, he killed or otherwise silenced witnesses who claimed that he had once been a KMT agent or a traitor to the Communist cause.

Chinese who had dealings with Kang are more reluctant to talk about him than about any other leader. People on the inside of the system realize he was so close to Mao that to expose Kang would risk the final collapse of China's entire socialist heritage, which is already reeling under the impact of disasters that date back decades. Kang's notoriety was such that when his career first came under posthumous scrutiny in 1977, his critics did not even name him but simply referred to him as "that adviser." Nevertheless, Byron was able to meet a number of Kang's former acquaintances and colleagues. Some of them, secure in their homes, reminisced about Kang as they unrolled pieces of calligraphy he had presented to them as keepsakes.

No one source could—or would—reveal Kang's whole story, but many people provided separate pieces of information. Among them

---

* For a full discussion of "Zhongkan" as a source, see Bibliography.

were senior Party historians; the sons and daughters of many of Kang's closest colleagues; figures from the world of Chinese culture, a world Kang both enjoyed and devastated; and scores of others who have never before been interviewed by Westerners. Kang was, in his own secretive way, a global figure; fragments of the map to his labyrinth are scattered everywhere, from the back streets of Peking to the KMT intelligence files stored in Taiwan to the libraries of the West. A major treasure trove of background about Kang is the U.S. National Archives, the storehouse for the records of the State Department, American military intelligence, the OSS, and the CIA; likewise, the files of the Special Branch of the Shanghai Municipal Police (SMP), which have also found work their way into the National Archives, throw much light on Kang's time as a young revolutionary activist in China's largest city.

Valuable material about Kang (in some cases, written by Kang himself—often under pseudonyms) has also been published in a variety of places: magazine articles from Hong Kong and Taiwan, standard histories, and brief references in the biographies of other Chinese leaders. Comparing standard accounts of modern Chinese politics with "Zhongkan's" version of Kang's life illuminates both: Kang is the missing piece in many of the jigsaw puzzles of twentieth-century China.

What emerges is the portrait of a ruthless conspirator who combined extraordinary sadism with a refined taste for traditional art and a scholar's knowledge of history. Many Chinese have described Kang as "two-faced"; the writer Lin Qingshan compared Kang to Robert Louis Stevenson's character who was both Dr. Jekyll and Mr. Hyde. Kang was a product of the past who became part of a modern political organization and then helped to corrupt it from within: at once a Chinese Bolshevik and a rogue mandarin.

The Chinese Revolution is often presented as an example of how a desperately backward nation can break the shackles of oppression and poverty, but Kang's story reveals how the leaders of any noble cause may yield to corruption, greed, and lust. After the first few years, the lofty ideals of this revolution were distorted by the spinning of ever bloodier and stranger fantasies by men like Kang and his lord, master, and bewitched listener, Mao. Mao and his colleagues proclaimed, "We are the people"—but, as Kang typifies, "We" meant that very limited number of potentates who lived high while the masses suffered unbearable deprivations. The corruption that now, in the 1990s, is such a pressing issue in China, as leaders and bureaucrats use special privileges and family connections to improve their own lot, flows directly from the example set by Kang and his comrades.

Kang's love of culture—his exquisite calligraphy, his delicate painting, his passion for art collecting—was an instance of divided sensibility, the product of mind without heart. He had the face of an antiquary; encountering him at a party, one might have mistaken him for nothing more than a genial professor of art. Other than the fact that he spoke at least two foreign languages—German and Russian—with some fluency, there appeared to be nothing remarkable about him. A slender man about five-foot-eight—slightly shorter than Mao but about the same height as Zhou Enlai and Lin Biao—Kang wore thick-lensed glasses, liked to eat peppers and play poker ("as most Chinese Communists do, sometimes gambling for a chicken or some other small 'treat' "), and was a chain-smoker (during the 1930s, Kang preferred the brand Golden Rat).

Inside, though, was the heart of a killer—not surprising for someone who had mixed with gangsters in his youth and mastered kung fu and other martial arts in addition to his classical studies, run a team of Communist hit men during his early days in Shanghai, and functioned for most of his career as investigator, prosecutor, judge, jury, and lord high executioner. Charming as he could be, it was best to stay on his good side: during the Cultural Revolution, Kang put on a dinner for Liu Xiao, an old friend since their student days more than forty years earlier at Shanghai University; professed his goodwill over food and wine; then, at the end of the evening, packed his guest off to languish for months in a secret prison, in the hope that Liu would incriminate one of Kang's rivals.

Today Kang Sheng is considered an enemy of the Chinese people. He was expelled posthumously from the Communist Party in 1980, and his ashes were removed from their place of honor at Peking's Babaoshan Cemetery. Party cadres and ordinary intellectuals alike condemn him in terms that are a kind of tribute to his protean monstrosity—"Trotskyite," "Kuomintang special agent," "opportunist," "sadist." Such epithets are apt, for Kang's story reveals the dark and terrible inner history of the Chinese Communist movement. Kang was close to every one of its legendary figures: Li Lisan, Wang Ming, Zhou Enlai, Deng Xiaoping, Jiang Qing, and, most notably, Mao Zedong.

As they each boosted him toward the summit of the Party, the shadows emanating from his life stain their reputations, too.

Kang espoused an ideology that purported to be the leading edge of modern and progressive thought, but his instincts and attitudes were heavily colored by tradition. Like the Confucian officials of earlier dynasties, he was obsessed with enunciating the orthodox philosophy of statecraft; like those men, he was also an amateur painter of considerable ability; like the court favorites who repeatedly emerged at the emperor's side and conspired with eunuchs and concubines and empresses to wield power at the expense of ministers and magistrates outside the palace, Kang plotted with Mao's wife and friends to block the orthodox CCP commissars and administrators. He guided a faction at the court of the new emperor that stimulated a popular upheaval, which he used to destroy his political and bureaucratic enemies. Using a montage of formulas and code words, Kang whipped the Chinese people on to believe in a magical capacity to achieve scientific and technological breakthroughs, just as the Boxer chiefs had promised a century earlier that sacred rites would protect their followers from the bullets of foreign troops. Even his sexual relationship with his wife's sister evoked the convoluted erotic conspiracies celebrated in a long line of tales originating with the Han dynasty novella *The Emperor and the Two Sisters*.

Kang's status as a figure who synthesized the Chinese people's capacity for high culture and civilized living with their reputation for inflicting such tortures as "death by a thousand cuts" makes him altogether more compelling, however grimly so, than the heroes of the Long March and the Civil War. Mao was a self-described revolutionary who, in coping with the modern world, preserved the mentality of the past, but Kang was something much more profound. His was the hand—largely unseen, for all of Kang's infamy—that unlocked the gates of darkness and exposed China to the same forces of anarchy and chaos which since the Bronze Age had periodically overwhelmed China.

The value of Kang's history lies less in its colorful, chilling episodes than in its power to illuminate the fundamental dynamics of Chinese politics and government. Kang's story reveals China's continuing struggle to come to grips with tradition so that the nation can enter the modern world. Kang was both product and prisoner of the past; it is his equal devotion to relentless revolution and to the ways of the ancients that fascinates and frightens.

It seems fitting that Kang Sheng was such a creature of the past. To explore his origins, we must be transported to nineteenth-century China—a world of anarchy shot through with fanaticism, tempered by tyranny, and haunted by the greatness of a dying culture; a world that existed long before there was a Communist Party, a "People's Republic," or a leader named Mao Zedong.

Part 1

CAUGHT BETWEEN TWO WORLDS

Chapter I

FROM THE
PROVINCE OF
CONFUCIUS

IN 1898, as the Chinese empire entered its final stages of decay, the wife of an affluent landlord gave birth to a baby who would grow up to be a fearful symbol of twentieth-century China, a man whom millions of terrified Chinese would come to know by the name Kang Sheng.

For almost a century before Kang Sheng's birth, China had been plagued by poverty, peasant rebellions, ethnic revolts, and foreign invaders. But now, as the nineteenth century drew to a close, so did the empire, in a last outburst of blind frustration, impotence, and disintegration. "The Old Buddha," the Empress Dowager Cixi, had increasingly dominated court politics since the death in 1861 of her syphilitic consort, the Xianfeng Emperor. In 1898, the year Kang Sheng was born, the Empress Dowager crushed "the hundred days of reform"—the final attempt to reinvigorate the dynasty from within. Backed by a clique of eunuchs and conservative mandarins, she executed six of the high court officials behind the reform movement and arrested the young Guangxu Emperor, who had blessed the goal of modernization, and imprisoned him within the Forbidden City.

That same year, German military forces seized from China yet another "concession," the euphemism foreign governments used for Chinese territories they could rule as their own. A squadron of the German Imperial Fleet entered Jiaozhou Bay—twenty miles from Kang's birthplace—to enforce the Kaiser's demands upon the ever weakening regime in Peking. The German action was nothing new—the British, French, and Japanese had used force to gain control of

Chinese ports and trading centers for five decades—but it underscored the apparent irreversibility of China's decline.

The year 1898 also saw a prodigious upsurge in the Society of Righteous Harmony. This xenophobic and messianic secret order, known in the West as the Boxers, drew international attention in 1900 when its fanatical adherents rampaged through northern China, killing foreign missionaries and Chinese Christians alike and laying siege to the foreign legation quarters in Peking. The Boxers' mission was to preserve the Qing dynasty, the regime that the Manchu invaders had imposed on China in 1644. Nevertheless, the Manchu regime was swept away once and for all in 1911. After that, China became a vast cockpit where venal warlords who dreamed of sitting on the Peacock Throne within the Forbidden City in Peking fought against radicals who wanted to bring the nation into the twentieth century. Kang, in short, was born into a society spinning out of control.

Shandong, where Kang was born, is a huge peninsula that protrudes into the Yellow Sea like a finger pointing at Korea. In a single province, Shandong displayed the most obvious symptoms of China's afflictions. Overpopulated, poverty-stricken, and infested with bandits, Shandong was a hotbed of the Boxer movement, as well as the target of German, British, and Japanese aggressors bent on exploiting the long-predicted wreck of China. Shandong and its thirty million inhabitants seemed part of a doomed world.

But Shandong was also a symbol of China's glories, rich in both nature and history. Its long coast is lined by scenic bays and gentle bluffs, and much of its hinterland is taken up by rugged mountain ranges filled with springs and ancient goals of pilgrimage, including China's most sacred mountain, Tai Shan. The Kingdom of Lu, the home state of Master Kong (Confucius, in the West), lay in Shandong. The influence of Confucian philosophy, with its respect for family, authority, and moral rectitude, continues to permeate Chinese life, and the descendants of Confucius (still surnamed Kong) make their homes in the ancient town of Qufu in the southern quadrant of the province, a living connection with the past. Shandong also had close ties, dating back to the fifteenth century, with the imperial court in Peking—so close that in 1911, when the combined forces of the nationalistic Kuomintang party and military strongman Yuan Shikai overthrew the last Manchu emperor, Xuantong,* many officials fled

---

* Known in the West as Henry Pu Yi.

from Peking to Shandong, seeking refuge in the homes of the provincial gentry.

Kang Sheng spent the first quarter-century of his life in this province of anarchy, violence, poverty, superstition, foreign aggression, and memories of former grandeur. Many of his attitudes—his unrelenting chauvinism, his unscrupulous elitism, his will to amass power, even at the expense of human life—were spawned in the conservatism, xenophobia, and desperation of Shandong.

Kang Sheng was born in Dataizhuang ("Large Tower Village"), a small rural settlement on the outskirts of Wanggezhuang, just in from the coast about fifty miles southwest of Qingdao, the German colonial outpost that became the main center of modern commerce and culture in Shandong. Known today as the Datai Production Brigade of the Wanggezhuang Commune, Jiao County, Dataizhuang was at the time of Kang's birth an obscure part of an unchanging and conservative rural world.

In villages like Dataizhuang, life was dominated by customs and traditions more than a thousand years old. The cult of ancestor worship was strong; the living believed that their forefathers' souls kept a watchful eye over them at all times. Life was punctuated by a series of rituals designed to satisfy the ancestral spirits: clouds of incense swirled around sacrificial meals, graves were zealously swept clean, animals were offered up to the dead. The peasants believed strongly in witchcraft, magic, and an invisible but potent world of kitchen and temple gods, fox spirits, water fairies, and ghosts. So strong was their faith that in the last years of the nineteenth century, many Shandongese accepted, to their misfortune, the Boxers' claims that magic formulas and spells could protect them against the rifles and artillery of the round-eyed foreign devils.

Kang's original family name was Zhang, but in keeping with a literary fashion followed by some educated Chinese, he changed his name several times before settling on Kang Sheng when he was thirty-five. Despite the poverty of his native province, Kang came from a family that had moderate-sized landholdings scattered across Jiao and Zhucheng counties in southern Shandong Province. The size of the family estates had diminished with each generation, but Kang's father, Zhang Faxiang, inherited 170 acres, which made him one of the larger landowners in a county where ownership of as little as 40 acres indicated economic success. Unlike many of Shandong's rural gentry, who farmed their own land, Zhang avoided performing any agricultural labors. Most of his land was leased to tenant farmers who paid him with half their produce, enabling Zhang and his family to enjoy a comfortable life. Besides Kang's mother, who came from a family named Li, Zhang also kept a concubine—a rare sign of prosperity in rural Shandong. Their relative affluence gave Zhang Faxiang and his two equally well-to-do brothers prestige and power in Dataizhuang and beyond. The hamlet's entire population was surnamed Zhang—in theory, at least, every male inhabitant of the village was descended from a single ancestor—and Kang's father and uncles were some of the most influential members of the local branch of the Zhang clan. Kang was truly a son of privilege.

Kang spent the first sixteen years of his life in Dataizhuang, where his family had a single-story, thirty-two-room house enclosed by earthen ramparts as protection against roving bandits. Outside the ramparts huddled the tenant farmers' simple dwellings of stone and mud brick. The Zhang family owned the house until 1938, when invading Japanese troops occupied Jiao County and the neighboring town of Zhucheng, causing many of the wealthier inhabitants to flee to safer parts of the country.

The privileged character of Kang's childhood was reinforced by the size of the Zhang family's household staff. In a village like Dataizhuang, to have even one domestic servant was a rarity; Kang's father employed an accountant to keep track of his rents, a man to grow vegetables, a servant to do odd jobs, and five women to cook and perform other household chores and look after the Zhang children.

Kang had three older brothers: Zhang Zongyi, Zhang Zongkai, and Zhang Zongru. Being the youngest, Kang was at least as spoiled as any other youngest son in a Chinese household; a corollary of the Confucian cult of ancestor worship was the indulgence of young male children. The clashes Kang had with his father on reaching adolescence suggest that his childhood had left him with the expectation that at home—and possibly beyond—he could have anything he wanted.

Descended from a long line of Confucian scholars, Kang was raised according to the principles of Confucian learning. At the beginning of the nineteenth century, Kang's great-grandfather, Zhang Hongyi, had been a student at the Imperial Academy in Peking, a mark of exceptional scholastic achievement. Kang's grandfather, Zhang Baoyuan, was also an industrious and recognized scholar of

Confucian culture. Kang's father had passed the imperial civil-service examination at the county level and qualified for the degree of *xiucai* ("flourishing talent"), an accomplishment that identified him as an unusually well-educated member of the local gentry and set him apart from the vulgar and barely literate landlords who ruled many of China's rural regions.

The Confucian tradition contributed more than intellectual atmosphere: the Zhang home was filled with artifacts like antique porcelain, paintings, calligraphy, furniture of the finest wood, inkstones, and brush holders. As the years passed and he joined the Communist Party and moved up its hierarchy, Kang never lost the tastes he had acquired as a young man, becoming a formidable expert on art and antiques.

In keeping with convention, Kang's father gave the family home in Dataizhuang the rather poetic Confucian name of Nan Shu De Tang ("Virtuous Hall of the Southern Tree"). The same devotion to words and word games led Zhang Faxiang to call his son by several names. Kang's name at birth, Zhang Zongke, meant "the Zhang fit to be a Great Master." He subsequently received the formal adult name of Shaoqing ("Young Minister"). His nickname at home, however, was Zhang Wang ("Flourishing Zhang").

China had no standard system of public schooling in the early twentieth century; at the age of seven, Kang joined his brothers and cousins in studying at home with a tutor in his father's pay. As in all traditional Chinese education, the emphasis was on rote instruction. To a modern-day Westerner, the process would seem extraordinarily tedious, with the students learning to recite and write out the entire texts of *The Three-Character Classic* and *The Thousand-Character Classic*—simple primers that provided the rudiments of Chinese politics, history, and philosophy—even before they knew the meaning of the words. With respites only for festivals and family celebrations, Kang was obliged to copy out, time after time, books written in an archaic language no child could fully understand. After mastering these primers, he graduated to the Confucian classics, *The Four Books* and *The Five Classics*—collections of stories, fables, poetry, histories, and philosophical tracts supposedly compiled and edited by Confucius and his followers. Boys as young as Kang were able to make only limited sense of the old-fashioned passages they were forced to read, but they did gain a grounding in the literature that refined Chinese had studied for centuries. Despite his exposure to the teachings of the ancients, Kang Sheng never showed much respect for the Confucian moral code. However, he was so conscious of Confucius's historical symbolism that he later incorporated the name Lu (as in "Kingdom of Lu") into the art name with which he signed his paintings and calligraphy.

The training Kang received in the family school did little to prepare him for a world already visibly passing away. In 1901, a decree issued in the name of the Guangxu Emperor brought an end to the traditional examination system used for selecting entrants to the bureaucracy. Modern, Western-style instruction was promoted in its place. Classical education, then, had lost its value as the foundation of social status and the path to office even before Kang began his studies—which did not deter Kang's father from hoping to see his son become a Confucian gentleman, a princely man.

The Revolution of 1911 caused profound changes in Kang's life. Followers of Sun Yat-sen (who was in the United States at the time) instigated a military revolt that ended in the overthrow of the Manchu regime and the collapse of the imperial system. One result was that Kang was delivered from the routine of classical education. But the traditional culture he had already absorbed under the Zhang family tutor had instilled within him the makings of a gifted calligrapher and painter, which not even half a century in the Communist movement, in places as remote from centers of Chinese art as Moscow and Yan'an, could erase.

In 1911, Kang Sheng turned thirteen. After five years of the routine of copying out, practicing calligraphy, and rote learning, he was exploding with energy. He was also on the verge of puberty. For the next three years, he led an unsettled, troubled life in a rural environment still governed by tradition. The fall of the Qing dynasty might have brought new Western ideas to China's coastal cities, but daily life in the hamlet of Dataizhuang was unchanged. Kang wore the gown and skullcap of a scholar and kept his hair in a queue, the so-called pigtail style that most Chinese men had jubilantly abandoned with the fall of the Manchus, who had forced it on them as a mark of subjugation. Kang maintained his conventional affectations for most of his teenage years. He passed much of his time playing the flute and the *banhu*, an ancient stringed instrument, and loved to watch local plays, the basis of his later fascination with Chinese opera.

As a teenager, Kang also started to explore the world of sexual pleasure, acquiring a reputation for "picking blossoms and stealing willow branches," a Chinese euphemism for womanizing. Youths with money chased women at market fairs, held every two weeks or so in the town squares, where people gathered to trade and to enjoy the color and fun. The fairs provided opportunities for entertainment as well as commerce. Troupes of acrobats, sword fighters, and players who performed the local Shandong opera—Shandong *bangzi*—entertained the crowds of traders, peasants, peddlers, and idle youths. On market days smartly attired young men like Kang paraded up and down, flirting with the actresses in the itinerant theatrical troupes and striking up conversations with girls whose hair was dressed in long plaits braided with red ribbons—signifying that a girl was unmarried. Some fairs were held inside temple grounds, where enterprising monks occasionally rented out rooms for discreet assignations or sometimes acted as go-betweens for people looking for sexual gratification and able to pay for it.

During his wild adolescence in rural Jiao County, where most families had no choice but to send their children off to toil in the fields, Kang was a member of a select set made up of the sons of the gentry. He and his privileged friends passed the time in teahouses, restaurants, and theaters, as well as at the local market fairs. The ties that developed between the boisterous young men were based on the age-old tradition of swearing blood brother relationships in ceremonies that usually took place either in winehouses or before a natural landmark, such as a cave or an ancient tree. Both parties took pledges of eternal friendship in these rituals, swore to help each other in times of trouble, and sealed their vows with toasts of wine mixed with chicken blood. "We were born under different stars but hope to die together" went one of the oaths. Kang swore blood brother relationships—bonds not much different from those which held together the criminal gangs evolved from the long-established secret societies—with many young men from the villages around Dataizhuang.

Kang also mingled with the local *liumang*, the opium-smoking, brothel-haunting hooligans and ruffians who were part of the province's network of gangs and secret societies. Banditry was deeply rooted in the province: Shandong had been the setting of a fourteenth-century novel, *The Story of the Marshes*, which celebrates the adventures of 108 heroes driven into lives of crime by unjust and corrupt officials. It was the bandit heritage and its accompanying cult of secret societies, combined with the widespread antiforeign sentiment of the 1890s, that helped make Shandong so hospitable to the Boxer movement.

Under the tutelage of his gangster friends, Kang became an expert at traditional techniques of combat with sword, knife, iron staff, and fists—martial arts now popularized in the West by kung fu movies from Hong Kong and Taiwan. Some of Kang's older friends among the *liumang*, survivors of the Boxer movement, often told tales of the brutality of the foreign troops who had helped suppress the uprising, and of missionaries who, so some stories went, gouged out the eyes of Chinese children to make medicine.

As Kang grew up, he became increasingly rebellious. His sexual escapades and his penchant for fighting deeply offended his father's Confucian sensitivities. In 1914, when Kang was sixteen, his outrages finally drove Zhang Faxiang beyond the limits of his tolerance. By then, the village was filled with gossip about the scandalous behavior of Zhang's youngest son. In a desperate attempt to prevent further loss of face, Zhang and his wife decided to lock up the unruly Kang in the family home.

Some of Kang's blood brothers were little more than drug addicts and gangsters, but others were much better influences. One was Chen Shunting, who approached Zhang Faxiang and finally persuaded him that a more effective and farsighted remedy for Kang's misbehavior would be to allow him to join Chen as a student at the German missionary middle school in nearby Qingdao. Although Zhang Faxiang feared that his son might be indoctrinated with foreign ideals, he reluctantly agreed to send Kang off to school. After all, he could not have kept Kang locked up forever. So in 1914 Kang left his family and for the first time ventured beyond the immediate environs of Dataizhuang, traveling with Chen Shunting to attend the Qingdao German School.*

Besides sending Kang to school in Qingdao, Zhang Faxiang took another, more time-honored step to curb his son's restlessness. Confucian teachings emphasized the observance of social ritual and propriety, but they also had an earthy sense of the sexual origins of

---

* Chen took his oath of brotherhood very seriously, but Kang lost any sense of obligation as time passed. A half-century later, during the Cultural Revolution, Chen was a school principal. Like many school officials, he became a target of the radical Red Guards. By that time, Kang wielded enormous power, but he made no attempt to protect his sworn brother from the outrages of the Red Guards.

human misconduct. Zhang found a girl with enough social status to marry his son, and in 1915, when Kang came home for his holiday from school, he was married off to Chen Yi, the daughter of Chen Yuzhen, a landlord in Chenjiazhuang, a nearby village.

Chen Yuzhen had every reason to be satisfied with the match he had made for his daughter. Kang would have been a prize for any local young girl to win in matrimony. Son of a prominent and wealthy family, he was brilliant and properly educated and showed every promise of a bright future. Moreover, he was exceptionally handsome, with a high forehead, fleshy, sensuous lips, and a strong, well-formed nose.

Although Kang had two children by Chen Yi between 1916 and 1924—a daughter, Zhang Yuying, and a son, Zhang Zishi—the marriage, like many arranged unions, did not last. Chen Yi, unlike Kang, was decidedly old-fashioned, and had even had her feet bound as a child. Girls with bound feet were able to wear shoes only a few inches long; Chinese raised under the old ways believed that such small feet were delicate and beautiful, giving a woman extraordinary sexual appeal. But this ancient custom meant pressing a girl's toes and heel together until the bones broke, hobbling her for life. By the early years of the twentieth century, Western influence had led to campaigns in the cities to discourage the practice, and most educated Chinese condemned foot binding as a barbarous vestige of China's past. Kang may have found small feet alluring—many men of his generation did—but he did not want a wife who in many ways could have come straight out of the tenth century. His relationship with his first bride ended in 1924, nine years after their wedding, when he moved to Shanghai, leaving Chen Yi and their two children with his parents.

Qingdao and the German middle school gave Kang his first view of the dazzling modern world, which was fast overtaking China's ancient civilization. Qingdao was only fifty miles from Kang's hometown, but it was like a foreign country. Located on a headland that separated the beautiful natural harbor of Jiaozhou Bay from the Yellow Sea, Qingdao was colonized by the Germans in 1898 after local Chinese bandits had murdered two German Protestant missionaries. For centuries, Qingdao had been no more than a fishing village, but under German administration it developed rapidly into a Western-style modern city known popularly as "Little Germany in the East" and "China's Lido." The Germans built red-roofed residences that nestled among evergreen foliage imported from northern Europe, along with churches surrounded by picket fences and grand public buildings that featured towers, colonnades, and imposing façades. Except for the oriental features of most of its inhabitants, Qingdao might have been mistaken for a late-nineteenth-century European seaport, with its broad, clean streets, public utilities, tramway lines, and even an up-to-date telephone system—all of this completed in less than a decade. The Germans also established a brewery that drew its water from the natural mountain springs of nearby Lao Shan; to this day it continues to produce China's internationally famous Tsingtao Beer. The city—still filled with architectural evidence of its foreign-dominated past—continues to serve as a resort for Communist cadres seeking relief from the torrid summers of northern China's inland cities beside the cool waters of the Yellow Sea.

Qingdao demonstrated the extraordinary dynamism of the Germans, but the German dream of colonial glory was shattered in 1914. With the outbreak of the Great War, the Japanese saw the European conflict as an opportunity to seize the German-occupied territory in Shandong. In mid-September 1914, shortly after Kang's arrival in the town, the Japanese laid siege to Qingdao, which was defended by a string of forts and artillery emplacements. The battle dragged on until early November, when the superior Japanese forces broke the German defenses and sank the warships *Jaguar* and *Kaiserin Elisabeth*, forcing the enemy to surrender. In the course of the fighting, Qingdao was shelled, its electric works damaged, and a number of civilians killed. This spectacle of foreigners struggling for control of China no doubt contributed mightily to the xenophobia that marked Kang's years as a Communist leader.

For the Chinese living in Qingdao, including Kang, the change in colonial masters made little difference in their daily lives. The Japanese continued to administer the city as a modern municipality. After repairing the damage caused by the siege, they expanded Qingdao in accordance with plans meticulously drawn up by the German administration. The Japanese occupation was also benevolent in other respects; German residents were permitted to remain and were not persecuted. Among those who stayed was Richard Wilhelm, the missionary-scholar who had founded and continued to run the school Kang attended.

Wilhelm was an exceptional and gifted man with a wide range of intellectual interests. He had come to China as a Protestant missionary but had fallen under the spell of China's ancient civilization. A passionate admirer of Chinese culture, Wilhelm actively supported attempts to defend the wisdom and beauty of the past from what he saw as the nihilistic forces of modernity. He was a prominent member of some of the conservative political clubs, such as the Literary Society to Respect Confucius, which fought rearguard actions against the influence of the West. Wilhelm's reputation as a defender of orthodox Confucian values—recognized by the imperial court in 1906, when he was honored for "meritoriously teaching the classics and methodically running the school"—encouraged fathers like Zhang Faxiang to send their sons to study under him in Qingdao.

Besides entering the battle over Chinese culture, Wilhelm was a scholar, a prolific writer on Chinese history and culture, and the translator of a number of classic texts into German. His own books—among them, *The Soul of China, Chinese Economic Psychology*, and *A Short History of Chinese Civilization*—gave him stature in European cultural circles. He became a close friend of leading intellectuals like C. G. Jung, who met Wilhelm in the early 1920s and wrote the foreword to Wilhelm's most important work, his translation into German of the *I Ching*, an ancient book of philosophy also known in the West as *The Book of Changes*. Much more than just a translation, Wilhelm's rendition of the *I Ching* incorporated extensive explanatory notes on the meaning and symbolism of an obscure yet fascinating document. Even today, the most authoritative version of the ancient Chinese view of the world remains Wilhelm's.

Under Wilhelm's direction, the Qingdao German School (since 1949 the Number Nine Middle School) was different from the scores of other Western academies that had sprung up in the coastal cities where foreign influence was strong. The school syllabus, partly Western and partly Chinese, in many ways reflected the nineteenth-century Chinese concept that Western knowledge was essentially utilitarian and Chinese knowledge was the source of wisdom and moral virtue. Instead of the usual liberal arts, Wilhelm's faculty (twenty-eight Germans and nine Chinese) imparted practical Western courses in science, geography, and German, while using the Confucian texts—*The Four Books* and *The Five Classics*—as a basis for instruction in politics and government. A strict disciplinarian, Wilhelm kept his students confined to the school grounds and banned newspapers, political discussions, and unsupervised contact with the city. The result was that Kang and his fellow-students developed only a glancing familiarity with Western ideas and acquired a rather narrow, distorted view of the world. They were aware of contemporary events in China but isolated from and ignorant of developments elsewhere.

Wilhelm's respect for Chinese civilization left an indelible imprint on Kang. Years later, he often boasted that as a student of Wilhelm's he had met some of the most eminent officials of the old Manchu regime, such as Lu Ruxiang, the tutor to the last emperor, and Wang Shoupeng, who had been awarded first place in the highest civil-service examination. At Wilhelm's invitation, Lu and Wang had taken refuge at the school after the collapse of the Qing dynasty.

While Kang was at the Qingdao German School, Wilhelm was working on his monumental translation of the *I Ching*. Containing, in Wilhelm's words, "the seasoned wisdom of thousands of years," the *I Ching* places great emphasis on the fluidity of human affairs and on the role of chance, rather than consistency, in nature. Wilhelm almost certainly lectured Kang and his fellow students on the *I Ching*; this ancient classic's assumptions about the way the world works are echoed in Kang's later approach to life and politics. The emphasis of this book on change and fortuity presages the sudden twists and turns of Kang's career: his ability to switch sides at decisive moments; his tendency to fluctuate from indolence to frenetic activity according to opportunity; and his willingness to take risks, leaving his future to chance and his own skill in guiding events. Years later, Kang was still quoting from the *I Ching* and citing it as a source for strategy in espionage.

By the time he graduated from Wilhelm's school in the summer of 1917, Kang had studied a variety of technical subjects and developed a working grasp of German. But much as the modern world fascinated Kang, his ties to family and home were stronger. After graduation, he returned to live in his father's house in Dataizhuang instead of staying in Qingdao or going farther afield to enjoy the charms of larger and more westernized cities like Shanghai.

When Kang reappeared in 1917, Dataizhuang was far from an idyllic place to live. Since the fall of the Manchu regime in 1911, law and order in the Shandong countryside had disintegrated rapidly. Rural poverty, declining government vigor, and the successive German and Japanese occupations had removed the last barriers to violent disorder. Criminal activity, always a problem, had increased sharply, finally affecting Kang's own family. One autumn night several months after his return, a gang of bandits, intending to earn a hefty ransom by kidnapping a landlord, stormed the Zhang family's walled compound. As one of Kang's brothers tried to escape over a rampart, the bandits shot him dead.

Before the year was out, the shaken family moved to the more secure walled town of Zhucheng, fifty miles due west of Qingdao. Kang's maternal grandfather lived in Zhucheng, and the Zhang family owned several parcels of land there. Zhang Faxiang chose a site on South Street in the center of the town and built an imposing home, complete with a two-story tower and a stout wall with a gatehouse for his family's protection.

Zhucheng was an ancient village of thirty thousand people, a far cry from both Dataizhuang and Qingdao. Kang's new hometown was as much exposed to Western influence as any other part of Shandong; still, it was practically medieval in its conservatism. Its economy remained based on the cultivation of barley, millet, sorghum, wheat, and vegetables. Zhucheng's narrow stone streets were crowded with sedan chairs, coolies, donkey carts, beggars, and peddlers; its marketplace was filthy, packed with jostling animals, peasants, and traders.

But the town was not without entertainments. Gaudy plays and operas were staged regularly by roving troupes of actors who painted their faces and performed dramas from Chinese history and romance. Hawkers sold Shandong fare like *bauzi* and *mantou*, the traditional dumplings and bread of northern China. In restaurants, wine shops, and opium dens, sing-song girls sweetened the life of local gentlemen and affluent travelers with their music and humor, lighting opium pipes for them and sleeping with a favored few. Outside the eastern gate, an occasional spectacle, applauded by crowds, was the beheading of criminals. In later life, Kang would flaunt a taste for several diversions he had first encountered in Zhucheng: keeping a special cook, patronizing traditional theater, and personally supervising the torture of his victims.

Once he and his family had settled in Zhucheng, Kang studied for a year at a local training academy for teachers. Then, from 1918 until 1924, he taught music, among other subjects, in a primary school run by the county government. The school was quite old-fashioned by his standards; once again, Kang was drawn back into a way of life that had hardly changed since the mid-nineteenth century.

In 1917, Kang reached his twentieth year and thus, by Chinese reckoning, attained adulthood. Like many young men coming of age, he adopted a new name, Zhang Yuxian ("The Zhang Who Is Affluent First"). Two years later, he changed his name again, becoming Zhang

Shuping ("Zhang the Peaceful Uncle") until 1924, when he departed for Shanghai.

Tradition encouraged scholars, artists, and officials to adopt many pseudonyms, usually with significant meanings or poetic overtones. Painters and artists often hid behind a bewildering array of art names, and dictionaries were compiled to help identify the authors whose signatures appeared on paintings and works of calligraphy. As the years went by, Kang's revolutionary career demanded secrecy; changing names helped him sever links to his past.

Kang's years in Zhucheng further corroded his faith in the old, dynastic world. Although daily life still lumbered on in its archaic pattern, popular confidence in the old ways was diminishing and people were overcome by a sense of drift, decay, and decline. Part of their foreboding of imminent disintegration sprang from the rising tide of violence etched so vividly in Kang's memory by his brother's murder and reflected generally in the forces of political and intellectual discontent seething below the surface of Chinese society.

In 1919, these forces exploded into the open. On May 4, students in Peking rioted in protest over the warlord regime's weakness in the face of Japan's demand to be granted legal title to the former German territories in Shandong. The riots tapped a huge and proud nation's frustration over its internal chaos, its increasingly apparent backwardness, and its powerlessness to challenge foreign aggression. The demonstrations inspired calls for national rejuvenation and for a new culture to replace the decadent customs that had survived from the last century of Manchu rule. The May Fourth Movement, as it came to be known, was one of the watersheds of modern Chinese history.* It released a generation of educated young Chinese from the hypnotic grip of their ancestors' ways and gave modern form and content to their disappointment. What followed was a period of intense excitement as young people rejected classical language, literature, art, and philosophy and discovered scientific, literary, and philosophical traditions that offered alternatives to the crumbling icons of antiquity. To dramatize this rejection, some young Chinese went to the extent of

---

* The May Fourth demonstrations have posed a difficult problem for subsequent Chinese regimes. No Chinese government, including the Communists', has dared to deny the nationalistic credentials of the May Fourth Movement, but its antiauthoritarian tendencies have worried China's modern-day rulers. The May Fourth tradition was an important precedent for the student protests in 1989.

severing all ties with their families, changing their surnames or, in some cases, refusing to use a surname at all.

Propelled by anticolonial fervor, the May Fourth Movement cut deep in Shandong. The international status of the province had been the original issue behind the student riots in Peking; moreover, nationalism, xenophobia, and especially antipathy toward Japan ran at a fever pitch in Shandong. Zhucheng and the surrounding towns and villages were the site of extensive student activity. Wang Jinmei, one of the radical leaders of the day and later a prominent figure in the fledgling Communist Party, came to Zhucheng to help direct protests against the warlord regime and the foreign imperialists.

The tumultuous events of the May Fourth Movement reawakened Kang to the humiliations inflicted on China by foreign powers. Kang had previously been isolated in the Qingdao German School or absorbed in pursuing pleasures, but he suddenly realized that the country and civilization he had taken for granted were in danger of collapsing. Enraged by the same patriotic impulses as his contemporaries, he began participating in local demonstrations, reading the revolutionary books and magazines distributed in Zhucheng, and experiencing the sense of destruction at the heart of the movement.

In later life, Kang cited the year 1919 as the point when he parted with his family and joined the revolution. In 1965, he told a Communist leader from New Zealand, G. V. Wilcox, that he had broken with his "landlord family" at this time and discarded his family name of Zhang in favor of Kang Sheng. Kang's claims were only fictions to enhance his revolutionary credentials; he wanted to create the impression that he had been among the first Communist leaders to take up the cause of revolution. Kang had not repudiated his family, as he asserted to Wilcox, nor had he left Zhucheng for one of the more modern cities where he could have immersed himself in a new culture and escaped from his father's old-style household. On the contrary, Kang remained in Zhucheng and taught in the county primary school for five more years after the May Fourth Movement had inflamed the hearts and minds of China's youth. He continued to enjoy many of the more decadent pastimes of the well-to-do, attending plays, gambling, and flirting with actresses and girls in the sing-song houses.

Kang also continued to read the radical literature that was becoming increasingly popular with educated young people and to discuss China's problems with progressive friends. He grew particularly close to his maternal cousin Li Yuchao and to a young writer and native of Zhucheng, Meng Chao. Both men had radical aspirations. Meanwhile, Kang's relations with his father worsened: Zhang Faxiang disapproved of both his frivolity and his rebelliousness.

During this period, as Kang was discovering the modern world, he struck up a relationship that would endure almost until his death fifty years later. Reinforced by regional origins and a common dialect,* this alliance proved to be of great importance not only to Kang's role as a Communist grandee but also to the course of Chinese Communist history. In his last year in Zhucheng, Kang, then twenty-six, met a girl in her early teens† called Li Yunhe. Fourteen years later, as Jiang Qing, she became Chairman Mao's fourth wife and Kang's special channel of communication with Mao.

There are several versions of how Kang Sheng and Jiang Qing first met. According to "Zhongkan," the Zhang residence on South Street in central Zhucheng was only ten minutes by foot from Jiang Qing's impoverished quarters in the eastern part of town. Although Kang and Jiang Qing were not quite neighbors, the proximity of their homes led to their initial meeting as the young girl walked to school along South Street. By another account, the pair met at Kang's primary school: Jiang Qing told Roxane Witke, the American scholar who in effect wrote her authorized biography, that she spent a semester at a "primary school run by the county." The Zhucheng county government probably established only one such school, and the likelihood that she attended Kang's school is great.

Perhaps the most intriguing version of how the future Kang Sheng and the future Jiang Qing first met was provided by Zhu Zhongli, a Chinese writer who is the widow of Wang Jiaxiang, a senior Communist leader and onetime ambassador to Moscow. Jiang Qing's mother took a job as a maid in the Zhang household, she said, and Jiang Qing came to live in the servants' quarters of Kang's home. If

---

* The Chinese spoken in Shandong is, in theory, a version of the Mandarin or *putonghua* ("common speech") that represents the national language and is based on the Peking dialect. In fact, however, like the Mandarin spoken by many of the older Chinese leaders who do not come from Peking itself, Shandong Mandarin is clearly differentiated by its own idioms, expressions, tones, and accent. In its purest form, Shandong dialect is almost incomprehensible to other Chinese. Kang retained a heavy Shandong accent throughout his life.

† There is some uncertainty about the date of Jiang Qing's birth. She told Witke that she was born in 1914, but Edgar Snow and other sources have put it at 1912.

this indeed was the case, the claims by Kang's critics in the late 1970s that he had had an early sexual relationship with Jiang Qing become more plausible. As classical novels like *The Dream of the Red Chamber* showed, maidservants and their daughters were often expected to grant sexual favors to the master of the house and his sons. But Zhu Zhongli's account was presented in traditional Chinese literary form, as a casual history, and many of the incidents she reports may be fictitious.

There are also other lurid accounts of the origins of Kang's relationship with Jiang Qing. China watchers in the Soviet Union have asserted that as a teenager Jiang Qing spent some months as the concubine of a landlord named Wang, through whom she met Kang, a frequent visitor to Wang's residence. This claim, however, was made in 1970 and may have been disinformation spread to embarrass China at the height of the Sino-Soviet split, when the Russians had few scruples in making assertions that reflected badly on Mao's colleagues, especially Kang Sheng, who by then had evolved into Russia's archenemy.

Highly placed sources in Peking insist to this day that Kang's relationship with Jiang Qing had a sexual dimension. Even Hu Yaobang's confidential denunciation strongly hinted at it. Perhaps they are simply attempts to further blacken the names of two disgraced leaders, but such claims are plausible. There was a significant difference in their ages, but Jiang Qing was a precocious girl. Moreover, in China at that time, both men and women started their sexual lives at an early age. A pretty girl from a humble background, Jiang Qing surely was well aware that sex could be her ticket to a better world.* Kang, for his part, had a reputation for sexual escapades and might have slept with her, even if she was a schoolgirl or a friend's concubine, but especially if she was the daughter of one of his family's household servants.

The evidence that Kang Sheng and Jiang Qing were once lovers is strong but not conclusive. If the accounts of a sexual relationship are true, it is entirely possible that Kang Sheng was the first of Jiang Qing's many lovers—that the man who in a sense was instrumental in

---

* Jiang Qing told Roxane Witke in 1972 that "sex is engaging in the first rounds, but what sustains interest in the long run is power," a tacit admission that she saw a connection between her capacity to appeal to men and her efforts to secure position and influence.

deflowering the Chinese Communist Revolution also deflowered its future first lady. Kang Sheng carried to his grave the true story of this remarkable relationship, and it is probable that Jiang Qing did the same.

When the two first met, their friendship must have been nothing more than an incidental pleasure. Kang was growing tired of life in a country town far removed from the fabled excitement and stimulation of China's modern cities. In the summer of 1924, after a quarter-century in his home province, he left for Shanghai, leaving behind his parents and his wife and children, and paving the way for his life in the Communist movement. Kang's cousin Li Yuchao and his progressive friend Meng Chao accompanied him on the journey to Shanghai.

The increasing friction in his relationship with his father precipitated Kang's decision to leave Zhucheng. According to rumor, Kang was driven away by his father for accumulating debts through inveterate gambling. Stories also circulated that he had been caught in bed with his father's concubine. There had to have been some problem between Kang and his father, because when Kang reached Shanghai, he was forced to count his pennies. Normally, as the son of an affluent landlord, he would have received a handsome allowance; nothing less than a grave offense against Confucian propriety would have caused his father to drastically limit financial support.

Except for a brief visit two years later, Kang did not return to his native province until 1947. Large tracts of Shandong had been occupied by the Communist armies by then, and he was appointed head of the Party organization there. But Shandong left a lifelong mark on him. In later life, Kang would present himself as an expert on Marxist theory, international communism, and modern security techniques, but he never entirely divested himself of the legacy—the callousness, the resentments, the chauvinism, the tastes in theater and music, the ambivalent sense of the grandeur of China's past and the promise of the future—of having grown to manhood in the province of Confucius.

Chapter II

SHANGHAI,
HAVEN FOR
REVOLUTIONARIES

IT WAS IN SHANGHAI that Kang completed his transformation from wayward son of the upper class into committed Communist activist. He was involved in some of the landmark events of the Party's formative years—widespread protests against the British in 1925, urban uprisings in late 1926 and early 1927, and the KMT's devastating purge of Communists on April 12, 1927. Kang also laid the basis for his reputation as an expert on security and espionage during the nine years he spent in China's largest city.

Shanghai would have appealed to anyone with a sense of adventure. By July 1924, when Kang first wandered down its streets and alleys, Shanghai had become China's most populous city and the largest Western-style city in the Far East. To a bright young man of twenty-six, Shanghai offered spectacular possibilities: a free-wheeling commercial system, a dynamic and creative population, and an underworld economy of gambling, drug smuggling, and prostitution. Observers described Shanghai variously as "a city for sale"; a paradise for gamblers, chiselers, and other adventurers; and a place where a fortune could be wasted with ease. Or stolen: an abundance of wealthy people attracted equal numbers of thieves. Shanghai was truly a city of opportunity—ranging from the commercial to the cultural, from the criminal to the revolutionary—that lured and then held people even after their dreams had faded.

The most cosmopolitan city in the world at that time, Shanghai had a foreign population embracing Englishmen, Americans, Frenchmen, Germans, Russians, Japanese, Mexicans, and Filipinos. No other city in Asia could match its variety or sophistication. Stylish art deco skyscrapers lined both the Bund—the broad boulevard running beside the muddy Huangpu River—and Nanking Road, the teeming shopping street that led inland. Spacious mansions, set in walled compounds filled with flowerbeds and trees, graced residential areas. Comfortable apartment buildings housed the growing middle class of businessmen and professionals. Acres of Parisian-style row houses sprawled across "French Town," and Packards, La Salles, Oldsmobiles, Fords, and other chauffeur-driven foreign motor cars threaded their way through dense jams of coolies and rickshaw boys.*

A racetrack and dozens of nightclubs and cabarets presented an endless variety of entertainment for people with money. Restaurants served practically every form of cuisine from around the world, but the most popular was the local Shanghainese style of cooking, with specialties like crab and other seafood delicacies. For the pleasuring of other senses, Shanghai also offered a life of decadence. Brothels were almost as plentiful as restaurants; some Chinese establishments served as both. Lavish villas staffed with beautiful young girls catered to the wealthy, but almost anyone could afford a visit to one of the many hovels filled with the sick and the haggard. Opium dens flourished, although they were technically illegal and most of the opium had to be imported by criminal gangs. Glowing with luxury, pleasure, and every modern convenience, Shanghai certainly deserved its reputation as "the Pearl of the Orient."

But the patrons of the villas and apartments, the private clubs and restaurants, the chauffeur-driven motor cars, and the man-powered rickshaws represented a minuscule proportion of Shanghai's two million souls. Multitudes of coolies and factory workers existed amid grinding and inescapable poverty. Shanghai was a city of paupers; in winter, when icy winds whipped across gray skies, the corpses of beggars were gathered from the streets like excrement. Disease and crime were rampant, and death was a casual matter.

Some Chinese were offended by Shanghai's crass foreign values,

---

* In 1930, rickshaws outnumbered motor vehicles by almost five to one. There were 4,508 cars, 1,008 trucks, 263 horse-drawn carriages, 6,707 private rickshaws, and 17,792 public rickshaws in the city of Shanghai, apart from the French Concession and the International Settlement.

but Kang's three years in the modern, German-built seaport of Qingdao allowed him to settle in with ease. Hailing from nearby Shandong, he could count on the assistance of fellow provincials who had come to Shanghai to make their fortunes. Indeed, the Shandong community represented a sizable faction, many of them active in the city's notorious Red Gang and Green Gang, the criminal syndicates that lived by an ancient code of honor and controlled the city's thriving underworld. Kang's funds were tightly limited by his father, but his family connections, his education, and his good looks combined to guarantee that he could live tolerably well. Kang led a student's modest existence, but he never faced real economic hardship.

Soon after his arrival, Kang again changed his name. He retained the surname Zhang but adopted a new personal name, Yun, which he wrote with the character for "to weed," suggesting that he meant to use his time in Shanghai eradicating metaphorical weeds from his private garden. Kang also took another, more profound step. Together with his two friends from Zhucheng, Li Yuchao and Meng Chao, he enrolled at Shanghai University, which had gained a reputation as the most radical campus in China.

Shanghai University was a product of the political freedom that grew out of the city's complex and unique legal status. Shanghai was governed by three separate administrations—British, French, and Chinese; the resulting legal ambiguities and loopholes helped account for the city's flamboyance. The heart of the city, the International Settlement, was run by the British-dominated Shanghai Municipal Council on behalf of an eleven-nation consortium in which both the United States and Japan had a major say. Adjacent to the southern boundary of this anglicized enclave was the smaller, more elegant, and more corrupt "French Town," the concession the French had retained, in defiance of the British, as a separate entity from the International Settlement. Encircling both foreign sections was Greater Shanghai, a sprawling patchwork of slums, mansions, factories, mills, muddy creeks and canals, market gardens, and temples under Chinese administration.

Local warlords administered Greater Shanghai until 1927, when the KMT unified most of China under a Nationalist government based in Nanking. The military governor for most of the 1920s was Marshal Sun Chuanfang, whose ultraconservative administration ruled Shanghai and the surrounding provinces with the utmost ruthlessness and cruelty. Radicals and agitators who fell into the hands of Sun's soldiers were often treated like murderers or pirates and summarily beheaded.

The International Settlement and the French Concession, by contrast, were islands of freedom and due process in a sea of medieval despotism. The Chinese population in the two foreign districts was insulated from the brutalities of the warlords, allowing Shanghai to develop a new, hybrid mode of culture and politics. To Chinese of the day, "Shanghai style" meant anything that was modern, foreign, original, and bold, as opposed to the stale and archaic "Peking style," which was more prevalent across the country.

Shanghai's foreign enclaves attracted drug smugglers, adventurers, carpetbaggers, swindlers, gunrunners, and spies, along with a collection of dissident Chinese intellectuals, artists, poets, novelists, revolutionaries, defeated warlords, and retired politicians. By Kang's time, much of China's most daring cultural and intellectual activity was centered in these pockets of Shanghai. The city's publishing houses, bookshops, and newspapers generated an enormous quantity of modern literature, and many of China's most celebrated modern writers worked there at one time or another. The most renowned among the literary community were perhaps Lu Xun, a critic, essayist, and short-story writer; Mao Dun, a Communist novelist who was later minister of culture; Ba Jin, an anarchist writer; and Guo Moruo, a poet, historian, and scholar.

Shanghai's eclecticism proved the ideal breeding ground for the Chinese Communist Party, which was founded there in 1921 by thirteen men, including Mao Zedong. The organizers held their initial meeting at a Shanghai girls' school, but fear of police surveillance forced them to move to a pleasure barge on a nearby lake. From 1924 until April 1927, the Communists were allies of the KMT—then a nationalistic and revolutionary party with strong ties to the Soviet Union.*

Kang's school, Shanghai University, began as a teachers' college

---

* The KMT's relationship with the Soviet Union fluctuated over time. Bound together since 1917 by an anti-imperialist outlook, the two sides fell out when Chiang Kai-shek attacked the Communists in 1927. Ties between the KMT and the Russians were restored in 1932, when Stalin saw the KMT as a useful ally against Japan. After the defeat of Japan in World War II, civil war erupted between the KMT and the CCP; the Soviets sided with the Communists, although Stalin had not expected a KMT defeat.

but was transformed in 1923, when Communist-inspired students mutinied and seized control. The CCP relocated the college from the Chinese suburb of Zhabei to the International Settlement, where classes were held in two Western-style villas surrounded by gardens. The students, including Kang, lived in dormitories in the nearby lanes and alleys. The chancellor of the university was a scholarly and highly venerated KMT elder, Yu Youren. Ordinarily, Yu was absent, however, and the school actually was run by Shao Lizi, who in name was a member of the KMT but was very close to the CCP. Shao was not the only left-wing influence in the university. Two dedicated Communists, Qu Qiubai, a writer and theorist, and Deng Zhongxia, an organizer and agitator, set up a curriculum that would appeal to prospective Party members.

One of Kang's teachers, Qu Qiubai was known for his stormy personal life as much as for his intellect. Qu was one side of a love triangle with a woman writer named Ding Ling and a student of his, Yang Zhihua, whom he later married.* Qu's combination of romanticism and revolutionary fervor was a strong lure to China's youth. Having spent three years in Soviet Russia, he could speak from direct experience about Marxism–Leninism in action. Qu was a compelling, passionate speaker; Yang Zhihua, a fellow student of Kang's, later recalled that Kang took such careful notes of her future husband's lectures that students who missed classes always came to him for help. It was Qu's vivid and entrancing picture of the inevitable Bolshevik victory that converted Kang into a professional revolutionary.

Kang chose the school's social-science course, which was more politically oriented than the other two fields of instruction offered, Chinese literature and English literature. He soon immersed himself in studies of dialectical materialism, political economy, Marxism, and the history of social evolution—subjects designed to undermine belief in traditional society and provide a blueprint for a brave new future. Lacking all but the haziest notion of Marxist theory when he arrived at Shanghai University, Kang set out to cultivate his reputation as an intellectual. Years later, Mao told Anna Louise Strong, an American journalist and Communist propagandist, that Kang was one of the

---

* Qu's private life was part of the extensive web of personal ties that held CCP leaders together. Yang Zhihua had previously been married to Shen Jiannong, the son of Shen Dingyi, one of the founders of the CCP along with Mao Zedong. Yang left Shen to marry Qu, but Qu and Shen remained close allies.

few college graduates among the early revolutionary leaders. In reality, Kang was a scholar only when measured against his fellow Party leaders; it was not academic accomplishments that gave him standing as an expert on ideology but his verbal agility and his willingness to exploit his position to silence his critics.

But Shanghai University, after all, was a training ground for revolutionaries, not scholars. Formal lectures were just one element in the syllabus. Study meetings to discuss contemporary issues—the threat of imperialism, the plight of the workers, official corruption—were combined with practical experience in agitation. Students were encouraged to regularly conduct propaganda work, distribute handbills on street corners, and run discussion groups in factories. Their objective was nothing less than to harness the latent power of Shanghai's enormous working class.

While Kang was at the university, his radical sentiments crystalized into deep identification with the Communist cause and completed his break with tradition. The cumulative effect of the May Fourth Movement, the foreign ideas he had absorbed at Richard Wilhelm's school in Qingdao, and the bitterness of the quarrel with his father had combined to alienate him forever from the old order. Influenced by the oratory of men like Qu Qiubai and Deng Zhongxia, Kang discovered in Marxism an intellectually and emotionally satisfying substitute for his lost Confucian world.

The CCP appealed to Kang also because it had the potential to become a global cause that could bring him power and prestige. The Party's emphasis on secrecy, too, intrigued him; throughout his career, Kang was a secretive, power-craving man who enjoyed, as historians said of the Empress Dowager, "issuing orders from behind the curtain."

Early in 1925, after about six months at the university, Kang became one of the first new recruits in the CCP.* Joining the Party was not the dangerous step it became two years later, because the Communists still were allied with the KMT, Sun Yat-sen's party, which had been behind the Republican Revolution of 1911. Previously outgunned by the warlords, the KMT had acquired prestige and

* Party membership grew from about forty to nine hundred between 1924 and May 30, 1925. Within two years, there were sixty thousand CCP members; another forty thousand belonged to the Communist Youth League. By 1930, KMT aggression against the CCP had reduced the number of Communists in China to seventeen thousand.

influence. Not only were Sun and his fellow leaders recognized as men with a vision for China's future, but the KMT had built up a military base in Canton that forced rivals to take it seriously. Aided by Vasili Blyukher, a young Russian general who operated in China under the name of Galen, the KMT ran a military school at Whampoa, just outside Canton. The Whampoa Academy, staffed by about forty Soviet advisers, produced hundreds of well-trained officers who formed the core of the most modern army in China. The KMT's combination of national standing and armed force gave a measure of protection to its sympathizers, including members of its Communist coalition partner. Kang was merely joining the radical wing of the Nationalist movement.

The circumstances of Kang's admission to the CCP remain unclear.* Kang gave several conflicting accounts of how he had joined the Party, at various times naming three different sponsors. One was Wang Youzhi, a cadre from Shanxi Province in northwestern China, who later rejected Kang's claim, insisting that as a lowly member of the Communist Youth League at the time, he was not qualified to sponsor anyone for Party membership. The second person named was Li Puhuan, but like Wang Youzhi, he strenuously denied responsibility for Kang's entry into the Party. The third sponsor cited was Kang's own cousin, Li Yuchao, who equivocated whenever the question was put to him.

Within weeks after Kang joined the Party, the local Communist leaders assigned him to work as an organizer of the city's left-wing labor movement. In Shanghai, with its swarms of poverty-stricken workers, the creation of a mass labor movement was a top Communist priority. Shanghai was the only city in China with an authentic proletariat, and the Chinese Communists of the day, heavily influenced by Soviet thinking, expected that the country's revolution would be born there.

In February 1925, Kang participated in organizing a mass strike against Japanese companies. Along with trade union cadres and members of the "volunteer squad," he swore alliance in a traditional ceremony that involved drinking the blood of a slaughtered animal mixed

---

* Hu Yaobang revealed that the investigation of Kang conducted by the Party during the late 1970s failed to turn up any evidence that illuminated this mystery. Kang had removed all the papers from his personal file, substituting a version of his career that he had written himself and that was silent as to his entry into the Party.

with a fiery grain alcohol. In an intense, highly charged atmosphere, Kang and the other labor agitators shouted an oath as they swallowed the bloody spirits:

> *Oppose the Japanese to the end,*
> *Don't resume work before winning;*
> *Support the union, root out scabs,*
> *Face life and death together.*
> *If we are false-hearted,*
> *May celestial thunder strike us dead.*

The strike lasted for three months, until a foreman in a Japanese-owned factory shot and killed one of Kang's fellow students, Gu Zhenghong. Gu was masquerading as a mill worker in order to agitate the workers against "foreign dwarfs"—the Chinese term for Japanese. Gu's slaying on May 15, 1925, provoked a crisis, culminating on May 30 in a huge, Communist-organized demonstration of workers and students in the International Settlement. These protests were a milestone in popular opposition to foreign exploitation, as well as the first major Communist action in which Kang was involved.

Initially, the Japanese had been the main targets of the uprisings. But when mobs of angry demonstrators milled around the Louza Police Station off Nanking Road, a contingent of the Shanghai Municipal Police (SMP)—the British-run force that maintained a surprising measure of law and order in the International Settlement—panicked and opened fire, leaving ten dead and over fifty wounded. The police action wrenched the focus of the Communist activity from the Japanese to the British, releasing a torrent of fury throughout China. A protracted strike and trade embargo against British commercial interests swept the major coastal towns and cities, including Hong Kong. Hostility ran so high that the domestic staff of the British legation in Peking refused to report to work.

Kang's involvement in the May Thirtieth Movement gave him direct contact with three of the Party's top leaders: Liu Shaoqi, Zhang Guotao, and Li Lisan. In later years, Kang had occasional but limited dealings with Zhang, a founder of the CCP who abandoned the Communist cause in 1938, but he worked closely with both Liu, a tireless and methodical organizer who became Mao's deputy in the 1950s, and Li, a romantic and reckless activist who was the chief architect of Communist strategy in the late 1920s.

In the tense aftermath of the May Thirtieth Movement, the police began to pay closer attention to the radicalism of Shanghai University. Increasingly conscious of the dangers of Bolshevism in China, the British administration forced the university out of the International Settlement, and the campus was shifted back to Zhabei, where it occupied some cramped premises on Qingyun Road, not far from its original location. Kang continued to attend classes after the move; years later, he was still impressed by the attentiveness of the students in such crowded conditions. "When we had classes at the old Shanghai University in Qingyun Road people were always jammed together tight," Kang recalled. "The building was old, there were a lot of people, and the upper floors shook as if about to collapse. But everyone just listened quietly, right up to when the class ended."

After the crisis caused by the May Thirtieth demonstrations had passed, the Party managers assigned Kang to work as a secretary in the Shanghai General Union—an appointment that initiated his steady progress up the Party hierarchy. In 1926, he graduated from street-level organizer and joined the committee that controlled Communist activity within Shanghai University. Given the university's role in mobilizing student support, Kang had landed an important job, which he used to build a network of contacts among the young intellectuals who were being inducted into the Party. He also started to develop a wide-ranging knowledge of the Communist organization in Shanghai and the cadres who led it. Many of its early leaders either taught or studied at the university.

Several of Kang's teachers, including Deng Zhongxia, Yun Daiying, and Zhang Tailei, were captured and shot by the KMT; Kang later boasted of his personal ties with the Party's early martyrs. A number of Kang's fellow students who had survived the danger of the times went on to illustrious careers. His contemporaries included scores of bright, dynamic, and angry young Chinese like Qin Bang-xian, a magistrate's son from Zhejiang Province, who styled himself Bo Gu; Wang Jiaxiang, a graduate of St. Jacob's Senior High School in Anhui Province, who had protested against compulsory Bible reading and prayer; a Hunanese named Liu Xiao, who was educated by the American Christian Reformed Church and introduced to Marxism by a Chinese Christian pastor; and a veteran of the May Fourth Movement named Yang Shangkun, who came from a rich landed family in Sichuan Province. Kang was getting to know the young men who would one day rule China.

Kang was also involved in Communist campaigns of urban agitation after the anti-British strike finally ended. These demonstrations grew ever more ambitious, climaxing in late 1926 and early 1927 in a trio of armed uprisings against the warlord rulers of Greater Shanghai. Kang was at the forefront of the reckless attacks on conservative authorities, starting on October 26, 1926, when he led a detachment of students in the first workers' revolt.

This uprising, however, was short-lived. The warlord troops smashed the poorly prepared workers and students in several bloody encounters. A number of Communist leaders, including Tao Jingxuan and Qi Zuoyao, were executed, along with ten other Party workers. The revolt was the first in a series of violent actions planned to assist the so-called Northern Expedition, the political and military campaign launched from Canton by KMT forces to push the warlords out of central and northern China and unite the country under a new, Nationalist administration.

Unlike his more bookish fellow students, Kang had been adept at fighting with swords, staffs, and bare hands since his youth in Shandong, and he was well qualified for violent undertakings. In modern terms, he was street-smart—a perfect urban guerrilla. Kang's combat skills led to a new assignment in the fateful year of 1927: he was to run the eastern Shanghai branch of the Party, one of three in the city, with responsibility for the main muscle of the Shanghai revolution, the urban workers. Kang's promotion brought him closer to the top Communist leaders; the three Shanghai branches reported to the Jiangsu–Zhejiang Regional Committee, the powerful office directly below the Central Committee, which directed all Communist activity in Shanghai and the nearby provinces.

Kang was also at the center of the next two uprisings. The second, which broke out on February 19, 1927, was larger than the October riot, but was brutally suppressed by the troops of Marshal Sun Chuanfang's ally, the colorful warlord Zhang Zongchang, known as the Dog Meat General. A giant of a man, Zhang was renowned for his international harem as much as for his skills on the battlefield. A squad of Zhang's sword-wielding executioners roamed Shanghai, slicing off the heads of any strikers or agitators they encountered and hanging these gory trophies from city lampposts.

The third revolt was carefully planned and far more effective. Starting on March 21, 1927, with a general strike of over 100,000 workers, it was timed to coincide with the approach to Shanghai of

the Nationalist KMT armies. After months of fighting and politick-
ing, the KMT forces began extending their hold over the entire Lower
Yangtze region. The attack on the warlords in Shanghai meshed perfectly with the broader KMT strategy of using propaganda, political
agitation, urban revolts, and labor unrest to undermine the forces of
archmilitarists like Marshal Sun and General Zhang.

The more conservative KMT leaders like Chiang Kai-shek saw
the Shanghai insurrection as part of their overall campaign, but the
Communists hoped the armed revolts in China's largest city would
transcend the Nationalists' narrow objectives. Realizing that the insurrection, if successful, would give them power over all but the
foreign-controlled sector of the city, they anticipated an explosive
revolutionary situation. The CCP leaders, inspired by the Bolshevik
victory in Petrograd and the Soviets' doctrine that revolution would
start in the cities, believed themselves to be on the crest of a historic
movement that would sweep away the conservative forces, including
the right wing of the KMT.

The March rebellion was commanded by three well-known
Shanghai Communists: Zhao Shiyan, Luo Yinong, and Wang Shouhua. Also among the leaders was a suave and skilled administrator
named Zhou Enlai. Born in 1898, the same year as Kang, Zhou had
led an unsettled and poverty-stricken early life. A child when his
father died, Zhou was passed around among relatives in Huai'an,
Shenyang, and Tianjin. In spite of his grim childhood and adolescence, Zhou had a lighter side. Conspicuous for his extremely fine
features and high-pitched voice,* he had made a name for himself
playing female roles in dramas during his school days. Offstage, Zhou
courted Deng Yingchao, a student who belonged to the Awareness
Society, a radical discussion group; their six-year romance was to lead
to marriage in Canton in 1925.

After completing his education, Zhou moved to Japan in 1917
and lived there until 1920, when he returned to China and within the
year got arrested for participating with radical students in antigov-
ernment demonstrations in Tianjin. Still frustrated by his family's
financial problems and China's degradations at the hands of foreigners, Zhou went to France in 1920 as a worker-student. He helped

---

* Years later, an Indian newspaper, *The Statesman*, observed that Zhou "retains his
high contralto voice, which seems hardly to belong to this great revolutionary and
statesman."

establish the European branch of the CCP in Paris, where he became a full-time revolutionary. For three years, he traveled across France, Belgium, and Germany, recruiting members for the tiny movement. He returned to China in 1924 to take up the post of deputy political commissar at the Whampoa Academy, where he became the center of a network of young Communists who worked secretly to give a more revolutionary orientation to the KMT. After taking part in a KMT military campaign against warlord forces around Swatow in 1925, Zhou made his way to Shanghai, where he worked with local Communists to organize an armed revolt.

Kang's mission in the March uprising was to mobilize and command the workers from the factories, shops, newspaper publishers, tramway company, and postal and government offices of the eastern part of the city. This dangerous work put him on the front line of the fighting. At 7 A.M. on March 21, he received secret orders from the regional committee to concentrate the combat forces at his disposal. Within an hour, he had met two dozen or so of the picket organizers under his command in a small house on the rue du Siemen in the French Concession, just outside the west gate of the old Chinese city. By 10 A.M., when his men were armed and ready, Kang reported to Communist headquarters in the four-story Commercial Press building on Pao Shan Road in Zhabei, just across the boundary of the International Settlement.

Zhou Enlai and the other leaders assigned Kang the task of attacking the Fifth District Police Station, capturing its arsenal, and then joining an offensive against the Northern Railway Station. The action against the police station started in the early afternoon. "After a member of the Workers Pickets threw a hand grenade at the entrance of the Fifth District Police Station," Kang wrote ten years later, "a salvo of gunshots followed in quick succession, and the action started immediately." By 4 P.M., when the fighting ended, many of the strategic locations in Greater Shanghai had fallen to the workers.

After his victory, Kang led his forces, re-equipped with police weapons, to the Northern Railway Station. One of the key strategic targets in Shanghai, this was a large, fortified brick building strongly defended by warlord troops not only armed with machine guns, artillery, and armored cars but also supported by a unit of White Russian mercenaries. The battle, which directly involved Kang, took place mainly in the surrounding streets and alleys, as the two sides fought from block to block. On the evening of March 21, the warlord troops torched the buildings nearby, so that the Communists had to fight the fires as well as the station's defenders. The rebels tried to rush the station the following morning, but the soldiers had planted land mines in the main entrances, and the Communists were beaten back with heavy losses.

By the evening of March 22, the armed workers had overwhelmed the warlord outposts in most of Shanghai. The Northern Railway Station remained the sole center of resistance. Kang and his men charged again in the early evening, finally forcing the defenders to retreat. The White Russians escaped into the adjacent International Settlement, while the Chinese soldiers did their best to flee the city.

At 11 that night, Kang and his colleague Guo Bohe, who led the Communist organization in western Shanghai, reported to Zhou Enlai, Zhao Shiyan, and Luo Yinong in a newly established command center on Canton Road. After discussing the capture of the station, the group turned to the next tasks facing the Communists—establishing a "citizens' government" and holding a public meeting of Communist activists in the Huzhou Guild building.

The strategy session lasted until after 1 A.M. Kang and Guo finally made their way back to their posts through the empty streets. Fires burned through the night, illuminating the revolutionary banners that fluttered from buildings. Kang and Guo stopped at a late-night restaurant on Jukong Road and had two bowls of rice porridge and a bottle of Shaoxing rice wine. Ten years later, Kang wrote that he never again matched the happiness of that midnight supper.

During the two earlier uprisings, the warlord armies had successfully massed against the rebels; but this time, under pressure from approaching KMT columns commanded by Chiang Kai-shek, they collapsed. Many soldiers defected to the Communists; others fled in disarray; any units that remained intact retreated. By the time Chiang Kai-shek's gunboat sailed up the Huangpu River on March 26, almost the entire city was in the hands of the Communist-led workers. Only the International Settlement and the French Concession, guarded by foreign troops behind their sandbagged barricades, had not fallen to the radicals.

The Communist leaders were convinced that victory over the warlord administration in Shanghai was the beginning of a revolutionary upsurge that would bring about a new social order. They organized a commune in Zhabei, took over key government buildings, and worked to establish a citizens' administration. But while seeking to consolidate their hold and advance the revolutionary process before the conservatives could intervene, the Communists failed to take adequate measures to protect themselves. However suspicious they might have been of Chiang Kai-shek and the right wing of the KMT, they remained confident that their victory in Shanghai would guarantee their safety.

On top of that, the Communists would have had difficulty making overt preparations to use force against their Nationalist allies. Stalin issued orders through the Comintern—the Soviet-controlled organization that directed the international Communist movement—emphasizing the need to maintain a common front with the KMT. From Stalin's perspective, it was more urgent to undermine Western influence to the east of the Soviet Union than to spread communism, and the KMT appeared to offer the best bet for accomplishing his goal. Sun Yat-sen, the founder of the KMT, had been a staunch supporter of Soviet views. Many young Kuomintang cadres had studied in the Soviet Union, so Britain and the United States saw the KMT as part of a dangerous anti-imperialist movement hostile to Western interests. Most important of all, the expanding but still tiny six-year-old Chinese Communist Party was clearly, in many ways, at a disadvantage vis-à-vis the immensely more prestigious and powerful KMT.

The rising star in the KMT was Chiang Kai-shek. Stalin believed there was nothing to fear from him and promised his colleagues that although Chiang was playing a cunning game with them, he would be crushed: "We shall squeeze him like a lemon and then get rid of him." But Stalin and the Chinese Communists grossly underestimated the iron-willed Chiang's capacity to cross them and his ability to generate a following. With his shaven head, bristling dark mustache, and penetrating stare, Chiang certainly looked born to lead men. He would be a thorn in the side of the Communists, Soviets and Chinese alike, until 1949.

Chiang was a decade older than Kang, Zhou, and most of the Communist leaders, and he shared the aspirations and anguish of the educated men of his generation—intense patriotism, suspicion of foreigners, and a commitment to modernization tempered by a profound sense of family loyalty and Confucian values. But Chiang had rebelliously cut off his pigtail in 1905, when China's Manchu rulers punished such conduct as a sign of disloyalty. Attracted to the army, he went to military schools, first in Baoding in Hebei Province, and later in Tokyo. When the Qing dynasty fell in 1911, Chiang, along with many of his nationalistic friends, returned to China to take part in the Republican Revolution. He mixed with Kuomintang figures of all political persuasions, although the assassination of his mentor, General Chen Qimei, in mid-1916 seemed to sour his taste for politics. About that time, Chiang became a Shanghai stockbroker, befriending wealthy bankers and businessmen as well as leaders of the Green Gang, but he failed to make his fortune and joined Sun Yat-sen in Canton as a military adviser in 1920. When Sun started developing contacts with the Soviet Union, Chiang went to Russia in 1923 for almost six months to study with the Red Army. Sun's Russian military and political advisers established the Whampoa Academy in 1924, and Chiang, the only KMT soldier who had studied in Moscow, was the logical choice to head it. As commandant of China's equivalent of West Point, Chiang emerged as the personal sponsor of the cream of the KMT officer corps, including many who later transferred their loyalties to the Communists.

Chiang was first and foremost a patriot—he was to call his autobiography *China's Destiny*—and he worried that the CCP was becoming a cat's-paw for Moscow. Because he was familiar with Bolshevik practices, Chiang's suspicions of the Communists grew during the Northern Expedition in late 1926 and early 1927. He had staged a minor anti-Communist coup in Canton in 1925, the so-called Chung Shan Gunboat affair, and was worried by the increasingly obvious Soviet alignment of the KMT's Communist partners. Chiang was prepared to learn from the Russians and deeply impressed by Lenin's integration of party, army, and government into a centralized and omnipotent regime, but he had no desire to see Soviet agents run China.

In late 1926 and the first weeks of 1927, Communist-inspired mobs rampaged through the British enclave in Hankow (today part of Wuhan), a port city on the south side of the Yangtze River that had British, Japanese, and French concessions. Communist activities in Shanghai, especially the establishment of a commune, confirmed Chiang's fears that a radical grab for power was imminent. Now was the time to act.

The leftist riots provoked a diplomatic crisis. Enraged Western governments filed outspoken notes of protest with the KMT, which had nominal authority over the Communists at the time. Although resolved by diplomatic negotiations in February, the crisis set off a radical swing within the Nationalist movement. In early March, a few weeks before the Shanghai revolt, radical agitators in Nanking, which the KMT had just captured from the warlords, once again terrorized and pillaged the foreign community. Chiang Kai-shek and his conservative colleagues believed the Communists were behind the disturbances, as shown partly by the increasingly radical public stance of the Comintern representative, Mikhail Borodin. A Russian political exile who had studied for a time at Valparaiso University in Indiana and run a school for émigrés in Chicago, Borodin returned to the Bolshevism of his youth and became a professional revolutionary. He served as an organizer in Mexico, Spain, the Netherlands, and Scotland before ending up in China. In theory, Borodin had been sent to advise the KMT and help mold it into an anti-imperialist force, but he also had the undeclared objective of spreading communism and setting the East ablaze. As the KMT armies chased the warlords from the Yangtze Valley, Borodin began giving fiery speeches against the conservative wing of the KMT. Before long, the Chinese Communists were glorifying him as "the Revolutionary Tutor."

Meanwhile, just when riots and looting in the Yangtze Valley drew attention to the Communist strategy, a serious diplomatic incident orchestrated by conservatives in the north aroused the specter of a leftist conspiracy. On April 6, 1927, ten days after the fall of Shanghai, Marshal Zhang Zuolin, the Manchurian overlord of Peking, raided the Soviet legation there. Despite its dubious legality (Zhang claimed that the diplomatic corps had authorized his action), his attack uncovered further evidence linking the Communists to the radicals in the KMT. A cache of documents found in the Soviet military attaché's office revealed some of the covert aims of the CCP. Moreover, Li Dazhao, a professor at Peking University and the best-known Communist leader in northern China, was caught hiding in the Soviet legation. Hanged by the warlord troops, he became the first notable Communist martyr in China. Li's presence inside the Soviet diplomatic offices increased fears among moderate and conservative Nationalists that the Soviet Union, the left wing of the Kuomintang, and the Communists were conspiring to seize power.

To Chiang Kai-shek, then based in a villa in Shanghai's French Concession, the Communist threat grew day by day. But with only about three thousand troops in the vicinity of Shanghai, there was little Chiang could do at the time. Most of his army was three hundred miles away, restoring order in Nanking, in the wake of Communist-inspired riots. Chiang sought to strengthen his forces by enlisting the aid of Du Yuesheng, a flamboyant strongman in the Shanghai underworld. Du, an illiterate orphan from the slums, controlled the most powerful secret society in Shanghai, the Green Gang, and thus had hordes of thugs and gunmen at his disposal. Du's fortune was based on his status as the high chief of Shanghai's black economy of brothels, casinos, and drug dealing, but he posed as a millionaire philanthropist and civic leader. Confronted with the choice between a worldly yet patriotic military adventurer like Chiang and a working-class party whose puritanical bent threatened his own interests, Du had little trouble making up his mind.

In the early morning of April 12, 1927, more than a thousand of Du's Green Gang hoodlums, clad in blue denim with white armbands bearing the character for "labor," crept through the International Settlement and attacked Communist strongholds in the Chinese sectors of the city. The Communists were not taken completely by surprise—tensions between them and their conservative partners had been mounting for weeks, and they had their own contacts among the mobsters. Even so, with the scope and swiftness of the gangster onslaught, the Communist ranks broke quickly. The larger groups were soon isolated and besieged in Zhabei's fortified strongholds, the Commercial Press and Huzhou Guild buildings—only weeks before, the headquarters for their victorious uprising.

By afternoon, resistance had petered out. Hundreds of Communists surrendered large stocks of arms to the gang members, including three thousand rifles, twenty machine guns, two hundred convertible Mauser pistols, and four hundred automatic pistols. Many Communists died fighting, and many more perished in the wave of executions and random killings that followed as squads of gangsters and KMT troops roamed the streets in search of Communist activists. In their sweeps through the city, Chiang's men did not forget Shanghai University; KMT troops entered the campus, which had been shifted out of Zhabei to a new location in the far northern district of Jiangwan, and shot a large number of students. After confiscating all books and equipment, the KMT declared the university closed. Zhou Enlai subsequently claimed that five thousand Communists were massacred on or immediately after April 12. The actual figure, however, was much lower; the Shanghai Municipal Police reported that four hundred workers had died, while others put the figure between six hundred and seven hundred.*

Many Communist leaders perished—including Zhao Shiyan, Wang Shouhua, and Chen Yannian, the son of Party general secretary Chen Duxiu—but some eluded the squads of gunmen and escaped to safety outside the city or in underground cells within the foreign enclaves. Zhou Enlai, trapped in the Commercial Press building along with a large number of workers, was especially lucky. The leader of the surrounding KMT detachment turned out to be the younger brother of one of Chiang Kai-shek's generals, Bai Chongxi. A onetime cadet at the Whampoa Academy under Zhou, the younger Bai recognized his former instructor and gave Zhou, along with four others, safe passage out of the building. Zhou immediately made his way to a hideout on the outskirts of the city.

A highly visible frontline leader in the March uprising, Kang should have been easy to track down and capture. His counterpart in western Shanghai, Guo Bohe, who had fought alongside him during the attack on the Northern Railway Station and shared that happy midnight supper with him, was arrested within weeks and forced to betray his colleagues. But the events of those days were extremely chaotic. Although one Communist leader, Wang Shouhua (who was also a gangster), seems to have been trapped on Du Yuesheng's personal orders, Du's men apparently did not have lists of individual targets. The pandemonium worked to Kang's advantage, and he managed to escape.

Kang now entered a new world. For his first two years as a Communist, from 1925 until April 12, 1927, Party work had been relatively safe, at least in Shanghai, where the International Settlement and the French Concession offered some refuge from the oppressive warlord regimes. Even in the Shanghai suburbs outside the foreign enclaves, the risk of arrest was slim because the warlord police were corrupt and lacked the specialized security apparatus required to combat underground political movements.

The Communists' heyday in Shanghai ended with the attack led

---

* Harold Isaacs, an American journalist, estimated that the casualties totaled six hundred and fifty. André Malraux, in his novelized account of the anti-Communist coup, *The Human Condition*, described Communist prisoners being thrown into the furnaces of steam locomotives. But no evidence supports Malraux's grisly claim, which is not surprising: the closest Malraux got to Shanghai in those days was Canton, eighteen hundred miles to the south.

by the Green Gang on April 12. After the carnage of that day, Kang, like every other Communist, was forced to lead a secret, menaced life. The KMT, which replaced Marshal Sun Chuanfang's administration in Greater Shanghai, started a relentless hunt for Communists in hiding; Communist propaganda would call it the White Terror. Authorities in the foreign enclaves, first alarmed by the workers' uprisings and then reassured by Chiang Kai-shek's suppression of the Communists, started to cooperate with the KMT by arresting suspected Communists and extraditing many of them to the Chinese-ruled areas.

Many Communists fled, but Kang remained in Shanghai, learning to live in a dark and deadly world. For a man as devious as Kang, the environment was perfect. He was to emerge from it as a man to be reckoned with in China for half a century.

Chapter III

LIVING
DANGEROUSLY

CHIANG KAI-SHEK'S PURGE of Communists in April 1927 set off a witch-hunt that lasted until the Japanese invasion of China in 1937 drove the Kuomintang and the Communist Party into another uneasy embrace. Confident until then that revolution was about to roll across the Chinese stage, the Communists instead found dangers pressing in on all sides. The threats forced some CCP members to flee, either to inland cities like Hankow, where the KMT's left wing still welcomed them, or to Hong Kong, where British law provided a measure of protection against the KMT secret police. But many Communists went underground in Shanghai, protected only by caution and false identities. Among the leaders, Li Lisan, the youthful labor firebrand who had burst to prominence in the May Thirtieth Movement, passed himself off as an antique dealer, and Deng Zhongxia, one of Kang Sheng's teachers at Shanghai University, masqueraded as a barber.

Kang remained in Shanghai, living the secret life of a Communist in "French Town," surviving by his wits and knowledge of the city and growing ever more cautious and street-wise. He knew the lanes and alleys of Shanghai and the entrances and exits of its grand hotels and emporiums so well, he later boasted, that no one could catch him. It took six years before Shanghai became so dangerous that Kang had to retreat to Moscow.

Kang was familiar with more than the city's physical layout. According to a leftist writer who later moved to Hong Kong, Kang lived like many of the other wealthy young men who had come to

Shanghai to study. Cinemas and dance halls were still rare in the mid-1920s, so they passed their time in middle-class brothels, where custom allowed them to drink with the madams while they flirted with the prostitutes in the hope of free sex. The male students at Shanghai University sought the same amusements as colleagues from less ideological campuses, although they justified their hunt for pleasure as "investigating the diseases of society." Kang, or so this source claimed, was no exception.

Once involved in underground Party work, Kang turned his knowledge of Shanghai's night life to good use. When he found himself in danger of being apprehended by Kuomintang agents he would sometimes retreat to a brothel, where he could disappear for an hour or a night, safe in the knowledge that the security forces seldom raided establishments that had paid off the local police. Kang also used Shanghai's numerous billiard halls and bath houses as emergency refuges and as locations for discreet meetings. These places of entertainment stayed open all night, offering the perfect venue for Party cadres to rendezvous in secret.

After the April 1927 debacle, Kang set out to build a new life that would provide for his day-to-day needs—food, money, and sex—and make him invisible to KMT agents. His first move was to find a new wife so that he could pass as an ordinary married man. Nothing in China is more conspicuous than bachelorhood; in the CCP's early days, so strong was the pressure for senior male cadres to at least appear to be married that they often had young female Party workers assigned to live with them as a cover.* Kang, to be sure, already had a wife and children, but the arranged marriage with Chen Yi was already far behind him.

Kang had last seen Chen Yi in June 1925, when he returned to his family home in Zhucheng, together with his close companions Li Yuchao and Meng Chao. After that, he simply ignored her. At first, Chen Yi relied on Kang's father for support, and after his death she lived with Kang's son, Zhang Zishi. When she died is unclear, but in

---

* The case of a young woman named Wang Xiuzhen illustrates how Communist leaders ordered female members to act as "wives." Wang was assigned to be Li Lisan's domestic companion around 1928. She acted as his wife until he left for Moscow in 1930. She was then ordered to live with Luo Fu (Zhang Wentian), who had just returned from Moscow. Wang Xiuzhen played the role of wife in the complete sense, bearing her Communist "spouses" three daughters between 1928 and 1930. She was arrested on November 19, 1932, by the Shanghai Municipal Police.

any case, she had long since vanished from Kang's life. Kang's daughter, Zhang Yuying, eventually married into a landlord's family in Zhucheng but divorced her husband and went to work in a tobacco factory.

Kang himself, unconcerned with legal niceties, never bothered to get a formal divorce. His conduct was not unusual by the standards of the time. After the May Fourth Movement had popularized modern Western ideals of individualism and freedom of choice, many young Chinese, Communists and non-Communists alike, repudiated parentally mandated unions. The CCP later enforced a puritanical code, but during the 1920s and 1930s the Communists accepted informal marriages and espoused a theory of free love known as the "glass-of-water" principle—that sex was like a drink of water. Some Chinese men practiced polygamy, others changed partners when it suited them—including Mao Zedong, who rejected a childhood bride (the marriage was never consummated) and went on to have a string of three other marriages. Mao's marriage to his third wife, He Zizhen, typified the casual attitude the Communists had toward marriage in that era. Mao met He Zizhen following the Communists' 1928 capture of the central China town of Rongxin (a place where KMT posters offered a twenty-thousand-dollar reward for the arrest of "notorious bandit leader" Mao).* Shortly after the Communist forces entered Rongxin, a group of students brought pork and vegetables to the Communist headquarters as a token of welcome. He Zizhen, "a bright-eyed girl of eighteen," was one of those students; the next day, she called on Mao and presented him with two chickens and two bottles of wine. She stayed on to dine with him, and they became "fast friends." A day passed; she and Mao had "a long talk" in his bedroom, and she began staying overnight with him. Within a couple of weeks, her nightlong visits had become so "habitual" that she and Mao were "generally regarded as 'married.'"

Chiang Kai-shek, though he lived much more conservatively than Mao, had a similar record. In December 1927, Chiang fell madly in love with Song Meiling, the beautiful younger sister of Song Qingling, Sun Yat-sen's widow, and left his first wife, Mao Fumei, the mother

---

* About eight thousand five hundred dollars in U.S. currency at the time. The value of Chinese currency has fluctuated greatly over the years. This estimation of its American equivalent, like those that follow, is merely a very approximate calculation.

of his favorite son, Chiang Ching-kuo. Chiang never formally divorced Mao Fumei; nevertheless, he considered himself married to Meiling. That union caused much controversy. Madame Sun adamantly opposed it, and Meiling's father, Charlie Jones Song, consented only when Chiang Kai-shek agreed to convert to Christianity. And not least, Du Yuesheng, boss of the Green Gang, feared that marrying into Sun Yat-sen's family might make Chiang forget his obligations to the Shanghai mafia. Not long after the gorgeous Meiling "married" Chiang Kai-shek, she stepped into a limousine that she thought was going to deliver her to her sister's house but was instead transported to an unfamiliar, if comfortable, villa and held there. Chiang's brother-in-law, T. V. Song, finally approached Du Yuesheng, who explained that his concern for Meiling's safety had prompted him to keep her in a secure place. Chiang had no trouble understanding Du's message: he could never afford to neglect paying his proper dues to the master of the Green Gang.

In 1927, Kang married a young woman he had met at Shanghai University, where she was studying Chinese literature. Born Cao Shuying, Kang's new bride changed her personal name to Yi'ou ("Surpassing Europe")—a chauvinistic sentiment entirely to Kang's liking. She, too, came from Shandong and was a typical modern Chinese woman. Cao had been raised with natural, unbound feet and educated at the prestigious Shandong Girls School in Jinan, the provincial capital. Swept up by the radical notions of the May Fourth Movement, she joined the Communist Party in 1926. Like Kang, Cao Yi'ou had been married before, and it was a mark of her rebellion that she abandoned her first husband to marry Kang.

Cao Yi'ou never bore Kang any children, but their relationship involved much more than many other Communist "marriages" of convenience during that era. Petite, small-boned, and outwardly jovial, Cao in fact was fully prepared to join Kang in the most devious and dangerous—and politically rewarding—conspiracies. She was a worthy partner for a man living a secret life, and Kang eventually helped her launch a political career of her own.*

---

* For Kang's wife to have had a role in politics was not unusual. In the Chinese Communists' elitist power structure, it was common for senior officials' wives to occupy prominent posts. Jiang Qing, Mao's wife and confidante and later the dragon lady of the Cultural Revolution, was the most obvious one. Among others were Deng

Kang changed his name again in late 1928, a year after his marriage, abandoning Zhang Yun in favor of Zhao Rong ("Tolerant Zhao"). For the first time, he concealed his connection with the Zhang family, taking another step away from the name he had been born with. Kang set out to make his new identity complete by securing employment as a personal assistant to Yu Qiaqing, head of the Chinese Chamber of Commerce in Shanghai. Yu Qiaqing, who commanded a far-flung banking and shipping empire, was one of the city's most influential and wealthy Chinese entrepreneurs. A controversial public figure, he had been a key supporter of the anti-British strike of 1925; as a businessman with nationalistic leanings, he could be expected to hire a young man from Shandong with progressive, antiforeign attitudes. With such high standing among Shanghai's Chinese citizens, Yu was chosen several times to act as their community representative in negotiations with the Shanghai Municipal Council. He was a strong advocate of Chinese interests—some suspected him of having "Communist sympathies"—yet was part of the old order. Yu was an intimate of the archgangster Du Yuesheng and was one of the main financial benefactors of Chiang Kai-shek.

But it was for Kang's calligraphy, not his politics, that Yu Qiaqing hired him. For all his wealth and power, Yu was still a comprador, one of a special breed of Chinese businessmen who made immense fortunes by trading with Westerners but were widely despised by Chinese outside of Shanghai who took a dim view of the modern business world and its questionable ethics. Residents of the provinces mistrusted Shanghai wheeler-dealers like Yu, much the way many Americans today regard Wall Street fortune hunters. "To the comprador even a foreigner's fart is fragrant," observed Wu Jianren, an early-twentieth-century writer.

Seeking to demonstrate that he was a man of culture, Yu Qiaqing maintained the customs of a nineteenth-century gentleman, going so far as to dress in the traditional Chinese cap and gown. In keeping

---

Yingchao, the wife of Zhou Enlai; Kang Keqing, the wife of Marshal Zhu De; Ye Qun, the wife of Marshal Lin Biao; and Wang Guangmei, the wife of President Liu Shaoqi. Deng Yingchao and Ye Qun became members of the Politburo; Kang Keqing was a Central Committee member; and Wang Guangmei was a presidium member in the National People's Congress. This was not inconsistent with a strain in Chinese culture of a sacrificing proletariat manipulated by a prodigiously rewarded elite—just a century ago, the Taiping rebels established a compulsorily celibate mass movement whose leaders maintained large harems.

with his mandarin image, Yu issued countless hand-written messages to friends and business associates: invitations, acceptances, greetings, congratulations, condolences. Yu needed an accomplished calligrapher on his payroll, and Kang, the child of a family of scholars with literary traditions centuries old, was skilled with the brush.

By the late 1920s, Kang was living a double life. To the outside world, he was a young man in the employ of one of the city's wealthiest businessmen and living in the French Concession with his wife. In Shanghai, where thousands of young men worked for large firms, his way of life did not seem unusual. But Kang and his wife were dedicated Communists, and he was a cadre on the rise, with power over much of the Party apparatus in Shanghai.

Conveniently disguised as secretary to a leading capitalist, Kang worked feverishly within the Party to expand his power and make his way up the Communist hierarchy. There was no shortage of opportunities. Chiang Kai-shek's 1927 massacre of the Communists ignited ten years of feuding and factionalism within the CCP. Accusations were exchanged over the April disaster, strategies were debated bitterly, and cadres competed for command of the Party, each one ascribing the defeat to his rivals and promising to recover lost ground. Some, like CCP general secretary Chen Duxiu, blamed the disaster on Stalin's ill-informed, self-serving policies and turned to Leon Trotsky for political inspiration, forming a Chinese Trotskyite movement. Others were so disillusioned with the Party leadership and so frustrated in their attempts to oust it that they tried to establish parallel communistic organizations. Some turned to the KMT. Still others simply wearied of the squabbles and dangers inherent in radical politics and drifted back to their former lives.

Kang was one of the faithful who never abandoned the Party. Living in Shanghai, where CCP headquarters was transferred from Hankow shortly after the worst of the White Terror, he was well placed to profit from the factional struggles. By then, Kang was completely familiar with the local Communist organization and able to exploit any opportunity for advancement that presented itself as the Kuomintang caught, kidnapped, imprisoned, or murdered senior Communists.

During this period of bitter infighting and crumbling idealism, Kang's position improved rapidly. At the time of the Third Workers Uprising in 1927, he was a municipal-level organizer—the Party leader of one of the three sectors into which the Communists had divided Shanghai. By early June, a mere two months later, he had been promoted to membership on the Jiangsu Provincial Committee, a new unit created to run CCP activities in Shanghai and the surrounding area in the wake of Chiang Kai-shek's purge.

Kang had little contact with the first CCP general secretary he served under, Chen Duxiu, a forty-eight-year-old veteran of almost every radical movement since 1900, who was removed as leader in August 1927, or with Chen's successor, Qu Qiubai. Qu, a powerful influence on Kang at Shanghai University, had such a recklessly naïve view of revolution that his reign as general secretary was too short, and his style of leadership too secretive, for a low-level cadre like Kang to improve his position. At the CCP's Sixth Congress in July 1928, Comintern officials, disillusioned with Qu's disastrous mishandling of several armed uprisings, orchestrated his removal.

The delegates to the Sixth Congress, which was held on the outskirts of Moscow,* installed the Soviets' candidate, Xiang Zhongfa, as general secretary. Xiang, a Yangtze bargeman by trade, had begun his political career as a labor agitator in a mine. His proletarian origins got him selected for training in Moscow; in those days, he was one of the few workers in the Party's top echelons. China hands in Moscow also approved of Xiang's pliability and his riveting oratory.

But Xiang struck his Chinese comrades as poorly educated, foulmouthed, and stupid. Faced with the tedium of organizing and planning, he preferred to spend his time in Shanghai's dance halls and brothels. His ineptitude left a power vacuum for others to exploit—principally, Li Lisan, the impetuous activist who had been a key leader in the May Thirtieth Movement of 1925.

Born into a Hunan landlord family in 1899, Li spent several years studying in France, where he befriended Zhou Enlai and other young Chinese radicals who were founding a Chinese Communist movement in Europe. Li was expelled by the French for his radical politics in late 1921 and returned to China to serve as a labor organizer. By the time of the 1928 congress in Moscow, he had earned a reputation as a charismatic leader with the qualifications to guide the Chinese Communist movement back onto the path of victory. In Moscow, he mesmerized his Soviet hosts, earning himself special

* The fact that this congress was held in Russia rather than China shows how much power the Soviets held over the CCP at the time.

treatment and three meetings with Stalin. The Russians were confident that Li could reinvigorate the Chinese revolution, so they had him elected to the Politburo and appointed head of the Propaganda Department.

In spite of the good impression he made on the Comintern, Li was essentially a rabble-rouser. He was more cosmopolitan and polished than Xiang Zhongfa, but he had little stomach for administration or strategy. When he planned campaigns, his passionate romanticism clouded his understanding of the conditions around him. He lived in a fantasy world, with the tide of revolution always on the rise. Other Communists spoke of him as "a big cannon"—noisy but unreliable in hitting the target. Zhang Guotao recalled that many cadres viewed Li as "a hornblower, lover of pomp, and destructionist."

Under Li's leadership, the CCP apparatus, already badly hurt by the massacre in April 1927 and Qu's brief but incompetent reign, degenerated into complete paralysis. Party cells started to fade away: often, they received no instructions from above, ignored them when they did, or failed to pass them on to subordinate cells. Some Party units simply lost contact with the rest of the apparatus, as addresses and contact arrangements were mislaid or forgotten. Membership fell sharply. In the all-important Shanghai area, the Party recovered to about three thousand members after the April disaster; but under Li's direction, membership plummeted to five hundred.

Li's strategy was not even new. Though widely referred to as "the Li Lisan line," his program for revolution imitated that of his discredited predecessor, Qu Qiubai, by placing a lopsided emphasis on urban insurrection. Li paid lip service to the revolutionary potential of the countryside, but his willingness to include peasant troops in his plans was nothing more than a nominal concession to the rural-based Communists. Adventurous to a fault, Li presided over a string of defeats within his first twelve months in power.

Kang did not attend the July 1928 congress in Moscow, but Li Lisan's installation in office accelerated Kang's climb up the Party hierarchy. Several months after the congress, Kang was named director of the Organization Department of the Jiangsu Provincial Committee, a post with control over patronage and other personnel matters. After the Communist headquarters, which included the Politburo and the Central Committee units, the Jiangsu provincial apparatus was one of the most important components of the CCP. It oversaw Communist activities in Shanghai and in the Lower Yangtze as far afield as Nanking, the new KMT capital. Furthermore, with the Party headquarters based in Shanghai, the Jiangsu cadres had every opportunity to catch the eye of more senior Communist leaders.

In his new post, Kang actively supported Li and enforced his policies on the Party's ever shriveling grass roots. Near the end of 1929, he helped Li oust his opponents and critics from the Jiangsu Provincial Committee. Kang's support of Li did not go unrewarded: in February 1930, Kang was appointed secretary-general of one of the main instruments of Party control, the Central Organization Department.

Kang now supervised a wide range of administrative tasks, including management of finances and the Party archives. He also gained the power to discipline members who disobeyed orders or were careless about security. In March 1930, Kang issued a rebuke to a young, Soviet-trained cadre named Wang Ming for flagrant disregard of the Party's security procedures. The Shanghai Municipal Police had arrested Wang Ming two months earlier at an ostensibly secret meeting of labor agitators and imprisoned him in the Louza Police Station. Wang Ming established contact with his CCP comrades by bribing one of the many Sikh constables in the SMP to deliver a letter to Pan Wenyu, a Communist propaganda worker; as a result, the Comintern representative in Shanghai paid several thousand Chinese dollars in bribes* and Wang Ming was released. Whether Wang's action compromised the safety of Pan's office remains unclear—Pan moved to a new location before any police raided his old quarters—but high cadres charged Wang with placing a Party cell in danger. The Politburo decided to discipline Wang because he had "ignored political vigilance and seriously deviated from the discipline of secret work." But Wang was not intimidated for very long; at a meeting four months later, he openly blasted Li Lisan's policies. The Politburo suspended his Party membership and placed him on six months' probation. In both cases, Kang was the whip responsible for punishing Wang Ming.

Kang flourished in Shanghai's world of factional rivalries, making his way into the select circle of high cadres around Li Lisan. But that environment of opportunity—as Wang Ming had learned—carried

---

* About seven hundred dollars in U.S. currency of the time.

with it the risk of imprisonment, torture, and death. The police finally caught up with Kang in 1930, arresting him and some of his colleagues at a Communist meeting.

Kang's luck did not run out completely, however. One of the young Communists taken into custody with him was Ding Jishi, whose uncle, Ding Weifen, was a well-connected Kuomintang elder. By coincidence, Ding Weifen came from Rizhao, a village on the Shandong coast not more than fifty miles from Kang's hometown of Dataizhuang. At the time of Kang's arrest, Ding Weifen was dean of the Central Party School in Nanking, where KMT cadres were indoctrinated in the principles of non-Communist nationalism. One of Ding Weifen's aides at the school was Chen Lifu, then the head of the KMT secret service. With Chen's help, Ding Weifen was able to arrange the release of Ding Jishi and his friends. Ding Jishi was bundled off to study in Germany, but Kang returned to work in the Communist underground.

Despite Ding Weifen's intercession, Kang still had to make some deals with his jailers. According to Lu Futan, a Communist who was arrested by the KMT secret police in 1933 and forced to talk,[*] Kang "was arrested and betrayed the party" in 1930, when Kang "sold out his comrades."

Fearful that reports—true or not—of his treason to the Communist cause would leak out, Kang did his best to keep his arrest secret. In fact, he lied about it ever after, dismissing as "nonsense and rumors" a 1968 report from Taiwan that "Kang Sheng was once arrested in Shanghai and immediately released." "I have never been arrested," Kang commented, adding, "If I had been arrested I would have been executed long ago." Word of his arrest by itself would have placed him under suspicion in CCP circles. One of the Kuomintang's favorite tactics with the Communists they arrested was to recruit them as KMT agents—a fate their victims considered far preferable to death. Most defectors were integrated directly into the KMT, but a few were released and fed back into the Communist ranks as double agents. So Communists taken into custody by the KMT were often

---

[*] Lu Futan was a Cantonese worker who became a Central Committee member and the director of the Communist organization in Shandong. An ally of Wang Ming's, Lu was named the CCP's acting general secretary in July 1931, when Wang resigned after just four weeks as CCP head and returned to the Soviet Union. Six weeks later, on September 1, 1931, Lu Futan stepped aside in favor of Bo Gu, another of Wang Ming's associates, who was installed as permanent general secretary.

distrusted by their former confederates once they emerged from jail.

None of the sources that report Kang's arrest disclose treasonous cooperation with the KMT. Even the exact location of his capture remains unclear. The files of the Special Branch of the Shanghai Municipal Police that are now held in the United States National Archives contain no record of Kang's being caught in the International Settlement. He may have been detained in the French Concession, where he lived for much of the time, or in KMT-controlled Greater Shanghai. The SMP Special Branch records reveal that Communist suspects were often released for lack of evidence. In one instance, the SMP arrested ten people at a Communist meeting but failed to advance the case further. One of the suspects was an informer, another was a minor Communist functionary who told a series of confusing lies, and the remaining eight professed to know nothing. According to one SMP report, the police were extremely reluctant to use informants in court, which suggests that if Kang provided information on a regular basis, no formal action would ever have been taken against him. Moreover, the SMP records that survived the fall of Shanghai are incomplete; a number of files fell overboard while being hurriedly loaded onto a U.S. Navy ship in the desperate last days of Kuomintang rule in 1948. Others were removed by Communist agents.

The Shanghai Municipal Police records reveal numerous cases of Chinese arrested for distributing "communistic literature," but most of the people captured were "coolies, carpenters, linesmen, brass smiths, painters, cable fitters, [and] unemployed butchers." Top Party officials were sometimes caught (usually on information provided by the KMT secret police),* but none of the surviving dossiers suggest that Kang was one of them. As the SMP files disclose, the Special Branch was aware that a well-organized Communist machine existed but the bulk of the operation remained underground. The police oc-

---

* Some of the intelligence passed on by the Kuomintang police was of less than the highest quality. On November 8, 1929, the KMT forwarded to the SMP details from the confessions of two Communist detainees: "They have confessed that the dress of the Communists are [sic] all in white short shirts and trousers with straw hats. The badge sign of the chief is colored in red and that of the member in white. Their secret sign is a letter 'Goong' written under the left arm with a chemically made pen . . ." Noting the ludicrousness of that information, Chief Detective Inspector Robertson scrawled on the margins of the KMT report, "Raids on bath houses would seem to be indicated although washing is not one of the necessities of the doctrine."

casionally caught rank-and-file activists but rarely penetrated the maze of compartmentalized channels linking the street workers with the Party's top policymakers. If Kang was in fact arrested in the International Settlement, it probably was a minor affair not considered worthy of a permanent record in the central police registry.

Kang's arrest in itself is no proof that he was turned by his captors or forced into long-term cooperation with them. KMT prisons were notoriously chaotic and corrupt. Many a Party member bribed his way out or was released because the police failed to discover substantial Communist affiliation. The police may have ascertained nothing more than that Kang worked for Yu Qiaqing, an extremely wealthy businessman with radical leanings, and had a link with Ding Weifen, a KMT leader; but while Kang may conceivably have named a couple of suspected Communists, the police had no record of his involvement with the CCP.

Li Lisan rode high throughout the summer of 1930 but was unable to sustain his power. Concocted in a fantasy world, Li's policies led to a string of calamitous defeats. Kang and others supported Li, but opposition to his leadership grew, largely among a group of experienced, pragmatic, Shanghai-based cadres. The leader of the anti-Li faction was He Mengxiong, a labor organizer who, like Kang, served on the Jiangsu Provincial Committee. He Mengxiong, from Mao Zedong's home district of Xiangtan in Hunan Province, had been a Communist since 1922, when he helped organize one of the first Communist-led strikes.

Li Lisan's adventurism also provoked opposition from Zhou Enlai. In the summer of 1930, Zhou, then working in Shanghai, broke with Li and made a special trip to Moscow to appeal for Comintern approval of a change in leadership. The Comintern, alarmed by Li's failures as well as his frequent statements that the Soviet Union was subsidiary to Chinese interests, took note of Zhou's message.

Li's downfall finally came several months later, when he ordered uprisings in Wuhan and Changsha. Believing that China was on the verge of an upsurge in revolutionary fervor, Li planned a revolt in the central provinces of Hubei and Hunan. He ordered rural Communist forces to attack Changsha and Wuhan while the urban proletariat rose and seized control of both cities. Communist troops under Peng Dehuai captured Changsha on July 27, 1930, and held it for about a week. But the KMT armies soon routed them, and the urban revolt Li had wishfully forecast as the main engine of the Chinese revolution turned out to be a pipe dream.

Tension among the various factions turned into open struggle after the Changsha debacle. In late September, Zhou Enlai—already acting as an intermediary and troubleshooter—secured the Comintern's blessing to call a CCP Central Committee meeting to resolve the problem of leadership. The committee met in a villa on Medhurst Road in the International Settlement, although for security reasons word was put out that the meeting would take place in the Lushan mountain resort of Jiangxi Province. For three days, about twenty Communist leaders argued over the leadership question, at times growing so boisterous that Zhou had to warn them to keep their voices down.

The Medhurst Road meeting ended Li Lisan's rule but failed to pick a successor. The upper-level splits within the Party widened into two main factions. One clique supported He Mengxiong and the Jiangsu veterans; the other side, a group of young, Moscow-trained cadres later known as "the Twenty-eight Bolsheviks" or "the Returned Students," backed their leader, Wang Ming.* Kang, who by that time had distanced himself from Li Lisan, remained neutral. Though very familiar with He Mengxiong and his followers, he waited to see who would emerge with the most influence and to make his decisions accordingly.

Wang Ming had clashed twice with Kang earlier in the year. Born Chen Shaoyu, Wang Ming was an ambitious, twenty-three-year-old intellectual, son of a wealthy merchant in Anhui Province. He had gone to Moscow in 1925 to study at Sun Yat-sen University, the Soviet-founded school for training Chinese revolutionaries. There he caught the eye of the Soviet officials who managed Chinese affairs. When a number of the Chinese students at Sun Yat-sen University rallied to support Trotsky in his battle with Stalin, the Soviet authorities assigned Wang Ming to spy on them and made him their agent

---

* The Twenty-eight Bolsheviks included a number of important CCP leaders in addition to Wang Ming. Luo Fu (Zhang Wentian) became vice foreign minister and ambassador to Moscow; Bo Gu (Qin Bangxian) was general secretary for four years; and Wang Jiaxiang was also ambassador to Moscow and head of the International Liaison Department. But the most durable was Yang Shangkun, who became president of China; he earned the title "Butcher of Peking" after the June 1989 protests in Tiananmen Square.

in wiping out sympathy for Trotsky within the CCP. Wang Ming hoped to win even greater favor with his patrons and quickly evolved into a ruthless disciplinarian. As it turned out, his calculations were correct: impressed by Wang's abilities and his loyalty to the Kremlin's view of revolution, the Comintern Stalinists concluded that he was the ideal man to communize China.

Wang Ming was a glib speaker adept at Marxist jargon. Both a political activist and an intellectual, he had written, in the tradition of Lenin, a number of articles on the theory and practice of Communist revolution. He reinforced his image as a leader in November 1930 by publishing *The Two Line Struggle*, an analysis of communism in his homeland (it appeared in Moscow under the title *The Two Lines: The Struggle for the Bolshevization of the Chinese Communist Party*). His revolutionary credentials were enhanced when he married Meng Qingshu, a young Chinese Communist who had been a student with him in Moscow. Wang Ming, a sturdily built, debonair young man, and Meng Qingshu, a slim, demure woman with finely molded cheekbones, made a striking couple.

When Meng Qingshu was arrested in Shanghai at a meeting of factory workers in 1930, the brokenhearted Wang Ming set aside everything else until he could arrange her freedom. She spent six months in Shanghai's Longhua Prison before Wang finally persuaded the local CCP committee to raise two to three thousand dollars in Chinese money (very roughly equal to fifteen hundred American dollars) for bribes to secure her freedom. Many Communists discovered on their release from prison that their partners had taken up with someone else, but Meng Qingshu emerged into Wang Ming's open arms. Theirs was one of the true love stories of the revolution.

When Wang Ming returned from the Soviet Union in 1929, he was driven by an inflated notion of his own destiny. He turned down his first assignment, a relatively junior post as Party secretary in the Nanyang Tobacco Factory in eastern Shanghai. Wang was reassigned to propaganda work, but he continued to clash with local Communist officials who resented the ambition and pretensions of all the young, Moscow-trained intellectuals. A contemporary of Wang Ming's described him and his coterie as "mindless and arrogant young bureaucrats, who had never done a thing for the Chinese revolution and who had only gained control of the party organization at [Sun Yat-sen] University by toadying to their Comintern superiors."

Wang and the rest of the Twenty-eight Bolsheviks had few allies

among the Communist rank and file, but they did have one crucial
advantage over their rivals: the backing of the Comintern. Soviet
patronage increased dramatically in importance in October 1930,
when Pavel Mif, the head of the Far Eastern Bureau of the Comintern,
arrived in China. Born into a Russian-Jewish family in 1899, Mif had
joined the Communist youth movement after the Revolution of 1917.
His first important contact with Chinese affairs came in 1925, when
he was appointed deputy chancellor of Sun Yat-sen University under
Karl Radek, a famous revolutionary. Mif succeeded Radek as head of
the university in 1927. That same year, he made a brief visit to China,
writing several in-depth essays on the revolution in China and returning to Moscow with the overbearing confidence of a firsthand observer.

Mif became one of the most influential directors of China policy
in Moscow. An obedient and heartless follower of Stalin, he enforced
political discipline on the Chinese student community in Moscow and
specialized in hunting down pro-Trotskyite dissidents. In Wang Ming,
Mif saw all the qualities the Stalinists demanded of foreign revolutionaries, first and foremost a proper respect for the preeminent role
of the Soviet Union. When Mif returned to China in late 1930, he was
determined to install Wang Ming as the leader of the Chinese Communist Party.

Mif's first step was to order Li Lisan back to Moscow, where Li
made a self-criticism and admitted to being a "semi-Trotskyite." (By
day, Li studied at the Lenin Institute; at night, he compensated for his
political failures by seducing a succession of Russian women.) By
early January 1931, Mif had suppressed opposition to Wang Ming
from local cadres and felt confident enough to convene a meeting of
the Central Committee. This fateful and bitter session was held in a
hideaway in the International Settlement on January 13. The Central
Committee met upstairs while several young women from the Communist secret service played cards and listened to gramophone records
downstairs. Communist gunmen, disguised as chefs and domestic servants, stood guard, ready to protect their leaders from harm.

In his capacity as general secretary, the incompetent and vulgar
Yangtze bargeman Xiang Zhongfa chaired the gathering. However,
according to one participant, Xu Binggen, Mif dictated the outcome
by having men armed with pistols enforce his directives. Mif and
Wang Ming had drawn up a list of candidates for leading posts;

although He Mengxiong and his group of Shanghai-based veterans tried to promote a separate slate, Mif's list was accepted in its entirety. Xiang Zhongfa remained general secretary, but the Politburo was dominated by Wang Ming and his associates.

Even before the meeting began, Kang had grasped the new political currents and set out to tie his fortunes to Wang Ming's. His sense of purpose seemed to evoke the philosophy of the *I Ching*, with its portrayal of a world in endless flux where the key to success lies in acting while a situation is still gestating. Kang's main obstacle to reaching an accommodation with Wang Ming was the bitterness between them over their hostile encounters the previous year, when Kang had twice disciplined Wang Ming on behalf of Li Lisan. Indeed, the probationary period that Kang had imposed on Wang Ming's Party membership had barely expired when Wang was appointed to the Politburo—a startling indication of how fast the situation, including Kang's perceptions and allegiances, had changed.

Confronted with the reality that Wang Ming had leapfrogged over him, Kang set out to ingratiate himself with his former victim. He managed to convince Wang Ming that their earlier problems had resulted simply from his following Li Lisan's orders. In reaching an accord with Wang Ming, Kang was not without allies. A number of the Twenty-eight Bolsheviks, including Yang Shangkun, Bo Gu, and Wang Jiaxiang, had been fellow students of Kang's at Shanghai University. Wang Ming was well aware that he needed the services of a tough cadre with knowledge of Party affairs and personnel in Shanghai, and Kang was the obvious choice. Wang Ming knew from personal experience that Kang could be brutally effective at handling enemies within the Party. By the time the Central Committee assembled on January 13, their relationship had undergone a fundamental shift, and Wang Ming placed Kang's name on the list of new Central Committee members. More important, he promoted Kang from secretary-general to director of the Central Organization Department. To his great profit, Kang had switched sides at the right time.

Mif had used his status as a ranking Comintern official to place Wang Ming and his Soviet-trained clique in control of the CCP, but Mif's high-handed style sparked widespread discontent. His barely concealed assumption that Chinese Communists should take orders from white-skinned revolutionaries moved some of the more overtly patriotic delegates to walk out. Serious opposition came from the

veterans around He Mengxiong, who felt that their courageous resistance to Li Lisan's adventurism should have been rewarded by a
share of the spoils of office.

But Mif's dogmatism allowed for no compromises. The result
was that the Shanghai-based Party split into two warring camps. He
Mengxiong and his allies denounced Wang Ming, broke with the
Central Committee, and set out to establish a separate, competing
organization. Determined to reduce Mif's influence, the He Mengxiong faction distributed statements among the Party rank and file
attacking Comintern interference, Mif, and Wang Ming.

On January 17, 1931, several members of He Mengxiong's
group, including Lin Yu'nan and Li Qiushi, met to discuss opposition
to Wang Ming and the Twenty-eight Bolsheviks at the Eastern Hotel,
a middle-class, Western-style establishment at 666 Hankow Road,
one of the busiest parts of the International Settlement. By defying
Wang Ming, however, they were entering a deadly world where anything was permissible, no matter how dirty or deceitful. The following day, a joint party of SMP Special Branch officers and KMT secret
police, acting on a "secret report," placed the Eastern Hotel under
surveillance. One of the police officers, disguised as a teaboy, entered
room 31, where He Mengxiong and his followers were holed up.
Deciding that the occupants of the room looked like they might be
Communist agents, the officer alerted other police, who burst into the
room and caught eight men. After taking their prisoners to the Louza
Police Station, the KMT detectives and SMP officers lay in wait and
caught three more Communists trying to enter room 31. Later that
afternoon, they raided the Zhongshan Hotel on Tianjin Road and
arrested He Mengxiong and another seven suspects. Raids continued
throughout the night; by morning, a total of thirty-six Communists
had been rounded up.

Once routine legal procedures had been attended to in the International Settlement, the prisoners were handed over to the KMT
security forces and taken to the Garrison Command Prison in Longhua on the southern outskirts of Shanghai. Late on the night of February 7, 1931, prison authorities informed He Mengxiong and
twenty-three other captives that they were to be transported to Nanking. Twenty-one men and three women were secured with handcuffs
and leg irons and marched out of the prison yard. As soon as the
column was beyond earshot of the jail, their escorts abandoned all
pretense. Waiting beside a nearby bridge was a judge who pronounced

the death sentence. As a firing squad prepared to execute them, the prisoners burst out singing "The Internationale." Their corpses were still in shackles when they were buried.

Although the KMT had tried to keep the massacre a secret, news soon leaked out. The local and foreign press reacted with anger. Among those executed were five aspiring young left-wing writers and poets: Li Weisen, an essayist and the editor of *The Shanghai Red Flag*; Hu Yepin, a novelist; Rou Shi, a short-story writer; Yin Fu, a minor author; and Feng Keng, a woman writer. The work of all five had been introduced to the West by the American journalist Edgar Snow, and the dead writers quickly became immortalized as "the Five Martyrs." Progressive writers condemned the slayings, entirely disregarding the quintet's connection with the Communists and alleging a general suppression of writers and artists.* The international reaction played into Wang Ming's hands: the focus on the Five Martyrs served as useful propaganda against Chiang Kai-shek's White Terror and obscured the political realities behind the incident.

The KMT was blamed in the news stories of the day for killing the Five Martyrs, but the man actually responsible for masterminding the whole series of arrests was . . . Kang Sheng! As Wang Ming's newly acquired ally, Kang was determined to prove his effectiveness in the murky world of factional politics. This incident was shrouded in rumor for decades, but recently uncovered evidence reveals that Kang informed the KMT secret police where He Mengxiong's group was meeting. In 1967, Wu Bingshu, a former KMT secret-service agent captured by the Communists in 1949, disclosed to his captors that the KMT police had had detailed biographical information on every member of He Mengxiong's group before their arrest— including the date each had joined the Party, the outlines of their Communist careers, and small but intimate details that the prisoners themselves had sometimes forgotten. As a result, Wu said, the interrogation of the group involved no more than asking each prisoner to verify a predetermined set of facts. Wu Bingshu believed that the information had come from a source in the Communist Party. But he did not know who. As head of the Organization Department and the

---

* Among the 104 American writers who later protested against "the torture and execution of writers in China for their political opinions" were Sinclair Lewis, Robert Frost, Thornton Wilder, Edna St. Vincent Millay, Edna Ferber, Theodore Dreiser, Will Durant, Lewis Mumford, John Dewey, Edmund Wilson, and Malcolm Cowley.

custodian of files on Party members, Kang had ready access to the damning information.

There is stronger evidence against Kang than Wu Bingshu's testimony. Another KMT intelligence officer who fell into Communist hands after 1949, Wang Yuncheng, bore explicit witness to Kang's betrayal of He Mengxiong and the Five Martyrs. Originally a Moscow-trained Communist (he was one of the Twenty-eight Bolsheviks and later head of the Communist Youth League), Wang Yuncheng joined the KMT intelligence service after his capture in 1933. Three weeks after his arrest, Wang Yuncheng wrote a "declaration of submission" dated February 24, 1933. "In its factional struggle," Wang declared, "the communist party uses assassination and the disclosure of secrets as methods, such as in the case of He Mengxiong and his twenty-odd colleagues who all died under the Red Terror led by Zhao Rong [Kang's name at the time] and others."

Wang Yuncheng could speak about "the Red Terror" as one of Wang Ming's most trusted aides. At the time of the Five Martyrs incident, Wang Yuncheng, a worker by background, belonged to the Wang Ming clique on the Central Committee. Wang Ming had always used him to bully and intimidate his rivals. Wang Yuncheng had first met Wang Ming in Moscow, serving as one of his bodyguards at Sun Yat-sen University. As a confidant of the young pro-Soviet leader, Wang Yuncheng had direct knowledge of the treacherous schemes and conspiracies Wang Ming and his allies used against their Party rivals. He also knew Kang, and described him to the SMP.

While ingratiating himself with Wang Ming, Kang advertised his capacity for underhanded operations, yet skillfully concealed his treachery from other eyes. Several days after He Mengxiong's execution, Kang met Zhang Guotao, who had just returned to Shanghai from Moscow. Zhang found Kang "distressed" over He's execution and "fearful" that it would endanger other Party members. Zhang, in earlier days a friend of He Mengxiong, would certainly have voiced any suspicion if he had detected anything odd in Kang's demeanor.

Resistance to Wang Ming and the new CCP regime continued after the extermination of He Mengxiong and his allies. Wang began weeding out his rivals while he reorganized Party units in ways that increased their efficiency and firmed up his control over them. As head of the Organization Department and one of Wang's main hatchet men, Kang increasingly became identified with the Twenty-eight Bolsheviks and their Soviet patrons. He helped them suppress dissident cadres and revamp the Party, bringing it closer to the Soviet model.

Backed by the Comintern and helped immeasurably by Kang and others, Wang Ming kept building up his influence. Within two years after his return from Moscow, he became head of the entire Chinese Communist movement. He had also begun to foster a personality cult within the Party rank and file. Young Communists spoke in admiration of their leader, describing him as "brilliant and far-seeing" and quoting from his "classic" work, *The Two Line Struggle*. Battle-hardened veterans like Zhou Enlai, head of the Communist Military Commission, and Mao Zedong, a mere Central Committee member and commissar of a rural base, were required to follow Wang Ming's directives.

Wang Ming had one spectacular weakness that rendered him unfit to lead the CCP: fear of discovery and arrest sent him into a panic. In Soviet eyes, he may have been the ideal cadre, but in stark contrast to Kang, Wang lacked the nerve and resourcefulness necessary to function as an underground Communist in a city as dangerous as Shanghai. He had already had a close call in January 1930, when he was detained briefly, which terrified him. With the KMT, the SMP, and other security forces hot on the trail of the Communists, Wang Ming found Shanghai increasingly intolerable. Kang, who was responsible for organizational matters, did his best to protect Wang Ming and his wife, Meng Qingshu. In the time-honored Chinese tradition of pretending illness during times of crisis, the couple hid in a sanatorium on the outskirts of Shanghai; it was Kang who made the arrangements. Together with Chen Yun, a Shanghai-based labor organizer who was Wang's aide-de-camp,* Kang hired an entire floor for the couple, enabling them to avoid contact with other occupants of the sanatorium. Even so, Wang suffered from uncontrollable fear. In late July 1931, after only a month as general secretary, he quit his post and departed for Moscow, where he took up the much safer and (at that time) even more prestigious position of chief Chinese representative to the Comintern.

Wang Ming's retreat to the Soviet Union by no means ended his influence within the CCP. Nor did it discourage Kang from continu-

---

* A natural survivor, Chen Yun emerged from the Cultural Revolution as an important critic of Maoist economics. Modern Chinese historians have conveniently forgotten Chen Yun's role as Wang Ming's aide, which may help explain why China watchers in the USSR have often attributed pro-Soviet sympathies to him.

ing to work for him. Many of the young, Soviet-trained Communists promoted by Wang held high Party office, which gave him an extraordinary measure of influence over Communist affairs. In early September 1931, one of Wang's most trusted and able lieutenants, Bo Gu, was named general secretary; Wang's faction remained in control of the Party. Moreover, Wang's position in Moscow, where he was a member of the Executive Committee of the Comintern, imbued his orders with all the authority of the office that, in theory, exercised supreme leadership over the Communist movement.

Kang still identified himself with Wang Ming's cause, advocating its underlying policies. He helped to create the type of well-organized, disciplined Bolshevik political machine favored by Soviet-trained Communists. Ever on guard, he used his authority to intimidate any cadres who challenged the Politburo's directives.

The devoted service Kang rendered to Wang Ming during their years in Shanghai disguised Kang's true approach to politics. He paid less attention to the substance of policy than to tactical acts that could increase his own power. By the early 1930s, Kang's chief political skill was that of identifying, and then hitching his fortunes to, any leader who happened to be the rising star within the Chinese Communist movement at the time. His opportunism may now seem recklessly transparent, but Kang acted with enough finesse to safeguard his reputation as a dedicated revolutionary. However insincere his support for any particular leader or policy, he always managed to convince his comrades that his uppermost priority was the Communist cause. These were the same tactics of sycophantic and unscrupulous courtiers known in China and portrayed in official histories and classical novels like *The Romance of the Three Kingdoms*, for over two thousand years. There is a common saying in the Shanghainese dialect, *jian mao bian se* ("to change color on seeing the cat"). Kang's protean allegiances thus followed a well-established pattern. In fact, the Shanghainese expression refers to an animal that has every reason to avoid cats: the rat.

Chapter IV

SECRET DANGERS,
SECRET SERVICE

BY GRABBING on to Wang Ming's coattails, Kang managed to land himself in the midst of the Chinese Communist elite. But his promotion to leader of the secret service—a role that was to become synonymous with the name Kang Sheng—had less to do with his skill at exploiting Wang Ming's patronage than with a crisis following a major Communist defeat in the dirty war against the Kuomintang. To the extent that Kang owed his promotion to any senior Party leader, rather than to luck, it was Zhou Enlai who helped him make the crucial transition from underground Party organizer to chief of spies and assassins.

After its decisive victory over the Communists in April 1927, the KMT gradually tightened its grip over most of China's cities. In Shanghai, Nanking, Peking, Tianjin, Hankow, Canton, and many smaller municipalities, the KMT controlled the instruments of government and used the police, army, and secret service to fight the Communists. A war of attrition followed, the KMT usually enjoying the advantage. Even in polyglot Shanghai, with its political, diplomatic, and legal loopholes favoring secret organizations, the CCP's chances of long-term survival might have seemed slim.

But the Communists did not make easy targets. Surrounded by deadly enemies, they had learned how to conceal themselves in the turmoil of Shanghai. The Special Branch files of the Shanghai Municipal Police paint a dramatic picture of the shadowy world Kang and his comrades inhabited. The CCP evolved into an endless network of cells, highly compartmentalized to ensure that no single arrest would provide more than a minimum of information to the police. The Communists devised an elaborate code of rules, many of them copied from the Russians: cadres were not to talk politics in the street; meetings should neither involve more than five people nor last longer than three hours; a meeting place should not be used more than three times a week; no more than seven people were to be present in any party "organ" at any time; if a comrade was arrested, everyone connected with him should move immediately (a rule that explains why police occasionally raided fully furnished apartments whose occupants had vanished). Communists also mastered the use of disappearing ink to write hidden messages on what appeared to be everyday correspondence between friends or lovers.

As the Communists became more elusive, the KMT established a professional security or "special service"* organization, the Investigation Section, which operated independently of the police and the army. The Investigation Section started out as a small cell within the KMT Organization Department, but it soon expanded into a sprawling, nationwide system of spies and agents. Its first chief was Chen Lifu, who was Chiang Kai-shek's secretary and the younger of the famous Chen brothers. The Chens headed "the CC Club," a powerful Kuomintang faction. Like many up-and-coming KMT leaders, Chen Lifu had studied in America, earning a master's degree in mining engineering at the University of Pittsburgh and then going to work in the Pennsylvania coal mines. Chen's experience in the United States convinced him that science and technology held the key to China's future, but when he returned to China in 1925, he became involved in politics at his brother's behest.

By 1929, Chen Lifu was devoting much of his time to other jobs, so he placed management of the secret service in the hands of his cousin Xu Enceng, although Chen was still nominally in charge of the Investigation Section. Xu, known in the West as U. T. Hsu, had graduated in electrical engineering from Shanghai's Communication University, then joined Chen Lifu in Pittsburgh, gone to work for Westinghouse, and attended the Carnegie Institute of Technology

---

* The Chinese term *tewu* ("special service") has a very broad meaning, combining the Anglo-American concepts of "intelligence," "secret intelligence" (i.e., collected covertly), and "security" with the concept of "special operations"—that is, paramilitary operations ranging from reconnaissance missions to assassinations.

before returning to China in 1925. Soft-spoken and smiling, Xu was in fact cunning, ruthless, greedy, and lascivious.

Menaced by the Investigation Section, the Communists decided to establish their own secret service. Zhou Enlai, as chief of the Party's Military Commission, was responsible for security matters. In November 1927, he formed a "Special Section"* out of a small, covert unit created after the April 12 massacre and a group of survivors of the worker pickets. At first, the Special Section concentrated on two basic functions—organizing safe meeting places and assassinating Communist renegades—but it rapidly grew into a comprehensive security and intelligence organization. Within a year, it had four subsections, each with its own specific tasks.

The most ordinary of the Special Section's assignments were the responsibility of the General Affairs Cell, which handled financial matters, logistics, and living accommodations for the top Communist leaders. It developed connections with photo studios, antique shops, furniture stores, and other commercial enterprises that could be used to hide weapons, pass secret messages, and provide fronts for its operations. The General Affairs Cell rented apartments in ways that could not be traced to the Communists. Cadres from the cell sometimes lived and worked in these safe houses. The unit's leader, Hong Yangsheng, occupied an apartment in the French Concession where Zhou Enlai and his Special Section deputies would assemble, thus avoiding the need to know each other's home addresses. Hong later rented an apartment on Avenue Road where Party leaders and Comintern representatives could meet, posing as local traders and foreign businessmen.

The General Affairs Cell also served as the Party's link with socially prominent Communist sympathizers scattered throughout Shanghai's intellectual and professional classes. When Party members were arrested, the General Affairs Cell would approach radical lawyers for help. Pan Zhenya, a well-known law professor, volunteered his services free whenever the Communists asked. Another lawyer, Fei Guoxi, also helped out but usually charged a small fee. The General Affairs Cell also had on call a doctor, Chen Jiakang, who treated wounded Communists.

---

* The full title of the Special Section was the Special Service Work Committee of the Central Military Commission, sometimes abbreviated to Central Special Section.

To carry out its most violent work, the Special Section employed a group of skilled gunmen. Known as the Red Squads or, in SMP parlance, the Assassination Corps, they provided bodyguards for senior personnel in Shanghai and security for meetings; they also targeted agents of the Investigation Section known to be particularly effective against the Communists. But the most important function of the Red Squads was to discipline, and sometimes even murder, Communists who had wavered in their commitment to the cause or defected to the KMT—a task that earned the Red Squads the name "Dog-Beating Corps." The Red Squads often were unable to find men and women among the Party rank and file who could use firearms, so they recruited operatives from the drug smugglers and gangsters of Shanghai's underworld.

The Red Squads conducted operations using a wide range of subterfuges and disguises. Gunmen at times passed themselves off as beggars and itinerant peddlers. Female squad members sometimes dressed as domestic servants. More elaborate schemes involved disguising gunmen as film crew cameramen and technicians. But the theatrical nature of the Red Squads' tactics never obscured their life-and-death missions or the brutality of their actions.

Beginning in mid-1927, Communist gunmen carried out a succession of attacks and assassinations. SMP dossiers report that in the International Settlement alone, the Red Squads shot at least forty people between 1927 and 1931—a minimum figure, because many victims of the Red Squads were never discovered. Often, they were buried secretly so that their fate would remain unknown. Besides, many assassinations took place in the French Concession and in Chinese-administered Greater Shanghai and so were not recorded by the SMP.

The police records of the assassinations reveal the confused loyalties and shifting alliances of Kang and his fellow Communists. Of the forty Red Squad victims detailed by the SMP, at least thirteen were Communists who had either turned police informant or defected to anti-Communist organizations. Traitors were often shot, but the Red Squads also suffered heavy losses; twenty-six of the gunmen responsible for the assassinations were arrested by the SMP. For a clandestine organization, the Communist casualties were high, a consequence of operating in a society where tipoffs and private deals were a way of life.

Zhou Enlai was usually too busy to pay much attention to the Party's secret work, so he entrusted day-to-day management of the Special Section and the Red Squads to a flamboyant gunman named Gu Shunzhang. Gu, a short, plump man expert at both pistols and the traditional Chinese staff, had caught the eye of the Communist leaders in 1925 during the May Thirtieth demonstrations and strikes. He went to the Soviet Union a year later for training in security work—investigations and interrogations, shooting, the use of explosives, and hand-to-hand combat. After returning to China, he served briefly as bodyguard for the Comintern representative, Mikhail Borodin, then began working closely with Zhou Enlai. Gu commanded some of the Communist forces in Shanghai during the 1927 uprising, eluded death in the April massacre, and was reportedly one of those who escaped along with Zhou shortly before KMT forces attacked the workers trapped in the Commercial Press building. Gu went on to gain election to the Central Committee in 1928.

Gu Shunzhang, a child of Shanghai's slums, craved political and social recognition. As a member of Du Yuesheng's infamous Green Gang, Gu had quick access to information from Shanghai's various police forces, all of which had been penetrated by Green Gang agents. He also frequented nightclubs, smoked opium, and gained celebrity as a magician, performing under the name Hua Guangqi in amusement centers like the famous Great World. This was a tall, wedding cake-like building on avenue Edouard VII that provided every form of entertainment from dancing and prostitution to target shooting, fan-tan, and roulette. Zhang Guotao, who worked with Gu during the May Thirtieth Movement, noted that "there was something of the Shanghai playboy in his appearance and mannerisms." Sheng Yue, a former Communist who had also known Gu, spoke of his "spendthrift private life and conduct" but observed that Zhou Enlai seemed to overlook that aspect of Gu's personality.

As the Shanghai police grew increasingly adept at detecting "Bolsheviks," spying on the Party's enemies became crucial to the Communists' survival. In April 1928, Zhou Enlai established the Intelligence Cell, a unit within the Special Section tasked with infiltrating hostile security services. The first head of the Intelligence Cell was Chen Geng, a twenty-five-year-old Hunanese who had studied assassination techniques along with Gu Shunzhang in the Soviet Union. After returning to Shanghai, he became involved in security work; always on edge, he slept with a pistol under his pillow. Like many of the Party workers in Shanghai, Chen was well known to Kang, sometimes staying in his house.

No sooner had the Intelligence Cell been established than the SMP Special Branch struck a blow at the Party, underscoring the importance of penetrating the enemy secret police. In late April 1928, the SMP raided an underground CCP office and arrested Luo Yinong, one of the leaders of the 1927 uprising. Chen Geng was frightened by the police's discovery of a safe house that Party cadres thought had never been compromised, and he set out to learn how it had been done. Through Gu Shunzhang's Green Gang contacts with the police, Chen Geng found that a pretty, German-speaking Chinese woman had approached a Special Branch officer at the Louza Police Station, offering to sell the names and addresses of 350 Communists in return for fifty thousand Chinese dollars and a passport to a foreign country. As a token of her bona fides, she had divulged the location of the office where Luo was caught.

Chen Geng identified the betrayer as He Zhihua, a former wife of Zhu De, the indestructible Communist general who was later depicted by the foreign press as always at Mao's side. He Zhihua had accompanied Zhu De to Germany in the mid-1920s, but afterward they broke up. After a period in Moscow, she went to work in the Party headquarters in Shanghai. Quickly disillusioned with communism, she plotted to escape to a new life. Upon discovering her identity, Chen Geng, Gu Shunzhang, and several Red Squad operatives raided He Zhihua's house at dawn and caught her and her new husband, He Jiaxing, asleep in bed. They recovered the list of 350 names and addresses, which had not yet been handed over to the police, then shot the couple while one of their men in the street drowned out the gunfire by setting off a string of firecrackers. He Zhihua survived the shooting (the Communists usually carried Mausers that fired 7.65mm ammo—a caliber that was too small to make death certain), but the SMP was no longer interested in her without the list. After recovering from her wounds, she vanished into anonymity in Sichuan Province, where she was from.*

---

* This incident had a sequel in 1983, when the Chinese authorities launched a wide-ranging anticrime campaign. In order to make the point that the children of high cadres were not above the law, the authorities executed one of Marshal Zhu De's grandsons, Zhu Jianhua, alleged to be a notorious criminal in Tianjin. That Zhu

Under Chen Geng's guidance, the Intelligence Cell cultivated a network of agents within the anti-Communist forces. The central figure in Chen's operations was a Cantonese, Bao Junfu, who worked at the Shanghai office of the KMT's Investigation Section. Educated in Japan, Bao returned to China during the May Fourth period and plunged into the hectic social world of Shanghai. He got to know a cross-section of society, ranging from Japanese journalists to SMP officers to Shanghai University students. Bao never actually joined the CCP, but he sympathized with the revolutionary cause. Through a Communist friend, he arranged to meet Chen Geng, who agreed that Bao would work for the Special Section. Recognizing Bao's value as an agent inside the KMT, Chen Geng spared no expense to assist him. He provided Bao with a car and assigned him a CCP cadre named Lian Desheng to act as both bodyguard and contact with the Intelligence Cell.

Bao's entry into the Investigation Section had been sponsored by a fellow Cantonese, Yang Jianhong. After Yang committed suicide over a corruption scandal, Bao was named the Investigation Section's "special representative" in Shanghai. He turned out to be an extraordinary asset to the Communists, providing a wealth of information about the KMT security forces. Bao also grew close to an SMP Special Branch officer, Detective Inspector Robertson,* who regarded Bao as an expert on communism in Shanghai and freely shared intelligence with him. Bao had even better access to the Chinese staff of the SMP, including another fellow Cantonese, Tan Shaoliang, who was a "clerical assistant" in the Special Branch section dealing with Communists. In the evenings, Bao and Tan dined and smoked opium together at the famous restaurant Yipin Xiang ("Supreme Fragrance"). Intoxicated by both Bao's charm and the opium, Tan talked openly about the Special Branch's operations.

Besides exploiting Bao as a source of knowledge about the enemy's plans, Chen used him to eliminate Communists who had turned

---

Jianhua was descended from He Zhihua mixed an element of revenge into what was already a highly political use of the judicial system.
* Detective Inspector Robertson was not the only SMP Special Branch officer on whom the Communists spied regularly. As the conflict with the Red Squads intensified, an American named Ross was assigned by a "U.S. intelligence bureau" to the Special Branch to strengthen the fight against the CCP. But according to Chinese accounts, Ross habitually confided in an unnamed "intimate" who provided information to Chen Geng's men in return for five hundred Chinese dollars a month.

renegade after arrest by the KMT. Chen would provide Bao with evidence purporting to show that a defector was a Communist "plant"; this he could then pass on to the KMT police, who often ended up doing the CCP's dirty work of executing the lapsed Communist.

Another Chen Geng agent, Song Zaisheng, landed a job as a "secret political investigator" in the Wusong Shanghai Garrison Command by bribing his former tutor, who had also taught the newly appointed garrison commander, Xiong Shihui. As an official in the garrison command, Song could expect to receive about a case of opium a month in bribes from the Green Gang; sharing 30 percent of his booty with his old tutor got him a glowing recommendation. Xiong himself hired him, and Song became known throughout Shanghai as a prominent KMT security official. He was especially close to a key Chinese policeman in the French Concession, Fan Guangzhen, who often tipped off Song about raids on the Communists. Disaffected left-wing activists occasionally approached Song, seeking to betray Communists like Li Lisan for a reward. With the help of Chen Geng and Gu Shunzhang, Song saw to it that none of the turncoats survived.

Even though the Communists had a number of highly placed agents, over time the Investigation Section started to win most of the battles in the secret war. By infiltrating Communist cells, recruiting renegades, and squeezing information from prisoners by torture or bribery, the Investigation Section smashed one Communist unit after another. In January 1928, not long after the Party had recovered from the massacre of April 1927, KMT agents raided over twenty Communist hideouts throughout Shanghai; according to the SMP, 125 Communists were arrested in the International Settlement and 186 in the French Concession and Greater Shanghai. The following year, an important peasant leader, Peng Pai,* was among 295 Communists captured. In 1930, another 572 Party members were arrested in Shanghai, many more than in any other part of the country. The year Wang Ming gained control of the Party, 1931, was an especially bad one for the Shanghai Communists. Only 345 were arrested, but they

---

* Peng Pai was executed, but his son, Peng Shilu, rose to be a senior Party cadre. In the mid-1980s, he was a member of the Central Committee and vice minister for water resources and electric power.

included a number of high officials—among them Paul and Gertrude Ruegg, a Swedish-born couple who were then Comintern representatives in China.*

The worst crisis of all hit on April 25, 1931, when Gu Shunzhang, for all his skills at covert work and his various disguises, was captured by Investigation Section agents in Hankow. An opportunist at heart, Gu agreed within hours of his arrest to cooperate with the KMT. His defection posed the greatest danger to the Shanghai Communists since 1927. In the days of panic after Gu's capture, Kang was promoted to head the CCP secret service.

Gu's defection could have crippled the Communist movement. His loss jeopardized the safety of many key CCP leaders, including Zhou Enlai, Wang Ming, Chen Yun, and Kang Sheng. A disaster that might have changed the course of Chinese history was thwarted only by the courage and coolness of two Intelligence Cell agents who, guided by Chen Geng, had infiltrated the KMT security services.

The more strategically placed of the two agents was Qian Zhuangfei, a thirty-five-year-old physician who worked in the Investigation Section headquarters in Nanking. Qian, a CCP member since 1925, was perfectly suited to be a Communist spy: tall and dapper, with a mischievous smile, a broad range of interests (painting, calligraphy, acting, filmmaking), and an effortlessly achieved image of a polished capitalist. Chen Geng, knowing that Xu Enceng picked many of his intelligence workers from the Zhejiang Radio and Telegraph Bureau, arranged for Qian to join a radio training group. Qian's special qualifications—not to mention his origins in Xu's hometown, Huzhou, in Zhejiang Province—made a good impression on Xu, who

---

* Ruegg, who called himself Hilaire Noulens, headed the Comintern's organization branch in China, handling financial and operational affairs. The SMP, who arrested Ruegg and his wife on June 15, 1931, after a tip from the Singapore colonial police, discovered documents in Ruegg's office revealing that the Comintern's Shanghai operation was the nerve center for Communist activity throughout the entire region. A total of $130,000 a month was budgeted out of Shanghai for organizing the Dutch East Indies, the Straits Settlements (which included Singapore, Malacca, and Penang), Formosa, Indochina, Korea, the Philippines, and Japan. Only $15,000 of that went to the Chinese Communist Party. The Ruegg affair caused a public sensation and led to Gerhardt Eisler, head of the CCP's political branch, fleeing China. The Rueggs were extradited to Nanking, but the Communists bribed the judges and the couple avoided the death sentence. They were released a year later, shortly before Chiang Kai-shek and Stalin established diplomatic relations. Within a year, a German named Arthur Ewart had reestablished the Comintern presence in Shanghai.

recruited him into the rapidly expanding Investigation Section in 1928. Moreover, Qian provided Xu with discreet accommodations for one of Xu's mistresses and became his confidential secretary and personal assistant.

The other undercover Communist who helped save the Party from the danger created by Gu's treason was Li Kenong. Inspired by the radical ideals of the May Fourth Movement, Li joined the Communists in 1926 in Wuhu, where he helped set up a Party training center, the Minsheng Middle School, and got to know the city's community of pro-Communist writers and poets. Transferred to Shanghai in the spring of 1928, Li worked on cultural matters, helping to radicalize local novelists, journalists, and magazine editors.

Like Qian, Li was ideal for espionage work. In his suit, tie, and thick round glasses, he could easily pass for a Shanghai journalist. He was a witty speaker with a talent for mimicry, and his engaging personality naturally elicited confidence. In 1929, with Qian's help, Li went to work at the Shanghai Radio Control Bureau, another of the units from which Xu picked recruits for secret work. As Qian had hoped, Li was invited to join the KMT intelligence service. Li spied on the KMT in Shanghai and also served as the intermediary between Qian (who dared not have contact with Communists at his base in Nanking) and Chen Geng. Chen, as head of the CCP Intelligence Cell, coordinated the work of Qian and Li and passed on their findings, first to Gu Shunzhang and then to Zhou Enlai.

The first report of Gu's defection was telegraphed to the Nanking headquarters of the Investigation Section on Saturday night, April 25, 1931. Minutes before the telegram arrived, Xu Enceng had left to spend the evening prowling cabarets and nightclubs. Using a codebook he had secretly copied, Qian deciphered the telegram and sent his young son-in-law, Liu Qifu, to warn Li Kenong late that night. The trains were slow, and Liu Qifu did not reach Shanghai until Sunday evening. When he tracked down Li Kenong in the Eastern Hotel, a popular haunt for Communist operatives, Li hastily arranged to contact the Special Section to pass on the news from Nanking.*

On hearing that Gu had changed sides, Zhou Enlai straightaway

---

* Qian escaped to Shanghai and from there to the Communist stronghold in Jiangxi; he died four years later during the Long March. Li Kenong also had to abandon his position within the KMT Security Office in Shanghai, but he continued in intelligence work and became a legendary figure in the Communist secret service.

ordered a series of drastic countermeasures. With the assistance of Chen Yun and Kang, who ran the Organization Department at the time, Zhou sent out the word for all important Party elements—the headquarters, the Jiangsu committee, and the Shanghai offices of the Comintern—to shift to a new base that night. Confusion took over the CCP hierarchy as files, equipment, clothing, and personal belongings were hastily packed and moved to different locations.

On Monday, April 27, as the Shanghai Communists were frantically trying to find new hiding places, Gu Shunzhang arrived by boat in Nanking under police escort. As soon as Gu reached the Kuomintang capital, Chiang Kai-shek granted him a personal audience. Gu swore to renounce communism, began revealing everything he knew about CCP operations, and proposed a plan for capturing Communist leaders in Shanghai. Xu Enceng ordered a squad of agents under the command of two of his subordinates, Zhang Chong and Gu Jianzhong, to go to Shanghai that evening and prepare a joint operation with the French and British police. On Tuesday morning, a series of raids began. But they were too late—the Communist leaders had already fled.

Nonetheless, Gu Shunzhang's treachery was a serious blow. A number of cadres were arrested, not only in Shanghai but also in Nanking, Peking, Tianjin, Hangzhou, Hankow, and other cities. Gu's information led to the capture of Xiang Zhongfa, the CCP general secretary who had been installed under Soviet auspices at the Sixth Congress in Moscow in 1928. On June 21, he was caught in the company of his mistress, a cabaret girl, Yang Xiuzhen, at the jewelry shop he used as a cover on avenue Joffre in the French Concession. Xiang then made a detailed confession to the Investigation Section interrogators and offered to work for the KMT, but he was executed two days after his capture. According to rumors at the time, Xiang was put to death because his captors considered him too stupid to be a useful defector, but the real reason was that Chiang Kai-shek's telegram of reprieve arrived only after the security police, showing unusual efficiency, had already shot him.* Gu also fingered many of the Communists arrested earlier, including two of Kang's teachers at

---

* Xiang's execution was a major blunder by the KMT, at once depriving them of a potent propaganda weapon (the capture and defection of the Communist general secretary was extremely humiliating for the CCP) and allowing the Communists to present Xiang as a martyr.

Shanghai University, Yun Daiying and Deng Zhongxia. Both were executed.

The arrests and executions that followed Gu Shunzhang's defection were not the only problems he caused. He wrote a book, *The Theory and Practice of Special Agent Work*, which for the first time gave the KMT a comprehensive inside picture of how the CCP secret service operated. The information he gave to the KMT almost devastated the Special Section: the network of spies Chen Geng had so artfully set up was destroyed; Bao Junfu, one of the Communists' most important assets, was arrested; Song Zaisheng had to run; other, less significant sources also disappeared.

At this moment of crisis, with the Party in Shanghai on the brink of destruction, Kang Sheng took his first step toward becoming the dominant figure in the Communist security and intelligence community. Zhou Enlai still headed the Military Commission, and as part of his effort to protect the Party against further damage, he reorganized the secret service. He formed a group of trusted senior cadres, the Special Work Committee, to manage the Party's intelligence and security operations and overcome the problems in the Special Section revealed by the Gu Shunzhang case. Zhou also ordered Chen Geng and the other Communist agents with blown covers to leave Shanghai, replacing them with new personnel.

Chairing the new committee personally, Zhou appointed four other members: Pan Hannian, a twenty-five-year-old cadre who had worked as an agent of influence in Shanghai's literary world and had befriended many of the local writers; Guang Huian, a Cantonese gunman and alternate member of the Central Committee; Chen Yun, Wang Ming's personal aide; and Kang Sheng.* Kang lacked the specialized Soviet training of Gu Shunzhang and Chen Geng, but he was qualified for the task by his years of operating covertly in the dangerous environment of Shanghai.

---

* Three members of this group—Zhou, Kang, and Chen Yun—would exercise a profound influence on Chinese Communist politics over the next four decades. As for the other two, Guang Huian vanished after his arrest by the Kuomintang in September 1934, and Pan Hannian, Shanghai's vice mayor after 1949, was arrested on April 3, 1955, while attending a Party meeting in Peking. Pan was accused of having been an agent of both the Kuomintang and the Japanese during the war and of having protected a group of KMT agents from Taiwan in the 1950s. He died in 1977, having spent the last twenty years of his life in a succession of prisons and labor camps.

Within months of organizing the new secret service, Zhou Enlai faced increasing risk of arrest. The Investigation Section, following up the many clues provided by Gu Shunzhang, got closer and closer to him. Fearing for his safety, Zhou left for the rural Communist base in the mountains of Jiangxi in August 1931. Before his departure, though, Zhou completed the first stage of Kang's elevation to China's security czar, giving him command of the Special Work Committee and placing him in charge of the entire Communist security and espionage apparatus—not only in Shanghai but throughout KMT China. Not one to ignore such an opportunity to wield power, Kang held this crucial post for two years until he was reassigned to Moscow.

Zhou Enlai reshuffled the personnel of the Special Section and established new operating procedures, but its structure remained intact. When Kang took over the secret service, the Intelligence Cell, the Red Squads, and the General Affairs Cell still performed the same functions. But a Liaison Cell had been newly created to manage the sensitive task of communications, both within the secret service and between Party headquarters in Shanghai and the rural base in Jiangxi. By the time Kang was in charge of security, the Liaison Cell used clandestine radios for much of its work.

In the course of establishing the Special Work Committee , Zhou put an entirely new management team in place. Guang Huian, a colleague of Kang's on the Special Work Committee, replaced Gu Shunzhang as chief of the Red Squads. Known as the Third Section, the Red Squads by then had between thirty and forty gunmen divided into nine teams. Guang Huian worked closely with Kang, although the Red Squads as a group remained separate from the rest of the secret service. Pan Hannian, another member of the committee, succeeded Chen Geng as head of the Intelligence Cell, or Second Section, and started to reestablish a set of agents inside the KMT.

Unlike Zhou, who had supervised the Special Section from afar, Kang involved himself directly in the work of the secret service. He assumed command of the Liaison Cell, or Fourth Section, from its previous head, Li Qiang, one of the men sent away from Shanghai by Zhou. This position put Kang in control of almost every facet of Communist security operations. With responsibility for communications among the four sections of the secret service, he had direct knowledge of most of the Party's clandestine activity. As the man in charge of radio communications, Kang could monitor the messages transmitted among the various Party bases. He also supervised contact with Comintern representatives in Shanghai; although the Comintern had its own radio operator in Shanghai, its agents still had to rely on Kang's Fourth Section to communicate with the Communist headquarters in Jiangxi.

In his new role, Kang entered a hidden Communist elite that enjoyed extraordinary powers and privileges. The Special Work Committee and its four sections were independent of the normal Party structure; few cadres knew this secret organization existed, let alone who its members were. The agents of the Special Work Committee had few duties except to carry out their covert work, for which, by CCP standards, they were highly paid. Indeed, Kang usually had first call on Party funds. Handsome bribes were paid to police in the International Settlement and the French Concession, while money for other activities often was hard to come by.

Kang's control of the Party's bank accounts sparked heated debate among the Communists in Shanghai. As the secret service became ever larger and more costly, its critics began making veiled references to greed and corruption. Some even hinted that the police posed no great threat and only arrested a few Communists at a time so that the corrupt policemen who sold tips to Kang's men could better milk the CCP for money. The relative luxury in which secret-service agents lived added to the controversy. Many of them led glamorous, flamboyant lives. Two of Kang's desperado-operatives in the Red Squads, Ding Mocun and Li Shiqun, habitually wore expensive suits, spent their time in restaurants, gambling dens, and brothels, and socialized with gangsters and cabaret girls.

High living helped set the secret service apart, but more telling was the power it exercised with utmost harshness over other Communists. After Gu Shunzhang's arrest, for example, no sooner was his defection confirmed than every member of his family—wife and infant son, mother-in-law, and wife's sister and brother-in-law—was murdered by the Red Squads on Zhou Enlai's orders and buried secretly. Except for Gu's infant son, all the victims worked in the General Affairs Cell, and none showed any indication of wanting to follow Gu's example and defect. Their deaths were not intended as a deterrent to others—their bodies were buried in a garden in the French

Concession and not discovered for several months—and can only be explained as an act of revenge.*

The murder of Gu's entire family exposed the brutality and bloodlust of Kang's professional hit men and epitomized the life-and-death power he came to exercise over his comrades and their families. Kang looked harmless enough, peering through his thick glasses at documents and people like a nearsighted bookworm, but the history of the Red Squads shows he had no qualms about inflicting pain.

The Communists survived Gu's betrayal, but the Party's situation in Shanghai remained precarious.† The KMT Investigation Section arrested a number of Party officials but only a few of much importance. Comintern representative Otto Braun laid the blame on Kang for the Party's losses, asserting that "the security department established by Kang Sheng ... had proved a total failure—culminating in the arrest of numerous leading functionaries and the confiscation of the radio station, severing the central committee's contact with the outside world." The truth is that the damage had been inflicted before Kang became the secret-service chief; Gu Shunzhang's treason was the decisive blow. In the words of Xu Enceng, Gu "was a living encyclopedia of communist underground activities" who provided the key to the Communists' secret world.

The Communists became further imperiled in April 1932, when the KMT set up a new security agency. On April 1, Chiang Kai-shek established the Special Agent Section of the Rejuvenation Society, a right-wing organization usually known in English as the Blue Shirts or Blue Gowns and modeled, somewhat loosely, after Hitler's Brown Shirts and Mussolini's Black Shirts. The leader of the Special Agent Section was Dai Li, a graduate of the Whampoa Military Academy, who had proved his loyalty to Chiang Kai-shek by carrying out a variety of dangerous and sensitive missions.

Dai Li's Blue Shirts steadily expanded their authority, eventually gaining command of much of the KMT police and military. Blue Shirt

---

* Gu himself worked for the KMT Investigation Section until 1935, when evidence emerged that he had resumed clandestine contact with the Communists—largely, it would seem, out of boredom with a settled life. The KMT executed him that spring.
† A debate continues to this day over how much damage Gu's defection caused. It certainly cost the Communists the lives of several important leaders and dislodged the most important Communist agents within the KMT at the time, but it never developed into a complete disaster.

special agents monitored the conspiracies of the militarists (the war-lords and semi-independent generals who threatened Chiang Kai-shek's power), spied on critics of the KMT like the widowed Madame Sun Yat-sen, and ran a private war against the Communists. Dai Li's men relentlessly pursued their targets, kidnapping and assassinating at will. Free from legal constraints, they were always prepared to torture their victims. One of their common methods of extracting information from a male prisoner was to bind his hands behind his back, tie a rope to his two thumbs, and then slowly hoist him from the ground, jerking the rope suddenly at every sign of resistance. If that failed to loosen the prisoner's tongue, he was tied to a wall and his ribcage was pressed to squeeze his internal organs and cause extreme agony with little outward sign of injury; or water was forced into the prisoner's nose and throat, inducing a sense of drowning. Female prisoners had their nipples punctured with needles, sticks forced into their vaginas, and bamboo splinters inserted under their fingernails.

Dai Li's Blue Shirts had no major impact on the Communists for almost a year, but the Investigation Section and Shanghai's police forces continued their campaigns with notable success. Faced with the growing KMT threat, Kang's secret service began a violent counter-offensive. The Red Squads, armed with automatic pistols, unleashed a campaign of terror to intimidate Investigation Section operatives, KMT secret agents, and defectors. On April 22, 1932, two male Chinese dressed like foreigners shot and killed Detective Superinten-dent Wang Bin, the operative from KMT military headquarters in Shanghai who had arrested Xiang Zhongfa, the Communist general secretary, the previous year. On November 25, 1932, six Red Squad gunmen led by Guang Huian and assisted by a KMT defector raided an underground office of the Investigation Section in Zhabei, killing one agent and wounding three others. On April 11, 1933, five Red Squad gunmen sitting in a café in southern Shanghai opened fire on four Investigation Section agents they had spotted in the street. One of the KMT men died, and two were seriously wounded; the Com-munists vanished into the crowds. The following month, an Investi-gation Section agent on his way to give evidence in court was ambushed by the Red Squads; he died in an ambulance en route to a hospital. The feud between the Red Squads and the KMT security men was starting to turn Shanghai into a Wild West town or gangland Chicago.

Despite the Communist counteroffensive, the Party's security continued to deteriorate, and the leaders decided to move their head-quarters out of Shanghai near the end of 1932. Equipment and records were transported along a secret route that went by steamer from Shanghai to Swatow and then by small boats up the Han River into the heart of Fujian Province, about 180 miles from the Communist stronghold in Jiangxi. Most of the senior Communists retreated to Jiangxi, but Kang stayed in Shanghai. He had two major tasks: to run the newly established Shanghai Bureau, which supervised Communist activity in China's main city, and to lead the Special Work Committee in the clandestine war with the KMT.

Amid this life-and-death struggle, Kang still found time to turn out copious articles for secretly distributed propaganda papers and magazines such as *Red Flag Periodical*, *Struggle*, and *Compass of the Workers' Movement*. As his writings show, even then he understood the place of secret-service work in the CCP's overall structure and recognized that no matter how useful brute force was, anyone who wanted to reach the highest rungs of the Party must also be both propagandist and policymaker.

Ever since the reorganization of the Communist headquarters following Gu Shunzhang's defection, Kang had also managed the Labor Department. That job lacked the instant and direct power that flowed from the assassin's pistol, but in a political party that exalted the proletariat it carried great prestige. By publishing articles on labor issues, Kang participated in Communist debates on Party policy, trade union affairs, and, perhaps most significant of all, foreign policy. Between December 1931 and July 1933, he wrote about twenty articles, a figure that shows how much importance he attached to literary warfare.

For security reasons, Kang always wrote under one pseudonym or another. Sometimes he used names such as Luotuo or "Camel," but his favorite pseudonym had a prophetic ring: Xie Kang ("Gratitude for Health") was a step toward his adoption of "Kang Sheng" when he reached Moscow in 1933. Despite all of Kang's aliases, the Communist cadres who mattered to him, especially Wang Ming and his lieutenants, knew that he was the author—a guarantee that his literary efforts would bring political rewards.

Nominally, Kang's articles were concerned with labor matters, but as often as not he turned his attention to the central issues of Communist policy. Support for "the accomplishments of the fourth plenum"—the code word for Pavel Mif's selection of Wang Ming as the dominant leader of the Politburo—was a regular feature of his essays. Kang's writings gave Wang Ming unreserved backing, thereby endorsing Soviet policy at a time when the Comintern faced growing resistance from some elements in the Chinese Communist movement.

The main issue at the time was Japan's aggression against China and what attitude the Chinese Communists should adopt toward it. Chinese police had arrested a Japanese army officer, Captain Naka-mura, and three other Japanese in a restricted military zone in north-eastern China in June 1931. All four had been wearing civilian clothes, so Chinese authorities executed them as spies on July 1. This was what the Japanese militarists had been waiting for. On September 18, 1931, Japanese troops seized Mukden (as Shenyang was then known) and occupied Manchuria, which covered China's three northeastern provinces. Outraged, most Chinese declared that they would oppose the Japanese by any means possible. The same nationalistic impulses were voiced by many Communists who criticized Chiang Kai-shek's cautious response to the Japanese. Under Wang Ming's leadership, however, the official line—which Kang propagated zealously—was an anti-Japanese stance designed primarily to serve Soviet interests.

Kang's articles depicted "the Mukden Incident" not so much as an attack on China as "imperialism carrying out the carving up of China and starting its assault on the Soviet Union." This pro-Soviet perspective distanced Kang from the nationalistic Chinese Commu-nists who wanted the labor movement to unite against Japan. Kang insisted that correct Party policy was to arm the labor force and "mobilize the workers to support the soviets"; nationalistic Party members, in direct opposition, wanted an alliance between the Com-munist ("red") unions and the KMT ("yellow") unions to bolster the country's anti-Japanese cause. In this, Kang loyally echoed the policy of the Stalin-dominated Comintern and unwaveringly defended the Moscow-oriented policies of his patron, Wang Ming.

Meanwhile, threats to the Communists in Shanghai, and to Kang in particular, increased steadily. The Investigation Section tightened its net around the CCP and began arresting cadres close to Kang. On February 1, 1933, Wang Yuncheng, Wang Ming's former bodyguard who later revealed Kang's perfidy to the Communist cause, was de-tained by a KMT detective in a house in the International Settlement and forced to divulge details about a number of Communist leaders.

One of these was Kang, whom he referred to as Zau Yoon, a transliteration of the Shanghainese pronunciation of Zhao Rong, the name Kang was then known by. The police dossier summarized Wang's comments on Kang: "Native of Jiangsu, age about forty, height five foot two inches. Slim build, deep set eyes. Wears glasses. Known to be a heavy smoker of Golden Rat cigarettes. Member of 'Central' and of the Special Party (G.P.U.)."

Wang Yuncheng's description did nothing to apprehend Kang. It incorrectly listed his home province as Jiangsu and underreported his height by six inches, but it did highlight Kang's prominence, especially in the eyes of the police, always on the watch for anyone from the Communist security unit.

The SMP got a big step closer to Kang one month later, when they captured Chen Geng, former head of the Intelligence Cell. Chen had come back to Shanghai after losing contact with his comrades in the field. A turncoat, Zhang Liansheng, spotted him inside the Peking Theatre in the International Settlement; Chen was arrested on March 24, the night before he was to have left for a Communist base in Sichuan. Chen's arrest was a stark warning to Kang, in whose home Chen had spent the previous few days. Once Chen fell into the hands of the Investigation Section, there was no guarantee that he would not reveal Kang's whereabouts. Chen later said that he had divulged none of the names of his Communist cohorts, although he was whipped and tortured with electric shocks.*

The Red Squads continued to have their successes under Kang, even though more and more Communist leaders were being caught. On June 14, four Communist assassins shot and killed the head of the Shanghai bureau of the Investigation Section, Shi Jimei—also known as Ma Shaowu, Lu Keqin, and Zhou Guangya—as he alighted from a car in the heart of the International Settlement. Shi, a former Red Squad agent, had defected to the KMT and won the reputation of being the most effective Investigation Section agent in Shanghai. He had masterminded a number of schemes, including the kidnapping of

---

* Chen told Edgar Snow that he was tortured during his detention in the International Settlement, before he was handed over to the Chinese authorities. That seems doubtful, since the bulk of evidence suggests that the British-run police avoided brutal methods of interrogation. Indeed, when a Chinese newspaper reported that Chen Duxiu had been beaten by the SMP, the head of the Special Branch, T. P. Givens, noted on the report, "Not even Chen Duxiu could be guilty of such a monstrous lie." The paper finally published a retraction.

Ding Ling, by then a widely read left-wing woman writer. Operating out of the East Hun-chi Hotel, Shi led a team of shady detectives, many recruited from Shanghai's underworld. Shi's men, according to a Chinese journalist, Li Jiezhen, spent their spare time "gorging themselves with food and drink, gambling, sleeping with prostitutes, and taking salversan injections."

True to his dissolute lifestyle, Shi Jimei was on his way to a dinner party in an elegant brothel (euphemistically described by *The Shanghai Evening Post and Mercury* as "a sing-song house known as Sweet Heart") when Communist agents gunned him down. Shi's killing set off a citywide manhunt. At first, Shi's mistress was suspected of having set him up for ambush, but attention soon focused on another guest at the dinner—Kang's underling Ding Mocun, a member of the Red Squads who worked by day as a journalist and editor of *The Social Daily News*. Ding was taken into custody. Friends in the KMT secured his release, in a gesture typical of the tangled relationships of Chinese politics, but Ding's arrest sounded another warning that the KMT was closing in on the Communist secret service in Shanghai.

Even so, the Special Section continued to wage war on the KMT. Red Squad gunmen assassinated Shi Jimei's successor, Qian Yizhang, shortly after his arrival in Shanghai, as he waited for an elevator on the third floor of the Chunghua Hotel. But now the tide was running against the Communists, and the losses inflicted by the KMT mounted. Soon after the slaying of Shi Jimei, Kang's colleague Sheng Yue concluded that Kang was too well known for his own safety, a judgment supported by a story in *The Shanghai Evening Post and Mercury* on July 19, 1933. According to this news item, "a mysterious document purporting to emanate from the secret Blue Gown or Chinese Fascist Organization and containing orders for wholesale assassinations has been circulated in Shanghai. . . ." The third name on the death list—dated June 15, the day after Shi Jimei's assassination—was Zhao Yun, another Shanghainese version of Zhao Rong, Kang's *nom de guerre*. Dai Li's Blue Shirts had recognized Kang's importance in the Communist movement in Shanghai. It was time to go.

Instead of retreating to the Communist base in rural Jiangxi, Kang went to Moscow to join Wang Ming. Accompanied by Cao Yi'ou, Kang followed a route that many other Party members had taken before him: by steamship from Shanghai to the Japanese-occupied port of Dalian on China's northeast coast, then across Manchuria by train to the small border town of Manzhouli, and from there by a Russian train across Siberia to Moscow.

Kang entrusted Li Zhusheng, a supporter of Wang Ming and a Moscow-trained Communist, with running the Party's operations in Shanghai. Li survived for about a year. On June 14, 1934, KMT agents acting together with police forces of the International Settlement and the French Concession raided four dozen Communist hideouts and netted fifty-four senior leaders, including Li Zhusheng, who soon defected to the KMT. Seven radio transmitters were also seized by the police, which effectively stopped all but the most limited communication between the few Communists remaining in Shanghai and both the Comintern in Moscow and the CCP base in Jiangxi.

The final blow to the Party apparatus in Shanghai was struck three months later. On September 27, 1934, an all-out KMT campaign against the Red Squads succeeded in arresting their leader, Kang's former henchman Guang Huian, and thirty-five of his comrades. This series of arrests marked the KMT's final victory over the Communists in Shanghai. It is significant that the Red Squads, then under Kang's control for two years, were the last of the Communist organizations to be cracked by their archenemy, the KMT Investigation Section.

Kang's years in Shanghai directing the Party's clandestine work and its assassination teams had initiated him into a secret and powerful elite. The period had also cleared a path for Kang's future advance in CCP ranks; it had brought him face to face with the darkest side of the Party's activities and inured him to treachery, violence, and brutality. Kang's Shanghai experience was ideal preparation for his next destination, Moscow, where there were unusual opportunities for a man of his temperament and talents.

Chapter V

MOSCOW,
FINISHING SCHOOL
FOR SADISTS

KANG SHENG spent the next four years in Moscow completing his political education and earning postgraduate degrees in every aspect of political terror. He had frequent and intimate dealings with the Soviet secret police,* lived through the darkest and most terrifying days of Stalin's Great Purge, and came to understand in detail the value of secret police in a Communist state. Within five years of his return, Kang was boasting that he had learned nothing in Moscow; to Soviet officials he would add, tauntingly, that otherwise he would have sunk into "dogmatism"— Maoist jargon for slavishly following Russian theory. Nevertheless, what Kang learned in the USSR helped him climb to the highest levels in the Chinese Communist Party during the next twelve years as the CCP fought the KMT for control over the mainland.

When Kang reached Moscow in July 1933, it was the radical capital of the world, "the Holy City of Socialism"—tangible proof that revolution could succeed, sweep away the old order, and create

---

* Although Lin Biao and others have compared Kang Sheng to Stalin's dreaded secret-police heads, Feliks Dzerzhinski and Lavrenti Beria, Kang had no direct dealings with either one. Dzerzhinski died in 1926, when Kang was still a fledgling member of the CCP in Shanghai. Beria was not transferred from Georgia to Moscow until 1938, the year after Kang left Russia for China. By the time Kang returned to Moscow in 1956, Beria had already been executed. Mikhail L. Titarenko, director of the Soviet Institute of Far Eastern Studies of the Academy of Sciences, told the authors in a 1989 interview that Kang "certainly was a disciple of Beria's, using perversion and very subtle cruelty and in some instances even surpassing Beria's cruelty."

a new society under Communist rule. Ever since the Bolsheviks had toppled the czar and seized power in October 1917, Moscow's revolutionary aura had lured hundreds of young Chinese, many of them Communists sent for special training. But there were also young members of the KMT, in those days a revolutionary, anti-imperialist party; among them, for instance, was Chiang Ching-kuo, son of Chiang Kai-shek. Still others were idealistic, free-floating radicals.

Apart from its promise of utopia, Moscow possessed few charms when Kang and Cao Yi'ou arrived there. The suburbs were filthy; the people wore drab, unwashed clothes that took on "an unendurable odor of sheep's dung" from the sweat of their owners; long lines waited outside the shops; restaurant menus mostly listed unavailable dishes. The Chinese visitors, accustomed to filth and poverty, were not shocked by Moscow's physical appearance. But the Russian diet, especially the lack of fresh vegetables, was hard on them. Soviet economic policy, as it did until recently, placed priority on armaments and heavy industry, at the expense of the citizens' well-being. Then as now, Russian products were shoddy: locks either shut and would not open, or opened and would not shut, or else neither opened nor shut; doors fitted so badly that the cracks had to be filled with paper and rags to stop drafts; buses fell to pieces on the roads; elevators were always "out of order." Life was bad enough for Soviet citizens, but foreigners had the additional burden of being viewed with suspicion. The growing menace of European fascism and Japanese aggression reinforced Russian xenophobia; ordinary citizens shunned foreigners. Few officials responsible for international affairs deigned to talk to visitors like Kang and Cao Yi'ou, whose alien origins were obvious.

Moscow did have its pleasures—ballet, theater, museums, and art galleries all were splendid. So were the Kremlin, with its stately grandeur, and the onion domes of the Russian churches, rising like tarnished moons out of the industrial wasteland. After Shanghai, though, with its bustling population, well-stocked stores, and countless restaurants, Moscow seemed gray, bureaucratic, and run-down.

The drabness of the Soviet capital did not dim the enthusiasm of Kang and true believers like him. The nearly spiritual fervor of most radical visitors to the Soviet Union made it easy for them to disregard the long lines, the shabby apartments, and the daily hardships. Besides, living in Moscow as a leader of a foreign Communist party, Kang was granted privileges enjoyed by the Soviet elite. Together with Cao Yi'ou, he settled into the Hotel Lux. The Lux had accommodated a transient population of self-proclaimed revolutionaries from all over the world since the 1920s. Few of the hotel's occupants left their traces on history, but Kang had some interesting neighbors, including Japanese Communist leader Nosaka Sanzo, who eventually followed Kang back to China, and the Yugoslav Communist Josip Broz, as Tito was then known.

The Lux was dark and dingy, but its Bohemian atmosphere made for a pleasant haven. The apartments, large and comfortable, came furnished with beds, sofas, tables, and chairs—every amenity except telephones. Located on Gorky Street, a main shopping thoroughfare in those days, the hotel stood amid a bustle that reminded Chinese of their homeland.

The Lux was a watering hole for foreigners. Agnes Smedley, a radical American journalist who had worked in China, visited the Lux and met both Wang Ming and Kang Sheng in 1933 and 1934. Senior Comintern officials often attended social events there, as did many overseas visitors seeking to consult on advancing the cause of world revolution. Chinese studying at the University of the Toilers of the East, the Lenin Institute, and the military academies around Moscow also called at the Lux from time to time. Language was not a major problem for Kang; from his years at the Qingdao German School, he knew enough German to communicate with the Lux's German contingent, and he soon acquired fluent if ungrammatical Russian. Many Russian officials habitually worked late into the night and held parties at 10 or 11 P.M. That suited Kang, who was something of a night owl.

To mark still another new phase in his life, Kang changed his name for the last time. He dropped Zhao Rong, which had served him for the previous five years, in favor of Kang Sheng. The literal meaning of his new name was "Healthy Life," but when Kang chose it he undoubtedly had in mind that in classical Chinese the character "sheng" also means scholar and that he was thus styling himself "the Healthy Scholar." Although foreigners had no difficulty in pronouncing Kang Sheng, which was sometimes rendered in the Comintern English-language propaganda as Kon Sin or Kang Sin, it was a strange name to Chinese eyes and ears. It reflected the traditional Chinese desire for longevity, but its blunt expression of concern with physical well-being betrayed an intense anxiety about health. Some of Kang's old friends from his Shanghai days continued to call him Zhao Rong until the 1960s, but he used the name Kang Sheng for the rest of his life.

Kang arrived in Moscow at the right moment. It was summer, the rain and mud of spring had given way to warm, comfortable weather, and the city's parks were green and fresh. More significant, it was high summer in the CCP's relations with the Soviet Union, so Kang could use his time in the socialist motherland to improve his standing within the CCP.

There was no question which of the two Communist powers reigned supreme. The Soviets had ordered a succession of changes in the CCP leadership between 1927 and 1933. The Comintern had blessed Chen Duxiu's ouster and Qu Qiubai's rise and fall, and had actually orchestrated the ascent and decline of Li Lisan, as well as the installation of Wang Ming as CCP head. By 1933, the Comintern no longer tried to direct policy implementation in China itself, but it still had a say in the Party's general political line. Some Chinese, including those who had turned to Trotskyism after the massacre of April 1927 and those who had resisted Mif's installation of Wang Ming as CCP leader, had challenged Moscow's influence (unsuccessfully) as early as January 1931. But the first serious disruption in relations between the CCP and the Russians was caused by simple communications problems. The Soviet radio link with the Shanghai Communists was severed by KMT Investigation Section raids on Party hideouts in 1934. Several months later, the Chinese Red Armies lost their codebooks, and thus contact with Moscow, while setting out on the chaotic Long March through the mountains and gorges of western China.

Fortunately for Kang, Wang Ming, his patron in Shanghai, was now head of the Chinese delegation to the Comintern. The original plan had been for Wang Ming to move to the Communist headquarters in Jiangxi and for Kang to replace him as delegation chief in Moscow, but because of the deteriorating security situation in China, Wang Ming could not—or would not—run the risks involved in the journey. So Wang Ming stayed in Moscow and Kang was named deputy leader. Kang may have been disappointed, but he also knew he could profit from Wang Ming's continued presence in the Soviet Union. Wang, an experienced operator in the dangerous world of Soviet politics, had close ties to both Pavel Mif, the chief of the Comintern's Far Eastern Bureau, who had installed him as Party chief in 1931, and Georgi Dimitrov, the tall, robust, serious Bulgarian who advised Stalin on international Communist matters.

The Comintern connection was especially important to Kang. In theory an independent bureau representing the Communist parties of the world, the Comintern became, in the early 1920s, an instrument of Soviet policy. Its operatives enjoyed special status in Russian society: they had access to senior Soviet officials; they could obtain tickets to the theater and the ballet and to military parades in Red Square; they could shop in the stores reserved for the elite.

As a body dedicated to leading a world revolution, the Comintern gave its members a sense of playing a unique role in history. The conspiratorial dimension of the Comintern accentuated its mystique. The secret agents who represented the Comintern in cities as diverse as Barcelona and New York, Berlin and Shanghai, came to see in their own clandestine existences the makings of a new world; associating with them, Kang also grew convinced that he was part of destiny.

As Kang found his way around the corridors of the enormous old mansion in Ozhod-Niriat that housed the Comintern offices, his connection with Wang Ming was a potent talisman in this alien environment. Other Chinese had discovered that survival in Moscow's ever shifting political currents was not easy; not even a senior post on the Comintern guaranteed against trouble. Factional rivalries had reached a frightening level since Lenin's death in 1924. Stalin had emerged as supreme leader, but he was surrounded by enemies, both real and imagined—principally Leon Trotsky, the father of the Red Army, until his exile from the USSR in 1929. But even after Trotsky's defeat, to voice the wrong line could mean prison or execution. An atmosphere of threat and apprehension paralyzed official circles in Moscow as struggles at the top led to the arrest and disappearance of anyone who had aroused suspicion.

At first, the Chinese in Moscow had no direct interest in the struggle for succession, but they were inevitably swept up in it after Trotsky blamed the April 1927 massacre in Shanghai on Stalin. Almost without exception, the Chinese students in Moscow had been distressed by Chiang Kai-shek's suppression of the Communists in China. Many Chinese viewed Stalin as the root cause of the CCP's setbacks. Naïve and ignorant about the intricacies of Russian politics, a number of Chinese openly blamed Stalin for the Communist defeat in China, only to be arrested and imprisoned. The hunt for Trotsky's "agents" had abated temporarily by the time Kang arrived in Moscow, but in such a potentially hazardous place Wang Ming was a sure and steady beacon.

In return for Wang Ming's patronage, Kang maintained his highly vocal support of Wang's claim to be the supreme Chinese Communist leader. Soon after he reached Moscow, Kang made a round of speeches in the role of "a central leader who had just arrived from China." He visited the University of the Toilers of the East, the Lenin Institute, and other schools and academies with large numbers of Chinese students learning how to take Marxism back to China; at each one, he gave glowing reports of the Chinese Communist Revolution. In his talks, Kang praised Wang Ming for his leadership of the CCP, and for Wang's booklet *The Two Lines: Struggle for the Further Bolshevization of the Chinese Communist Party*, which Kang described as a "realization of the party's line."

Kang also recounted Wang's achievements to the Comintern. In November 1933, four months after Kang's arrival, Wang Ming addressed the Thirteenth Plenary Session of the Comintern's Executive Committee. Kang also spoke, painting an optimistic picture of the Chinese Revolution and conveying the misleading impression that the CCP had suffered no reverses under the Moscow-trained Communists Wang Ming had left in charge. Kang recited a litany of Wang Ming's alleged victories. Over the previous year, he reported, Party membership in the "White Areas" (controlled by the KMT) had grown from thirty thousand to sixty thousand. Kang's claim was a lie, but it flatteringly attributed the "increase" to Wang's "lively leadership." Kang was especially eloquent on the Communists' urban successes. "Despite the horrible conditions of police terror," Kang declared, "the Chinese proletariat and toiling masses have performed marvels of heroism, have applied flexible means of struggle, and have been able to overcome all difficulties."

Besides advertising Wang Ming's achievements in China, Kang's speech endorsed the Soviet line on almost every issue. At the strategic level, he unequivocally stated that China would assist the Soviet Union if Japan invaded the USSR. "In the event of a military attack by Japanese imperialism upon the Soviet Union," Kang declared boldly, "the Chinese toiling masses and the Chinese Red Army under the leadership of the Communist Party and in alliance with the Soviet and Japanese proletariat will . . . decisively . . . repulse the

Japanese and other imperialist plunderers, will . . . defeat Japanese imperialism and . . . [will] convert military-fascist, monarchist-police Japan, the Japan of the Mikado and of Araki, into a free, soviet workers' and peasants' Japan." Putting aside his own nationalistic passions, Kang implied that the Soviet Union's fate was more important than China's: "The national revolutionary war . . . organized by the CCP against the Japanese . . . is not only a struggle for the national liberation of China but has already in actual fact become a factor delaying the offensive of the Japanese imperialists against the USSR."

In keeping with the Russian view of China as a bastion against a Japanese attack on the USSR, Kang displayed a special interest in Manchuria, China's resource-rich northeastern region that served as a strategic buffer between Japanese-occupied Korea, to the south, and the Soviet Union and its puppet state, Outer Mongolia. Kang praised the success of the Communist partisans in Manchuria and reproved the KMT's alleged tendency to compromise with the Japanese. Indeed, he condemned Chiang Kai-shek as "the open agent of Japanese imperialism and traitor to the national interests of China."

Kang's first speech to the Comintern endorsed an ideological framework that pleased Soviet ears. Instead of glorifying peasant uprisings, the specialty of Mao Zedong and other Chinese Communists who had never been to Moscow, Kang implied that the Chinese proletariat, not the peasantry, was the most reliable and sophisticated class. He lauded the peasant movement for its spontaneous character but noted that once it had fallen under the leadership of the proletariat and the CCP, it had degenerated into nothing more than a struggle to develop "soviets"—self-contained rural Communist bases.

The 1933 plenum of the Comintern Executive Committee gave Kang a prominence in Moscow's political community that ordinarily took new arrivals years to achieve. Kang's and Wang Ming's speeches were published in 1934 in a co-authored book titled *China's Present Situation and the Mission of the Communist Party*, allowing Kang to link his name with Wang Ming's in Comintern propaganda distributed widely throughout the Soviet Union and beyond.

Kang's praise of Wang Ming and his clear endorsement of Soviet policy brought quick rewards. In January 1934, when the CCP Central Committee met in the town of Ruijin in Jiangxi Province, Kang was elected in absentia to the Politburo, the Party's supreme policy-making body.*

Kang had no cause to regret working with Wang in Moscow. His own prestige and power grew ever greater, and his cocoon of privilege insulated him from the irritations of daily life. But being in Moscow also excluded Kang and Wang Ming from the drama that was unfolding in China at the time.

Routed from China's cities, the Communist armies had moved to the wild terrain of China's central provinces—in Jiangxi; in the borderlands between Hunan, Sichuan, and Guizhou provinces; and in northern Sichuan. In October 1934, after months of fighting the Kuomintang's crack, German-trained troops, the Communist forces started the epic retreat that came to be known as the Long March. This trek, which saw a hundred thousand troops and camp followers cover between six thousand and seven thousand miles in about twelve months, at a cost of thousands of lives, transformed the Chinese Communist movement. By creating a sense of commitment and sacrifice, it converted a ragtag army of peasants, bandits, deserters, and disaffected intellectuals into an efficient fighting machine. Their mettle was tested by nearly insuperable obstacles—a bitterly cold winter; severe shortages of food, medicine, and ammunition; savagely inhospitable mountains, ravines, and rivers; and pursuing armies that forced the Communists to march night and day without sleep. A profound change started to take place. The men Wang Ming had left behind to run the Party in China were shunted aside, and the voice that took precedence spoke in favor of peasant revolt. It was the voice of Mao Zedong.

The chaos that overtook the Party as a result of the Long March

---

* Many accounts of Kang's career place his promotion to the Politburo at a much later date, but "Zhongkan" is adamant that Kang joined the Politburo in 1934. Given "Zhongkan's" access to Party records, there is no reason to doubt this claim. Moreover, it is clear from other sources, such as Zhang Guotao, that after Kang's return to China in 1937, he regularly attended Politburo meetings.

The prestige of the Comintern, combined with the practical influence of Bo Gu and the rest of the Twenty-eight Bolsheviks on the Communist forces in Jiangxi, gave Wang enough say in Party affairs to secure the election to the Politburo of key supporters like Kang. So great was Bo Gu's power in the CCP at the time that he removed Liu Bocheng, a prominent general who became one of China's eight marshals, from the post of chief of staff of the Red Army on the advice of Comintern representative Otto Braun.

and the CCP's communications problems made it almost impossible for cadres in Moscow—Chinese and Soviets alike—to direct events in China. The first unmistakable sign of Moscow's decline in influence came at a meeting of the CCP Politburo in the tiny town of Zunyi in January 1935, after the Red Army had suffered heavy casualties on the first leg of the Long March. Zunyi is located in Guizhou, a province made inaccessible by the mountains of southern China, and it was there that the Red Army had holed up. Mao used the occasion to attack Bo Gu, Wang Ming's most effective lieutenant, and Zhou En-lai; Zhou had aligned himself with the Soviet-trained cadres who formed the basis of Wang's clique. Arguing that the Red Army's losses were due mainly to the tactical blunders of Bo Gu, Zhou, and the Comintern military adviser, Otto Braun—a German soldier known to the Chinese as Li De—Mao was elected chairman of the Party's Military Commission in place of Zhou Enlai. Mao's triumph at Zunyi represented a major step on his road to supreme power.

Mao and his supporters succeeded in forcing Bo Gu out of the general secretary's post, replacing him with Luo Fu. Luo was one of the Twenty-eight Bolsheviks, but even so, he was willing to compromise with the Maoists (a trait that enabled him to become a successful diplomat in the 1950s).* Mao's victory in Zunyi was so significant that the Soviet masters of the Comintern took note of it and elected him in absentia to the Comintern's Executive Committee six months later, an honor he shared with only three other Chinese—Zhang Guo-tao, Zhou Enlai, and, of course, Wang Ming.

To Kang, the Zunyi conclave was an ominous event. Mao did not win a total victory—the Twenty-eight Bolsheviks still held a few important posts, and Mao had a way to go before he consolidated his hold on the Party—but the meeting warned that Wang Ming's position was not impregnable, and that Moscow's power over the CCP was weakening. This posed a threat to Wang Ming's effectiveness as Kang's patron, while Mao Zedong, a man Kang had never met, was clearly on the rise. Far from welcoming the Zunyi outcome, Kang did everything he could to conceal its meaning from the Chinese officials and students in Moscow.

---

* "Luo Fu" was the Party name of Zhang Wentian, who served as ambassador to Moscow and vice foreign minister during the 1950s. To minimize confusion, we have used "Luo Fu" throughout the text, although he reverted to his original name after 1949.

Rather than publicly acknowledge the expansion of Mao's power, Kang seized on the removal of Bo Gu from the general secretaryship (he stubbornly ignored Luo Fu's promotion) and feverishly spread the impression that Wang Ming was about to resume that important post. In the months following the Zunyi meeting, Kang called Chinese students to the Hotel Lux and encouraged them to write to the Comintern demanding the reappointment of Wang Ming as general secretary. On November 15, 1935, at a reception celebrating the success of the Comintern's Seventh Congress, he even proposed a toast with the words "Support Comrade Wang Ming as the General Secretary of the CCP in China."

Kang continued to tout Wang Ming's claim to the general secretaryship into 1936, proclaiming Wang Ming's preeminence at every opportunity. In March, while introducing Wang to a young Chinese Communist about to return to China, he referred to Wang as "the general secretary of our party." Nor was it just on private, Chinese-only occasions that Kang promoted the fiction that Wang was the supreme Chinese Communist. At a July 1, 1936, reception attended by senior Soviet and Comintern officials to celebrate the fifteenth anniversary of the establishment of the CCP, Kang praised Wang in a passionate speech concluding with cries of "Long Live Comrade Wang Ming!" The rhetoric of a personality cult was familiar in Moscow, where the words "Three cheers for great Comrade Stalin!" inevitably elicited tumultuous and jubilant shouts of "Stalin! Stalin! Stalin!"

Soviet officials may have had an incomplete understanding of events in China, but Kang soon faced further challenges to his advocacy of Wang Ming and his distortion of what had happened at Zunyi. In mid-August 1936, Chen Yun, who had been Kang's colleague on the committee that ran the CCP secret service in Shanghai, arrived in Moscow. Chen had witnessed Mao's victory at Zunyi. Indeed, although he had once served as Wang Ming's personal aide, Chen had supported Mao against Bo Gu. Chen Yun had come to Moscow as a CCP delegate to the Comintern congress, but Kang saw him as a potentially troublesome visitor.

Chen Yun was not the only new arrival from China who threatened Kang's interpretation of the Zunyi meeting. In early 1936, Wang Jiaxiang, a Red Army political commissar who had been wounded on the Long March, was sent to Moscow for medical treatment. Originally one of the Twenty-eight Bolsheviks, Wang Jiaxiang had deserted the Wang Ming camp. When he reported to the Comintern, he brought more details of internal CCP politics and of Mao's ascendancy.

Wang Ming's influence was fading in much of China, but there was one notable exception: Manchuria. Kang played a key role in maintaining Wang Ming's authority there. After the Mukden Incident on September 18, 1931, the Japanese had occupied China's three northeastern provinces, and Communist ranks grew as rapidly as anti-Japanese feelings in that region. The Communists gained a much stronger foothold in Manchuria than in the southern parts of the country, where nationalistic sentiments had not yet been inflamed by brutal foreign intervention.

Once the Red Army had embarked on the Long March, the Manchurian Communists lost contact with the CCP leadership, which was playing hide-and-seek with Chiang Kai-shek's troops in the distant mountain ranges of southwest China. The Manchurians looked instead to Moscow for leadership. Wang and Kang were quick to exploit the situation. In June 1935, five months after the Zunyi council had handed Wang his first serious setback, he and Kang sent the Manchurians an order that later became known as the Wang–Kang Directive. Wang and Kang warned them that they could expect help from neither the Soviet Union, which was anxious to avoid war with Japan, nor the main Chinese Communist armies. They should conserve their strength, wait for opportunities to act, and, if necessary, abandon their bases. It was a message of caution, designed to maintain the Party's manpower while holding back on any action that might provoke a Japanese attack on Soviet territory.

Upon receiving the Wang–Kang Directive, the Manchurian Communist leaders assembled in the town of Zhuhe in northernmost Heilongjiang Province. After some debate, they rejected the directive as an expression of "rightist opportunism." In the face of their mutiny, Wang Ming and Kang summoned a succession of small groups of Manchurian Party leaders to the USSR—ostensibly for training and liaison—but once on Soviet territory any cadre who had defied orders was disciplined. Their Manchurian victims included Wang De, a Party secretary who had come to Moscow to work on *The Salvation Times*, a Chinese-language newspaper produced in Moscow and Paris and then smuggled into China. In spite of his status, Wang De was arrested in 1937 and never seen again. His wife, Tang Guofu, a propaganda worker who had also joined the staff of *The Salvation Times*, was forced to become a domestic servant in a Russian household near Moscow, later vanishing in the turbulence of World War II. One of Wang De's Manchurian colleagues, Yang Guanghua, was more fortunate. Kang accused Yang of being an "international spy" and had the NKVD arrest him.* Yang was exiled to the Arctic Circle for twenty-one years but survived and was repatriated to China in 1956.

Wang and Kang used cruel methods to seize control of the Manchurian Party organization, but their military strategy was appropriate in the circumstances. Western experts have concluded that the Wang–Kang Directive reduced Communist casualties by averting the catastrophe that almost certainly would have followed a direct challenge to the Japanese army.†

Kang also helped organize a contingent of cavalry and motorized troops that operated from bases in Outer Mongolia. About four thousand strong, the force was drawn from the community of Chinese students and workers in Moscow, Korean radicals who had been forced to flee Japanese-occupied Korea, and assorted European Communists. Kang's army was never called on for its declared purpose: to assist the Chinese Red Army if the KMT forces pursued it into Outer Mongolia at the end of the Long March. It was the closest Kang ever came to being a military commander.

Kang spent much of his time in Moscow on public activities— delivering speeches that were published in Comintern booklets and magazines; writing for *The Salvation Times*; holding discussions with Chinese students; attending Comintern meetings. But he also led a hidden life as the head of a security apparatus that persecuted, imprisoned, and sometimes executed Chinese in Moscow suspected of being politically unreliable. Some of his highly placed comrades knew of his activities against "counterrevolutionaries," but his work as a secret-police agent in Moscow was never publicized. There were no

---

* The Soviet secret police was then known as the NKVD. It had been called the Cheka from 1917 until 1922 and the OGPU from 1922 to 1934. It was known as the NKVD until 1953, and since then as the KGB.

† The Wang–Kang Directive became the subject of heated controversy during Mao's campaign against Wang Ming in the 1940s. Mao charged that Wang Ming had aborted Manchuria's revolutionary potential. Unable to justify the directive, Kang simply denied that it had ever existed. To guard against exposure of his connection with it, he began intimidating, and in some cases exterminating, Party members who knew the truth.

public trials of his victims nor any announcement about their fate; the unfortunates simply disappeared.

Kang entered this sinister world in early 1936, after Stalin had mounted the first show trials, the public events that signaled the outbreak of the Great Purge that ravaged the Soviet political, bureaucratic, and intellectual classes. From these events Kang learned how to use the secret police for purposes he had never dreamed of. Having survived the KMT's hunt for Communists in Shanghai, Kang was no stranger to terror. But the police state he encountered in Moscow was qualitatively different from the regime of Chiang Kai-shek. The lessons Kang mastered were not the simple technical details of arresting, torturing, and executing opponents—he discovered how to use panic as a means to suppress political dissent, how to turn the most ridiculously false confessions into potent tools, and how to silence enemies who might otherwise denounce him or attempt to oust him.

No event in Soviet politics during Kang's Moscow years matched the horror of the *Yezhovshchina*. Stalin's series of mammoth purges took its name from Nikolai Yezhov, who headed the Soviet secret police when the purges reached their climax. Stalin methodically set out to destroy every human obstacle to a despotic state in which everything from military theory to music became an extension of his own personality. Kang watched this nightmare overtake the entire nation.

On December 1, 1934, Sergei Kirov, a veteran Bolshevik and longtime supporter of Stalin, was shot in the back of the neck by an assassin at the Smolny, the headquarters of the Communist Party in Leningrad. The murder of such a high official reverberated throughout the USSR. "The Hotel Lux seethed from roof to basement," recalled one of its occupants. "No one stayed in his room. There were questions on every side and all of us eagerly devoured *Pravda* and *Izvestia* . . . There was equal commotion in the Comintern."

Kirov's assassination, almost certainly instigated by Stalin, led to the show trials and the mass purges. During 1935, almost all the old-time Bolsheviks, including such legendary colleagues of Lenin as Grigori Zinoviev and Nikolai Bukharin, were rounded up, forced to confess to crimes they could not possibly have committed, and executed.* Their deputies and assistants then suffered the same fate.

---

* The trials of Zinoviev and Bukharin illustrated how ludicrous false confessions could be. The prosecutor produced a witness named E. S. Holtzman, who swore that

Several years later came a purge of the upper echelons of the NKVD itself, the instrument of this massive exercise in state murder. The purges climaxed in the execution of the NKVD's chief, Henry Yagoda, in 1936. In 1938, the year after Kang left Moscow, Yezhov, Yagoda's successor, was himself swallowed up by the creature that had taken his name as its own, the *Yezhovshchina*.

Kang had been in Moscow for less than eighteen months before Kirov's assassination. Many foreigners viewed the murder as simply the untimely and dramatic death of one of Stalin's comrades, but Kang grasped the true meaning of the ensuing show trials. The role of the NKVD in Soviet society soon became much more visible—the "secret" police on the street could hardly have been more conspicuous, with "their leather coats, fat faces, and shorn heads." As if to impress the overseas contingent with the new reality, the NKVD established an operations center at the Hotel Lux and began identifying and processing candidates for arrest.

Heeding the NKVD's example, and with Wang Ming's support, Kang established a small security unit within the CCP organization in 1936. He called it the Office for the Elimination of Counterrevolutionaries. Kang himself directed the operations of the Elimination Office, as it came to be known, using his power to purge large numbers of Chinese as "counterrevolutionaries," "renegades," "special agents," "spies," or "Trotskyites." He worked closely with the NKVD, which was responsible for arresting, imprisoning, torturing, banishing, and executing anyone Kang had identified as a suspect, investigated, and designated as "guilty."

Kang gained great power from the Elimination Office, which he used to silence opponents and witnesses to any embarrassing episodes in his past, especially his arrest in Shanghai. Anyone familiar with his alleged collaboration with the KMT and his betrayal of other comrades was target. Many Chinese in Moscow were arrested, imprisoned, exiled, or shot on Kang's orders. The information currently available is still too sparse for an accurate calculation of how many Chinese perished in Moscow, but the figure ran into the hundreds, most of them cadres of some importance. This was not the first time the Chinese in Moscow had fallen victim to purges. Soviet authorities had made numerous arrests at Sun Yat-sen University during the late

---

he had met with Leon Trotsky's son Sedov in the Hotel Bristol in Copenhagen in 1932 on behalf of the old Bolsheviks. In fact, the Hotel Bristol was demolished in 1917.

1920s; students disappeared in the night, never to be seen again. But Kang worked his own variation: in the past, the Chinese had been purged by the Soviets; now, under Kang, they were liquidated by their fellow Chinese.

The personal motives that drove Kang to eliminate "counterrevolutionaries" are best revealed in the cases themselves. In the spring of 1935, several months after Kirov's murder and the opening rounds of the Great Purge, four young Chinese secret-service officers arrived in Moscow to study security and intelligence practices. The KMT-inspired White Terror was gradually crushing the CCP's urban networks within China, so the Chinese Communists needed training on how to protect themselves. Three of the new arrivals had worked under Kang in the secret service in Shanghai. One of them, Ouyang Xin, had led the Second Section (the Intelligence Cell) when Kang had headed the Fourth Section and supervised the entire security machinery. Kang met the quartet in Moscow and set out to cultivate Wu Hujing and his wife, Hou Zhi. But something in Kang's manner aroused the couple's suspicions, and they rejected his approaches. Kang had the entire group arrested in 1936 as "Trotskyites" and "spies." The four men were executed the following year. Hou Zhi alone survived to tell her story in Peking in the late 1970s, after Kang's death.

Kang was operating in a terrifying environment. If security chiefs as powerful as Yagoda and Yezhov could disappear into the executioner's cellar, everyone was at risk. Kang took special care to ensure that his operations conformed with Soviet trends. The case of a Manchurian Communist, Wang Runcheng, illustrated Kang's efforts to pander to Stalin's prejudices. Until 1936, Wang was the political commissar of Communist forces in Manchuria. That year, while leading a group of cadres to the Soviet Union, he met a Korean woman named "Miss Jiang," who was fleeing from the Japanese with her family. Told that she was a member of the Korean Communist Party, Wang agreed that she could travel with him to Moscow. Shortly before, however, Stalin had turned the *Yezhovshchina* against a number of foreign Communist parties, including the Korean. As soon as Kang learned that Wang Runcheng had been accompanied by a Korean Communist, he saw an opportunity to score points with the Stalinists. Kang branded Miss Jiang a traitor and, without even the pretense of an investigation, ordered her and Wang Runcheng arrested. Wang Runcheng was sentenced to eight years' imprisonment and sent to a coal mine in the Arctic Circle. After completing his sentence, he served another eight years there as a laborer. He returned to China in 1953. The fate of Miss Jiang is unknown.

Kang's so-called elimination of counterrevolutionaries among his countrymen in Moscow was an important stepping-stone. The issues had been easy to define in Shanghai, where his management of the Party's secret service had involved the assassination of renegade Communists. Kang could dismiss the violence of his methods in the name of protecting the Party from danger. In Moscow, by contrast, the charges of treachery and treason behind the execution or imprisonment of Party members lacked any basis; the Party was not under threat, and very few, if any, of his Chinese victims were actually "Trotskyites" or "international spies." Their "crimes" were the product of a fantasy Kang imposed on the Party.

Kang's impulse to construct a make-believe world full of evil and alien forces flowed naturally from the events around him. Stalin's Great Purge itself grew out of nothing more than the grotesque delusions of a paranoid dictator. The real triumph of NKVD chief Henry Yagoda was his success in convincing the Soviet public that any opposition to Stalin must come from enemies of the state. Kang learned from Yagoda's charade, realizing that if charges against supposed hostile conspirators were presented with conviction, backed by physical force, and confirmed by confessions, even the most bizarre and outrageous claims would eventually be accepted. He never forgot this lesson.

At the time Kang and the Soviet secret police were purging the Chinese community, representatives of other Communist parties in Moscow were relatively untouched. But in 1937, the Great Terror broke over the foreign Communist community like a tidal wave. The first omen came in May, when Hungarian Communist leader Béla Kun was condemned before the Comintern Executive Committee by Soviet representative Dimitri Manuilsky. Wang Ming, a member of the committee, watched as the unfortunate Kun was escorted from the room. Kang, as an alternate member of the Executive Committee, undoubtedly was there, too. Kun was held in Lefortovo Prison and forced to stand on one foot for up to twenty hours at a time—a torture that Kang himself applied in later years. Kun was finally executed in 1939.

The Hungarian Communists were not Stalin's only victims. He also exterminated many top officials of the Polish, Romanian, Bulgarian, German, Korean, and Yugoslav parties. (Tito later recalled that he had lived in constant fear of a "fatal knocking" on the door at midnight.) The Comintern apparatus itself was decimated, starting with the Soviet representatives on the Executive Committee. The Comintern's entire communications staff, for example, was either executed or imprisoned. Only a handful of pliant men at the top like Dimitri Manuilsky and Georgi Dimitrov survived.

Kang witnessed the beginnings of this purge of Comintern officials and foreign Communists firsthand. Those arrested included many of his fellow occupants of the Hotel Lux, which "became something like a frontier village raided nightly by bandits." One of the victims was Heinz Neumann, a German Communist whom Kang almost certainly knew. Neumann had connections to China, where he had worked as a Comintern agent, succeeding Borodin. He had played a leading role in the disastrous Canton commune and the Nanchang uprising in August 1927.

The Chinese Communists in Moscow had more to fear from Kang than from Stalin. Stalin, feeling increasingly threatened by a militaristic Japan, was reluctant to jeopardize his influence over the Communists in China. Many foreign Communist parties existed only in Moscow, but the CCP had a functioning army, which Stalin was counting on to help divert the Japanese militarists from invading Soviet territory. Rather than approve the execution or imprisonment of Wang Ming—the Chinese equivalent of Béla Kun—Stalin embraced him as a favored protégé, reasoning that he could serve Soviet interests.

Kang's status in Moscow rested on his claim to be a leader of the Chinese Revolution. But he acquired extensive power from his capacity to make the most of the shifts and trends in Soviet politics. When Stalin started to review policy toward China in mid-1935 and realized that Chiang Kai-shek could better protect the USSR's flank against Japan than the CCP could, Kang quickly fell in line. By the end of that year, he had become a vocal supporter of a united front between the Communists and Chiang Kai-shek, whom he had earlier reviled as an agent of Japanese imperialism. In late 1936, Kang visited CCP representatives in Paris, the European center of Chinese Communist activity ever since Zhou Enlai, Li Lisan, and other young Chinese had studied there fifteen years earlier. While in France, Kang sent an emissary to Shanghai with a series of messages that revealed the extent of his support for Stalin's position. Kang directed the Party cells in Shanghai to merge Communist interests with the KMT's in a united front against Japan, cooperate with Chiang Kai-shek against the Japanese, combine with the "yellow" (KMT-controlled) unions, employ legal methods of struggle, and dissolve Communist unions. Kang's orders completely contradicted his earlier position in Shanghai and his statements upon arrival in Moscow—in both places, he had outspokenly advocated a struggle to the death against the KMT.

The outbreak of full-scale war between China and Japan ended Kang's stay in Moscow. A minor incident at the Marco Polo Bridge outside Peking—set off by an argument over the fate of a Japanese soldier allegedly kidnapped by Chinese while he was urinating—became a pretext for the Japanese to occupy the area south of the Great Wall in July 1937, then to invade Shanghai a month later. In November, Japanese troops captured the Chinese capital, Nanking, where at the least tens of thousands of Chinese were shot, bayonetted, beheaded with samurai swords, raped, sliced to pieces limb by limb, and in many cases left to die from horrible wounds.* This infamous incident, which came to be known as the Rape of Nanking, confirmed Stalin's worst fears about the danger of an attack from the east; he started to plot to have China distract Japan by drawing the imperial armies south instead of west. As a gesture to Chiang Kai-shek, Stalin had already allowed Chiang's son, Chiang Ching-kuo, who had been a virtual hostage in the Soviet Union, to return to China.† With the situation deteriorating, Stalin's next step was to send Wang Ming, accompanied by Kang, to consolidate the CCP–KMT united front.

Before leaving for China, Wang Ming and Kang had an audience with Stalin. Wang Jiaxiang, the political commissar who had come to Moscow to recuperate from his wounds, was also present, as was Georgi Dimitrov, who remained Stalin's assistant on international Communist matters. At the meeting, Wang Ming, backed by Kang, exaggerated the CCP's influence in China. Stalin asked how many troops the Communists had; when Wang Jiaxiang replied that in

---

* The number of deaths resulting from the Japanese atrocities in Nanking has never been established. Western estimates place the figure at about 40,000; KMT sources speak of over 100,000; Chinese Communist historians claim that 300,000 were killed.
† Chiang Ching-kuo, who went to Moscow as a radical young student in 1924, was prevented from returning to China after graduating from Sun Yat-sen University in 1927. Stalin kept him in Russia, in the most difficult circumstances short of imprisonment, as a sort of ace-in-the-hole, to be played at the appropriate time.

northern Shaanxi Province there were only 30,000, Wang Ming immediately interrupted to place the number at 300,000 or more. Kang supported Wang Ming's figure; Stalin seemed reassured.

Kang also used this conference to settle personal scores. He informed Stalin that Klavdiia Kirsanova, head of the Lenin Institute, had protected two Chinese Communists, Zhou Dawen and Yu Xiusong, who had serious "political problems." By then, Zhou and Yu had fled to Dihua (known today as Ürümqi), the capital of Xinjiang or Chinese Turkestan, but Kang's charges led to Kirsanova's removal as head of the Lenin Institute. Kang bided his time in catching up with Zhou and Yu.

Kang and Wang Ming had engineered the execution and imprisonment of countless Chinese and made enemies during their stay in Russia. To guard against vendettas coming back on them, Kang orchestrated the arrest of the one Chinese in Moscow with the standing to pose a threat: the famous radical Li Lisan, who had led the CCP from 1928 until 1930. After his recall to Moscow in late 1930, Li had cooperated with the Soviet authorities, conceding that he had made mistakes. He was stripped of influence but remained a member of the Central Committee. Li performed propaganda and translation duties in the Chinese section of the International Workers Publishing Company and worked for several years on *The Salvation Times*. He married a Russian woman, Lisa, in February 1936, further tying himself to the Soviet Union.

Wang and Kang had good reason to mistrust Li Lisan. Li hated Wang for replacing him as CCP leader, and he hated Kang for switching allegiance to Wang Ming. Moreover, living in the Hotel Lux gave Li and his Russian wife front-row seats to the spectacle of Wang and Kang purging their countrymen. Wang and Kang conspired to silence Li Lisan permanently. In November 1937, on the night before he flew back to China, Wang Ming abruptly informed Li, who had hoped to make the trip on the same aircraft, that he must remain in the Soviet Union. Kang played his part behind the scenes; as his final act before departure, he informed his NKVD contacts that Li was one of the dread "Trotskyites." On February 23, 1938, three months after Kang and Wang Ming left for China, the Soviet secret police arrested Li, accusing him of being both the head of a Chinese spy ring in Moscow and a Japanese agent tasked with assassinating Stalin.

Acting on Kang's information, the NKVD had Li taken into custody without any preliminary investigation—by itself an indication of how much faith the Soviet secret police placed in Kang's reports. But Kang had concealed Li's membership on the Central Committee of the CCP, fearing that otherwise Kang's NKVD contacts would seek higher authorization. In the end, Kang's omission backfired on him; when Li disclosed his identity to the startled Soviet interrogators, a more careful investigation began. Zhou Enlai (then in Moscow recuperating from a riding accident that left him with a permanently crooked arm) intervened on Li's behalf. The Soviet Ministry of the Interior finally ordered Li's release.*

On November 14, 1937, Kang and Cao Yi'ou left Moscow for Yan'an aboard a Soviet plane specially provided for the journey. Their fellow passengers included Wang Ming and his wife, Meng Qingshu; Chen Yun; and a less senior official, Zeng Shan (who later became one of Chen Yun's deputies). The first stop they made in China was at the garrison city of Dihua, the Chinese Turkestan capital, where Wang Ming and Kang called on the local warlord, Sheng Shicai. A slippery general whose affiliations changed with the wind, Sheng had an alliance at the time with the Soviet Union and the CCP.

Wang Ming and Kang also dropped in on Deng Fa, a flamboyant labor leader from Canton who headed the CCP unit in Dihua. Deng had commanded the Political Security Bureau in the Jiangxi Communist base and had worked as a secret agent in northern China after the Long March, operating out of the household of Manchurian warlord Zhang Xueliang. Deng Fa still had some responsibility for security matters, so Kang ordered him to arrest and execute three Communist cadres then in Dihua. The three men—Yu Xiusong, Zhou Dawen, and Dong Yixiang—had crossed Kang in Moscow, where, as students at the Lenin Institute, they had encouraged other Chinese to resist Wang Ming's bid for influence. Using Soviet rhetoric, Kang told Deng Fa that the three were Trotskyites. Yu was arrested almost immediately and transferred to a prison in the Soviet Union in 1938, where he died before the year was out. Zhou and Dong presumably suffered similar fates.

After ordering the three murders, Kang and Wang Ming flew to

---

* Li Lisan was not the only victim of that particular NKVD operation. Nosaka Sanzo, a Japanese Communist, was arrested at the same time; by ironic coincidence, so was Pavel Mif, who had deposed Li Lisan in order to install Wang Ming in 1931. Li and Nosaka survived, but Mif was executed.

Yan'an, the headquarters of the Communist-controlled region established in northern Shaanxi at the end of the Long March. Kang arrived in China a seasoned Party leader with incontestable qualifications for high office. During his four years in Moscow, he had completed the political education he had begun as a student and agitator in 1924 in Shanghai. He had consolidated his standing as an intelligence and security expert, emerging as a Communist "internationalist" and a specialist on Soviet politics and foreign policy.

After his Moscow experience, Kang returned home with high hopes. He was not disappointed. The lessons he had learned in Russia did indeed help him acquire immense power—but not until he bit the hand that had once fed him.

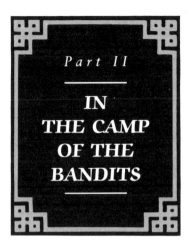

Part II

IN
THE CAMP
OF THE
BANDITS

Chapter VI

MAO'S MAN

NOVEMBER 29, 1937, began the most fateful period in the life of Kang Sheng. Late that afternoon, a Soviet airplane appeared in the cloudy skies over Yan'an, the town in northern China where the Communists who survived the Long March had established Party headquarters earlier that year. At first, those on the ground, including Mao Zedong, feared that the plane was a Japanese bomber making a periodic raid on the Communist base. But as the aircraft circled in search of the town's primitive airstrip, its identity was verified. A large crowd, led by Mao (riding in the only motor vehicle in the town—an old ambulance),* streamed to the airfield, curious about the plane and its passengers. It was the first aircraft to land in Yan'an in nearly two years.†

---

* Colonel David D. Barrett, commander of the Dixie Mission, a U.S. Army team sent to Yan'an in 1944 to establish relations with the CCP, said that when he arrived there in July of that year, Mao often rode in a "battered truck, with enclosed cab, which as far as I ever knew, constituted the Communists' sole motor transport." Barrett reported that the main form of transportation in the region was by mule-drawn cart and said he took Mao and Zhou Enlai for their first ride in a Jeep, which the U.S. Army had shipped in for Barrett's use. Making vehicular transport even more difficult in Yan'an was the fact that the primary fuel was vegetable oil. Any gasoline in Yan'an had to be brought in, primarily by camel, in ten- and twenty-five-gallon drums—which, moreover, had to be provided in advance, because the available drums in China (too few, in any case) had not been tested for leaks.

† Yan'an was not easily accessible to aircraft. It was in "the narrowest of valleys" and "exceedingly hard to find from the air." It was especially unusual for a plane to try to

Kang and his companions, including Wang Ming, received a warm greeting when they stepped off their plane. The Yan'an Communists were generally suspicious of new arrivals, but they were also eager to have CCP leaders long absent from China bringing the latest news from Moscow. In true Chinese style, a feast was held that night, and Luo Fu, the Soviet-trained intellectual who had been elected CCP general secretary at Zunyi in January 1935, gave a welcoming address. Luo praised each of the new arrivals: Wang Ming had raised the CCP's international standing with the Comintern; Chen Yun had accomplished his mission in Moscow; and Kang Sheng had protected the Party in Shanghai during the White Terror.

Mao Zedong also saluted the travelers in a speech laced with Chinese aphorisms. Then forty-four, Mao was surprisingly corpulent and reportedly had a somewhat effeminate air about him—an impression accentuated by his small hands and his high-pitched voice. In his address that first night, Mao paid homage to Wang Ming's status as a Comintern spokesman. But for all his homespun courtesy, Mao carefully avoided conceding any of the authority he had acquired during the Long March; his wariness of the newcomers was clear.

The strains between Mao, on the one hand, and Wang Ming and the Comintern, on the other, surfaced occasionally during the evening. Someone asked at one point whether the air link between Yan'an and the Soviet Union would remain open so that weapons and other supplies could be flown in to the Chinese Communists. Wang Ming replied that the flight was illegal and secret. According to Stalin's understanding with Chiang Kai-shek, he explained, the Soviet air force in China was there to assist the KMT government. All military supplies would be delivered to the KMT troops, not the Communists.* "If so much can be given to Chiang Kai-shek," Mao sighed, "why can't we get a small share?"

If Kang had any illusions that he would enjoy living in Yan'an, he quickly lost them. His family heritage of wealth and education made him an outcast among the Communist rank and file. He had had no trouble blending into the urban environment of Shanghai—his fellow

---

land in late November; the best flying conditions were from April to October, and high winds were a hazard to aviation at other times.

* Among the primitive equipment the Communists at Yan'an were forced to rely on was their two-way radio for communicating with the outside world. The generator that powered it was run by a worn-out truck engine; for a resistor in the circuit, they used a steel rod in a barrel of water.

CCP members there had been intellectuals, university students, or factory workers with at least some measure of sophistication. But now that the Party had expanded into China's rural areas, an ever larger element came from the peasant class; 90 percent of all Party members boasted a peasant background.* Kang's high birth was not the only thing that set him apart. Early on, he antagonized (among others) Mao, who initially disliked Kang for his dogmatism and his stubborn refusal to yield on any argument.

Moreover, Yan'an and the countryside of northwestern China was a disagreeable environment for Kang: barren and desolate, with its already uncomfortable summers aggravated by frequent sandstorms blowing off the Gobi Desert and its winter temperature plunging far below freezing. The CCP base was in a valley almost completely surrounded by hills, allowing the sun to penetrate only briefly each day. The worst time was from March to May, when spring thaws swelled the rivers to flooding. Built on a narrow plain to the south of the sluggish Yan River, the town itself was little more than a few acres of buildings encircled by ancient earthen ramparts and dominated by a nine-story pagoda.†

The Communists lived in caves cut into the steep brown cliffs of loam that circled Yan'an. Each cave was a single room ending at the wall of a tunnel. A door and a window covered by white paper in place of glass admitted some light, and candles provided the only other illumination; there was neither electricity nor running water. But the caves were reasonably warm in winter and cool in the summer. Short-term visitors stayed in a Communist-run establishment called the Northwest Hotel, a series of caves about nine feet deep, eight feet wide, and nine feet high. The Party's offices also were housed in caves during the late 1930s, at a place called Yangjialing just outside the walls of Yan'an.

When the Communists first occupied the small, unpromising town, the population had been about three thousand, with no more

---

* The hallowed oath taken by soldiers in the Yan'an-based Eighth Route Army ("We, sons of workers and peasants, swear . . .") must have added to Kang's sense of estrangement.

† The pagoda was one of the few pleasant sights in the bleak Yan'an environment. In the words of one visitor: "Late in the evening, about an hour after sunset, when the light of the glorious Shensi moon was making the mountain peaks and gorges look still more beautiful and fantastic, we suddenly saw about a mile ahead of us a tall graceful pagoda glittering in the moon-light. It announced our arrival at Yenan."

than a couple of shops and restaurants in operation. Within two years, the Japanese invasion and Yan'an's reputation as a stronghold of nationalism lured many young Chinese with leftist or nationalistic sentiments to the town, and its population mushroomed tenfold. Nevertheless, Yan'an was a far cry from Shanghai, with its skyscrapers, gardens, cosmopolitan population, and crowded streets. Even the Shandong of Kang's youth had little in common with this bleak, undistinguished land of rock, sand, and dust—it had "the sameness of the sea."

Shaanxi, the province surrounding Yan'an, had played a major role in Chinese history. It had been the home of the ruthless Qin dynasty, which had unified China two thousand years earlier. A frontier where China intersected with Mongolian and Turkish states, Shaanxi had frequently attracted invaders from the north. The local people, whose narrow eyes and flat faces showed the influence of non-Chinese blood, were physically very different from the inhabitants of Kang's native Shandong.

Many of the Communists found Yan'an oppressive. Zhu Qihua, a onetime CCP member, wrote an account of the Party's early years describing Yan'an as "a purely medieval, disagreeable small town" where "Mao Zedong established his Platonic kingdom. This was not accidental . . . Mao Zedong's backward mind could only find nourishment in this backward, earthen town."

Since the Long March, life in Yan'an had taken on the regimented ambience of a military camp. Strict sets of rules governed living arrangements and routines, down to the sex lives of CCP members. Husbands and wives were separated except on Saturday nights. Even at the height of the White Terror in Shanghai, couples had lived together and temporary sexual liaisons had been common. But in Yan'an, the Party tried to impose the puritanical sexual mores of a revolutionary military organization.* According to one observer, "Everyone is asked to sacrifice his personal [romantic] interests and inclinations to the common effort." When one CCP cadre lost his girlfriend to another man living in Yan'an and shot her in revenge, he was found guilty of lacking "devotion to the Cause" and executed.

---

* David Barrett said that he once saw Zhou Enlai kiss his wife goodbye before Zhou departed Yan'an on a trip; it was "the first time I had ever seen a Chinese man kiss anyone."

Everyone from Mao to the lowliest member of the Party was required to spend several hours a day at manual labor. Central Committee members were assigned a quota of grain to produce each year; in compliance, Mao and his guards farmed a plot in front of his residence. They planted vegetables in season and did spinning, weaving, or metalwork. The Party provided housing, food, clothing, medical care, and "normal living expenses"—which amounted to twelve dollars a month for Chairman Mao. Other CCP leaders were paid five dollars a month, but in the Communists' egalitarian society, factory workers received thirty dollars a month, which allowed them to "live better than the generals and officials"—a policy intended to "encourage industrialization."

For all the discipline and straitlaced asceticism enforced in Yan'an, however, the economy of the so-called Border Region surrounding it relied largely on the production and export of opium. The Communists were aware that opium symbolized the society they were trying to eradicate, but the profits were too tempting. The CCP tried to keep opium cultivation a secret, but reports inevitably filtered out to Soviet and American observers.

Kang, always regarding himself as "more equal than others," tried to adapt to his new environment, but in his own way. One concession was his style of dress. Rather than outfit himself in the blue-dyed quilted cotton garments that most civilians wore, however, Kang opted for khaki military fatigues, similar to the uniforms of the Eighth Route Army—although he had never served in the military. A contemporary of his in Yan'an recalled Kang's fondness for wearing high leather boots, riding horses, and hunting with foreign-bred hounds. His dress at that time had other marks of distinction. Photographs show him wearing not the peaked military hat worn by most of his comrades but the sort of felt cap popular with European motorists in the 1920s and 1930s—and a scarf flung stylishly around his neck.

Kang also started to sport a small, clipped mustache of the type affected by British dandies or European professors, as well as several of Stalin's closest comrades, including Molotov and Mikoyan. Very few Chinese Communists wore a mustache, and Kang's distinguished him from his colleagues, suggesting a genteel and cosmopolitan air. His usual crew of four bodyguards made him almost as conspicuous as Mao, driving around in his ambulance. Kang also hired a chef who had worked in the imperial kitchen of Henry Pu Yi, the last Manchu emperor, and enjoyed lavish meals while the Communist rank and file subsisted on a diet of millet, salted turnips, pickled vegetables, and occasional eggs.*

Several observers of the Yan'an scene noted that Kang had few friends and kept aloof from most social activity, especially when it involved foreigners. He occasionally played musical instruments in public theatrical performances[†]—one of the hobbies of his youth—but in general, he led a secluded and secret life. Kang soon developed a reputation as a sinister, dangerous figure, and most people avoided him.

A year after his arrival in Yan'an, Kang removed himself from the caves of Yangjialing and shifted his residence to Zaoyuan ("Date Palm Garden"), a small settlement several miles west of town. Zaoyuan was the most attractive spot in the Yan'an area. Although date palms were rarer than its name suggested, Zaoyuan was filled with groves of plum, apricot, and pear trees that blossomed from spring until early summer, attracting butterflies and bees. During May and June, Kang's enclave hummed with the pleasant sounds of life.

Before long, other leaders, starting with Mao and his staff, vacated their caves and joined Kang in Zaoyuan. Acknowledging the scarcity of palms, Mao and his fellow leaders decided to rename it Yanyuan ("Yan'an Garden"). Kang Sheng, the onetime professional calligrapher for Shanghai capitalist Yu Qiaqing, wrote the characters for the new name and had them carved into the stone wall beside the entry gate.

During Kang's four years in Moscow, the status of the Chinese Communists had changed dramatically. The CCP was no longer a secret underground organization, the target of repeated KMT military campaigns and police dragnets. By the terms of the united-front agreement reached between the Communists and the KMT in 1937, Yan'an

---

* According to a Polish journalist who visited Yan'an in 1938, "Rice could not be got for gold. No oil or fats of any kind; no sugar; no fruit; no milk, of course. Bean curd, so common all over China, was here a delicacy. And peanuts were the only luxury; they at least were abundant."

[†] In quality, the instruments available at Yan'an fell short of those from Kang's youthful days of affluence; still, ingenuity carried the day. A bass cello, improvised from "a Standard Oil gasoline tin, a long piece of what looked like mahogany, a backboard of unfinished pine, and regular cello strings," reportedly had "a really beautiful liquid tone."

and the Border Region were under Communist administration. Yan'an was the capital of a state within a state, the government and military headquarters for the CCP. For the first time, Kang had close contact with the Communist generals. Powerful commanders like Zhu De, He Long, Peng Dehuai, and Lin Biao—not to mention Mao Zedong—had merely been names to Kang until his arrival in Yan'an.

The Long March had also changed the CCP's relationship with both the Comintern and the Soviet Union. As Kang quickly discovered, the CCP enjoyed a measure of practical independence that had not been apparent from the Hotel Lux in Moscow. Through the Comintern, Soviet leaders continued to exercise a form of authority over the Chinese Communists and to shape overall policy, but their influence was on the decline and they could no longer bring about changes in Party leadership as they had done up until 1931.* Mao, Zhu De, and the other Long March heroes did not lack opponents within the Party. Among their rivals were Zhang Guotao, a veteran leader with his own military following, and some of the Twenty-eight Bolsheviks like Bo Gu who had made the Long March and still challenged Mao's power. But the new breed of Communist leaders grouped around Mao tended to have a narrow, nationalistic perspective. Their power, they knew, rested on their familiarity with chaotic local conditions, especially their capacity to tap the resentment of superstitious and conservative peasants in China's vast, heavily populated, and economically depressed rural areas. They distrusted directives from Moscow. Mao had already started to speak of the need to sinicize Marxism.

The situation was still fluid when Kang arrived, and Wang Ming's presence raised the possibility of expanded Soviet leverage. As a member of the Comintern's ruling body, Wang Ming could claim to be a world figure, an international Communist leader, with interests far

---

* The so-called Xian Incident illustrates how the CCP continued to conform to Soviet guidance. In December 1936, two warlords, Zhang Xueliang and Yang Hucheng, kidnapped Chiang Kai-shek at a hot-springs resort on the fringes of Xian, Shaanxi's provincial capital, in an effort to force him to establish an anti-Japanese alliance. At first, the Yan'an Communists vengefully demanded Chiang's execution, but Stalin, concerned with the strategic need to oppose the Japanese and mindful of Chiang's importance to establishing a united front against Japan, telegraphed Mao and argued for Chiang to be set free. Mao finally deferred to Stalin and sent Zhou Enlai to negotiate an anti-Japanese alliance with Chiang that led to his release on Christmas Day 1936.

beyond the parochial issues that consumed the Maoists. Wang had come directly from a meeting with Stalin, who had immense prestige among Chinese Communists. No matter how nationalistic the Yan'an Communists were, they continued to attach portraits of Stalin to the walls of their caves beside pictures of Mao Zedong and Zhu De and to applaud loudly whenever they saw Stalin in newsreels.

Kang ignored the shift in power away from the Comintern-backed leaders and joined with Wang Ming in an attempt to guide the CCP back in line with Soviet thinking and help Wang replace Mao as the preeminent figure of Chinese communism. Within days after his arrival from Moscow, Kang attended a Politburo meeting at which thirteen of the most senior CCP leaders discussed the messages he and Wang Ming had brought back from the USSR. Wang Ming relayed the importance that Comrade Stalin, the supreme revolutionary commander, placed on a united front against Japan. Kang also spoke, echoing Wang's emphasis on cooperating with the KMT and talking at length about his own work with the Comintern. He solidly identified himself with Wang Ming and confirmed his opposition to the more China-oriented cadres around Mao.

Armed with Stalin's endorsement, Wang Ming carried the day at that December meeting, accomplishing personnel changes that strengthened his hand. Kang Sheng, as Wang Ming's chief lieutenant, benefitted significantly. He was appointed to the Party Secretariat, the executive office that managed day-to-day affairs at the highest level, and was named head of the Party School, which provided him with a platform for lecturing on ideological matters.*

Kang Sheng and Wang Ming also set out to sovietize the CCP and apply the issues and techniques of Russian politics to China. The dominant theme of Soviet politics since the late 1920s had been Stalin's relentless campaign to eliminate the influence of Leon Trotsky. China had spawned a Trotskyite movement after the Communists' setbacks at the hands of the KMT in the late 1920s, but the Chinese Trotskyites never grew beyond a small clique on the fringes of radical politics in Shanghai. By 1937, the fear of Trotsky had subsided and few Chinese Communists saw him as the embodiment of evil, but Wang and Kang set out to impose on the Yan'an Communists the

---

* Although the Party School has few tangible powers, in Chinese Communist politics it can confer ideological legitimacy on senior leaders and generate considerable influence. Kang exploited the school's ideological authority to gain greater power.

doctrine that there could be no compromise with this notorious enemy of both the Soviet Union and the international Communist movement.

The December 1937 Politburo meeting served as the perfect opportunity to turn Trotskyism into a major issue. Among other matters for discussion was whether Chen Duxiu, a former CCP general secretary who had led the Chinese Trotskyites in the late 1920s, and now a radical professor, should be readmitted to the Party. To Mao and his colleagues, removed as they were from Moscow politics, it appeared that Chen Duxiu's prestige among Chinese university students could prove useful. They were willing to overlook Chen's old Trotskyism as a passing fancy with an obscure doctrine that had no relevance to China. Indeed, Zhou Enlai and Dong Biwu, a Communist elder close to Mao, had already taken steps to readmit Chen to the Party.

In January 1938, Kang, whose role in the Elimination Office in Moscow had turned him into a hardened warrior against the scourge of Trotskyism, published in two successive issues of the Communist magazine *Liberation* a virulent attack on Chen Duxiu. This piece of unadulterated Stalinism soon achieved notoriety and helped quash any hope of reenlisting Chen. To prove that Trotskyism was no less insidious an influence in China than in the USSR, Kang made the startling allegation that Chen Duxiu was a Japanese secret agent. Kang's charges could easily be rebutted—and nine distinguished professors in KMT-controlled Hankow did exactly that. They wrote an open letter of protest to the left-wing newspaper *Da Gong Bao* in March 1938, accusing Kang of slander. But Kang, drawing on his Soviet background, put a veneer of credibility on his charges by disclosing that Trotsky headed an international espionage organization dedicated to the defeat of the USSR. Asserting that Trotsky was prepared to pay any price to overthrow Stalin, Kang added that Trotsky viewed Japan as a natural ally in his anti-Soviet campaign. Given Trotsky's international plans and his followers, Kang argued, it was only natural for Chinese Trotskyites like Chen Duxiu to form an alliance with the Japanese; both the Trotskyites and the Japanese were anti-Soviet, and a Japanese foothold in China would enable them to exert more pressure on the Soviet Union.

Kang painted a dark picture of the Chinese Trotskyite movement, depicting it as part of an international network of terrorists, saboteurs, and assassins. He quoted a Shanghai daily to the effect that "Trotsky had personally dispatched an American Trotskyite to Shanghai to be the leading figure of Trotskyism in the Far East." Kang identified the "foreign special agent" as Frank Glass, an American who lived in the French Concession, worked in the advertising section of *The Shanghai Evening Post and Mercury,* and called himself V. T. Robertson. Glass and other American Trotskyites, including "Yi Luo-sheng" (Harold Isaacs), editor of *The China Forum,* were, according to Kang, in contact with Japanese secret-service organizations and Chinese Trotskyites like Chen Duxiu, Peng Shuzhi, Ye Qing, and Liu Renjing.*

Although he was importing a personal phobia of Stalin's as exotic in China as Russian culinary tastes, Kang electrified the situation in Yan'an. Mao and his comrades had used similar Russian jargon in 1930 while liquidating opponents they dubbed " the A–B Group," or "Anti-Bolshevik Group." Kang again injected Soviet slogans into Chinese politics. The result, in the words of a Chinese writer, was that the dreaded Trotskyism "floated like a slow cloud from the horizon until it covered the heads of all those communists gathered in Yan'an and at every front of the struggle against Japan."

Playing on his reputation as an espionage expert, Kang imposed his claims, groundless though they were, on the senior councils of the Party. Many Chinese Communists had been prepared to disregard the evils of Trotskyism, but once Kang had revealed the supposed links between the international Trotskyite organization and the Japanese war machine, other CCP cadres agreed that they threatened China as well as the Soviet Union. The CCP's negotiations with Chen Duxiu quickly collapsed and Trotskyism remained a political crime in China until 1991.

Kang continued to support Wang Ming in every way possible. As head of the Party School in Yan'an, Kang praised Wang Ming in his lectures to the elite student body. He invited Wang Ming to address the school, introducing him with the words "This is Comrade Wang Ming, initiator of the united front against Japan." If not for Wang Ming, Kang suggested, the Chinese Communists never would have cooperated with the KMT against their common enemy—the implication being that Wang was a leader of the entire nation, not just the Communist element within it.

---

* Kang's allegations about American connections with Chinese Trotskyites was accurate at least in that Liu Renjing, who once visited Trotsky in exile in Turkey, had helped Harold Isaacs write *The Tragedy of the Chinese Revolution.*

Reassured by his victories, Wang Ming left Yan'an to head the Communist delegation to Hankow, the temporary KMT capital, and to lead the Communist organization in the Yangtze region. Wang's assignment distanced him from the CCP headquarters in Yan'an, but it seemed an astute move. In many respects, the KMT capital, even after its transfer, first to Hankow and then to Chongqing, was the center of Chinese resistance to Japan. The United States, the Soviet Union, and Germany all maintained diplomatic missions there, making the KMT the main contact between China and the outside world throughout World War II. During much of the war, despite their propaganda to the contrary, the Communists played a marginal military role, conducting guerrilla activity in northern China while the KMT armies bore the brunt of the Japanese offensives.

While Wang Ming hurried off to the national capital, Kang remained at headquarters in Yan'an. Watchful as ever, in 1938—Kang's fortieth year and his first back in China—he soon decided to make a major political shift; it was to become a watershed in his career. Sometime between January, when he saw Wang Ming off on his journey to Hankow, and August, when he was appointed head of the Communist security-and-espionage apparatus, Kang, the cultivated and worldly scion of Shandong gentry, and Mao Zedong, the ungainly guerrilla leader and son of a Hunan peasant, reached an arrangement to their common benefit.

Like his shift of allegiance from the dangerously impractical adventurer Li Lisan to the Soviet-trained Wang Ming seven years earlier, Kang's decision to court Mao reflected both crass opportunism and shrewd insight into the political dynamics of the Chinese Communist movement. Once again, Kang's actions seemed patterned after the traditional Chinese wisdom of the *I Ching*, which teaches that a superior man can succeed by flowing with the current of the times. Just as Mao was gaining his grasp on supreme power, Kang saw what was happening, realized the advantage of switching sides, and decided to risk breaking with one force and identifying with another.

It was an affair of the heart that sealed Kang's lifelong alliance with Mao. Jiang Qing, the Shandong beauty and Shanghai actress, had arrived in Yan'an in August 1937, three months before Kang's return from Moscow. She claimed that she was only twenty-three, but she already had a past strewn with scandal. In Shanghai, where she had performed on stage and screen for the past four years, Jiang Qing was notorious for her promiscuity. By the time she met Mao, she had had numerous love affairs, including one with Zhang Min, a prominent film director, and had been married at least three times. Shanghai's gossip columns brimmed with stories of her romances, especially her stormy marriage to Tang Na. A Shanghai actor and critic, Tang had tried to kill himself several times during the marriage, frustrated that not even he, her husband, could ever fully possess this handsome and strong-willed woman.

Jiang Qing's reputation was more than enough to make her seem dangerously bourgeois to the staid Communists; in addition, she had a record of working with the KMT. In October 1934, KMT security agents in Shanghai had detained her as a suspected Communist. After eight months in jail, and terrified at the prospect of serving more time, she indulged the whims of Hei Dahan, a former Communist who had defected to the KMT and taken over as head of the KMT security unit. Jiang Qing dined with Hei in the prison's reception room, sang for him, and did everything a nightclub hostess would do to pamper a wealthy patron—except, as far as is known, sleep with him. She also signed a declaration disavowing her past leftist associations, criticizing communism, and promising to sever all her links with the CCP. After her release from prison in mid-1935, Jiang Qing sent Hei Dahan a keepsake: a photograph of herself in costume.

Jiang Qing's release may have entailed more than renouncing communism and flirting with Hei Dahan. For a former political prisoner, she received surprisingly favorable reviews in some of Shanghai's KMT-run newspapers. Her performance in *Blood on Wolf Mountain* in 1936, her first leading role, was proclaimed by the prominent KMT *Central Daily News* "the most significant and outstanding work among nationally produced films." She also participated in KMT propaganda activities. In September 1936, two years after her arrest, the KMT staged elaborate festivities to mark the acquisition of eighty bomber aircraft, a celebration that coincided with Chiang Kai-shek's fiftieth birthday. The Shanghai Film Commission organized an "Aircraft Purchase and Birthday Extravaganza," in which Jiang Qing played a role: she performed in the one-act drama *In Search of Marriage*. Cui Wanqiu, a journalist who was also a KMT intelligence agent, praised her performance and loyalty in *The Great Evening News* and also published an interview with her, in which he described her as "a model northern Chinese woman." There is no firm evidence that Jiang Qing was a KMT convert, but in the days of the White

Terror, less intimate dealings with the KMT were often sufficient to merit CCP disciplinary action.*

Tall, slim, and vivacious, Jiang Qing would have attracted men anywhere. But in Yan'an, where most women were peasant soldiers unschooled in dress and deportment, she shone as an exceptional beauty.† Mao, whose marriage to his third wife, He Zizhen, had degenerated into a series of domestic quarrels, quickly fell under Jiang Qing's spell.

By the summer of 1938, Mao's passion for the notorious femme fatale had begun to draw relentless criticism from other CCP leaders. To many of the battle-hardened survivors of the Long March and the Shanghai underground, Jiang Qing was suspiciously bourgeois. Some Party leaders resented her successes in the capitalist world of Shanghai. Others, puritanical elders who saw sensual pleasure as the corruption of the privileged classes, were displeased by Mao's self-indulgence. Even more damning was Jiang Qing's history of public association with the KMT; some openly regarded her as a KMT "mole." Mao's enemies, led by Wang Ming's protégé and ally Bo Gu and Wang Ming's former aide Chen Yun, pounced on the Chairman's romance, hoping to discredit him and remove him from the Party leadership.

Mao's salvation came from an unexpected quarter. As Mao attempted to fend off criticism by branding his opponents' thinking "feudal," Kang Sheng turned against Wang Ming's cronies and came to Mao's rescue.

Shortly after his return from Moscow, Kang had renewed his friendship with Jiang Qing, a student at the Party School he headed. Many years had passed since their last encounter. Kang had left Zhucheng in 1924; it is possible that they met again in Shanghai, but

* This account of Jiang Qing's arrest and contact with the KMT is based on "Zhongkan" and differs from Jiang Qing's version, as reported by Roxane Witke. Jiang Qing did concede during her interviews with Witke that she had been arrested, but she insisted that she had courageously withstood the intimidation of Hei Dahan and finally been released after an unnamed foreigner intervened on her behalf. Once the Cultural Revolution got under way, Jiang Qing went to extraordinary lengths to suppress documents about her past and rewrite her history.
† David Barrett observed that "the rather shapeless jacket and baggy trousers worn by women in the Border Area, as well as their severely plain hairdo, did little to enhance feminine charms." He said that Jiang Qing, by contrast, showed "all the grace and polish traditionally associated with an actress . . . I remember her as being much better looking and more chic than most of the wives of the other Communist leaders."

any contact there would have ended with Kang's departure for Moscow in July 1933, just a few months after Jiang Qing had reached the city. They quickly resumed their rapport, however, and by May 1938, when Jiang Qing performed in the Peking-style opera *The Fisherman's Tragedy*, Kang accompanied her on the *xiaogu* ("small drums")—a remarkable display of intimacy, and also, perhaps, a clean bill of political health. It was unusual, to say the least, for a forty-year-old Politburo member to provide musical accompaniment for a young actress, especially one with Jiang Qing's past.

Kang remained intrigued by Jiang Qing's feminine charms and sultry, seductive air. In dusty Yan'an, the company of an actress from the film studios of Shanghai was a pleasant diversion. Whether they resumed or developed a physical relationship in Yan'an remains a mystery, but a sexual liaison would help explain Kang's support for Mao's marriage to Jiang Qing: Kang would have known that for Jiang Qing to proceed from an intimate relationship with him to one with Mao would give him the power of *zhentou feng* ("wind on the pillow") to influence Mao's thinking through his consort. Moreover, the scholarly Kang was aware that Chinese history featured many cases of ministers and courtiers who presented their wives and concubines to other, more powerful men in order to smooth the way for their personal advancement. Etched on Kang's mind, as on the minds of all educated Chinese, were the legends of China's "Four Great Beauties"—Xi Shi, Diao Chan, Wang Zhaojun, and Yang Guifei—each of whom was a gift from one man to another.

In any case, no sexual relationship between Kang and Jiang Qing in Yan'an could have lasted more than a month or so. She was involved with Mao by mid-1938, and Kang would not have dared jeopardize his political advantage by continuing a physical relationship of his own with her. Unlike Mao, whose romantic temperament allowed him to be overwhelmed by passion for an actress even as he was attempting to win control over the most populous nation on earth, Kang was cool, calculating, and self-controlled. Their tastes in art reflected the difference: Mao's poems and calligraphy were stormy and impetuous, while Kang's paintings and calligraphy were marked by reserve, elegance, and discipline.

Kang acted decisively to protect Mao and rebut the charges against Jiang Qing. Invoking his background as head of the Organization Department and as an expert on security and espionage matters, Kang vouched for Jiang Qing. She was a Party member in good standing, he declared, and had no affiliations that would bar marriage to Mao. Kang's personal knowledge of Jiang Qing's past was fragmentary and certainly insufficient to allow him to prove that she was not a KMT agent, but he doctored her record, destroyed adverse material, discouraged hostile witnesses, and coached her on how to answer the probing questions of high-level interrogators who hoped to discredit Mao.

Kang's intervention in the controversy soon silenced Mao's political rivals and critics. Jiang Qing moved in with Mao, and although her enemies insisted that the marriage was conditioned on her promise to the CCP never to participate in public life, she worked as Mao's personal assistant from the outset. Jiang Qing kept out of the public eye until the 1960s, but she was a Party insider from 1938 on.

As Kang developed intimate ties with Mao and Jiang Qing, he burned his bridges with Wang Ming and the Soviet-oriented faction. In the highly regimented community of Yan'an, marriage was not a personal affair. The Communist rank and file were admonished that even personal acts had ideological meaning; for the leadership, that rule was magnified. The implications of Mao's marriage to Jiang Qing were clear; everyone knew that by vouching for her loyalty to the CCP, Kang had saved Mao from a damaging scandal.

This episode inaugurated the relationship so crucial to Kang's later success. With both Mao and Jiang Qing in his debt, Kang became the couple's confidant and ally. Mao grew to rely on Kang's advice on a wide range of matters and entrusted him with responsibility for checking and revising drafts of many important statements.

Within months after Mao's marital problems had been resolved, Kang was named the supreme chief of the Communist secret service. In a major shake-up of the security organs in August 1938, he was appointed head of the two most powerful and sinister organizations in Yan'an: the Intelligence Department of the Military Affairs Commission, which coordinated all military intelligence work, and the harmless-sounding Social Protection Department—commonly referred to as the Social Affairs Department—which conducted internal security work and espionage against the Party's enemies.

Kang rapidly became more than Mao's matchmaker and security chief. By 1939, he had joined the inner circle of leaders always at the Chairman's side. He often accompanied Mao on his tours around Yan'an, introducing him to other officials and providing a running commentary on what Mao was inspecting. Regularly but unobtrusively, Kang guided Mao through the tangle of his day-to-day relations with people.

Despite their differences in social origin, Mao and Kang had some surprisingly similar traits. They both hailed from rural China, and Mao's father—though a peasant, unlike Kang's—had managed to pay for his son's schooling in the classics. So Mao and Kang shared a vibrant interest in classical culture—poetry, painting, and calligraphy—which continued to feed the relationship; at times, Mao referred to Kang as his *yi-zi-shi* ("one-word teacher") because he polished the Chairman's poetry and writing by changing a word here and there. Their friendship lasted for the rest of Kang's life, with Kang always the self-effacing sycophant—downplaying suggestions that he helped Mao, humbly declining Mao's praise, and taking care never to offend his leader.

Deserting Wang Ming and assisting Mao and Jiang Qing paid off handsomely for Kang. Mao had every reason to dismiss Kang's past support for Wang Ming. Not only had Kang engineered a happy ending for Mao's love affair, but, having spent four years with Wang Ming in Moscow, he was able to provide Mao with tales about Wang's subservience to the Russians that Mao could use against his rival. These services to Mao kept Kang well protected. But in consolidating his new position, he had to repudiate his outspoken support for Wang Ming over the last decade. A number of senior cadres knew the extent of that relationship; Chen Yun, for one, had been in Moscow when Kang was publicly touting Wang Ming as CCP general secretary. Those who had not heard Kang praise Wang Ming in person had read his articles in the Party's broadsides and magazines, essays that supported the Soviet-oriented side and showed that he had been one of Wang Ming's most zealous lieutenants. Still, Kang was able to switch sides and erase his personal history.

In obscuring his earlier factional alignments, Kang displayed his well-practiced capacity for deceit. First, he issued frequent and flat misrepresentations of his past, declaring that he had consistently resisted Wang Ming during his stay in Russia. In speech after speech, Kang repeated the lie that he had always opposed Wang Ming, even boasting that during Stalin's purges he had risked his life trying to protect fellow CCP members from Wang Ming and his brutal Soviet backers. Kang, of course, had been one of the main hatchet men who terrorized other Chinese in Moscow. But no one dared challenge the revisionist version of his life.

Kang also forged documentary evidence that obscured his previous affiliations. In earlier days, Wang Ming had presented Kang with a copy of his famous booklet, *The Two Lines—Struggle for the Bolshevization of the Chinese Communist Party,* as a personal memento. Now Kang doctored his copy in ways that "proved" his allegedly bitter dispute with its author. He added a note beside the words "two lines" that read, "Actually it is one line, which is the left opportunist line." He changed one character in the title, converting the Chinese transliteration of "Bolshevization" to read "Menshevization"—a reference to the moderate social democrats who had opposed the Communists in Russia on the eve of the October Revolution. Kang also added the comment, "It should read 'Struggle for the Menshevization of the Chinese Communist Party,' for then the title would reflect the reality of the book." Kang displayed his doctored copy of the booklet prominently, allowing visitors to discover for themselves documentary "evidence" of his long-standing differences with Wang Ming. As late as the 1960s, while Kang was overseeing the preparation of articles attacking Soviet revisionism, he left his annotated copy of *The Two Lines* on the desk of his Peking office. By then, Wang Ming was ill, powerless, and in exile in Moscow, but Kang continued to guard against ghosts from the 1930s.

Mao, who had never visited Russia, had always harbored suspicions about the Soviets. To him, there was no question that within China the CCP owed nothing to foreign Communist parties. Seizing upon the Soviet issue, Kang insinuated himself into the debate on policy toward Moscow. By 1938, Kang was well qualified to pass himself off as an expert on Soviet affairs. He had spent four years in Moscow, knew many Soviet leaders, and spoke enough Russian to handle Soviets who visited Yan'an. His position as chief of security and espionage also involved him in Soviet affairs. The CCP had no foreign ministry at the time, so it fell to Kang, as intelligence chief, to interpret international trends for Mao and other Party leaders, especially as to the Soviet Union.

Kang had turned against the Russians within a few months after his arrival in Yan'an. By 1942, when Tass reporter Peter Vladimirov reached the CCP headquarters, Kang was well established as a venomous critic of the Soviet Union. In his diary, Vladimirov repeatedly described Kang's hatred for the Soviet Union. "Wherever you find Kang Sheng, there is no respect for the Soviet people or the Comintern," he wrote in one entry. At another point, Vladimirov quoted Kang telling other Chinese on their return from Moscow to "forget that you ever worked there. This is China. You must work Chinese-style. Remember that you were spoiled there, not taught. I forbid you to hobnob with the Soviets."

Kang was the official liaison between Vladimirov and the CCP leadership in Yan'an. He greeted Vladimirov and his assistants with polite smiles and went through the motions of cooperating with them—but, in Vladimirov's view, did his best to isolate the Soviet envoys from Chinese leaders. Kang even forced Wang Ming to avoid Vladimirov. Kang fed the Russian visitors false information about events in China, stalled their requests to travel beyond Yan'an, and taunted them about Mao's genius as a Marxist revolutionary.

Not surprisingly, Vladimirov arrived at a bitter and sarcastic estimation of Kang. He conceded that Kang always smiled, but he added, "It seems that the smile has been glued to his thin, bilious face. When he listens, he inhales the air noisily, in a Japanese manner, to show that he is glad to hear the voice of his interlocutor." Vladimirov, who had known Kang in Moscow, declared that Kang "remained the way I have always known him—gnarled of features and energetic in a nervous way. The impression he gives is that of a wooden puppet suspended on strings. . . ."

Vladimirov's main complaint, however, was that Kang kept the Soviet delegation under surveillance. "Kang Sheng's ubiquitous men are amazingly light of foot. Their very presence clams shut the mouths of anyone we want to talk with." Vladimirov claimed that his cook and other domestic staff were informants for Kang; he even alleged that Kang tried to plant a beautiful Chinese girl in his post on the pretext that she was a language teacher who needed to practice Russian. Kang kept a close watch on Vladimirov and other foreign visitors to Yan'an,* but he never bothered to arrest any of them. With so

---

* Kang was responsible for keeping track of any foreigners who called in Yan'an. From Kang's arrival there in late 1937 until 1944, when United States delegations started to visit with some frequency, the foreign community in Yan'an was both small and transient. The largest component was made up of exiled Asian Communists, including a number of Koreans, several leading Japanese Communists such as Nosaka Sanzo, and the Vietnamese revolutionary Ho Chi Minh. The only American who lived full-time in Yan'an before 1944 was George Hatem, a North Carolina–born, Swiss-

many of his countrymen under his scrutiny, Kang had little time to waste chasing foreigners.

Kang did everything in his power to disrupt relations between Yan'an and Moscow during the early stages of World War II, according to Vladimirov. Kang delivered biased, inaccurate accounts of Soviet affairs to Mao, consistently giving the gloomiest reading of the Soviet military situation. When Vladimirov arrived at Yan'an in May 1942, pessimistic assessments seemed reasonable, since the German army was inflicting enormous casualties on the Soviet Union. Even so, Kang was especially negative in evaluating Soviet reverses on the battlefield and only too happy to confirm Mao's prejudices and prove his personal hostility to Wang Ming's ideological camp.

Kang's attempt to create trouble between the Chinese Communists and the Soviets had a major impact, but not until years later. For the time being, his greatest influence on the Communist movement was his backing of Mao, so vital while Mao was consolidating his position as supreme leader of the CCP.

Although Wang Ming remained a member of the Politburo until 1945, he had long since lost out to Mao as a result of the infighting in the caves and meeting halls of Yan'an. Mao had Kang Sheng to thank for much of his success.

---

educated physician who in 1937 had "stopped off in China on the way around the world, and . . . remained." Hatem married a Chinese woman, adopted the Chinese name Ma Haide, and advised the Chinese on how to eradicate leprosy and venereal disease.

From time to time, foreign journalists visited Yan'an. In 1938 a Polish writer, Ilona Ralf Sues, spent a week or so there, and the following year, Roman Karman, a Soviet filmmaker, visited Mao. Western journalists did not reach Yan'an until 1944, when a group of foreign and Chinese reporters accompanied the first American military team to Yan'an (the Dixie Mission). The only journalists based permanently there during Kang's time were Vladimirov and his assistants.

Chapter VII

LORD OF
THE SNAKES

AS HEAD of Mao's secret service, Kang never lost sight of one essential lesson from his Soviet experience: that by inventing a world full of spies and enemy agents, it was possible to acquire enormous influence. Kang also borrowed the imagery he had first been exposed to in Moscow; like a good Stalinist, he continued to vilify Trotsky. Trotsky's status as public enemy number one was a product of Soviet politics, but Kang conjured up the discredited leader's specter in Yan'an and used it to arouse fear of traitors and saboteurs. Only he, Kang Sheng (or so he implied), was able to guard China against Trotsky's international network of spies and assassins.

Besides invoking Trotsky as a symbol of the imminent dangers facing the CCP, Kang laced his conversations and speeches with references to "special agents," "secret agents," "spies," "traitors," "double agents," "international espionage organizations," and "secret agent running dogs"—and used every opportunity to present himself as uniquely aware of the threats posed by clandestine opponents. "The danger of the secret agent," Kang wrote in his article blasting Chen Duxiu and the Chinese Trotskyites, "is not that he is outside opposing you. The greatest danger of the secret agent is that he is hidden in your bedroom and often licking your boots."

Kang was eager to become the supreme Communist spymaster, but taking over the Party's clandestine agencies in Yan'an brought some daunting challenges. Not only did he have to create a system that could protect the Communists in wartime, but he had to assert control over seasoned, often unruly survivors of the White Terror and the Long March. The personal authority Kang gained from Mao's support needed reinforcement from a display of professional competence and tough-mindedness. The fearsome aura he had acquired as a secret-police chief ordering assassinations in Shanghai and the imprisonment and execution of Chinese of allegedly suspect loyalty in Moscow now became a potent asset.

The difficulties Kang faced went far beyond the need to impose himself upon a corps of strong-willed cadres; there were also technical and managerial problems. The CCP's defeats since the early 1930s had left its security-and-intelligence apparatus fragmented and disorganized. The KMT Investigation Section and the Blue Shirts had broken many Communist cells in Shanghai, Tianjin, Peking, and other cities. Meanwhile, the confusion of the Long March had caused extensive damage to the Political Security Bureau, the rural arm of the Communist secret police.

Soon after the CCP had set up headquarters in Yan'an, the Party leaders established a new organization, the Social Affairs Department, with the idea of consolidating the three distinct security or espionage agencies that existed in one form or another at the time. The decision to form an integrated security system had been made before Kang returned from Moscow, but the task of molding its constituent parts into a single unit fell to Kang.

The urban secret service that had answered to the Shanghai-based Special Work Committee was a major element of the Social Affairs Department. Kang had led the Special Work Committee before his departure for Moscow and still knew many of its operatives who had survived mauling by the KMT secret police. Some of these agents came to Yan'an and continued their secret work, while others remained as underground workers in Japanese- or KMT-occupied territory.

Another major component of the Social Affairs Department, the Political Security Bureau, operated in villages and small towns under Communist control. This para-military body was originally established in the early 1930s at the Communist base in the mountains of Jiangxi to maintain order, enforce land reform, exterminate landlords who tried to keep their fields, and counter KMT subversion. The bureau's additional task of guarding senior Party leaders during the Long March had conferred on it the status of an elite corps.

Along with those two groups of security and espionage workers, the Communist administration in the Border Region around Yan'an had established its own special detachment, the *Baowei Chu* ("Guard Unit"), which was locally responsible for everything from routine police work to arresting subversive elements and enemy spies. The Guard Unit was closely associated with the Yan'an Garrison Regiment, made up of soldiers who ensured public safety in the Communist capital. The Garrison Regiment furnished the rank-and-file manpower for work assigned by the Social Affairs Department: posting sentries, arresting suspected enemy agents, and providing physical protection for Mao and other top Communist officials. As commander of the Garrison Regiment, General Wang Zhen—a crude, tough-talking peasant from Mao's province of Hunan—took orders from both Kang and the Military Commission.

"Social Affairs" was an innocuous title—unintentionally suggesting that a revolution might be a dinner party, after all—but under Kang's direction the department evolved into an agency modeled upon the Soviet secret-police system at its harshest. Like the OGPU and the NKVD, the KGB's forerunners, the Social Affairs Department integrated the two classic functions of secret services: conducting counterespionage and countersubversion, as well as collecting intelligence by all available means about the Party's enemies, both external and internal. The department's jurisdiction ranged from spying on foreigners to investigating and arresting anyone suspected of spying for other nations or subverting the Communist system. The scope of its functions was reflected in the names of the four principal branches: military security, political security, economic security, and international intelligence. To carry out such broad responsibilities, the Social Affairs Department expanded into a large bureaucracy, with a sizable but often covert presence in every province under Communist control.

In spite of its size, the Social Affairs Department did not have all-embracing power. Its military-security branch, for example, had to share responsibility for army intelligence with the Military Commission, which ran its own Military Intelligence Department. But this particular overlap did not curtail Kang's influence—he was head of both departments.

The Social Affairs Department also had close links with a number of other organizations that had at least some covert functions. The United Front Work Department, tasked with promoting the CCP's image as a nationalistic party keen to cooperate with other

Chinese patriots, maintained a system of agents within the KMT structure, many of whom also served Kang's organization. In theory, the Urban Work Department was supposed to administer the cities and towns that came under Communist control, but it also had a substantial covert role and worked in close cooperation with the Social Affairs Department.

Kang's bureaucratic kingdom continued to spread through the early 1940s. In 1943, five years after Kang had assumed command of intelligence work in Yan'an, the Communists established a new organization with the cumbersome title of Commission for Work Behind Enemy Lines to supervise intelligence operations in hostile territory. This agency included representatives from both the Social Affairs Department and the Intelligence and Liaison departments of the Military Commission. Kang's appointment as chairman of the new commission reinforced his dominance in the work of infiltrating and subverting enemy organizations.*

Control over both the Social Affairs Department and the Military Intelligence Department gave Kang immense influence. His position had no analogue even among intelligence and security chiefs in the Soviet Union, where the military-intelligence apparatus remained in the hands of the army's supreme command, separate from the civilian-dominated organizations like the OGPU, NKVD, and KGB. No one could compete with Kang's control over covert power. By the mid-1940s, he was virtually the second most powerful man in Yan'an, and one Social Affairs Department operative believed Kang was at least as powerful as Mao.

Already a man with many enemies for having betrayed Wang Ming, Kang generated even more hatred as he amassed power, frustrating the ambitions of men who thought they had greater claim to

---

* Hu Yaobang claimed in 1978 that Kang coordinated Communist intelligence work during the final stages of the Chinese Civil War. No available information supports Hu's claim, however. At the war's climax, Kang had been ousted from both the Social Affairs Department and the Military Intelligence Department and was working on matters of land reform and Party organization in Shandong. Hu asserted that in March 1948, Lin Boqu and Ren Bishi had proposed that Kang should manage intelligence operations against the KMT. But Ren Bishi, one of the most outspoken critics of Kang's work in Yan'an, would hardly have backed Kang for a job of that magnitude. Hu Yaobang probably confused times and dates, attributing to the late 1940s the power Kang wielded from 1943 until 1945 as chairman of the Commission for Work Behind Enemy Lines. Given the paucity of material published in China on Communist intelligence activities, such a mistake would not be surprising.

the posts he held. By becoming head of military intelligence, he shoved aside Luo Ruiqing, the general in charge of security during the Long March, even though Kang had only a limited understanding of army matters. Kang's sudden rise also thwarted the hopes of Deng Fa, the original commander of the Political Security Bureau in Jiangxi. Other, more obscure men lost opportunities similarly, but Kang seemed to be fearless of making enemies. He preferred to stake his future on power, not friends.

The major beneficiary of Kang's reign as espionage czar was the "devious and crafty" Li Kenong, who had helped the Party weather the impact of Gu Shunzhang's defection during the Shanghai era. Experienced in almost every aspect of intelligence work from covert operations to codes and cryptography, Li was named Kang's deputy in both the Social Affairs Department and the Military Intelligence Department in 1941.

To put his stamp on the Social Affairs Department, Kang changed its location as well as its personnel. By early 1939, he had shifted its headquarters from the caves at Yangjialing to Zaoyuan, where he lived. Along with offices and residences for his staff, Kang built a jail at Zaoyuan where he could detain, interrogate, and torture certain prisoners without outside interference.

During his first few years as head of the Social Affairs Department, Kang managed to create what amounted to his personal secret service. Kang himself insisted on better living standards than most other CCP leaders, and to strengthen the commitment of Social Affairs Department cadres to him and him alone, he made sure that his agents had better food, clothing, and housing than other CCP staffers. Kang's men earned a reputation for their "privileged status and cocky mannerisms."*

China had made remarkable headway since Kang's years in Shanghai. Millions upon millions of people still suffered from intermittent famine, natural disasters, and extreme poverty; but by the mid-1930s, China had achieved a level of prosperity suggesting that the country was at last on the road to modernization. Large cities like

---

* One informant noted that by the late 1940s, Kang's men had "cameras, good pens, watches, phonographs ... and large expense accounts. Outsiders, knowing that a certain man is of the Social Affairs Department, are constrained to treat him well, to curry his favor. Social Affairs Department agents frequent the restaurants and hotels. They are developing a zest for good living which sets them apart from the austere existence forced on the average party members."

Shanghai and Nanking thrived, and the pool of Chinese with foreign educations was growing fast. Chinese politics also seemed promising. Chiang Kai-shek had defeated or co-opted many of the warlords who had jeopardized China's unity in the decades following the Republican Revolution in 1911. The Communist rebels had survived the Long March, but by 1936, holed up in northern Shaanxi, they played only a small part on the national stage.

While the Kuomintang and the Communists continued to struggle, Japan looked at China with renewed greed. Japanese adventurers had dabbled in Chinese affairs since the nineteenth century; by the 1930s, the increasingly chauvinistic regime in Tokyo again saw military aggression against China as a way to expand the Japanese empire. The KMT–CCP united front against Japan, formed in early 1937, was shaky from the outset. Both parties paid lip service to cooperation, but endless jockeying for advantage took place behind the scenes, at times erupting into armed clashes.

By the time Kang had gained control of the security-and-intelligence apparatus, the Chinese Communists were surrounded by two sets of formidable enemies: well-armed Japanese troops occupied the area to the north and east of Yan'an, while the Communists' KMT "allies," quietly seeking to undermine any gains made by Mao's forces, held the territory to the south and west. Of these two foes, the Japanese posed the more serious espionage threat during Kang's first year as secret-police chief. Driven by an ideology that combined emperor worship and a callous contempt for China, Japan's militarist rulers implacably opposed the Chinese Communists. After their full-scale invasion of the Chinese mainland in July 1937, the Japanese started to clash with the Communists, periodically bombing Yan'an. The Japanese bombs caused few casualties, but they heightened fears of an all-out Japanese assault against the Communist stronghold and flattened the town into piles of rubble. In their final raid in 1941, the Japanese sent ninety planes over Yan'an and "bombed until they could not see a building standing up."

Kang's Social Affairs Department had to be constantly on the alert against Japanese clandestine activity. As Kang had observed in his article about Chen Duxiu and the Chinese Trotskyites, the Japanese were notorious for their use of spies and special agents. In Kang's words: "Agents and spies are an inseparable part of . . . the Japanese invaders' arsenal. In war this type of tool is the most fierce, dangerous, and most inexpensive; it is also the most difficult weapon to counter." The history of Japanese espionage in China dated back to the Sino-Japanese War of 1894, and, Kang asserted, it took every conceivable form. "In conducting espionage work in China the Japanese invaders use every method. Some are overt—military attachés' offices in embassies, intelligence organs based in military garrisons, and local intelligence units. Some are partially covert—shops, societies, chemists, newspaper companies, photographic studios, investigative groups, 'cultural' organizations, brothels, and every type of gang of vagabonds and drifters."

Japanese military-intelligence units, known as special-service organs—*tokumubu kikan*—proliferated throughout China after the Mukden Incident in 1931. These units were led by flamboyant adventurers like General Kenji Doihara, dubbed "Lawrence of Manchuria" by local English-language papers, or Kawashima Yoshiko, a Japanese-educated Manchu princess famous for her sexual appetite. Many Chinese became Japanese spies and special agents; Kang let it be known that he was always on guard against them.

The Japanese, as part of their strategy against China, also used opportunistic and pro-Japanese Chinese to set up puppet regimes in Manchuria, Peking, and Nanking, each with its own secret police. The Manchukuo government in Manchuria, nominally ruled by the last Manchu emperor, Henry Pu Yi, ran three secret services: a centralized security bureau, a special-service unit attached to the police force, and another special-service unit within the Manchurian Railway Administration. Supervised by Japanese agents, these organizations recruited Chinese criminals and soldiers of fortune who operated in a political no-man's-land and thus were vulnerable to pressure from both Communist and KMT intelligence services.

By the end of 1939, when the Japanese offensive bogged down because of China's sheer size, the threat of a Japanese assault against Yan'an became less likely. At the same time, competition intensified with the KMT, which remained the Communists' major rival for control over China. Both sides had always viewed the united front against Japan as a temporary expedient demanded by Chinese nationalism; now the Communists and the KMT started to launch paramilitary operations against each other. The KMT stationed a crack military force under Hu Zongnan, one of Chiang Kai-shek's most trusted generals, across the southern approaches to Yan'an to blockade the Communist-controlled Border Region. Meanwhile, the Communists launched guerrilla campaigns in areas nominally under

Japanese control where they could establish "liberated zones." Pitched battles often flared up between the opposing Chinese forces. In January 1941, the Communist New Fourth Army, operating in the Yangtze Valley, was almost annihilated in an engagement with KMT troops. Each side accused the other of provoking the battle. Both the KMT and the Communists turned increasingly to clandestine intelligence campaigns as part of their efforts to gain an advantage during this period.

Changes in Soviet policy also fueled the old KMT–Communist rivalry. The Soviets were providing extensive aid to the KMT when Kang arrived in Yan'an in late 1937, but that support had shrunk dramatically by 1939, freeing Chiang Kai-shek from any concern that operations against the Communists might curtail Moscow's largesse. Moreover, the Soviet defeat of Japanese forces in the battle of Nomohan in Mongolia that lasted from May until September 1939 eased Stalin's fears of Japan. The subsequent signing of the Soviet–Japanese mutual nonaggression pact in April 1941 reduced the pressure on the Russians to maintain close ties with the KMT as a precaution against a Japanese invasion of the Soviet Union.

By 1940, the undeclared war with the KMT posed a serious challenge to Kang. The KMT Investigation Section, the nemesis of the Communists when Kang worked in Shanghai, had evolved into the Central Statistics Bureau, a sprawling organization that operated throughout KMT China and bore the brunt of the secret war with the Communists. Another gigantic intelligence organization, the Military Statistics Bureau, also emerged out of the KMT in 1938. As its name suggests, the bureau originated in the army, but it soon had a tentacle in almost every facet of intelligence work; much of its effort was directed at political and civilian targets, including both the Communists and the pro-Japanese puppet regimes. Just as the CCP's Social Protection Department had little to do with protecting society, the KMT's two statistics bureaus were responsible for much more than gathering statistics.

The Military Statistics Bureau was headed by the notorious Dai Li, who, as chief of the Blue Shirts, had put together the death list that contained Kang's name and forced him to flee Shanghai in 1933. Dai had been accumulating power ever since. While the Sino-Japanese War raged on, he became one of the most powerful and feared men in China, gaining control of some of the most important elements of the KMT administration, from military police and intelligence to customs, taxation, and opium suppression. Dai Li's Military Statistics Bureau indulged in every imaginable ploy—training beautiful women to seduce enemy officials; setting up a radio interception and decoding unit; using torture to extract information; and running a concentration camp for political prisoners just outside Chongqing. Dai Li even established a network of agents in India and America and developed close ties with U.S. Naval Intelligence. Under Dai Li, the Military Statistics Bureau scored a number of successes, especially against the Japanese puppet regimes, managing to place agents at the highest levels of the pro-Japanese Wang Jingwei regime in Nanking and to assassinate many well-known Chinese collaborators.*

The array of secret services operating in China created a shifting, rootless, and unstable world for Kang and his comrades. Dangers could be invisible, and the loyalties and motives of one's friends often were open to question. In this period of extraordinary chaos and turbulence, many Chinese changed political affiliations with the circumstances, swept from group to group—from KMT to Communist, from Communist to Japanese puppet regime—by conflicting impulses of ambition, honor, disillusionment, shame, greed, and fear.

A complicated web of temporary friendships, betrayals, and expedient reconciliations linked many of the secret services. The infamous secret-police organization of the Wang Jingwei puppet regime in Nanking typified the confusion and opportunism that extended throughout this netherworld. The Wang Jingwei intelligence unit, headquartered in a spacious villa at 76 Jessfield Road in Shanghai, came to be known simply as Number 76. Recruiting its personnel from the underworld of gangsters, renegade Communists, KMT spies,

---

* Dai Li died in 1946 when an American-made C-47 carrying him from Tianjin crashed in a storm as it attempted to land in Nanking. Some writers have blamed Kang for Dai Li's death. In fact, Kang had been removed as security chief by that time, so he lacked the power to sabotage the aircraft. Any evidence of sabotage points to Dai Li dying at the hands of his own side. U.S. Naval Intelligence records show that one month before Dai Li's death, his rivals within the KMT were plotting to kill him by "the usual accident, either in a plane or a car." Other evidence, including eyewitness accounts, supports the assessment that the crash resulted from a severe storm that forced the pilot to divert the plane to Nanking from Shanghai, where Dai Li had planned to visit his lover, Hu Die, an actress who was known in English as Butterfly Wu. The pilot tried to land in low clouds and heavy rain but overflew the airfield and rammed into a mountain. Claims that the aircraft exploded mysteriously in midair, presumably as a result of a bomb planted by Kang's agents, are merely further examples of the myths that came to surround both Dai Li and Kang.

and assassins, the unit brought together in one organization a trio of men who had started as dedicated Communists but ended their careers as unprincipled tools of the Japanese militarists. The political director of Number 76 was Zhou Fohai, who, like Mao Zedong, Zhang Guotao, and Liu Renjing, had been one of the thirteen founders of the CCP in 1921. Zhou Fohai eventually turned into a compulsive conspirator; by the end of his life, he was working for the Japanese while maintaining clandestine contact with Dai Li. The day-to-day management of Number 76 was in the hands of Ding Mocun, who had worked directly under Kang as a member of the Red Squads in Shanghai. Ding's chief assistant was Li Shiqun, another graduate of Kang's Red Squads. Both Ding and Li had been trained as Communists in the Soviet Union, but they defected first to the KMT and then to the pro-Japanese puppet regime. Instead of furthering the cause of Communist revolution, they spent the war years kidnapping wealthy Shanghai residents for ransom and assassinating Chinese nationalists. The political histories of Zhou Fohai, Ding Mocun, and Li Shiqun typify the depravity that came to drive many of those who worked for Kang over the years.

Soon after he was installed as head of the secret police, Kang began involving himself directly in the investigation of spies in Yan'an. During the first half of 1939, Kang intervened personally in one case that aroused anxieties over the threat of enemy agents and accented his importance. This episode occurred at a time when the Communists, at Mao's instigation, were again preparing to invade KMT territory. By manufacturing evidence of KMT espionage against the Communists in the Border Region, Kang laid the groundwork for Mao to override the so-called united front and secure a consensus in favor of aggressive action against the KMT.

The first casualty of Kang's intrigues was Qian Weiren, a minor official in the Border Region bureaucracy. Qian's job of building and repairing roads in the Yan'an area required him to meet occasionally with KMT officials responsible for public-engineering work in the areas adjoining Communist territory. Such contacts were not unusual, but even so, Kang accused Qian of being "an internal traitor." To strengthen his case, Kang intimidated Qian's wife, threatening to treat her, too, as an enemy agent. Terrified of what Kang might do to her, she agreed to spy on her husband, report on his activities, and help prove his guilt.

Qian was arrested and hauled before a "public interrogation meeting," one of the political institutions used to maintain psychological control over the community. About one hundred cadres from the Social Affairs Department and the local security units attended the session. Kang presided over the interrogation of Qian; when it was over, he declared that Qian was a traitor and special agent, and sentenced him to seven years' imprisonment.

In Kang's hands, the Qian Weiren affair appeared to justify a more aggressive approach toward the KMT. Within weeks, Kang intervened in another case, this time implicating both the KMT and one of the pro-Japanese puppet regimes in a joint espionage operation against Yan'an. Kang's newest victim was Wang Zunji, a young woman who had fled Japanese-occupied Peking. Wang Zunji, the niece of Wang Kemin, a leader of the pro-Japanese puppet regime in Peking, had left the city in disgust over her family's collaboration with the Japanese. Like Jiang Qing and many others, she was drawn to Yan'an by the Communists' reputation for being staunch opponents of the Japanese. But Kang, instead of welcoming her as a valuable defector, saw her as a useful pawn in his broader scheme. Accusing Wang Zunji of being "a Japanese agent and KMT special agent," he ordered her arrest. Security officials held her in Yan'an in one of the dark caves he used as prisons; then, under Kang's personal supervision, they pried a confession out of her.

In the first stages of the interrogation, Kang's men forced Wang Zunji to remain standing and sleepless for three days and nights, until her feet swelled and she began suffering attacks of dizziness. When Kang saw that she was still unwilling to cooperate, he threatened to throw a pair of poisonous snakes into the cave with her. The ploy worked; Wang Zunji made the confession. Prompted by terror and sleeplessness, she concocted an elaborate tale of her recruitment as a special agent, going so far as to claim that she communicated with her alleged spymasters through a code represented by a pattern woven into the fabric of her clothes.

With Wang's confession in hand, Kang promptly spread the word throughout Yan'an, comparing her to the notorious Manchu adventuress Kawashima Yoshiko, who had become a symbol of the sinister virtuosity of Japanese espionage. Kang transferred Wang Zunji to the Social Affairs Department prison at Zaoyuan and then established a "Special Case Group"—an institution that was to plague Chinese politics until the Cultural Revolution and beyond—to further investigate her supposed crimes. Kang wrote to the group on May 31, 1939, instructing it to establish proof that Wang had belonged to the Blue Shirts Society, the unofficial KMT intelligence unit run by Dai Li. Kang's assertion had no basis, but it made the point that the CCP's enemies were working simultaneously for the Japanese and the KMT. Despite the lack of evidence against her, Wang Zunji was imprisoned until 1946 and released only after Kang had lost control of security work.

A few months later, Kang involved himself in another espionage action, which he handled with great fanfare. The suspect this time was Li Ning, a beautiful young woman from Manchuria. She had worked in the CCP's underground organization in the northeast and had arrived in Yan'an in 1938 after escaping from Japanese-occupied territory. The ever vigilant Kang ordered her arrest in July 1939 on the grounds that she "walked like a Japanese woman" and possessed "a Japanese style undergarment"—an accusation indicative of the mindset he brought to his investigations. Kang conducted the public interrogation of Li Ning, finally fashioning a charge against her that, if nothing else, stands as a classic non sequitur: "Miss Li," he declared, "you're very attractive, so if you're not a special agent, then who is?" Succumbing to the relentless pressure applied by Kang and his secret police, Li Ning finally admitted that she had "turned against the party and joined the enemy as a special agent." Kang's success in breaking Li Ning enhanced his reputation as a spy catcher with an almost supernatural ability to detect hidden enemies.

Kang conducted his persecutions with full publicity—an uncommon feature of counterespionage work in closed, authoritarian societies. But the Moscow show trials had taught Kang how espionage cases could be used to control political debate. Suspects were arrested on the flimsiest evidence, or at times on none at all. Kang frequently accused people of espionage for meeting certain criteria he deemed typical of spies and traitors: they were related to a Japanese collaborator, for example, or they were said to possess Japanese-style underwear!

The Wang Zunji and Li Ning episodes set a precedent; over the next few years, Communist counterespionage operatives became increasingly haunted by the notion that KMT and Japanese agents had flooded into Yan'an along with the young people fleeing Japanese oppression. Thanks to Kang's emphasis on catching enemy agents, the Social Affairs Department acquired a new nickname: "the Department for Hoeing Traitors."

Deep in the bowels of the Social Affairs Department, Kang established a bureau known as "the Trial Office," which was responsible for "liquidations"—everything from setting time of arrest to executing sentence. Trial offices were established throughout the areas under Communist control. They usually included a section that specialized in obtaining confessions. According to one Social Affairs Department operative, "medieval tortures and the cruellest cross-examination methods are utilized as a matter of course." Some of the men who served as interrogators and torturers had been at their jobs for many years and become "indifferent to suffering" and prone to "torture victims when not necessary."

For their punishments and interrogation techniques, the Social Affairs Department's professional inquisitors drew on thousands of years of Chinese tradition and adapted it to the twentieth-century Stalinist model of fabricating a new "reality" out of bogus confessions. The procedure usually began with the prisoner being ordered to reveal everything about his life. If his jailers concluded that he was holding something back, or decided to make an example of him, or simply were in a sadistic mood, they would place him in a tiny cell where it was impossible to stand or lie down. Some prisoners spent as long as twenty days in these cells. When they got out—if they got out—many of them were no longer able to walk. If a prisoner's confession was not up to Kang's standards, a range of techniques was applied, either to force cooperation or just to finish off the victim:

- *The bamboo cut:* bamboo spikes were driven under the fingernails.
- *Passing horsehair through the eye:* a hair from a horse's tail was inserted into the penis.
- *Passing through a woman:* water from a narrow hose was pumped into the vagina at great pressure.
- *Giving the guest a drink:* a large quantity of vinegar was forced down the throat; after the first few retchings, the pain was excruciating.
- *Beam pulley:* the victim was suspended by his arms and lashed with leather thongs.

- *Pressing incense:* with the prisoner suspended from a rafter by his arms, smoldering incense was applied to the armpit; when withdrawn, it tore out a piece of burning flesh.
- *Pulling down the road:* the prisoner was bound and tied to a horse's tail, then dragged to his death as the horse was whipped.
- *Assisting production:* the prisoner dug his own grave and was pushed in and buried alive.

Starting with the detention center Kang established at Zaoyuan, the Social Affairs Department created its own prison system. Inmates were usually organized into groups of five; if one of the group escaped, the other four were executed. It was an effective deterrent, as individual escapes almost never occurred. Prisoners were not allowed any contact with friends or family members on the outside. The prisons also used the "report-to-the-comrade system," whereby an inmate had to ask permission from a guard before moving a limb or even shifting position, or else risk a beating from "the comrade." (The guards alone were referred to as "comrades"; the prisoners, because of their status, were denied this title.) Prisoners could tend to the needs of nature only at three set times each day.

Much as Kang must have relished identifying and catching "enemy agents," he also had to conduct intelligence operations against the KMT, the Japanese, and the Japanese-dominated puppet governments in China. The nation's wartime capital, Chongqing, an ancient city on the Yangtze River, symbolized the intrigue of the times, with spies and conspirators flourishing in a society of corrupt generals and avaricious officials. Growing disillusionment with Chiang Kai-shek and his henchmen afforded the CCP's Social Affairs Department plenty of opportunity to plant agents inside KMT party and government agencies.

It is surprising that Kang did not achieve greater success in this. The Social Affairs Department created a series of underground networks in the Yan'an area, with operatives and secret-communications networks in cities like Peking, Xian, and Lanzhou. The Communists also placed several moles close to Hu Zongnan, the KMT general whose troops blockaded the southern approaches to Yan'an. Both Hu's secretary and a journalist with the North West News Agency, a propaganda unit run by Hu, were Communist spies. The Social Affairs Department recruited many agents within the upper levels of the

KMT, including Chen Lian, the daughter of Chen Bulei, Chiang Kai-shek's personal secretary and trusted adviser.* A number of KMT politicians and generals, including Fu Zuoyi, Long Yun, and Shen Zui, defected on the eve of the Communist victory in 1949, but none had worked for the Communists until then. Given the explosive mixture of opportunism and idealism so characteristic of the times, Kang should have been able to accomplish more.

Nor was the secret war one-sided. The KMT's counterespionage operatives broke several spy networks that the CCP Social Affairs Department had established in KMT organizations and territory. The most important KMT successes occurred in 1947, after the outbreak of the Chinese Civil War, when a series of intelligence cells in northern China were shattered by KMT security services. Dozens of Communist operatives were arrested, including Zhao Yaobin, who had been one of Kang's top aides.

The KMT also managed to infiltrate Communist headquarters in Yan'an with a Dai Li operative named Shen Zhiyue. The inconspicuous and hardworking Shen penetrated Mao's office, where he worked as a clerk and processed documents. On realizing that he was in grave danger of exposure, he persuaded Mao to post him to the Jiangsu–Zhejiang region as leader of the local underground Communist organization. From there, he eventually made his way back to Chongqing.

Besides running operations against the KMT, Kang maintained the links with traditional Chinese secret societies that the Communists had forged almost at the Party's inception. Some of the CCP leaders in Shanghai, such as Gu Shunzhang, had been members of the Green Gang, an urban secret society, while veteran Communist military commanders Zhu De and He Long, among others, had belonged to rural secret societies like the Red Spears. Kang himself had consorted with gangsters in his native village of Dataizhuang and had often encountered Green Gang members in Shanghai, especially when he headed the Special Work Committee after Gu Shungzhang's defection.

---

* The fate of many of the Communist agents is unknown, but it is worth noting that Chen Bulei's niece Weng Yuwen subsequently married Qiao Shi, who became the supreme CCP official responsible for China's security-and-intelligence activity in the 1980s.

Under Kang, the Social Affairs Department consolidated its previously haphazard links with the secret societies into a more formal structure. According to Tass representative Peter Vladimirov, this system was set out in a 1942 document entitled "Instructions for Work with Secret Societies." As managed by Kang's deputy Li Kenong, the CCP's relations with secret societies helped Kang systematically monitor developments in many parts of the country. The rural secret societies were well placed to observe enemy troop movements, and agents among the Green Gang enabled the Communists to keep abreast of events in such far-flung cities as Shanghai, Mukden, Nanking, and Chongqing.

No matter what setbacks the Social Affairs Department had, and for all his dislike of Kang, Vladimirov expressed a grudging respect for the intelligence chief and his ability to organize the collection, assessment, and interpretation of intelligence data. Vladimirov quoted Mao as saying that Kang was the best-informed man in China. The Russian noted with irritation that Kang boasted endlessly that he had warned Moscow of German plans to invade the Soviet Union in June 1941. (The Chinese Communists had acquired their information from Chongqing, where a member of Zhou Enlai's entourage had heard it from a KMT contact, who had in turn seen a report from the Chinese embassy in Berlin.) Kang's message had no effect, however—Stalin ignored it, just as he disregarded similar warnings from the British and from Richard Sorge, a Soviet agent in Tokyo. Stalin's refusal to heed the Chinese warnings must have perplexed Kang and contributed to his animosity toward the Soviet Union.

The methods Kang put in place in Yan'an shaped the Party's public security work through the Cultural Revolution and beyond. Many of his colleagues later expressed outrage at the treatment they received during the Cultural Revolution, but they had witnessed, and in some cases applied, similar techniques during the Yan'an period without voicing a word of protest. The persecutions Kang began conducting in 1939 were a mild, relatively harmless preview of the nightmare he created and presided over for nearly forty years.

What had started out as an attempt by the Communists to create a Marxist Shangri-la in the valleys and caves of northern China degenerated within a few years into a reign of terror. The pioneers at Yan'an had arrived "fired with a zeal to . . . erect a democratic utopia in China." For many of them, this zeal was soon quenched by the hardships of daily living and the disillusioning Communist policy of growing and selling opium to raise funds. A lot of cadres "wished to desert Yenan as quickly as they had come," which they found impossible to do. Impossible because there was no way to elude the omnipresent "Chinese Communist 'Gestapo' " headed by Kang Sheng.

Chapter VIII

CONNOISSEUR
OF TERROR

BY 1940, KANG SHENG wielded immense influence over the lives of others. But he lusted for more. During the next few years, he expanded his authority with such ruthlessness that he became a symbol of terror among the Communists, from the rank and file up to the Party's most senior officials.

Kang consolidated his control over the Social Affairs Department in 1939 and spent the first half of the 1940s as both secret-police chief and Mao Zedong's favorite courtier, greatly enhancing his stature as a Party leader. Kang worked on security and intelligence matters, lectured at the Party School, attended meetings of the Party's highest councils, mixed with Mao and Jiang Qing, and systematically applied Stalinist methods to the Communists in Yan'an.

Exploiting the Party's growing authoritarian tendencies—already encouraged by the White Terror, the Long March, the war with Japan, and the fear of KMT attack—Kang made the secret police the final arbiter of what was fact and what was fiction. The perfect opportunity to do so came in the early 1940s, when Mao deputized him to oversee the Rectification Movement, the thought reform campaign that came to shape the techniques of political control the Communist leaders have used in various forms and with varying degrees of success ever since.

As Mao tightened his grip on the Party, he intensified his campaign to undermine Wang Ming. Wang had continued to use his network of Soviet-trained supporters and his Comintern connections to challenge Mao's position as supreme Party leader. In one instance, a single word literally sufficed for Kang to move against his former patron Wang Ming. In late December 1940, Mao drafted an essay, "On Policy," which included the claim that "Chen Duxiu [and] Wang Ming committed mistakes of the right opportunist line." When the majority of the Central Committee persuaded Mao to reword the passage without using "line"—an omission that weakened the impression that Chen and Wang Ming were consistently wrong—Kang went to Mao and told him that "not to write the word line was a problem of principle." Whispering his views in Mao's ear became a favorite tactic of Kang's, one that enabled him to operate without the knowledge of other leaders while he positioned himself as Mao's most trusted adviser.

In late 1941, Mao began preparations for a campaign to spread a view of the Party's history that would inflate his own contribution to the cause of communism in China. That September, the Politburo debated the political and strategic errors from the early stages of the Long March, when Wang Ming's followers had dominated Party councils, outvoted Mao and his allies, and set Communist strategy. The Politburo concluded that serious mistakes had indeed been made—in itself a victory for Mao—and decided to launch a movement to purify the thinking of senior leaders and overcome "misunderstandings" about the past. In other words, the rank and file would be indoctrinated with Mao's view of Party history. The Rectification Movement officially started on February 1, 1942, when Mao laid it out in his address at the Party School's annual opening ceremony.

Mao and his closest supporters designed the Rectification Movement to instill in all Party members a single-minded loyalty to Mao. In the early stages of Rectification, anyone who questioned Mao's place was subjected to intense group pressure—and, as the process gained momentum, to torture and imprisonment. Among the Maoist goals was to discredit Wang Ming and his Soviet-oriented faction, the Twenty-eight Bolsheviks. Mao's side, in the obscure lexicon of Communist Chinese ideology, "had to remove the damage and dangers to the party created by first the rightist and later the leftist mistakes of Wang Ming." Mao was glorified for devising the shrewd policies that had rescued the CCP and the Red Army after the Twenty-eight Bolsheviks had led them to the brink of defeat and destruction. Coupled with praise of the tactical virtues of Mao's ideals was an emphasis on his philosophical accomplishments, bringing a new, Chinese dimension to the Marxist-Leninist tradition. Unlike Wang Ming, who relied on the prestige of the Comintern and the Soviet Union, Mao appealed to China's sense of nationalism and its xenophobia.

To disguise the partisan motives and inhuman methods of the Rectification Movement, it was presented as a process of Marxist education. Party members had to study and discuss selected documents and then participate in endless sessions of criticism and self-criticism, in which all members were expected to reveal instances when they had deviated from the ideological standards set forth in the texts and to reprimand less forthcoming comrades. The declared goals of this process were to improve the Party's "work style," overcome "misunderstandings about ideology" (a code phrase for sudden shifts in the Party's policy), and help "remold the bourgeois mentality" of (i.e., demand absolute loyalty from) younger cadres. This relatively benign interpretation of the Rectification Movement still has wide acceptance in the West, where many experts continue to insist that the movement was nothing more than an attempt to subject wrong-thinking CCP members to psychological stress instead of purging them. The purpose, in the words of Mark Selden, author of a major academic study of the Rectification Movement, was to reform and reincorporate faltering cadres into the Party, "rather than to eliminate them as enemies through exile, concentration camp, or even expulsion from the party or public office."*

Mao, together with his ghostwriter, Chen Boda, drafted many of the texts studied during the Rectification Movement. Kang, however, was assigned to organize and conduct the program. In August 1941, one month before the Politburo authorized the rectification process, Kang was named chairman of the Cadre Investigation Commission, a powerful agency that, like the Social Affairs Department, vetted cadres to ensure that they met the required political standards. Kang's appointment signaled his status as one of the most powerful CCP

---

* Selden wrote, "I am familiar with no cases of cadres who were imprisoned or excluded from the party in the course of the intensive study and criticism which began in the spring of 1942 ... So prominent a 'sick man' as Wang Ming, Mao's former rival, apparently in Moscow at this time, retained his Central Committee membership ... The writer Wang Shiwei, the object of the most virulent public campaign of denunciation and a man adamant in his refusal to admit his 'errors' and reform at the party's behest, eventually renounced his membership rather than accept the legitimacy of the criticism against him. But such cases were rare." In fact, Wang Ming, who was in Yan'an and was the main target of the campaign, claimed that Mao and Kang attempted to poison him, while Wang Shiwei was imprisoned for five years and then beheaded.

leaders. The three vice chairmen who helped Kang run the commission were themselves extremely influential: Gao Gang, who headed the Party apparatus in northwest China; Chen Yun, the Politburo member responsible for organizational work; and Peng Zhen, an important leader in northern China who later became mayor of Peking.

Appointment to the Cadre Investigation Commission involved Kang directly in the Rectification Movement and put him working side by side with Mao. Kang's control over the Rectification Movement and his close relationship with Mao became more obvious in July 1942, when a new body, the General Study Commission, was established to supervise the Rectification Movement. Mao chaired the commission, but day-to-day power rested in the hands of its sole vice chairman, Kang Sheng. Kang also headed the commission's most influential subcommittee, the one responsible for restructuring the central Party organs and deciding who would work for them. Kang was by then perhaps second to Mao in power, if not in the formal hierarchy; with Mao's help, he had come to occupy some of the most important posts in Yan'an. Peter Vladimirov aptly described Kang as Mao's "claws and teeth."

Not only did Kang use the Rectification Movement to discredit Wang Ming, but he figured centrally in an alleged attempt to poison Wang with mercury. Wang Ming fell seriously ill in 1942. The medicine prescribed by one of the doctors who looked after the Communist leaders, Jin Maoyue, aggravated his condition. By March 1943, Wang's health had so deteriorated that his life seemed in danger, and his wife, Meng Qingshu, asked a Russian doctor attached to the Soviet delegation in Yan'an for advice about the medicine Jin had prescribed. The Russian told her that over time one of the ingredients, mercury, could react with other substances and seriously harm her husband.

Wang Ming claimed that a guilt-ridden Jin Maoyue had admitted to him that he had been ordered to prescribe a poisonous compound by Li Fuchun, deputy head of the Organization Department (and one of Mao's fellow-Hunanese). Vladimirov, who recorded the same episode in his diaries, concluded that Mao and Kang had devised a plot to poison Wang Ming.*

---

* If true, Wang Ming's claims that Li Fuchun ordered Jin Maoyue to poison him makes it almost certain that Kang was involved. The Social Affairs Department had

Wang Ming's claim that Kang, Mao, and Li Fuchun sought to poison him remains controversial. Chinese Communist historians refuse to consider Wang Ming's charges at all. Soviet sinologists, by contrast, believe that an attempt was made to poison Wang Ming and see the incident as an example of Kang's "exquisite cruelty." Some Western experts skeptically insist that it was out of character for Mao to order the death of an opponent. Yet during the Cultural Revolution, Mao made no attempt to interfere with Kang's use of medical mistreatment—prescribing the wrong medicine or no medicine at all—to ensure that rivals like President Liu Shaoqi and Marshal He Long would die. Not that Mao needed to be brought into the picture; any attempt to kill Wang Ming could have been initiated by Kang alone. No one would find this particular method inconsistent with his taste for inflicting pain.

Mystery still surrounds this incident, but Wang Ming's accusations stirred up an embarrassing debate inside senior Party councils. A three-man committee established to investigate "the Jin Maoyue affair" concluded that Jin had attempted to poison Wang Ming on the orders of Chen Lifu, a senior KMT spymaster. Chen, according to the investigators, conveyed instructions to Jin through the chairman of the KMT Red Cross organization. Jin made a "confession" that supported the investigators' conclusion, but in Yan'an during the 1940s such avowals rarely corresponded to truth. The Jin committee's findings bear the fingerprints of Kang Sheng, who was one of its three members, along with Liu Shaoqi and Li Fuchun. The probers sentenced Jin to five years' imprisonment but, at the same time, allowed him to remain at liberty and practice medicine—a privilege accorded to few CCP members found guilty of working for KMT intelligence services. In 1945, when the excesses of the Rectification Movement were being redressed, Jin recanted his confession, insisting that he had simply made a mistake in drawing up the prescription and had not deliberately sought to injure Wang Ming's health.*

Wang Ming remained sick for three years, unable to participate in regular political debates in Yan'an or to attend the Seventh Party

---

close links to the Organization Department, and Li Fuchun was part of the committee Kang chaired that coordinated the activities of the Social Affairs Department and the Organization Department.

* The fact that Wang Ming made charges in Yan'an that he was being poisoned was confirmed in a September 1981 conversation between a Chinese journalist and George Hatem, the American physician in Yan'an at the time of Wang's poisoning.

Congress in April 1945. Mao finally allowed him to travel to the Soviet Union for medical treatment. Whether Jin Maoyue prescribed mercury deliberately or not, the damage to Wang Ming's feeble physical condition speeded up Wang's eclipse by curtailing his ability to respond to Mao's well-timed attacks.

Soon after Kang was placed in charge of the Rectification Movement, he stepped up his efforts to weed out alleged enemy agents in Yan'an. By late 1943, with Rectification already under way for a year and a half, Kang had converted it into an all-out witch-hunt, with the Social Affairs Department emerging as the ultimate judge of political reliability. Kang argued that "we have discovered so many spies that all comrades must be on guard . . . Now you must increase your vigilance . . . and help those who wish to confess to the party to repent and save them from the trap of the enemy's fifth column. This is your sacred duty."

Kang began turning the Rectification Movement into a brutal purge in December 1942, when he arrested a young male student at the Shaanbei Academy, a training school run by the Social Affairs Department that many of Kang's aides and protégés attended. The student, nineteen-year-old Zhang Keqin, had worked with the underground Communist resistance in Gansu Province. But Kang declared Zhang to be a typical espionage suspect, charging that the Gansu organization was a "red-flag" group—his term for a group conducting anti-Communist activity under a progressive cover, or "red flag." Kang pointed out that Zhang's father had been arrested by enemy forces in Lanzhou, Gansu's capital, and was thought to have "political problems." To confirm his suspicions that Zhang Keqin was an enemy agent, Kang adduced Zhang's record of voicing dissident opinions to senior cadres—even though such conspicuous conduct could hardly be expected of someone involved in covert activities.

Kang had no substantive evidence against Zhang Keqin. But that did not stop him from subjecting Zhang to his standard repertoire of psychological pressure and physical torture. Zhang gave in within days, admitting that he was a KMT spy. Kang immediately staged a public meeting, forcing Zhang to repeat his confession to a large audience. Zhang's humiliation gave Kang his first example of a youthful "enemy agent" who had been "rescued"—that is, blessed with Kang's special kind of "salvation."

Zhang Keqin's case set in motion a wild search for enemy agents who could be "saved." Kang declared that KMT secret agents had penetrated not only every department and organization in Yan'an but the underground Communist cells and organizations operating in KMT- and Japanese-occupied areas as well, and had turned them into "red-flag" groups. Kang's hunt for spies gathered tremendous momentum, turning 1943 into a year of terror. On April 1 of that year, Hu Zongnan, the KMT general who was blockading approaches to the Border Region, sent a representative to Yan'an. Kang exploited the envoy's visit and, on the pretext of keeping traitors from contacting the KMT, had security operatives detain over two hundred suspects in one night. Challenged by some of his more sober-minded colleagues who doubted that so many secret agents had actually worked their way into Yan'an, Kang replied, "We can talk about that after their arrest. When they're locked up we can interrogate them."

A more prominent victim of Kang's dragnet was Wang Shiwei, a well-known writer who had been in Yan'an since 1939. Although he had joined the Communist Party as far back as the mid-1920s while studying at Peking University, Wang had irked a number of the high leaders in Yan'an. He was a sincere, serious, passionate intellectual with no interests apart from literature and the rejuvenation of China. "He never smoked, drank, or watched movies; his only pastime was walking," according to his wife. Wang lost patience with the elitist system in Yan'an; he began criticizing the heads of various organizations for helping themselves to more nutritious meals and better clothes than were available to ordinary students and workers. He also spoke out against the selection of Rectification committee members by the senior leaders instead of through democratic elections.

Wang Shiwei expressed his heretical views in a series of talks and wall posters and in a famous essay, "The Wild Lily," published in March 1942. No sooner had Wang's treatise appeared than he and his criticisms of Yan'an society dominated everyone's conversation. But celebrity was dangerous. Within weeks, a number of literary workers in Wang's department at the Central Research Academy, the Party's supreme intellectual body and forerunner of the Academy of Social Sciences, began to condemn him for pursuing "egalitarian" ideas.

Kang Sheng took no part in the initial criticism of Wang Shiwei, but less than a month after "The Wild Lily" appeared, Li Yan, the head of the Central Research Academy, reported to Kang on developments in the case. Kang's response took Li by surprise. Kang knew all about Wang and warned Li to be careful of him: "Wang Shiwei is a Trotskyite element; he is organizationally active; he is also a Blue Shirt special agent. He is different from other people. His is not a problem of ideology."

Kang's cousin Li Yuchao, who had also been his fellow student at Shanghai University, charged Wang Shiwei with Trotskyism at an open meeting of literary workers on May 27, 1942. In response, Wang conceded that he had been friendly with a number of the literary figures among the Chinese Trotskyites but protested that he had never belonged to their organization. He did acknowledge his agreement with the Trotskyites that the Communist revolution in April 1927 had failed because of the policies dictated by Stalin and his agent Borodin. Once again, Wang was making a dangerously provocative gesture in a disciplined, authoritarian society.

At Kang's direction, the Social Affairs Department sent some operatives to the Central Research Academy to gather information about Wang. By the time of Wang's arrest on April 1, 1943, the charge against him had been switched from "Blue Shirt special agent" to "Trotskyite." He remained in jail in Zaoyuan until 1947, when the entire Communist community evacuated Yan'an in the face of a KMT offensive. Wang was escorted by Social Affairs Department guards to Xing County, a desolate little town in Shanxi Province, and there beheaded by Dai Youqiao, a local Social Affairs Department operative.* Kang has been credited with ordering Wang's execution, but the latest research in China suggests that the men directly responsible were Li Kenong, Kang's successor as head of the Social Affairs Department, and General He Long, the most senior Party and military official in the region at the time.†

By July 1943, Kang had been conducting "sudden strikes" for several months and had detained over a thousand "enemy agents." On July 15, at a meeting of cadres from the central Party organs, he gave a

---

* Wang's executioner, Dai Youqiao, became the deputy director of the Sichuan Provincial Public Security Office after the Communist victory. He later went insane and is now in a mental hospital in Chengdu, reportedly obsessed by fears that the ghosts of the men and women he killed are seeking vengeance.

† In a statement issued on February 7, 1991, the Public Security Ministry cleared Wang Shiwei of involvement with Trotskyite organizations and admitted that his execution had been a mistake.

lengthy report entitled "Rescuing Those Who Have Lost Their Footing." Kang's speech, epitomizing the air of suppressed hysteria he cultivated, sent waves of dread through the audience. Having declared that he was speaking "at a time of emergency, a time of military mobilization . . . when the Kuomintang . . . is tightly enveloping our southern front and awaiting the order to attack," Kang continued:

> Here, three months ago, we informed everyone that the Japanese invaders and the KMT had trained a large number of spies and agents to destroy us . . . Therefore, after April 10 the central Party organs once again adopted a lenient policy and called on those young people to renew and reform themselves, to break away from the special agents' trap. In the last three months the efforts of the Party and non-Party members have spurred many of those who had lost their footing and been injured to accept the Party's call to rise and speak out against the Japanese bandits and the Kuomintang for their murder of China's youth. So far 450 people have confessed to the Party and repented.
>
> Why does the Communist Party take so many pains to rescue you? Simply because it wants you to be Chinese, and not be cheated into serving the enemy. Those of you who have lost your way, be conscious, take a firm decision, repent to the party, and cast off the special agent's garb, cast off the uniform of the fifth column, put on Chinese clothes, and speak out about the deception, the insults, and the injuries you have suffered, and confess to the crimes you have committed. The Communist Party welcomes those of you who have lost your footing to become Chinese and oppose Japan and serve the country . . . You who have been raped, cheated by the Japanese invaders and the KMT, and won over to the fifth columnists, because you're juvenile and ignorant, because you wish for fame and profit, fear death and have sunk into the morass of the special agent. . . . We are concerned about you, afraid you will commit suicide. . . . When a person confesses to the Party we immediately remove the evidence about him, remove his name from among the ranks of special agents, and we are happy that he has become conscious. The Communist Party has saved another person! . . .
>
> Finally, I warn those people who don't wish to confess, we have maintained a lenient policy, but leniency has a limit . . . We warn those special agents who stubbornly refuse to wake

up. Wake up, wake up quickly and change. We have the heart
of a Bodhisattva in saving the young who have lost their footing, but we have an iron will to suppress confirmed agents, and
if they . . . prefer to serve in the enemy's fifth column, then we
must use stern methods to stamp them out.

Kang's speech set off a succession of hunts for spies and special agents.
Most Party members accepted the claim that "KMT agents," "Japanese agents," "traitors," "renegades," "red-flag parties," "CC
agents," and "Blue Shirts Society" agents* had subverted every arm
of the Communist organization; many felt that safety lay in making
accusations against their comrades or in admitting their own "political problems" to preempt any charges against them. "Salvation" and
"confession" meetings at which frightened and confused youths disclosed remote links with the KMT through family or friends—the sort
of affiliations that senior Communists overlooked in their own lives—
were common. Party members were arrested, interrogated, and tortured into confessing. The terror perpetuated itself: the more cadres
who made voluntary confessions, the more real the danger of enemy
subversion appeared and the easier it became to justify the arrest and
torture of other suspects. Kang finally declared that on the basis of
careful security work, he calculated that 70 to 80 percent of the young
cadres who had joined the Communists in Yan'an were politically
unreliable.

In some units, almost everyone was branded an enemy agent. Of
some 200 students at a military-communications school, Kang arrested 170 as special agents; of 88 students at one teachers' college
who participated in the Rectification Movement, 62 were taken into
custody; at another school for teachers, 73 percent of the students
and staff were apprehended. The surge of arrests spilled over into the
security organs themselves. Between 80 and 90 percent of the Yan'an
Guard Corps, a security unit attached to the local administration,
were detained as KMT agents. Within a span of two weeks, Kang had
uncovered an alleged espionage network of over 200 people in Longdong. The arrests also touched cadres in the Party headquarters, al-

---

* "The CC Group" was the popular name for the KMT faction led by Chen Guofu
and Chen Lifu which, among other things, ran the KMT Investigation Section and its
successor, the Central Statistics Bureau. "The CC Group" and "the Blue Shirts"
collectively called up the specter of Chiang Kai-shek's secret agents.

though senior levels had fewer casualties; only 10 out of 60 officials in the Party Secretariat were charged as "special agents."

The victims of the roundups were placed under extreme pressure to admit to working for the KMT, the Japanese, or both. Kang and his henchmen held out the prospect of salvation for anyone who cooperated, but those who resisted were subjected to savage psychological and physical torture, including the tactics he had used in 1939 of depriving victims of sleep and then threatening them with snakes. Other common techniques were "car wheel wars,"* solitary confinement, offering rewards for confessions, and mock executions. Especially prominent throughout the "salvation" campaign was the use of public meetings. These sessions often took on a ghoulish theatrical quality, with a bayonet, a rope, and a glass of poison being placed in front of the suspect, while the masses shouted, "Confess that you are a counterrevolutionary or die immediately!" or "There are three ways of dying. Choose one!" Those who denied the demands of the masses risked the most painful treatment, even execution.

In eliciting false admissions, Kang knew the truth was being distorted, but it appears to have satisfied some impulse in him. He brushed aside objections, commenting that if "false evidence is what the criminals want to say, let them say it." When a fourteen-year-old girl confessed to training by special agents to seduce and entrap Party cadres, Kang seized upon her statement to declare that his counterespionage work had "created a new line" of approach to the enemy. But he also emphasized the unreliability of many confessions, warning that since the truth of any particular one was impossible to determine, further interrogation must be conducted.

Although he promised "salvation," Kang was reluctant to release people after their arrest, whether they confessed or not. When one interrogator asked him whether a suspect could be set free once he had admitted his crimes, Kang directed him to tell the prisoner, "You have not confessed thoroughly, you have not explained clearly, your task is incomplete." He told another interrogator, "Ask ten thousand questions. Make it impossible for them ever to respond fully."

Kang's conduct of the Rectification Movement introduced a new element into Chinese politics: an emphasis on eliciting false confessions. For over two thousand years, Chinese emperors and their min-

---

* Mildly defined in *A Chinese-English Dictionary* (Peking: Commercial Press, 1982) as "the tactic of several persons taking turns in fighting one opponent to tire him out."

isters had been known to execute opponents for political crimes, but they rarely sought to manufacture groundless confessions. In 221 B.C., Qin Shihuang, the first emperor to bring political unity to China, buried hundreds of scholars whose theories might have threatened his newly founded empire, but he did not try to compel them to admit guilt. The Chinese legal system has traditionally used torture to obtain evidence, but only on the assumption that evidence produced under duress is true. The Rectification Movement, under Kang's guidance, marked a major break with custom. Applying Stalinist concepts to Yan'an, Kang deliberately extracted false confessions from anyone unlucky enough to be branded a suspect, which gave credibility to his fantasy world of counterrevolutionaries and secret agents.

The Chinese Communists began to use crude methods of thought control in the late 1920s, when military commanders had to develop solidarity and commitment among their troops. But thought reform attained a new level of refinement in Yan'an, setting the course for decades to come. Kang was not the only Communist responsible for adapting Stalinist techniques to China, but he was the most important. His work in Moscow had given him an unmatched opportunity to observe Soviet practices, and as head of the Social Affairs Department and master of the Rectification Movement, he was ideally placed to apply the lessons in China.

The human cost of the Rectification Movement was extremely high. Jacques Guillermaz, a French sinologist, estimated that between forty thousand and eighty thousand Party members were expelled during the movement. Many people went insane, while others committed suicide, either by hanging or by drowning in rivers or wells. Many more were imprisoned and held until the Seventh Party Congress in 1945 rehabilitated a large number of them. Although nothing worse than physical and psychological torture befell the majority, executions were still being carried out as late as 1947. In March of that year, when KMT armies invaded Yan'an and forced the Communists to retreat, Kang ordered the secret execution of the one hundred or so prisoners held since the Rectification Movement.

For many victims of Rectification, release and rehabilitation in 1945 after the Seventh Party Congress did not protect them permanently against Kang. During the Cultural Revolution, he searched many of them out, arrested them, and charged them again with being traitors or renegades. A standard item of evidence used against them was a record of their arrest in Yan'an during the Rectification

Movement—phony charges from the 1940s reappeared twenty years later as "proof" of an individual's disloyalty.

Outraged Party leaders finally began whispering against Kang and his campaign of terror, but none except the most powerful dared challenge his methods and discuss them with Mao. Ren Bishi, an influential and independent-minded Politburo member, tried unsuccessfully, just before he died in 1950, to draw Mao's attention to Kang's abuses. Another of Kang's antagonists, Zhou Enlai, while based in the wartime capital of Chongqing, ridiculed Kang's claim that Communist organs in KMT China were "red-flag" parties.

As a response to the dissenters, the Party issued a directive on August 15, 1943, about "the investigation of cadres," which sought to limit the use of violence and intimidation. But Kang's "salvation" movement, going at full tilt, had already resulted in so many Party members admitting to contacts with the KMT that the need to act against enemy agents was obvious to all. In spite of the August 15 directive, 280 Communists at a mass meeting held a few weeks later as part of the continuing witch-hunt acknowledged being spies; another 190 confessed under pressure after their comrades implicated them by voluntarily giving statements.

Kang justified his tactics by presenting lists of self-avowed spies and special agents. Moreover, he could invoke the authority of Mao Zedong, who had declared as early as 1940 that "we must firmly suppress the confirmed traitors and anti-communists, or otherwise we shall not be able to protect the anti-Japanese revolutionary forces." Amid the Salvation Movement controversy, Mao issued a dictum that "killing no one, and not arresting the majority, is the policy which must be maintained in the struggle against special agents." Yet even these carefully chosen words acknowledged a need to "struggle against special agents"; in the double-talk of Chinese propaganda, Mao's prohibition against "arresting the majority" was heard by loyal Party members as a clear endorsement for detaining the minority. Mao left Kang with ample scope to set his own quota of arrests; he had decreed that no one should be killed, but his order could be interpreted loosely.

Mao's position as supreme leader was further strengthened by Kang's work. The Rectification Movement, by popularizing Mao's theories, bestowed on him a reputation as an expert on Communist doctrine, which helped to undermine Wang Ming's standing as an authority on Marxism. Meanwhile, Kang's activities were doing more direct damage to Wang Ming's position. Underneath Kang's speeches and articles on the dangers of enemy agents lay the notion of KMT–Japanese cooperation against the Communists. This claim challenged the concept of a united front that Wang Ming had brought back from Moscow and, as "intelligence" to that effect came to light, served to discredit Wang Ming. At the same time, Kang continued to rewrite his history of having served as Wang Ming's lieutenant in Shanghai and Moscow.

Kang's brutal Rectification operations lasted until late 1943, but the controversy over his methods continued for many more months. Generals like Nie Rongzhen and Ye Jianying joined Zhou Enlai and Ren Bishi in criticizing Kang's excesses. Most of Wang Ming's Soviet-oriented supporters condemned Kang, too, in revenge for his betrayal of their leader, Kang's former benefactor.

The course of World War II also worked against Kang. He had assured Mao that the Soviet Union would succumb before the German army, but by 1944, with the Russians on their way to a victory over Germany, Mao could no longer disregard Stalin and the Soviet Union. To prepare for the struggle with the KMT that was likely to follow Japan's defeat, he needed to patch up his differences with Moscow. Mao required a sympathizer, not a critic, of the Soviet Union among his personal retinue; so notorious was Kang's hostility to the Soviet Union that Mao had to choose between endorsing Kang and clearing the air with Stalin and other Soviet leaders.

At the very moment when Mao and his colleagues needed to strengthen ties with the Soviet Union, they found themselves receiving representatives of another country powerful enough to be a crucial player on the Chinese scene: the United States. And Kang, in his contacts with the Americans who started to come to Yan'an in the summer of 1944, proved as devious as he had with the Russians.

As the war against Japan dragged on in the Pacific, diplomats and soldiers in the United States embassy in Chongqing persuaded Chiang Kai-shek's government to permit them to send "an observer team" to Yan'an, which had been out of bounds for Americans since 1940. The Americans hoped that CCP intelligence on the Japanese war machine would hasten the end of the conflict. The first group of Americans to reach Yan'an, known as "the Dixie Mission," arrived in the summer of 1944. One of the U.S. Army's foremost China hands, Major David Barrett, led the eighteen members of the Dixie Mission:

sixteen servicemen plus two civilians from the embassy, John S. Service and Raymond P. Ludden.

The Dixie Mission men formed a highly favorable opinion of the people they encountered in Yan'an. CCP leaders, they found, "were open, direct, and friendly" toward Americans. Barrett and his colleagues were equally impressed by the quality of "the outstanding communist soldiers and statesmen," who struck one American as "a body of vigorous, mature, practical men—young, and physically and intellectually tough." The American assessment portrayed the Communists as "unselfishly devoted to high principles, and possessing great qualities and gifts of leadership. They made no attempt to wrap themselves in the inaccessibility of a closely-held power group."

Indeed, the Chinese Communists gave their American visitors an avid welcome, granting them access to some of their top leaders, including "the most dominant figures, Mao Zedong and Zhou Enlai," who laid out to their visitors these cardinal points of the Communist program:

(1) Adherence to the United Front.
(2) Full mobilization to fight Japan.
(3) Recognition of the Central Government and the leadership of the Generalissimo (Chiang Kai-shek).
(4) Democratization of the Kuomintang.
(5) Establishment of freedom of speech and political activity for all China. (Communist leaders, believing the word "communist" to be misleading in regard to their program, are considering abandoning it and referring to their party by its Chinese name, Kungchantang, or Common Goods Party.)

The members of the Dixie Mission believed that the Communists were providing them with extremely good intelligence. The Communists agreed to set up several weather stations in northern China that could help U.S. air units based in Kunming plan bombing raids on Japan. Although the Communists failed to provide the Japanese order of battle, as the Americans had hoped they could, Barrett felt confident that he had fulfilled his mission.

In fact, Barrett and his team were taken in by the Communists.*

---

* Several years later, a Communist intelligence operative revealed to an American diplomat that Barrett's group was "effectively isolated from seeing the realities of

A primary purpose of the Dixie Mission was to make contact with the CCP intelligence system, but none of the Americans ever met the CCP intelligence head, Kang Sheng. If the Americans viewed their mission as a way to tap into the Communist secret service, the Communists had different ideas. To them, the Dixie Mission presented a chance to manipulate United States policy by misleading the visitors while pretending to comply with their wishes and needs.*

Even though the Communists kept the members of the Dixie Mission away from Kang, he did not remain invisible forever. On December 14, 1944, at the suggestion of Chinese officials, John K. Emmerson, an expert in Japanese affairs who was in Yan'an on a brief visit from the embassy in Chongqing, called on Kang Sheng ("Mr Kon Seng" in Emmerson's record) to discuss the war against Japan and, as it turned out, other issues. In keeping with Communist concerns about allowing outsiders access to the intelligence apparatus, Kang was introduced as "a member of the Central Executive Committee"; he never bothered telling Emmerson what his actual role was.

After a brief discussion of "political warfare" against Japan (Kang suggested that "reconditioned prisoners of war" might be sent from Yan'an to the United States or elsewhere to help prepare for the invasion of Japan), Emmerson asked Kang whether the CCP, which had been "successful in solving the problems of agrarian society," would have difficulty governing large cities. Kang told Emmerson he appreciated the question, which, he said, posed a problem of great concern to the Communists. At least three factors would help the Communists manage urban areas, Kang said: they recognized the gravity of the problem; they were even then training cadres in municipal administration; and many Communist cadres had gained experience in governing cities by living in them. Kang, always conscious of culture and literature, referred Emmerson to a book by radical writer and scholar Guo Moruo that "described the failure of a revo-

---

communist rule. . . . Careful precautions were taken that they should come in contact only with politically 'trustworthy' people."

* Reports from the United States embassy in Chongqing reveal that some of the Americans were aware from KMT intelligence reports that Kang Sheng was head of both the Social Affairs Department and the Military Intelligence Department. Nevertheless, it apparently did not occur to anyone from the Dixie Mission, which was supposed to establish links with CCP intelligence organs, to insist on being allowed to meet Kang.

lutionary hero to adapt to the cities tactics which had succeeded in villages."

Kang turned next to the question of relations with the KMT. A settlement between the KMT and CCP was probably not in the cards, he told Emmerson, because "Chiang refuses to give up his principle of one-party dictatorship." But Kang claimed that the outbreak of civil war was unlikely since "neither the Communist Party, the Chinese people, nor the United Nations want it."

Kang expressed his concern that many Americans in China did not understand the Communist attitude toward cooperation with the KMT. "Even if Chiang offered the communists posts in the Military or Executive Councils, these would be refused." Participating on that basis, he explained, would not bring about a genuine coalition government. Chiang was banking on a United States victory against Japan. "He will wait," Kang predicted; "he will not relinquish one-party dictatorship." If the Communists were to join a coalition with Chiang under those conditions, they would miss their "objective: a democratic China."

Having spelled out the Communists' alleged goals, Kang commented approvingly to Emmerson that "Americans were frank"—claiming with a straight face, as he built lie upon lie, that candor was "a trait which he liked." He assured Emmerson that he thought many Chinese Communists also were frank, then added that he hoped American technicians might come to China after the war to aid in modernizing and developing Chinese industry.

Utterly bamboozled by Kang's "candor," Emmerson asked him about relations with Russia, pointing out that "many people believe the Chinese communists to be dominated by the Soviet Union." Kang replied in pure Maoist terms: "One of the characteristics of Marxism [is] that it must be adapted to local, individual circumstances. What will work in one place can never be transplanted to another place and be expected to flourish." He went on to say that "the Chinese communists have always worked out their own policies, programs, and problems independently, without consultation or direction from outside. This was a fact even before the dissolution of the Comintern."* Lapsing into his habit of crediting everything to his patron, Kang continued, "Chairman Mao is constantly telling the party leaders that they must evolve practical programs suited to the people and to the

* Stalin dissolved the Comintern in 1943.

local regions. For example, even if they so desired, it would be impossible to practice communism in Yan'an."

When Kang Sheng met with John Emmerson, he was still the unchallenged head of the Communist secret-police and intelligence service. But the opposition sparked by his atrocities during the Rectification Movement continued to dog him. In early 1945, Kang found himself under increasing pressure. He never expressed any remorse over his cruelties, and his grip on power steadily weakened.

Kang's real crisis erupted at the long-overdue Seventh Party Congress in April 1945. This congress, the first held since the one in Moscow in 1928, had been postponed by Mao until he could be assured of routing the forces of Wang Ming and his Soviet-trained allies. The main purpose of this congress was for the Party to formally acknowledge Mao's supreme position, which was accomplished partly by rewriting CCP history to conform with the mythology Mao had invented.

None of the delegates dared question Mao's reinterpretation of the Party's history, but heated debate occurred on other issues. Kang's opponents vented their anger at his conduct of the Rectification Movement. Kang addressed the congress on two topics—the Party's line on peasants, and the work of the Military Intelligence Department—but omitted mention of the campaign against enemy agents in need of "salvation." Several delegates protested his omission; written demands called for the congress to discuss the issue publicly. Vladimirov described Kang's reaction: "He was a picture of an offended intellectual. Expressively raised eyebrows behind the spectacles, delicate, refined gestures, pursed lips ... The very [picture of] innocence offended!" To fend off his rivals, Kang argued that all he had done was to implement "the Mao Zedong line." This explanation outraged Kang's already irate critics to the point where Mao himself was required to intervene and calm them down.

One of Kang's most outspoken opponents was the former Party strongman Li Lisan, whose arrest Kang had ordered just before leaving Moscow in 1937—the victim of his farewell conspiracy. Li, who knew a great deal about Kang's activities in Moscow, sought to expose his duplicity and cruelty toward his Chinese comrades in the Soviet Union. But the congress was too preoccupied with other matters to take his accusations seriously.

Kang still had Mao's support, and all the opposition to him did not prevent his reelection to both the Central Committee and the Politburo. But the controversy over the Salvation Movement raged on. In response to growing pressure from senior cadres, the Party's central leadership removed Kang as head of both the Social Affairs Department and the Military Intelligence Department in late 1945. His deputy, Li Kenong, replaced him in both positions.

After his transfer from the security-and-espionage apparatus, Kang was in effect banished from the Party's central organs. For once, he had failed to adjust to the realities of the times. Mao was still master of the Communist movement, but by then he had many other supporters and could afford to deprive Kang of some of his influence. Having enjoyed an intimacy that made him Mao's "shadow, his will, his desire," Kang had now fallen somewhat out of favor. He remained one of the Chairman's companions and continued to appear with him on public occasions, but Mao no longer blessed Kang with command over the organizations that had made him such a powerful and feared man over the previous six years.

In spite of Kang's decline, his influence on the security-and-intelligence system was visible for decades to come. The methods he popularized in Yan'an shaped public-security work through the Cultural Revolution and beyond. His proclivity for introducing questions of espionage into routine politics recurred often. Kang moved on to other tasks, but doing away with the secret police who had risen under his patronage was never even attempted; his henchmen and protégés in the Social Affairs Department remained in control of the dark side of the Party. One of the Social Affairs Department interrogators in Zaoyuan in the 1940s, Ling Yun, was appointed minister of state security in 1983. Many other institutions Kang helped create have survived with minimal change. As recently as 1990, Chinese jails bore a striking resemblance to the prison system established under the auspices of Kang's Social Affairs Department.*

---

* Although Chinese prisons today are somewhat less draconian than in Kang's time, many of the practices ingrained in the system under Kang's direction remain in effect. According to Yao Yongzhan, a Hong Kong resident imprisoned in Shanghai in 1989 for his part in the student unrest, wardens and interrogators commonly use violence and torture against prisoners, beating and kicking them until they vomit blood; political prisoners are often beaten up by other prisoners, at the guards' instigation; standard legal procedures are ignored; and prisoners can relieve themselves only three

Nor has there been any sustained effort to abandon Kang's methods as inappropriate in the new China. Throughout the 1950s, when Kang had no direct connection with security-and-intelligence work, thousands of Chinese both in the country and abroad, along with many foreigners who had stayed on the mainland after 1949, were charged with being "foreign agents" or, even worse, "KMT spies." Millions of others were arrested simply for falling into the wrong social category.

At least 20,000,000 residents of the People's Republic of China were imprisoned or sent to labor camps soon after the 1949 Communist takeover of the mainland, according to a 1984 report by the New China News Agency. All 20,000,000 were convicted of belonging to one of four categories—landlords, rich peasants, counterrevolutionaries, and "bad elements"—and imprisoned for remolding or "salvation." Of this group, the final 79,504 had their designations removed in 1979 (four years after Kang's death) as part of the de-Maoization process initiated by Deng Xiaoping and his reformist allies. But 20,000,000 is the minimum figure for the victims of mass terror in the first decade of Communist power. This figure still leaves out of account cadres who were summarily executed as KMT officials, as well as the people slaughtered *en masse* during the land reform programs in some parts of China.

Politics in Yan'an led to Kang's partial eclipse in 1945, but he had already bequeathed a bitter, bloody, and enduring legacy to the Chinese Communist movement.

---

times a day. In fact, the only substantial change in Chinese prisons since Kang's days in Yan'an is that wardens now carry electric batons and frequently give prisoners shocks for minor infractions.

Chapter IX

PARTIAL
ECLIPSE

KANG SHENG remained a member of Mao's inner circle following his ouster as chief of security and intelligence, but the views of men like Liu Shaoqi, Ren Bishi, and Yang Shangkun carried at least as much weight as Kang's.

Immediately after the Japanese surrender in August 1945, the Chairman and the Generalissimo began talks about establishing a new coalition regime. With encouragement from a series of American envoys, both sides engaged in a long-drawn-out shadow play of offer and counteroffer. But neither Mao nor Chiang was prepared to yield; each was simply jockeying for political and tactical advantage and waiting for the right time to resume hostilities. By December 1945, negotiations had all but broken down and warfare seemed imminent. The long-anticipated civil war between the Communists and the Nationalists finally erupted with a fury in March 1946.

As Mao and Chiang parried with each other, Kang took every opportunity to advertise his expertise in secret warfare, hoping Mao would realize that he could be indispensable against the KMT, but Mao ignored him. The Chairman finally assigned Kang to an area he had never before been involved in: land reform.

Ever since the late 1920s, when China's Communists had first questioned whether the urban proletariat could be the driving force of revolution in China that it had been in Russia, the concept of land reform—confiscating the land of wealthy landlords and rich peasants and redistributing it among hundreds of millions of poor peasants, hired laborers, and landless squatters—had been a cornerstone of

CCP strategy. It was disagreement over land reform policies, in fact, that had destroyed the early coalition between the KMT and the CCP and caused civil war to erupt in 1927. That year, Mao Zedong wrote that "several hundred million peasants will rise like a mighty storm ... [and] sweep all the imperialists, warlords, corrupt officials, local tyrants, and evil gentry into their graves." Mao understood that in order to tap into the discontent of the poverty-stricken peasants, the Communists needed to offer them something; and the most compelling prize for them was land.

Large tracts of rural China were ripe for exploitation by a revolutionary party that appealed to a rural population gripped by inescapable poverty. In many places, landlords ruthlessly mistreated their tenants—demanding exorbitant rents and extracting excessive rates of interest when they could not pay, raping wives and daughters, and hiring thugs to beat up anyone who caused trouble.

On December 10, 1946, bearing orders from Chairman Mao, Commander-in-Chief Zhu De, and the CCP's chief civilian administrator, Liu Shaoqi, Kang set off from Yan'an with a party of seven for Longdong, in the desolate borderlands in eastern Gansu Province, about one hundred miles west of Yan'an. His mission was to review the land reform program the Communists had instituted in the region since gaining control several years earlier. Kang spent only five weeks in Longdong, but his time there left him optimistic about land reform and its place in the Communist revolution.

Communist land reform policy varied greatly from place to place. In the more deprived areas under CCP control, where economic hardships, banditry, warlordism, and drought had reduced the peasants to intense squalor and misery, the Communists often used extreme measures, eliminating the rich peasants much as Stalin had liquidated the kulaks, the landowning farmers of the Ukraine and southern Russia. In regions of fertile soil and temperate climate, the Chinese Communists had more difficulty inciting hatred toward the wealthier peasants and landlords; usually, the landholders lost their land but escaped with their lives.

Not surprisingly, Kang advocated the most severe methods in conducting land reform. In Longdong, he armed himself with criticisms of the way the program was being run, and then, upon his return to Yan'an, accused the Longdong leadership of "right deviations"—meaning a tendency to be lenient and to compromise with the landlords. On February 2, 1947, after less than a week back in Yan'an, Kang delivered a tough speech to the Party School, the first of a series of talks he made on the need for radical land reform. He called for a new, populist approach of "arousing the masses and then passing all problems over to the masses to handle. That way problems can be resolved."

Kang's formula translated into countless acts of revenge at the village level. Instead of merely confiscating the landlords' houses and goods and dividing their land among the peasants, Kang whipped up hatred for the landlords and their retainers. In the name of social justice, he encouraged the peasants to settle scores by killing landlords and rich peasants. Kang's affluent background never inhibited his enthusiasm for drastic methods of land reform; undoubtedly, he would have been no less cruel on the other side. At any rate, it was the landlords who had the misfortune of being Kang's targets. As Mao explained the following year, "Our task is to . . . wipe out the landlords as a class, not as individuals."

In March 1947, five weeks after Kang's return from Longdong, a KMT military offensive against Yan'an forced the Communists to evacuate the ancient town. As KMT aircraft bombed and strafed the troops streaming out of Yan'an, Kang and Cao Yi'ou marched west with the main Communist forces as far as the banks of the Huang He (Yellow River). At that point, he received orders to take control of an experimental agrarian-reform program in Shanxi Province, several hundred miles to the east. Splitting off from the main Communist armies, he made his way to the northwest corner of Shanxi and set up headquarters in the town of Haojiabo in Lin County. Kang stayed there almost four months, spending most of the summer reviewing the land reform program already in place and correcting the local cadres' mistakes in his own way. As a standard method of separating landlords and their families from the land, he ordered their murders.

Savagery toward landlords went hand in hand with land reform throughout Communist-controlled China, but Kang even terrorized fellow CCP members. In Shanghai, he had used the Red Squads to betray and assassinate Communists who supported his Party rivals; in Moscow, he had directed the power of the secret police against Chinese Communists studying in the Soviet Union; in Yan'an, he had used the Social Affairs Department to arrest large numbers of young Communists he could misrepresent as enemy agents in need of "salvation." Now, in northwestern Shanxi, Kang consciously set out to victimize landlords who were recognized as Communist sympathizers.

In Lin County, the region under Kang's rule, two wealthy land barons were well known for their support of the Communists during the war against Japan: Niu Youlan and Liu Shaobai. Kang ordered his armed henchmen to seize Niu, then abused and humiliated him before the assembled peasants. Kang joked that since the landlord's name, Niu, also meant "cow," he should be made to look like a cow. To give practical effect to his pun, Kang ordered his men to cut a hole in Niu's nose, attach a ring through it, and tie a rope to the ring; then he forced Niu's son to lead his father, blood streaming down his face, through the narrow, dusty streets of Haojiabo. Liu Shaobai, alerted by Niu's fate, got word to Party headquarters, which sent orders to leave Liu alone.

Kang also turned on the low-level Communist cadres who had worked in the district long before his arrival. Some were simple men who had joined the Party organization in that particular area and understood little of the broader goals of the Communist movement, while others were young intellectuals not of a temperament to carry out Kang's vicious policies. Kang coined an expression for his victims, "stones": stones that pressed on the peasantry, stones that impeded the restructuring program, stones that needed to be cleared away. In the name of eliminating the "stones," Kang purged many local Communists, subjecting them to mass "struggle-and-criticism" sessions, where peasants abused and beat up hapless cadres.

Kang also investigated the backgrounds of the "land reform teams"—the groups largely composed of ruffians, bandits, and illiterate Communists who were responsible for the mechanics of the land reform process—and conducted "struggle" sessions against members not of proletarian or peasant birth. He confiscated minor personal items under the guise of eradicating private ownership—and forced any cadres from slightly better social origins than other team members to eat at separate tables.

Kang justified his actions by invoking the ancient Chinese notion that officials posted to an area inevitably formed alliances with the wealthy and influential local gentry. Unless those officials were eradicated, Kang argued, land reform would never work. But Kang's record suggests that he simply used this argument as a pretext for greater violence; his persecution of fellow Communists in Shanghai, Moscow, Yan'an, and Haojiabo consistently points to an overriding concern with wielding power over his own camp.

The "stone" theory so vigorously propounded by Kang influenced land reform agencies all across China. During the 1950s, when the policy was implemented nationally, local Party officials often disappeared along with the landlords as part of the attack on "local bullies." (Even though Kang conceived the assault on "stones," he was to make a complete about-face during the Cultural Revolution and accuse Liu Shaoqi, China's state president, of having "moved stones" during the land reform movement twenty years earlier. The contradiction didn't appear to bother Kang one bit.)

The CCP Central Committee had decreed that the main criterion for confiscating land was whether the owner had a record of exploiting hired laborers and poor peasants. But Kang dismissed that standard as too moderate. He added three other measures—"history, life, and political attitudes"—which made it easy for him to lump landlords and rich farmers together with ordinary peasants who had served in Chiang Kai-shek's army or had some other KMT connection, however vague. His targets were deprived of their land, publicly humiliated, beaten, and sometimes shot, beheaded, or buried alive. As one statistical example of the effect of Kang's policies, the village of Chaijiaya in Lin County had 124 of 552 households classified as rich peasants—over twice the number actually in that category. And despite his atrocities in Haojiabo, Kang earned Mao's praise for his work; in April 1948, Mao singled out "Comrade Kang Sheng" for having overcome "the right deviations" that had impeded land reform in the Haojiabo district.

In this way, Mao showed continued support for his former security chief. At a time when Mao was arguing in public against the sorts of abuse perpetrated by Kang and others, his praise of Kang had special meaning. Mao knew that land reform had gotten out of control in the region around Haojiabo (in the essay commending Kang, Mao acknowledged that "left deviations" had taken place), but he was clearly indicating that he did not hold Kang responsible for the "deviations."*

Under the influence of Kang and many other hard-line cadres, agrarian reform cut a bloody swath through much of rural China. Squads of Communist enforcers were sent to the most remote villages

* The sensitive nature of Mao's relationship with Kang during the land reform period is reflected by the fact that Lin Qingshan's *A Casual History of Kang Sheng*, which in effect was authorized for public distribution, makes no reference to Kang's record on land reform.

to organize the local petty thieves and bandits into so-called land reform teams, which inflamed the poor peasants and hired laborers against the rich. When resentment reached fever pitch, peasants at staged "grievance meetings" were encouraged to relate the injustices and insults they had suffered, both real and imagined, at the hands of "the landlord bullies." Often, these meetings would end with the masses, led by the land reform teams, shouting, "Shoot him! Shoot him!" or "Kill! Kill! Kill!" The cadre in charge of proceedings would rule that the landlords had committed serious crimes, sentence them to death, and order that they be taken away and eliminated immediately.

Mercy was no more a part of the execution process than it was of the judicial proceedings. Many landlords were shot, hanged, beheaded, battered to death, nailed to the walls of buildings, or buried alive. The more inventive and grotesque means of death inspired a macabre slang: dressing an individual in a thin cotton garment in winter and pouring water over him until subzero temperatures froze him to death was "wearing glass clothes"; burying a victim alive in snow was "refrigeration"; smashing the skull and exposing the brains of a man buried up to his neck in a pit was "opening the flower."

After inflicting four months of terror in northwestern Shanxi, Kang attended a major conference on land reform at the small town of Xibaipo in Hebei Province, about two hundred miles southwest of Peking, where Liu Shaoqi and Zhu De had established a new Communist headquarters after the retreat from Yan'an. Many senior cadres attended the meeting, which was chaired by Liu Shaoqi, the leader in charge of nonmilitary issues such as land reform. The conference, which lasted from July 17, 1947, until the middle of September, formally authorized a harder line toward landlords, setting a pattern that stayed in effect for years to come. Kang actively expounded his extremist views. On September 9, as the conference drew to a close, he delivered "A Report Concerning the Problems of Land Reform and Party Rectification," advocating "a policy of thoroughly equal land distribution" that would reduce the landholdings of middle-class peasants and meet the demands of the landless and hired workers. What sounded like a plea for equality and land for everyone was in fact a program for widespread human slaughter.

Two months later, in November 1947, as the Communist armies prepared to launch their final offensive against the KMT, the Politburo transferred Kang away from both Party headquarters and the front lines of the civil war, assigning him to inspect land reform in his native province of Shandong. The KMT still controlled several parts of Shandong, including the capital, Jinan, but the Communists ruled northern Shandong and eastern Hebei, where Kang was posted.

After an absence of over two decades from his home province, Kang found that the local Communist apparatus was well established, and that extensive land reform had already been implemented. Confronted by a local Party machine whose cadres, he suspected, resented any leaders sent to oversee them, Kang used his authority to put them in their place. Not surprisingly, he measured the performance in Shandong by the harsh standards he had applied in Shanxi, discovering that in many cases the local Communists had been lax and indulgent. He detected a clear bias in favor of the gentry. As soon as Kang had assembled enough evidence, he announced a predictable finding: the Communist organization in Shandong represented "a landlord and rich-peasant party" and included many "stones" that needed to be cleared away.

The first "stone" he dealt with was a young man named Jing Xiaocun, the Communist chief of the Bohai district in the western sector of Kang's area. Jing had some local influence, but he was an easy target for a Politburo member like Kang, who sarcastically observed that Jing was both inexperienced and ignorant of Marxism-Leninism: "You're a party secretary at the age of twenty-odd! What do you know about Marxism-Leninism?" Making a pun on Jing's personal name, Xiaocun ("Knowing the Villages"), Kang continued, "How do you know the villages when you don't even know yourself?"

Jing was sacked, but he fared better than Kang's next victim. Zhao Jizhou, a local Red Army leader who had ignored Kang's directives, was arrested on his orders and threatened with execution for breach of discipline. The local cadres were paralyzed. Resistance to Kang crumbled as everyone came to see that the choice lay between submitting to Kang and imprisonment or perhaps death.

Kang chose his targets carefully, using the tactic of divide and conquer. At the same time he deliberately crushed some cadres, he recruited others to his cause, constructing a network of allies who included Wang Li and Guan Feng, members of the local propaganda department; Wang Xiaoyu, a district Party chief; and Liu Geping, who had just been released from a KMT jail in Peking.* Kang's clique in Shandong remained intact until the Cultural Revolution.

Once he had imposed his authority over the provincial Communist organization, Kang introduced a much more radical land reform program. Proclaiming the slogan "Let the poor peasants lead everything," he set about examining the land redistribution already carried out by previous Communist officials. The blood of landowners and rich peasants again flowed freely as Kang made the indiscriminate killing of landlords an integral part of agrarian reform.

Party headquarters publicly supported the balanced and flexible implementation of land reform, but Kang's work in Shandong drew no criticism. His political fortunes began to improve; early in 1948, he was appointed deputy chief of the East China Bureau of the Party, one of six high-level geographic organs that collectively governed all territory under Communist control. At the time, the East China Bureau had its headquarters in Shandong, an increasingly secure Communist area, but the bureau had responsibility for the entire eastern China seaboard, starting near Peking in the north and stretching almost as far south as Hong Kong. Kang's appointment restored some of his status in the Party machinery, giving him direct control over people, policy, and territory. He was no longer a Politburo member without portfolio, standing outside the Communist chain of command, performing routine missions, supervising land reform, attending endless conferences, and giving advice that might or might not be heeded. He seemed to have weathered the controversies of 1945 and to be well on his way back toward high office.

Kang's appointment as deputy chief of the East China Bureau also, however, meant private humiliation for him. The head of the East China Bureau, and his immediate superior, was Rao Shushi. Rao had studied at Shanghai University with Kang and joined the Party at the same time but for many years had been Kang's subordinate. Rao was working on *The Salvation Times* in Paris during the 1930s when Kang was already a Politburo member and a senior Comintern official. But Rao was an energetic and sociable man who steadily developed a wide circle of friends among the top leadership, including Zhou Enlai, Deng Xiaoping, and Li Lisan. Rao had also spent time in Moscow and then in New York, where he worked in a Chinese res-

---

* Liu Geping had allegedly completed his sentence, but he is now said to have been a KMT agent sent to infiltrate the Communist ranks.

taurant and helped run a Chinese newspaper. After returning to China in the late 1930s, he served as political commissar to the New Fourth Army, a Communist force in the Yangtze Valley. Though captured by KMT troops in 1940, Rao managed to escape and make his way back to Communist lines. Rao's broad network of personal contacts helped him reach Politburo rank in 1945—twelve years after Kang.

Kang fumed privately over Rao's success, but he was careful to hide his feelings. Rao Shushi was oblivious to Kang's envy; on the eve of the Communists' final victory in 1949, the two men conspired to expand their power in Shandong. They first schemed together on an attack against the senior Party elements in Shandong. Their primary target was Party chief Li Yu, who combined a grass-roots following with Party status: he was an alternate member of the Central Committee. For newcomers like Kang and Rao, Li Yu stood in the way. To destroy him, Kang and Rao charged Li Yu with following "the rich peasant line." They also accused him of "localism," "mountain-strongholdism," and "kingdomism"—Communist jargon for the political crime of using local power to resist central Party directives. Unable to defend himself against opponents as formidable as Kang and Rao, Li was forced to undergo six months of intensive criticism, a form of persecution that alternated supervised confinement with sessions of verbal abuse. He was then transferred out of Shandong. As often happens when a leader falls in China, Li Yu did not go down by himself; without Li's umbrella of patronage, a number of local cadres were also criticized, transferred, or dismissed.*

Kang and Rao Shushi worked together, but all the while each was trying to further his own cause. After the Communists had captured the final KMT strongholds in Shandong in late 1948, the Central Committee, agreeing to a joint call from Kang and Rao, combined the four regional units in Shandong into a single body. Kang was appointed secretary in charge of the new organization, but he still remained subordinate to Rao, who continued to head the East China Bureau.

For the moment, Kang was less concerned with Rao Shushi than with advancing his wife, Cao Yi'ou. He had her installed as head of

---

* Although Kang and Rao later parted ways, Li Yu's troubles continued for many years. Transferred to work under Rao in Shanghai, he was dismissed from his post. He rose to the rank of vice minister after Rao's fall in 1954 but saw his standing decline once more in the late 1950s, when Kang regained power.

the provincial organization department, a unit that controlled the personal files and political fates of provincial Party members. Moreover, while in charge of the Party machine in Shandong, Kang misused his authority to obtain sexual favors from the wives of men in political trouble, promising that the women, or their husbands, would thereby escape a dreadful fate.

Kang's insistence on special privileges was further illustrated when he arranged to be reunited with Zhang Zishi, his son by his first wife. When he approached the young man late in 1948, Zhang was in his early thirties, working for a KMT public-relief organization in Qingdao. Father and son had last met in June 1925, when Kang had visited family and friends in Zhucheng. Contact between the two had been limited ever since to intermittent correspondence. Kang's stay in remote places like Moscow and Yan'an and the chaos caused by the Japanese invasion and the ensuing civil war—events that divided millions of Chinese families—made communication almost impossible.

Zhang Zishi remained Kang's only son; Cao Yi'ou had never borne him any children. After their reunion, Kang sponsored Zhang Zishi for membership in the Communist Party to protect him from the potential dangers of his KMT affiliation and make a place for him in the glorious Red future. In keeping with the traditional Chinese preference for male heirs, Kang showed no interest in his daughter, Zhang Yuying, whom he had long since left to spend her life working in a Qingdao tobacco factory.

Kang stayed in Shandong throughout the final stages of the civil war, as the KMT troops deserted or were defeated in battle and Chiang Kai-shek's administration disintegrated. Communist troops occupied Peking in January 1949, after the KMT garrison commander, Fu Zuoyi, surrendered to avoid a devastating siege. Little did Fu suspect that the new regime's economic policies would rapidly disfigure the city's historic beauty. Three months later, the Communist armies crossed the Yangtze; in May, they marched into Shanghai, putting the outcome of the epic struggle beyond doubt.

Kang tried desperately to escape his marginal role. During a March 1949 meeting of the Central Committee at Communist headquarters in Xibaipo, a session that shaped the administration the Communists would put in place once they had vanquished the KMT, Kang met with Mao, Liu Shaoqi, and other leaders. Nevertheless, he failed to gain a promotion; when the conference ended on March 13, he had no choice but to return to Shandong. The East China Bureau headquarters was relocated to the newly liberated city of Shanghai three months later, and Rao Shushi was assigned there. Kang repeatedly hinted to members of the Politburo that he, too, should move to Shanghai, hoping that the leadership would get his hint and appoint him head of the East China Bureau in place of Rao Shushi. But Mao and other key leaders, preoccupied with their dramatic victory over the Nationalists, ignored Kang. He was left in Shandong, the ruler of his native province but for all intents and purposes out in the cold.

Kang was elected chairman of the provincial government at a meeting of the Shandong People's Congress in August 1949,* making him head of Shandong's Party and government apparatus. Kang's response to his rather hollow triumph cannot be described as jubilant: upon learning that the vote for him was ten short of unanimity, he ordered a secret investigation to determine who had been against him. The CCP leadership in Peking also appointed him to the Sino-Soviet Friendship Association—ironically, given his hostility toward Moscow throughout the 1940s—and named him to the Military Commissars' Committee of the East China Bureau in December, making him political commissar of the Shandong Military District.

The posts Kang held at the end of 1949 would have satisfied many veteran cadres: head of the Party and government in Shandong; political commissar of the Shandong Military District; senior official in the East China Bureau; and a Politburo member. But these accomplishments fell far short of Kang's expectations.

It had become abundantly clear by then that the Communist Party had made a permanent transition. No longer a collection of outlaws, rebellious peasants, and discontented intellectuals, the Communists were now the sole and legitimate government of mainland China. But it was also clear that, for the short term at least, Kang could not expect to hold any meaningful office. After twenty-five frantic years spent mostly as a rising star in the Communist camp, Kang Sheng found himself abandoned in a dead-end local job.

---

* Provincial people's congresses were among the rubber-stamp legislatures created by the Communists to legitimize the new regime.

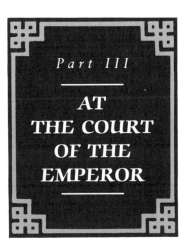

Part III

AT
THE COURT
OF THE
EMPEROR

Chapter X

A FAMILY
AFFAIR

WITH THE DEFEAT of Chiang Kai-shek's forces in 1949, China saw the dawn of a new era. The Chinese Communists were no longer a bandit army; like the rebel forces led by Zhu Yuanzhang, the monk-adventurer-emperor who had founded the Ming dynasty six centuries earlier, the CCP established a new government, a new court, and a new empire. Party members, regardless of rank, looked forward with excitement to the prospect of a new and flourishing China, to an era of progress and growth, a golden age reminiscent of the brilliant dynasties of years past. But Kang, unmoved by the national sense of joy, shunned the celebrations and displayed no public satisfaction over the Communist victory. Indeed, for almost six years thereafter, he hardly ever appeared in public.

The portraits of Kang produced by China specialists in the outside world are vague about his activities during the early years of the People's Republic, simply listing his official posts in Shandong and the new capital, Peking. Some Western journalists suggest that Kang was assigned to recruit scientists and experts for developing China's first nuclear weapon, a mission so sensitive that he lived in absolute secrecy.*

* Deacon, as well as Faligot and Kauffer, allege that Kang masterminded the development of the Chinese atomic bomb during this period, but they cite no credible sources. A 1952 report prepared by Howard Boorman, then a diplomat at the United States consulate in Hong Kong, commented on Kang's absence at every public occa-

Although Kang's absence from public view during the early 1950s inspired much speculation among foreign correspondents, it resulted from something far more mundane than a grand feat of espionage. Infuriated by his failure to regain a significant post in the Communist regime, Kang declared in late June 1949 that he had fallen ill. He retreated to Qingdao, the coastal resort town where he had attended Richard Wilhelm's school, and took up residence in a German-style villa at 4 Rongcheng Road, which overlooked the entrance to Jiaozhou Bay and was surrounded by a stand of pines.

Kang pointedly remained in Qingdao the whole time preparations were under way in Peking for the October 1 declaration of the founding of the People's Republic. Every Communist functionary who could make the journey heard Mao intone the historic announcement of a new nation from the ramparts of Tiananmen Square. Kang's conspicuous absence lent credibility to his claims of ill health. Finally, in mid-October, Kang set out by train for Peking, where he explained his unexpected arrival by insisting that he needed medical attention. Again pronouncing himself unwell after a short stay in the capital, he returned to Qingdao, where the warm currents of the Yellow Sea provided a milder winter than the northern city of Peking.

Kang spent the next six years almost totally inactive in Communist affairs, abandoning his official work and leading the isolated life of an invalid. In name, Kang occupied several prominent offices, but he made no public appearances, performed no tasks for the Party, and received no official visitors.

For the first year of his self-declared illness, Kang lived in seclusion in the seaside villa at Qingdao that had become his retreat in June 1949. In early May 1950, he traveled by train south to Shanghai, where he stopped for a week or so and called on Rao Shushi, who still headed the East China Bureau. Carefully concealing the rage and jealousy he felt toward his former colleague, Kang pumped Rao for the latest news about East China Bureau politics. Then he continued on to Hangzhou, the garden city with its ancient pagodas and temples on the edge of the West Lake, for two months of purported convalescence. In late July, he headed north, stopping in Shanghai en route

---

sion and concluded that he either had been demoted or was ill. Boorman astutely observed that if Kang was involved in some form of "secret police or underground work," the Party would have provided a more effective cover than Party boss of Shandong.

to meet again with the East China Bureau leaders. After several days in Shanghai, he took the train to Peking, adding credibility to his claim of poor health by checking into a private ward reserved for high cadres at Peking Hospital. This would be his home for the next five years.

Kang's years of seclusion, first in Qingdao and Hangzhou and later at Peking Hospital, were in keeping with Chinese tradition. There are countless stories of ministers who retired to their sickbeds in times of adversity at court, thereby avoiding the duties of office, distancing themselves from the world of politics, and increasing their odds of survival until an opportunity to return to power presented itself.

Although Kang lived as an invalid for the better part of six years, details of his medical condition are elusive. Throughout the time he pleaded illness, he kept hinting to the highest leaders in Peking that he was willing to ignore his medical problems and return to active service if the right post was offered to him. But the call never came.

Both political and psychological reasons entered into Kang's retreat from the public eye. Being denied greater power and prestige enraged him. With so many years of experience at the top levels of the Party, he found himself passed over in favor of peasant generals and unlettered commissars who had risen to prominence during the final years of the civil war, when Kang had been banished to a provincial assignment. Most exasperating of all for Kang was being forced to serve in the East China Bureau under Rao Shushi, but whenever the two met, Kang continued to treat Rao as his trusted friend.

Kang's failure to gain an influential post triggered his fears that the most senior Party leaders might suspect him of having once been a Kuomintang agent. After the Party meeting in mid-1949 at the Communist headquarters in Xibaipo, anger and indignation over his political marginality began to overwhelm Kang. As the Communist armies won their final victories, Kang worried that he might even be under surveillance. During his trip to Peking in October 1949, Kang stopped in Jinan, where he informed public-security officials that his secretary, a young man named Sha Tao, was opening his mail. Kang reported to others that Sha Tao—the only member of his personal staff with enough education to work as a spy—was "Rao Shushi's little running dog." But Kang hid his suspicions from Sha Tao himself. On the contrary, he boasted to Sha that he knew Shanghai so well that during the White Terror of the 1930s the KMT secret police never were able to catch him.

While in Hangzhou in June 1950, Kang confided to Rao Shushi and Marshal Chen Yi, then the mayor of Shanghai, his fear that he was suspected of being an enemy agent, and asked them to intervene on his behalf. Rao, unaware that Kang meant to stab him in the back at the earliest opportunity, reported Kang's declarations of innocence in a July 22 telegram to Mao:

> After the expanded meeting of the East China Bureau concluded, Chen Yi and I quickly went to Hangzhou to call on Kang Sheng. He repeatedly said to me: "Perhaps I made mistakes in my work, but I certainly am not a special agent. Ask the organization not to misunderstand me." Today Kang Sheng left Shanghai for Peking and I spent another hour in his place. Comrade Kang Sheng repeatedly requested that I explain to the Chairman that he certainly is not a spy or special agent, and [to] ask the organization not to misunderstand him.

Having to relay his plea through a man he secretly viewed as an enemy revealed the depth of Kang's desperation.

During the same period, Kang was frequently plagued by nightmares in which masked assassins sneaked into his quarters and attacked him with daggers. As evening approached, he would make a point of checking the lock on each door and window. He also started to live in fear of ghosts, reasoning that since the human body was much more complex than the most sophisticated scientific instrument, God must exist, and that if God existed, so must ghosts and devils.

Some of Kang's phobias may have been absurd, but the possibility that he was under suspicion as an enemy agent gave him good reason to be afraid. After all, the KMT had arrested him in 1930, and disclosure of his capture might have caused his comrades to suspect that he had been compromised and forced to betray the Communist cause, since both sides commonly turned prisoners. The lengths to which Kang had gone to suppress this incident would only have worked against his credibility. Moreover, details of how Kang had double-crossed some of his fellow Communists like He Mengxiong and the Five Martyrs during the factional struggles in Shanghai would have strengthened any rumors that he was a turncoat. Kang's treacheries in Shanghai, conducted on behalf of Wang Ming and not the

KMT, would not have led to charges of treason but would not have reduced his embarrassment, either.

Kang knew only too well that evidence linking him with the KMT secret police had a far greater chance of surfacing after 1949. The defeat of the KMT opened the way for the Communist security organizations to discover which Party members had cooperated with the enemy. As Communist forces overran cities like Peking, Nanking, and Shanghai, they confiscated extensive intelligence archives abandoned by the fleeing KMT forces. The Communists also captured several high-ranking KMT security officials, whom they persuaded to assist in rounding up other agents. Among the KMT operatives arrested were Lu Futan and Wang Yuncheng, Kang's colleagues in Shanghai during the late 1920s and early 1930s before they defected to the KMT security services. Kang understood that a wealth of new information was falling into the hands of the Communists; what he did not know was whether any of it incriminated him.

From his years in Moscow and Yan'an, Kang was well aware that in a totalitarian state charges of treason can be "proved" without a shred of evidence. As a secret-police director, he himself had instigated countless false cases of espionage. Kang also knew that secret-police chiefs could themselves become victims: Henry Yagoda, the head of the NKVD at the outset of Stalin's Great Purge, had been executed while Kang was in Moscow, and his successor, Nikolai Yezhov, had disappeared not long afterward.

Paralyzed by his fantasies, Kang began imagining the consequences of his own misdeeds. Many of his victims in Yan'an had survived and prospered in the Party—and were now in a position to seek revenge. The obsessiveness of Kang's dread and the distortions it wrought on his behavior suggest a deep psychological disorder. His personality underwent a distinct change; in place of the cool, confident Kang of earlier days, when he had worked underground in Shanghai, operated in Moscow and Yan'an, and implemented land reform so ruthlessly, he was now a man haunted by fears. In later years, Kang would regain his insatiable appetite for power; but during the early 1950s, he seemed drained of all energy and vitality.*

---

* Kang's condition cannot be positively identified, but several diagnoses are plausible. He might have suffered from manic-depressive psychosis. He exhibited at least a few of the symptoms of this disease—his sudden collapse followed years of believing that he was destined to be one of China's most powerful men. Kang's fear that he was a suspect

*   *   *

Passing himself off as an invalid was not the only aspect of Kang's life in the early 1950s that fitted easily with Chinese tradition. He also indulged in the predominant vice of eighteenth- and nineteenth-century China, opium smoking. Chinese society was awash with the drug at the time of Kang's birth in 1898. Foreign observers estimated a decade later that in China's cities as many as 50 percent of the men and 20 percent of the women smoked opium, while in the countryside 25 percent of the men and 5 percent of the women did.* Exactly when Kang first smoked opium is uncertain, but both Shandong and Shanghai were notorious centers of opium consumption. In any case, he had used opium long before he began his hospital retreat. Li Mingfang, a free-lance journalist in Guilin, told United States intelligence operatives in 1944 that Kang was "an opium addict."

It would not be surprising if Kang had smoked opium as a youth in Shandong or Shanghai, where the gangsters and others he dealt with as an underground Communist agent would have included many users of the drug. But he had also spent years in Moscow and Yan'an, both strongholds of public puritanism where opium smoking—a habit that produces a distinct and powerful fragrance, along with what was known in China as "the big smoke color" ("the peculiar duskiness of visage that comes from heavy use of opium")—would have been impossible to keep secret.

Kang resumed his opium use during his retreat at Peking Hospital. One of Kang's old friends who visited him there discovered him in his ward surrounded by the implements the smoker needs: a small

---

coincides with the tendency of manic-depressives to be driven into despondency by a sense of guilt about misdeeds or sins, illusory or otherwise. An alternative explanation is that he suffered from temporal lobe epilepsy, TLE. Kang displayed a number of traits commonly associated with TLE: his passion for calligraphy showed a compulsive urge to write; his fear of ghosts suggested a religious fixation; and several episodes in his life revealed unlimited aggression. Other traits associated with TLE—paranoia, a sense of destiny, and grandiosity—were also present in his behavior.

* U.S. intelligence sources also concluded that opium use was extremely high in China. U.S. Military Intelligence reported in 1936 that the Chinese "regard smoking opium as a very minor vice," and estimated that "about one person in five may be expected to be a drug user," adding that "today as in the past the common narcotic of China is cooked opium." An American diplomat reported that at the end of World War II, China's Opium Suppression Commission estimated that there were more than forty million opium addicts (defined as "regular smokers of opium") throughout China.

lamp, brass boxes to store the opium pellets, wirelike needles used to hold the boiling opium over the flame of the lamp, and, of course, a pipe. By then, the CCP was using drastic means to create a new, drug-free China, executing opium smokers who refused treatment, but Kang continued to enjoy the drug inside his exclusive ward. Indeed, it is doubtful that he gave up opium even after his return to the political arena in 1955. Ye Hongsheng, a Hong Kong writer, has reported that Kang smoked the drug right up to the 1960s and was known to Lin Biao and his clique as "Old Opium Pipe."

When Kang took Cao Yi'ou as his second wife in Shanghai in 1927, he married into her family in every sense of the word. Cao's younger sister, who called herself Su Mei, was among his new in-laws. Presumably, Su had abandoned the family name of Cao for security reasons; she, too, was a CCP member and a survivor of the White Terror.* Soon after Kang and Cao Yi'ou were married, Su Mei moved into the "Party organ" they inhabited—a residence in the French Concession.

Kang's domestic arrangement was not unusual on the surface; family members often moved into conjugal homes. But Su Mei became his lover. The rumors following Kang's departure from Zhucheng that he had slept with his father's concubine seem more credible in view of his relationship with Cao Yi'ou and Su Mei. In China's feudal past, men often took a pair of sisters as wife and concubine—a practice celebrated in a long line of tales of sexual conspiracy and power that date back two thousand years to the Han dynasty novella *The Emperor and the Two Sisters*. But in the twentieth century, Kang's family situation had the potential to attract criticism from puritanical Communists eager to condemn anything that smacked of China's feudal and bourgeois past. Disregarding all risks, Kang acted as Su Mei's patron in the Party. Su Mei never attained her sister's prominence, but she did hold a succession of executive posts in the key area of ideological education.

Politics and sex linked the two sisters to Kang, but their personalities were noticeably different. While Cao Yi'ou was ebullient, ruthless, and ambitious, prepared to join Kang in his devious and

* "Zhongkan" does not explain why Su Mei used a different surname from her sister, but it unambiguously states that they were sisters, referring to Su Mei as Kang's *xiao yizi* (the little sister of one's wife) and *qi mei* (one's wife's younger sister), at pages 47 and 289. One of Su Mei's friends has also confirmed, in a 1990 interview with the authors, that she was Cao Yi'ou's sister.

dangerous conspiracies, Su Mei was a nervous figure with suicidal tendencies, always in the shadow of her elder sister. Lacking Cao's robust capacity to carry out Kang's malevolent schemes, Su Mei was the obedient lover, the source of flattery and pleasure.

Both Cao and Su Mei accompanied Kang wherever he went— Moscow, Yan'an, Shandong, and finally Peking. It is unclear when Su's sexual involvement with Kang began, or whether it produced any children. When Su Mei returned from Moscow with Kang and Cao in late 1937, she brought with her a young Chinese girl called Ren Neiya. This child was passed off as Su Mei's daughter and Kang's niece, but her true identity remains a mystery. She may have been the orphaned child of a Chinese couple who vanished in the Moscow purges; she may have been Su's child, fathered by a Chinese in Moscow; or she may have been Kang's daughter. In any case, to this day Ren Neiya denies knowing why she bears the family name Ren.

In an attempt to distance herself from Kang, Su Mei married in 1945. Her husband, Huang Huoqing, was then a midlevel cadre who, like Kang, had worked as a labor agitator in Shanghai during the 1920s. Huang had studied in the Soviet Union but retuned to China in time to participate in the Long March. Most of the war years he spent in Yan'an; by marrying Su Mei, he was choosing the sister-in-law of a powerful colleague of two decades' standing. In 1946, Su Mei and Huang Huoqing had a son, who took his mother's name and was known as Su Han. Huang Huoqing and Su Mei soon split up— according to some accounts, under pressure from Kang.

Neither Su Mei's marriage nor Kang's mysterious illness—not to mention his own marriage to Cao Yi'ou—diminished Kang's lust for his sister-in-law. Confining himself to his quarters, he gave himself over increasingly to his passion for Su Mei, totally disregarding the risk of scandal. A number of cadres noted that wherever Kang and Cao Yi'ou went, Su Mei was sure to follow; they speculated maliciously about her role in Kang's household. Until his retreat, there had been no evidence to support the rumors that Kang enjoyed sexual relations with both sisters. But now Kang's discretion turned to abandon, so that by 1950 his affair with Su Mei was an open secret within elite circles.*

---

* Under a new code on marriage that the Chinese Communists imposed on May 1, 1950, polygamy and the taking of concubines were specifically banned. But the CCP leadership turned a blind eye to Kang's domestic arrangements.

Cao Yi'ou had remained silent in the past about Kang's relationship with Su Mei; as long as the affair was hidden, it caused her no public embarrassment. But while the three of them were in Qingdao and Hangzhou, Kang began flaunting his sexual alliance with Su Mei, causing a storm of gossip and innuendo. Cao exploded in a jealous rage. She bickered constantly with Kang, and a highly emotional quarrel broke out between the two sisters, fueled by decades of suppressed envy and frustration. In May 1950, while the three of them were in Hangzhou, the struggle reached a climax: Su Mei jumped off the upper floor of a building. She survived, but word that she had tried to kill herself spread quickly.

Kang tried to cover up Su Mei's attempted suicide by charging that his secretary and whipping boy, the unfortunate Sha Tao, had deliberately pushed her through the window. But public-security officials in Hangzhou rejected Kang's charges against Sha (indicating how far Kang's influence with the security apparatus had eroded). Kang's only recourse was to use the incident as an excuse to dismiss his aide. Sha Tao left Kang's employ and returned to Peking, where he enrolled at the People's University. Even there, however, after Su Mei had recovered and family tensions subsided, Kang pursued Sha Tao relentlessly. Kang viewed Sha as a former spy in his household, one who knew so many details of Kang's life that he must be discredited if not actually destroyed.

When Kang heard in December 1950 that Sha was a student at People's University, he instructed Cao Yi'ou, then the deputy director of the East China Bureau's organization department, to report to Party headquarters that "political problems" made Sha an inappropriate candidate for the school. Cao recommended that Sha be transferred to the liaison department of the Central Military Commission, where his political attitudes could be monitored.

Upon resuming his official duties in late 1955, Kang found to his dismay that not only was Sha still attached to the Military Commission but he had been promoted. Kang personally contacted the Military Commission, warning the nervous officials who received his message that Sha was "a bad person" and demanding that they transfer him to some less sensitive job. Kang's order placed the Military Commission staff in a quandary: they saw no reason to persecute Sha Tao, but they were reluctant to cross Kang, with his dangerous reputation. The officials appealed to higher authority, reporting the matter to Liu Shaoqi, who then supervised the work of all central Party offices. Liu wrote two short sentences on the submission from the Military Commission: "Kang Sheng's mind is not normal. Do not pay attention to him." Kang could do little at the time, but when the Cultural Revolution erupted a decade later, Kang personally ordered Sha Tao's arrest. Sha was finally released in 1978, three years after Kang's death and nineteen years after he had unwittingly incurred Kang's wrath.

After her failed marriage and failed suicide attempt, Su Mei tried again to establish her own life. In 1958, she married Zhang Dingcheng, a former Red Army commander who was deputy head of the Organization Department and procurator general (a post that Su Mei's first husband, Huang Huoqing, was to occupy after the Cultural Revolution). Zhang had known Kang, and presumably Su Mei, for many years; he had been deputy head of the Party School in Yan'an during the Rectification Movement and had served under Kang in the East China Bureau during the late 1940s. He was the same age as Kang, so in marrying Zhang she was once again becoming involved with an older man. Like her earlier marriage, Su Mei's union with Zhang collapsed after a year or so—again, it was said, largely because of pressure from Kang.

As the Cultural Revolution took hold, tragedy finally overtook the Kang Sheng–Cao Yi'ou–Su Mei triangle. One morning in mid-April 1967, Su Mei was found dead in her Peking apartment. Then in her mid-fifties, she had served for several years as deputy head of the political department of the Academy for Political and Legal Cadres, an elite training center run by the Public Security Ministry. She was maintaining a separate home in the academy's residential quarters, where she lived with Ren Neiya and Su Han, Kang's "niece" and nephew. While eating dinner at home with them the night before her death, Su Mei had shown no sign of distress or illness; but during the night, she died in her sleep.

Kang immediately charged that Su Mei had been a victim of foul play. He directed public-security officials to detain and interrogate everyone who lived near Su Mei's apartment, and ordered physicians at Peking Hospital to perform an autopsy. The doctors concluded that she had killed herself with an overdose of barbiturates. Investigations conducted by the Public Security Bureau turned up no evidence that contradicted the medical findings.

With the outbreak of the Cultural Revolution in 1966, Su Mei had again been consumed by anxieties. Charges of being a "special agent" or "renegade" were hurled at people on the slightest provocation; many were arrested; and many more were subjected to horrifying abuse at the hands of the Red Guards. Su Mei, having lived with Kang through the White Terror in Shanghai, the purges in Moscow, and the Yan'an Rectification Movement, was all too aware that the skeletons in his closet could place her in jeopardy. Like Kang, she had been arrested by the KMT in Shanghai, which made her vulnerable to charges of being a KMT agent.

Neither Kang nor Cao Yi'ou accepted the judgment of suicide. Both were furious at the findings of the postmortem that a member of their family had killed herself. In Communist China, suicide is considered a distinctly unsocialist act; moreover, Chinese tradition associates suicide with protests against injustice that can be corrected only in the afterworld. Kang insisted that Su Mei had been the victim of homicide, and that some of the doctors who had investigated her death were attempting to cover up her murder. He presented a grotesque explanation of the autopsy's results, claiming that the hospital staff had substituted the contents from the stomach of another corpse for the fluid allegedly extracted from Su Mei's body. Flaunting his powers, Kang assembled his own team of investigators. They produced the conclusion Kang wanted, implicating eight main suspects in Su Mei's "murder." Among them were Shi Lei, the vice president of the Academy for Political and Legal Cadres, and Gu Xichun, a woman doctor who had performed the original autopsy. Fifty others were listed as "secondary suspects." Despite the rigorous probe Kang instigated, no one was ever identified formally as Su Mei's killer, and the verdict of suicide was never overturned. Still, at the hands of Kang and his operatives, one "suspect" died, four went insane under torture, and seven were imprisoned for long periods.

In the eyes of some cadres in Peking, Kang had good reason to cover up the true cause of Su Mei's death. One of her friends, a senior Chinese academic who for obvious reasons wishes to remain anonymous, suspects that Kang himself murdered Su Mei, fearing that she would crack under the strain of the Cultural Revolution and reveal secrets from his past. Su Mei's friend also believes that Kang saw Su Mei as an obstacle to Cao Yi'ou's prospects in an age when Jiang Qing and Ye Qun (the wife of Marshal Lin Biao, Mao's designated political heir) were becoming national figures in their own right.

*   *   *

In his six-year retreat from public life, Kang played no role in the formation of the Chinese Communist state and was overtaken by several leaders previously subordinate to him, or at most equal in rank. The rising Communist stars included Rao Shushi; Deng Xiaoping, who was appointed CCP general secretary in 1954; and Peng Zhen, who became Peking's mayor and Party chief.

Even in his own area of security and espionage, Kang's contribution during the early 1950s was limited. A newly created nationwide internal-security police organization, the Ministry of Public Security, took over many of the functions formerly in the domain of the Social Affairs Department. Social Affairs continued to exist as a Party organ free from government supervision, but it mainly collected intelligence about foreign countries. It was further transformed during the mid-1950s into the Investigation Department, which spied abroad on behalf of the Party. Some of Kang's former colleagues gained influential positions during the reorganizations, including Li Kenong, who became head of the Investigation Department. But many posts went to men from different backgrounds who had no reason to like Kang. The new minister of public security, Luo Ruiqing, was the intelligence expert Kang had displaced when he took over the Military Intelligence Department in 1938.

Kang's absence from Party affairs cost him any chance of retaining a circle of allies within the security and espionage services. He also missed an opportunity to exploit a slew of major challenges facing the Communists. China entered the Korean War in 1950 on the side of the North Korean regime of Kim Il-Sung against the American-dominated United Nations forces that supported the South Koreans. That conflict, right on China's borders and accompanied by debate in the United States about whether to attack China itself, made extensive demands on the Chinese security services. The fledgling U.S. Central Intelligence Agency, in conjunction with the Taiwan-based KMT intelligence services, began conducting covert operations against the mainland, flying agents into remote airstrips in an attempt to create a network of anti-Communist military units that might eventually overthrow the CCP. But Kang made no attempt to join the battle. Even without him, the newly formed Public Security Ministry foiled many of the CIA–KMT clandestine operations.

Kang also chose to stay on the sidelines during the CCP's war on landlords and "counterrevolutionary elements" in the early 1950s.

Once the Communist forces had won control over the mainland, the Party set out to remold society in the image of Communist doctrine. Landlords in areas previously under KMT control were completely wiped out. Rigorous measures were also introduced against "counterrevolutionaries"—KMT officials, secret-society members, religious leaders, and any Chinese who had had intimate dealings with foreign governments. These operations, too random and uncoordinated to reshape China in any lasting way, did result in extensive bloodshed. Millions died as Communist ideologues sought to bring the country under control.* Kang had done as much as anyone to set the pattern for the measures now being imposed all across China, but he missed the opportunity to participate in the butchery by retiring to his sickbed. His rage was so deep that not even the prospect of terrorizing China's landlords and opponents of the regime could assuage his hatred for Rao Shushi.

Kang's withdrawal from public life also excluded him from the first major power struggle within the Party after the Communist victory. During the early 1950s, a confrontation developed between Chairman Mao and Manchuria's CCP boss, Gao Gang. Mao was suspicious of Gao Gang's links with the Soviet Union and also worried about Gao's independence from Peking. Gao Gang, a Party veteran of almost as many years as Mao, resented the Chairman's domineering style of leadership as well as his claim of being primarily responsible for the Communist victory. If the clash had reached a climax several years later, when Mao's abuses were more widely recognized, Gao might have succeeded in overthrowing Mao. Gao was the first Communist leader to challenge Mao after the People's Republic was founded in 1949. Only one other member of the ruling clique had enough nerve to go along with Gao Gang: Rao Shushi. The outcome of their premature challenge was predictable. At secret meet-

---

* Estimates of the numbers killed by the Communists as they established control during the early 1950s vary greatly. Mao Zedong claimed that 700,000 "counterrevolutionaries" were executed between 1950 and 1952, while Luo Ruiqing, who was minister of public security at the time, reportedly said that 4,000,000 were killed between 1948 and 1955. The U.S. State Department generally accepted a figure of about 2,250,000 as having been killed in the first half of 1951, when the purges were at their worst. Newspapers in Hong Kong and Taiwan have claimed that 10,000,000 to 20,000,000 executions took place in 1950 and 1951. These figures, however, are not based on hard data but were arrived at by multiplying by a factor of five or more the number of deaths documented in one way or another.

ings in 1954, the rebels were accused of plotting against the Party leaders and arrested by security guards. Gao Gang committed suicide in detention, while Rao Shushi served a life sentence, dying in jail on March 2, 1975. Soon after Rao's imprisonment, Kang declared that "the root of my disease" had been eradicated.

If Kang had wished, he could have stayed in retirement permanently. But his quest for high office and for power over people's lives had already consumed him for more than a quarter of a century; a man with his passions was unlikely to remain the prisoner of morbid and paranoid fears forever. Rao Shushi's demise removed the central focus of Kang's frustrations and envy, and Kang's realization in late 1955 that a major Party shakeup was in the offing induced him to forsake the passive life of a convalescent and return to the tough, competitive world of Party politics.

Once Kang gave up his isolated lifestyle, he discovered his loss of position and privilege. Kang did the best he could to regain his former stature, but success came only in fits and starts. He spent the next decade alternating between frantic, nihilistic attempts to destroy his rivals and periods of relative withdrawal from the high councils of the Party, when he concentrated on his lifelong artistic pursuits.

Given Kang's six years of seclusion, it is not surprising that he should have faced obstacles on his return to politics. He was a menacing and widely hated figure whose misdeeds in Shanghai, Moscow, and Yan'an had earned him many enemies. What is astonishing is that Kang was given another chance; in virtually any other system, his prospects would have been nil, and in most regimes as ruthless as the one that had taken over mainland China, he would have been lucky even to survive.

But survive Kang Sheng did. The eastern mountain, to quote a Chinese idiom, would rise again.

Chapter XI

COMEBACK
OF A
COURTIER

SIX YEARS after he had retired from public life, ostensibly with a mysterious illness, Kang Sheng made an equally miraculous recovery. No physician had been able to find anything wrong with him, and there was no medical explanation for his sudden return to good health. Kang himself started to talk about diseases that afflicted "patients of the Socialist Age." He warned that "if [you] doctors only understand those who are physiological patients, and not those who are social and political patients, then you are only half doctors." Declaring that doctors had to study Marxist theory if they wanted to cure people, Kang provided himself with an ideological explanation for both his long hospitalization and the physicians' failure to detect a cause.

On the last day of January 1956, in the dead of Peking's winter, Kang appeared unexpectedly at a meeting of the Chinese People's Political Consultative Conference, a largely symbolic institution that provided a forum for prominent non-Communists to air their views on national affairs. Low-key as his first public appearance in over five years was, it signaled a readiness to get on with the next phase of his career.

Kang explained to inquisitive comrades that his health had at last improved enough for him to withstand the rigors of regular work. All along, in fact, his physical condition had been as good as could be expected for a heavy smoker of both tobacco and opium in his middle to late fifties. Kang was reluctant to tell his colleagues the real reason for his comeback: staying on the sidelines any longer, he knew, would have forever jeopardized his future prospects. The Eighth Party Congress, the first since 1945, was scheduled to be held in late 1956, and Kang, like the rest of China's leadership, expected it to be a watershed in CCP affairs. Kang's failure to return at that point would likely have seen him pensioned off if he was lucky, or, if not, simply demoted into the ranks of the anonymous, powerless masses.

After Kang left the hospital, the Party's General Office assigned him a large house in Small Stone Bridge Lane, a narrow side street just northwest of the Drum Tower, one of Peking's ancient landmarks. In his spacious, sprawling mansion, which featured an artificial hill crowned by a small pavilion and a succession of courtyards leading to a bamboo forest that was alive with chirping cicadas in the summertime,* Kang lived the life of a scholarly official. He collected art and antiques, painted, and produced calligraphy. He told one guest that he hoped eventually to leave official life, live in the forests and mountains, and devote himself to art. But for the present, he yearned to be back in a position of power.

Although he had spent five years in Peking as a patient, when Kang moved out of the hospital he was starting a new life in a city unlike any other place he had lived. Peking represented both the new and the old China. By the time Kang rode its streets, the Communists had started demolishing the castellated walls that for centuries had endowed the empire's heart with an air of strength and grandeur; as they flattened the once magnificent fortifications, the engineers of the new China were covering acres of the city with oversize Soviet-style office buildings, meeting halls, hotels, and exhibition centers. These large, square structures lent a sense of cosmopolitanism and modernity to the capital. Behind its socialist mask, however, the ancient city of lanes and alleys, palaces and pavilions, temples and pagodas, gar-

---

* After the Cultural Revolution, Kang's residence was converted into the Bamboo Garden Hotel, a thirty-nine-room hostelry for Western tourists. A promotional brochure recently produced by the hotel management describes the Bamboo Garden as "a Chinese garden, unique and of classic beauty," containing a "densely wooded" courtyard "with bamboo groves while rocks and fountains are embellished with varieties of exotic flowers and rare plants." There are two dining rooms: a Chinese restaurant known as "the Drunken Beauty Verandah" and a Western restaurant called "the Studio of Tending the Pines." The circular declares that the building was once the home of "Shen Xuanhuai, the then minister of post [sic] of the late Qing dynasty," but it discreetly avoids any mention of Kang's occupation of the property from 1956 until his death in 1975. According to sources in the Peking tourist industry, the hotel is now owned and operated by a subsidiary of the Ministry of Public Security.

dens and lakes, and mansions concealed by high walls and moon gates, survived in a state of gentle decay.

The new regime did more than scatter construction projects across the face of Peking; it also imported a new elite to staff the various government ministries. Handing out jobs to the most promising and most loyal of the cadres who had fought in the revolution, the CCP rulers created a new society that appeared to have few links with the city's past. But just as the Russian-style department stores and hotels could not entirely overshadow the architecture of old China, the Communist regime had to come to grips with the conspiracies and intrigues that had been a part of life in Peking for centuries. If Shanghai was a flashy, commercial metropolis that lived for money, then Peking was a city of backroom politics and private deals. To be sure, it was often the site of majestic ceremonies in Tiananmen Square, but power lay in the hands of men who transacted business across the bridge table or in exclusive restaurants and traveled in black sedans with curtains over the rear windows.

The challenges Kang faced during the early months of 1956 underscored the dangers he would have risked by continuing his retreat. As soon as he reappeared, Kang encountered serious problems that caused his position in the hierarchy to fluctuate dramatically. After the purge of Gao Gang and Rao Shushi in 1954, he had ranked sixth, below Chairman Mao, Liu Shaoqi, Zhou Enlai, Zhu De, and Chen Yun. But in February 1956, just weeks after his return to public life, he was listed below Peng Zhen. By the end of April, he was reported in tenth place, below even Luo Fu, the only member of the Twenty-eight Bolsheviks who still held a Politburo seat. Yet on May Day of 1956—the international socialist celebration—Kang was suddenly back in sixth place. His position, at least going by public reports and official bulletins, remained unchanged from then until the Eighth Congress four months later.

Behind Kang's shifts in rank lay a controversy over whether he should retain the elevated status granted him almost as a courtesy during his hospital stay. No one was prepared to set the risky precedent of questioning the situation of a sick colleague, but Kang's comrades were less considerate once he reappeared in the flesh. To reward him for six years of inactivity and deny advancement to men who had meanwhile worked relentlessly for the People's Republic threatened to cause morale problems. Some cadres were disgusted by Kang's rumored amorous escapades during his period of ill health; others coveted his position and power; few had reason to welcome him back warmly. Despite Kang's long absence from politics, he was widely seen as a dangerous man with links to the security services. Many people had suffered at his hands, and some of them, such as Li Lisan— then the minister of labor—actively spread stories of Kang's duplicity and sadism. Kang's social mannerisms added to his unpopularity. One witness who saw him in Peking at a film show for elite cadres in the second half of the 1950s compared him unfavorably to another member of the audience, the ebullient and gregarious military veteran Marshal He Long. This observer recalled Kang strutting in and surveying the audience with a look that was half smile and half scowl, a manner he described as *yinyang guaiqi* ("enigmatic and ambivalent"). A man like Kang was a natural target, though a dangerous one.

Kang's first move to advance his position was to seek out a specialty that would give him a platform. He was still a Politburo member, which afforded him prestige but not control over any Party or government machinery. Gradually, he had lost all the posts that had given him authority over people, leaving him much worse off than in 1946. Even his home province of Shandong was no longer in his hands by 1955, when Shu Tong, a Long March survivor and former member of the Social Affairs Department, officially replaced Kang as provincial chief. Until then, Kang had held the title in name, although his status as an invalid prevented him from doing any work.

Kang's quest for a new and influential mission was not easy. In six years, politics had changed. As the economy recovered from twelve years of constant warfare, government policy shifted focus to the mundane tasks of economic construction and socialist transformation. The talents required when the Party was struggling for survival counted for less in the new era. Now that the Party had its grip on power, the Politburo agenda was no longer dominated by issues of security and espionage; the regime needed people with backgrounds as economists, engineers, and administrators. Only one civilian member of the Politburo was needed to supervise the security-and-espionage community in the broader context of police and legal affairs. For much of the time between the early 1950s and early 1960s, this responsibility fell to Kang's former underling Peng Zhen, in his role as vice chairman of the Committee on Political and Legal Affairs.

Cut off from his natural base of power, Kang took on a series of diverse assignments, none of which was very promising. In early 1956, he was named to the Commission for Popularizing Putonghua—that is, "the common spoken language," the form of standardized Mandarin Chinese the Communists were seeking to impose on the population. Putonghua used simplified characters and a number of new, socialist terms to replace the "feudal" vocabulary of the past. Even in this relatively unimportant area of expertise, Kang was merely vice chairman below Marshal Chen Yi, the soldier-turned-administrator who was now the mayor of Shanghai.

Foreign affairs provided Kang with more opportunity. He went to East Germany in March 1956 as head of the Chinese delgation to the Third Congress of the East German Socialist Unity Party. The month Kang spent in East Germany marked his first personal contact with other Communist parties in the post-Stalin world and revealed to him the political implications of the attacks on Stalin that were sweeping Eastern Europe. The Socialist Unity Party session was held just one month after the Twentieth Congress of the Communist Party of the Soviet Union, at which Nikita Khrushchev had delivered his famous "secret speech"—his outspoken condemnation of Stalin, Stalin's secret-police techniques, and his "personality cult." The East German Communists, sick of the terrible costs of Stalinism, were eager to follow Khrushchev's lead; in Kang's presence, they adopted measures designed to introduce "liberalization from above," emphasizing socialist legality instead of the deification of individual leaders.

New trends in the East German Communist movement were enough to disturb Kang or any cadres who had acquired power from the Stalinist system of a tightly controlled society motivated by an extravagant personality cult. The limitations being placed on the role of the Party had alarming implications for China; for Kang's patron, Chairman Mao; and for Kang personally. Kang's methods—the use of terror, the extraction of false confessions, the manipulation of espionage charges, and the glorification of a supreme leader—were all derived from Stalin's rule. Kang's sense that his world was slipping away deepened when he stopped in Moscow en route home, his first visit there since 1937. Over the two intervening decades, Moscow had changed tremendously. "The Holy City of Socialism" had emerged from the war as the capital of a large empire in competition with the United States for global supremacy. The cause of world revolution had been sacrificed to the national interests of the Soviet Union. The new forces at work had become even more pronounced after Khrushchev's landmark speech unleashed the first officially endorsed wave of anti-Stalinism.

Kang continued to try to rebuild his influence, but the currents of change that were lapping at the edges of China's Communist machine gave him little help. With the Chinese elite taking ever more care to avoid the mistakes of Stalinism, Kang's record as a security chief made his predicament even more acute. By the opening of the first session of the Eighth Congress on September 15, 1956,* he found himself the target of ambitious colleagues envious of his seniority. Kang sought to fight back, but six years of living as an invalid had undermined his defenses.

Kang was made even more vulnerable by the problems that Mao himself was facing. Mao's supremacy was not in jeopardy, but many Party leaders wanted to make sure that no Stalin-like personality cult developed around the Chairman. In response to pressure from nervous functionaries, the Congress passed a resolution deleting all references to "Mao Zedong Thought" from the Party constitution. Mao was too busy placating his own critics to worry much about delegates lobbying against Kang.

Kang suffered one of the most humiliating reversals of his career at the Central Committee plenum that followed the first session of the Eighth Congress. He was demoted to alternate or nonvoting membership in the Politburo, plunging from sixth to twenty-second place in the hierarchy—a painful insult to a man who had been a full Politburo member for twenty-two years. Experts on China in the U.S. Consulate General in Hong Kong observed that "the day is not far off when he will be consigned to limbo."

Above Kang on the Party ladder were several cadres who had once been his subordinates. The fat little philosophy professor Chen Boda, once a mere lecturer at the Party School in Yan'an, now ranked higher than Kang. So did propaganda boss Lu Dingyi, who had not even been named a member of the Central Committee until 1945.

Kang had little choice but to mask his unhappiness and pretend to cooperate with his superiors. Even with the muted debate over Mao's status, Kang viewed Mao as the key to his future and maximized every opportunity for contact with the Chairman. In 1956, the Politburo set up a Political Research Office, nominally under the guidance of Chen Boda, where Mao often held discussions with pro-

---

* The Eighth Congress met in two sessions, in 1956 and 1958.

vincial secretaries. Kang persuaded the General Office of the Central Committee to assign him a room near the Chairman's. By late 1956, Kang had become a champion of Mao's views on how China should respond to de-Stalinization in the Soviet Union and the rising tide of hostility toward communism in countries like Poland and Hungary.

The Chairman's approach to these disturbing trends in the socialist world marked a departure from the way he had previously faced challenges to Party control. Mao's regime had dealt ruthlessly with its enemies ever since the founding of the People's Republic: the CCP had killed several million Chinese citizens while consolidating its hold on the mainland in the early 1950s; Mao's henchmen had arrested high officials like Gao Gang and Rao Shushi who had plotted against him; China's non-Communist scholars had been humiliated and silenced; a famous Marxist literary critic, Hu Feng, had been imprisoned for pointing out the narrowness and superficiality of Mao's cultural and artistic theories.

Faced with the risk that events in Eastern Europe might ignite discontent in China, Mao took a completely new tack. Instead of ordering additional purges, he proposed a more liberal approach. Mao spoke of "letting a hundred flowers bloom and a hundred schools of thought contend," arguing that non-Party intellectuals should be encouraged to criticize the high-handed authoritarianism and bureaucratic style of cadres who, according to Mao, had tarnished the Party's reputation. To his wary comrades Mao explained that by allowing citizens who did not belong to the CCP to express their grievances, China could achieve national harmony and avoid the troubles that threatened other Communist governments.

Kang, who had never shown the slightest sympathy for liberalism of any kind, suddenly declared himself to be resolutely in favor of public criticism of the Party's dogmatic and despotic practices. The need to make a dramatic change in attitude did not deter Kang for a moment: he had made many about-faces in the past. In fact, he flaunted a philosophy of politics that assumed that day-to-day continuity did not exist—and that inconsistency was the norm. Kang once opened a talk by pointing at a tape recorder and telling his audience that he had "three fears:—tapes, notes, and records of slogans and concepts." He explained that whatever he said related only to that time and place and therefore might not be correct in other circumstances. "I will not acknowledge tomorrow what I say today. So a tape recording is useless!"

Kang worked closely with Mao in introducing the concept of free expression and justifying it to the Party. In a speech on February 27, 1957, Mao stated his views on the question of internal criticism, or, as he put it, on how to handle contradictions among the people. The Chairman argued that conflicts within society fell into two categories—antagonistic and nonantagonistic—and concluded that public debate of the latter was the best way to achieve social cohesion. Kang sat on the podium listening approvingly to Mao's speech—in marked contrast to Liu Shaoqi, Zhu De, and Peng Dehuai, who made a point of being absent from the podium, if not the meeting, when Mao took the microphone. According to unofficial accounts, a number of dissenters in the audience stalked out of the hall in protest at Mao's ideas.

Kang unhesitatingly echoed the Chairman's call for non-Communists to expose the faults they saw within the Party. In early March 1957, Kang helped run a seven-day conference in Peking on propaganda work, turning it into an opportunity to advance Mao's ideas. Mao addressed the conference and also explained to small groups of delegates why writers, journalists, and artists should bring to light any shortcomings of the CCP. Kang interjected occasional sarcastic remarks about those entrenched officials who feared that such widespread criticism might weaken their grip on power. The task of summing up at the end of the conference fell to Kang. Sensing that he could exploit the differences between Mao and the opposition, Kang dwelled on the philosophical significance of Mao's formula for resolving the problems facing socialism. The Chairman's thinking represented an original and creative development of Marxism–Leninism, Kang told the audience.

Kang's persistence in playing the part of an expert on Marxism whose views accorded with the Chairman's paid off on March 15, 1957, when he was appointed deputy head of a small "internal" or secret committee, the Central Group on Culture and Education. This agency had great influence—it reported directly to the Politburo and supervised the work of the Propaganda Department, the Party School, and the Ministry of Culture. If Kang was to escape political stagnation, he desperately needed such a job, one that formalized his authority over a major element in the Chinese political system: ideology.

Mao traveled to Tianjin, Shanghai, and Nanking later in March, explaining the "hundred flowers" policy at each stop and meeting with publishers, editors, and local leaders. Kang did not go to Tianjin, but at Shanghai he joined Mao and performed the introductions when a group of newspaper people called on Mao; Kang acted as the master of ceremonies, inviting the visitors to ask any questions they might have about the Chairman's wish to have open discussion of the Party's performance.

The continued calls to let "a hundred flowers bloom" that followed Mao's speech on contradictions gradually spread. Many intellectuals had been afraid to voice their objections to the Communist government, but starting in early May 1957, people from almost every sector of society began to speak out against the regime. Newspaper and magazine articles used ever harsher language to lambast China's rulers and the bureaucrats who served them. Former KMT officials who had stayed on the mainland after 1949 out of a sense of patriotism began attacking the closed system of the CCP; highly respected professors and student activists called for a removal of the intellectual straitjacket the CCP had imposed on society; workers demanded the right to strike and demonstrate, and students in Wuhan even attempted to mount a Hungarian-style revolt. The Party found itself surrounded by hostile voices, all uttering variations on the theme that the Communists had created a one-party state that prohibited dissent. In the words of one highly placed dissident, Chu Anping, the editor of *The Guangming Daily,* China had become "the party's world."

As the protests increased, Mao gave an indication that his original purpose in proposing the campaign was perhaps more sinister than he had let on. In mid-May, he circulated a note to high Party cadres: "Things are just beginning to change. The rightist offensive has still not reached its peak. [The rightists] are still very enthusiastic. We want to let them rage for a while and climb to the very summit." The fact that Mao kept his words secret from the public at large suggests that from the outset he wanted to incite non-Party figures to excess. If Mao was truly worried about dissent getting out of hand, he could have curtailed it immediately by publicizing his note. Many writers and scholars would have been much more reticent if they had known that the Chairman no longer welcomed the campaign.

Clearly, Mao was waiting for the attacks on the Party to become stronger. Yet even today, his reasons for doing so remain uncertain. Perhaps he simply wanted to see more pressure applied to the rank-and-file cadres before he halted the protests. But many Chinese observers believe that he wanted the Party's bourgeois enemies to expose themselves completely before he permitted a crackdown. His speech on contradictions, with its distinction between antagonistic and nonantagonistic conflicts, offered a neat justification for dealing severely with anyone who went beyond pointing out the mistakes of individual Communists and challenged the place of the CCP. Liu Shaoqi and other cadres who emphasized discipline were almost certainly not taken into his confidence.* But Kang had supported Mao's calls for criticism of the Party from the outset; Dai Qing, a journalist who has investigated the period, has suggested that Kang was probably privy to Mao's plans from the beginning. Dai Qing wrote that although Mao's thinking was too obscure for propaganda boss Lu Dingyi to follow, "Kang Sheng was perhaps on top of it. At that time he was no longer living as an invalid and had enthusiastically and with great spirit taken part in every step [of Mao's campaign]."

In an abrupt reversal, the ruling commissars and ideologues began a broad purge of "rightists" on June 8. Peng Zhen and other cadres who had argued against Mao's methods seized on this turn of events to chastise Mao in barely disguised terms. Mao's vulnerability might not have been so great, however, had not *The New York Times* obtained a copy of his speech on contradictions from an East European source in Warsaw. The publication of the text of Mao's speech in a bourgeois American newspaper on June 13 forced Mao's hand. The Party leadership had to release its own version of the speech to end speculation about Mao's remarks, but the recently commenced campaign against the "rightists" required that some embarrassing changes be made in the authorized text. In the eyes of orthodox cadres, the revised version of Mao's speech as printed in China on June 19 underscored the concessions he had been forced to make to his hard-line colleagues. The "hundred flowers" campaign led to a devastating attack on those who had spoken out against the CCP, but the crude way that the much-vaunted open debate had turned into widespread repression pointed to a double failure for Mao. Not only had he been unable to resolve China's "nonantagonistic contradic-

---

* Li Weihan, who was head of the United Front Work Department and directly involved in the "hundred flowers" campaign, wrote shortly before his death in 1984 that the first indication he got that an attack on "rightists" would follow the period of free expression came from remarks Mao made in mid-May 1957. If Li Weihan, one of Mao's close colleagues since 1918, was kept in the dark as to the Chairman's true intentions, then probably so were Liu Shaoqi and other Party stalwarts.

tions," but the sudden reversal of policy had enabled his opponents within the Party to expose his shortcomings.

In response to this flood of hostility, the Communist Party launched a short but savage campaign that saw 550,000 imprisoned or exiled to labor camps. The leaders of the small non-Communist democratic groups who had been made government ministers to enhance the image of a tolerant, multiparty regime were sacked and forced to make self-criticisms. The most important casualties were the tens of thousands of intellectuals—professors, writers, journalists, students—who had had the courage (or the naïveté) to take Mao's invitation at face value; many were sent to prison farms to reform their deviant thoughts through manual labor. Student leaders who had organized the uprising in Wuhan were executed. Other Communist governments were searching for ways to overcome the problems expressed in Khrushchev's attack on Stalin, but China, after only six weeks of free speech, had reverted to classical Stalinist methods to suppress dissent.

The crackdown on "rightists" followed the general pattern Kang had established in Yan'an, with police, prisons, and labor camps used to crush a purely political threat. On this occasion, Kang showed little interest in purging the bourgeois intellectuals and non-Communist politicians who had embarrassed the regime. He focused his efforts on rooting out cadres in the Party School who, he charged, espoused rightist opinions. Rather than join most of his comrades in destroying the Party's opponents, Kang exploited the antirightist campaign to attack targets inside key Party institutions and expand his own influence.

Besides making himself one of Mao's personal troubleshooters, Kang started to build his own circle of allies and co-conspirators. Among them was Chen Boda, the editor of Red Flag magazine, the Party's newly established mouthpiece on ideological matters. Chen had earned Kang's envy by being promoted above him at the Eighth Congress, but Chen was the sort of man Kang believed he could use to his own advantage. Chen was close to Mao—he had served as Mao's political secretary in Yan'an—but only the Chairman thought him especially clever. Known among his friends as Lao Fuzi ("Old Scholar"), a term that implied an honest but absent-minded professor, Chen was not so intelligent that Kang needed to fear him. Another new member of Kang's circle was Ke Qingshi, previously Kang's comrade in Shanghai and Yan'an. Ke had succeeded Chen Yi as Party boss in Shanghai in 1958 and turned China's largest city into a Maoist stronghold. Much more astute politically than the bumbling Chen Boda, Ke was another perfect ally for Kang: as the CCP leader in Shanghai, he was not a rival of Kang's for power. Kang also renewed his ties with Shandong protégés like Wang Li and Guan Feng, who occupied influential posts in the Propaganda Department and the Chinese Academy of Sciences, and cultivated former colleagues from the intelligence world such as Li Kenong, head of the Investigation Department.

Mao remained the object of all of Kang's moves—his tactics and his choice of colleagues. By regaining Mao's favor, Kang recognized, he could outstrip the earnest bureaucrats who had gained influence during his years of hospitalization. He became a courtier in Mao's palace, a chamberlain who knew the rules of the system and derived special stature from his relationship with the emperor.

Meeting regularly with Mao was far from easy, however. No longer the approachable peasant rebel whom Kang had befriended and helped in Yan'an, Mao had become the Chairman, an icon, a legendary colossus who led a removed, distant existence. He lived in a pavilion in Zhongnanhai, an exclusive compound adjacent to the Forbidden City in the heart of Peking, retired to secluded villas in the south when the weather in the capital turned cold, even traveled by special train. Jiang Qing, the woman who had aroused Mao's passion and had been Kang's bridge to the leader, now led a separate life. During the early 1950s, Jiang Qing spent several years in the Soviet Union receiving medical treatment for a range of illnesses: tonsillitis, a liver problem, and finally cervical cancer. She and Mao were together far less than during the late 1930s and 1940s.

Kang arranged to travel frequently with Mao, which gave him a chance to flatter the Chairman and probe the direction and orientation of his thoughts. Mao left frigid Peking in January 1958 for the southern climate of Hangzhou and Nanking, taking with him a number of senior officials, including Kang. During discussions of national policy for the coming year, Mao condemned the cautious planners and technocrats who took issue with his proposals for rapid economic progress. He repeated his attacks in March in Chengdu, where he praised two provincial leaders—Kang's ally Ke Qingshi, from Shanghai, and Li Jingquan, from Sichuan—for their support of his call for economic transformation. Over the following months resistance to Mao's objectives lessened and in mid-year China embarked on the Great Leap Forward, a program designed to create a modern state almost overnight. Although it touched every aspect of Chinese life, from urban construction to housing arrangements for the peasantry, the main objectives of the Leap were to double steel production, replace private land holdings with collective farms or communes, and dramatically increase grain production.

Kang came away from Chengdu appreciating Mao's fascination with the idea of creating a pure Communist society. Identifying himself with the Chairman, Kang argued strenuously that Mao's vision of rapid economic transformation demanded radical change in the education system—an area Kang directed through the Central Group on Culture and Education. By March 30, 1958, months before the Central Committee endorsed Mao's economic program for communizing Chinese society, Kang had proclaimed that "education needs a Great Leap Forward."

To spread his radical ideas on education, Kang began visiting universities and technical and secondary schools in Shanxi, Sichuan, Shanghai, and other places throughout China. At each stop, he declared that true revolution required education to be integrated with labor—that this combination underlay the "Great Educational Leap Forward," which would parallel progress in agriculture and industry. He rejected the commonly accepted ideas on education with sarcastic comments about pet targets like the Ministry of Education. Current educational policy, he complained, was fundamentally wrong because the ministry passed off anti-Marxist teachings as Marxist. Moreover—according to the originator of the "stones" concept—the disciplinary rules and regulations enforced by the ministry were "ropes" that tied the students down and should be discarded.

Kang ridiculed standard school instruction as "dogma, nonsense, and trash" and questioned the basic procedures of the entire educational system. He rejected as unscientific the idea that classes should last for forty-five minutes; in some cases, he argued, ten minutes was quite enough to transfer the message from teacher to pupil. He also singled out long school holidays as further evidence of the ministry's stupidity and, even worse, its bourgeois tendencies. "I have asked many physiologists and doctors, and they cannot understand it either," he declared at one meeting. "In fact there are two reasons. One is that school is considered to be mental labor, and therefore there should be holidays. But there is a question they can't answer—what [about] the Party Center? I think the Party Center also performs mental labor, so why don't we have holidays? There is also another reason, which is that the students are young and need rest. But children in rural villages, if they don't get to middle school, cannot rest, and why is that?" Rather than abolish holidays, Kang proposed, classroom time should be limited, since physical labor was just as important as standard education. His comment on a school that had followed his guidance and abandoned classes in favor of physical labor summed up his attitude: "Don't call this stopping classes. Call it shifting classrooms!"

Wherever he went, Kang ridiculed the education system, yet he maintained the public image of a respected scholar. After Kang had visited Tianjin's Nankai University in 1957, one of the students, Yang Dechun, composed a prose poem that ascribed to Kang the sort of gentle curiosity usually associated with men like Albert Einstein:

Just as the school bell stopped
An old man entered.
Softly, he
Sat down on the last seat. . . .
During the rest period
He was so friendly with the teacher,
Asking this and that
As if they were intimate friends
Chatting and laughing.
He listened until the end of the literary history class
And then walked out.
Inside the classroom laughter and debate arose.
Everyone eagerly said: "I dare guarantee
That was the central leader who visited once before—Kang Sheng."
The entire classroom was excited, moving like a river in spring.
The students squeezed together near the window
And poked their heads outside,
Gazing as that humble figure
Grew ever more distant, until he was out of sight. . . .

Kang based his philosophy on the principle that workers should become intellectuals and intellectuals should become laborers, so that the distinction between manual and mental labor would vanish as

China moved toward a state of pure communism. Implicit in his analysis was the belief that China's intellectuals were hostile to the masses, which presented an obstacle to the great educational leap forward and the transition to communism.

Kang also proposed "readjusting" the living accommodations of urban workers, which meant relocating managers and workers to hostels adjacent to the workplace; forcing male and female workers, including husbands and wives, to live in separate dormitories; and moving children into state-run nurseries so that family responsibilities would not distract workers from their duties.

Kang justified the separation of husbands and wives, parents and children, on the grounds that cutting travel time and directing commitment to the work unit instead of the family would increase industrial efficiency. But his fundamental objective was to tighten social controls. "When some workers return to their quarters they eat and drink, engage in low amusements, read pornographic novels, and even have promiscuous sex," said a *People's Daily* article published in connection with Kang's travels. Under Kang's direction, Party trusties would register guests and conduct security patrols; residents of dormitories would dine in a mess hall, reducing the danger of excessive private consumption; and cadres would study political texts together, exercise together, and attend plays and films together.

Kang thought that by directly controlling the family lives of the common people and regulating the time they could spend with their sexual partners through a dormitory roster administered by the commissars, the Party could transform the workers into mindless robots entirely at the disposal of the nation's rulers. In the guise of calling for pure communism, Kang advocated a slave society. In October 1958—at the zenith of the Great Leap Forward—while inspecting Yangquan, a coal-mining town in Shanxi where sexually separated living quarters had been introduced, Kang claimed that the new living arrangements "created the preconditions for establishing urban communes." All of which, he insisted, amounted to "revolutionary measures for urban social life, a good method for cultivating the new Communist man." And to cadres at People's University in Peking, he praised the realignment of society, using a prophetic phrase: "This is cultural revolution. Cultural revolution is not mystical. Carrying earth, digging up mud, constructing artificial lakes is also part of cultural revolution."

As his visionary policies gained momentum, Kang's personality changed. No longer bedridden, and propelled by a strong sense of self-confidence, he delighted in shocking his audiences with demands for irrational and reckless action. His outrageous comments clearly had an unsettling effect on the committed midlevel cadres who attended his lectures, and he enjoyed their amazement as he set himself apart from the prosaic planners and technocrats.

One of Kang's favorite themes was the need to "do things recklessly" without regard to scientific reality. "What is science?" he provocatively asked teachers in provincial Zhengzhou. "Science is simply acting recklessly. There is nothing mysterious about it." His disregard for the applied sciences came out even more bluntly at a meeting in Hefei, when he declared, "There is nothing special about making reactors, cyclotrons, or rockets. You shouldn't be frightened by these things; as long as you act recklessly you will be able to succeed very quickly . . . You need to have spirit to feel superior to everyone, as if there was no one beside you. . . . You shouldn't care about any First Machine Building Ministry, Second Machine Building Ministry, or any Industrial University or Qinghua University, but just act recklessly and it will be all right." He informed a meeting at Shanghai that "at national day next year if Shanghai's schools are able to launch a third-grade rocket to an altitude of three hundred kilometers they should get three marks . . . A third-grade rocket with a satellite would get five marks. This is very easy. At new year the Shanghainese fire skyrockets, so surely the schools can launch rockets!"

Kang's inflammatory statements echoed Mao's utopian sentiments, but Kang took care to make them seem a logical product of Marxist doctrine. "We should be like Marx, licensed to talk nonsense," he announced to a gathering of educational workers on January 20, 1959. He often repeated that line, without any elaboration or justification as to this supposed license of Marx's. Kang relied instead on his seniority and the cadres' respect for position; those who heard him speak never dared challenge his view of Marx.

His outspoken support for Mao paid off. Kang was an important participant at the second session of the Eighth Party Congress in May 1958, when Mao's proposal for a Great Leap Forward received its final endorsement. Whereas the first session of the Eighth Congress had been the occasion of Kang's demotion, this time he addressed a plenary session of the congress—a signal to all delegates that he had regained his standing as a senior leader.

Further evidence of his rise was presented in August 1958, when he attended the Politburo meeting at the beach resort of Beidaihe. This former colonial playground, graced with rather run-down bungalows built at the turn of the century along the wooded shore of the Bo Hai Gulf, has been the unofficial summer capital of the People's Republic for many years. At the Beidaihe conclave, Chairman Mao's personal vision, the Great Leap Forward, became wildly adventurous. The Politburo decided that China should double its steel production within a year and begin establishing rural communes. Kang's growing influence manifested itself when the concept of educational reform was written into the final resolution adopted by the CCP leaders, sanctifying his field of special interest at the highest level.

Unfortunately, however, the economic policies that flowed from Mao's utopian schemes were based on nothing more than fantasy. As 1958 drew to a close, signals began to appear that the Great Leap Forward and all it represented was plunging China into a world of disasters almost as terrible as the Taiping Rebellion a century before, when a fourteen-year-long uprising led by Hong Xiuquan, a visionary who saw himself as a latter-day Jesus Christ, turned much of central China into a wasteland. During the first phase of the Great Leap Forward, bogus statistics encouraged euphoric leaders to believe that their policies had forged miracles. As turmoil started to engulf China, though, the failure became undeniable. The central leaders decided to slow the establishment of rural communes in late 1958—in effect, shelving a major part of the Great Leap program. Mao made a tactical retreat, leaving the task of economic management in the hands of Liu Shaoqi, Zhou Enlai, Chen Yun, and other technocrats.

Having advocated the Great Leap Forward with such extraordinary energy, Kang found that the calamity it had visited upon China threatened his position. But this time he was lucky. Whereas in the 1942–1944 period Kang alone among the senior leaders had been identified with the terrifying witch-hunt for spies, he now carefully avoided drifting too far from Mao's position. As a result, he did not become a target of other cadres, many of whom were busy covering up their own records as ardent supporters of the Leap.

Kang expanded his influence further in March 1959, when he proposed that a "Theoretical Small Group" should be established to handle ideological matters under the auspices of the Central Group on Culture and Education. As deputy director of the Central Group, Kang got himself appointed head of the new body. For the next few years, he invariably described himself as "director" of the Theoretical

Small Group. He avoided revealing that his unit was subject to the Central Group on Culture and Education. This sleight of hand enabled him to exaggerate his importance in the eyes of Party cadres. He was also appointed deputy chairman of the committee supervising the publication of Mao Zedong's *Selected Works* (Kang edited the fourth volume)—a clear sign of the faith Mao had in him.

By the time the Central Committee met in Lushan in July 1959, most leaders recognized that their main task was to overcome the disasters sweeping the land; few saw any advantage in an open conflict over policy. Mao and his closest allies, including Kang, were prepared to lie low. The more pragmatic economic planners, who might have been expected to blame Mao for the failures of the Great Leap, had their hands full without attempting a challenge to the Chairman. Kang went to Lushan expecting to hear declarations of unity and exhortations to pull together to overcome the famine, waste, and economic dislocation crippling the country.

But the Lushan plenum unexpectedly exploded into controversy, cutting deep cleavages in the Party and setting the stage for the eruption of the Cultural Revolution seven years later. Behind the uproar at Lushan was Marshal Peng Dehuai, a courageous, outspoken, upright, but politically naïve general who had commanded the Chinese forces in Korea. Peng, a chubby, loose-jointed, round-faced man, came from peasant stock in Mao's home province of Hunan. He was one of Mao's favorite generals, and Mao had described him to the Russians as "the brightest star on the Chinese military horizon." Surrounded though he was by devious politicians, Peng never lost his farmer's innocence. Famous for sharing the hardships of his troops, he grew distressed over the suffering he discovered across the land as the toll of the Great Leap Forward started to mount. Misjudging the climate of the plenum, Peng wrote a letter criticizing the policies of economic development, self-reliance, and the distancing of China from the Soviet Union—the core of the Maoist program.

Peng Dehuai's letter to Mao was not intended to challenge the Chairman's authority so much as to candidly describe the pain he had found in China's villages. Nevertheless, Peng's blunt statements inadvertently revealed the nakedness of previous policies, which Mao could only regard as a direct threat. Peng had questioned the legitimacy of the Party, and not even the more pragmatic leaders—Liu

Shaoqi, Peng Zhen, and Deng Xiaoping, all of whom now recognized the deep flaws in Mao's economics—could countenance such an attack on the Party. Peng and his faction were branded "right-wing opportunists."

Peng Dehuai was not alone in criticizing Mao and the Great Leap Forward. He had the support of other Party leaders, including General Huang Kecheng, head of the general staff of the People's Liberation Army; Vice Foreign Minister Luo Fu, a onetime supporter of Wang Ming who had passed Kang in the hierarchy after 1956; and Zhou Xiaozhou, the Party boss in Hunan. The critics were powerless against the combined ranks of the senior leaders, however. Not even Marshal Peng, who as defense minister had day-to-day command of China's army, could defy the magical aura of authority that now surrounded Mao. In the face of united opposition, the dissidents soon lost the battle and were stripped of their offices.* The personnel changes ushered in by this battle were to influence the course of Chinese politics for two decades. Marshal Lin Biao, who had spent most of the 1950s as an invalid, succeeded Peng as defense minister and began carving out a position as a prominent advocate of "Mao Zedong thought." Hunan Party head Zhou Xiaozhou was replaced by Hua Guofeng, another junior member of Mao's circle of admirers.

Far from disturbing Kang, the unexpected turbulence within the Party's upper reaches created the sort of tense and suspicion-filled atmosphere that suited his manipulative style of politics so well. The dissident officials became the targets of four separate committees; assigned to the one that investigated Peng Dehuai, Kang gave a performance full of sarcasm and rancor. He ridiculed Peng's claim of good faith and launched a pitiless attack highlighted by a pun he made on Peng's name. "Dehuai" ("Embracing Virtue") should read "Dehua" ("Getting Hold of China"), according to Kang; his wordplay portrayed the unsophisticated general as a man of boundless

---

* The Chinese Communists were more subtle than their Soviet counterparts in disposing of purge victims. Peng Dehuai became a gardener in the western suburbs of Peking, while Luo Fu was assigned to work in an economic-research institute. The two troublemakers received harsher treatment during the Cultural Revolution. Luo Fu was exiled to a prison south of the Yangtze, where he died in disgrace in 1976; Peng was imprisoned and "struggled," i.e., was manhandled and beaten by Red Guards, in Peking—a process that involved criticism by his former wife, who had divorced him in 1962. He died in 1974.

ambition. At another session, Kang charged that "you have run a club, conducting conspiratorial activity. We also have a club, conducting revolutionary activity." Kang's themes were carefully designed to place the marshal and his allies on one side of the political line and Mao and the rest of the top leaders, including himself, on the other.

Kang used the furor over Peng Dehuai as an excuse to launch a rectification movement aimed at "rightists" and "rightist opportunism"—code words that singled out critics of the Great Leap Forward and anyone connected with them. Kang's campaign against "rightist" tendencies had a modest tally of victims, but it destroyed or disrupted the careers of many officials associated with Marshal Peng and his key allies. One of Kang's targets, Li Zewang (China's ambassador to Moscow during the 1980s), was removed from the Foreign Ministry because of his association with Luo Fu. Yang Xianzhen, a Marxist philosopher and president of the Party School, weathered Kang's attacks for the time being, but he was a marked man from then on.

By the end of the 1950s, Kang had greatly improved his political position. But the radical and utopian visions that had served as the basis for his rise were wearing dangerously thin. Indeed, in the final months of 1959, China faced an awesome crisis as economic disaster threatened to devastate large portions of the country, especially in the rural areas. Terrible drought, combined with Mao's attempt to collectivize all of the nation's farmland and cover the countryside with backyard furnaces where the peasants' tools supposedly would be smelted into first-grade steel, had destroyed the gains of a decade and convinced the peasants that the emperor's heavenly mandate was open to question. The result, already starting to become apparent that winter, was massive starvation. According to one meticulous analysis of population growth statistics, from "16.4 to 29.5 million extra people died during the leap, because of the leap."*

Kang was fully aware of the catastrophes China faced. Measur-

---

* A number of prominent visitors from the West somehow failed to notice the widespread starvation. Edgar Snow, who visited China in 1960, reported in the book he subsequently wrote, *The Other Side of the River,* that he "diligently searched, without success, for starving people or beggars to photograph." British Field Marshal Lord Montgomery visited the following year and declared that there was no malnutrition in China. Mao's idealistic and irrational bid to transform China into a Communist society had devastated the economy, but it still deceived many foreign observers.

ing the political currents carefully, he decided that his specialty should no longer be education, which was reverting to the systems in place before the fantasy years of the Great Leap. He had already discovered the perfect stage for his political magic act: China's dispute with the Communist Party of the Soviet Union.

Chapter XII

PLAYING
THE RUSSIAN CARD

KANG SHENG'S ROLE in the purge of Marshal Peng Dehuai and Peng's allies at Lushan further strengthened Kang's ties with Chairman Mao. By late 1959, however, Kang faced a new problem: Mao started to lose the energy and sense of mission that had driven him for the previous decade. Even though insulated from the realities of everyday life in China, Mao came to recognize the failure of the Great Leap Forward and its catastrophic effect on the country. Stunned by his nation's dire situation, he seemed to suffer a failure of nerve. Mao was so detached from government policy by 1960 that when a visiting American journalist, Edgar Snow, asked about economic-development plans, Mao shocked his guest by admitting, "I don't know."

Hard on the heels of the progress China had made during the first decade of CCP rule, the disaster of the Great Leap Forward devastated national morale. Mao was so depressed by China's internal difficulties that in early 1962 he made a self-criticism before an assembly of seven thousand Party cadres, acknowledging his responsibility for China's nightmare. No longer did he issue ideological directives or talk of a rapid transition to total communism. Mao's status as supreme elder statesman remained beyond challenge, but administrators and economists now ran the country. Mao seemed to be slipping into retirement, and his countrymen did not begrudge him that; he was a revered national leader who deserved a rest after the exertions of war and revolution.

But Kang—now in his early sixties and refreshed by his years in retreat—was hardly ready to join Mao in retirement. One of the few issues that still interested Mao was China's intensifying dispute with the Soviet Union. Kang's four years in Moscow during the 1930s had made him one of China's top Soviet hands. Moreover, much of the dispute with Moscow was expressed in ideological jargon—and Kang was renowned in China as an expert on Marxist theory.

The feud with Moscow enabled Kang to have extensive contact with another very senior official, whom he could cultivate as a secondary patron: the CCP general secretary, Deng Xiaoping. Deputized by Mao to manage China's relations with the Soviet Union, Deng was a man of extraordinary talents. Terse and crisp in speech, he could sum up complex issues in one or two sentences; though small in stature—barely five feet tall—he had enormous energy and willpower. But Deng's qualities did not always win him friends. Zhang Guotao allowed that Deng was "a very intelligent and articulate fellow who regards himself as a political figure of considerable importance" but added that he had "a difficult personality, is arrogant, argumentative, and something of a show-off."

By the time the Communists smashed the Kuomintang in 1949, Deng was political commissar of one of the largest Communist armies. Many of the revolution's military heroes were assigned to ceremonial jobs once the People's Republic was established, but Deng's abilities earned him a place at the center of the new regime. Mao recognized Deng's unusual qualities, pointing him out to Khrushchev when the Soviet leader visited China in 1958: "Do you see that little man over there? He is very intelligent and has a great future ahead of him."

Deng was combative, energetic, and pushy—all traits that helped in prosecuting China's case against the Soviet Union. Beyond that, he had the required balance of foreign and domestic experience. In the first half of the 1920s, in France, he had belonged to a group of Chinese Communists that included Zhou Enlai and Li Lisan. Deng devoted his time to political agitation, earning the nickname "Doctor Mimeograph" from his printing of radical pamphlets. From Paris he went to Moscow, where he attended Sun Yat-sen University for almost a year, then returned to China by late 1927, ready to match his experiences abroad with years of campaigning on the revolutionary battlegrounds of rural China. He led Communist troops in the southern province of Guangxi, joined the main Communist base in Jiangxi, made the Long March, and took part in the Zunyi meeting that opened the way for Mao to become supreme leader. Thoroughly steeped in the Chinese Communist movement when the dispute with the Soviet Union broke out, Deng was an obvious choice to represent the Maoist cause.

Both Kang and Deng had backgrounds in domestic and international affairs, and when they started to work together against the Soviet "revisionists," they discovered a natural affinity: their Russian experiences had left them both with a strong dislike of the Soviet Union. Deng's suspicion of Nikita Khrushchev and the rest of the Soviet leadership complemented Kang's hatred of almost everything Russian. But they agreed that the Soviet Union had one virtue: the legacy of Joseph Stalin.*

Tension between Chinese and Soviet Communists dated back to the 1920s. Many Chinese Communists had blamed their vulnerability to KMT treachery in 1927 on the tactics devised by Russian advisers like Mikhail Borodin. The controversy caused by one of Borodin's successors, Pavel Mif, when he installed Wang Ming as Party boss in 1931, added to anti-Soviet sentiment. The Long March was also punctuated by squabbles between the proponents of Soviet methods and Mao Zedong and his followers, who favored a more China-oriented strategy. By the late 1940s, many Chinese Communists suspected that the Soviet Union was attempting to erode China's independence. Some cadres feared that Soviet influence over the Social Affairs Department, especially in northeastern China, was growing to intolerable proportions. According to a Chinese intelligence officer stationed in Dalian, "When it comes to differences of opinion between the MVD [the Soviet internal affairs ministry] and the Social Affairs Department, the former gently reminds the Chinese that all communists are brothers and that elder brothers know best." Chinese cadres also suspected that Tass representatives in China were using their journalistic cover to investigate senior officials and gain leverage over them.

The atrocities committed by Soviet troops who occupied Manchuria after the Japanese surrender further enraged the Chinese. Russian soldiers raped Chinese as well as Japanese and European women,

---

* Now that Deng has become the most revered figure in China, this phase of Kang's career, especially his connection with Deng, is a sensitive issue. Anything that threatens to tarnish Deng's reputation is extremely controversial. Mainland sources such as "Zhongkan" and Lin Qingshan carefully omit detailed discussions of Kang's contribution to the Sino-Soviet dispute, let alone the relationship he developed with Deng.

plundered shops, and shot the Chinese mobs who challenged them—on one occasion killing 750 Chinese. Meanwhile, at least one Russian general in China made a fortune trading in diamonds. Soviet forces also stripped the Japanese-built factories in Manchuria of almost every piece of machinery before they withdrew to Russian territory.

But during the early years of the People's Republic, the antagonism that many Chinese felt toward Moscow gave way to a warm camaraderie. Russian experts came to China to help rebuild the shattered economy, and large numbers of Chinese went to Moscow to study engineering and electronics and learn how to build dams, factories, steelworks, and aircraft. Trade between the two states grew rapidly, and hundreds of contracts and agreements were signed. Many Chinese even gave their children Russian-sounding names like Sasha, Nana, Lisha, and Doya.

Although economic and personal relations between the two countries flourished, Khrushchev's repudiation of Stalin and his crimes at the Twentieth Congress of the Soviet Communist Party in February 1956 released a new and dangerous element that in time turned the warmth to ice. Many Chinese leaders viewed de-Stalinization as an implicit challenge to the legitimacy of both the collective system they were seeking to create in China and the international Communist movement. Mao and his allies had sometimes disagreed with Stalin's policies, but they had never questioned the methods he used to build a modern economy or his position as Lenin's rightful heir.* In particular, the Chinese leaders recognized that the Soviet attack upon Stalin jeopardized Mao's position in China.

Compounding the problem was Mao's naïve belief that China could accelerate its economic progress and catch up with the Soviet Union and the West. Soviet leaders began complaining in private to their Chinese counterparts that Mao's adventurous ideas and policies would bring ruin to China. To the Soviets, the Great Leap Forward, the establishment of communes, and the obsession with village steel production reflected an arrogant and hopelessly unrealistic revolutionary fervor. Moreover, Chinese foreign policy, which was militantly hostile toward the United States and one of its Asian outposts,

* So abiding is Stalin's place in the Chinese Communist firmament that his picture is still displayed on National Day next to portraits of Mao, Marx, and Engels—decades after his image disappeared from billboards in his own country.

Taiwan, seemed dangerously reckless to military planners in Moscow. In 1958, the Chinese began bombarding Quemoy and Matsu, two small islands just off the mainland coast held by KMT troops, adding to Russian worries about China.

When China's economic policies began to fail, relations with the Soviet Union deteriorated even further. Mao had gloated during the early, heady stages of the Great Leap that China was ideologically more progressive than the Soviet Union—a boast that made the failure of the Great Leap a doubly painful loss of face. As they watched Chinese animosity grow, Soviet leaders started to fear that the gigantic country to Russia's east, the source of massive invasions in centuries past, might rise against them yet again.

The two sides dressed up the quarrel in the convoluted language of ideological debates about "the inevitability of war," the role of "national revolutions," and "the validity of Lenin," but essentially the conflict was over national security. The Chinese feared that the Soviets did not respect their interests and tended to treat China as a second-class citizen in the socialist community. The Chinese saw the United States—which had military bases in Japan, Taiwan, and Korea—as a hostile imperialist. Khrushchev and his Russian colleagues, by contrast, believed that the United States was in an accommodating mode, and that Soviet interests called for tensions with Washington to be reduced in the name of "peaceful coexistence." Khrushchev's lack of regard for Mao's demands for a hard-line anti-American posture made it appear to the Chinese that in the Soviet view of the world only the United States and the Soviet Union really mattered.

Conflicting approaches to various regional problems added to the fundamental disagreement between the two Communist powers. In 1959, China became embroiled in a border conflict with India, which had given refuge to the Dalai Lama in the aftermath of China's bloody suppression of a revolt by Tibetan nationalists. The Soviet government, ignoring what China saw as the demands of socialist fraternity, refused to blame India and support China. Soviet sympathy for "bourgeois" nationalists rather than the "socialist" Chinese was also reflected in Russia's support for Indonesia when China fell out with the Sukarno regime over its treatment of the Chinese community there. The leaders in Peking concluded that the Soviet Union was competing with China for influence in Asia, which they believed should be their exclusive sphere of influence.

*   *   *

Kang had impressive credentials as a general in the war against Soviet domination. He had spent four years in Moscow; he had been an alternate member of the Executive Committee of the Comintern; he knew enough Russian to follow what was being said on the other side of the table; he understood, or so he boasted, how the Soviet system worked; he knew many senior Soviet officials; and after his return to China in 1937, he had treated the Soviet representatives in Yan'an with enough contempt to show that his experiences in Moscow had not seduced him in favor of the Russians. In Mao's eyes, according to Mao's longtime associate Dong Biwu, Kang was the only Moscow-trained Communist who remained Chinese in thinking and reasoning.

Kang had been involved with the delicate question of China's relations with the Soviet Union and the socialist bloc practically from the instant he returned to public life in January 1956. His selection as the Chinese Communist representative at the Socialist Unity Party Congress in Berlin in April 1956 indicated that he was seen in Peking as a man with a background in East European and Soviet affairs.

In mid-November 1956, Kang received another assignment, which solidified his reputation as an expert on the ideological issues threatening China's relations with the Soviet Union. He was commissioned by the CCP Politburo to oversee the drafting of a pivotal article that appeared in *The People's Daily* on December 29, 1956, under the title "More on the Historical Experience of the Dictatorship of the Proletariat." More than ten thousand words long, Kang's article was the sequel to a much shorter report published eight months earlier; together, the two documents expressed the Chinese response to Khrushchev's accusations against Stalin and an assessment of other dramatic events during 1956, such as Soviet suppression of the anti-Communist revolt in Hungary. These issues were extremely important to the Chinese, touching as they did on China's relations with the Soviet Union and the place of Mao, who was open to charges of creating a personality cult similar to Stalin's.

Under Kang's supervision, the Chinese document avoided direct criticism of Khrushchev, but its defiant assertion that Stalin's achievements overshadowed his mistakes left no doubt that China's rulers disagreed with the Soviet leader. Stalin was "a great Marxist–Leninist revolutionary. . . . [He] always stood at the head of historical developments and guided the struggle; he was an implacable foe of imperialism." But Stalin had also made mistakes: he had "a tendency towards great-nation chauvinism" (a reference to his attempts to impose his policies on the Chinese Communists), and he had committed abuses in "the suppression of counterrevolution" (the mass purges he had inflicted on Soviet society). Bringing up the purges could have embarrassed Kang, who himself had been in charge of liquidating "counterrevolutionaries" among the Chinese community during his four years in Moscow. Kang was also seen in China as one of the grand architects of the equivalent Chinese campaigns to eradicate any elements that could not fit into the new society—landlords, enemy agents, bourgeois intellectuals, and corrupt officials—starting with the Yan'an Rectification Movement.

Kang deftly endorsed the need to suppress enemies of the new order: "Stalin . . . punished many counterrevolutionaries whom it was necessary to punish." At the same time, Kang conceded that Stalin had "wronged many loyal communists and honest citizens." Kang's commentary did more than affirm the need to root out the opponents of the revolution; it suggested that in some ways Stalin had not gone far enough in imposing his system on his own country. According to Kang, Stalin had only "in the main" succeeded in his task—a carefully qualified wording implying that some Soviet reactionaries had escaped. Fear of spies and enemy agents who had eluded the purges, establishing the need for continued vigilance, was exactly the atmosphere Kang wanted to create in China.

Kang struck again in June 1958, with a stinging attack on Yugoslav "revisionism," blasting Tito as a lackey of the United States. Kang's article—"Yugoslav Revisionism Exactly Meets the Needs of the American Imperialists"—utterly condemned Tito and his policy of seeking an accommodation with Washington. Kang accused Tito of betraying the socialist camp, of having supported the "counterrevolutionary rebellion"* in Hungary, and of defending American imperialism at a time when it was in retreat and "the East Wind was prevailing over the West Wind."

Kang's words warned of the growing differences between Moscow and Peking. He ridiculed Tito's claim that Yugoslavia was seeking "peace and international cooperation"—the sort of language the

---

* Some of the language Kang used in the Sino-Soviet dispute is still part of the Chinese political lexicon more than thirty years later. "Counterrevolutionary rebellion" was the term China's leaders used to describe the student demonstrations in Tiananmen Square as recently as 1989.

Soviet Union was using to justify a relaxation in tensions with the United States. Kang also quoted liberally from American newspapers and the *Congressional Record* in order to prove that the United States viewed support for Yugoslavia as a way to subvert communism. Kang wrote, "The spokesman of the American bourgeois classes, [political commentator Walter] Lippmann, said . . . that to let so-called 'Titoism' spread among the socialist countries is in America's real interests." Tito was obviously selling out to American imperialism, and, Kang implied, so would any other Communist governments that cooperated with the United States.

Aware that several leaders, including Liu Shaoqi, Zhou Enlai, and Canton Party chief Tao Zhu, favored a more cautious and moderate approach toward the Soviet Union, Kang moved in 1959 to intensify divisions within the Chinese elite, inflame passions, and flaunt his nationalistic credentials.* Above all, he wanted to impress upon Mao that he, Kang Sheng, and only he, had enough courage and insight to successfully defend the interests of both China and the Chairman against the increasingly outrageous demands of the Soviets.

Mao's clash with Peng Dehuai at Lushan in August 1959 gave Kang his first chance to play on the differences among his colleagues. Peng had close ties to many Soviet officials and generals—he had worked with the Russians as commander of the Chinese forces during the Korean War, and as defense minister he had traveled extensively in the Soviet Union. Indeed, Peng had returned from Moscow imme-

---

* Mao, Deng Xiaoping, Peng Zhen (the mayor of Peking), and Kang were the Chinese rulers most suspicious of the Russians. Other Chinese leaders, like Liu Shaoqi, viewed the Soviet Union more pragmatically, as a source of much-needed economic help. Liu, who was free of the emotional antagonism toward Moscow that motivated men like Kang, argued for moderation in internal debates about the course of relations with Russia; he was regarded by the Soviets as a friend within the Chinese leadership, according to Soviet officials interviewed in Peking in 1990. Liu had not experienced some of the events that shaped the outlooks of his comrades. He had not participated in the dispute with the Twenty-eight Bolsheviks that led to Mao's victory at the Zunyi meeting. He also had personal ties to the Soviet Union. After 1949, several of Liu's children studied in Moscow; one son, Liu Yunbin, married a Russian; and another, Liu Yunruo, had a Russian lover whom he wished to marry. Neither relationship lasted beyond 1960—Yunbin divorced his wife, and Yunruo never married his girlfriend—but the romantic ties showed an openness on Liu's part toward the Russians that many Chinese leaders did not share. Moreover, although Liu and his sons remained in China, one of his brothers-in-law, Zhang Fan, defected to the Soviet Union in 1960.

diately before the meeting in Lushan. Moreover, Marshal Peng's main ally at Lushan, Vice Foreign Minister Luo Fu, had been one of the Twenty-eight Bolsheviks and was ambassador to Moscow in the mid-1950s. In the aftermath of the Lushan plenum, Kang seized on Peng's links with the Soviet Union to insinuate that he was a stooge of the Russians. Peng's attack on Mao was not simply an internal challenge to the Chairman's authority, Kang implied; it was the work of a conspiratorial clique that stretched all the way to Moscow.

Kang also accused Li Lisan, then a Party leader in northeastern China, of "maintaining illicit relations with a foreign country"—Chinese Communist jargon for acting as a Soviet agent. Kang's charges did not lead to Li's persecution until the Cultural Revolution, but Kang used them in 1959 to spread suspicion that Soviet spies had penetrated the Chinese hierarchy. It was a rerun of events in Yan'an twenty years earlier: Kang knew that his claims would make Mao wary of spies and traitors within his own camp and look to colleagues like Kang whose loyalty had been tested.

Several months after the Lushan plenum, Khrushchev visited China for the tenth anniversary of the establishment of the People's Republic. Although mutual suspicion was already eroding trust between Mao and his guest, the Chinese gave the Soviet leader the correct, full red-carpet treatment. On October 5, however, while Khrushchev was still in Peking, Kang delivered an address filled with anti-Soviet rhetoric to a group of students who had recently returned from Moscow. In his speech, Kang boasted of China's achievements over the decade following the Communist victory. Well aware that living conditions in China were even more primitive than those in the Soviet Union, Kang asserted that China should be judged by its ideological perfection instead of by economic standards or statistics. He placed special emphasis on China's eradication of the capitalist system of ownership—an implicit claim that China had reached the same stage of socialist development as the Soviet Union. He also expanded on the theme that although private ownership had disappeared in China, class struggle continued in the realm of political thought, suggesting that the Soviet Union, despite its socialist economy, was potentially a class enemy.

In Kang's view, anything Russian deserved disparagement. Soviet policy was not the only sign of Russia's inferiority to China; even its art and literature were second-rate. Discussing the contents of textbooks at a conference on the social sciences, Kang introduced the theme of eradicating "superstitious faith in foreigners" and singled out Russians as his main examples. "The poems written by our workers and peasants," he declared, "surpass Mayakovsky and Pushkin a billion times."

Kang made a bald attempt to use the dispute with Moscow to underscore his loyalty to Mao when he discussed Mao's role and the question of "personality cult" at a December 1959 meeting of cadres from the Academy of Military Science and the Supreme Military Academy. Kang insinuated that anyone who argued for a softer approach to the Soviet Union was allied with Mao's Chinese critics. Two types of people, Kang said, resisted Mao Zedong Thought. One faction (Kang cited Chen Duxiu, Wang Ming, and Peng Dehuai as examples) opposed Mao openly, while another faction fought Mao secretly. Kang did not name the members of the second group, but the phrases he attributed to them—"respecting Marx" and "it is impossible to surpass Marx"—pointed to anyone who supported the Soviets. Whoever adhered to the orthodox Soviet view of Marxism in the post-Stalin era, in short, was Mao's secret enemy. Once again, Kang's address was specially directed to the ears of the Chairman, who, as Kang knew, would receive a transcript of his remarks.

China's leaders began secretly reassessing relations with the Soviet Union toward the end of 1959. Before long, in January 1960, Kang flew to Moscow as head of the Chinese observer delegation to the Warsaw Pact Consultative Conference—his first public identification as a key player in China's feud with the Soviet Union.

Exactly how the Chinese happened to attend the 1960 Warsaw Pact meeting has never been fully clarified. Public statements at the time fudged the question of whether the Chinese observer delegation was formally invited or sent on China's initiative. As to two other observer states, Mongolia and North Korea, the Soviet press at first reported that they were there "by invitation," which later was changed to "at their own request," as if to finesse any possible controversy over the apparent failure to invite China. If the Russians had deliberately snubbed the Chinese, Kang was an excellent choice for gate-crasher—his ruthlessness and anti-Russian bias qualified him to state China's views forcefully.

Two other cadres with an extensive background in Sino-Soviet matters accompanied Kang. One was General Wu Xiuquan, whose connections with Soviet officials dated back to the 1920s. Wu, a burly and gruff intelligence expert, had studied at Sun Yat-sen University in Moscow and later interpreted for Otto Braun, the Comintern military adviser attached to the Red Army during the Long March. During the early 1950s, Wu was the vice foreign minister responsible for Soviet and East European affairs and, more important, a deputy director of the International Liaison Department of the CCP. The other member of Kang's mission was Liu Xiao, then the Chinese ambassador to Moscow. Liu had been a colleague of Kang's since Shanghai, where Liu participated in the workers' uprisings of 1926 and 1927. Arrested twice, first by the French police and then by the British, Liu spent several years in Shanghai jails. After his release in 1931, he moved to the Communist stronghold in Jiangxi. Liu finally returned to Shanghai, where he was one of the top Communist agents during the war against Japan.

Kang addressed the Warsaw Pact conference on February 4, 1960, delivering a subtle, almost sarcastic critique of Russian foreign policy that became a milestone in deteriorating Sino-Soviet relations. His speech was the first statement that publicly outlined the differences between the two sides; while the Soviet press did not publish it, *The Peking Review*, China's foreign propaganda magazine, printed the full text. The ideas expressed had been approved at a conference of CCP leaders in Shanghai in late January, but the total skepticism about Soviet motives in Kang's remarks was consistent with the views he had been promoting since reaching Yan'an more than twenty years earlier.

The tone and implications of Kang's Moscow speech were profoundly anti-Soviet, but to establish his revolutionary credentials he began with a blistering attack on the United States. "The actions of the United States prove fully that its imperialistic nature will not change. American imperialism still remains the archenemy of world peace," he declared. Not only was America undeniably an aggressor, "but United States imperialism, hostile to the Chinese people, has always adopted a discriminatory attitude against our country in international affairs."

Kang's condemnation of United States foreign policy contained nothing new. Since the Communist conquest of the mainland in 1949, Mao and his colleagues had viewed the United States as the most formidable threat to China's security. The United States had sent an army to Korea that had fought the Chinese "volunteers" in a war that seemed likely to spill over into Chinese territory. The United States had also deployed ships and warplanes to stop Mao's armies from invading Taiwan and smashing Chiang Kai-shek and the KMT. Besides its direct confrontations with the Communist government in Peking, Washington was actively expanding its influence in other parts of Asia: helping to rebuild China's most bitter twentieth-century enemy, Japan, and conducting a wide range of anti-Communist activities in Thailand, Vietnam, and Laos.

But Kang did not stop at identifying the United States as a dangerous adversary of China. He introduced a new theme that gave a completely unexpected direction to his speech. "The United States ruling circles," Kang observed, "do not try to hide the fact that . . . their . . . 'strategy to win victory by peace' " meant "wrecking the unity of the peace forces of the world and disintegrating the socialist camp. . . . They are even dreaming of a so-called 'peaceful evolution'* in the socialist countries." Everyone present knew that Kang was referring to Khrushchev's dialogue with President Eisenhower; no one at the meeting could have understood his words as anything but an absolute rejection of Soviet policy and of Moscow's attempts to reach an understanding with Washington. Kang held back from spelling out the full implications of his argument, but his message was clear: the Russians were selling out China for the sake of peaceful coexistence with the Americans.

Kang also elaborated on the internal threat to the socialist countries—"revisionism," as he called it. Citing Yugoslavia, he declared that "the Chinese people . . . have always considered that the modern revisionists of Yugoslavia are renegades to the Communist movement, that revisionism is the main danger in the present Communist movement and that it is necessary to wage a resolute struggle against revisionism." Kang's statement was aimed directly at Khrushchev, who had gone to great lengths to cultivate Tito.

Kang's absolute rejection of the Soviet world view infuriated the Russians. A heated exchange followed between him and Khrushchev, who launched a personal attack on Kang's status. "You don't have the qualifications to debate with me," the irate Khrushchev shouted. "I am general secretary of the Communist Party of the Soviet Union, but you are just an alternate member of the Chinese Communist

---

* "Peaceful evolution" is another phrase in the Communist lexicon that has stood the test of time. The Chinese leaders used it to describe the encouragement the Western countries gave to the 1989 democratic movement in China.

Politburo." Kang fired back immediately in his ungrammatical Russian, "Your credentials are much more shallow than mine. In 1931 I was a member of the Politburo standing committee. In 1935 I was an alternate member of the executive committee of the Comintern. At that time you were not even a member of the Central Committee!"

Kang's personal relationship with Mao enabled him to misreport the course of this and other meetings any way he liked. He used his brief to provide Mao with accounts—often grossly distorted—that intensified rather than eased the dispute with Moscow. At the Warsaw Pact meeting, for instance, Khrushchev had turned to his colleagues, pointed at the aged Otto Kuusinen (a member of the Politburo responsible for international affairs), and commented, "We have some old boys here, and we should say goodbye to them as we do an old shoe." When Kang returned to China, however, he told Mao that Khrushchev had referred to Mao himself, not Kuusinen, as "an old shoe"—a version of events that reinforced the Chairman's expectations and fears. As a result, Mao took delight in referring to Khrushchev after that as "the bald-headed one." By late 1961, "Old Baldy" had become a pet term for Khrushchev in Chinese ruling circles.

In his duplicity, Kang succeeded in igniting a personal feud between the supreme leaders of the two major Communist powers. One of the Russians present along with Kang at three meetings between representatives of the two countries, Mikhail L. Titarenko, declared in 1989 that Kang "played a very evil role, poisoning the atmosphere and subverting confidence between the USSR and China." Whenever Kang attended Sino-Soviet meetings, according to Titarenko, he was introduced to the Soviets as Mao's personal representative. Titarenko attributed two objectives to Kang's mission:

- To cause trouble between the two sides and prevent them from reaching an accord, especially when the naturally conciliatory—and, in Mao's mind, less perceptive—Zhou Enlai was there.
- To act as the eyes and ears for Mao, who never attended such sessions.

Other Chinese delegates, according to Titarenko, dared not contradict whatever story Kang related to Mao, who believed that Kang alone—given his ability to speak Russian, his years in Moscow, and his insight into human nature—understood the nuances of what was happening and could read between the lines. Moreover, Titarenko speculated that Kang always foresaw what Mao wanted to hear, rarely paid attention to what was actually taking place at meetings with Russian leaders, and reported things according to his own caprices. Mao personally testified to Kang's central role as the medium for his views. In an interview with American journalist Anna Louise Strong in January 1964, Mao introduced Kang to Strong and five other foreigners, including Sidney Rittenberg, an American who worked at Radio Peking. "Khrushchev says I am full of empty talk," Mao said. "Well, I want you to meet my Minister for Empty Talk, Comrade Kang Sheng."*

In Soviet eyes, Kang became a diabolical figure. Titarenko recalled that Kang spoke in a strange way, keeping his upper and lower teeth together, "which gave one a very unpleasant feeling. He had a very stern and heavy look; he could freeze you with his stare. Everyone was afraid of him. On the Soviet side we compared him to Beria. You could see at first glance that he was a very evil and ruthless person." Kang usually had cigarette ashes scattered on his mustache or his upper lip, according to Titarenko: a touch that might have made Kang look like a fatherly, absent-minded professor. But Kang's overall demeanor, enhanced by his thick eyeglasses, was very different from that.

"I am not a strong advocate of Sigmund Freud," Titarenko declared, "but what Freud said matched Kang Sheng one hundred percent. Although Kang was not unusually short by Chinese standards, he somehow *looked* small," primarily because he was very thin and had an extremely narrow face. "He was a true example of a small man with great ambition. He was extremely envious of healthy, handsome, attractive people. The Chinese have a saying that when a man

---

* Sidney Rittenberg told the authors that Mao meant "Empty Talk" as a compliment to Kang in the context of the Sino-Soviet fight. Ironically, Khrushchev was ousted from power nine months after Mao's conversation with Strong, while Kang rode higher and higher. Rittenberg first went to China in 1945 as a U.S. Army interpreter but stayed on to work with the CCP. He spent two long periods in prison (1949–1955 and 1968–1977). His first imprisonment came after Stalin arrested Anna Louise Strong, who was planning to collaborate with Rittenberg on a biography of Mao, and told the Chinese that both Rittenberg and Strong were American spies. Next, Rittenberg was jailed for supporting a losing faction during the Cultural Revolution. Nevertheless, he was always on good terms with many senior Communist officials. He left China in 1979 and now lives in the United States.

is old, all of his qualities come out. I think all of Kang Sheng's evil qualities came out as he grew old."

Another Soviet observer at talks between the two sides gave a somewhat different account. Fyodor M. Burlatsky remembered Kang as a very homely and gloomy individual who "usually just sat there and spoke nothing" but never missed a trick.

Once he had made public China's political differences with the Kremlin at the Warsaw Pact meeting, Kang moved to intensify the dispute and to increase his capacity to exploit it. Neither side was prepared to go beyond Kang's double entendres; neither Mao nor Khrushchev wanted to be the first to breach socialist unity. But China had seized the public initiative. To keep pressure on the Soviet Union, the Chinese published a series of articles attacking the Soviet ideological position and seeking to justify China's stance by portraying Khrushchev as a heretic who had forsaken the Marxist–Leninist tradition. A number of writers helped compose these articles, but Kang was the editor in charge and responsible for circulating drafts to Mao and other senior leaders.

The first essay Kang edited after the Warsaw Pact conference was "Long Live Leninism!" which the Chinese theoretical journal *Red Flag* published on April 16, 1960, six days before the ninetieth anniversary of Lenin's birth. Beyond repeating many of the points Kang had made in Moscow, this article gave extensive consideration to whether technological change had outmoded Leninism. Central to Khrushchev's theory was the proposition that modern military technology—nuclear weapons in particular—had rendered obsolete Lenin's belief that war with imperialism was inevitable. In "Long Live Leninism!" however, Kang and his scribes argued that weapons were not as important as "the People," and that war with the imperialists was not necessarily to be feared.

Although "Long Live Leninism!" asserted that China loved peace, it rang with apocalyptic prophecies of a world war: "On the debris of a dead imperialism, the victorious people would create very swiftly a civilization a thousand times higher than the capitalist system, and a truly beautiful future for themselves." Under Kang's analysis of global developments, many millions of human casualties would be an acceptable price to pay for the creation of a "beautiful future."

At the same time that they scorned Soviet fears of a mutually destructive nuclear war, Kang and his group presented Mao, not

Khrushchev, as the legitimate heir of Lenin. As if that did not sufficiently glorify Mao, they also emphasized the absolute correctness of Mao's pet projects: the Great Leap Forward and the people's communes. "Long Live Leninism!" appeared during a period when Mao's policies of the late 1950s had combined with unusually harsh weather to cause a famine that killed between sixteen and twenty-five million people; nevertheless, Kang and his staff praised Mao's policies for having "inspired the initiative and revolutionary spirit of the masses throughout the country." In short, the article was riddled with Kang's illusionist tricks: while denying China's economic problems, he promised a "beautiful future" following a global holocaust—and still managed to pander outrageously to Mao.

Together with Deng Xiaoping and Peng Zhen, Kang spent the next five years plotting the outlines and implementation of the feud with the Soviets, who made it clear that they reciprocated China's hostility. In July 1960, the Russians suddenly withdrew all of the thirteen hundred experts and advisers they had sent to work in China—a totally unexpected gesture that even today the Chinese characterize as an act of betrayal. That November, all but six of the world's eighty-seven Communist parties gathered in Moscow to celebrate the anniversary of the Russian Revolution, but the occasion produced only a cosmetic and temporary truce between Moscow and Peking. Deng did most of the talking for the Chinese side at this meeting, once engaging Khrushchev in an exchange of recriminations. Kang again served as Mao's personal envoy, keeping a close eye on the proceedings and making sure that the Chinese side agreed to no compromises.

The November 1960 meeting in Moscow, which showed that there was no easy way to bridge the suspicion and resentment separating the two sides, marked the end of a phase. Within months, the Chinese and the Russians each began visibly recruiting advocates from the international Communist movement. Kang actively sought the support of other Communist parties for the Chinese position, participating in international conferences, receiving visitors, and supervising the development of ideological arguments that justified China's stance.

Kang's relationship with Deng Xiaoping grew ever closer during this period. The two journeyed in September 1961 to Pyongyang, the North Korean capital (founded, legend claims, by an ancestor of Confucius) on the banks of the Taedong River. Ostensibly, Deng and

Kang were attending the Fourth Congress of the Korean Workers Party, but they used their visit to ensure that this strategically located state, bordering on China's eastern frontier but heavily dependent on Russian assistance, did not support the Soviet cause. They achieved some success: Kim Il Sung, the North Korean dictator, maintained a careful balance between the two contending parties for more than ten years.

Kang, Zhou Enlai, and several other Chinese leaders escalated the quarrel with the Russians at the Twenty-second Congress of the Soviet Communist Party held in Moscow in October 1961. While in the Soviet capital, the Chinese representatives dramatized their differences with the Russians by laying a wreath in memory of Stalin at the mausoleum in Red Square where both Lenin and Stalin were buried. The Chinese tribute to Stalin did not prevent Khrushchev from using the congress as an occasion to publicly expose the extent of the dead dictator's appalling crimes. A few days afterward, perhaps intending to embarrass the Chinese delegation, Khrushchev had Stalin's corpse removed from the tomb.

Khrushchev's catalog of Stalin's crimes and the subsequent desecration of his tomb were not the only provocations the Chinese envoys experienced. Vyacheslav Molotov, Stalin's trusted colleague and a longtime friend of the CCP, was humiliated and expelled from the Soviet Communist Party while Zhou and Kang were in Moscow. Molotov's final fall from grace was a further reminder that China had no allies among the new generation of Soviet leaders.

Khrushchev goaded the Chinese delegates even further by launching a vitriolic attack on Albania, the Balkan state that by then fully backed China's defiance of the Soviets. In his fury, Khrushchev called Albania's leaders "murderers and criminals"; Zhou, regarded by foreigners as "the brainiest" of the CCP leaders, responded sarcastically that the Russian's words "cannot be regarded as a serious Marxist–Leninist attitude." Zhou and the rest of the Chinese group, including Kang, then walked out of the congress. They returned to Peking several days ahead of schedule—as Sino-Soviet bonds continued to unravel.

Kang's reputation was greatly enhanced at home by his continuous verbal assaults on the Soviet Union, and in September 1962 the CCP Central Committee appointed him to the Party Secretariat, the key office that managed day-to-day affairs. CCP general secretary Deng Xiaoping, who directed the Secretariat, could have vetoed any appointment, so Kang's promotion was additional evidence of the growing relationship between the two men.

The Sino-Soviet dispute brought Kang further rewards in November 1962, when he was assigned the sensitive task of drafting a series of articles opposing "revisionism." These essays were written by a special group of propaganda writers, including Zhou Yang, Deng Liqun, and Wu Lengxi. Much of their writing was done in the Diaoyutai State Guesthouse, a collection of large, square, Soviet-style residential villas and offices built in the 1950s on the grounds of an ancient imperial hunting park in western Peking. Kang occupied the Number Eight Villa, a white, two-story structure with high ceilings and cavernous rooms. In these quarters, he had an office with a large desk and filing cabinets; a meeting room furnished with sofas crowned with embroidered antimacassars; a dining room; and a small cinema. The villa also contained bedrooms that Kang sometimes used instead of returning to his home in Small Stone Bridge Lane. Kang's servants, drivers, cooks, and guards usually lived in the villa, while his secretaries would sleep there overnight whenever he required their presence. It was in this well-equipped building that Kang worked up the case against "Soviet revisionism."

Deng Xiaoping was the nominal supervisor of the propagandists, but Kang was the man in practical control. Kang performed this task for two years, consulting closely with Deng but always incorporating Mao's views. The polemical essays Kang and his group produced were tough, argumentative, and aggressive, further blocking any attempts to repair the Sino-Soviet relationship. Together with "Long Live Leninism!" the new ideological broadsides against the Soviet Union were known as "the Nine Criticisms"—final proof of the break between the two Communist giants. With their publication, there was no going back.*

Kang accompanied Deng to Moscow for further Party-to-Party

---

* Hu Yaobang attempted to conceal Kang's contribution to "the Nine Criticisms" and advanced a series of convoluted arguments that derided but did not deny Kang's involvement in what the Chinese still regard as a positive achievement: China's campaign against Soviet ideological domination. Hu avoided an outright disavowal of Kang's role, citing instead a series of rhetorical questions posed by other Chinese leaders and insinuating that Kang had had no part in the dispute. Hu's remarks were designed to prevent Kang's ghost from haunting current Chinese policy. Hu also seemed eager to conceal Kang's association with Deng Xiaoping, Hu's own patron at the time. Deng, of course, emerged in 1978 as China's preeminent leader.

discussions in July 1963. A photograph taken by the New China News Agency at the Peking airport upon their return from Moscow shows Kang, dressed in a neat gray Mao suit, cigarette in hand, smiling happily at the applauding crowds. The Sino-Soviet talks had failed to bridge the gap between the two nations; no wonder this photo is one of the few that shows Kang grinning.

Kang made his final visit to Moscow in November 1964 to observe the forty-seventh anniversary of the Russian Revolution. With Khrushchev ousted a month earlier, the Chinese, led by Zhou Enlai, sought to explore whether the new Soviet regime was any more sympathetic toward China. The two sides made some progress, reaching limited agreement on bilateral cooperation. Kang, however, was up to his old tricks. Marshal Rodion Malinovsky, the Soviet defense minister, noting that "the two old men"—Mao and Khrushchev—had disliked each other, called for the two sides to negotiate in a spirit of friendliness. But Kang seized upon Malinovsky's words to halt further progress. Upon returning to China, he told Mao that Malinovsky had referred to the deposed Khrushchev and had suggested that the Chinese should follow their example and overthrow Mao.

The collapse of China's relations with the Soviet Union made the early 1960s good years for Kang Sheng. As usual, he was able to gain the most for himself at the expense of others. This time, strife between the two leading nations in the Communist bloc allowed him to manipulate Mao and lesser Chinese leaders for his personal benefit.

Chapter XIII

OPERA LOVER

FOR CHINA, its people, and its rulers, the early 1960s were painful years. The aftermath of the Great Leap Forward threatened to ruin the economy and starve millions of people, and the deterioration of Sino-Soviet relations left China isolated internationally. Mao, mortified over China's dreadful circumstances, spent long periods in seclusion, usually in his villa at Hangzhou. In Peking, Liu Shaoqi, Zhou Enlai, Deng Xiaoping, Chen Yun, and other mainstream leaders struggled to put the economy back in order and save the country from total collapse.

For Kang Sheng, these years were almost idyllic. The feud with the Russians had given him the perfect opportunity to flaunt his nationalism and his Soviet expertise and thereby restore himself to prominence. The Sino-Soviet dispute was not so demanding, however, that it deprived him of time for pleasure. Kang had claimed on the eve of the Great Leap Forward that CCP leaders engaged in as much "mental labor" as any students but, unlike students, had no holidays from work. During the early 1960s, though, Kang got his share of relaxation, travel, and entertainment. He toured China's scenic and historic sights and collected antiques. But one activity fascinated him above all others: watching traditional plays and operas and imposing his views on the country's stages.

The theater had been a form of popular entertainment in China for more than a thousand years. Combining singing, acting, dancing, acrobatics, and instrumental music into a single spectacle, Chinese theater was enjoyed by every sector of society in every province. Each area produced a style of its own, using different dialects and reper-toires and catering to local tastes and customs. Peking opera was perhaps the most refined form of theater, but what regional schools of acting lacked in sophistication they often made up for in vitality and bawdiness.

Playwrights frequently drew upon the glorious and tragic legends of Chinese history and literature, but also upon folktales of love, sex, and the supernatural. In Peking, the earthier themes were usually treated with restraint, but elsewhere actors and audiences alike rev-eled in salacious stories filled with double entendre, suggestive scenes, and risqué puns and jokes from regional dialects. The stage also became associated with homosexual prostitution. During the seven-teenth century, the Manchu regime had banned women from per-forming in public; and so in many parts of the country where this rule had been enforced, male actors still portrayed empresses, princesses, widows, prostitutes, and countless court ladies on the Chinese stage well into the twentieth century. In Peking, men who played female roles were chosen for their delicate features and feminine personali-ties, and less successful actors often supplemented their incomes by entering homosexual brothels or servicing Manchu rulers. An aura of homosexuality continued to linger around Peking opera up to the Cultural Revolution and beyond, providing the background to an espionage case involving She Peipu, a classical Chinese actor who passed himself off as a woman so successfully that for many years his French diplomat lover did not realize that he was a man—an episode that served as the source of the play M. Butterfly.

The moral ambiguity permeating the traditional theater pre-sented complicated problems for the Communists. China's new rulers knew they could win greater public support by glorifying Peking opera and its regional equivalents; a "People's Republic" could hardly suppress such a beloved and distinctly Chinese form of entertainment. Yet many of the plays exuded a sense of decadence completely at odds with the Party's puritanical values. So the cultural commissars set out to reform the time-honored repertoire, championing productions that celebrated patriotic themes while banning the obscene, the erotic, and the supernatural.

Kang's passion for the stage dated from his youth in Shandong, a province with a strong and vital regional theater. The area around Qingdao, where Kang had spent his first nineteen years, had its own style of drama, which combined earthy vernacular dialogue with long and melodious librettos. Kang had often seen plays in Dataizhuang and Zhucheng; his opportunities for amusement increased with his move to Shanghai, which supported a multitude of playhouses, often featuring the most famous and talented performers of the day. Kang was so fascinated by the theater that he learned to play several musical instruments, including the flute, the fiddle, and the small drums—percussion instruments that provided the rhythm flowing through each show. As late as 1938, he had accompanied Jiang Qing's performances in Yan'an.

When Kang ended his hospital retreat in 1956, he resumed indulging his passion for live drama. By that time, the Communist cultural police had eradicated many of the "bourgeois" and "feudal" elements from the traditional repertoire. But Kang did not accept the Communist line like a disciplined cadre; he vigorously defended the bawdy and superstitious plays of the past. Addressing a group of actors in Peking in 1956, he rejected the slogans the CCP's cultural departments used to condemn the old plays—"deviating from politics," "back to the ancients," and "purely artistic viewpoint"—as obstacles to cultural freedom. He insisted that the old plays should be performed, and specified several titles, including *Four Visits to Hell*, an erotic ghost story combining sex and the supernatural that had been banned since 1950.

Kang enjoyed erotic shows so much that he was known to pressure famous actors into giving private performances of salacious scenes in his home. Zhao Yanxia, a renowned Peking opera actor who specialized in playing beautiful young ladies, called at Kang's residence on Chinese New Year early in the 1960s. To Zhao's mortification, Kang asked him to sing a pornographic song. Zhao protested, but Kang finally overcame his objections and wound up accompanying him on the Chinese violin.

Kang also sent one of his actor friends to Shanghai to find someone who could perform a notorious form of skit known as a "noisy-bed play" or a "next-room play." Before 1949, Shanghai playhouses sometimes put on brief comedies in which an actor would imitate the sounds of a couple having sex in the next room. Kang's friend was unable to find a single entertainer in Shanghai who knew a "noisy-bed play," but Kang located a Sichuanese actor familiar with the genre and arranged a performance at his home—which he tape-recorded.

A devotee of other forms of Chinese erotica, Kang also collected "spring palace pictures"—scroll paintings and woodblock prints that depicted couples, threesomes, and at times as many as ten men and women, engaged in every form of sexual activity. Kang stored his art works in his house on Small Stone Bridge Lane and examined them at his leisure, using a magnifying glass so as not to miss a single detail.

Kang's interest in erotica extended to literature as well. Shortly after the beginning of the "antirightist" campaign, the harsh attack on intellectuals that the CCP launched in mid-1957, Kang approached Shanghai Classical Literature Publishing Company with a startling request. He ordered its editorial staff to find him early, uncensored editions of several highly erotic novels: *Jin Ping Mei* (*The Golden Lotus*), a rich, detailed, and engrossing Ming dynasty novel about a well-to-do Shandong rake; *Jiuwei Gui* (*The Nine-tailed Tortoise*), a nineteenth-century novel about sing-song girls and prostitutes; and *Liuye Xianzong* (*Fairies in the Wilderness*), a tale of high-class corruption and depravity. *The Golden Lotus*, filled with explicit sex—its chief character, Ximen Qing, copulates his way through the female population of his hometown—stands as a remarkable work of literature, containing sympathetic and moving portraits of a large cast of characters. *The Nine-tailed Tortoise*, by contrast, has few redeeming features. Written in the Wu dialect of Shanghai, it describes life in the brothels of the late nineteenth century. Hu Shi, an eminent twentieth-century scholar, dismissed it as "a guide to the world of prostitution." *Fairies in the Wilderness* contains long passages of unadorned pornography. Kang's desire to add these works to his private collection showed a defiant rejection of the prudish values the CCP sought to impose on society at large.

Increasingly, Kang grew preoccupied with protecting and reviving old-style drama. In the summer of 1960, he heard that the China Peking Opera Theater, a major company, had revised (i.e., bowdlerized) two classical plays in preparation for a foreign tour. Bursting into a tirade against the leaders of the company, Ma Shaobo and Ma Yanxiang, Kang declared that "the two Ma's are crude" and threatened to cancel the Party membership—in those days, a serious sanction that could limit a person's access to accommodations, employment, and even food—of anyone who favored staging modern plays.

A number of works banned by the Communists found a sponsor in Kang. After returning to Peking from celebrating the anniversary of the Russian Revolution in Moscow in November 1960, he endorsed a production of *The Eight Mistakes of the Flowery Field*, which is filled with double entendre and racy scenes. Kang defended his action with an argument that combined patriotism and the finer points of dramatic technicalities. Male actors, he noted, continued to play female parts in Peking opera, and the prohibition of suggestive works had greatly reduced the number of *hua dan* ("coquette roles")— vivacious and dissolute female characters such as prostitutes, unfaithful wives and concubines, or sensual widows. The increasing rarity of such performances, he claimed, represented a loss to China's cultural heritage and justified staging plays such as *The Eight Mistakes of the Flowery Field*.

As Kang understood very well, he was challenging the orthodoxy of the day. He recognized that some actors, afraid of controversy, were reluctant to perform *The Eight Mistakes*, with all its overtones of sensuality and sexual ambiguity. Before the performance, he went backstage and gave his advice to the cast: "Act with a free hand. Perform it now just as you performed it in the past. Perform the entire play. If there is any problem, then consider it mine!" With Kang's support, a series of erotic plays were staged in Peking during the winter of 1960–1961.

Kang also helped to write and direct plays. He involved himself in the production of *Li Huiniang*, an adaptation by Meng Chao of a popular Ming dynasty drama, the *Story of the Red Plum*. Four years younger than Kang, Meng Chao was one of Kang's oldest friends; after studying at Shanghai University with Kang, Meng had served a stint as a labor activist and later devoted himself to literary work, a popular calling for many young leftists. Instead of proceeding to Yan'an to join the main Communist forces, Meng moved south during the war with Japan and worked as a journalist in the areas under Kuomintang control, although he was never a KMT sympathizer.

In 1959, the Peking Kun Opera Theater commissioned Meng Chao to write a play based on the tale of Li Huiniang, the heroine of the *Story of the Red Plum*. In the course of developing the play, Meng received considerable support from Kang, who attended the dress rehearsals in 1960 and suggested a number of changes in both the dialogue and the costumes of the players. Kang took an interest in the most minute details, down to the color of the actresses' earrings. When the play was finally performed in the summer of 1961, he was delighted. Kang not only wrote a letter congratulating Meng Chao on his success, he also ordered the Peking Kun Opera Theater to "develop along these lines in [the] future, and don't play around with modern drama again."

Although Kang praised *Li Huiniang* for its traditional character, its story line coincided with Kang's view of a world of high politics populated by spies and traitors. Set in the Song dynasty, which ruled China from the tenth through the thirteenth centuries, the play was a tale of betrayal with a distinctly modern ring to it. The central character was Li Huiniang, a beautiful young woman who came back from the dead after being murdered. Together with her lover, Pei Shunqing, she saved China from the schemes of Jia Sidao, a corrupt minister bent on seizing power at court. Kang undoubtedly saw in Li Huiniang's story more than a passing relevance to modern Chinese affairs. In a loose way, Li and her lover could be seen as ancient equivalents of Jiang Qing and Mao Zedong—a parallel that made the audience wonder who could be the modern Jia Sidao. Kang, of course, was on the side of the lovers, so Jia Sidao must have been someone else: Deng Xiaoping, Zhou Enlai, or even Liu Shaoqi.

In search of local operas that never appeared in Peking, Kang traveled the length of the land. Shortly after the lunar new year in 1961, he led several companions to Yunnan and then to Sichuan, ostensibly on an inspection tour, but performances of Yunnan and Sichuan opera were staged for Kang and his group almost every night.

Kang and his friends decided to travel some sixty miles southeast of Kunming, the provincial capital of Yunnan, to Shi Lin, the famous "Stone Forest," a panoramic formation of jagged rocks and scarred cliff-faces over one hundred feet tall that spreads across the landscape like a forest of disfigured and petrified trees. This extraordinary natural phenomenon was promoted as a tourist attraction in the 1930s by the military ruler of Yunnan, Long Yun, who wrote the characters "Shi Lin" in his own hand and had them carved on a large slab of stone set into the face of a tall outcrop at the entrance to the forest. Upon seeing the general's calligraphy, Kang criticized it as a blot on the beauty of the place; he ordered it removed from the cliff-face by local authorities and replaced with the same two characters in his own handwriting. Kang's new characters remained at the entrance of the Stone Forest until the mid-1980s, when they in turn were replaced by Long Yun's. By China's standards, it was as if an American president had ordered one of the likenesses on Mount Rushmore replaced with his own.

Travel also became a way of maintaining contact with Chairman Mao. Following Mao's confrontation with Peng Dehuai at Lushan in July 1959, Mao, Kang, and Chen Boda visited a number of the historic and scenic landmarks in the surrounding mountains. Among their destinations was the famous Cave of the Immortals; to commemorate the occasion, Kang composed a set of lyrics to be sung to an old melody:

> *The Cave of the Immortals—a cave opened by Heaven,*
> *The spring flowing in drops—a pure stream from Earth.*
> *The depths of the green shadows hide red pavilions.*
> *Step on the white clouds, walk beyond the Heavens.*
> *Gaze at the Long River, flow on the horizon.*
> *The immortals are everywhere.*

This verse conjured up images of the dramatic visions glimpsed from Lushan, with its jagged, cave-ridden peaks penetrating the clouds and scarlet pavilions rising out of the wooded mountains. For more than a thousand years, educated Chinese had written poems during travels with friends; Kang's lines followed the custom, strengthening the bonds between him and his two companions.

Kang's enjoyment of the stage helped him reinforce other political and personal ties. During the early 1960s, he reestablished one of the most important relationships of his life: his friendship with Jiang Qing.

Jiang Qing and Kang had rarely met during the years following the 1947 evacuation of Yan'an; he returned to their native Shandong, and she followed Mao. Nor did they meet often during the 1950s, when she spent long periods in the Soviet Union trying to overcome her health problems. Jiang Qing divided much of her time between Chinese and Soviet medical institutions. Not until 1959 had she recovered enough to socialize regularly.

Jiang Qing had become one of Kang's regular theater companions by the early 1960s. After the Meeting of Seven Thousand Cadres in March 1962, Kang and Jiang Qing withdrew together to Hangzhou for rest and recreation. They spent almost two months in the southern city, whose mild climate was more congenial than Peking's, with its biting, sand-laden winds so common in the middle of spring. During their stay, Jiang Qing covered her face with a gauze mask to bolster her claim that she was convalescing from a bout of flu, and watched operatic plays with Kang almost every evening. Taking advantage of their status, they commanded the local theater group to perform plays suppressed since 1949. Twice they forced the Hangzhou drama troupe to send a driver on the 240-mile journey to Shanghai and back to collect props necessary for the plays they wanted to see. Imperiously, they ignored the difficulties the local officials encountered in attempting to stage dramas that had not been performed for over ten years.

The works Kang and Jiang Qing chose were bawdy and erotic, completely in keeping with the art Kang had been fostering since the mid-1950s. Their favorite plays challenged the values and morals promoted by the Communist regime, celebrating court plots and sexual intrigues that had no place in the new China. Jiang Qing especially enjoyed *Rainbow Pass*, a story of love and revenge set in the early-seventh-century interregnum between the Sui and Tang dynasties. The melodrama's heroine was Dongfang, the wife of a general slain by an assassin named Wang Bodang. True to the custom of revenge deeply ingrained in popular Chinese culture, Dongfang donned a suit of armor, disguised herself as a warrior, and set out to avenge her husband's death. But on discovering what a handsome young man Wang Bodang was, she fell in love with him, abandoned her vendetta, and revealed herself—in a flirtatious dance that drew enthusiastic praise from Jiang Qing—as a beautiful and seductive young woman. Even when performed with decorum, this tale of sexual betrayal undermined the basic precepts of Confucian culture, putting sensual satisfaction above loyalty to a dead husband. It was even more out of place in a Maoist setting, where literature was supposed to have the viewpoint of the workers, peasants, and soldiers.

Another of Jiang Qing's favorite operas was *Cutting the Yellow Gown*, which related the story of Han Sumei, a concubine in the harem of Zhao Kuangyin, the founder of the northern Song dynasty. Through various conspiracies, Han Sumei acquired the position of "Imperial Consort of the Plum Flower Palace," using her influence to slander an upright general, Zheng Ziming, and imperil the stability of the state. That play, too, undercut the Communist Chinese emphasis on placing the state's interests before those of the individual.

The unorthodox tastes Kang and Jiang Qing flaunted in Hangzhou did not go unnoticed. Several years later, a bulletin that recorded the proceedings of a theatrical conference in Peking included an item alleging that in 1962 two "central leaders" had watched "old plays" in Hangzhou. The Party's Propaganda Department investigated the incident, discovered that Kang and Jiang Qing were the central leaders in question, and submitted a copy of the report, along with its own conclusions on the matter, to each of them for comment.

Jiang Qing panicked when she saw the report. She wrote extensive comments on her copy, claiming that she had merely watched the "intolerable" plays advertised in the local paper and insinuating that local officials were out to harm her reputation. Pretending outrage, she suggested that her critics should look to themselves and conduct self-criticisms. Kang, by contrast, took the matter in his stride. He declined to respond to the Propaganda Department's accusations and simply placed a circle beside his name, indicating that he had read the document. He did not forget the episode, however; the Hangzhou officials who had informed on him and Jiang Qing met with Kang's revenge during the Cultural Revolution. They were accused of "bombarding the proletarian headquarters," a catchall crime that encompassed everything from criticizing radical policies to making oblique attacks on Mao Zedong; twenty of them were arrested, beaten, and jailed. Several died in prison.

Kang's patronage of suppressed opera seemed to provide him with a feeling of power, as if his disregard of socialist mores proved his membership in an elite group. He once spoke of his participation in a performance in Yan'an of *The Fisherman's Tragedy* in terms that revealed considerable pride in his defiance of the Party's cultural policies:

> Position has its advantages. I am a Central Committee member, and I play the drums, so who will criticize? Will anyone criticize? Yes, but they will only curse me behind my back. They are not really game to do so openly, for to speak in public means that they are suspected of opposing the party center. Chairman Mao also gave political support, and went to watch the play we performed. You say that Peking opera has feudal consciousness, but can you say that Chairman Mao has feudal consciousness? By using this method we can get away with it.

Kang's theatrical diversions ended in August 1962, when he attended a top-level meeting in the coastal town of Beidaihe in preparation for the approaching plenary session of the CCP's Central Committee. Mao spoke at length; instead of dwelling on his own responsibility for the economic problems facing the country, as he had done at the beginning of the year, he was unexpectedly robust and aggressive. He reaffirmed the importance of "class struggle"—the conflict between "the workers, peasants, and soldiers" on the one hand and the bourgeoisie and remnants of the old ruling circles on the other. Although supposedly the Communist victory had opened the way to eliminating all classes and thus any struggle between them, Mao announced that class struggle was still "the key link." In doing so, he was reemphasizing the importance of ideological issues in general, displaying a decisiveness and determination that foreshadowed a new and active phase in his career.

For Kang, Mao's performance at Beidaihe presaged a drastic change in the political atmosphere. Mao's renewed vitality and his desire to talk about more than the Soviet question showed Kang that the Chairman had returned to the sort of politics that favored theorists rather than technocrats. Ideology was back in fashion.

Mao's unexpected emphasis on class struggle, as Kang realized at once, required a public rejection of all things feudal, bourgeois, and capitalist. To free himself of any such taints, Kang immediately set out to obscure his record as a patron of ideologically deviant theater and started to criticize China's modern dramatists. Works he had praised to the skies a year or two earlier he now belittled as "fit for Taiwan or Khrushchev." "In fifteen years," he declared, "there have been no good plays written. On the contrary, there have only been bad plays like *Li Huiniang* and *Xie Yaobei*." The reason, he added, was simple: the playwrights' "thinking and viewpoint is not serving the workers, peasants, and laboring people, and is not serving socialism, but on the contrary is propagating feudalism, capitalism, and a small group of people."

Kang took particular pains to distance himself from Meng Chao, his old friend from Zhucheng, who had written *Li Huiniang* with so much encouragement and help from Kang. Before Kang left Beidaihe, he summoned Meng Chao's daughter, Lu Yuan, and gave her a message for her father: "Don't just write *Li Huiniang*, write other things as well." A short time later, Kang wrote directly to Meng Chao, "Please tell the other comrades in the Dramatic Association that from now on they should not perform any more plays about ghosts."

The sudden transformation of Kang's official tastes in drama augured serious trouble for Meng Chao and the others involved in the production of *Li Huiniang*. The play was branded "a poisonous weed" during the Cultural Revolution, and a special-case group was established to investigate it. The concept of "special case" dated back to the Yan'an period, when Kang had controlled the Social Affairs Department; its use against Meng Chao reflected Kang's habit of introducing security and police techniques into ordinary government and cultural activity. Meng, unaware that the director of his special-case group was in fact Kang, sought to defend himself by presenting two letters from Kang praising the play; the letters immediately disappeared without a trace. Imprisoned on Kang's orders, the playwright remained under attack until he died in March 1976, a casualty of the Cultural Revolution.

Kang may have forsaken public advocacy of the traditional theater, but he retained his delight in the smell of greasepaint and the company of actors and actresses. In 1964, when Jiang Qing started a campaign to radicalize Peking opera, Kang supported her zealously, openly identifying himself with the new revolutionary plays. Photographs of Kang started to appear in the media, together with the cast of a play or ballet, his thin, pallid face surrounded by heavily painted actors and actresses, often holding hands with one of the girls. Kang watched across the footlights, mounted the stage after the show, and mingled with the cast, but he surely knew that the revolutionary operas he now applauded were a poor substitute for the ancient and varied repertoire he had denounced as ideological trash.

Kang wasted no time in turning his back on the bawdy operatic voice of China in all its uncensored native glory. Much as he loved the traditional stage, he was not about to let it keep him from high office. Kang Sheng could watch the entire world unravel as long as he continued to thrive.

Chapter XIV

DRESS
REHEARSAL
FOR
DESTRUCTION

KANG SHENG, along with his wife and his sister-in-law, stepped down from a first-class carriage onto the platform of the Beidaihe railway station one warm day in August 1962. He was completely unaware that Chairman Mao was about to resurrect the concept of "class struggle" as the touchstone of all policy debate. But Kang had such a keen instinct for guessing the Chairman's intentions that as soon as Mao declared that class struggle was still "the key link," Kang started to make his plans. Recognizing that China was again on the verge of internal strife, he began to rearm in preparation for warfare at the top of the Party.

Sensing at once that the radical ideologues who surrounded Mao would inevitably clash with the pragmatic administrators who had run China since 1959, Kang moved to advance his own interests by exploiting the controversies and confusion that would arise from any attempt to impose class uniformity on China. Neither Kang nor Mao foresaw at the time that their latest attempt to reshape Chinese society would lead to the turmoil of the Cultural Revolution, but even if they had, Kang certainly would have pressed on.

Unsure how far Mao would carry his new ideological campaign, Kang took out insurance against any unexpected events, cultivating warm relations with orthodox leaders like Liu Shaoqi and Deng Xiaoping even as he secretly stirred up trouble that might sweep them from power. Right up until the Cultural Revolution erupted in 1966, many of Kang's comrades failed to recognize his sympathy with the radical cause or his capacity to condemn anyone, including them, as "class enemies."

Kang's chameleon qualities led some foreign observers to portray him as an "ambiguous" figure with a foot in each camp. But that picture of Kang was far from true: he would happily have sacrificed anyone—even Mao—for his own cause. After decades at the summit of the Party, however, Kang knew only too well that his chances of success were never better than when China was dominated by the fantasies that Mao imposed all around him.

Within days of Mao's talk at Beidaihe, Kang began intervening in cultural matters. His first act of aggression against the world of literature and art was to denigrate an as yet unpublished novel, *Liu Zhidan*, the fictionalized biography of an early Communist revolutionary. Since 1949, most Chinese literary criticism had judged writers by ideological standards: books praising capitalists were bad, those praising workers and peasants were good. By that lone criterion, *Liu Zhidan* was an admirable work; but Kang, integrating his security expertise with his avocation as literary critic, charged that *Liu Zhidan* was the product of a conspiracy of disgruntled cadres who had plotted to use the novel to damage Mao's reputation.

Liu Zhidan, the central character in the novel, had been a real-life figure, the leader of a secret society in the late 1920s. Resisting oppressive landowners and petty warlords, Liu turned to communism and emerged as one of the outstanding Party leaders in northern Shaanxi. He expanded his forces into a sizable peasant army, aligning himself with two dynamic Communist organizers, the famous northern Chinese leader Gao Gang and his lieutenant, Xi Zhongxun. Liu died in combat against the Japanese in 1938, but not before arousing Mao's jealousy.

Mao deeply resented the men who had first liberated zones in Shaanxi in the name of the Communist cause. To Mao, the success of other Communist leaders in northwestern China weakened his claim to be *the* genius of the Chinese Revolution. Liu Zhidan, Gao Gang, and the others, achieving military successes that had eluded Mao in the south, had created a haven for the survivors of the Long March. Mao's resentment set the scene for his clash with Gao Gang and Gao's fall from power and suicide in 1954.*

---

* Xi Zhongxun, one of the masterminds of Communist success in Shaanxi, speaks with contempt to this day about Mao's overblown reputation.

Kang had first heard of *Liu Zhidan* six months before the Beidaihe meeting, when a contact in the literary establishment told him that the Workers Publishing House was preparing to print a novel about the revolutionary hero. Even before he read the book, Kang recognized that it could be construed as an attempt to overturn the verdict rendered against Gao Gang in 1954. Kang immediately ordered the publishers to print six hundred copies of the fifth draft and three hundred copies of the third draft so that officials could find political meaning in the discrepancies between the two versions. But although Kang saw the novel's potential as a political weapon, there was nothing he could do until Mao emerged from his passive state. Meanwhile, Kang bided his time.

Kang started to act in August 1962, even before the summer retreat at Beidaihe came to an end. While other CCP leaders were mixing business with the resort's pleasures of swimming, basking in the sun, and eating fresh crabs and fish, Kang seized the initiative. No sooner had Kang heard Mao talk about class struggle than he invoked his authority as deputy head of the Central Group on Culture and Education to write to the Party's General Office, the unit responsible for the security of the Communist elite and the appropriate body to investigate a plot against the Chairman. "This is not a question of pure literary writing," Kang told the General Office. "It appears to be a question with political tendentiousness."

Liu Zhidan was nothing more than a bit of propaganda designed to celebrate the revolutionary spirit and courage of one of the Party's early leaders. It eulogized the shining deeds of a man who had helped the Communists triumph over the vicious warlords and corrupt Kuomintang officials who had ruled China for four decades. But the author of the novel, Li Jiantong, and the people who had assisted and encouraged her had been close to Liu Zhidan himself. This web of personal relationships was the "evidence" Kang needed to give his charges of conspiracy the ring of truth.

Li Jiantong had married Liu Zhidan's younger brother, Liu Jingfan. Even under communism, family ties are extremely important for Chinese, and Liu Jingfan was named vice minister of geology, a fairly important post, thanks to his brother's posthumous prestige. Li Jiantong started working on the novel in 1956; by the time her research was finished, she had interviewed scores of veterans who had served with her famous brother-in-law. One of her key advisers, and certainly the most senior cadre to take an interest in her research, was

Vice Premier Xi Zhongxun, who had been Liu's chief lieutenant during the 1930s. Xi was not mentioned in the novel, but his role in founding the Communist base at Shaanxi was portrayed collectively by several characters.

Kang quickly seized on Xi's connection with the novel to show that it was a dangerous plot, labeling Xi "a big anti-party conspirator" who was "the leading personality" behind the novel. Xi had "colluded" with Li Jiantong and her husband, Vice Minister Liu Jingfan, "in a partnership to concoct the anti-party novel, *Liu Zhidan*, in order to reverse the verdict on Gao Gang"—or so Kang claimed. Kang dramatized Vice Premier Xi's contribution by charging Xi with introducing a new kind of dissidence: "using a novel to carry out anti-party activity." Kang outlined his criticism in a note he submitted to Mao, who read the message and simply returned it to Kang, implicitly allowing him to claim that the Chairman endorsed his judgment.

After his return to Peking in October, Kang secured Central Committee approval to create a special-case group to investigate the "conspiracy" behind *Liu Zhidan*. Kang himself was placed in charge of the group and given control over the course of the inquiry. The establishment of the special-case group alone predetermined the outcome: branding the situation a "special case" confirmed in advance the "guilt" of the main "suspects."

Kang's first step as head of the special-case group was to confront the author, Li Jiantong, and to confiscate the notes of her interviews with the men who had fought alongside Liu Zhidan. Kang and his interrogators questioned everyone named in Li's notes—senior cadres and simple folk alike—and wove their findings, no matter how innocent, into a barrage of serious charges. Kang's first high-level victim, Xi Zhongxun, was removed from his post, subjected to a lengthy investigation, and jailed for eight years. Liu Jingfan was sacked as vice minister of geology. Other leaders once prominent in the northwest Communist apparatus were Kang's next targets. Jia Tuofu, a ministerial-level official in the Economic Commission, was dismissed, sent to the countryside, and finally persecuted to death during the Cultural Revolution. Bai Jian, vice minister in the First Machine Building Ministry, was struggled to death by Red Guards in his own ministry because he was said to have provided "ammunition" for the novel.

Under Kang's direction, the special-case group also persecuted the officials of the Workers Publishing House. The original publisher, Gao Lisheng, was tortured to death. Other staff members were badly beaten or, in some cases, tormented with electrical devices. The book's editor, He Jiadong, was sent to a faraway village, where he and his family of six had to subsist on a monthly income of thirty yuan.* He Jiadong's wife and two of his children died as a result. Ordinary people who had had casual or indirect contact with Li Jiantong also found themselves swept up in Kang's dragnet. The manager of a restaurant where Vice Premier Xi Zhongxun had dined several times was arrested and accused of being Xi's "underground messenger." His detention led to the arrest on conspiracy charges of the managers of the Peking Duck and the Hunan, at the time two of the capital's leading restaurants. Kang's vicious crusade reached its peak when a couple of elderly people whom Li Jiantong had once helped to cross a road in the course of her research were persecuted to death. As Kang continued his purge, numerous cadres from China's northwestern provinces were transferred to Peking for "study"—a euphemism for intensive brainwashing—and criticized as members of "an anti-Party clique." The victims of the *Liu Zhidan* affair numbered in the thousands over the next four years.

Kang's investigating team disbanded in 1966, but after the Cultural Revolution broke out later the same year, Kang melded several Red Guard divisions into what was known as "the Sixty-two Special-Case Company," which had units in Peking, Shanghai, Xian, Lanzhou, Shenyang, Changchun, Changsha, and Yan'an—the main areas where Gao Gang had been active at one time or another. The dossiers that Kang's original special-case group had collected, Kang handed over to the Sixty-two Special-Case Company with instructions to apprehend everyone named in them. Practically anyone who had had any association with Li Jiantong, no matter how trivial, was tracked down and persecuted.[†]

The *Liu Zhidan* controversy represented a victory of sorts for Kang, as it helped make the populace more receptive to incredible and

---

* Approximately twelve dollars in American money.
† *Liu Zhidan* was finally published in 1978, three years after Kang's death. The following year, Li Jiantong was admitted to the Chinese Writers Association, a mark of distinction for authors in China. After surviving for eight years in prison, Xi Zhongxun was appointed Party chief in Guangdong in the late 1970s. Later promoted to the Party Secretariat and Politburo, Xi remained an influential figure and a leading reformer through the mid-1980s.

extravagant accusations and raised the threshold of political skepticism. Even though the *Liu Zhidan* case brought down a vice premier and several ministers and vice ministers, however, it did not affect the balance of power in Peking—it increased Kang Sheng's influence without dramatically altering his position.

Flush from exposing the "literary conspiracy" behind *Liu Zhidan*, Kang embarked on a search for ways to destroy as many orthodox administrators and economists as he could. As the problems between China and Russia continued to fester, few more serious charges could be made against a CCP cadre than that of being a "revisionist"—jargon for being sympathetic toward the Soviet Union. Kang, well aware how effective charges of revisionism could be in internal power struggles, recruited in 1963 a number of writers and theorists to form what he called "the Anti-Revisionist Philosophy Writing Group." The group produced articles under Kang's supervision, but its manager was Guan Feng, a propaganda operative who had been one of Kang's stalwarts in Shandong during the late 1940s and had emerged in the 1950s as a Communist intellectual and "philosopher." Guan, a senior cadre in the philosophy and social sciences department of the Academy of Sciences, prolifically turned out sleep-inducing articles with titles like "The Law of the Negation of Negation," "Marxist Dialectical Discussion of Universal Relationships and Development," and "Oppose Revisionism in the Methodical Discussion of Philosophical History." His writings were abstract and tedious, but with Kang's backing Guan Feng developed into a swaggering bully in Peking's intellectual circles.

Literary units like the Anti-Revisionist Philosophy Writing Group figured prominently in Chinese politics from the early 1960s onward. The writing groups served as polemicists, speechwriters, propagandists, and literary provocateurs, and could be major weapons in a system where propaganda played a key role in molding popular thinking, which they were originally intended to do. But in Kang's hands these groups also became instruments for trapping and crushing rivals.

Kang began to use his detachment of propaganda writers to turn an abstruse philosophical debate into an attack against one of his ideological foes during the summer of 1964. He orchestrated the episode like a puppeteer, and his meticulously planned conspiracy wrecked the reputations and influence of several orthodox theorists at the Party School, China's wellspring of Marxism.

The Party School had a sizable staff of instructors and lecturers regarded as experts on all ideological and philosophical questions. Kang himself had once run the Party School in Yan'an, where it was first established. It had since moved to a compound at the foot of the Fragrant Hills on the western outskirts of Peking. The campus, graced with rows of poplar and willow trees, provided an oasis far from the city's noise and distractions so that faculty members could indoctrinate students and ponder the philosophical issues that faced the Communists. For years, Kang had had several agents there, including Cao Yi'ou, who served as director of short-term courses and was a member of the CCP committee that supervised the school. Until Kang could place the Party School entirely under his control, though, it threatened his claim of being a top Chinese authority on Marxist theory.

Keenly aware of the Party School's importance, Kang had criticized its head, Yang Xianzhen, in the wake of Mao's clash with Marshal Peng Dehuai at the Lushan meeting in 1959. Yang had gone to study in Moscow during the 1920s, then stayed on to teach Chinese at the Soviet Foreign Languages Institute for almost twenty years. Unlike many Chinese Communists, Yang was a scholar with a detailed knowledge of Marxist theory. Appointed to the Central Committee in 1956, he later became one of the leading critics of the ideologues around Mao, deriding the Great Leap Forward as "99 percent romanticism and 1 percent realism" and ridiculing Mao's economic policies as "beggars' communism." Kang fastened on Yang's contempt for the Great Leap and other visionary policies of Mao's and branded Yang a "rightist" lacking any trace of revolutionary enthusiasm. As a result, Yang was demoted to head a bureau within the school and replaced by one of his rivals, Ai Siqi, who had previously been a teacher at the Shaanbei Academy, a training school in Yan'an run by Kang's Social Affairs Department.

Even demoted, Yang proved more resilient than the other casualties of the Lushan meeting, returning to head the Party School again in 1962. He was shunted aside once more, in 1963, but managed to hang on as a vice president of the Party School, where he organized resistance to the irrational policies the Maoists were pushing in the name of Marxism.

Yang's ups and downs kept Kang from gaining firm control over the school during the early 1960s. Another chance presented itself in April 1964, when two philosophy lecturers at the Party School, Ai

Hengwu and Lin Qingshan, wrote a short but highly esoteric essay on Hegelian theory. The tract was brief, but its title was not: "The Division of One into Two and the Synthesis of Two into One." The subject matter was every bit as inviting as the title promised: the function in dialectical materialism of the formula of thesis-antithesis-synthesis.

The theme presented by Ai and Lin was that after the process of "one splitting into two" had culminated in the Communist victory, the process of "two combining into one" ushered in a period of national integration. Their argument could be construed as counter to Mao's view that class struggle remained the key issue in Chinese politics, but it was a far cry from the direct criticism that had caused trouble in the past for men like Marshal Peng and Vice Foreign Minister Luo Fu. Indeed, such an abstract article would otherwise have disappeared without a ripple. Kang understood, however, that to take an essay that obscure and turn it into heresy required nothing more than a pronouncement of some sort from Mao.

Ai Hengwu and Lin Qingshan played into Kang's hands by submitting a draft of their essay to *The Guangming Daily*, the newspaper that specialized in philosophical and cultural matters. *The Guangming Daily*'s editorial department had no authority to make political decisions, so it routinely submitted sensitive articles for approval at higher levels. One copy went to Kang as director of the Theoretical Small Group, another to Guan Feng as head of the Anti-Revisionist Philosophy Writing Group.

Kang realized as soon as he read the draft that it could lure his adversary, Yang Xianzhen, into a compromising position. Together with Guan Feng, Kang formulated a lethal but deniable scheme to embroil Yang in a controversy over the synthesis of opposites. Instead of rejecting Lin and Ai's paper, Kang suggested to the editors of *The Guangming Daily* that China's experts on Marxist theory should debate the subject. The Lin–Ai essay was published with his approval in *The Guangming Daily* on May 29, 1964. Meanwhile, Kang secretly instructed his agents at the Party School, including Cao Yi'ou, to collect evidence implicating Yang in the work Lin and Ai were doing. Kang, confident that he could get Mao to condemn the synthesis theory, wanted to compile a dossier that, when the time was ripe, he could produce to show Yang's responsibility for spreading such deviant thought.

Kang made his next move one week later, when a rebuttal entitled "The Synthesis of Two into One Is Not Dialectical Materialism" appeared in the same paper. On the night of June 5, Kang attended a special performance of several new revolutionary operas in the Great Hall of the People, the gigantic shoebox of a building on the western side of Tiananmen Square that was one of the few lasting accomplishments of the Great Leap Forward. He sat beside Jiang Qing, and during the intermission, when they and the other high officials in the audience retired to a private lounge for refreshments, he handed her copies of both articles. Hinting at their significance, Kang asked her to pass them on to Chairman Mao. As Kang had anticipated, Mao returned the two articles to him without comment three days later, in effect giving Kang license to assert that Mao approved his position. Kang went ahead and publicly quoted the Chairman as saying that the synthesis of two into one amounted to the terrifying specter of "class compromise."

With great care and cunning, Kang—through Guan Feng and the Anti-Revisionist Philosophy Writing Group—orchestrated an ever widening debate over the trivial question of two into one. Kang, master editor and wordsmith, checked the phrasing of each item prepared by Guan Feng's scribes but took pains to conceal his personal involvement. He also went so far as to inspect the layout of the pages in *The Guangming Daily* where the stories were published. By keeping the debate alive, Kang hoped to trick Yang and his protégés into thinking that it was safe to continue publishing commentaries in support of their position.

The controversy gained considerable momentum, inspiring correspondence in the pages of major newspapers. Kang directed the editors of *The Guangming Daily, The People's Daily*, and *Red Flag* to keep track of the names of everyone who wrote letters in support of the synthesis argument. Not only was Kang preparing a trap for Yang Xianzhen—as if luring a snake out of its hole—but he was also identifying a large number of low-level cadres and intellectuals who he could show were themselves being lured into joining an extensive conspiracy headed by "revisionists" within the Party School.

After allowing the discussion to simmer in the pages of *The Guangming Daily* for a month, Kang dropped the pretense of academic debate and went straight after Yang. Early in July 1964, he instructed *The People's Daily* (as the Party's official paper, it was more authoritative than *The Guangming Daily*) to prepare an article criticizing Yang by name for promoting the revisionist doctrine of the synthesis of two into one. Yang's concept, Kang told *The People's Daily*, obscured class struggle and contradicted everything the Chairman had proposed since September 1962.

Kang took a keen interest in the article prepared for *The People's Daily*. He chaired meetings at his office in the Number Eight Villa in the Diaoyutai State Guesthouse on July 15 and 16, going over the manuscript word by word with members of his writing group and redrafting various passages to sharpen criticism of Yang. He took special care in choosing the byline. After consulting his assistants, he finally decided that the essay should appear to have been written by two Party School officials totally unconnected with the debate.

The People's Daily carried Kang's article on July 17 under the title "Discussing the Problem of the Synthesis of Two into One with Comrade Yang Xianzhen." Once a Party School faculty member as well known as Yang was named publicly, the discussion ceased being purely academic and became a clash between personalities. Moreover, publication of the article in *The People's Daily* clearly implied that the Party leaders had rejected Yang's interpretation. Its appearance of having been written by two cadres from Yang's own organization further strengthened its validity, suggesting that the Party School was divided over the issue, with Yang opposed by his own subordinates.

Next, Kang enlisted the support of *Red Flag*, the main journal on theoretical affairs. In early August, he briefed its editor, Chen Boda, on his plans. Chen had risen to the top of the CCP structure because of his obsequious but close relationship with Mao. Anything that might be interpreted as criticism of the Chairman was anathema to Chen, so he willingly accepted Kang's advice. Chen instructed his editorial board to draft an argument that the synthesis of two into one was an indirect call for combining the bourgeoisie and the proletariat and compromising the all-important class struggle. Kang, with his customary attention to detail, chose the byline for the *Red Flag* article. "This Magazine's Commentator" he rejected as too serious for *Red Flag*'s first entry into the battle. On the other hand, Kang believed, "This Magazine's Reporter" would make the article seem nothing more than a junior staffer's personal view. He finally settled on "This Magazine's Leading Reporter." The article itself was headed "A New Theoretical Struggle on the Philosophical Front."

Kang continued to press his campaign against Yang, arranging the first of a series of mass meetings in the Party School's main auditorium on August 24. The theory of synthesis came under strong criticism, along with Yang and everyone who Kang claimed was associated with him. Kang's agents dominated these meetings, which soon deteriorated into sessions of verbal abuse and intimidation that often lasted well past midnight. These grueling confrontations produced statements naming Yang as the mastermind behind the articles that advocated the synthesis of two into one. By late August, most of the Party School's senior officials either had been co-opted by Kang or were too intimidated to oppose his schemes, leaving defenseless the ones accused of being members of Yang's clique. However intense the pressure upon them and their families, Kang's targets, being idealistic academics rather than slippery politicians, stood their ground and suffered the consequences.

Yang's position was beyond hope. Now that the Party's main theoretical organs had come out against him, everyone knew that the leaders were united in their opposition to him. Only a few cadres still refused to acknowledge that Yang had deliberately set out to challenge Mao's decree that class struggle was now paramount. As the perpetrator of an act of great disloyalty to the Chairman, Yang had to be punished; he was transferred from the Party School to a much less important job in the philosophy department of the Chinese Academy of Sciences. That was just the beginning of his decline. At the outset of the Cultural Revolution, he was beaten by Red Guards and subjected to a year of criticism-and-struggle sessions. Finally, on May 18, 1967, Kang ordered him locked up in Building Number Fifty-two at the Party School compound. After four months, Kang had Yang moved to a prison, where he was put in solitary confinement, even though by then he was seventy-one years old. Yang spent eight years in prison; then, broken in body if not in spirit, he was sent to rural Shaanxi to work as a laborer. He was finally rehabilitated in 1978—more than two years after Kang's death.

Yang was far from the only casualty of the theoretical debate contrived by Kang. Lin Qingshan, one of the authors of the original article, was expelled from the Party, exiled to Jilin in northeastern China, and assigned to work as a vegetable seller. He survived; in the early 1980s, he published a number of articles exposing Kang and his crimes. Ai Hengwu, Lin's co-author of the two-into-one essay, was exiled to his native province of Liaoning and forced to work on a commune. The vice president of the Party School, Hou Weiyu, was accused of supporting "an anti-Party clique" because he had worked with Yang. Hou experienced a string of political problems, culminating in his arrest during the Cultural Revolution. Another victim was Sun Dingguo, a soldier-turned-theoretician from Shandong who had been a protégé of Kang's in the late 1950s, drafting speeches for him, dining in his mansion, and discussing philosophical issues with him for hours. In 1964, at Kang's direction, Sun was placed under severe pressure to make him identify Yang as the architect of the synthesis theory. Rather than betray his colleague, Sun drowned himself in the artificial lake in the western corner of the Party School compound.

Many others also suffered. One hundred and fifty-four cadres and students had undergone criticism by the end of 1964. Seven were expelled from the Party or suffered harsh "administrative penalties" such as forced labor or imprisonment. Forty-five were severely "criticized"—harangued and beaten at mass meetings. Fifty were "helped" by small groups—that is, subjected to tirades by committees instead of at mass meetings. Another fifty-nine had adverse comments written in their personal files, a sanction that could wreck a career.

The number of casualties from this episode mushroomed at the start of the Cultural Revolution, when people previously under political suspicion often became the first targets of the Red Guards. For some, the ideological controversy later became an issue of life and death. One was a common soldier named Chen Bo. An ardent student of Mao's works, Chen had been honored as an exemplary member of the People's Liberation Army for five years in a row. But in 1964, he wrote an essay supporting the concept of "the synthesis of two into one"—an ideological crime that led to his arrest and execution during the Cultural Revolution. Not even death ended Chen Bo's problems: his corpse was hacked to pieces by the Red Guards.

The debate about synthesis consolidated Kang's grip on the Party School. He was increasingly free from then on to use school officials and students as his personal emissaries and agents. With the help of Cao Yi'ou, he recruited research assistants and speechwriters from the school. The Party School became the base of another writing group, "Tang Xiaowen"—a name chosen to make it sound like an actual person. Under Kang's direction, the Tang Xiaowen authors penned cynical propaganda articles to stir up minor controversies Kang could use in his quest for greater power.

Kang's victory in the synthesis debate marked another stage in his search for a key to unlock the gates of darkness and admit waves of chaos that would sweep him to the very summit of the Party. A year or so later, Kang found exactly what he was looking for: a seemingly innocuous historical play that he put to his own use, at what would prove to be a terrible cost to his party and his people.

Part IV

GODFATHER OF THE CULTURAL REVOLUTION

Chapter XV

THE PLAY'S
THE THING

AS KANG CONTINUED to work in the shadows, the discrepancies between Mao's dreams of perpetual revolution and China's harsh economic realities became increasingly obvious. Liu Shaoqi, Deng Xiaoping, and Peng Zhen tried to steer the nation on a moderate course, but after Mao announced his political comeback in 1962, mass campaigns began extolling the ideal of a selfless Communist hero completely at home in a collective society. Countless urban cadres, intellectuals, writers, artists, and students were sent to the countryside for "socialist education"—that is, to emulate the simple lives of the peasants. The propaganda of the era had its spiritual roots in Yan'an. Some of Mao's essays from two decades earlier were presented as models of Communist morality. And photographs from Yan'an showing Mao and other senior officials digging vegetable patches outside their cave dwellings reminded the masses that the Chairman had labored with them.

Against that background, a spectacular controversy came to a head in late 1965, when Defense Minister Lin Biao instigated the arrest of his rival, General Luo Ruiqing, chief of the General Staff Department of the People's Liberation Army. Kang became involved in the Luo Ruiqing affair late the following year, when he helped fabricate charges that Luo was "a hidden traitor" who had had "illicit relations with foreign countries." Until Lin Biao turned on him, General Luo had seemed invincible. Though a veteran of the Long March, a member of the Secretariat, a vice premier, and a former minister of public security, Luo Ruiqing had made the mistake of deviating from Mao's military theory and calling for a professional army equipped with modern weapons and trained in advanced tactics—he had disregarded the Chairman's beloved icons of guerrilla warfare and ideological fervor. Luo became a symbol of resistance to Mao's concept of the military, as well as to Lin Biao's control over the PLA. Lin Biao and his wife, Ye Qun, a woman with unlimited ambition and a taste for daring conspiracies, coaxed a number of army and air force officers into accusing Luo of plotting to seize power in the military. Luo was arrested in November 1965 and subjected to years of persecution.

While the struggle between Lin Biao and Luo Ruiqing moved toward a climax, Kang returned to literary controversies. This time the focus was the play *The Dismissal of Hai Rui,* a retelling of the story of a sixteenth-century Ming dynasty courtier, Hai Rui, who was removed from office for openly opposing the Jiajing Emperor's misguided policies. Jiang Qing had first tried to persuade her husband to criticize this play in 1962, but Mao had shrugged off her advice—had, in fact, proceeded to invite the play's star, Ma Lianliang, to dinner at his residence in the Zhongnanhai compound and to praise his performance throughout the evening.

Two years passed before Kang got involved. Rather than follow Jiang Qing's example and condemn *The Dismissal of Hai Rui* as a challenge to Mao's literary theories, Kang worked on the Chairman's suspicions, planting the idea that the play attempted to rehabilitate Peng Dehuai. Essentially, Kang repeated what he had done in the *Liu Zhidan* case, characterizing a work as the vehicle for a conspiracy aimed at Mao.

Kang's role in this incident was so devious that to this day many observers believe *The Dismissal of Hai Rui* really was what Kang made it out to be. Actually, the inspiration to glorify Hai Rui had originated with Mao himself. At a Shanghai meeting in early 1959, when China's leaders first grasped the disastrous consequences of the Great Leap Forward and started calling for truthful reports from the provinces, Mao made a plea to emulate "the spirit of Hai Rui." His secretary, Hu Qiaomu, relayed these remarks to Wu Han, a respected non-Communist historian who had been appointed vice mayor of Peking in 1951 as part of the CCP's efforts to improve relations with the country's intellectuals.* Hu Qiaomu suggested that Wu base an essay or a play on Hai Rui's life story.

In response to Hu Qiaomu's message, Wu Han wrote an article, "Discussing Hai Rui," which was published in late 1959—not until after the bitter fight at the Central Committee meeting at Lushan and the purge of Marshal Peng. Nevertheless, his essay was well received; no one accused him of having ulterior motives or of defending Mao's fallen critic. Wu Han then began turning the story of Hai Rui into a play. The early drafts he called simply *Hai Rui,* but a friend, Cai Xitao, the director of the Yunnan Biological Research Institute, pointed out that many literary works over the centuries had appeared under that name, and suggested expanding the title to *The Dismissal of Hai Rui.* From the fourth draft on, the play was known by its new and ultimately disastrous name.

The Dismissal of Hai Rui, first performed publicly in 1961, two years after the Lushan plenum, was warmly applauded by Peking audiences, which often included senior leaders. Kang, then involved in promoting traditional operas about ghosts, traitors, and sex, gave no sign that he detected any problems with Wu Han's drama.

Three years later, however, Kang began a campaign worthy of Iago, preying upon Mao's fears and suspicions. He suggested to Mao that what betrayed the play's conspiratorial purpose was the word "dismissal" in the title. This word, Kang insinuated, established a spurious parallel between the courageous Hai Rui and the mutinous Peng, both of whom had been *dismissed* from office.

While the controversy over the play about Hai Rui was heating up, Jiang Qing lost her husband to a younger woman. On a visit to the provinces in the mid-1960s, Mao had had a chance encounter with a young railway attendant, Zhang Yufeng. Zhang was a lively woman

---

* Wu Han's relationship with the Communist Party remains unclear. Officially, he was a member of the non-Communist China Democratic League, an organization that opposed the KMT before 1949, but he was probably an undercover Communist. According to Zhang Guotao, the China Democratic League was infiltrated by Communists from the moment of its inception in 1942. Communist agents who had been prominent in the so-called democratic parties retained their identity as "democratic personalities" after 1949 in order to help the Communist leaders project an image of political pluralism while avoiding any risk of genuine opposition.

in her early twenties with a short fringe of hair, a somewhat square face, and an intriguing smile; combined, these gave her a Mona Lisa look.

Mao flirted with Zhang Yufeng and several of her coworkers during his trip, but he did not pursue a relationship with her at the time. After his return to Peking, Mao idled away his leisure hours with calligraphy—a pastime not a few Chinese believe improves health as well as artistic skills. Unable to get Zhang out of his mind, Mao wrote her name over and over again in his calligraphy exercises. Mao's chief bodyguard, Wang Dongxing, chanced upon some handwritten pages left lying around the Chairman's study, realized that Mao was infatuated with Zhang Yufeng, and began investigating her background. Learning that Zhang was married to a young army officer in the Jinan military region, Wang arranged for him to be transferred to the Central Guard Regiment, the select force in Peking responsible for the Party elite's physical security. Zhang accompanied her husband to the capital, where she was assigned to the General Office, the agency that looked after the needs of Mao and other senior leaders.

Zhang Yufeng started out in the General Office as a junior cadre, but Wang assigned her tasks that put her in frequent contact with Mao. As Wang had expected, Zhang's youth, ebullience, and desire to serve "the Chairman" soon overwhelmed Mao. She quickly became his lover as well as his main female companion, even as Jiang Qing had done nearly thirty years earlier. Senior cadres explained to Zhang's husband that his wife had been blessed by the Chairman's favor, and the young army officer readily agreed to accept a sum of money as compensation for his loss. Wang arranged for Zhang's husband to be shifted to a military unit outside the capital, where he was free to look for a new wife. Zhang Yufeng bore Mao two daughters in the mid-1960s; from then on, high cadres in the know regarded her as the Chairman's fifth wife.

Zhang Yufeng's presence in Mao's life jeopardized Kang's channel to the Chairman via Jiang Qing. Fortunately for Kang, Jiang Qing eventually adjusted to the new situation, even getting on good terms with Zhang Yufeng by giving her a color television set and other gifts. In the protocol-conscious Chinese state, Jiang Qing retained her official status as Mao's wife and continued to have regular contact with

Richard Wilhelm, headmaster of the German middle school Kang attended in Qingdao. Wilhelm was one of the foremost sinologists of his day, translating the I Ching into German and introducing European intellectuals like C. G. Jung to the arcane aspects of Chinese thought. CENTER: *Shanghai's Bund, the bustling waterfront at the heart of the International Settlement, in the 1920s. Kang Sheng lived in Shanghai from 1924 until 1933 and later described it as his "second home."* BOTTOM: *Communist prisoners being paraded in the streets of Shanghai before execution; when Kang Sheng was arrested in 1930 he used personal connections to avoid a similar fate.*

1

2

3

Kang Sheng in Moscow in the mid-1930s, when he was deputy leader of the Chinese delegation to the Comintern. During his time in the USSR, Kang worked closely with the NKVD, the Soviet secret police, and led a security unit that hunted down and purged suspected "counterrevolutionaries" among his fellow Chinese. BELOW: *A recent photo of the Lux Hotel in Moscow, where Kang Sheng, his wife, Cao Yi'ou, and his sister-in-law and lover, Su Mei, lived in a ménage à trois from 1933 until 1937. The Lux housed the leaders of the Comintern, the semi-clandestine organization that was supposed to set the world ablaze with Communist fervor.*

4

5

6

LEFT: *The Soviet-oriented Wang Ming, who was Kang Sheng's patron in Shanghai and Moscow. This photograph, taken with Bishop Logan Roots, shows Wang Ming (seated in center), Madame Wang Ming (right), Bo Gu (front row, far left), Zhou Enlai (front row, second from left), Luo Ruiqing (back row, second from left), Ilona Ralf Sues (back row, center), Madame Zhou Enlai (top right), and Agnes Smedley (seated behind and to the right of Wang Ming).*

7   8

FAR LEFT: *Li Lisan, CCP leader from 1928 until 1930, was Kang Sheng's first high patron. After his policies failed, Li was called to Moscow, where he worked with Kang. But in 1938, Kang had the NKVD arrest Li as a "Trotskyite."* LEFT: *The film star Jiang Qing, who married Mao Zedong in 1938, but only after Kang Sheng guaranteed her political loyalty. Kang had known her since she was a teenager, and, it was rumored, had had a sexual relationship with her.*

RIGHT: *Kang Sheng lecturing in Yan'an in 1938, the year he abandoned Wang Ming and joined Mao Zedong in an alliance that would last the rest of his life.* BELOW: *Sharing a meal in Yan'an in 1937 were Mao Zedong, United Press correspondent Earl Leaf, General Zhu De, and Mao's third wife, He Zizhen, who was soon to be replaced by Jiang Qing.*

9

10

11

12

The cave dwellings (TOP) and the pagoda (BOTTOM) that look down upon Yan'an—"a purely medieval, disagreeable small town" where, according to former Communist writer Zhu Qihua, Mao Zedong established his "Platonic kingdom." It was in Yan'an, the Party's base from 1936 to 1947, that Kang Sheng founded the Social Affairs Department, a precursor of the Communist security system.

Kang Sheng's terror campaign against "enemy special agents" in Yan'an stirred up strong criticism at the Seventh Party Congress in April 1945 but, as this photograph shows (RIGHT), *he still managed to smile.* BELOW: *Kang Sheng with Mao Zedong in Yan'an in April 1945. Despite criticism for the excessive terror of his "salvation" campaign, he still had direct access to the Chairman.*

13

14

15   16   17   18

ABOVE, LEFT: *Lin Biao, perhaps the most brilliant Communist strategist of the Sino-Japanese War, in about 1944. Lin showed signs of hypochondria in the 1950s and gradually retreated into a fantasy world, finally attempting to overthrow Mao in a botched coup in 1971.* SECOND FROM LEFT: *Zhou Enlai in the 1940s, when he spent much of his time in Chongqing as the CCP representative in the Kuomintang capital.* SECOND FROM RIGHT: *Zhu De, the legendary Communist military commander, in the mid-1940s. Zhu was closely associated with Mao, but had no political ambitions and so remained a senior but totally ineffective official until his death in 1976.* RIGHT: *Mao Zedong in 1944, when he was consolidating his domination over the Chinese Communist movement.*

RIGHT, *left to right: Zhou Enlai, Mao Zedong, and Zhu De in Yan'an in the mid-1940s. In Western eyes this trio represented the supreme Communist leadership, but in fact Zhu's influence did not extend beyond the army and Zhou was a debonair executive officer who in policy discussions was usually outgunned by men like Kang Sheng.*

19

*Kang Sheng addressing a Central Committee meeting in March 1949.
He was en route from Shanxi, where he had terrified locals by
butchering the landlords. Mao praised him for correcting "right
deviations," and he returned to take over Party work in his home
province of Shandong.*

ABOVE, LEFT: *Kang Sheng liked to pore over documents, pen in hand, polishing his reputation as a wordsmith and editor, a master of subtle theoretical issues and not just a dispenser of state terror.* ABOVE, RIGHT: *A monochrome bearing the inscription "Late in the season fragrance comes," which Kang Sheng painted in the 1950s. Recognized by Chinese intellectuals as an artist who produced original and delicate paintings and elegant calligraphy, Kang used the pseudonym Lu Chishui ("Red Water of Lu").*

LEFT: *The entrance to the Stone Forest, the exotic rock formation near Kunming, bearing Kang's characters shi lin ("stone forest"). When Kang's name came into disrepute in the 1980s, the characters were replaced.*

ABOVE AND RIGHT: *The large courtyard house in Small Stone Bridge Lane, Peking, where Kang Sheng lived from 1956 until his death in 1975. It is now the Bamboo Garden Hotel. This Qing dynasty residence provided Kang with an old-world environment that complemented his scholarly interests.*

Kang Sheng listens attentively to a lecture at "The Red and Expert University," a machine factory in Shanxi that was converted into a school as part of the lead-up to the Great Leap Forward in September 1958.

28

LEFT: *Mao Zedong with Deng Xiaoping in the early 1960s. Mao singled Deng out for praise in a conversation with Khrushchev, but after the Cultural Revolution was under way he decided that Deng was an obstacle to his plans. Deng returned to office in early 1973, much to the displeasure of Kang Sheng, who accurately warned Mao that Deng would try to "overturn the Cultural Revolution."*

ABOVE: *In a show of solidarity, China's top leaders gather at Peking airport to welcome home Chinese delegates from an abortive meeting with Soviet officials in Moscow in the summer of 1963. Second from left, front row, is Marshal Zhu De (holding hat); next to him is Liu Shaoqi, Mao's designated successor; then come Deng Xiaoping, general secretary at the time and delegation leader; Chairman Mao; Peng Zhen, Peking Party boss and one of the delegates to Moscow; and, on the far right, Zhou Enlai and Kang Sheng, who had also been a member of the delegation. The man standing behind and between Zhu De and Liu Shaoqi wearing sunglasses and a hat is Foreign Minister Chen Yi.*

ABOVE: *Yao Dengshan (third from the left), the chief Chinese diplomat in Indonesia, was hailed as a hero when he was expelled from Djakarta in May 1967. Kang Shang is at the far right. Zhou Enlai (left), Jiang Qing (second from left), Mao Zedong (center), and Lin Biao (to the right of Mao) welcomed him in Peking, but Yao's easy familiarity with Mao and Jiang Qing did not prevent his dropping from sight within twelve months.*

ABOVE: *Sidney Rittenberg, an American translator at Radio Peking, with Mao Zedong, who introduced him to Kang Sheng in 1964. "Khrushchev says I am full of empty talk," Mao told Rittenberg. "I want you to meet my Minister for Empty Talk, Comrade Kang Sheng." RIGHT: One of the rare photographs of Kang Sheng smiling shows him at Peking airport in July 1963 after returning from talks in Moscow that marked a further step toward a total break between the two Communist giants.*

LEFT: *This montage was already out of date when published in 1967. Deng Xiaoping, Liu Shaoqi, Peng Zhen, Luo Ruiqing, and Lu Dingyi had been purged by then; Tao Zhu, the then propaganda boss, disappeared a month later; and Lin Biao, Chen Boda, and Yang Chengwu were all to fall before the end of the Cultural Revolution. Only Kang Sheng, Jiang Qing, Zhou Enlai, Zhou's lieutenant Li Fuchun, and, of course, Mao did not fall victim to the "Ten Years of Chaos."*

33

RIGHT: *Kang Sheng, conspicuous in his white suit, checks a draft while Lin Biao (second from right) reads a speech during the Cultural Revolution. The others are Mao Zedong (far right), Zhou Enlai (center), and Jiang Qing.*

34

35

ABOVE: *The first four prominent victims of the Cultural Revolution are humiliated by Red Guards who parade them with huge placards bearing their names around their necks. Kang Sheng had a hand in the fall of each one. Left to right are Yang Shangkun, former security and intelligence overlord; Luo Ruiqing, former public security minister and PLA chief of staff, who attempted to kill himself; Lu Dingyi, former propaganda boss; and Peng Zhen, former Party boss in Peking.*

RIGHT: *Kang Sheng, Jiang Qing, Zhou Enlai, and Chen Boda review Red Guards from a jeep in the early stages of the Cultural Revolution.*

36

37

ABOVE: *Kang Sheng, a pace behind Mao, meets with Red Guards during the Cultural Revolution. Lin Biao is to Mao's left, while Zhou Enlai, Chen Boda, and Jiang Qing bring up the rear of the Chairman's entourage.* RIGHT: *Kang Sheng at an assembly of Red Guards in 1968.*

38

LEFT: *Zhang Yufeng, Mao Zedong's "secretary" and constant companion from the mid-1960s, assists the Chairman in greeting a foreign visitor in 1976, the last year of his life.*
BELOW: *Jiang Qing with members of a theatrical group from the People's Liberation Army in 1970.*

39

40

LEFT: *At the Tenth Party Congress in August 1973, Kang Sheng looked frail, but through his control of organizational matters he was able to make the meeting a personal triumph, being promoted to the post of Party vice chairman, which placed him just one rung below Mao. He never appeared in public again.*

41

ABOVE: *A cartoon captioned "Left-handed Kang Sheng" from the late 1970s that facetiously compared Kang's famous left-handed calligraphy with his ultra-leftist politics.*

ABOVE: *Photograph of Kang Sheng from the front page of* The People's Daily, *which reported his death under the banner headline "The Chinese People's Great Proletarian Revolutionary, Glorious Anti-Revisionist Warrior, Comrade Kang Sheng, Is Immortal!" This claim is less fanciful than it seems: Although Kang was posthumously expelled from the Party in 1980, his legacy of terror was plainly visible in the behavior of former comrades like Deng Xiaoping, Yang Shangkun, and Wang Zhen at the Tiananmen massacre.*

Kang Sheng's family at the memorial service for him on December 21, 1975. Front row, right to left: Cao Yi'ou; Zhang Zishi and Zhang Yuying, Kang's son and daughter by his first wife; Madame Zhang Zishi, Kang's daughter-in-law; Kang's two granddaughters; Ren Neiya, Kang's niece; and Ren Neiya's two children. Second from right, back row, is Su Han, Kang's nephew.

LEFT: *Peng Zhen addressing the Tokyo National Press Club in 1985. Although Kang Sheng had been instrumental in Peng's removal in 1966 as Party boss in Peking, the two men had worked closely over the years. Peng had been Kang's deputy during the Yan'an Rectification Movement in 1942 and 1943, and later worked closely with Kang on the dispute with Moscow in the early 1960s.*

RIGHT: *President Yang Shangkun at the opening of the Asian Games in September 1990. Dubbed the "Butcher of Peking" for his role in the Tiananmen massacre, Yang had a long association with Kang Sheng. A Moscow-trained Communist, he survived being purged at the outset of the Cultural Revolution, when he was charged with having bugged Mao's office.*

RIGHT: *Chen Yun, a Party veteran with close links to Kang Sheng, was, as of late 1991, second only to Deng Xiaoping in the Party hierarchy. Chen Yun became one of Kang's deputies in the Communist secret service in Shanghai in 1931. He joined Kang in Moscow in 1935, and they returned to China on the same plane in November 1937. Taken in 1978, this photograph shows Chen shortly after he had been rehabilitated following the Cultural Revolution.*

him. But now Jiang Qing was one of Mao's professional associates, no longer a spouse in whom he confided secrets.*

Ironically, Wang Dongxing, who acted as Mao's matchmaker and pimp, had ties to Kang that dated back to the Yan'an era. When Kang was in charge of the Social Affairs Department, Wang had been a junior cadre in one of the units under Kang's command, the squad of bodyguards who protected the Chairman and other Politburo members. Wang had become a vice minister for public security by 1955, but in the close-knit Chinese security elite, he continued to respect and admire Kang. Wang had earned the nickname "the Devil's Clutch" for spotting and catching several people who made the mistake of speaking out against Mao. He was exactly the sort of man who approved the brutal measures Kang had used in Yan'an to suppress "traitors" and "secret agents."

As Kang adjusted to Mao's new domestic arrangements, he continued to incite Mao's suspicions about Wu Han's motives in writing *The Dismissal of Hai Rui*. He also schemed secretly with Jiang Qing and several other cadres to openly attack the play. Kang and Jiang Qing assumed that the Propaganda Department in Peking would stifle any attempt to publish a critique of the play there; instead, they chose to launch their assault from Shanghai. Despite the Communist regime's monolithic image, China's two largest cities had vastly different political and cultural atmospheres. Peking was still in many ways a medieval imperial capital with a seductive air of cultural refinement. Labor leaders—many of whom had started out in life as gangsters—had dominated Shanghai's politics since 1949. The city was a hotbed of radical ideology, formed over years of battling against foreigners, capitalists, and the KMT. Kang and other Communists who had spent their early years in the Party as agitators amid the squalor of Shanghai's mills and factories had an appetite for hard-line ideological rhetoric that set them apart from the more pragmatic soldiers and bureaucrats who ran Peking.

Ke Qingshi, one of Kang's comrades from the late 1920s, con-

* Mao's relationship with Zhang Yufeng was a closely guarded secret within his inner circle. Word leaked to well-informed Chinese during the late 1970s, following the Chairman's death. The first American to report on Zhang Yufeng was probably Fox Butterfield, a journalist based in Peking during the late 1970s.

trolled the city's Communist machine, providing Kang with another reason to choose Shanghai as his base. Ke, only four years younger than Kang, shared his gentry roots and had worked with him in Shanghai's Communist underground during the days of the White Terror. Known to his friends as "Big Nose" and "Ke the Strange," Ke Qingshi made a fetish of studying Mao's writings. Ke had a set of Mao's slogans under the glass that covered his office desk, kept Mao's collected works beside his bed, and always carried with him at least two copies of Mao's thoughts. After serving as mayor of Nanking, Ke moved back to Shanghai in 1954. By the late 1950s, he was both mayor and first secretary of the Party apparatus in Shanghai.

Ke Qingshi filled Haig Mansions, the elegant, colonial-era structure that housed Shanghai's Communist headquarters after 1949, with cadres who shared his radical fire.* Ke's most trusted aide was a journalist named Zhang Chunqiao, a man who almost never smiled and who, unlike most Chinese, shunned social contact.† Zhang Chunqiao, like Kang, came from a wealthy and prominent family in Shandong, where he was born in 1917. At the age of eighteen, Zhang went to seek his fortune in Shanghai. There he started as a proofreader, punctuating and annotating classical texts for publication in modern form. Earnest and hard-working, Zhang soon became a widely read journalist under the pseudonym "Dick." He socialized in Kuomintang circles and was a protégé of Cui Wanqiu, the editor and KMT special agent who fawned over Jiang Qing when she was an actress in Shanghai. As a member of the KMT camp, Zhang penned many vitriolic attacks on Lu Xun, China's most brilliant satirical writer, whom the Communists had co-opted and turned into a symbol of intellectual disenchantment with Chiang Kai-shek's regime. Zhang later severed his KMT affiliations, and when the Japanese invaded China in 1937, he fled to Yan'an. There he joined the Communist Party and studied at the Shaanbei Academy, the school run by Kang's Social Affairs Department. Zhang began working closely with Ke Qingshi a decade

---

* Haig Mansions has had a varied history. Built by Germans in the 1930s, it was the center of Nazi activity in Japanese-occupied Shanghai during World War II. From 1949 until 1977, Haig Mansions served as the Communist Party headquarters. It was converted into the Jing'an Guest House, a hotel for foreigners, in 1979.

† Zhang Chunqiao, along with Jiang Qing, became a member of the Cultural Revolution's infamous Gang of Four. As an example of how self-contained and sullen Zhang was, he did not utter a single word during the trial of the Gang of Four, which lasted from November 1980 until January 1981.

later, followed him to Shanghai, and became one of the rising stars in the municipal bureaucracy. By 1965, he was the Shanghai propaganda chief and a member of the committee that ran the city.

Jiang Qing, like Kang, had strong feelings for Shanghai. She had many fond memories of her days as a young actress, and she spent much of her time there after 1962. From her suite in the Jinjiang Hotel, a prewar complex of luxurious apartment buildings filled with polished wood paneling and brass fittings, she cultivated close relations with Ke Qingshi and some of the local propaganda workers. Ke Qingshi had worked with Kang and Jiang Qing in the 1963 offensive against Meng Chao's play about ghosts and traitors, *Li Huiniang,* and the city's cultural bureaucrats always promoted Jiang Qing's revolutionary operas.

About a year after Kang had begun his crusade to convince Mao that there was poison hidden in Wu Han's historical drama, Jiang Qing spoke to Ke and Zhang about the need to criticize the play. They agreed, and in February 1965 Zhang assigned Yao Wenyuan, a young journalist on the staff of *The Liberation Daily,* one of the city's two main newspapers, to spend all his time preparing an attack.

Only thirty-four at the time of this assignment, the round-faced and rotund Yao Wenyuan was a product of the same world of corruption in Shanghai that had helped to shape Kang and many of his confederates in the late 1920s and early 1930s. Yao's father was Yao Pengzi, a successful Shanghai writer who had joined the Communist Party in 1927 and been recruited as a special agent four years later by one of Kang's secret-service colleagues, Pan Hannian. Yao Pengzi worked as a "communications officer" in Kang's organization, passing messages to clandestine Communist networks in northern China. But in December 1933, when the KMT Investigation Section arrested him in the port city of Tianjin, Yao Pengzi renounced communism and became a KMT agent of influence in literary circles under the KMT security chief, Xu Enceng. In spite of his father's checkered past, Yao Wenyuan was admitted into the Communist Party in the early 1950s and gradually established himself as a minor but ideologically reliable journalist.

Yao Wenyuan ran into serious obstacles once he started to write his attack on *The Dismissal of Hai Rui.* Educated in the early days of the People's Republic, he had only a hazy knowledge of Ming history, let alone Hai Rui himself. Seeking expert but discreet assistance, Yao turned to two sources. Zhu Yongjia, a history professor at Fudan

University in Shanghai who had always wanted to involve himself in politics,* provided Yao with some of the historical details of Hai Rui's story. Yao's second source was his father, by then a retired writer and secret-service agent and only too happy to assist his son in preparing an article that might win him favor with national leaders like Jiang Qing and Ke Qingshi.

Tutored by his father and Professor Zhu, Yao Wenyuan mastered the intricacies of Ming history. But before he could publish his first article, he lost one of his two main patrons. On April 5, 1965, Ke Qingshi paid a visit to Chengdu, Sichuan's provincial capital. Ke topped off a heavy meal of spicy Sichuan food with several handfuls of peanuts; minutes later, he was stricken by excruciating stomach pains and started to bleed internally, apparently from his pancreas. Minister of Health Qian Xinzhong and a team of specialists made an emergency flight to Chengdu, but Ke died four days later.† Yao Wenyuan and his backers feared that the political situation in Shanghai might become more subdued as a result of Ke's death, with the radical spark that set it apart from Peking being extinguished by his successor.

These fears proved correct. Ke's successor was Chen Pixian, a conservative cadre with close links to the men in charge in Peking. However, Zhang Chunqiao retained his post as municipal propaganda chief. That gave Yao the cover necessary to continue his work, and the article, "A Criticism of the New Historical Play *The Dismissal of Hai Rui*," finally appeared on November 10, 1965, in *Wenhui Bao,* a Shanghai daily newspaper.

Nothing in Yao's critique suggested the earth-shattering impact it was to have on Chinese politics. Yao charged that Wu Han had deviated from Marxist–Leninist theory; that Wu, contradicting Mao's assertion that the people were the driving force of history, had instead portrayed history as a process determined by individual "saviors"; and that Wu had sought to replace the theory of class struggle with one of class harmony. Noting that Hai Rui had called for land to be

---

* Once the Cultural Revolution broke out, Zhu became the central figure in a Shanghai-based writing group, Luo Siding ("Screw"), which turned out leftist propaganda. He later served on the Revolutionary Committee that controlled Shanghai.
† It was later rumored that Kang Sheng had poisoned Ke Qingshi, but given Ke's fervent Maoism, it is hard to see why Kang would have done away with such a staunch ally. Ke's health had been uncertain for some time; he had undergone an operation for lung cancer the previous year.

returned to its rightful owners, Yao raised rhetorical questions about whether Wu Han was challenging the Communist Party's land reform process.

Though filled with political arguments, Yao's article did not accuse Wu Han of plotting to rehabilitate Peng Dehuai or of being involved in any other conspiracy. In fact, Yao did not go beyond the sort of ideological criticisms that had been leveled at a number of other writers over the previous year or so. What made Yao's critique so controversial was less its substantive points than its censure of a work by Wu Han, who was not only a respected scholar and playwright but also a prominent official. Wu had long been under the protection of the Party boss in Peking, Peng Zhen, so Yao's attack on Wu had the potential to tarnish Peng's image.

Cutting Peng Zhen was exactly what Kang wanted. Peng Zhen had been Kang's subordinate in Yan'an, but his rapid rise during the 1950s had highlighted Kang's declining fortunes. Although he had worked with Peng Zhen in the struggle against Soviet revisionism, Kang had ranked lower in the protocol order at the international conferences they had attended together, and that had stoked Kang's resentment.

The decision to launch their attack from Shanghai had been a master stroke by Kang and his coconspirators—they caught Peng Zhen and the other leaders in Peking completely off guard. Without warning, an illustrious scholar-official who was a prominent member of the Peking municipal government came under attack in one of China's main newspapers. Given Wu Han's status as a vice mayor of Peking, this incident represented an unbearable slap in the face for the Party establishment that governed the capital. Yao Wenyuan may have been just a minor Shanghai journalist, but his lack of stature made what he had written no less provocative. *The Liberation Army Daily,* which Lin Biao controlled, quickly reprinted Yao's article, giving it much greater prominence. Before long, a steady flow of literary commentaries, both for and against the play, started to appear in the national press.

The orthodox leaders responded by using *The People's Daily* and *The Peking Daily* to try to stop the attack on Wu Han and his play. To Peng Zhen and his colleagues, Yao Wenyuan's criticism of one of their vice mayors amounted to a personal challenge. Wu Han published mildly self-critical articles on December 27, 1965, and January 12, 1966, in which he acknowledged having made several mistakes.

Wu's gesture set the scene for a compromise under which he made a symbolic retreat, leaving the matter for others to debate. Peng Zhen then raised the issue with his Politburo colleagues. With their approval, he referred the controversy to the Central Cultural Revolution Group of Five, commonly referred to as "the Group of Five," to investigate the charges and report to Mao.

The Group of Five had been established in 1964 as part of an effort by Peng Zhen and other Party conservatives to answer criticism from some of Mao's protégés over the allegedly "revisionist" tendencies of Peking's cultural scene. A range of activities conducted under the auspices of Peng Zhen and his allies—publication of writings by the essayist Deng Tuo, resistance to Jiang Qing's operatic reforms, and the promotion of several plays, films, and novels—had come under attack for their bourgeois leanings. Ostensibly, the Group of Five's mission was to implement a "cultural revolution" in Peking. In reality, Peng and his allies viewed the group as a device that would enable them to boast that a "cultural revolution" was under way, when, in fact, nothing would be changed. In the words of one sinologist, empowering the Group of Five to report transgressions to Mao was the same as if "the task of drawing up the prosecution dossier was handed over to the chief defendant."

The orientation of the Group of Five was reflected in its makeup. Peng Zhen, the target of much of the criticism directed at the Peking cultural scene, was himself the chairman. Three other members also represented the Party establishment: Lu Dingyi was minister of culture, head of the Propaganda Department, and a member of the Secretariat; Zhou Yang, one of the CCP's veteran literary hatchet men, was a deputy director of the Propaganda Department; and Wu Lengxi was editor of *The People's Daily,* which made him the chief spokesman for the conservatives. One lone member of the group—Kang Sheng—was affiliated with the CCP's radical wing. However, Peng Zhen had known Kang since the Yan'an days and did not view him as a threat.

Kang's position on the Group of Five gave him the perfect opportunity to exploit the controversy over Wu Han. As the unsuspecting Peng Zhen threw up a string of defenses around the play, and as Peng's subordinates investigated every aspect of the play, including Wu Han's political background, Kang sat back and waited like a tiger for the moment to pounce. Peng Zhen was cautious; although Yao Wenyuan had not drawn a parallel between Wu Han's protagonist, Hai Rui, and former Defense Minister Peng Dehuai, rumors had started to link the two, and Peng Zhen wanted to cover every base. Peng's investigation concluded that there was no "organizational" tie between Wu Han and Peng Dehuai, that the two men had never met and had no personal links similar to those between Li Jiantong, the author of *Liu Zhidan*, and the family of the revolutionary hero celebrated in her book. Once the probe was complete, Peng Zhen felt he could refute any suggestion that *The Dismissal of Hai Rui* was the work of conspirators seeking to rehabilitate Peng Dehuai.

Peng Zhen submitted his conclusions to the Group of Five on February 3, 1966, proposing that discussion of the play be left to scholars and historians—a sure way of turning the controversy into a harmless academic exercise. Kang did not utter a word the entire time, but his silence failed to alert Peng Zhen, who had no cause to suspect Kang's association with Yao Wenyuan's article.

Peng Zhen continued to believe that he had the situation under control. He ordered two propaganda writers, Xu Liqun and Yao Qin, to prepare an outline of the Group of Five's discussions; it was printed on February 4 and distributed to the principal participants in the previous day's meeting. Once again, Kang raised no objections, refraining from even the briefest comment on the outline report. The following day, Peng presented the outline to the Politburo. Liu Shaoqi, acting as chairman in place of Mao (then wintering in the south), asked Peng Zhen whether any evidence pointed to "an organizational connection" between Wu Han and Peng Dehuai. Behind Liu's question was the concern that the play might have been written in protest at Peng Dehuai's purge, as it was rumored among Peking's elite at the time. No such evidence had come to light, Peng Zhen assured Liu. Kang remained silent.

Kang, Peng Zhen, and the other three members of the Group of Five flew to Wuhan three days later to present their conclusions to Mao. The Politburo had accepted their report, but the Chairman still had to approve the handling of the controversy before the case could be closed. Under questioning by Mao, Peng Zhen declared that the investigation had uncovered no evidence of a link between Wu Han and Peng Dehuai.

Peng Zhen was amazed by Mao's reply. "I have said that the important danger of Wu Han's article is 'dismissal.' This is what Kang Sheng told me. Kang Sheng has the patent to this discovery." Kang, still unsure of Mao's attitude and anxious to avoid a premature clash with Peng Zhen, interjected hurriedly, "No, I don't have the patent to the discovery. That belongs to Chairman Mao." Mao later repeated that "Kang Sheng has the patent to the discovery"; this time, Kang declined to contradict the Chairman.

On February 11, after returning from the conference with Mao in Wuhan, Peng Zhen distributed the outline report, together with a separate sheet of comments, to the members of the Group of Five, seeking their approval before it was circulated more widely within the Party. Kang was watching a film in his residence at Diaoyutai when the papers arrived, so he instructed one of his secretaries to read them and make a short notation on his behalf. Kang simply placed a circle on the cover note, indicating that he had read them, and returned the papers to Peng Zhen.

Kang traveled to Shanghai the next day, ostensibly to attend a forum sponsored by Jiang Qing to promote radical art and culture within the PLA. But he stayed for almost two weeks in Shanghai, most of the time in a suite at the Jinjiang Hotel reviewing recent trends with Jiang Qing, Zhang Chunqiao, and other Shanghai-based radicals. The outline report of the February meeting of the Group of Five—called "the February outline" for short—was distributed to Politburo members and other senior cadres during his absence from the capital. The Wu Han affair seemed about to vanish into the political no-man's-land of scholarly debate, no longer to threaten the balance of power in the capital.

Just when Kang's opportunity to profit from the Wu Han controversy seemed to be slipping away, Mao intervened. A month after Kang's return from Shanghai, on March 28, Kang, Jiang Qing, Zhang Chunqiao, and several others were summoned to Wuhan to speak to the Chairman. Kang and his radical comrades spent two days with Mao, who spoke at length about Peng Zhen's handling of the controversy over *The Dismissal of Hai Rui.*

Obviously, Mao was leaning toward the radicals' position, so Kang seized the chance to shore up the Chairman's suspicions about Peng Zhen. Kang gave Mao a misleading account of the drafting of the outline report, implying that Peng had prepared it behind his back. Mao responded by calling the February outline a "mistake" that had "confused class divisions and did not distinguish between right and wrong." Given that Mao viewed class struggle to be "the key link," his statement made clear his strong disapproval of the report.

Now, at last, Kang dropped his mask of civility. At a three-day Secretariat meeting starting on April 9, he attacked Peng Zhen in the presence of Deng Xiaoping, Yang Shangkun, Lu Dingyi, and other officials. Avoiding mention of the February outline so as not to expose his role in its preparation, Kang accused Peng of having committed "a series of crimes" as chairman of the Group of Five. Kang's sudden outburst warned Peng to prepare for trouble. At the same time, it alerted the other Secretariat members that the mayor was likely to come under attack. They knew that a man as cautious as Kang would never make a move without strong backing; they also knew that Kang was one of Chairman Mao's few intimate companions. Peng Zhen's colleagues started to trim their sails.

Kang spent a day and a half with Mao in Hangzhou in late April to report on his work. Their conversations satisfied Kang that Mao accepted his view that Peng Zhen was deliberately trying to use Wu Han's play to limit Mao's influence. Emboldened by the Chairman's attitude, Kang resumed his offensive against Peng at an enlarged meeting of the Politburo that opened on May 4. This time, he made no secret of his opposition to Peng Zhen, delivering a marathon speech that lasted for two and a half days. Kang wove together every ideological phrase he could summon to prove that Mao's thought had far surpassed the philosophy enunciated by Marx. Besides flattering Mao, Kang also brought up the investigation of Wu Han and accused Peng of a range of political crimes. The most serious of Kang's charges was that Peng had secretly prepared the outline, which was an "anti-Party, anti-socialist poisonous weed."

According to Kang's account, Peng had instructed Xu Liqun and Yao Qin to lock themselves away in the Diaoyutai State Guesthouse to draft the outline and keep it secret from the rest of the Group of Five, "even including Kang Sheng, who lived in the same building." Kang presented the Politburo with a fabricated chronology that claimed Kang had fought Peng Zhen's proposals through bitter arguments at meetings of the Group of Five. So Kang was completely absolved of any blame for the outline, while Peng's manipulation of the Wu Han issue was presented in the most unfavorable light.*

---

* Kang enlisted a still unidentified colleague to assist his secretary in fabricating a chronicle of events that highlighted Peng's alleged duplicity. "Zhongkan" referred to Kang's ally as "X X," implying a two-character name. While both Wang Li and Guan Feng qualify, they are unlikely candidates, because "Zhongkan" would hardly protect such discredited figures. Presumably the reason "Zhongkan" refused to identify Kang's confederate is that he was politically active after the Cultural Revolution. Three possibilities are Zhou Yang, Hu Sheng, and Yao Qin.

The Politburo meeting lasted twelve days, finally breaking up on May 16. Thanks to Kang, Peng was humiliated: the Politburo dissolved the Group of Five and declared the outline report invalid. On the final day of the session, Kang and Chen Boda jointly drafted an internal Party document, known subsequently as the May 16 Communiqué, which criticized Peng Zhen and recorded the decisions made by the Politburo.

During the next few weeks, Kang continued to falsely accuse Peng Zhen of having prepared the outline in secret. North Vietnamese leader Ho Chi Minh paid a call on Kang on June 3 (the two had first met when Ho worked with the Chinese Communists in Yan'an twenty years earlier) and got a briefing on the outline. Kang declared, "I was a member of the Group of Five, but he [Peng] did this behind my back and I was dissatisfied." Ho interrupted Kang, saying, "You were also at fault." Kang, never at a loss for words, immediately replied, "Yes. My fault was that I was watching a film when his secretary delivered it to me to read. I was unhappy and told my secretary to draw a circle for me, and continued to watch the film. I must say now that I was not being responsible toward the party." Kang's conversations with Ho and other foreign dignitaries were recorded by clerks and circulated among senior officials, spreading the lie that Kang had steadfastly resisted Peng.

Peng Zhen was removed from all his posts, as were three other members of the Group of Five: propaganda chief Lu Dingyi, deputy propaganda head Zhou Yang, and *People's Daily* editor Wu Lengxi.* Their ousters were announced on June 3—by coincidence, the same day Kang met with Ho Chi Minh. In place of the Group of Five, the Politburo established what was known as the Cultural Revolution Group (CRG), which was immediately given extremely high status and almost total political freedom. It reported directly to the Standing Committee of the Politburo, then dominated by Chairman Mao, Defense Minister Lin Biao, and Premier Zhou Enlai.

Kang declined to join the CRG. But that did not curb his influence on it: the members were Jiang Qing, Chen Boda, Zhang Chunqiao, Wang Li, and Guan Feng—and each one had close ties with

---

* Support for Peng Zhen's management of the Group of Five was not the only charge brought against the trio. Lu Dingyi came under pressure from Lin Biao because Lu's wife, Yan Weibing, had written several anonymous letters alleging that Ye Qun, Lin's wife, had once been the lover of Wang Shiwei, the dissident writer whom Kang had arrested in 1942 as a Trotskyite. Wang was finally executed in 1947.

Kang. Kang did agree to serve as the group's "adviser," a title that suited his style perfectly. His post gave him an identifiable place in the newly emerging political order while allowing him to distance himself from any mistakes the CRG might make. Kang got exactly what he had always desired: maximum power with minimal risk.

By luring Mao into the debate over *The Dismissal of Hai Rui*, Kang had laid the groundwork for the Cultural Revolution. After three years of false starts in the form of various ideological campaigns, Kang and his network of radical and opportunistic associates had finally destroyed one of the top leaders of the Party establishment. Peng Zhen, Liu Shaoqi, and Deng Xiaoping constituted the supreme triumvirate of pragmatic mandarins; Peng's fall represented a crucial step as Kang and his allies moved to gain power over the entire country.

Four members of the Group of Five had been disgraced. Only one survived with his reputation and authority intact. To China's misfortune, that man was Kang Sheng.

Chapter XVI

"DON'T FEAR
CHAOS!"

DESTROYING PENG ZHEN was by far Kang Sheng's most daring operation since his return to the political scene in 1956. His triumph propelled Kang into a frenzy of conspiratorial activity. Aided by several women, including his wife and the ever present Jiang Qing and a university lecturer notorious for her sexual opportunism, Kang spent almost every waking minute plotting ways to incite turbulence that would sweep more of his rivals from power.

During the last few days before the formal ouster of Peng Zhen, Kang moved to expand his offensive. Using Guan Feng as his cutout in order to avoid exposing himself to risk, Kang passed a discreet message to Wu Chuanqi, one of Guan's colleagues in the philosophy and social-science department of the Academy of Sciences. Kang suggested that Wu write a big-character poster accusing Peng Zhen of "political crimes."*

Kang's advice frightened Wu, who did not know that Peng Zhen was about to go down. Nevertheless, Wu understood that Guan was acting on behalf of a powerful official, so he prepared a poster. In place of the mayor, though, Wu attacked a much less prominent

---

* "Big-character posters" are a common Chinese means of political expression. A prominent part of the student demonstrations during the 1920s and 1930s, they also were used after the Communist victory in 1949, although within strict guidelines. Big-character posters sprang up all across the nation again during the Cultural Revolution.

figure, Yang Shu, a deputy director of the Propaganda Department in Peking. Yang Shu did not have enough importance to cause much controversy, however, so the first wall poster of the Cultural Revolution was little noted and soon forgotten.

Kang quickly deployed Cao Yi'ou to start an offensive on another front, at Peking University—then as now, China's most prestigious institution of higher learning and a breeding ground for protest activity. Kang told Cao to contact radical lecturers and students and goad them to criticize the university administration—and, by implication, the Peking municipal apparatus, which was responsible for education in the capital. To provide an excuse for her presence on campus in case things went wrong, Kang used his position as director of the Theoretical Small Group to give Cao a commission to "investigate" student politics.

Cao Yi'ou, accompanied by six aides, checked into the West Summer Palace Guesthouse, a series of pavilions the Empress Dowager had had built during the nineteenth century near the front gates of Peking University. The campus occupies several hundred wooded acres, once the grounds of the Rockefeller-financed Yenching University. The elite character of the university is reflected in its architecture: pagoda-style buildings are topped with glazed tiles, moon gates open on to quiet courtyards, and a scenic lake meanders through classical gardens. China's newer schools and colleges, by contrast, tend to consist of barren compounds crammed with square, gray cement buildings.

Cao made secret contact with radical activists at Peking University, inviting them to call on her for "consultations." The most energetic of her visitors was Nie Yuanzi, a plump woman of forty-five who was a lecturer in Marxism and a member of the Party committee that ran the department of philosophy. Politically active since the early 1960s, Nie was a sufficiently outspoken Maoist to serve Kang's purposes. Her private life generated whispered tales of sexual intrigue. She had divorced her first husband after he was branded a "rightist" and then married a very highly placed Party leader, Wu Gaizhi, twenty years her senior. Wu, who had joined the CCP at the same time as Kang, belonged to the Central Discipline Inspection Committee, a watchdog unit that rooted out unorthodox cadres; Nie used her second husband's connections to advance her career. Her marital opportunism aroused much hostile comment among university colleagues, but her reputation did not faze Kang. "Even if Nie is a tortoise we should support her," Kang commented sarcastically to Cao.*

Nie Yuanzi tended to favor extreme measures. She suggested a wall poster exposing the alleged crimes of the central Party apparatus, starting with Liu Shaoqi and Deng Xiaoping. But Cao Yi'ou, on Kang's advice, warned Nie not to be so reckless. Kang had Cao tell Nie to select a more modest target, such as the Party Committee for the city of Peking. Kang designated three potential scapegoats: Song Shuo, the municipal Party secretary for education; Lu Ping, a veteran revolutionary and president of Peking University since 1959; and Peng Peiyun, deputy head of the CCP unit at the university. All three were associated with the Party structure in Peking, yet each had a role in education. Nie and her group could go after the entire municipal Party if the attack succeeded; if not, Kang could disown the movement as nothing more than a misguided case of campus politics. Come what might, he ran little personal risk.

Following Cao Yi'ou's advice, Nie Yuanzi and six radical students from the philosophy department pasted up a wall poster on May 25, 1966. As Kang had suggested, Nie targeted Song Shuo, Lu Ping, and Peng Peiyun, along with the municipal committee as a whole. Modest as Nie Yuanzi's approach was, it set off an unexpectedly hostile reaction among the students. Angry mobs tore the poster from the wall, and various student groups argued and fought with each other. That night, in response to reports of disturbances, Zhou Enlai sent several representatives to pacify the students and investigate the sudden outbreak of trouble. The premier's agents reminded the students that wall posters must conform to established guidelines, restored order, and rebuked Nie Yuanzi and her fellow agitators—but failed to discover who was behind her actions.

Kang learned within hours of Zhou's intervention and moved to protect his flanks. Student turbulence was a key element in his plans, but now he faced the prospect that Zhou, with his vast public prestige and bureaucratic influence, might succeed in restoring calm at the university. Even more disturbing, if Zhou were to find out about

---

* "Tortoise" has unpleasant overtones in Chinese. It has a vulgar meaning normally translated as "cuckold" and derived from the belief that a female tortoise's eggs are fertilized by a number of males. But it also represents the male sex organ, which is suggested by the shape and movement of the tortoise's neck and head. Branding a woman a "tortoise" is the ultimate condemnation of her morals.

Kang's responsibility for the poster, Kang could be severely embarrassed, or worse.

To some extent, Kang had painted himself into a corner. He decided to ignore established procedures and take a policy question straight to Mao, then in southern China. Liu Shaoqi was supposed to review every document submitted to the Chairman, but Kang bypassed Liu, sent the text of Nie's poster directly to Mao, and asked for his endorsement.

Several days passed before Mao replied. Kang had spent a quarter-century flattering Mao, doing personal and political favors for the supreme leader, and engaging him in conversations about art, literature, politics, and Marxist philosophy; but as he waited for Mao's word, he felt uneasy. Kang's maneuver required the Chairman's support of the poster, and Kang had no guarantee of that. The suspense ended on June 1, when Mao telephoned Kang from Wuhan. As Kang explained to a rally at Peking University several months later, Mao was delighted; the Chairman's words "liberated" him. Just as he had endorsed Kang's conspiratorial interpretation of the play *The Dismissal of Hai Rui*, Mao approved Nie's poster and ordered the Central Radio Station to broadcast the text.

Until then, news of the poster had spread by word of mouth to a limited audience of students, lecturers, and university officials. Once Central Radio carried the message, however, everyone knew about it. Listeners besieged the radio station with telephone calls, furious about the abuse directed against the municipal committee. The station kept records of the calls, but without backing from senior leaders, public opinion had little impact. On the contrary, Kang cited the protest calls as evidence of how cleverly the municipal authorities were manipulating the city's population. Any sense of objective reality was slipping away.

The following day, June 2, Kang had the text of Nie's poster published in *The People's Daily*. Under the banner headline "Big-Character Poster Exposes a Large Conspiracy," the nation's leading newspaper carried a front-page attack on the Peking municipal committee. To strengthen the impact of the poster, Kang assigned Chen Boda, Guan Feng, and Wang Li, a deputy editor of *Red Flag*,* to draft

---

* Wang Li, born into a Jiangsu landlord family, was a KMT member before he turned to the CCP. By the late 1940s, he had become one of Kang's protégés in Shandong, where Wang worked closely with Guan Feng.

a "commentary"—a sort of informal editorial expressing the views of senior leaders.

The critique prepared at Kang's direction, "Welcome the First Big-Character Poster," signaled to the public that Nie had powerful backers. *The People's Daily* carried a lead story about the broadside and wholeheartedly endorsed its message on the editorial page. The newspaper's support amounted to a call for rebellion against the municipal authorities. Before another day passed, Party officials announced that Peng Zhen, Lu Ping, and Peng Peiyun had been sacked. Even so, Kang was not yet confident of a major victory. Mao, absent from Peking much of the time at his villa in Hangzhou, continued to keep his own counsel. The Chairman had revealed a desire for change but had never stated how far he wanted the trend toward anarchy to go.

The first violence of the Cultural Revolution erupted on June 18, 1966, when Nie Yuanzi, secretly backed by Cao Yi'ou and Kang, organized a mass movement to criticize and humiliate senior members of the university administration. Nie and her youthful lieutenants set up an open-air stage—dubbed "the Ghost Fighting Platform"—and assembled a crowd of rebellious students. The demonstrators, convinced that the university management had been conspiring with the Peking municipality to frustrate Mao's wishes, sent out search parties to grab university cadres and professors and drag them to the meeting to account for themselves. Tempers flared; angry students, carried away by the unexpected opportunity to defy authority, started to kick and punch the sixty or so professors, lecturers, and Party cadres who had been rounded up. The young rebels forced their victims to wear dunces' hats, pinned insulting placards to their clothes, smeared their faces with black ink, manhandled them into kneeling postures, and in many cases shaved the hair off one side of their heads. Some of the professors were badly injured, and a number of women had their clothes torn and their breasts fondled—treatment almost unheard of in the puritanical atmosphere of socialist Peking.

The June 18 riot, the first unplanned violence since the Communists had marched into Peking in 1949, was a shocking challenge to a regime preoccupied with public order. Kang himself, fearing that the disturbances could thwart his plans by provoking military intervention or by making Mao more cautious, joined in criticism of the day's outrages.

Within a few weeks, though, seeing that the June 18 outburst had not incited a dangerous backlash, Kang emerged from behind his screen of intermediaries and began openly advocating mass mobilization. "Don't fear chaos!" he exhorted a crowd of sympathizers on July 27, 1966, at Peking Normal University. The next day, he told a student audience at Peking University that the June 18 incident amounted to "a revolutionary mass movement" with "basically good people striking bad people." Although the outbreak of disorder had violated Party guidelines, Kang promised that the students involved would be forgiven for "the product of a moment's indignation." He defended the way the victims were compelled to wear dunces' hats and carry placards listing their crimes, insisting that the punishments were "as light as anything."

The juggernaut of the Cultural Revolution had been set in motion. By the end of July, more than 120 senior cadres and prominent intellectuals would be chased from office. Liu Shaoqi, Mao's heir apparent, came under attack in August. But that was just the start. Within eighteen months, casualties would number in the millions.

In Nie Yuanzi, Kang had an agent in place at Peking University. But as the clouds of violence and disorder gathered, he searched for ways to expand his influence—Peking University was not exactly a power center in the Chinese political structure. Aware that he needed to add to his authority, Kang turned to his stronghold at the Party School. He had transformed the school into a battlefield two years earlier with his attack on its vice president, the prominent Marxist philosopher Yang Xianzhen; now he plotted to tighten his grip on this key institution.

Kang mapped his strategy from his office at the Diaoyutai State Guesthouse. Once a hotel for foreign dignitaries and high officials, the guesthouse became the radical leaders' headquarters, converted into a fortified compound where they could live, work, and hold discreet meetings in comparative safety. Jiang Qing, now living completely apart from Mao, resided in Diaoyutai, as did Guan Feng, Wang Li, Zhang Chunqiao, and Chen Boda. They let weeds overrun the previously immaculate gardens and planted wheat and sunflowers in front of some of the buildings. At the same time, windows and doors were sealed to keep intruders out.

Kang started putting his plans in motion by summoning a Party School official, Li Guangwen, to his office. Li was another member of Kang's Shandong mafia, one of several Communist organizers and propaganda workers who had first joined Kang's circle during the late 1940s, when Kang took charge of land reform in his native province. Ever since, Li had held Kang in awe; Kang had been a Moscow-trained revolutionary when Li was still a child. After transferring to the Party School in 1963, Li came to view Kang as a potential bene-factor. He was especially pleased that Kang had turned to him at a moment of crisis.

Kang let Li look at a copy of a paper the Ministry of Posts and Telegraphs had submitted to Mao. The document reported that Party School head Lin Feng had taken extraordinary measures to prevent a student* from sending a criticism of him to Mao. "Lin Feng is just too much of a dictator," Li Guangwen protested as soon as he glanced through the document. "[Imagine] checking personal mail in this way in order to deprive a youth of the right to write to Chairman Mao," Li added, genuinely outraged by evidence of Lin Feng's high handed-ness.

Li's indignation was exactly what Kang had hoped for. He gave Li his orders: "Return quickly to the school. The leadership of the Party committee at the school is very weak. Everywhere else the Cul-tural Revolution is being conducted with great enthusiasm, but the Party School seems cold and quiet. It can't get itself started." Kang was deliberately vague, but Li went away convinced that any action he took would receive his mentor's blessing.

Li's first opportunity for action came a few weeks later, when Zhi Chun, a young woman student, hung a wall poster that criticized school head Lin Feng. Li Guangwen prepared to defend Zhi Chun; before he could act, though, Lin Feng had mobilized his own follow-ers against her. Lin Feng, a tough veteran who had lost an arm on the battlefield before becoming Liu Shaoqi's secretary, had little trouble outflanking Zhi Chun's clumsy offensive; Li did nothing.

Kang telephoned Li a few days later and asked him to bring three confederates to Diaoyutai. They were Zhi Chun; Jia Zheng, deputy head of the Party School; and Wu Baohua, a young graduate of Peking University who worked at the school. Kang listened while his visitors reported how Lin Feng had quashed Zhi Chun's poster; then he declared cryptically, "Lin Feng's main problem is not at the Party School. It concerns the Northeast. You should send your people to the People's University and other units to investigate this."

---

* The name of the student was Li Taiyou.

Li knew nothing about Lin Feng's record in the northeast, where Lin had been posted in the late 1940s, finally becoming head of a Communist university in Jiamusi, near the Soviet border. Immediately, however, Li saw that Kang meant Lin's political past deserved special attention. Lin Feng must have skeletons in his closet, Li knew; even so, the prospect of such an offensive scared him. Young people could parade through the streets and shout slogans at mass meetings, but Li was in his mid-fifties. A political blunder could cost him his job and his ability to support his family. As a result, Li again declined to act.

One month later, when Mao wrote his famous poster—"Bombard the Party Headquarters"—Kang again summoned Li, along with Jia Zheng. "Even Chairman Mao has written a big-character poster. What are you waiting for? You should take some positive action!" declared Kang. Li Guangwen finally abandoned his caution and drafted a broadside attacking Lin Feng's suppression of Zhi Chun. When Li pasted up his poster on August 15, the students rallied to his cause. Li was a senior cadre at the school, so his criticism of Lin Feng carried much more weight than the views of a young student like Zhi Chun. Hordes of students, frustrated by the Party School administration's attempts to curb the Red Guard movement, gathered to support Li and his criticism of the increasingly dictatorial and unpopular Lin.

Lin Feng did not give up without a struggle. On August 18, 1966, the day of the Red Guards' first enormous parade in Tiananmen Square, Lin Feng joined Mao, Kang, and other leaders on the parapet of the vermilion gatehouse, where they watched the surging masses of young people who had gathered in hopes of glimpsing the Chairman. To be seen publicly in such company was a sure sign of status. Or so Lin Feng thought. As soon as he returned to the Party School that afternoon, students and teachers from one of the school's Red Guard factions surrounded him, then beat and kicked him, forced him to wear a dunce's hat, paraded him around the school grounds, and showered him with abuse and ridicule.

By nightfall, Lin Feng's power was broken. Li Guangwen headed the new ruling group at the Party School, with Wu Baohua as his deputy. Through Li and Wu, Kang had gained uncontested control over the school. Now he could use its brightest lecturers and teachers to produce propaganda that would help justify the Cultural Revolution; and he could enlist hundreds of its students, who formed his personal corps of Red Guards—the brawn of the Revolution.

*   *   *

In response to Mao's call to rebel, young activists all across China formed Red Guard organizations and poured into Peking during the late summer and autumn of 1966. Between August 18 and China's National Day, October 1, four huge rallies were held in Tiananmen Square. An estimated one million Red Guards, clad in green uniforms and red armbands, participated in each one. A sea of adoring youths, waving the red book of Mao's quotations in frenzied tribute to their idol, filled the hundred-acre square.

Kang's position at the August 18 demonstration showed how much his fortunes had improved since the fall of Peng Zhen. He had ranked twentieth in the hierarchy at the beginning of 1966; by August, he was seventh. Only six men outranked him, according to news reports of the rally: Tao Zhu, a southern strongman-turned-propaganda-boss, who was soon purged from the Party's top echelon; Chen Boda, the former editor of *Red Flag,* now the leading radical spokesman; Deng Xiaoping, under attack from the radicals but still clinging to the post of general secretary; the unsinkable Zhou Enlai; Marshal Lin Biao, Mao's heir apparent in place of Liu Shaoqi; and Chairman Mao himself.

Kang was one of the few leaders to sit among the official entourage at each rally. He chaired the rally on September 15, introducing the speakers, praising Mao, and echoing the Chairman's call for a total "cultural revolution." As if his presence beside Mao, Jiang Qing, and other leaders was not enough to draw attention to him, Kang wore a white tropical suit with a high collar. Amid the baggy and creased army uniforms and the dull blue-and-gray outfits of his comrades, Kang's dress was conspicuously stylish.

While men like Kang plotted to purge their rivals, vast numbers of young Red Guards disrupted the daily life of Peking and eventually the country at large. Originally conceived as a force of shock troops whose ardor and sheer numbers reflected the Chairman's charisma, the Red Guards ran barbarically out of control and started terrorizing every corner of the land. The young men and women who made up their ranks were intoxicated with Mao and oblivious to opposition; remorselessly, they began attacking the mandarins and professors and factory managers whom Kang and his fellow radicals singled out as symbols of "revisionism" and bureaucratic oppression.

The Red Guards tapped into the malaise bred by nearly two

decades of Communist rule. As the "hundred-flowers" campaign in 1957 had shown, discontent was rampant at almost every level of society. The Communists had brought peace and temporary prosperity and promised freedom from the Kuomintang. But the commissars and ideologues who replaced Chiang Kai-shek's magistrates and policemen had become immensely more intrusive than any previous regime, interfering in every aspect of social and intellectual life. Their economic policies, which had caused mass starvation in some provinces after the catastrophic Great Leap Forward, brought the situation to a boiling point. Widespread frustration was fanned by Maoist propaganda, which spoke of shared happiness and prosperity for all—if "revisionist" cadres and intellectuals who stood in Mao's way were removed.

Once the call to destroy Mao's enemies went out, groups of self-styled rebels sprang up inside schools, universities, and factories throughout China. Accusing their superiors of belonging to "black gangs" or other reactionary organizations, the protesters dragged them from their homes and offices, ridiculed them at mock trials, paraded them through the streets, and sometimes even beat them before packing them off to the countryside to plant rice or shovel manure. Almost every Chinese somehow set apart from the masses was a potential target. A college education, a brother or cousin abroad, a middle-class lifestyle before the Communist victory, membership in a church or religious organization, a supervisory post in a school or factory or shop—any of these could mark ordinary folk as class enemies.

The movement to eradicate even the smallest privileges had a terrible impact. As parents were sent to the countryside, their children had to fend for themselves—often by joining one of the Red Guard bands that had attacked their mother or father. Writers were forced to burn their libraries, book by book; art collectors saw their paintings ripped to pieces and their porcelain smashed; women from middle-class families had to cut their fashionable garments to shreds, saw the high heels off their shoes, and flush their gold jewelry down the toilet to hide evidence of an affluent past; family photographs were torn up as "bourgeois playthings."

No one was immune from accusations of ideological deviation or hostility to the workers, peasants, and soldiers. Ordinary laborers could be cast as villains if they made enemies among their comrades or were found to be descendants of a landlord's family. Even soldiers in many parts of the country abandoned military activities to devote their time to studying Mao's thoughts and working on farms and in factories in place of the workers and peasants swept away by the chaos.

As the Red Guards tore apart the Party and government apparatus in Peking, China teetered on the brink of almost total disorder. Countless blocs competed for control over schools, factories, and government units. The nation's leaders were losing their grip on the monster they had created. Kang again retreated behind a curtain of intermediaries and cutouts, increasingly exploiting his title of "adviser" to the CRG and his reputation as ideological expert to conceal his manipulation of the Red Guards. His esoteric pronouncements on Marxist theory became a means of diverting attention from his true role as one of the commanders.

Kang still appeared in public—an essential way of proving that he remained a top leader of the nation —but he adopted the bookish image of Chairman Mao's mild-mannered confidant, an aged and absent-minded intellectual. He continued to sport thick, horn-rimmed glasses and a sparse mustache and started leaving his long, cadaverous face unshaven for days to enhance the gaunt look that Chinese often associate with a dedicated scholar. Few within Kang's inner circle of friends, favorites, trusted secretaries, and servants recognized that Kang had the look of an opium smoker; even during China's years of crisis, he still took time to enjoy at least an occasional pipe.

Kang parlayed his reputation as an expert on theoretical matters into major influence. In China, no system of law stands above politics; instead, theory and philosophy are of paramount importance. Starting in 1949, CCP doctrine had celebrated the Party's role, given the Party credit for the victory over the Kuomintang, and provided policy guidelines for governing the new state. The rise of radical thinking in the early 1960s directly challenged Communist orthodoxy. Kang's mission as adviser was to justify Mao's rejection of the policies of the 1950s and to construct a rationale that would sanctify a new program and a new elite. It was Kang who built the rhetorical and ideological façade that gave the Cultural Revolution an appearance of legitimacy to crucial segments of the population: students, urban youth, and soldiers.

Mao needed Kang in this role because Mao could not deify himself alone and weave the sophistry that would make the Cultural

Revolution's abuses acceptable to the masses. Kang perceived Mao's needs and exploited them to the full. There was no one else to fill a philosopher's shoes. Members of the Cultural Revolution Group were Jiang Qing, an actress-turned-court-concubine-and-conspirator; Chen Boda, who was so filled with his own importance that he lacked credibility; and Zhang Chunqiao, who was too junior to carry much weight with the people. Kang alone among the surviving Party veterans had a reputation as an intellectual, so the job of theoretician fell to him partly by default.

To reconcile the destructiveness of the Cultural Revolution with its claim to be a progressive movement, Kang came up with this piece of doublespeak: the brutality of the Cultural Revolution was a small price to pay for China's historic attempt to remake the nature of mankind and raise it to a higher level of existence. It followed that anyone who opposed the nation's progress toward the fulfillment of Chairman Mao's utopian vision must be thwarted.

Prominent in Kang's logic was the notion that China's internal crisis somehow reflected its position among the nations of the world. In the international context, Kang pointed out, China was a bitter foe of "revisionism," the infatuation with capitalism that emanated from Moscow and Belgrade and infected every socialist state except China, North Korea, and Albania. The forces of revisionism, Kang argued, were conspiring to poison China not only internationally but also from within, like an ideological virus coursing through her political veins. Kang named many of the Red Guards' targets, notably Liu Shaoqi, Deng Xiaoping, and Peng Zhen, as Chinese representatives of the dread "international revisionism." It was difficult, to be sure, for Kang to brand this trio as Russian agents; Deng's and Peng's anti-Soviet credentials were obvious, and Liu had never challenged the CCP's policy toward the Soviet Union. So Kang charged them with the next most serious offense, insisting that they had followed policies that were Chinese versions of Khrushchev's "goulash communism," a doctrine that was allegedly indistinguishable from capitalism in that it was mainly concerned with economic production. Liu, Deng, and Peng, Kang claimed, were traveling down "the capitalist road."

Another recurring theme of Kang's was that the Cultural Revolution amounted to nothing more than a new chapter in China's civil war. In Kang's eyes, there was a battle raging between the Communist Party led by Mao and the KMT-oriented opposition, by which he meant Liu Shaoqi and almost all other conservative leaders. Here Kang applied one of his favorite tactics, spy phobia, to the Cultural Revolution. He hurled charges of KMT collusion against his enemies, especially the Party cadres who (like him) had been arrested by KMT security forces years earlier but who (unlike him) had not been able to destroy the evidence of their capture.

In addition to blatantly falsifying history, Kang used the personality cult around Mao to give more credibility to the theoretical basis for the Cultural Revolution. Like emperors of old, Mao was beginning to have mystical powers attributed to him. Many people, including Mao himself, promoted the myth, but it was Kang who worked subtle metaphysical concepts into a way of elevating Mao to superhuman proportions. The integration of Mao's thought with the power of the masses, Kang argued, had produced a new and invincible political force capable of marvelous deeds; even the faltering national economy would prosper under Mao's influence.

To further glorify the Chairman, Kang anointed him the supreme Marxist theoretician of the century. Mao's unique contribution to the "development" of Marxism made him the "transcendental" figure of the Marxist pantheon, the one who had carried Communist theory far beyond the stage reached by Marx, Lenin, and Stalin, according to Kang. In the eyes of Mao's adoring followers, it was only proper that his critics should be chased from office and treated like dogs.

The Chairman's concept of "perpetual revolution" lay at the core of Kang's apotheosis of Mao as the ultimate Marxist philosopher. In his August 1962 speech on "taking class struggle as the key link," Mao had declared that the CCP triumph in 1949 had ushered in a socialist phase in the march toward total communism, a phase in which classes and class struggle would continue to exist. Mao implied that revolutionary conflicts would cease only when the advent of Communist society ended forever the process of class struggle. According to Kang, this was an epiphany of such remarkable proportions that it set Mao above all other twentieth-century thinkers.

To justify the persecution of many categorically loyal Communists, Kang took Maoist thought one step further and turned the materialist framework of Marxism upside down. During the socialist era of history, Kang argued, classes were no longer defined in economic terms; they were determined by mental attitude. Party members who had no bourgeois or capitalist attributes at all—the ones from neither rural landlord society nor the world of urban commerce—could be branded class traitors solely on the basis of their ideological attitudes. By placing this gloss on Mao's concept of "perpetual revolution," Kang produced a brilliant justification for waging war against the CCP establishment. Even peasants and workers—typical members of the Maoist proletariat—might be class enemies, by Kang's logic. The overthrow and persecution of Party and government leaders became legitimate conduct.

Kang also had to rationalize the damage the Cultural Revolution was inflicting on China's economy. The danger of mass starvation if harvests failed or if the transportation system collapsed limited the extent of the Cultural Revolution in rural areas, but Red Guard factionalism disrupted the manufacturing sector in the cities and towns and destroyed much of China's foreign trade. Many factories closed; others operated only part-time; endless hours were wasted studying Mao's writings, as if familiarity with them would automatically raise production standards. The railway system was disrupted by Red Guards traveling from one end of the land to the other, ostensibly in pursuit of class enemies but more often than not just looking for a good time. Unlettered peasants were placed in charge of agricultural affairs, and foul-mouthed workers rose to be ministers in the government. The country's management system collapsed as laborers and farmers were put in charge of factories and shops simply for having the correct class background. At all levels, China's economy was run by the ignorant and the stupid. So living standards plummeted: meat and chicken could be found on the market only once or twice a month; staples like rice and wheat were always scarce and sometimes unavailable; other necessities—soap, toilet paper, sugar, tea, and even material for clothes—were either unavailable or strictly rationed.

Kang, one of the few Chinese spared a life of great deprivation, made a special effort to justify the cavalier neglect of the country's economic needs and to head off arguments from conservative administrators that economic necessity required setting a limit on the scope of Mao's revolution. Central to Kang's rationale was his claim that in economics, just as in politics, there were "two lines": one line gave primacy to ideology, the other to economics and technology. The advocates of the second line were, in Kang's eyes, "bad people" who automatically aligned themselves with the reactionary opponents of Mao Zedong Thought. In Kang's idiom, his adversaries' doctrines amounted to "productivism"*—the theory that only production mattered—which he called "the root of revisionism" in industry, agriculture, and the economy. Kang's theory of "productivism," dovetailing neatly with his view that mental attitudes determined class identity, forestalled rational economic arguments from undercutting the authority of Mao and his radical followers.

Kang was well disguised as an "adviser" on theory, but his position began to be threatened as things spun further out of control. He had gained a hold over the Party School after the overthrow of Lin Feng in August, but the students started to break into competing gangs, making it increasingly difficult for Li Guangwen and the rest of Kang's agents to keep order. Two factions emerged: the Red Battalion and the Red Flag Squad. Only by acting sympathetic toward each side's leaders could Kang maintain command over them. His tactics worked; for the rest of 1966, as one national figure after another vanished from office, Kang operated from a secure base at the Party School.

Early in 1967, however, leaders of the Red Battalion, encouraged by the example of Red Guards who appeared to have the power to purge veteran cadres at will, attempted to throw off Kang's controls and assert their independence. Kang turned for support to the Red Flag Squad, over which Li Guangwen and Wu Baohua had a tight hold, persuading them that the Red Battalion was the tool of already toppled orthodox leaders. "The group that was in power has been overthrown, but it is like a centipede, and has a hundred legs. . . . The sons and daughters of some of those who have been overthrown are acting against me. Zhang Jichun's daughter is studying at [the Party School]. The sons of Su Zhenhua, Song Zhiguang, and of Ren Bin, Peng Zhen's crony, are all students there." His enemies, Kang warned, had lost so much ground since the start of the Cultural Revolution that they would seek revenge by using their children to attack him and his allies.

As part of their move to oust Kang, the Red Battalion leaders formed an alliance with Red Guards at Qinghua University, a re-

---

* "Productivism" is an inadequate translation of *wei shengchanli lun*, literally "the Theory of Productive Forces Only," which was used to ridicule the belief that economic development was the purpose of the revolution. "Productivism," however translated, was a serious charge in a society where it is believed that "politics should lead everything."

nowned scientific and technological institute near Peking University. Together with Kuai Dafu, a Red Guard who had rocketed to national prominence at the start of the Cultural Revolution, the Red Battalion set up a Committee to Investigate Kang Sheng. The first open challenge came in mid-January of 1967, when a series of anti-Kang wall posters appeared at Qinghua University. Crowds gathered to read the daring messages: "Kang Sheng is a big ambitionist, big conspirator, big butcher, and two-faced element. He is a cruel official whose hands are dripping with fresh blood." . . . "In daylight Kang is a man, but in darkness a devil." . . . "Kang Sheng is not an able minister who can rule the world, but a treacherous hero of a chaotic universe."

Lesser provocations had caused Kang to explode into rage in the past, but this time he waited silently to strike back. His chance came several days later. Toward evening on January 20, 1967, a poster suddenly appeared on the wall of the main auditorium at the Party School, addressed to "Cruel Official Kang Sheng." It challenged Kang, referred to as "an ambitious conspirator and butcher," to confess his crimes or meet the author, "Quan Wudi"—a pen name meaning "Completely Without Enemies"—in a fight to the death.

Li Guangwen and other of Kang's allies at the Party School rushed to Diaoyutai as soon as they heard of the latest outrage against their leader. They found Kang in Chen Boda's office in the Number Fifteen Building and gave a report on the day's events to Kang, Chen, Wang Li, and Guan Feng. After some general discussion, Kang abandoned his subtler habits of persuasion and issued specific orders to crush "the black wind" opposing him. "Declare immediately that the Red Battalion is a reactionary organization that should be disbanded," Kang ordered. "Second, the leaders of the Red Battalion should be arrested at once by Public Security Bureau officials. Third, let the rebel group of the philosophy and social science department participate and cooperate in attacking the Red Battalion. . . . Fourth, tell Kuai Dafu of Qinghua University that the Red Battalion is a reactionary organization and that he cannot have any contact with it."

Kang's operatives began putting his plan into effect the next morning. Chen Boda telephoned Kuai Dafu to inform him that Kang was "a respected member" of the Cultural Revolution Group; the move succeeded in isolating the Red Battalion by severing its ties with the Red Guards at Qinghua University. Red Guards from the department of philosophy and social science, Guan Feng's main base, assembled outside the northern gate of the Summer Palace, adjacent to the Party School, and helped the Red Flag Squad seal off the Party School compound and launch a police-style dragnet. Challenging anyone on the campus who did not belong to the Red Flag Squad, Kang's supporters tracked down the leaders of the Red Battalion.

The manhunt was followed by a mass meeting at which Kang's followers beat the leaders of the Red Battalion, leaving many of them bleeding and with broken bones. The three hundred or four hundred rank-and-file members of the Red Battalion were then investigated, criticized, and struggled individually until every trace of the Red Battalion had been obliterated. To help justify the operation, Kang instructed Li Guangwen, Wu Baohua, and other aides to investigate the defeated Red Battalion cadres and search for evidence associating them with an alleged network of the children of high officials, one-time victims of Kang's. By the time he finished, Kang had consolidated his grip on the Party School. Now, nothing could prevent him from using it as a source of propaganda workers and political thugs.

As the Cultural Revolution gained momentum, the Red Guards began to humiliate, harass, manhandle, persecute, torture, and imprison large numbers of cadres, intellectuals, artists, and anyone with links to the outside world. Although reports of abuse were common, Mao continued to endorse the movement, sanctifying his nation's lapse into chaos and barbarism.

The CCP establishment was shattered by Kang's witch-hunts, leaving China at the mercy of the radicals for most of 1967 and 1968. In this lawless world, Kang Sheng found the ideal opening to install himself as one of his nation's most powerful rulers.

Chapter XVII

THE SPIDER
WEAVES
HIS WEB

KANG SHENG, Jiang Qing, and the other radicals in the Cultural Revolution Group rode ever higher as the revolt wore on. By 1967, they had succeeded in bringing down the well-entrenched bureaucrats who had run China since the failure of the Great Leap Forward. Peng Zhen had been purged; Deng Xiaoping had been placed under house arrest; Liu Shaoqi was a virtual prisoner in Zhongnanhai; and hundreds of other important Communist leaders had been removed from office during the last half of 1966. As 1967 began, the rebellion against the Communist establishment spread to Shanghai, where Red Guards under Kang's friend Zhang Chunqiao seized power in an uprising known as "the January Storm." Within weeks, Red Guards began taking control in other provincial centers, extending the Cultural Revolution throughout the land.

The flood of anarchy created a range of tantalizing possibilities for Kang. One false step could have sent anyone, including him, to prison or a labor camp, but cadres who knew how to exploit the disappearance of every boundary and control had carte blanche to promote themselves. Especially for Kang, who could combine his supreme skills as conspirator and political infighter with his ties to Mao, the collapse of the old Communist order offered a wealth of opportunities.

Kang's preoccupation with his personal fortunes embraced Zhang Zishi, his son by his first marriage. Kang helped Zhang Zishi become one of the most influential leaders in Shandong, where Zhang had continued to live long after his father was transferred to Peking. Kang had a reunion with Zhang Zishi when Wang Xiaoyu, a radical official in Qingdao who had worked for Kang in Shandong during the late 1940s, sent Zhang to the capital in mid-January 1967. Zhang's mission was to gauge how much provincial disorder the rulers in Peking would tolerate.

The meeting between Kang and his son was strained—they had not met for many years—and Kang maintained an almost Confucian air of decorum. Kang received Zhang Zishi on January 19 in the highly formal setting of the Great Hall of the People, with Wang Li, Guan Feng, and several other of Kang's cronies present. Kang, seated on a sofa topped with an antimacassar, lectured Zhang Zishi on the significance of what was then taking place in China. "The Cultural Revolution is essentially [a matter of] struggling against those in power who take the capitalist road and criticizing the reactionary bourgeois academic authorities," Kang declared. "But don't forget that in a certain sense the Cultural Revolution is a movement to rectify cadres. All cadres need to be rectified, and not because they are all taking the capitalist road. Don't we speak of our desire to touch souls? Can't we touch your soul? Are you so clean?"

After observing coldly that no soul was so pure that it did not need to be cleansed—an obvious reference to his son—Kang gave Zhang Zishi the green light to rebel against the provincial authorities. "Tell Wang Xiaoyu to seize power at once," Kang said to his son. "Don't just think about the problem of seizing power in Qingdao. Think about seizing power throughout Shandong." Soon after Zhang Zishi returned to Shandong, the Cultural Revolution swept through the province, overturning the Communist establishment and creating a new, radical regime. Wang Xiaoyu emerged as provincial boss, but Zhang Zishi was a power behind the scenes, providing a direct family link to Kang.

Public order collapsed all across China during the next few weeks. Resistance to the Red Guards was sporadic and ineffective; thousands of national and local leaders were caught up in endless rounds of self-criticism sessions, placed under house arrest, or imprisoned. As brutality became more common and the Red Guards' savagery began to belie their high-sounding Maoist rhetoric, opposition stiffened. Local governors and Party secretaries tried to stop the slide into public disorder in many areas, with limited success.

The cruelty of the Red Guards to elderly cadres in Shanghai in

January 1967 triggered the first concerted resistance in Peking, by a group of top administrators and generals who had managed to avoid the radicals' firing line. Among them were some of the legendary names from forty years of Communist revolt in China: Marshal Chen Yi, who was also foreign minister; Marshal Xu Xiangqian; Marshal Nie Rongzhen; Marshal Ye Jianying; Vice Premier Li Fuchun; Vice Premier Tan Zhenlin; and Vice Premier Li Xiannian. Protected partly by their revolutionary credentials and partly by longtime links with the Chairman, these Party stalwarts had initially assumed that the Cultural Revolution was a repeat of the programs of mass mobilization that Mao had launched in 1963 and 1964. But as the Red Guards in Shanghai stormed Party headquarters and beat up local Communist leaders, Chen Yi and his colleagues realized that they were witnessing something unprecedented. Members of the Chen Yi faction, distressed that the Communist state seemed to be vanishing before their eyes, confronted the radicals at a February 1967 meeting in Peking. Zhou Enlai chaired the session, which was held at Huairentang ("the Hall of Cherishing Benevolence"), one of the Qing dynasty pavilions in the Zhongnanhai compound. Mao was absent, but most of the prominent extremists attended, including Jiang Qing, Chen Boda, Zhang Chunqiao, Wang Li, and Kang Sheng.

News from Shanghai of the fate of elderly comrades there had reached Peking, and Chen Yi and his allies were enraged. Across a table covered with teacups and ashtrays, the two sides started shouting at each other. Zhang Chunqiao tried to justify the violent treatment of aged cadres as the will of the masses, but Tan Zhenlin interrupted him: "What masses? You are always talking about the masses! Masses! But what about the party's leadership? You don't want the party's leadership! From morning till night it's just the masses liberating themselves, educating themselves, making revolution themselves . . . . Your objective is to purge old cadres, get rid of them one by one." Marshal Ye Jianying was so furious with the radicals that he broke several fingers as he pounded the table. But the moderates' rearguard action, instead of stopping Kang and his allies, exposed them to a counterattack that further weakened the orthodox cause. Kang, the master tactician of the Cultural Revolution Group, took the lead, hatching a plan to outflank the Chen Yi bloc and turn their defiance to his advantage.

Kang assembled Zhang Chunqiao, Yao Wenyuan, and Wang Li in his office in the Great Hall of the People on the evening of February

16. He directed them to prepare a record of the Huairentang meeting—an account which, under Kang's editorial hand, portrayed the remarks of Chen Yi and his colleagues as personal criticism of Mao. Kang sent the document on to Mao, knowing how sensitive he was to any slight.

As Kang expected, the Chairman accepted his version of the session. Mao called publicly for a strike against "the February Adverse Current," as the opposition came to be known. There were cries in response to protect "the heroes of the revolution," a code phrase for high-ranking veterans. Those protests were turned aside with the charge that "to protect the old cadres is to protect a small group of capitalist roaders, to protect renegades, traitors, [and] special agents," the labels that Kang habitually used to smear his enemies. Chen Yi, Li Fuchun, Xu Xiangqian, and Tan Zhenlin became the targets of vicious attacks during the spring of 1967, and one by one they fell from power.

Kang's influence with the Chairman went beyond an ability to persuade him to censure revolutionaries who had supported Mao in the past. During the first year or so of the Cultural Revolution, Kang grew as close to Mao as he had been in Yan'an during the 1930s and 1940s. Their intimacy was reflected in many ways. Mao appointed Kang deputy head of a committee to re-edit his works, making Kang one of the custodians of Mao's thought. Kang appeared regularly with Mao and was often present when Mao received Red Guard representatives from outside Peking. When the Chairman reviewed a gigantic parade of Red Guards in Tiananmen Square on May Day of 1967, Kang stood at his side, waving a copy of "the Little Red Book," the pocket-size volume of Mao's quotations that had become the Red Guards' sacred text. Ten days later, when Mao wanted to get a feel for the atmosphere in the streets, Kang and the Chairman drove around Peking in an unmarked sedan, their identities concealed by curtains covering the back windows, as they inspected the posters and slogans that adorned the city's walls and gateways. Hardly anyone outside Mao's household had as close contact with the Chairman during this period as Kang did.

As Kang's prestige and power skyrocketed, the Chinese state collapsed. High officials in local, provincial, and central governments were thrown out of their offices—sometimes literally. Cadres who had risked their lives for the Communist cause were detained or struggled and accused of "revisionism" or "maintaining illicit contacts with foreign countries." Terrified citizens watched as packs of Red Guards paraded their victims through the streets, abusing them, punching them, and forcing them to wear placards listing their crimes. Mao's goal of destroying Chinese society in order to remake it was coming all too true.

In the months since Mao had called upon the Red Guards to "bombard the party headquarters" and to rise up against the government apparatus, a firestorm had swept the country. As their hysteria grew, the Red Guards showed no mercy to anyone they suspected of betraying Mao's dreams. They attacked their own teachers—beating many of them in "struggle meetings," pushing some off buildings, nailing others to classroom blackboards. They searched out and persecuted "bourgeois" elements and destroyed or stole their personal property on the grounds that ownership constituted "political problems." They stole weapons from military arsenals, which they used to commit other crimes. Millions died as Red Guards carried the Cultural Revolution into China's farthermost corners, persecuting ethnic minorities in places like Xinjiang, Tibet, and Guangxi, which became the scenes of some of the worst fighting.*

The violence set off a series of wild uprisings, in the tradition of rebellious secret societies like the Taipings and the Boxers. In those days, large segments of the population, inspired by worship of a semidivine leader and unrestricted by any moderating organizational structure, had joined in a nationwide orgy of fighting and destruction. The Red Guards' abuses may have seemed to many observers, especially foreigners, simply a return to disorder, but to Kang, with his ingrained sense of the past, the Cultural Revolution had revived an aspect of ancient Chinese statecraft. Many times throughout China's history, emperors had sidestepped unresponsive mandarins and appealed directly to the lowest levels of society for support in attacking bureaucrats who displeased the rulers—most recently in 1900, when the Manchu Empress Dowager had called

---

* The number of casualties from the Cultural Revolution most likely will never be known. *The Free China Journal,* published on Taiwan, reported on October 7, 1989, that Communist officials admitted that 20 million people had died as a result of the Cultural Revolution. But this figure can be regarded as a maximum. A Chinese provincial-government source told the authors that extrapolations from statistics of the executions in several counties in Jiangxi Province suggest that perhaps 2.2 million Chinese were executed. At least that many more could have died from suicide, medical neglect, torture, beatings, and factional fighting.

on the Boxers to achieve what her ministers had failed to do: rid the kingdom of foreigners.

Along with cultivating Mao, Kang had to consolidate his own power base. In search of more authority, he moved to regain control over the Organization Department, the very influential Party agency he had headed nearly forty years earlier in Shanghai. Created in the 1920s as part of the Leninist system absorbed from Soviet instructors like Borodin and Mif, it supervised all personnel matters: appointments, promotions, dismissals, and transfers of Party cadres. Its most sinister potential lay in its being the repository of the personal files kept on each and every member of the Party, from Mao down to the most humble village official. The Organization Department, armed with reports from a nationwide network of cells attached to every Party and government unit, maintained records on Party cadres, including their political attitudes, personal lives, families, and travels.

Following the purge of hundreds of Party bosses during the early stages of the Cultural Revolution, the three men who ran China at the time—Chairman Mao, Defense Minister Lin Biao, and Premier Zhou Enlai—began a full-scale government shakeup. Kang gained the prize he was seeking in January 1967, when the ruling Chinese troika placed the Organization Department in his hands.

Before he could use the Organization Department as his personal instrument, however, Kang had to root out anyone within the agency who might resist his directives. He purged its staff with customary ruthlessness, creating an atmosphere of fear that ensured total obedience. To that end, on May 6, 1967, he assembled the department's cadres in the Great Hall of the People and declared in menacing tones that the department had many "problems" and was insufficiently critical of "the counterrevolutionary line" of China's two main "capitalist roaders," Liu Shaoqi and Deng Xiaoping. He indicated the direction he wanted his agents to take, commanding them to make use of the personnel records in their custody to "seize the renegades within the party." Kang also announced the establishment of "a professional group" headed by one of his loyalists, Guo Yufeng, a former military officer, to oversee the department and take responsibility for its day-to-day operation.

Kang continued to bully the cadres of the Organization Department, threatening to dissolve it for being "a black nest, a counterrevolutionary clique." In the process, he made it an instrument of great personal influence. In Kang's hands, the Organization Department provided seemingly credible material that portrayed many senior officials as "renegades and secret agents." The ability to use the department's files gave him the power to track the careers of his enemies, compile dossiers on their "political problems," and provide justification for their arrest and persecution.

Kang used the department's archives to discredit numerous members of the Communist establishment. Under his guidance, Guo Yufeng ran an operation against the five men who had headed the department since 1937: Luo Fu, Chen Yun, Peng Zhen, Deng Xiaoping, and An Ziwen. Guo assembled charts and reports purporting to show that they had been "renegades, special agents, and three anti-elements,"* and that most of them had indulged in "illicit dealings with foreign countries." Kang also instructed the department to work up cases against the twenty-two men who had served as deputy directors during the same period.

Kang also had Guo Yufeng prepare reports on "the political problems" of the 115 members of the Standing Committee of the National People's Congress, China's rubber-stamp legislature. Determined to destroy these individuals, Kang personally checked and revised Guo's reports, adding his own comments and allegations as he saw fit. In his final assessment, slightly more than half of the Standing Committee's members were "politically unreliable."

Judiciously sharing with fellow radicals like Jiang Qing and Lin Biao the material his Organization Department produced, Kang quickly gained a reputation as the expert who knew the most intimate personal and professional details about China's Communist elite. The department's records provided Kang and his colleagues with seemingly official and therefore irrefutable evidence for justifying the suppression and persecution of their enemies. Compared to Kang, with his skills at mining his precious files for dirt on his foes, his closest American counterpart, Federal Bureau of Investigation Director J. Edgar Hoover, was a rank amateur.

Kang also managed to extend his authority to the world beyond China's borders. To do so, he enlarged his role in the Sino-Soviet

---

* "Three anti-elements" was one of the most serious charges that could be made in the jargon of the Cultural Revolution. The three elements were anti-Party, anti-socialism, and anti–Mao Zedong Thought.

dispute until he came to dominate the International Liaison Department (ILD), the CCP bureau that coordinated business with Communist organizations in other countries. But Kang also used his power over international relations to persecute Chinese cadres who had crossed him in the past or might compete with him in the present or future. Once again, disciplining his own camp was more important to Kang than defeating enemies from abroad.

The ILD reported directly to the Central Committee and had an almost unlimited charter in external affairs during the 1950s and 1960s, wielding far greater influence than its government counterpart, the Foreign Ministry. In the eyes of Peking's Leninist rulers, foreign governments were much less significant than foreign Communist parties; the government was merely a tool of the Party in socialist countries. The ILD was responsible for contact with the Communist machines that governed China's allies, which made it an elite unit. The Foreign Ministry, which had little say in the dispute with the Russians, was left to manage embassies, send diplomats abroad, and handle relations with non-Communist governments.

As a department that operated both behind and above government, the ILD had a shadowy, almost covert side. The address of the ILD's heavily guarded compound—Number 18, Fuxingmenwai Street, Peking—was itself a secret for many years, known outside the CCP elite only to foreign Communists who had visited its quarters. As far as non-Communists were concerned, the ILD did not exist. But because it also had contact with certain overseas Communist parties not in power in their countries, the ILD developed a set of front organizations for its activities in Western countries. Many of China's peace organizations, trade unions, and "friendship" associations came under its jurisdiction. The ILD was also China's main conduit to Communist guerrilla units in Malaysia, Singapore, Thailand, and Indochina—a role that required it to maintain clandestine contact through underground agents in places like Hong Kong and Bangkok. In the words of the daughter of a Malaysian Communist leader, the ILD was a "very black" organization.

The head of the ILD for the first twelve years of its existence, starting in 1951, was Wang Jiaxiang, who had served as China's first ambassador to Moscow after the Communist victory. Wang had learned to speak flawless English as a student in a missionary school and was equally at home with foreigners and Chinese. He had attended Shanghai University at the same time as Kang, later studied in Moscow, and returned to China as one of Wang Ming's Twenty-eight Bolsheviks. Wang Jiaxiang tired of Wang Ming's adventurism during the Long March, however, and switched to Mao's side. Severely wounded on the trek to Yan'an, Wang Jiaxiang went back to Moscow in 1937 for medical treatment. He became the temporary Chinese representative to the Comintern when Wang Ming and Kang returned to China. He remained in Moscow until the summer of 1938; while there, he heard occasional tales of the outrages Kang had visited upon his fellow Chinese in the Soviet capital. By the time he set out for Yan'an, Wang was well aware of Kang's duplicity and ruthlessness. He was wary of Kang from then on.

Even so, Wang Jiaxiang unwittingly crossed Kang several years later. Discovering that He Zizhen, Mao's third wife, was in a Soviet mental hospital, Wang arranged for her and her daughter, Li Min, to return to China in 1947. He Zizhen had aged dramatically; she presented no threat to Jiang Qing for Mao's affections, but Jiang Qing bitterly resented Wang's rehabilitation of the woman who had preceded her in Mao's bed. Kang, as usual, lined up behind his protégé, Jiang Qing. At the time, there was nothing Kang could do to get even with Wang on Jiang Qing's behalf, but he filed Wang's kindness to He Zizhen away in his memory against the day he could use it to reinforce his relationship with Jiang Qing.

Kang and Wang had little direct contact until 1960, when the Sino-Soviet dispute emerged as the focal point of Chinese foreign policy. Kang began demanding to see top-secret ILD documents, but Wang insisted that without authorization from Mao, Zhou Enlai, or Deng Xiaoping, sensitive departmental papers could not be distributed to outsiders. Wang's reluctance to share material with Kang poisoned their relationship even further.

When China's economic problems and international isolation threatened to plunge the nation into deep crisis in 1962, Wang Jiaxiang, along with Wu Xiuquan and Liu Ningyi, the two deputy directors of the ILD, wrote to Zhou Enlai, Deng Xiaoping, and Foreign Minister Chen Yi. Wang and his lieutenants proposed that in the face of crippling economic difficulties, China should try to improve its relations with foreign governments and avoid needless warfare with countries like India, which Chinese troops had just invaded. In the uproar of the times, Wang's advice was lost—except by Kang, who used it as a pretext to undermine Wang's control over the ILD. Kang had Wang removed from the ILD in 1963, leaving Wang to spend most of his time at home reading.

Kang could do nothing more in 1963 than allow the former ILD head to retreat to his library, but the Cultural Revolution gave Kang the chance to translate his resentment toward Wang Jiaxiang into more extreme action. A few weeks after he had helped topple Peng Zhen from power in May 1966, Kang set about to purge Wang and his allies within the ILD. At a meeting of the entire ILD staff on June 21, 1966, Kang charged that Wang had turned the ILD into a department that "did not hold high the red flag of Mao Zedong Thought, but waved instead the white flag of Wang Jiaxiang." Kang also accused Wang of being "a time bomb" planted by "the revisionists." With a typically sarcastic turn of phrase, Kang added that he had examined himself to see if *he* was "a time bomb," but assured his audience that "if I am a time bomb, I shall blow up American imperialism, Lu Dingyi, Peng Zhen, and Luo Ruiqing." Besides encouraging the Red Guards within the ILD to join the battle, Kang mobilized outsiders to criticize Wang. One foreigner involved in helping radical Chinese try to oust Zhou Enlai from power actually struck Wang in the face at a struggle session.

Kang's persecution of Wang ran the risk of upsetting Mao, who had held Wang in high regard ever since the Long March. Zhou Enlai also tried to protect Wang. Zhou informed Wu Xiuquan that Mao had described Wang as "a person with a meritorious record. He is in bad health now. Don't struggle him. To kill a person only causes losses and brings no benefits." Wu Xiuquan, a rough, strong-minded cadre with many years' experience at the apex of the Party, tried to divert the Red Guards from Wang by quoting Mao's words of praise for Wang the next day at a meeting of ILD cadres. Even with the backing of Mao and Zhou, Wu's attempt to shield Wang failed miserably, backfiring on Wu himself. Kang heard about Wu's speech, branded him "a black cadre general of Wang Jiaxiang," and accused him of having had "illicit relations with foreign countries." Wu was arrested on Kang's orders and spent the next eight years in prison.*

Mao and Zhou were too distracted by other problems to shelter Wang Jiaxiang for long. Kang carefully hid his sponsorship of the Red

* Wu Xiuquan survived and returned to a senior military post in the late 1970s.

Guards who were struggling the long-entrenched ILD cadres and continued to incite Wang's enemies. In the spring of 1968, after a period of daily mistreatment at the hands of Red Guards within the ILD, Wang was thrown into a Peking prison, where he spent eighteen months in solitary confinement. In October 1969, on the pretext of preparing to defend Peking against a Soviet strike, the radical leaders sent Wang to a labor camp in Xinyang, a rural town in Henan Province. Zhou Enlai instructed the Party Committee in Henan to look out for Wang's welfare. But Wang contracted severe pneumonia in the winter of 1970, and Kang and other radicals in Peking denied permission for Wang to receive medical treatment. Despite this prohibition, local physicians who knew of Wang's illness persuaded the provincial committee to send a telegram to the Chairman. Mao then decreed that Wang must be given proper medication, and Wang was allowed to return to the capital, where he died of heart failure in 1974. To disguise his hand in Wang's fate, Kang sent a wreath to Wang's memorial service.

Most of Wang's family as well was wiped out during the Cultural Revolution. His son, Wang Mingxian, a lecturer at the People's University, could not stand the torture the Red Guards inflicted on him; he took his life by jumping into a river. Wang's nephew, Wu Baohua, a Party clerk in Beidaihe, drowned himself at sea to escape persecution. Wang's niece, Chuo Xinhua, a nurse in a maternity hospital, went insane after being persecuted for her link to Wang; she killed herself by swallowing poison. His sister and brother-in-law, exiled from Peking, eked out an existence as beggars until they starved to death in a deserted temple in Anhui. Wang's wife, Zhu Zhongli, survived, but not without being persecuted by Kang and Cao Yi'ou, who locked her up for six months in a dark cell in the ILD offices.

Kang closely monitored the politics of the ILD, at times intervening personally to undermine his enemies and ensure that the faction he supported emerged on top. His strategy for purging his opponents entailed posing as the guardian of foreign workers in the ILD and giving detailed instructions that turned their cases into weapons for clearing away opposition. When a wall poster appeared in the ILD offices in February 1967 exposing the crimes of a person named "Lin XX," Kang insisted that the character "Lin" was actually supposed to be "Ke," and that the correct reading, "Ke XX," referred to the

Chinese name of "an American expert."* Kang condemned the authors of the poster for trying to disrupt the CCP's relations with fraternal Communist organizations by labeling Ke XX "a black party." The "American expert" whom Kang had in mind was undoubtedly Frank Coe, known to Chinese as Ke Fulan. Coe, a former U.S. Treasury official and victim of the McCarthy era, had lived in Peking for many years before the Cultural Revolution and was one of very few foreigners trusted to work in the ILD itself.

The attack on Coe may have been a product of Kang's imagination, but Kang's defense of him was a marked exception to his instinctive xenophobia; he would hurl charges of espionage and treachery against foreigners, just as he did against his fellow Chinese. One of his victims was Sidney Rittenberg, an American who worked for Radio Peking and played an active role in the first year of the Cultural Revolution. Rittenberg was placed under house arrest in late 1967, causing Kang to boast in a speech that he had identified Rittenberg as "an imperialist spy" at the time they first met, in Yan'an in 1947. In fact, Rittenberg insists, he had never met Kang before 1964, when Mao introduced them at a meeting with Anna Louise Strong.

Kang impressed Rittenberg as being a strange, twisted man. Even before his arrest, Rittenberg sensed that Kang was not fond of him. "I always felt that Kang was one of the few people in the senior leadership whom I disliked and who disliked me." Kang was, in Rittenberg's mind, "a cold fish," always holding something back; besides bragging about his ability to spot foreign agents, Kang carried himself "as if he was wearing an invisible monocle," surveying others with a superior and suspicious gaze. Kang struck Rittenberg as more hardbitten and tense than other senior leaders. At banquets, Rittenberg recalled, Kang hardly ever smiled or joked like other senior cadres but acted furtively, constantly turning his head from side to side, firing short, nervous glances at those around him. Rittenberg looked upon him as a Rasputin—dark, devious, and sinister.

In spite of his malevolent aura, Kang could be affable and urbane. He was often called on to entertain visiting dignitaries and "foreign experts"—Communists from abroad and fellow-travelers

---

* The characters "lin" and "ke" are similar, and when written by hand can be difficult to tell apart. But without being able to examine the original wall poster, we cannot assess how contrary Kang was being when he saw "ke" and not "lin." "Zhongkan" believes that the character was "lin," and that Kang was deliberately misreading it.

who worked in Peking as translators and technical advisers. Returning to his residence from an April 1967 speech to one such group, Kang boasted to his aides that he had uttered only two phrases during his talk: "hold aloft" and "summit peak"—popular slogans about holding Chairman Mao's thoughts aloft as the summit peak of Marxism. A few stock expressions, Kang scornfully implied, satisfied the simple-minded foreigners who worked for the Communist cause.

Kang's four years in Moscow during the 1930s and his part in the Sino-Soviet dispute during the 1960s had given him an impressive mastery of Communist dogma. He had read enough of Marx, Engels, Lenin, and other Communist theorists to dazzle foreign and Chinese audiences alike with his knowledge. He spoke rusty German and ungrammatical Russian, but that was more than could be said of most of the other Chinese Communist leaders, who used interpreters even when they engaged foreigners in small talk.

Han Suyin, a Chinese-born British writer and author of *A Many Splendoured Thing*, spent two days with him in November 1969 and praised his wit and charm. Han testified to Kang's appeal, describing him as "a prestigious member" of the Party whose "integrity and ideological correctness have never been questioned, not even during the Cultural Revolution, when so many high officials were criticized."

Kang convinced many foreigners that China was engaged in serious social engineering. His guests never seemed to suspect that there was a dark, even monstrous, side to the Cultural Revolution, nor that they were in the presence of the man most responsible. Accounts of the horrible damage and suffering taking place in China reached the West—mainly from refugees who escaped to Hong Kong, often by swimming across Mirs Bay. But the bizarre collection of foreigners given audiences with Kang—ranging from theologians and trade unionists to professors and film stars—preferred to rely on his assurances that China's progress toward a new and happier society far outweighed a few minor "mistakes" by the Red Guards.

Assisted by his ILD aides, Kang helped "the foreign barbarians" who visited China see the uplifting side of the Cultural Revolution. Nevertheless, he was unable to prevent the Soviets from using the destruction taking place in China to discredit Mao. The Soviet propaganda machine unceasingly ridiculed China throughout the Cultural Revolution. A 1967 book by three Soviet sinologists, *On Events in China*, typified the more intellectual critiques of Mao and his rule. The authors, B. Zanegin, A. Mironov, and Ya. Mikhaylov, described the "so-called 'cultural revolution' " as "a frontal assault on the party."

Mao's regime had veered recklessly off the Communist path, in the view of China experts in Moscow. The Soviet analysts applied their own orthodox Marxist framework and characterized "the Maoist grouping" as "a petit bourgeois–nationalistic force" struggling against the world Communist movement. The "reactionary-utopian ideas" promoted by Mao were bound to fail. The economic reverses in China since the mid-1950s were due, the Soviets asserted, to Mao's "adventurist and voluntarist policies." China's failures were not surprising: "the Maoist group" was terrorizing "the best-known and most influential figures in science, art, and culture." The Maoists relied on "a kind of youth storm trooper detachment," the Red Guards, which comprised "adolescents drunk with power" and "immature youths . . . having neither political nor life experience, [who] had been brainwashed for years in the spirit of devotion to Mao Zedong."

Soviet critics also pointed out that Mao's personality cult had assumed "monstrous proportions," that it had reached "the stage of deification," and that it was propelled by the desire to "brainwash the masses . . . to carry out his every order without exception." The Soviets commented that the cult served also to reinforce "the military-bureaucratic dictatorship" generated by Mao's thirst for unlimited power. Mao-worship, in displacing China's cultural heritage, had created a spiritual vacuum, an ideological wall that prevented "the ideas of scientific socialism and the advanced know-how of the international working class" from penetrating China.

Soviet observers were most disturbed by Mao's obvious chauvinism on territorial questions. Back in the 1930s, they recalled, Mao had told "the American publicist" Edgar Snow that the Mongolian People's Republic—the Communist state established in Outer Mongolia by the Soviet Union in 1921—should be part of China. They also noted that in 1939 Mao had written that Korea, Burma, and the Ryukyu Islands had all been seized from China by the imperialists—Mao's implication being that China should recover these territories.

The Soviet analysts saved their name-calling for Mao, but their critique of the Cultural Revolution was littered with references to events and documents orchestrated by Kang. They pointed out, for example, that the Rectification Campaign of the 1940s, which was Kang's handiwork, had foreshadowed the terror of the Cultural Revolution. The Soviets also criticized the ideological basis of Maoism that Kang had expounded so loudly; they noted that the Maoist group sought to prove that Mao's ideas were even more important than those of Marx, Engels, and Lenin.

Many of the things that irked the Russians most about the Cultural Revolution could be traced to Kang. It was Kang who had declared that "to crush imperialism it is essential to crush modern revisionism," and he had said so in his 1960 speech to the Warsaw Pact conference; the article "Long Live Leninism!," which scorned Moscow for overlooking the inevitability of war, was produced under Kang's hand; and "the anti-Soviet, grossly slanderous articles during 1963–65" were "the Nine Criticisms" edited by Kang. Soviet commentators may have suspected that Kang, the man they considered the incarnation of evil in China, was behind every Maoist quirk that outraged Moscow. Aware of his actual role or not, the way they consistently fastened on events bearing Kang's imprint bespoke his influence on China's deteriorating relations with the Soviet Union.

By mid-1967, the Communist establishment had been shattered. Red Guard groups were so out of control that they began fighting with local units of the People's Liberation Army as the Cultural Revolution degenerated completely into bloodshed and factional violence. Never satisfied with his power, Kang set out to regain command of the police and espionage machinery.

Kang had had almost no contact with security work since losing his post as Communist spymaster in Yan'an. He recaptured a foothold in the world of the secret service in the early 1960s, however, when he joined the Political and Legal Group, a Party committee established in the 1950s to supervise everything from traffic police to intelligence collection. Even so, Kang's influence over the security-and-espionage apparatus remained limited. China's intelligence operation had grown from the relatively small organization he had run before 1945 into a nationwide bureaucracy; given its sheer size, Kang could have no more than a superficial say in its affairs. His authority was also curbed at first by his fellow committee members: Yang Shangkun, Peng Zhen, Luo Ruiqing, and Xie Fuzhi, the public-security minister.

From Kang's perspective, Yang Shangkun was the key. Besides chairing the Political and Legal Group, Yang headed the General Office, a central Party unit that oversaw the elite Central Guard Regiment and provided logistical, communications, and intelligence support for Mao and other Politburo members. Also known as Unit

8341,* the Central Guard Regiment performed a variety of extremely sensitive tasks. The regiment had some ten thousand crack troops at its disposal, which made it a pervasive presence in the capital. Along with supervising this elite force, Yang had overall responsibility for both the Investigation Department and the Public Security Ministry.

Kang's relationship with Yang Shangkun dated back to the mid-1920s, when they attended Shanghai University together. After the April Massacre in 1927, however, Yang went to Moscow to study at Sun Yat-sen University. He aligned himself with Wang Ming and returned to China as one of the Twenty-eight Bolsheviks. Yang worked beside Kang in Shanghai in the early 1930s as part of the Wang Ming machine, but, like Kang, he later switched to Mao's side. Kang often spoke approvingly of Yang during the Yan'an years, but by the 1960s Yang had become a close colleague of General Secretary Deng Xiaoping, whose pragmatic and down-to-earth politics set him apart from the more radical ideologues favored by Kang.

Yang had connections to some of the CCP's most powerful organs, but as the political crisis in Peking reached a climax in May 1966, he became an increasingly attractive target for Kang and his allies. Luo Ruiqing had been purged by Lin Biao in late 1965, and by May 1966 the controversy over *The Dismissal of Hai Rui* had all but destroyed Peng Zhen. Recognizing that Yang stood in the way of his plans, Kang went after him at an enlarged meeting of the Politburo's Standing Committee in late May 1966. Kang accused Yang Shangkun of being "on the same train" as Peng Zhen and Luo Ruiqing in opposing Chairman Mao and denying his status as the world's supreme Marxist thinker.

At the same session, Yang was also accused of having planted electronic listening devices in Mao's study so that he could spy on the Chairman's plans and pass the details to Peng Zhen and the Russians.†

* A source within the Foreign Ministry has told the authors that Mao Zedong chose the number 8341 after consulting a fortune-teller, who assured Mao that 83 and 41 were the magical determinants of his life. And so they were: Mao died in 1976 at 83, after being in power for 41 years, since the Zunyi conference in 1935.
† Although a *People's Daily* report in 1977 confirmed that Yang had bugged Mao's office, debate continues over his motive. Some Red Guard newspapers claimed that Yang did so to learn Mao's secret plans. A well-placed source in Peking has told the authors, however, that the listening devices were installed with Mao's knowledge, for the same reason Richard Nixon supposedly bugged his own Oval Office—to provide an accurate record of his conversations with visitors—and that the charges against Yang maliciously and deliberately perverted the facts.

It apparently was Wang Dongxing, Yang's deputy and Mao's longtime bodyguard, who discovered the taps in Mao's office. But Wang was not a Politburo member, so someone else had to have made the charges at the Politburo meeting. Whether Kang had engineered his problems or not, Yang was soon stripped of all his power, in the process acquiring a new nickname: "Big Ears."

With Yang out of the way, Wang Dongxing emerged as the unchallenged head of both the General Office and Unit 8341. Wang Dongxing was much more to Kang's liking. A fanatical admirer of Mao, Wang lacked the ties to Deng Xiaoping and the Party machine that had made Yang Shangkun such an obstacle to the radicals. Although sensitive to political issues, Wang was essentially a technician, an expert on security matters willing to do anything to help the Chairman. Wang's men handled the arrest and imprisonment of the leaders purged during 1966, including Liu Shaoqi, Luo Ruiqing, and Deng Xiaoping.

Kang by now was the dominant figure in the Political and Legal Group, and he inherited control of the various police and security organs under its supervision. One of these agencies, the Investigation Department, had evolved out of the Social Affairs Department to become China's main foreign-intelligence organization. Many of Kang's colleagues from the 1940s had remained in the Investigation Department, although his lack of contact with espionage work and the death of some former associates, like Li Kenong, had reduced Kang's influence. With the outbreak of the Cultural Revolution, however, the Investigation Department was disrupted by factional rivalries as Red Guards fought to get hold of its highly sensitive archives. By late 1967, unable to operate, the department was placed under military control, not to function as an independent entity until the 1970s.

Kang's next objective was to dominate the Public Security Ministry. Luo Ruiqing, a Long March veteran displaced by Kang while taking over the Communist intelligence system in 1938, had run the agency from 1949 until he returned to the military in 1959 as chief of the PLA General Staff Department. Luo's successor as public-security minister, the celebrated general Xie Fuzhi, was much like Kang himself: unprincipled, ambitious, and willing to back any leader able to advance his interests. Like Kang and many other Chinese leaders of the era, Xie viewed government as a family venture; he promoted the political fortunes of his wife, Liu Xiangping, who became minister of health during the Cultural Revolution.

Xie idolized Mao and was eager to curry favor with his political superiors. He willingly helped Kang gain control over the security-and-espionage machine, even though many top officials in the police establishment instinctively opposed the chaos unleashed by Mao, Kang, and the Red Guards. With Xie Fuzhi's backing, Kang charged that public-security employees had pursued "a revisionist counterrevolutionary line" and had cooperated with agents of both the Kuomintang and the KGB. He also claimed that the organization was "a headquarters for investigating the proletariat," not to mention "a dictatorship of special agents." Kang's allegations set the scene for attacks on any security officials who failed to toe his line.

Kang started arresting leaders of the Public Security Ministry toward the end of 1967. Except for Xie Fuzhi and Wang Dongxing, who remained a vice minister of public security, every senior official in the ministry was purged. Among them were Xu Jianguo, a security-and-intelligence officer who had been a vice minister since 1954 and had also served as ambassador to Romania and Albania; Xu Zirong, another vice minister who had been a loyal Party member and leader for forty years; and Ling Yun, the vice minister responsible for counterintelligence work and an underling of Kang's in Yan'an in the 1940s.

Another of Kang's prominent casualties was Liu Ren, a member of the Party committee in Peking responsible for security matters. In 1945, the Chinese Communists had invited three U.S. military intelligence officers, led by a Lieutenant Mackay, to inspect the newly occupied town of Kalgan (now known as Zhangjiakou), which controlled one of the passes in the Great Wall north of Peking. Liu Ren, then one of the local CCP security agents, had organized the visit; Kang now seized on the U.S. mission as evidence that Liu was "an American and Japanese spy." A special-case group on Liu Ren prepared a report under Kang's direction which concluded that "the special agent chief Liu Ren continued to provide intelligence to the American Central Intelligence Agency after Liberation." Liu, removed from office and persecuted by Kang, finally died of illness in October 1973. Many other officials in the Peking Public Security Bureau were arrested as well, including Director Feng Jiping, Deputy Director Xing Xiangsheng, and seventy other senior cadres. A total of sixteen hundred cadres were labeled "spies" or "renegades."

Kang orchestrated the punishment of the disgraced security administrators from the privacy of his office. After reading a report on a group of senior police and security officials, including Feng Jiping, Ling Yun, and Xu Zirong, Kang issued his first set of instructions on January 13, 1968: "This group of counter-revolutionary enemy special agents have sold inner-most secrets of the Party, government and army, betrayed the Party and country, and are so guilty that they deserve ten thousand deaths. The methods which are used on ordinary criminals cannot be applied to them." He prescribed the treatment they were to receive: "In order to prevent them from committing suicide and to strike at the enemy's stubborn attitude, they should be handcuffed and be subjected to severe, shock interrogation to make the enemy submit completely."

Kang received another report on the same men three weeks later, on February 2. He wrote his personal comments and directions in the margins of the report: "Liu Ren, Feng Jiping, Xu Zirong, Ling Yun, and the other counter-revolutionary elements have resorted to [forming] a group of so-called 'double agents.' Was this according to a decision of Luo Ruiqing and Peng Zhen? They frequently gave intelligence to the enemy, so what benefit did they get from the enemy?" The interrogation and torture of this group continued until May, when Kang and his protégé Xie Fuzhi proclaimed that their investigations had proved the existence of a conspiracy: "the old Peking Public Security Bureau Counter-Revolutionary Clique headed by Feng Jiping and Xing Xiangsheng." Members of the clique had "conspired with American and Chiang Kai-shek special agents and conducted special agent and espionage work," according to Kang.

Once they were politically discredited, Kang treated his victims like animals undeserving of even the slightest sympathy. They were locked up behind the high gray walls of Qincheng Prison, an hour's drive north of Peking, where they received the worst treatment imaginable. Vice Minister Xu Jianguo, who was kept in a "matchbox" cell less than eighteen square feet, died from a cancer left untreated while he was in prison. His son and daughter, Xinmin and Anli, were allowed to visit Xu only after four years of his incarceration. To their horror, they were confronted not by the robust man they had once known but by "a standing skeleton, sallow and emaciated." Throughout the visit, they did not stop crying. Vice Minister Xu Zirong died in prison as well.

There were also the survivors. Feng Jiping served his sentence and returned to a government post in the late 1970s. But he had spent four years in handcuffs, most of that time with one arm bent over his shoulder and chained to his other wrist. The handcuff scars remained on his wrists until his death in the early 1980s. Vice Minister Ling Yun also survived; he was named head of the newly created State Security Ministry in 1983.

Fresh from crushing resistance within the police and security departments, Kang launched a systematic search-and-destroy mission through four decades' worth of archival material, in pursuit of any records that might embarrass or incriminate himself or his allies. He initiated this process in late 1967 on the pretext of investigating the files of "enemy and puppet regimes"—namely, the ones left behind by the KMT, the Japanese, the pro-Japanese puppet administrations, and the Western powers who had administered territory in China before the Communist victory. On Kang's orders, seven hundred military clerks spent the next three years examining the archives at the Public Security Ministry's Peking headquarters. By the time they finished, the ministry's files were hopelessly disorganized.

Kang also mobilized thousands of people to inspect an enormous collection of documents in Shanghai, where he and many of his allies had spent their early years in the Communist Party. Among the friends Kang wanted to protect were Jiang Qing and Zhang Chunqiao. Both had been active in Shanghai when it was under foreign and Kuomintang rule, and both had entered into compromising relationships with the KMT intelligence services. Any evidence that linked Jiang Qing or Zhang with the KMT might have placed Kang in jeopardy. He had personally testified to Jiang Qing's political credentials when romance first bloomed between her and Mao; as for Zhang Chunqiao, he was one of Kang's closest allies.

Kang's central concern, of course, was to bury any evidence of his own dubious activities during his nine years in Shanghai. For one thing, he had betrayed fellow Communists to the KMT security police in the course of liquidating his rivals within the CCP. Much more ominous to him was his own arrest in Shanghai in 1930. If this incident became widely known, it could raise questions about whether he had been turned by the KMT and recruited as an anti-Communist agent.

Hunting for incriminating data in the Shanghai files was no easy task. Huge volumes of records, in English, French, and Japanese, had been abandoned in the confusion of China's civil war. They included files from the British-run Shanghai Municipal Council, the French Concession, and the Japanese administration. Kang's crew of six thousand—active soldiers, demobilized military personnel, students, and teachers, thirty-four hundred of whom knew one of these foreign languages—combed the city's archives and libraries for any material relating to "leading comrades of the proletarian headquarters," a code phrase for Kang Sheng, Jiang Qing, and Zhang Chunqiao.

The search through the records in Shanghai lasted from October 1967 until early 1970. According to Shanghai Public Security Bureau statistics, 519 municipal organizations surrendered their archives, and approximately 26,000 individual documents were removed in the name of "preventing distribution." Another 41,522 documents were confiscated from lower-level public-security offices. The investigation teams also pored through 600,000 editions of newspapers and magazines published in Shanghai before 1949.

Much of the confiscated material was destroyed at the time, so its contents will never be known. But how much of it referred to Kang was hinted at in a letter the committee overseeing the operation wrote to Zhang Chunqiao in March 1968, five months into the search. Ninety pages of material dealing with Kang, the committee reported, had been discovered among the archives of the KMT and the pro-Japanese regime run by Wang Jingwei—records that might well have been a matter of life and death for Kang during the Cultural Revolution. In true Orwellian fashion, Kang was controlling his future by erasing his past.

As anarchy consumed ever greater chunks of China, Kang grew more aware of the adage "He who rides the tiger dares not dismount." He plotted to guarantee his security against the increasingly menacing Red Guards: today they might be his, tomorrow he might be theirs. His final step in manipulating the secret-police and espionage apparatus was to create his own secret service, which he started to build early in 1968, recruiting five hundred agents from the central security units. He put them under the command of his personal office, which spread until it occupied three locations in Peking. Kang's secret agents also operated a torture chamber in Peking used for extracting confessions and information he needed for political purposes.*

---

* Kang was not the only leader to form a private secret service during the Cultural Revolution. The Shanghai Party boss, Zhang Chunqiao, established a similar unit known as "the Mine-Sweeping Column," which he used to impose his authority in Shanghai.

*   *   *

Stepping into the vacuum created by the Cultural Revolution, Kang Sheng came once again to wield enormous power over China's security and espionage organizations. Under his supervision, however, the secret police did little more than purge his enemies, guard him and his allies, and suppress popular discontent. He could boast of no major victories in the world of espionage to justify his claim of being a specialist in intelligence and security. In contrast to the Soviet Union, Chinese espionage successes abroad were rare. One well-publicized case involved Larry Wu Tai Chin, who was exposed in 1985 as Communist China's mole inside the U.S. Central Intelligence Agency. But Chin's work did not reflect much credit on Kang's skills as a spymaster. While Kang was riding high, Chin lost contact with his CCP handlers and had to resume his espionage activities on his own initiative after the Cultural Revolution ended and stability returned to China. Kang and his comrades were preoccupied with events at home, virtually to the exclusion of the outside world.

Kang had drawn his concept of the security services from the past. During the first years of the Ming dynasty, a period much admired by Mao and Kang, the emperor established two secret-police agencies—the Brocade Gown Guard and the Eastern Factory—that operated outside the system of magistrates and mandarins and had direct access to the court. Led by eunuch advisers to the emperor, the two police units removed troublesome officials and monitored the bureaucracy—a precedent for Kang's activities. The Brocade Gown Guard and the Eastern Factory often employed *liumang* ("hoodlums and ruffians") as informants and operatives, just as Kang used gangsters in Shanghai, secret societies in Yan'an, and Red Guards during the Cultural Revolution to further his own ends.

The exploits of the leaders of these ancient secret-police organizations, who gained enormous power over China, must have been tremendously inspiring to Kang. The most notorious of the old-time secret-police chiefs was Wei Zhongxian, a court eunuch who founded a gangster regime during the era of the Tianqi emperor in the seventeenth century. Much as Kang used his personal security service to counterbalance the Central Guard Regiment and the Public Security Ministry, Wei had created his own secret-police force, the Western Factory, three centuries earlier.

Whatever Kang's shortcomings as a spymaster in Yan'an during the 1940s and in Peking during the 1960s and early 1970s, they were more than offset by his ruthlessness and brutality. Under his auspices, China's security and intelligence operations imposed a reign of darkness and terror across the land. By the early 1970s, even the most menial officials in Peking lived in such dread of him that awareness of his activities spread to the city's isolated foreign community. His formidable reputation was encapsulated in a popular rhyme:

> *Prefer the city of those who met an unjust fate*
> *To passing through Kang the Venerable's gate.*

Chapter XVIII

THE KING
OF HELL

EXECUTING PEOPLE for political crimes was not easy after the establishment of the People's Republic in 1949. Mao had forbidden the killing of political prisoners. Men are not like chives, the Chairman declared; if you cut their heads off, they will not grow back. Stalin's custom of systematically executing the Party elite, of shooting members of his Central Committee and even Politburo, never caught on in China. The Chinese Communists butchered millions in the name of land reform and other exercises in social engineering, but the victims were usually landlords, common criminals, whoremongers, pimps, remnants of the KMT, or minor Communist functionaries—leaving the Party elite unscathed.

During the Cultural Revolution, many radicals, young and inexperienced activists intoxicated by their sudden success, were satisfied to accuse their enemies of ideological mistakes, of being "revisionists" or "capitalist roaders." But Kang had seen many cadres fall over the years, only to rise again; charges of political heresy, he knew, were rarely fatal. These were problems of "line," not crimes; in the endless flux of the Chinese world, cadres penalized for ideological errors might one day reappear as ministers or Politburo members.

Kang had often accused enemies of making ideological mistakes, but throughout his career he had also smeared his prey with more serious allegations, like being "renegades," "enemy agents," and "traitors." Instead of trying to capture the real spies sent by Taiwan, the Soviet Union, and the United States, or attempting to collect intelligence about foreign powers, Kang used the security organs to turn China into a chamber of horrors in which his rivals were forced to confess to imaginary crimes against the state.

Kang's charges of treason and betrayal were so serious as to make rehabilitation all but impossible—particularly, of course, when his accusations led to applying inhumane treatment that resulted in death by medical neglect or other administrative means. Kang did not have a free hand to execute his upper-echelon opponents, but he imposed a refined form of Stalinism: destroying a number of cadres by ostensibly official investigations that seemed to rely on genuine confessions and evidence.

The first victims of the Cultural Revolution quickly vanished from the Peking scene. Peng Zhen was exiled to Shaanxi; Lu Dingyi, Luo Rui-qing, and Yang Shangkun were ridiculed and abused at mass rallies and then sent to prisons and labor camps. As top CCP leaders continued to fall from grace, Kang, the mastermind behind the purge, found that his quest for the unholy grail of total power required him to blacken some of the most celebrated names on the honor roll of the Chinese Revolution.

Within two months of the fall of Peng Zhen and other early casualties of the Cultural Revolution, Kang decided that his plans and ambitions called for the ruin of Liu Shaoqi—president of the People's Republic, vice chairman of the CCP, and, since the mid-1950s, Mao's hand-picked successor. Liu was an extremely dangerous target; Kang knew he had to exercise extreme caution in any offensive against him. Unless he could get Mao's explicit support, Kang's best bet was to conceal his animosity toward Liu and let him believe he had nothing to fear.

Liu Shaoqi was born in 1898, the same year as Kang, and had known Mao Zedong since 1920, when the two helped found China's socialist-youth movement. After joining the Communist Party in 1922 as a student in Moscow, Liu returned to China and worked his way up from lowly labor organizer to supreme leader of Communist activity in the KMT-controlled "White Areas." For twenty years before 1949, he headed a far-reaching network of cadres that included many of the most talented Party members. Instead of the peasants who made up most of the Communist army, Liu surrounded himself with literate and intelligent men who occupied important posts after the CCP gained control of the mainland.

Given Liu Shaoqi's considerable power, Kang had assiduously

cultivated good relations with him. Kang went out of his way to flatter Liu after his return to the political arena in 1956; they were close enough by the early 1960s that Kang was picked to edit a selection of Liu's writings and speeches, a project Kang himself had proposed. As late as the crucial Politburo meeting in May 1966 that stripped Peng Zhen, Yang Shangkun, and Lu Dingyi of power, Kang continued to treat Liu with extreme deference. Indeed, a contrite Kang admitted to his colleagues at that very meeting that thirty-five years earlier he had written an article under the name "Xie Kang," criticizing Liu's trade union policies. Apologetically, Kang explained that he "had not realized that Comrade Shaoqi was the representative of the Mao Zedong line in the White Areas."

Liu's roots, like Mao's, were in Hunan, but he had little else in common with the Chairman. Industrious, colorless, unromantic—the consummate bureaucrat—Liu was characterized by Zhang Guotao as a man with "a pliable disposition" who always "avoided getting in the way" of his colleagues and who was "not a strong personality. He is not too aggressive for power. . . . He is not of the category of Stalin." In a word, Liu was boring. Mao viewed him as the harbinger of a China governed by a bureaucratic elite instead of by charismatic revolutionary leaders like himself and his Long March comrades. Liu never challenged Mao's orders, but the very smoothness with which he implemented them irritated Mao.

Sensing that Mao and Liu had their differences, Kang kept a close watch for any sign of Mao's dissatisfaction with his deputy. Kang prepared to strike against Liu at the earliest opportunity but took care not to expose his plans in advance. When Mao chaired an assembly of regional Party secretaries and the Cultural Revolution Group on July 25, 1966, Kang brought along a copy of a Party document, Abbreviated Report Number 9, quoting Liu Shaoqi as giving orders on campus politics that contradicted Mao's. Kang planned to produce this paper and criticize Liu to his face if the Chairman displayed any animosity toward Liu; if not, he would remain silent.

Liu sat next to Mao, acting as if no differences of opinion separated them. Kang, meanwhile, studied Mao's expression for the slightest hint of hostility to the president. Mao began discussing the question that Liu had commented on in the report Kang had in his briefcase. As he spoke, the Chairman directed several sideways glances at his deputy—which Kang recognized as signs of contempt for Liu. He slipped his hand into his briefcase, pulled out the document, but then had second thoughts. The moment passed, and Mao turned to other matters. "At the time I had the document with me," Kang later recalled, "and wanted to show it to Chairman Mao, but I lacked the courage, and after thinking for a long time I put it back in my case. I was afraid it would be said I was laying some charges. The next day I pointed out the danger of this document to its author, thinking of persuading him to mention it to the Chairman, but without result."

Kang continued to monitor the Chairman's attitude, but Mao kept silent on the subject of Liu Shaoqi for almost a week. Then, on August 4, Mao told a Central Committee plenum that "cow ghosts and snake spirits" were in the room. Turning toward Liu, Mao declared that the president had run "a dictatorship" in Peking. Liu made a self-criticism that very afternoon, conceding that he had committed errors while Mao was away from the capital and swearing that he was not seeking to avoid responsibility for his mistakes. Three days later, Central Committee members were shown a new and dramatic poster headed "Bombard the Headquarters—My Big-Character Poster." What made the broadside so explosive was the signature: "Mao Zedong." The Chairman's message was only about 230 characters long,* but it provided unequivocal evidence that he fully supported a purge of the Party establishment, starting with Liu Shaoqi.

Kang's caution, not to mention his obsequious respect for President Liu, vanished instantly. Within days, Kang started to assemble evidence that would, he hoped, serve to prove Liu guilty of some major act of treachery. As he launched this crusade, Kang fully recognized Liu's difference from the leaders who had already fallen: not even the victims of the Politburo meeting in May were on so high a plane. Peng Zhen, for all his influence, was a regional rather than a national figure, whereas Liu headed a network of cadres and administrators that covered the entire country. Kang knew that although charges of revisionism might be useful in the initial attack on Liu, they did not guarantee his permanent demise. So he looked for ways to portray Liu as an enemy of the state.

At the huge Red Guard rally in Tiananmen Square on August 18, 1966, Kang invited the leaders of a Red Guard contingent from Nankai University in Tianjin to an audience in one of the reception rooms in the gatehouse overlooking the square. Tianjin was where Liu had been

---

* A mere 158 words.

based when he led the Communist underground in northern China. Kang informed his guests that he was entrusting them with the crucial task of searching for evidence of "renegades" in the Party—among them, he specified, Liu Shaoqi. Overjoyed, the Nankai contingent had never expected the honor of meeting the adviser to the Cultural Revolution Group and receiving an important assignment from him when they left for Peking. Kang was pleased by their response, but to make sure that the sensitivity of their assignment did not frighten them, he took out his fountain pen and wrote a short note: "Please organize Red Guards to investigate the renegades who infiltrated every unit and department. Investigate the question of the arrest and treachery of Liu Shaoqi and others. Kang Sheng. August 18."

The Red Guards from Nankai University found no evidence that Liu Shaoqi had betrayed the Party in Tianjin, but they did discover some material about a group of senior cadres imprisoned during the early 1930s. At that time, sixty-one Communists had been locked up by the KMT in Caolanzi Prison, an imposing square compound surrounded by twenty-foot brick and plaster walls just west of Beihei Park in central Peking. Japanese occupation of Peking seemed ever more likely by 1936, and Liu Shaoqi had sent a telegram from his Tianjin base to the Communist headquarters in Shaanxi arguing that a rescue of the imprisoned cadres should be attempted. If the captives fell into Japanese hands, Liu pointed out, they would be executed.

In response to Liu's proposal, the Communist leadership ordered Ke Qingshi, then the head of the organization department in the CCP's North China Bureau, to establish clandestine contact with the inmates. Ke sent a secret letter to the imprisoned Communists instructing them to pretend to recant their radical beliefs, in hopes that the KMT would release them. Suspecting that Ke's message was part of a KMT plot, the leaders of the Party cell within the jail checked the handwriting against other documents and determined that the directive was genuine. They passed the word to their jailed comrades, and within weeks the Communists started to pretend submission to the KMT.

All sixty-one prisoners won their freedom by the end of 1936, but many Communists regarded their method of escape as extremely peculiar. By then, the Party boasted many martyrs who had died in prison. The suspicion with which released Communist prisoners were treated in case they had been recruited as KMT spies tended to discourage them from cooperating with their captors. But the course followed by the sixty-one Communists in Caolanzi Prison had been authorized by Liu Shaoqi in conjunction with the Communist headquarters in Shaanxi. Moreover, during the Rectification Movement in Yan'an several years later, Kang himself had approved the credentials of the Caolanzi prisoners. Addressing the Party School in 1944, he praised their courageous resistance to torture at the hands of the KMT.

With the Cultural Revolution under way and Liu Shaoqi vulnerable, Kang decided to use Liu's role in the Caolanzi affair to accuse him of masterminding the alleged treachery of these former prisoners, whom Kang now dubbed "the Sixty-one Renegades." "The little Red Guard generals" who had uncovered the supposed evidence against them were summoned by Kang to the Great Hall of the People, where he congratulated them for exposing "a large group of renegades. All of them are time bombs hidden inside the party."

Using the Caolanzi incident, Kang not only charged Liu Shaoqi with being a KMT agent but also implicated a number of the former inmates who had become senior officials with close ties to Liu—most prominently, Vice Premier Bo Yibo; An Ziwen, head of the Organization Department; and Yang Xianzhen, who had previously competed with Kang for influence at the Party School. "Bo Yibo and these sixty-one comrades have conducted resolute anti-communist renegade activity, but Liu Shaoqi's decision legalized this anti-communist renegade behavior," Kang wrote to Mao and other senior leaders on September 16, 1966.

Meeting the limited burden of proof required to establish his accusations was not easy, even for Kang. The prison experiences of Bo Yibo and his sixty associates had been widely touted as epitomizing the courage shown by Communists in the face of KMT abuse. On December 18, 1966, he established a special-case group. Together with Jiang Qing and Public Security Minister Xie Fuzhi, Kang directed the inquisitors to examine every aspect of Liu Shaoqi's past, especially episodes like Caolanzi that might provide proof of Liu's treachery.

The first target of the special-case group was Luo Fu, the former ambassador to Moscow and vice foreign minister whom Kang had previously helped purge at the Lushan plenum in 1959. Luo was sacked as vice foreign minister at that time and reassigned as a research assistant in a Peking think tank, the economics institute of the Academy of Sciences, a job he retained until the Cultural Revolution.

One of the Twenty-eight Bolsheviks and a close ally of Wang Ming, Luo Fu had been the Party's general secretary during the 1930s and therefore involved in the discussion of Liu Shaoqi's proposal to secure the release of the sixty-one Communists in Caolanzi Prison. Kang's special-case group threw Luo into jail and interrogated him relentlessly, seeking to squeeze out an admission that Liu had conceived the plan to liberate the prisoners without obtaining clearance from Party headquarters. Nevertheless, Luo refused to cooperate; Kang eventually had to drop the idea of using Luo as a witness against Liu.

Furious over his failure, Kang convened the members of the special-case group in his office and lectured them on how to play on a prisoner's hopes and fears, promising imminent release even while threatening endless imprisonment or worse. He also directed them to zero in on An Ziwen, head of the Organization Department before the Cultural Revolution and another of "the Sixty-one Renegades." The investigators acted immediately, promising An, who was under house arrest, "If you write some material certifying that Liu Shaoqi is a renegade then you can go immediately to Diaoyutai to meet a senior leader. A car is waiting to take you." An Ziwen was unmoved by their assurances. "Is this [offer from] central leader Kang Sheng?" he inquired. The investigators told him it was, but An held firm. "I have worked in the Organization Department for twenty-one years, but have never heard anyone say that Liu Shaoqi was a renegade."

Kang could not force An Ziwen to implicate Liu, so he took a different tack. He instructed the special-case group to focus on two incidents during the 1920s when Liu Shaoqi had fallen into the hands of anti-Communist police and to produce evidence that Liu had betrayed the Communist cause on both occasions. Under Kang's direction, the investigators tracked down several onetime Communists arrested with Liu, including Ding Juequn, a labor leader who had worked with Liu in Wuhan in 1927, and Meng Yongqian, who had helped Liu organize a strike in a Shenyang textile factory in 1929.

Kang's men used their customary blend of torture and blandishments on Ding and Meng to extract accusations that Liu had betrayed the Party. Ding, who had become a KMT intelligence agent after his arrest in Wuhan but failed to escape to Taiwan in 1949, gave a signed statement asserting that Liu had provided their KMT captors with information on the Communist labor movement. Meng succumbed after seven days and nights of interrogation and torture, testifying that Liu had provided intelligence to agents of Marshal Zhang Xueliang, the young warlord who ruled northeast China at the time. The special-case group next tracked down Liu Duoquan, a member of the police unit that had arrested Liu Shaoqi and Meng Yongqian, and forced him to state that Liu had made "a political agreement" with Zhang.

The web of accusations Kang wove around the fallen Liu Shaoqi enabled the CCP Central Committee to brand him "a renegade, a traitor, and a scab" and formally expel him from the Party in 1968. Liu, deprived of a proper diet and medication for his diabetes and insomnia during almost two years of imprisonment, was left a cripple. The regime turned fears of an allegedly impending Soviet attack in 1969 into an excuse to issue the infamous Directive Number One, which provided for Liu and other former leaders such as Deng Xiaoping, Chen Yi, and Wang Jiaxiang to be moved out of the capital lest they fall into the enemy's hands in the event of war.

Liu was taken to Kaifeng Prison, four hundred miles south of Peking, but his frail and battered body could not stand the strain of the journey and he developed pneumonia. Kang refused to permit doctors to care for him and Liu died in Kaifeng on November 2, 1969. When the news reached Peking, Kang and the rest of Liu's special-case group celebrated their success at a banquet.

Liu Shaoqi was never sentenced to death, let alone executed, but his treatment at Kang's hands amounted to a death penalty. Liu's history of arrests by enemy agencies and his marriage to an American-born woman had left him especially vulnerable, but, even with Mao's consent, it took Kang two years to bring this top leader down and keep him down.

Special-case groups had formed an integral part of the Communist secret-police system since the Yan'an period. The special-case units were staffed by experienced public-security cadres who employed all the methods of secret police—clandestine investigation, interrogation of witnesses, imprisonment, and torture—as they weeded out the ranks of the CCP during the Cultural Revolution.

Under Kang's supervision, the special-case groups compiled comprehensive dossiers purporting to prove that the cadres charged had committed serious crimes against the state and the Party. Threats, torture, and the promise of preferential treatment in return for cooperation were used as a matter of course. The arrest and investigation of one senior leader inevitably led to the imprisonment, torture, and blackmail of many others as the special-case groups searched for evidence—or, more often, fabricated it.

Kang rarely participated directly in the persecutions, leaving them to the special-case groups under his supervision. Two exceptions were Liu Shaoqi and his fourth wife, Wang Guangmei. Egged on by Jiang Qing, who was jealous of the glamorous Wang Guangmei, Kang declared the woman an American spy because she had been born in the United States and spoke English. Kang and Jiang Qing directed Xiao Ming, one of the group members investigating Liu, to prepare a report making out Wang Guangmei as an enemy agent. Xiao Ming submitted an assessment of Wang Guangmei couched in such reserved language that Jiang Qing had to ask the group to rewrite it. Xiao Ming approached Kang, who reprimanded the hapless investigator: "Your report is useless. You have not understood what Jiang Qing and I said. You have not presented the problem clearly." Unlike Jiang Qing, who had no claim to expertise in security matters, Kang hinted that he knew the inner truth of Wang Guangmei's past. "Don't bother about the report," Kang told Xiao Ming. "I will write it myself." Kang proceeded to compose a security report asserting that Wang Guangmei was not only a United States agent but a spy for the Japanese and the KMT as well. Once he had disposed of Wang Guangmei,* Kang turned on Xiao Ming and had him expelled from the special-case group, arrested, and jailed for five years.

It was Kang who ultimately decided the fate of most of the high cadres hauled from their offices by the Red Guards. He personally supervised ten special-case groups that investigated the "crimes" of 220 defendants from the very apex of the Communist Party—nearly 20 percent of the 1,260 senior leaders brought before the revolutionary tribunals.

The records surviving from the late 1960s show that as director of the ten special-case groups, Kang certified as criminals 33 "national leaders" (officials above the rank of government minister) and 210 government ministers, provincial heads, and army commanders. Adding to the list those cadres implicated as witnesses or accessories, the upper-echelon victims of Kang's special-case groups totaled 839. Long before Kang fulfilled his responsibilities as a master investigator

---

* Wang Guangmei spent several years in prison but survived and was appointed to a senior position in the Academy of Social Sciences after the Cultural Revolution.

during the Cultural Revolution, the highest ranks of the CCP were decimated.

Hardest of all for Kang and his cronies to destroy was Deng Xiaoping, the CCP's general secretary at the time Kang decided that his former friend and colleague must go.

Kang and Deng had worked closely together on the Sino-Soviet split just a few years earlier, but by October 1966 Kang had turned into an outspoken critic of Deng. Kang coined the term "Liu–Deng revisionist line" to link Deng directly with Liu Shaoqi, who had already been attacked by Mao, and then ordered Red Guards from the Party School to investigate "the Liu–Deng problem." Red Guards put Deng through a struggle-and-criticism session like the one that had marked the beginning of the end for Liu; but at that point Zhou Enlai interceded with Mao, who ruled that Deng was not to be subjected to any cruelties and would retain his post.

Since Mao and Zhou gave Deng a layer of protection, Kang and the radicals had to find more inventive ways to ruin him. Kang struck again in late 1966 and early 1967 but came up with nothing worse than that Deng was "very lazy," "has not properly studied Mao's works," and was "a Khrushchev-type person." Recognizing that these were hollow charges against a man of Deng's stature, Kang ordered his agents at the Party School to compile a collection of Deng's "revisionist" works. Once again, the difficulty of eliminating Deng was made clear: a painstaking search through every word Deng had either written or spoken yielded only one-third as many "revisionist" remarks as Liu Shaoqi had been accused of uttering.

Kang resumed his criticism of Deng at a March 1967 meeting of the Military Commission, claiming that Deng had delivered an anti-Mao speech at the Eighth Party Congress in 1956. According to Kang, Deng had in effect declared, "The Twentieth Congress of the Communist Party of the Soviet Union had a good result, in that it told us what serious consequences flow from making a cult of personality." This sentiment, Kang maintained, "maliciously attacks and slanders our great leader, Chairman Mao, and also maliciously attacks Marxism–Leninism and Mao Zedong Thought."

Kang's charges forced Deng to step down as general secretary, but Kang still had no grounds to justify a regimen of physical abuse that might have placed Deng's life in jeopardy. During his persecution of Liu Shaoqi, Kang had produced witnesses to swear that Liu was a "renegade" who had betrayed the Communist Party, but Deng's errors were essentially intellectual in character—problems of "line." And since Deng had never been arrested by the KMT, Kang could not accuse him of having been a traitor. Finally, in April 1967, Kang came up with enough evidence to charge that Deng had once been a "deserter." In 1931, or so Kang's story went, Deng had abandoned a column of troops under his command in the midst of a battle against the KMT general Bai Chongxi in Guangxi Province. Deng had fled first to Hong Kong, then to Shanghai, according to Kang. At the time, Deng had explained that he was reporting to central headquarters, but Kang now asserted that on reaching Shanghai, Deng had spent his time feasting, drinking, and sampling the city's luxuries. Kang's allegations had enough basis in reality to lend them some credibility: Deng had, in fact, traveled to Shanghai in 1931 after a military setback in Guangxi. Even so, the case against Deng was much weaker than anything Kang had manufactured against Liu and so many other victims. Deng may have abandoned his post, but he had not consorted with the enemy. Not even Kang could use Deng's alleged desertion to accuse him of having betrayed the Communist cause.

Although Deng was deprived of influence, the failure of Kang and his comrades to come up with more damning accusations kept Deng out of the hands of both the Red Guards and the special-case group investigators. Deng had worked closely with Mao for decades; he had been a member of the CCP's rural wing led by Mao, had made the Long March, and had supported Mao against the Twenty-eight Bolsheviks at the Zunyi meeting in 1935. Deng had cooperated with the urban-based cadres who had been part of Liu Shaoqi's organization in "the White Areas" during the 1950s, but he had still maintained close ties to Mao, leading Mao's defense against Gao Gang in 1954 and later supporting Mao in the face of Soviet criticism. The radicals had persuaded Mao to agree to Deng's removal from office, but he would not permit them to kill, torture, or imprison Deng. When the central leaders issued the Number One Directive, which led to Liu Shaoqi's transfer to Kaifeng Prison in 1969, Deng was sent to a small town in Jiangxi Province, where he spent three years, more or less unmolested, as a factory worker. Despite Kang's best efforts, Deng would live to fight again another day.

Kang could have taken it upon himself and persisted in having Deng struggled by Red Guards or tortured by special-case investigators, but he dared not do so without Mao's approval. Mao may not have acted in time to save Deng from the Red Guards' brutality, but Kang knew that the Chairman had the power to track down and punish anyone responsible for unauthorized mistreatment of a figure as important as Deng. Kang had personally supervised the interrogation and torture of many prisoners in Yan'an, but, mindful of the dangers posed by the Cultural Revolution, he usually operated at a distance from the detention centers and prisons. He continued to authorize the use of violence against many of his victims but carefully obscured his role, as he had done in the case of Marshal Peng Dehuai. In July 1967, Kang called in Qi Benyu, a Red Guard leader who had risen into the political elite. Kang told Qi to transmit a message to Han Aijing, the Red Guard leader at the Peking Aeronautical Academy, that Peng Dehuai was to be subjected to violent struggle. Peng was severely beaten and left with broken ribs and other serious injuries, but Kang's involvement remained a secret. The young Maoists had no idea that their seemingly spontaneous attack on the one-time minister of defense had originated at the highest level.

In arranging the execution of personal enemies who, unlike Deng, were not untouchable members of the Communist elite, Kang also followed the formalities of bureaucratic procedure. During the search for renegades and special agents that consumed his attention in the late 1960s, Kang discovered that two men who knew some of the truth about his own betrayal of Party rivals in the 1930s were in prison in Peking. Both men, Wang Yuncheng and Lu Futan, while working with Kang in Shanghai, had been arrested by the KMT and then recruited by the KMT security services.

Wang and Lu, like many Kuomintang intelligence officials, had failed to escape from the mainland after 1949. They were captured by the Communists, but their extensive knowledge of the KMT's clandestine activities made them more valuable alive than dead to China's new rulers. After hearing a special-case group report on Wang in late December 1968, Kang instructed the investigators to immediately write a report requesting approval for his execution. But Wang was not put to death then; a few weeks later, Kang pressed again for an early execution. Bureaucratic inertia, combined with the reluctance of individual public-security officials to take responsibility for killing prominent prisoners, delayed implementation of Kang's orders. "I have repeatedly told you that these men are responsible for many crimes and great evil," a fuming Kang wrote to his subordinates, "and allowed you to compile a report and execute them quickly. But you just don't do it." At last, both Wang and Lu were executed in secret in October 1969.

Kang also intervened to make sure that the treatment of Wu Han, whose play *The Dismissal of Hai Rui* had served as an excuse to ignite the Cultural Revolution, would guarantee his death. Having already branded Wu Han a "revisionist" who was seeking to overturn the verdict against Peng Dehuai, Kang needed to tarnish his reputation further in order to justify more savagery against him. Kang resurrected a claim from the initial controversy over Wu Han's play, insisting that Wu Han could possibly be Wu Xiaopu, a Communist who had defected to the KMT in Shanghai in the 1930s. Kang's allegations led to Wu Han's jailing in March 1968. The special-case group started an around-the-clock interrogation, depriving the playwright of sleep and beating him at frequent intervals. When it became apparent that Wu Han was not going to confess to any connection with the renegade Wu Xiaopu, the special-case group reported their failure.

An enraged Kang shouted at the investigators, "If Wu Han is not a renegade then he is a special agent!" Producing records on Wu Han's contacts with Soviet diplomats during the Chinese Civil War in the late 1940s, Kang insisted that Wu had once been a Russian agent. The special-case team, leaving Wu Han to rot in jail as an "enemy spy," subjected him to cruelties that ruined his health; he died in a Peking prison on October 10, 1969. Wu Han's wife, Yuan Zhen, and his daughter, Xiao Yan, also became indirect victims of Kang. Yuan Zhen, already seriously ill, was sent to a labor reform camp, where her health continued to deteriorate. She was allowed to return home to Peking on March 17, 1969, to seek medical treatment. That night, she went to a hospital but, because of her marriage to Wu Han, was ignored by medical personnel. She died at the hospital the next morning. Xiao Yan went insane over what had happened to her parents. She placed her mother's ashes beside the head of her bed; then, after Wu Han died seven months later, Xiao Yan took to asking the authorities for his ashes and wandering around and muttering such things as, "Father is not dead," and "If people die, can they still cry?" The radical leaders ordered Xiao Yan detained as a threat to their security; little else is known about what became of her except that she died in prison on September 23, 1976, seven years after her father's death. The only member of Wu Han's immediate family who survived the Cultural Revolution was his son, Wu Zhang.

Many of Kang's schemes reflected patterns deeply ingrained in Chinese history, but, at the same time, he violated one of the most fundamental Chinese values: the importance attached to relationships with longtime friends (although for years he had traded on this value in his alliance with Mao). One evening, as the Cultural Revolution was gaining momentum, Kang invited a crony, Liu Xiao, to dine with him. Kang and Liu had first met in the mid-1920s at Shanghai University and had kept in close touch over the years. After some casual conversation at the dinner table, Kang abruptly changed the subject: "There is a double agent, who at first was a KMT special agent and later a Soviet special agent. Do you think he should be arrested?"

Liu Xiao gathered at first that Kang was rambling on under the influence of the wine they had enjoyed together. But Kang started talking about Pan Hannian, who had been purged as a traitor in 1955 when he was vice mayor of Shanghai. Kang's mention of Pan aroused Liu's suspicion, because Pan, a former secret-police operative in Shanghai, had long been associated with both Kang and Liu.

"Zhao Rong [like Kang's other acquaintances from the Shanghai era, Liu still called him by the name he had used then], are you interested in a certain person named Liu? Are you talking about me?"

Kang laughed. "No, I am not thinking about you."

Liu let the matter drop, but after the meal, as he climbed into the car designated to drive him home, he was handcuffed and taken to prison. There he remained without being questioned for three months.

Liu Xiao was a ranking diplomat; he had served as ambassador to Moscow and still had ties to the Foreign Ministry. Marshal Chen Yi was foreign minister at the time of Liu's arrest; when Chen heard that Liu had disappeared after dining with Kang, he telephoned Kang to ask what had become of him. Kang shot back, "Liu Xiao has already confessed that he is a double agent. He is currently writing material exposing the former problems of the East China Bureau and the Shanghai Municipality"—and added menacingly, "I don't know who else was ganging up with him." Chen Yi understood that Kang's remark was aimed at him; Chen had headed both the East China Bureau and the Shanghai Municipality. Overcome by rage, he shouted over the telephone, "Kang Sheng, you should just drag me off and be done with it!"

Never one to rise to a direct challenge, Kang simply reported to Mao that Chen was interfering with an espionage case under investigation. Chen could not protect Liu Xiao, who spent years in prison.* Chen Yi escaped the fate that befell Liu Shaoqi and many other veterans, but he did come under increasing pressure and ultimately lost his post as foreign minister.

Kang took a special interest in Inner Mongolia, the massive, crescent-shaped strip of territory that, centuries before, had been part of an independent Mongolian kingdom. In April 1968, Kang, accompanied by Jiang Qing, received a delegation of Red Guard leaders who controlled the region. After listening to the group's report on conditions in Inner Mongolia, Kang turned the conversation to the Inner Mongolian People's Party, a long-defunct political organization active in the 1940s. The People's Party, under Soviet influence, had attempted to create an independent Mongolian buffer state between China and Russian-dominated Outer Mongolia.

"The Inner Mongolian People's Party is still conducting underground activity," Kang warned his visitors, and went on to give them their orders: "To begin with, the extent of detentions can be a little broad. Don't be afraid. Take a firm decision and continue to seize enemies and continue to seize them down to the very last one."

Thus Kang gave the Red Guards an excuse to wage an all-out campaign of terror against anyone allegedly connected with the Inner Mongolian People's Party, an operation that resulted in enormous casualties. An estimated 346,000 Inner Mongolians were persecuted as members of this underground party; 16,222 were killed, some of them in the most barbaric manner. When one young female suspect refused to admit that she had belonged to the banned party, her Red Guard interrogators stripped her naked and drove a wooden wedge into her vagina. She eventually died. The Red Guards were no easier on male suspects. They sliced off the sexual organs of a youth who declined to confess, even following a prolonged beating. He died soon after. One twenty-year-old suspect had his skin whipped to shreds and red-hot coals placed over his body. The Red Guards finally

---

* Liu Xiao was exiled from Peking in October 1969, one of the victims of the Number One Directive. He survived to write reminiscences in the 1980s about life as an underground Communist operative in Shanghai during the struggles with the KMT and the Japanese occupation troops. Liu died in June 1988 at the age of eighty.

doused him with cold water—but when it became clear that he still would not cooperate, they suspended him over a fire and roasted him to death.

Another area that attracted Kang's attention was the southern province of Yunnan, which borders on northern Laos and Burma and remained the scene of residual KMT secret-service activity. After the Communist victory, some of Chiang Kai-shek's troops had fled into Burma and Thailand, where they built an opium-growing empire in the so-called Golden Triangle and used it as a base for launching raids into southern China. What little anti-Communist activity there was in Yunnan by January 1968, when Kang focused on the province, posed no threat to the authorities in Peking—but that did not deter Kang.

Kang confronted Zhao Jianmin, a Party leader from Yunnan who was staying at the Jingxi Guesthouse on Chang'an Avenue in western Peking. Long used to accommodate provincial dignitaries in Peking, the Jingxi Guesthouse is a military hotel, a huge brick building set behind a high wall that keeps curious intruders out. During the Cultural Revolution, some of the guests at the exclusive hotel found it suddenly transformed into the site of their initial interrogation at the hands of Kang and his henchmen. So it was with Zhao.

Kang first accused Zhao of backing the Artillery Faction, a discredited Red Guard unit in Yunnan. "Zhao Jianmin, you supported the Artillery Faction and produced many bad ideas, didn't you?"

"I never supported the Artillery Faction's wrong behavior."

"Don't cheat me. Only Liu Shaoqi cheats us; only renegades and special agents cheat us. I ask you. When working in the White Areas, in which year were you arrested?"

"1936."

"How did you confess in prison?"

"I never confessed."

"You're still deceiving everyone. You're a renegade."

"I am not."

"I will repeat myself. You're a renegade."

"Truly, I'm not. I reserve my opinion."

"Good. You reserve your opinion," declared Kang. "Write a message. Your actions are not accidental. A renegade insinuates himself into our Party and thinks of using the Great Cultural Revolution to cause chaos in the border region. The Kuomintang special-service organization! I have seen their plans. I have over forty years of revolutionary experience behind me, and I have this sensitivity—it tells me that you have deep-seated class hatred towards us."

"The Party Center can investigate."

"It certainly will investigate. You are quite mad, and you are madly attacking the proletarian headquarters! Do you still demand that the Center investigates?"

"I still demand it."

"Write it down."

Zhao composed a document protesting his innocence and requesting the central Party authorities to explore the matter. The moment Zhao finished writing, Kang ordered his loyal lieutenant, Public Security Minister Xie Fuzhi, to arrest Zhao. He was dragged off to prison, where he remained for eight years.

One of the charges against Zhao, that he had connections with "the Kuomintang Yunnan Special Service Organization," provoked a wide-ranging investigation of his fellow cadres in the southern province. No evidence linked Zhao to any KMT activity, but Kang used the alleged KMT presence in Yunnan to justify an extensive witch-hunt. He was aided and abetted in his crusade by Xie Fuzhi, a former Yunnan Party chief who had personal scores to settle. Kang's operation ensnared tens of thousands of people and resulted in fourteen thousand deaths.

During the heady days of the Cultural Revolution, Kang managed to export his barbaric tactics to Cambodia. As the Chinese leader responsible for dealing with the international Communist movement, Kang developed close ties with the Cambodian Marxist organization, the Khmer Rouge, as well as its leader, a French-trained radio mechanic named Pol Pot. Kang adopted Pol Pot as a protégé during the late 1960s, when the Khmer Rouge was trying to overthrow Prince Sihanouk, an aristocrat whose regime maintained the privileges of the feudal elite behind a charade of progressive socialism.

By backing Pol Pot, Kang did more than express a desire to bring revolution to Cambodia: he advanced his own cause within the CCP leadership. The pragmatic Foreign Ministry bureaucrats, seeking to expand Chinese influence in Southeast Asia, had cultivated Sihanouk, who pursued a neutralist, anti-Western foreign policy so as to use the friction between Moscow and Peking to bolster his own position. As the Cultural Revolution gathered momentum, however, Kang touted Pol Pot as the true voice of the Cambodian revolution—thereby implying that the Foreign Ministry was backing a reactionary prince. High Chinese officials rarely publicize their differences over foreign policy, but Madame Deng Yingchao, Zhou Enlai's widow, was so outraged by Kang's meddling in Cambodian affairs that she told a Thai delegation to China in the early 1980s that Kang Sheng had been responsible for China's backing of Pol Pot.

China gave the Cambodian Communists financial and propaganda support in the 1960s; Kang himself helped shape the policies implemented by the Khmer Rouge after it overran Cambodia in 1975. These savage doctrines were molded by a number of factors, ranging from the example of Stalin's extermination of the kulaks to the abstract Communist principles Pol Pot had absorbed as a student in France, but Kang's influence also showed. Pol Pot's methods of class extermination and genocide bore a remarkable resemblance to Kang's land reform policies in Shanxi and Shandong during the late 1940s, when he had exterminated rich peasants and landlords alike in the name of an egalitarian revolution.

Kang was the Grand Inquisitor who directed thousands of persecutions during the Cultural Revolution. The special-case groups he supervised spread their tentacles across the land in a relentless search for witnesses and accomplices, intimidating and torturing an incalculable number of people. The system of persecution Kang helped create was self-perpetuating: each new victim implicated a network of accomplices to probe, and each of these new investigations exposed even more people to investigation and punishment.

Kang rarely issued formal death warrants, but huge numbers of deaths resulted directly from the campaigns he initiated. The confusion of those times makes it impossible now to calculate an exact death toll directly attributable to Kang during the Cultural Revolution, but the deaths between 1966 and 1970 for which documentary references can be found exceed 30,000.

Statistics as incomplete as these suggest the extent of Kang's crimes, but they fail to convey a sense of his barbarism. In pursuit of his enemies, he transformed China into a world of cruelty bereft of almost every trace of human sympathy. In his 1978 denunciation of Kang, Hu Yaobang described Kang's abuses:

"Before they died many comrades suffered greatly, both psychologically and physically. Some were tormented to death; some committed suicide; some were assassinated; others were poisoned; some died of hunger; others were locked away in mental asylums; some waited for death with their eyes open in hospitals."

Kang tried his best to conceal his role in the reign of murder and torture he instigated and carried to every corner of the land. But his lust for cruelty could never be completely hidden. So notorious was Kang's taste for inflicting pain that in the streets and alleys of China's cities, it earned him a title that could only be uttered in a whisper: "Yan Wang," the ancient Chinese name for the Indian demon Yama—"the King of Hell."

Chapter XIX

THE
KANG SHENG
COLLECTION

VISITORS WHO STOPPED by Kang Sheng's home in Qingdao after he pronounced himself an invalid in 1949 were turned away by his servants, who explained that he was comatose or otherwise unable to speak or to recognize anyone. But as his visitors were retracing their steps, Kang, in fact, was often amusing himself in the inner recesses of his villa, painting and practicing calligraphy and savoring his art collection.

As a young boy, Kang had received an excellent grounding in calligraphy from the family tutor. He had perfected his skills when he was personal assistant to the Shanghai business magnate Yu Qiaqing. Kang's life as an international Communist leader in Moscow and as a spymaster in Yan'an afforded him little opportunity to dabble in cultural pursuits. But after he virtually quarantined himself, he had more than enough time on his hands to resume his calligraphy and take up painting as well. He produced a sizable body of work in each medium during the next two decades.

Skilled artists who also serve as government officials have been a common feature of China's ruling elite for almost two thousand years. Much more than simply a devotee of traditional culture, Kang was a supremely talented craftsman in his own right, with the aesthetic abilities and outlook of a sixteenth-century magistrate and man of letters. He specialized in delicate monochrome paintings of flowers and birds. The Lone Cloud Studio, a famous gallery in Shanghai, made woodblock reproductions of some of his paintings in 1961 and sold them commercially.* Few of the buyers, however, suspected the artist's true identity, because Kang signed his work with a pseudonym, Lu Chishui.

Kang presented many of his works to friends and acquaintances—a traditional way in China of sealing and celebrating personal and political relationships. One large piece of Kang's calligraphy was prominently displayed for many years in the home of Guo Moruo, the historian and writer who served as the unofficial poet laureate of the Communist regime. Guo died in 1978, but members of his family left Kang's calligraphy in place until years later, when they discovered, to their disgust, whose work it was.

Kang's paintings were of professional quality, not extraordinary, but his calligraphy was magnificent. Fluent and full of vitality, the characters that flowed from his brush displayed great versatility, ranging from meticulous renditions of archaic ideograms based on oracle bones† to elegant, fluid versions of modern script. Within the Communist elite, Kang was renowned as a calligrapher; he produced the characters used as the title logos for a number of leading publications, including magazines such as *Wenwu* ("Cultural Relics") and *Kaogu* ("Archeology") and scholarly works like *A Summary of Historical Material on Ancient Chinese Music*. Like an artist-mandarin of old, he prepared countless inscriptions for friends, associates, and public institutions. Modern Chinese critics have tended to dismiss Kang's paintings as rather sterile, but even today, despite his posthumous disgrace, his calligraphy is praised for its elegance and beauty.

Kang's artistic pursuits were much more than casual therapy; after his return to public life, he continued to paint, produce calligraphy, cut seals, read obscure classical texts, and collect antiques and art works of every type and form. Kang had the attributes of a Renaissance prince: he was a match for the Borgias both in aesthetic refinement and in cruelty and deceit.

*   *   *

* One of Kang's woodblock prints has been shown to the authors by Pierre Ryckmans, a Belgian sinologist, and is reproduced in the photo section of this book (photograph 22).

† Ideograms are pictures that express an idea; Chinese fortune-tellers used "oracle bones" to make predictions three thousand years ago. The bones were heated white-hot, and the patterns they formed while cracking were interpreted as omens by a sage, who usually made comments on the cracked bones in an archaic script only one remove from an outright pictorial illustration of what he observed in the cracks.

By the outbreak of the Cultural Revolution, Kang had amassed an impressive hoard of art and antiques. He spent much of his time in his office-cum-residence in the Number Eight Building in Diaoyutai by then, but he still retained his home on Small Stone Bridge Lane and housed most of his collection there. Whenever he had the leisure, Kang retreated behind the gray brick walls of his Qing dynasty mansion on its two and a half acres and transformed himself from Marxist revolutionary into elegant and erudite mandarin. Thus locked away, he lived the genteel life of an artist, collector, and scholar. He diverted himself with his Pekinese terriers (in spite of strict taboos against keeping pets under the Communist regime), grew potted plants, and shared with a few select guests the pleasures of unrolling scrolls of paintings and calligraphy and opening small brocade boxes that contained exquisite porcelain, metalwork, and silk-bound books.

Kang also introduced foreigners to his private world of art and antiques. On occasion during the 1960s, he would instruct one of his lieutenants in the International Liaison Department to fetch some of the foreign Communists who worked in China as advisers and translators. Among them was Frank Coe, an American who worked for the ILD, and whom Kang once claimed he had kept out of the clutches of the Red Guards. Kang would show his privileged guests rare pieces of calligraphy, painting, and other works of art, then launch into monologues on Marxism and Maoist theory. His summons usually came after midnight; Kang liked to work late, keeping what Chinese Communists in the 1940s called "Stalin hours."

Culture and the arts are usually expected to sublimate if not tame man's baser instincts, but Kang's vindictiveness imbued his approach to painting and calligraphy. Kang followed custom by signing his paintings with an art name. By styling himself Lu Chishui, he took the name of the old Shandong kingdom of Lu as a family name and the words for "red water" (*chishui*) as a personal name. Kang's pseudonym reverberated with ideological rectitude—"red water" denotes the floodtide of Communist revolution—but the name also possessed a venomous double meaning. China's cultural cognoscenti recognized "Lu Chishui" as a deliberate insult to the leading Chinese painter living on the mainland at the time, and the most renowned Chinese artist of the first half of the twentieth century: Qi Baishi, a wizened and eccentric old man with a long, wispy beard, celebrated for his paintings of prawns. His name combined the title of another ancient kingdom, Qi, and the words for "white stone" (*baishi*). Kang's pseudonym implied that he was ideologically orthodox, and that Qi Baishi, however famous and revered, was a secret enemy of the Party, a supporter of the Kuomintang, or "white" forces.

The apolitical Qi was one of the darlings of the Communist regime in the early 1950s; Zhou Enlai and other senior Party leaders went out of their way to flatter the elderly painter, lionizing him as an outstanding artist with an international reputation who had chosen to remain on the mainland after the Communist victory. Qi's fame lent credibility to the new regime's claim of promoting a cultural renaissance in China. It also earned him the jealous attention of Kang Sheng.

Chinese students have been taught for thousands of years to write only with their right hand, but Kang could wield the calligrapher's brush with either hand—a talent possessed by only one or two major artists in a century. Using his unique skill as a political metaphor, Kang cut the motto *Zuo bi you hao* ("Left is better than right") onto a seal he reserved for examples of his left-handed brushwork.

In his calligraphy, Kang usually wrote out the text of a famous poem, essay, or tale from the Chinese classics, but he was still able to make points about politics. One example of his brushwork retold an ancient fable about a tiger that encountered a large, sturdy donkey on a mountain trail. The tiger, uncertain of the unfamiliar beast's strength, kept its distance, daring only to give the donkey a cautious prod from time to time. But the tiger soon noticed that the donkey was dimwitted and slow to react and had a ridiculously high-pitched bray. Having assessed the donkey's weaknesses, the tiger pounced and devoured its victim. A child's tale on the surface, Kang's version of the work vividly expressed his operational philosophy with an image of his circumspect way of biding his time, then pouncing on Peng Zhen, Liu Shaoqi, and other CCP leaders.

Several other members of the Politburo indulged in cultural diversions, foremost among them Chairman Mao, who was renowned for his poetry. Arthur Waley, the outstanding British scholar-translator, once remarked that Mao's poetry surpassed Hitler's paintings but did not compare to Churchill's paintings. In artistic talent, however, even Churchill was an amateur next to Kang.

*   *   *

Another ancient skill Kang mastered was the specialized craft of cutting seals, or chops: chiseling characters—usually names or pseudonyms but sometimes mottos or a line of poetry—onto semiprecious stone, jade, ivory, wood, or brass. Professional craftsmen cut the seals used in Chinese commercial life (bank checks were verified with chops, not signatures), but artists alone were entrusted with the delicate task of inscribing the highly prized pieces of stone used by painters or collectors to place names or poetic mottos on paintings or calligraphic works. Many famous Chinese artists had carved seals; Qi Baishi, the butt of Kang's satire, began his career as a seal cutter.

Both Mao and Kang were avid collectors and readers of early woodblock editions of China's literary and historical classics. Usually centuries old, these books were printed on rice paper, bound with silk thread, and sometimes enclosed in ornate brocade boxes. Kang's library included editions dating back to the Song dynasty, almost one thousand years before, and Mao had accumulated more than ninety thousand woodblocks by the time he died.

One of Kang's main interests as a collector was inkstones, or *yantai*, the slabs of river stone on which calligraphers and painters blended their materials. To the untutored eye, inkstones may seem like nothing more than ordinary pieces of rock, but Chinese connoisseurs have treasured them for centuries. Much of their charm comes from the beautiful patterns formed by the whorls in the rock, the decorations sometimes carved in their margins, and the satiny feel of their surfaces. Kang edited a text on the history of inkstones and published articles on other esoteric topics. Officials of the Cultural Relics Bureau (CRB) occasionally asked him to help decipher the archaic writing found on newly unearthed artifacts.

Widely known as both a mandarin and a scholar, Kang was often referred to publicly and privately by the deferential and ancient name Kang Lao ("the Venerable Kang"). This title, drawn from the language of China's Confucian gentry, reflected his artistic interests and mature years. It also showed his standing among many Chinese, who saw him as an expert with a comprehensive knowledge of everything from the minutiae of Chinese antiques to subtle questions about ideology and the international Communist movement.

Even with their stamping out of ribald plays, erotic pictures, and sexually oriented novels, the Communists began in 1950 to promote China's cultural heritage as a way of legitimizing their regime. They coddled painters such as Qi Baishi and Peking opera stars like Mei Lanfang; state-sponsored theater troupes performed classical dramas for the masses; archeologists explored the tombs of ancient emperors; and scholars conducted meticulous research into the costumes, tapestries, and fabrics of feudal China.

At the onset of the Cultural Revolution, however, Mao condemned what he termed "the four olds": old thinking, old culture, old customs, old habits. In response to the Chairman's call, the Red Guards began obliterating every vestige of Chinese culture, branding pre-Communist culture "revisionist" and rejecting the artistic products of the past as "poisonous weeds" that threatened the revolution. Mao's call to smash "the four olds" unleashed popular resentment against anything considered elitist; Kang dared not challenge Mao by continuing his open patronage of ancient art forms. Even so, he encountered criticism over his embrace of art. A provincial Red Guard delegation that visited Peking in 1968 asked Kang why, five years earlier, he had written the inscription "First Master of the World of Painting, Leader in the Garden of Art" in honor of the painter Pan Tianshou. Kang explained that it was intended to deflate the ego of another painter, Chen Banding, who had grown too arrogant. This confrontation with the Red Guards alerted Kang that his tastes in art could prove dangerous; just as he had forsaken his beloved plays about ghosts and lewd women, he heartily endorsed Mao's repudiation of China's cultural heritage.

The Cultural Revolution curtailed Kang's public interest in the arts, but the turmoil of the times also enabled him to quietly assemble perhaps the largest private collection of art and antiques in all of China. Kang's methods of acquisition were usually criminal—and his greed insatiable. The Red Guards committed repeated atrocities against the relics of civilization, razing temples to the ground, burning the contents of libraries, raiding museums, and confiscating and sometimes destroying all the privately owned paintings, porcelain, and calligraphy they could find.

As the Cultural Revolution raged out of control, Red Guard units stole priceless collections of art from many of Peking's wealthiest homes and hauled their booty to a central warehouse, where it was placed in state custody. Often, the first official of consequence to view the spoils was a man who had spent a lifetime developing an interest in his nation's various forms of art and accumulating a museum-quality trove of his own. Upon hearing of a new delivery to the main storehouse, Kang Sheng would rush over, examine the loot, and help himself to any treasures that caught his eye. With a cynical (or pragmatic) disregard for the ideals of the iconoclastic rebellion and its repudiation of the old culture, Kang contrived to add huge numbers of artifacts to his collections of rare books, seals, inkstones, bronzes, stone tablets, porcelain, ivory, jade, and works by ancient masters of calligraphy and painting.

The art Kang accumulated during the Cultural Revolution was grand in both scale and quality. He acquired thousands of pieces, many of them rare if not unique. His interests were nearly all-encompassing, but his pride and joy continued to be his inkstones. Some were huge—one was as large as a table—and he owned Tang dynasty items not known to exist in any other collection. Kang's inkstones certainly equaled, and maybe surpassed, the best museum holdings in China and the other Eastern lands that treasure calligraphy: Taiwan, Korea, Vietnam, and Japan.

Kang did purchase some items by legitimate means, but the vast majority he stole from state institutions and private collections. Before the Cultural Revolution, one of his favorite tricks was to arrange to borrow a particular work of art or set of books from a museum or library. He would sign receipts for his loans, but once an item came into his possession, he considered it his forever. Because of who he was, curators had no choice but to adjust their paperwork, converting "loans" to Kang into "transfers."

This method of collecting had its limitations. Kang could not commandeer the entire contents of a museum; many fine pieces, moreover, remained in private hands. So Mao's call for the Red Guards to smash "the four olds" was the perfect excuse for Kang to misappropriate truckloads of art and antiques. While the Red Guards were persecuting the intellectuals of Peking, Kang directed a detachment of leftist youths to seize the libraries and art collections of leading cadres, artists, and writers. These objects, he explained, symbolized the bourgeois mentality of their former owners, and some, such as erotic pictures and pornographic books, could "corrupt the party, corrupt the state, and corrupt the people."

Kang did not appropriate treasures haphazardly; he was discriminating and methodical. He monitored the Cultural Relics Bureau warehouse where the confiscated items were taken for storage, placing an agent there who informed him when Red Guards planned to pillage the home of a prominent connoisseur and told him whenever a new hoard of antiques had arrived. Kang would have inventories of the impounded goods drawn up, inspect the booty in person, and select the pieces he wanted. Sometimes, he personally initiated the raids on the homes of renowned collectors, directing his lieutenants to organize gangs of Red Guards to loot particular residences. Kang had often socialized with many of Peking's literary elite before the Cultural Revolution, so he could specify which items he wanted the Guards to steal for him, like a Western crimelord ordering the theft of a Van Gogh or a Picasso. Starting in late 1966, whole libraries, extensive collections of paintings and calligraphy, and antiques of every description were carted away by the Red Guards and handed over to the CRB. Bent on concealing his instigation of the raiding parties, Kang never intervened personally until the plundered treasures had reached the storehouse.

Kang made his initial foray to the CRB in the winter of 1966, shortly after one of Peking's rare snowstorms. He dashed to the warehouse as soon as he heard that a consignment of antiques had arrived, leaving his secretaries and the CRB staff to stand shivering in the ice-cold building while he sifted through piles of silk-bound books and boxes of antiques. Pretending to inspect the bureau's operations, Kang set aside objects that caught his eye, purportedly to check their authenticity and ensure that the victimized collectors had not passed off fakes and forgeries to the Red Guards in place of authentic treasures. Kang removed thousands of antiques and works of art from the Cultural Relics Bureau over the next four years, sometimes in his self-appointed role of "inspector," sometimes by paying for them at an outrageous "discount," and sometimes simply by taking whatever he wanted.

The first collection Kang helped himself to during the Cultural Revolution had been the property of Deng Tuo, a writer and former editor-in-chief of *The People's Daily* who later headed the Peking municipal propaganda apparatus. After arriving in Peking during the early 1950s, Deng Tuo was a regular customer of the shops in Liulichang, the lane in southwestern Peking that has housed the antique-and-curio trade for centuries. Kang got to know Deng Tuo during that period; when Kang visited the author's house, Deng Tuo showed him his art collection. Kang, full of praise for Deng's treasures, chatted with his host for hours about painting and calligraphy.

Deng Tuo was a widely read essayist with a telling turn of phrase. In the early 1960s, he wrote a string of essays that defended the conservative cultural policies advocated by Peking's municipal government against the radicals backed by Jiang Qing. As a result, Deng came under criticism at the same time as Peng Zhen. While the May 1966 Politburo meeting that resulted in Peng's fall from power was still under way, a group of radicals suddenly seized and attacked Deng Tuo. He became the very first victim of the Cultural Revolution, committing suicide on May 18, two days after the decision to dismiss Peng Zhen. Kang had long coveted Deng Tuo's beautiful little collection; late in 1966, when the Red Guards had swept away nearly every shred of law and order in the capital, Kang simply ordered one of his agents to raid Deng Tuo's home and confiscate his art and antiques.

This theft set a pattern. Other art troves that Kang stole belonged to Qian Xingcun, a Communist writer who published under the penname Ah Ying and was a longtime friend of Kang's colleague Li Kenong; Fu Xihua, the chief librarian at the Academy of Dramatic Research and an expert on the early texts of Chinese plays (one of Kang's keenest interests); Zhang Naiqi, an aged banker who had been minister of food from 1953 until the antirightist campaign got him sacked in 1957; and the family of Long Yun, a former military ruler of Yunnan who had crossed over to the Communists and moved to Peking during the 1950s. Kang's cultural bête noire, the painter Qi Baishi, escaped physical suffering at Kang's hand only because he died shortly before the Cultural Revolution erupted, but Kang subsequently plundered Qi's collection of art.

Kang kept his treasure hunting from the public, but he boasted about it within his own circles. Despite their avowed rejection of China's feudal past, many of the radical leaders became avid collectors when Mao made his statement repudiating everything old. Jiang Qing asked Kang for advice on what pieces to add to her own collection. Lin Biao, spurred on by his wife, Ye Qun, stole more than twelve hundred antiques from the Cultural Relics Bureau. (Ye Qun, who had delusions of her own artistic grandeur, tried to establish herself as a poet;* finally, forced to acknowledge her shortcomings at composing verse, she employed a succession of writers to fabricate poetry for her.) Several of the peasant-born generals close to Lin Biao, including Huang Yongsheng, Wu Faxian, Li Zuopeng, and Qiu Huizuo, began making expeditions to the CRB, where they overturned

---

* Not to be outdone, Kang's wife, Cao Yi'ou, also tried her hand at calligraphy, giving samples of her brushwork to political associates like Ye Qun.

cases and tipped out the contents of cupboards in their search for valuables. The generals' wives went along, helping themselves to gems and golden trinkets rifled from the homes of Peking's wealthiest families. Most of these army wives came from poor backgrounds and had no appreciation of art or antiques, but they did have a taste for ornate and expensive jewelry.

As the lawlessness ignited by the Cultural Revolution threatened to consume the last vestiges of Chinese culture, Kang assembled a treasure trove of art that would have stocked a small museum and fired the envy of any serious collector. Kang's thefts of artwork were quasi-bureaucratic, and records of his visits to the CRB's warehouses were often kept and filed away by nervous clerks and curators. Those records show that between 1968 and 1972, Kang worked his way through the libraries and collections of ninety-six members of Peking's cultural elite. He helped himself to 12,080 volumes of rare books—more than were taken by any other radical leader, and 34 percent of all the rare books removed—and 1,102 antiques, 20 percent of the total. Only Lin Biao, who, as Mao's designated political heir, ranked second in the land, appropriated more antiques than Kang.

In addition to what he stole outright, Kang made plenty of purchases at bargain prices. He once paid the equivalent of ten cents for a Song dynasty painting worth thousands of dollars. He paid 2,364 yuan for paintings valued at over 86,000 yuan, and only 252 yuan for antiques valued at 74,000 yuan. The total value of Kang's "purchases" was only about $80,000 in American money, but China was cut off from the international market at the time; the methods then used to value Chinese art grossly underestimated its commercial worth. The fair market price of the pieces Kang bought at discount was millions of U.S. dollars.

Officials of the Cultural Relics Bureau often were reluctant to part with their treasures at the prices Kang demanded, but they dared not refuse him. When one CRB administrator insisted that the figure Kang wanted to pay was much too low, Kang had his secretary reprimand the man for his "lack of proletarian sentiment"—a rebuke that cast doubt on the CRB official's ideological integrity and reminded him that Kang, as a proletarian leader, could set his own price scale.

Kang's fascination with the civilization of ancient China and its artifacts may seem completely at odds with his role as the godfather of the Cultural Revolution. But Chinese history is richly endowed with similar contradictions; Kang simply followed a long-established pattern. Since kingdoms first emerged in China about three thousand years ago, new dynasties have been created by rebellions that exploded like solar flares as regimes disintegrated. The peasants who provided the manpower for these volcanic upheavals rarely filled the highest offices in the imperial courts they helped found; those posts usually went to refined scholars who had cut their ties with the fallen ruler and passed instead as apostles of the next age.

Kang, like many courtiers of the past, had climbed higher than the peasant generals and commissars who had made the Long March, because he could put the learning and sophistication of the centuries at the service of the supreme rebel chief. His lust for power drove him to turn his back on the Confucian upbringing that qualified him to operate as a great mandarin. Yet the stronger Kang became, the less able he was to resist the aesthetic pleasures of the world he had renounced.

In the end, as his quest for power drove him to betray more and more of his comrades, Kang seemed to prefer the company of inkstones, chops, paintings, and works of calligraphy to that of people. He was at once a passionate antiquary and an accomplice to the destruction of the culture that had inspired the art he coveted. For all his influence over men and events, Kang was powerless to stay the nihilism that had made him a grand minister from destroying the beauty that brought him so much solace.

Chapter XX

THE
LIN BIAO
CONSPIRACY

WHAT A STRANGE PAIR THEY WERE: apart from displaying similar signs of hypochondria, Kang Sheng and Lin Biao had little in common, even to judge by photographs of Mao and his colleagues from the 1960s. Kang, the career civilian who never served in the military and had only tenuous links to the Red Army, looks every inch the ramrod-straight soldier, nearly always standing tall and square-shouldered—whereas Lin Biao and other military leaders slouch to one side, unable to conceal the paunches indicating that the People's Liberation Army commanders enjoyed traveling on their stomachs. The pictures also suggest that Kang alone among the Chinese hierarchy had access to an iron. His clothes were crisply pressed, his trouser creases sharp and straight, while Lin might have been living for days in his crumpled uniforms. Kang's wardrobe featured stylish tropical white and dark-blue Mao suits with the standard high collar; Lin Biao's military fatigues ran the gamut from dull green to dull green. Kang was usually bareheaded, with his high forehead and receding but becoming hair displayed; Lin Biao, hoping to keep outsiders from discovering that he was as bald as a billiard ball, never appeared in public without a shapeless army cap planted on his pate.

Equally different were the personalities of Mao's two closest confidants during the Cultural Revolution era. No matter what feelings he might harbor for the people he encountered, Kang could be a charming, gracious companion, capable of putting people in his presence at ease with a word, a look, or a touch. When a group of visiting foreign Communists lined up on the Tiananmen rostrum to be photographed with Mao and the rest of the CCP leadership in October 1969, Kang placed a chivalrous arm around the waist of a young and smartly dressed Swedish woman. By the Chinese mores of the day, he might as well have unbuttoned her blouse or fired up an opium pipe on the podium. Lin Biao, on the other hand, felt uncomfortable in the presence of other people. He was moody and aloof—Helen Foster Snow, an American writer who met him in Yan'an, described him as "the least friendly of any of the top officers."

A graduate of the Whampoa Military Academy, Lin Biao joined the Red Army in its earliest days. In many of the Communist uprisings of the late 1920s, he proved himself a brilliant general. Lin became the first Communist commander to win a battle against the Japanese when his 115th Division defeated a well-armed Japanese force in September 1937 at the battle of Pingxingguan.

Lin Biao was severely wounded in 1939, reportedly when troops of the warlord Yan Xishan mistook him and his escort for a Japanese patrol, and went to the Soviet Union for medical treatment. Remaining there after his recovery, Lin studied military techniques; he was said to have commanded a Soviet unit in the invasion of Poland in 1939. Returning to Yan'an in 1942, Lin began his rise through the upper echelons of the CCP military. Once civil war broke out in 1946, Mao transferred Lin Biao to Manchuria, where he won a series of victories that devastated some of Chiang Kai-shek's elite, American-equipped troops. Lin was named commander of the Fourth Field Army, one of the key units in the Communist armed forces, in 1948. He led his army south from Manchuria through the coastal provinces, capturing both Peking and Tianjin in a triumphant sweep that ended in Canton.

Following his successes against the KMT, Lin Biao headed the Chinese forces sent to aid the North Korean Communists in their struggle against the United States–backed regime in Seoul. The Chinese army under Lin almost broke through the U.S. defenses and nearly overran General Douglas MacArthur's headquarters.

After the initial Chinese drive had bogged down, however, Lin declared himself unwell and handed over command to Peng Dehuai.*
He returned to Peking and spent the next five years as an invalid—a

* Ironically, Lin Biao replaced Peng as defense minister after Peng was purged in 1959.

period that overlapped Kang's withdrawal supposedly due to mysterious and undiagnosable maladies.

Even more than Kang, Lin showed signs of extreme hypochondria. Terrified of sweating, he would stop whatever he was doing the
moment he began to perspire; afraid of both sunlight and wind, he
spent most of his time indoors, acquiring a shrunken, chalky appearance. For hours on end, he would pore over ancient Chinese medical
texts and then apply them in the most literal and bizarre ways; for
example, he refused to bathe, for fear that water might damage his
vital organs. Perhaps Lin's avoidance of water really was good for his
insides, but one thing was certain: on the outside, he exuded a body
odor that made social contact with him decidedly unpleasant.

Lin was also deathly afraid that too much activity might harm his
health, so he drastically cut his working hours as the years wore on.
He stopped reading official documents, relying instead on his secretaries to brief him on their contents. Apart from medical classics and
the dictionaries needed to decode them, the only books he read were
biographies of Chinese military heroes. Even then, he made sure not
to overextend himself, instructing his aides to read to him from piles
of books they had gathered on the generals of former dynasties. Vain,
obsessed with his health, and fascinated by deeds of ancient warriors,
Lin gradually withdrew into an imaginary world of martial heroes,
which spurred his ambition and lust for glory at the same time as it
dimmed his sense of the realities surrounding him.

Kang had spent years in the paramilitary world of spies and special
agents but never established close ties with the Chinese Communist
army. The Long March, the seminal military event in the early history
of the CCP and an experience that gave many civilians a claim to a
special relationship with the armed forces, occurred while Kang was
in Moscow. He headed the Military Intelligence Department for seven
years after his return to China, but this staff job did not allow him to
rub shoulders with the troops. Nominally, Kang was also the military
commissar for Shandong Province, but he spent his term in that post
as an invalid at Peking Hospital.

Still, Kang's lack of bonds with the military did not prevent him
from ascending to the top of the CCP's political structure. Mao purposely kept the army subservient to the Party; despite the Chairman's
widely quoted aphorism that power flows from the barrel of a gun,
his authority flowed from his control over the Party at large, which he

had built through his homespun charisma, his political acumen, and his peasant guile.

Kang, perceiving earlier than most of his colleagues that China was on the verge of a great upheaval, set out in the early 1960s to foster relationships with the military brass. Chinese history had taught him that during times of trouble the army, like the secret police, was apt to enlarge its power at the expense of the civil bureaucracy. Having exploited his intimacy with Mao to advance his fortunes ever since the late 1930s, Kang naturally sought as his allies the generals clustered around the Chairman.

Foremost among Mao's allies within the PLA on the eve of the Cultural Revolution was Lin Biao, who, despite his eccentricities, had become one of China's most powerful military and political figures. He had gained Mao's full confidence; in return, Lin promoted the Chairman's theories of guerrilla warfare and the superiority of men, when aroused by revolutionary spirit, over firepower and material resources. Lin did more than simply propagate Mao's ideals; by 1965, he had started to strike out against Mao's critics in the PLA—attacks that had many parallels with Kang's campaigns on the civilian side. Lin Biao's first prominent victim was Luo Ruiqing, chief of the General Staff Department of the army and former public-security minister, whom Lin purged as the Cultural Revolution was about to get under way.

Until the Cultural Revolution, Kang and Lin Biao had operated in separate worlds. They had not met before Kang arrived in Yan'an in 1937, and even after that Lin's frequent absences at the battlefield limited contact between them.

But in May 1966, when Kang's campaign against Peng Zhen reached a climax, Kang and Lin Biao found themselves on the same side. At the long and bitter Politburo meeting that set the Cultural Revolution in motion, Lin Biao delivered a landmark speech on military coups. After reviewing recent uprisings in Ghana, Indonesia, and other parts of Africa and Asia, he declared that in China, too, "you can smell a certain aroma, the aroma of gunpowder." Hearing the marshal's speech as proof that Lin, like himself, opposed the orthodox leaders, Kang started to court both Lin and his wife, Ye Qun.

Kang and Lin soon joined forces to fabricate charges against Marshal He Long, a flamboyant strongman and a potential obstacle to Lin's drive for control over the military. He Long was born in

Hunan in 1896, killed a government officer when he was sixteen, and fled to the mountains as the head of a group of bandits. Granted an amnesty, he then threw in his lot with the Nationalist cause of Dr. Sun Yat-sen and helped raise troops for the KMT. He Long joined the CCP in 1926 and participated in almost all of the early Communist military actions. He supported Mao in the intraparty squabbles on the Long March and gained prominence as a field commander in the wars with Japan and the KMT. A heroic, dashing figure with a clipped mustache—no other top Chinese Communist except Kang sported a mustache—He Long was promoted to marshal in 1955, at the same time as Lin Biao. He Long had remarkable influence in the armed forces throughout the 1950s; by the early 1960s, he was made executive head of the CCP's Military Commission (directly under Mao) and oversaw the military system.

Once he realized that Lin Biao was prepared to move against He Long, Kang twisted a series of totally innocent actions into evidence of a takeover plot such as Lin had warned of in his speech to the Politburo. Kang claimed that three months earlier, in February 1966, He Long and Peng Zhen had conspired to topple Mao, under cover of a program to reform the Peking militia. Using a raft of half-truths, coincidences, and circumstantial evidence, Kang smeared the old marshal as a leader of what Kang dubbed "the February coup." Kang seized on He Long's habit of sleeping with a pistol under his pillow (a leftover from his wilder days), plus He's encouragement of the Physical Education Commission to promote target shooting as a sport, to assert that He was plotting to seize power.

As usual, Kang had scrutinized his victim's history; he charged that He Long had betrayed the CCP as far back as August 1934, when a Kuomintang emissary, Xiong Shiqing, contacted He Long at his base in western Hunan and tried to persuade him to switch sides. Kang's suggestion that He Long had double-crossed the Communists perverted the truth completely—after hearing what Xiong Shiqing had to say, He Long had executed him as a spy. Yet Kang cited the incident as proof of illicit contact with the KMT.

One of Kang's primary coconspirators against He Long was Lin Biao's second wife, Ye Qun. After a brief, unsuccessful marriage in the 1930s to a certain Liu Mingxing, Lin remarried, making a fortunate choice: in Ye Qun, he had an unscrupulous woman with a flair for intrigue and years of experience in the Party. Since her arrival in Yan'an in the late 1930s, she had started out as a research assistant and worked her way up to a job as secretary on the Party committee that ran the Central Research Academy. Ye Qun acted as proxy for her reclusive husband, serving as a conduit to Jiang Qing and other civilian leaders of the Cultural Revolution and never missing an opportunity to advance her family's cause.

Ye Qun had long held a grudge against He Long's wife, Xue Ming. Back in 1943 in Yan'an, Xue Ming had accused Ye Qun of spying for the KMT. Ye Qun exacted her revenge by helping Kang find witnesses in the armed forces who could bolster the case against He Long. Under Kang's supervision, a special-case group started to investigate the old marshal's "crimes," and he was arrested. Kang used He Long's detention as an excuse to practice an especially subtle form of sadism on him. He Long suffered from diabetes, so Kang, in an apparently generous move, permitted him to be held in a hospital instead of prison. But under Kang's "care," He Long was denied sugar-free meals—which made completion of the investigation unnecessary. Without the proper diet and medication, He Long lapsed into a coma and died in June 1968. Thus Kang rid himself of a CCP stalwart without the need for a death warrant or the awkward spectacle of executing a legendary battlefield hero.

Kang and Lin Biao also combined to purge Minister of Culture Lu Dingyi. Between 1960 and 1966, Lu's wife, Yan Weibing, had written twenty-three anonymous letters alleging that Ye Qun had once been the lover of Wang Shiwei, the dissident writer executed in 1947 as a Trotskyite.* Lin Biao went to the extent of signing a statement that Ye Qun was a virgin when he married her, but Yan Weibing's accusations made Lin and his wife thirst for vengeance. At the direction of Kang and Lin, public-security officials arrested Lu Dingyi in 1966, threw him in prison, and tortured him, trying to extract a confession that Lu had used his wife to attack Lin Biao. To avoid the same fate, Yan Weibing had to pretend to be mentally ill.

Kang and Lin Biao shared many common causes, but they never became intimate friends. Kang was too sharp and quick for the reserved Lin; and Ye Qun, a cautious woman, had mistrusted Kang ever since Yan'an, where she had observed how ruthlessly he operated.

---

* No evidence is available to support Yan's charge that Ye Qun and Wang Shiwei were lovers, but in Yan'an they had worked together in the literature-and-art section of the Central Research Academy.

Zhang Yunsheng, one of Lin Biao's secretaries in the 1960s, reported that every member of Lin's staff was aware that Lin and Ye did not like Kang, although none of them knew exactly why.

Lin Biao and his inner circle were physically isolated from Kang and the other CCP leaders. Although invariably depicted during the Cultural Revolution as Mao's closest comrade-in-arms, Lin remained something of an outsider. Mao, Zhou Enlai, and several other leaders lived in Zhongnanhai; Kang, Jiang Qing, and the members of the Cultural Revolution Group had their main residences in Diaoyutai. But Lin Biao chose to make his home in Maojiawan, a spacious compound in western Peking at least a twenty-minute drive from the rest of the leadership.

Besides Lin Biao's wife and his son and daughter, Lin Liguo and Lin Doudou, the residents at Maojiawan included Lin's staff of more than twenty personal attendants, among them two doctors, two personal bodyguards, and six secretaries. Heavily armed soldiers guarded every entrance, discouraging other CCP leaders from dropping by for unannounced social calls. Accenting Lin's special status (not to mention his physical isolation), government and Party officials in Peking began referring to Lin as "Maojiawan," just as Americans call the President and his advisers "the White House."

Lin Biao was China's top general, but no one man could control an enormous and sprawling military machine like the PLA. As the Red Guards rampaged across the land and disrupted the daily life of much of the population, local army bosses started reacting to the growing disorder in ways that indicated the limits of Lin Biao's authority.

The most telling incident occurred in July 1967 in Wuhan, the largest industrial city in central China, as Red Guards clashed with groups of workers trying to maintain a measure of stability. The regional military commander, General Chen Zaidao, fearing that the situation was getting out of control, chose to disregard the directives from the capital and use troops to suppress the Red Guards.

Kang and his radical colleagues were shocked by Chen's resistance to the Red Guards. To coerce him into line and keep his defiance from spreading, they sent propaganda chief Wang Li and Public Security Minister Xie Fuzhi to Wuhan. Shortly after Wang and Xie arrived, however, groups of workers backed by the local military seized the two emissaries and paraded them through the city in an open truck. Wang Li was badly beaten in the mêlée, suffering a broken leg.

Chen's revolt, known as "the Wuhan mutiny," threatened to crack China apart. The leaders in Peking closed ranks, with Kang, Lin Biao, and the other radicals joining Zhou Enlai and the moderates to bring the rebellion to an end. After troops loyal to Lin Biao had parachuted into Wuhan and secured the airport and other key installations, Zhou Enlai flew to the city to pacify Chen Zaidao. It took him several days, but Zhou finally persuaded Chen that the nation's integrity was at stake. Accompanied by his deputy, Zhong Hanhua, and several of his officers, Chen flew to Peking with the Premier. Chen's surrender served to warn other regional commanders not to usurp local power and defy the central government.

Kang took advantage of the abortive Wuhan revolt to weed out senior military officers resistant to the Cultural Revolution. On the evening of July 24, 1967, twenty-four hours or so after Chen Zaidao's arrival in Peking, Kang organized a meeting in the Jingxi Guesthouse at which Red Guards interrogated and assaulted Chen Zaidao, Zhong Hanhua, and three other generals who had participated in the mutiny. Kang infiltrated several plainclothes security men into the meeting and directed them to beat and kick Chen and his fellow army officers; the violence lasted nearly all night. The Red Guards would have resumed the following day, but a PLA unit spirited away Chen and his companions, hiding them in an elevator and finally escorting them to another, more secure location.

Chen's escape was of little concern to Kang and the radicals; they intended mainly to use the Wuhan rebellion as a rationale for a public campaign against officers like Chen Zaidao and other army "counterrevolutionaries." Under Kang's supervision, a series of strongly worded articles was prepared for *The People's Daily, Red Flag,* and New China News Agency news bulletins. Kang's assistant Guan Feng wrote the articles, but Kang checked them personally and inserted the admonition to "resolutely drag out the handful of capitalist roaders in the army." In the name of preventing a repeat of the Wuhan incident, the stories called for strikes against "capitalist roaders, personalities like Chen Zaidao, and the small handful of counterrevolutionaries in the army." Such slogans signaled the Red Guards to resist any PLA commanders who opposed Lin Biao and who sought to protect the country's social and economic fabric during the Cultural Revolution.

Making a show of strength to intimidate their rivals in the military, the leaders of the Cultural Revolution Group staged a rally at Tiananmen on July 25, 1967. More than one million Red Guards and soldiers marched through the square, sending a message to the entire nation that the central leaders fully supported the radicals. In the absence of Mao, who was traveling in southern China, Lin Biao presided from the balcony on the Tiananmen gatehouse. Once the parade was over, Lin Biao took an elevator to the ground floor. Right away, Kang and Jiang Qing called Kuai Dafu, a Red Guard leader, to one side. They told Kuai that Mao himself had authorized the show of support for the Red Guards and also approved the call "to drag out the handful of counterrevolutionaries and capitalist roaders in the army." Kang and Jiang Qing ordered Kuai Dafu to tell other Red Guard units in the capital the gist of the Chairman's remarks, so that they could spread it throughout China.

The words that Kang and Jiang Qing put in Mao's mouth had an almost immediate impact. By early August, Red Guards across the country had started to confront the military—in some places, surrounding army headquarters; in others, attacking military officers, whom they branded as members of "the handful of counterrevolutionaries"; elsewhere, breaking into PLA arsenals and stealing arms for combat against the army and other Red Guard factions alike.

For once, however, Kang had miscalculated. The propaganda offensive against the PLA had intruded into forbidden territory, enraging many generals. The old marshals defeated in the battle over "the February Adverse Current" no longer had at their disposal men with guns and bayonets, but the regional commanders Kang had criticized in his articles did control powerful armies. Mao, returning to Peking in mid-August, soon recognized that a repeat of the havoc caused by the Great Leap Forward could endanger the entire regime. After hearing reports of Red Guard assaults on the army, Mao read one of the articles Kang had planted in *Red Flag* that endorsed the campaign against "capitalist roaders in the army." In his unmistakable handwriting, Mao wrote on the side of his copy of the article two fatal words: "poisonous weed."

Mao's disavowal of the campaign "to drag out the handful of counterrevolutionaries" stunned Kang and his allies. In the face of Mao's opposition, they had no choice but to abandon the campaign and seek some way to disguise their role in it. Fortunately for Kang, after the heady summer and autumn of 1966, he had reverted to his preferred modus operandi of using agents and operatives to conceal the true nature of his activities. His masterminding of the attack on "Chen Zaidao–like personalities" and "counterrevolutionaries" was known only to a select group of associates. He could disclaim responsibility for much of the antimilitary propaganda, confident that few people could contradict him.

After Kang, Jiang Qing, and Chen Boda had consulted Lin Biao, they decided to blame the affair on *The People's Daily, Red Flag,* and the propaganda apparatus. Kang Sheng remembered that Wang Li, Guan Feng, and Qi Benyu, a prominent Red Guard leader, had established "the May 16 Group"* to take on Zhou Enlai and further disrupt the army. The May 16 organization, Kang suggested, could be used as a scapegoat.

Jiang Qing and Kang called a mid-August meeting of the Cultural Revolution Group, which by now had formally taken over from the Politburo. The CRG leaders instructed Qi Benyu to attend as well; he had been busily collecting incriminating material about Zhou Enlai. Unlike most gatherings of the radical leaders, when banter and jokes set the tone for discussions, this one had a subdued atmosphere. When all the participants had arrived, Jiang Qing handed a bulky file of documents to Kang. Kang announced that a campaign to promote chaos in the army and the formation of the May 16 Group had caused "problems." Kang, Jiang Qing, and Chen Boda had decided before the meeting that the men responsible for these "mistakes"—Wang Li, Guan Feng, and Qi Benyu—should be relieved of their posts pending "self-examination." The other members of the CRG watched mesmerized as the three victims learned of their fate. Most astonished of all were Wang Li and Guan Feng, who had known Kang as their patron for almost twenty years; Chinese custom required Kang to champion his protégés for life. But before the trio could utter a word in self-defense, public-security officials entered the room, handcuffed them, and led them away. They were thrown into Qincheng Prison for twenty-one years and not released until 1988.

Tough provincial commanders continued to put down the Red Guards throughout September 1967. Kang, aware that he was still in danger, decided to retreat further and register his innocence in even more dramatic terms. To reinforce his claim that he had broken a ring

---

* May 16, 1966, was the date of the internal Party document announcing Peng Zhen's downfall.

of conspirators, he ordered the arrest of Lin Jie, deputy editor of *Red Flag,* and Mu Xin, editor of *The Guangming Daily,* both of them associates of Wang Li and Guan Feng. The quartet, Kang charged, had formed a conspiratorial clique. Any provincial generals with reservations about Kang were now reassured by his decisiveness in silencing the army's critics.

Kang feared with good reason that his betrayal of long-standing associates like Wang Li and Guan Feng might outrage their friends. He was especially leery of Li Guangwen, one of Kang's key agents and the leader of the main Red Guard faction at the Party School until his promotion in late 1966 to work as Wang Li's deputy on propaganda for the Cultural Revolution Group. To forestall any plotting against him by his subordinates in the propaganda apparatus and the Party School, Kang assembled them in late September. He lectured them on their fallen comrades' "crimes" and then staged a most bizarre performance. Kang accused Li Guangwen of having recruited propaganda workers for the CRG behind his back; to remove Li from the picture, Kang announced that Li would be returning to the Party School. Then, all at once, Kang exploded in a temper tantrum, smashing things and cursing. With one hand on his waist and the other pointing at Li, Kang screamed like a madman, "What sort of person are you! You are a rebel, daring to be so insolent!" Li Guangwen could only stare in astonishment at Kang's transformation from congenial ideological expert into foul-mouthed interrogator.

Afterward, Li sent Chairman Mao a letter protesting his innocence and telling of Kang's betrayal of Wang Li and Guan Feng. When six days had passed without a response from Mao, Li sought other means of exposing Kang's duplicity. About two weeks later, early on October 8, Li hung—and personally signed— wall posters on the main auditorium at the Party School calling for the overthrow of "the great careerist, conspirator, butcher Kang Sheng." Alerted to the posters by Wu Baohua, who had succeeded Li Guangwen as leader of the Red Guards at the Party School, Kang ordered Wu to remove them at once to stop Li's accusations from spreading beyond the campus. Kang also had Wu arrest Li; Red Guards seized Li and dragged him by the hair to a meeting, where radical students beat him until blood flowed from head wounds.

Wall posters against Kang continued to appear for several weeks. But Kang now had the situation under control; he dismissed them as the work of followers of Wang Li and Guan Feng, along with "the children of renegades, special agents, and the capitalist roaders" he had exposed in Yan'an. Even with all his enemies, Kang knew he had little cause to fear that the broadsides could threaten his position. Without support from behind the scenes, such campaigns quickly ran out of steam.

Midway through Kang's outburst against Li Guangwen, many of the cadres present had started to shout support for Kang. One man remained silent, however: Jiang Zichen, a chauffeur from the Party School. Kang turned on him and accused him of having worked for Jia Zheng, a disgraced former deputy leader of the Party School. When the lowly chauffeur replied that he had written a letter exposing Jia Zheng's ideological crimes, Kang insisted that Jiang reveal how he had sent his letter to the central leaders. Jiang Zichen replied that he had entrusted his letter to a certain Wang from the Marxist–Leninist Academy. Kang laughed sardonically; Wang, he declared, was a special agent. He demanded that Jiang Zichen explain his relationship with this "spy." But Jiang had no ambitions beyond driving cars and was not intimidated. Kang, for once finding his stock supply of false accusations unavailing, backed down and skulked away from the meeting. But he got his revenge before long. At Kang's direction, the impudent chauffeur was suspended from the Party for eight years and placed under observation—a fate that turned Jiang's daily life into a struggle for survival.

The Wuhan mutiny had revealed the limits of Lin Biao's influence, but the bald-headed, hypochondriacal marshal was far from a spent force. No other general wielded greater power than Lin, so Kang continued acting like an ally of Lin and the Maojiawan clique of military officers. In the aftermath of the Wuhan debacle, Kang helped Lin to purge generals who obstructed his power in the capital and gain a tighter grip on the troops stationed in Peking. Kang's most important contribution to Lin Biao's cause came at the CCP's Ninth Congress in April 1969, when he helped Lin formalize his position as Mao's successor.

The Ninth Congress was long overdue; the Party constitution mandated that a congress be held every five years, but the last one had ended eleven years earlier. The disasters of the early 1960s had discouraged the leadership from calling a new Party congress; the Cultural Revolution had delayed it even further. By 1969, however, convening the Ninth Congress appeared essential to restoring stability and legitimizing the radicals' newly won status.

The Central Committee had already ratified the purges of Liu Shaoqi and Deng Xiaoping, but a full congress was needed to decree that the Cultural Revolution had reached a successful conclusion. The purpose of the congress was to mark an end to the anarchy and to sanctify the gains made by the cadres who had emerged triumphant. To achieve those goals, the congress adopted a revised and much shortened Party constitution and elected a new Central Committee, which in turn chose a new Politburo and Politburo Standing Committee.

One of the key players at the Ninth Congress, Kang was responsible for drafting a long political report on the state of the nation, to be presented by Lin Biao to the thousand-odd delegates. Originally, Chen Boda was designated to write Lin's speech, but he had made no headway with it by mid-March, so Kang took over. Mao made extensive revisions to the draft, but Kang was still able to revel in the acclaim from supervising its production.

Kang had a hand as well in preparing the new Party constitution, which he used to advance the interests of both Mao and Lin Biao. Kang pushed to reintroduce the phrase "Mao Zedong Thought," which had been removed from the constitution at the second session of the Eighth Congress in 1958. He also eased his way into Lin's good graces by continuing several years of lobbying to have the marshal formally recognized as Mao's political heir. "Many comrades," Kang declared, "suggest that the Ninth Congress should enthusiastically promote Lin Biao as Chairman Mao's intimate comrade-in-arms and the Chairman's successor." Shortly before the congress convened, Lin Biao had suggested with false humility that references to him be deleted from the new constitution. A fawning Kang immediately registered objections: "Comrade Lin Biao is very modest. He demands that we remove the part mentioning him from the party constitution. Our opinion is that this part must be retained. Comrade Lin Biao is Chairman Mao's successor. This is publicly recognized throughout society."

Kang presented the new constitution as a document of unprecedented brilliance in the history of socialism. "The [Russian] communist constitutions of 1903 and 1919 are very long," he declared. "The party constitution of 1919 was . . . so long and complex [that] people could not remember it." He spoke as if communism in China had evolved completely beyond Engels and Lenin: the 1919 Party constitution "was possibly influenced by Engels's *Principles of Communism* . . . which is loaded down with trivial details and even talks about the problem of housing." Kang had no hesitation in criticizing such seminal socialist thinkers as Engels.

Kang also served with Zhou Enlai and the PLA chief of staff, Huang Yongsheng, on the working group that picked the members of the new Politburo. With an eye to Lin Biao's interests, Kang helped make sure that Lin's wife was promoted to the Politburo. Advancing Ye Qun was a delicate task; in the weeks before the congress, Mao had hinted that he doubted the wisdom of appointing either Jiang Qing or Ye Qun to the Politburo. Not that Mao (by now well settled in with his young lover, Zhang Yufeng) had any desire to destroy Jiang Qing's public career; but the prospect of cluttering the high councils of the Party with leaders' wives made him uneasy.

Kang had views of his own. Obviously, he did not want to offend Mao, but he saw advantages in supporting Jiang Qing and Ye Qun for Politburo membership. Both women exercised considerable influence, and Kang felt confident they would repay any favor he might do for them. Backed by Huang Yongsheng, Lin Biao's representative on the working group, Kang had his way: both women were on the list of new Politburo members submitted for Mao's approval.

Nor did Kang overlook his own future when he helped create the new Politburo. Mao, of course, remained chairman and Lin Biao vice chairman, but only three others—Zhou Enlai, Chen Boda, and Kang himself—joined them on the Politburo Standing Committee. It was now official: Kang was one of the five top leaders in the land.

Kang persevered in currying favor with Lin after the Party congress. He ordered researchers at the Party School to prepare articles that "gave prominence to Lin Biao," and suggested publishing a collection of Lin's sayings, similar to "the Little Red Book" of Mao's quotations. Kang also went out of his way to praise Lin Biao publicly with statements like this: "Comrade Lin Biao has conducted the Chinese revolution and Chinese revolutionary war with Chairman Mao over a long period. In both theory and practice he is the best student of Chairman Mao. In our party he is the model for studying and applying Mao Zedong Thought." Who could ask for anything more? Neither Mao nor Lin could fault Kang's attitude.

Unfortunately for Lin Biao, international developments began to intrude into Chinese politics—and foreign policy was not Lin's strong suit. The Cultural Revolution had begun at the same time as a coup in Indonesia and the outbreak of war in Vietnam, but Chinese leaders had been too preoccupied with their domestic problems to notice the outside world for almost three years. Then, in March 1969, Chinese and Soviet troops clashed over a strip of sand in the Ussuri River, the border between the two countries. The firefight over the frozen terrain, known as Zhenbao Island to the Chinese and Damansky to the Soviets, shocked leaders in Peking into the realization that they faced the prospect of war with their giant neighbor. Suddenly, policy debate in the Chinese capital centered on how to respond to the menace of Soviet military might. Kang and Mao soon perceived that Lin Biao, who remained detached from foreign policy, lacked the mettle to succeed the Chairman.

One aspect of Lin Biao's neglect of foreign affairs was his reluctance to entertain visiting dignitaries. Beqir Balluku, the minister of defense of China's closest ally, Albania, visited Peking in October 1968. The Soviets had invaded Czechoslovakia only two months earlier, so the Albanians were keen to bolster their international position. In an attempt to avoid meeting his eager Albanian counterpart, Lin pleaded poor health. Balluku finally suggested that he and Lin should at least have their photograph taken together. This compromise Lin could not refuse; the Foreign Ministry arranged a photo opportunity in the cavernous Xinjiang Room of the Great Hall of the People. Balluku embraced Lin warmly in front of a squad of photographers, but Lin excused himself after less than five minutes of small talk. Hurrying out of the room, he muttered to one of his secretaries, "I can't stand dealing with Westerners!"

Public indications that "Maojiawan's" distaste for foreign policy might create problems for him surfaced in 1970, when he botched several formal appearances. In May of that year, Mao chose Lin to read a statement of support for the Vietnamese struggle with "American imperialism." Lin seemed to lose himself almost immediately after he took the Tiananmen podium. "I want to talk about Vietnam. About both Vietnams. Half Vietnam," he muttered. Realizing that he was making a fool of himself, Lin switched from his extemporaneous and jumbled remarks and began reading from the prepared text of the Chairman's statement. He managed to get through the speech with only one other significant error, saying "Pakistan" instead of "Palestine." The incident may sound unimportant, but Chinese rulers never overlook such gaffes.

The early years of the Cultural Revolution had been good ones for Lin Biao. He had survived the military rebellion in Wuhan; the Ninth Congress had formally designated him Mao's successor; his portrait hung beside Mao's in factories, railway stations, schools, hospitals, and government and military facilities across China. All of that began to unravel, however, when the Party's Central Committee met in Lushan, the site of the 1959 showdown between Chairman Mao and Lin's predecessor as defense minister, Peng Dehuai.

The principal item on the agenda of the August 1970 Lushan gathering was whether to have a national or state constitution. The original constitution of the People's Republic, enacted during the 1950s, had been rendered totally irrelevant by the chaos of the 1960s. Together with the Party statutes ratified at the Ninth Congress in 1969, a new state constitution, once adopted by the National People's Congress, would formalize the political structure created by the Cultural Revolution. But before any action could be taken, the Party had to decide whether it wanted a state constitution or not.

In the months leading up to the Central Committee meeting, Lin Biao and Ye Qun saw the constitutional question as an opportunity to advance Lin's status. One side issue was whether to retain the presidency, vacant since the 1966 purge of Liu Shaoqi. Lin Biao lobbied forcefully in favor of keeping the position. He proposed that Mao should fill the post, but his real motive was to become president himself. Mao looked askance at the idea, though. Having held the title of president up to 1959, he had no interest in repeating the experience. Nor did Mao do what Lin Biao expected: suggest that Lin should be head of state. Instead, he declared that the nation was better off without a president.

Another controversy flared up at Lushan over "the theory of genius," an interpretation of history that stressed the role of exceptionally talented individuals. Lin Biao and his supporters wanted to insert a reference to the concept in the new constitution—ostensibly to flatter Mao but actually to dramatize Lin's destiny, implying that he himself was a genius whom fate had set above every other Chinese leader except the Chairman.

Kang, who drafted the new constitution with the help of Zhang

Chunqiao and Yao Wenyuan, followed Mao's lead and opposed Lin Biao's plans. In the weeks before the Central Committee assembled in Lushan, the debates about the state presidency and the theory of genius seemed to die away; the delegates anticipated that the Central Committee would meet for three days, endorse the draft constitution, and then close amid declarations of the blissful state of Party unity.

However, Lin Biao, Ye Qun, and their clique of generals wrong-headedly pressed on with their efforts to have the Central Committee endorse the theory of genius and write the post of president into the new constitution. Zhou Enlai opened the formal meeting on the afternoon of August 23, outlining the schedule of events for the days to come. Kang Sheng was to talk next and introduce the draft constitution. But Lin Biao, disregarding the agreed-upon order of proceedings, stood up and delivered a long speech full of praise for Mao and forceful arguments in favor of both the theory of genius and the retention of the presidency.

Kang was completely thrown off stride by Lin Biao's breach of protocol. He asked Chen Boda to speak next, but Chen refused, leaving Kang no choice but to proceed. He improvised an ambivalent speech, quoting some of Lin's remarks but taking care not to endorse them.

Having challenged the course set by Mao, Lin Biao and his disorganized followers had to carry the fight forward and try to persuade the Central Committee to adopt their proposals. Lin's men were generals and political commissars without any feel for producing the type of written material needed at Central Committee meetings, so much of the burden fell to Chen Boda. Chen had risen to high office on Mao's coattails, but he had started to gravitate toward Lin Biao as the Cultural Revolution wore on. Recently, though, he had sensed that he was being cut out of authority by his one time allies: Jiang Qing, Zhang Chunqiao, Yao Wenyuan, and Kang Sheng. Indeed, Chen was still infuriated by Kang's usurping his job of drafting Lin Biao's report for the Ninth Party Congress in 1969. And even before that, Kang's use of Wang Li and Guan Feng as scapegoats in the campaign against "the handful of counterrevolutionaries in the army" had made Chen start worrying about his own fate.

Chen's living arrangements also reflected his alienation from his old confederates in the Cultural Revolution Group. He moved out of Diaoyutai to a courtyard house in Miliangku Lane in western Peking, which separated him from Kang, Jiang Qing, Zhang Chunqiao, and

Yao Wenyuan. At the same time, Chen put out feelers to Lin Biao; before long, Chen was in regular telephone contact with Ye Qun, a fellow native of Fujian Province. Chen also began presenting works of calligraphy and other gifts to Lin Biao and Ye Qun, who hung the art in their bedroom. Still, concerned that too obvious a connection with Lin Biao might cause him trouble, Chen only rarely visited Maojiawan. When he did, he had his driver take roundabout routes to keep from being tailed.

By 1970, Chen Boda had become a full member of the Lin Biao group, providing the drafting and research skills that Lin Biao's army friends so conspicuously lacked. But Chen was ill equipped to outsmart Kang, Jiang Qing, and the other radicals. Chen was an absentminded professor with delusions of grandeur, rather than a master of court intrigue—his reputation as Mao's ghostwriter gave him credit for talents he never possessed. Worse, Chen's heavy Fujian accent made him incomprehensible to many people, forcing him to rely on an interpreter at large meetings. His failure to pass muster as a public speaker outside his native province would have mattered less if his mind had been more lucid. But, as one foreigner who lived in Peking throughout the 1950s and 1960s and translated some of Chen's writings expressed it, his "head was a total disaster. Every sentence he wrote seemed to have some fallacy or illogicality in it." Chen's mental shortcomings were no secret to Kang, who played games of intellectual one-upmanship with Chen. Once, when Chen remarked that the voluminous *Kangxi Dictionary,* a seventeenth-century compilation of over forty thousand Chinese characters, did not contain the Red Guard terms "smash" and "grab," Kang immediately checked and proved him wrong.

Oblivious to his weaknesses, Chen suddenly launched into the promotion of Lin Biao's ideas with great abandon. On August 24, the Central Committee meeting broke into small group sessions; at each one, Lin Biao's representatives spoke in favor of the marshal's support for both the theory of genius and the retention of the presidency. Chen Boda's speech was the most forthright, marking him as one of Lin's principal backers.

Mao, deciding to halt the systematic advance of Lin Biao's agenda, called a meeting of the Politburo Standing Committee the following day. Mao told his four colleagues that the Central Committee should adjourn, that discussion of Lin Biao's speech should stop, and that Chen Boda's speech in one of the small groups had blundered dangerously in deviating from the spirit of unity established at the Ninth Party Congress a year and a half earlier. Staring straight at Chen Boda, Mao declared, "If you carry on like this, I will just go down the mountain and let you argue. Don't mention the question of the president again. You want me to die earlier, so you let me be the national president! Whoever wants to establish the presidency can be the president. Anyway, I shall not be." By the end of the meeting, Lin Biao and Chen Boda knew they had lost.

Kang and Zhou Enlai moved quickly to solidify their victory. They forced Lin Biao's generals, Wu Faxian, Li Zuopeng, and Qiu Huizuo, to make self-criticisms for their statements to the Central Committee's small groups. Chen Boda, who had backed Lin Biao to the hilt, did not get off so lightly: he was ousted from the Politburo Standing Committee and forced to make a self-criticism before the Central Committee. To ensure that Chen stated his guilt sufficiently, Zhou and Kang agreed that Kang should draft the speech on Chen's behalf and Zhou himself should read it to the Central Committee, so that Chen could not use his incomprehensible accent to dodge embarrassment. After the final Central Committee session, Chen went across to thank Zhou, who was talking with Kang. Zhou acknowledged Chen's thanks and suggested that he also thank Kang for drafting the statement. Before Chen could utter anything else, Kang remarked curtly, "Don't be afraid of looking ugly!"— meaning that Chen should not worry about being shown up in front of other cadres.

Chen spent his first few weeks back in Peking reading and taking long walks. But toward the end of September, the authorities instructed him not to walk in public anymore lest foreigners see him, which would be "inconvenient." From then on, he was under house arrest.*

Though badly shaken by the events at Lushan, Lin Biao and Ye Qun felt relieved that Chen Boda had been made to take the fall for their bungled attempt to outflank Mao. Back at Maojiawan, they immediately removed from their bedroom wall all the works of calligraphy that Chen had given them.

Lin and Ye viewed Chen's tumble as a reprieve from further

---

* Chen Boda was imprisoned shortly after Lin Biao's abortive coup a year later. Put on trial in 1981 as a member of the Lin Biao clique, he was sentenced to life imprisonment but released in 1988. He died the next year of a heart attack.

trouble. But Kang saw it as a means of advancing another step. For all his shameless flattery and exploitation of Lin Biao, Kang never lost his sense of who had power; as long as Lin was Mao's sycophantic disciple, Kang would eagerly help the marshal improve his image. But at the first whiff of differences between China's two top leaders, Kang did not hesitate. In discussions leading up to the Lushan conference, he had consistently criticized both the retention of the state presidency and the theory of genius—as he took pains to point out to fellow top dogs. Kang was rewarded by being promoted to fourth place in the CCP hierarchy, behind only Mao, Lin Biao, and Zhou Enlai. He also inherited the Party's entire propaganda machine from Chen, expanding the base he already held with command of the ILD, the security system, and the Organization Department.

What might have been another step in Kang's rise to eventually succeed Mao himself became, instead, his high-water mark. Just when Kang's future seemed unlimited, he fell seriously ill in November 1970: the diagnosis, a malignant tumor in his bowel. Kang continued to exercise power and influence from home—drafting papers for Jiang Qing and others, and issuing directives to the departments under his supervision—but he never regained his former level of vitality.

Kang's illness kept him from attending the 1971 May Day parade at Tiananmen Square and deprived him of witnessing another of Lin's strange performances—one that helped bring the Lin Biao era to an end. Ever since the early years of the People's Republic, it had been customary for senior leaders to take their place on formal occasions in ascending order, with Mao always the last to appear. But when Mao's limousine pulled up to the Tiananmen gatehouse on May Day of 1971, he discovered that Lin Biao had not yet arrived. Lin did appear within a few minutes, explaining, "I was sweating. So I came late." Taken aback by Lin's faux pas, and pausing between each word for dramatic effect, the Chairman replied, "Who doesn't sweat!" The two supreme leaders rode together in an elevator to the viewing stand; the crowds assembled in the square greeted them with thunderous applause. Mao settled down to enjoy the proceedings, but Lin Biao got up and left within five minutes, telling some of the leaders present that he was worried about his health but explaining nothing to Mao. Nine weeks later, on July 6, Kang began distancing himself from the doomed marshal. He asked Cao Yi'ou to telephone the leaders of the

Party School and direct them to destroy every copy of *Lin Biao's Selected Works.* *

In the Byzantine ways of Chinese Communist politics, a hint of Lin Biao's trouble was made available to perceptive readers of *The People's Illustrated* and *The Army Illustrated*. In July and August, the two magazines published a photograph of Lin Biao taken by Jiang Qing (an amateur photographer, along with everything else). The composition of the picture was unexceptional: Lin seated, engrossed in reading Mao's works. One thing stood out, though: Lin Biao was "uncovered." The would-be emperor had no crown . . . nor any hair! For Lin, who had gone to great lengths to conceal his baldness, publication of the picture represented a painful embarrassment.

Nothing short of desperate action could save him now, Lin Biao knew. Aided by his son, Lin Liguo, who was head of the air force, and several other generals, Lin started laying plans to murder Mao. As early as March 1971, Lin Liguo had begun to expand the personal special-service unit he had created, "the Joint Fleet," into an organization with secret offices in Shanghai, Nanking, Canton, and several other cities. Working with a number of conspirators drawn exclusively from the military, Lin Liguo hatched a scheme he code-named "Plan 571," these numbers sounding the same in Chinese as "armed uprising."

Mao was soon alerted by intelligence reports that Lin Biao was trying to fashion alliances against him. The Chairman set off for the south of China on August 14. He called at a number of cities—Changsha, Wuhan, Canton, and Hangzhou—and at each stop, he questioned the local PLA commanders about their attitude in the event of a coup in Peking. Lin Biao received regular intelligence on Mao's activities from his army comrades, so he realized that the Chairman had guessed what he was up to and probably was taking countermeasures. For Lin, time was running out.

---

* A writer using the pseudonym Yao Ming-le has claimed that Kang worked closely with Zhou Enlai to help destroy Lin Biao. By Yao Ming-le's account, Kang used Guo Yufeng, his protégé who had taken charge of the Organization Department, to place agents in Lin Biao's inner circle. Yao combines accurate detail with so much sheer fantasy that it is difficult to assess his reliability. Yao's claim that Kang was aligned with Zhou against Lin Biao is consistent with all other creditable evidence. But even if Kang did direct Guo Yufeng to spy on Lin Biao, Kang's illness would have ruled out all but the most distant involvement.

On September 6, 1971, Lin gave the order to assassinate Mao, whom the conspirators had code-named "B-52," after the American bombers then devastating North Vietnam. Lin Liguo and his special-service agents planned to bomb the Chairman's train from the air as it approached Shanghai, blast it with land-launched rockets, and attack it with flamethrowers. As a final guarantee of success, Lin Biao had instructed Wang Weiguo, a military officer whom Mao knew and trusted, to board the Chairman's train in Shanghai and shoot him with a pistol. Lin would then blame Mao's death on Xu Shiyou, the commander of the Nanking military region, whose responsibilities embraced Shanghai, and declare himself head of an emergency government in Peking.

Mao's train reached Shanghai safely on September 10, before the plotters were ready to act. Mao remained in his railroad car and received a number of visitors, including Xu Shiyou. The Chairman asked Xu what he would do if a coup took place in Peking; Xu replied succinctly, "Lead my troops north and retake the capital!" Wang Weiguo, the designated assassin, came to the station but was kept in a waiting room and never got to see Mao. The Chairman's train left late on September 11. Wang Weiguo immediately reported Mao's departure to Lin Liguo's headquarters in Peking, but, for reasons that remain obscure, Lin's men made no move to attack the train. Mao reached the outskirts of Peking the following day at dusk. The presence in the capital of Unit 8341 under the command of his longtime bodyguard Wang Dongxing made an assassination attempt all but impossible.

Lin Biao had withdrawn to the relative safety of Beidaihe while he waited for Mao to be murdered. In case his plot failed, Lin had planned to fly to Canton, where an ally, Ding Sheng, was the regional military commander; once there, Lin would set up a separatist government, try to establish relations with foreign states, and start to negotiate with the powers in Peking. Lin and his associates planned to leave for Canton early on September 13, but that plan, too, came a cropper. Zhou Enlai had received word from sources (unidentified to this day) that the Lin Biao household was preparing for some unusual event. Zhou began making inquiries about a transport plane flown up to the town of Shanhaiguan, about twenty miles from Beidaihe, site of the airport nearest to Lin Biao's resort villa. Apparently, the Beidaihe guard bureau had also received reports of Lin Biao's plans to fly to Canton the next morning. As their enemies closed in around them,

Lin and Ye concluded that without the element of surprise, a rebellion in Canton was no longer possible. Instead, they decided to make a run for the Soviet Union.

Accompanied by their son, a bodyguard, an air force general, an assistant, and a three-man aircrew (including the pilot, Pan Jingyin), they took off late on the night of September 12 from the Shanhaiguan airport. Lin's party fled in such panic that during takeoff the undercarriage of his plane, a three-engine, hundred-passenger Trident, clipped the roof of a truck parked on the runway. The plane got off the ground anyway, but it was short of gasoline—there had been no time to refuel the craft before Lin had arrived, with the police in hot pursuit. His fuel gauges nearing empty, Pan Jingyin's only hope was a predawn emergency landing on a grassy field in Mongolia's Hentiy Province, about two hundred miles from the capital, Ulan Bator. In the last moments before the plane touched down, all the passengers removed their shoes, wristwatches, and any metal objects that could injure them. But Pan brought the plane in too fast—as he landed, the right wing hit the ground, the fuselage began to break apart, the fuel tank in the right wing burst open, and the remaining gasoline ignited. All nine on board were killed instantly, partly by impact and partly by fire.

News of the crash reached acting Foreign Minister Ji Pengfei in Peking a day later. Ji reported to several people present, "They all died in a plane crash. What a marvelous ending!" Zhou Enlai restricted news of Lin Biao's fate to a very small group of leaders and officials, including Kang, who received word of Lin's death the same day. He immediately had Cao Yi'ou telephone the Party School leaders, tell them what had happened, and assure them that "Kang Sheng hated Lin Biao."

Rumors in some quarters that Kang was involved in Lin's conspiracy have no factual support.* Nevertheless, the political intimacy Kang had pursued with Lin and his coterie of grasping generals proved

---

* During political infighting over Deng Xiaoping's return to power in the late 1970s, posthumous criticism of Kang sought to link him to Lin's coup attempt. In his secret denunciation of Kang at the Party School in 1978, Hu Yaobang alleged that Liu Xiangping, the widow of Public Security Minister Xie Fuzhi, claimed that before fleeing from Beidaihe, Lin had met Kang, who supposedly was driven to and from Lin's hiding place by Lin's son, Lin Liguo. Given the chaotic circumstances of Lin's departure, not to mention Kang's incapacitating illness, this account seems most unlikely.

embarrassing in the wake of Lin's bid for power. Mao's erstwhile warm embrace of Lin Biao now reduced the danger of Kang's past association with Lin, but Kang let no opportunity pass to misrepresent his relationship with Lin Biao and to insist that he had always distrusted and despised Lin. Struck down by a terrible illness and confronted by thoughts of his own mortality, Kang Sheng remained true to only one man: himself.

Chapter XXI

THE LAST
DOUBLE CROSS

ON FEBRUARY 21, 1972, five months after Lin Biao's death, the twenty-three-year break in relations between the United States and China officially ended when Air Force One, carrying President Richard Nixon, landed in Peking. From that time on, or so it seemed to the outside world, China was putting a decade of madness and terror behind it. Cadres purged in the late 1960s began reappearing at their desks. Even Deng Xiaoping, disgraced as "the number two capitalist roader" during the Cultural Revolution, was rehabilitated (much to the dismay of Kang Sheng, Jiang Qing, and other radical leaders). Deng had to write a long letter to Mao confessing to serious ideological mistakes, but little more than a year after Nixon's visit, Deng was installed as vice premier.

Things began to return to normal in 1972, but at first more in style than in substance. Within the Chinese Communist Party, the struggle for power continued. The Red Guards had chanted "Long Live Chairman Mao" countless times, but as Mao approached eighty, he was visibly aging; inevitably, his life would soon draw to a close. Leaders jockeyed for advantage, fighting among themselves for control of the ministries and departments that ruled the land. Even junior cadres felt they were witnessing the calm before another storm.

An almost surreal atmosphere hung over Peking. During the early years of the Cultural Revolution, battle lines had become clear very quickly as Red Guard factions fought each other or the army. But the Red Guards had disappeared, most of them sent to work on farms in a program begun as early as autumn 1968; big-character posters no longer announced which leading cadres were under attack; and an ominous silence fell over the land. China became the stage for a giant shadow play in which armies maneuvered behind a veil, only occasionally giving away their positions as their images flickered. Fact and fiction seemed to meld into one as scenarios made out of chatter and gossip took on a reality of their own.

Kang was a central figure in many of the rumors that circulated in Peking. By some accounts, Kang used Lin Biao's death to surreptitiously take over the personal secret service formed by Lin in preparation for seizing power. Appointing several of his most trusted aides to run Lin's clandestine network, Kang was said to have expanded his personal security organization into a force that had offices in Canton, Hangzhou, Shanghai, Hainan, Shenyang, and Beidaihe and was completely independent of the Party and the government.

In the immediate aftermath of Lin Biao's attempt to overthrow Mao, China retained all the hallmarks of a police state. Within days after Lin Biao's ill-fated escape, a group of generals suspected of being involved in the coup attempt were seized. Among them were Huang Yongsheng, the head of the PLA General Staff Department; Li Zuopeng, political commissar of the navy; Qiu Huizuo, chief of the PLA's Logistics Department; and Wu Faxian, commander of the air force. Arrests continued over the following year or so as teams of investigators explored every aspect of the Lin Biao incident and linked more and more junior officers with him.

A series of strange crimes intensified the fear and suspicion that permeated Peking. The most notorious case involved Li Zhen, the minister of public security. Li, a leftist general once based in the northeast, inherited the public-security portfolio after Kang's henchman Xie Fuzhi had fallen seriously ill in the summer of 1971 (Xie died the following March). In October 1973, after a little over two years in his new post, Li was found hanging from the basement ceiling in the ministry's headquarters on Peking's Chang'an Avenue. It appeared that Li had committed suicide, but some evidence pointed to murder: a mysterious telephone call that had summoned Li to a meeting in the ministry on the night of his death, and signs that sleeping pills had been forced into his mouth. Murder was the first official assessment, and Yu Sang, a vice minister of public security, was arrested as the chief suspect. But Yu was released and the authorities started to speak of Li's death as a suicide.

The true cause of Li Zhen's death has never been established. Chinese authorities have clung to the verdict of suicide in spite of protests from his family. Hu Yaobang, however, claimed that Jiang Qing had Li Zhen killed and then conspired with Kang to posthumously frame him for having shielded the perpetrators of the alleged murder of a former KMT president, Li Zongren.* Another theory, set forth by the Hong Kong magazine *Zheng Ming*, had Zhou Enlai responsible for Li Zhen's death. *Zheng Ming* suggested that Li died shortly after handing Jiang Qing the last existing copy of a compromising photograph long held in the ministry's secret archives. Taken during the 1930s, this picture supposedly showed her sitting naked on the lap of Huang Jinrong, a leading gangster and drug smuggler of the era. By turning over the embarrassing picture to Jiang Qing, the theory went, Li Zhen prevented Zhou Enlai from using it against Jiang Qing, and an enraged Zhou retaliated by ordering Li's death. *Zheng Ming* had previously linked Li's death to the investigation of the Lin Biao affair. But considering Li Zhen's strong leftist affiliations, it is unlikely that Kang and the radicals would have had him murdered.

The flashpoint of the intra-Party strife dominating Peking was an undeclared war against the ghost of Lin Biao—which threatened severe damage to Mao's reputation as well. By hand-picking Lin as his successor, the Chairman had destroyed his own reputation as an infallible leader possessing the mandate of heaven. Many ordinary citizens silently reflected, as they eventually read Lin's criticisms of Mao in propaganda reports intended to discredit Lin's character, that the dead conspirator had been right. Not that the views of the masses counted for much, but they were symptoms of a regime in disarray. Communist leaders who had cavalierly assumed that Maoist propaganda would always protect them from challenges to their power now faced an alienation of the citizenry caused by the endless repetition of meaningless slogans and the compulsory worship of an obviously flawed leader.

So sensitive was the matter of Lin Biao's treachery that word of his botched coup and subsequent death was withheld from rank-and-file Party members for two months after the event and not formally

---

* Li Zongren died in Peking in 1969. Hu Yaobang seemed confused about the time of Li Zongren's death, however, putting it before the Cultural Revolution.

announced to the nation at large until August 1973.* Until the time of Lin Biao's formal disgrace, however, the Foreign Ministry declined to give diplomats stationed in China any advice about his status except that he should not be toasted at state banquets.

Vilifying Lin Biao without smearing Mao was no easy task. The regime's refusal to publicly explain Lin's fate for almost two years after his death made it necessary to use innuendo and allegory to deny the rebel marshal's standing. Further complicating matters, scores of Lin's associates and protégés were chagrined at his death and disgrace, which ruined their own dreams of glory and power. Many of Lin's supporters rejected the account circulated inside the Party of his plot against Mao and subsequent disappearance; undoubtedly, someone in the Lin Biao camp was behind a mysterious book entitled *The Conspiracy and Death of Lin Biao,* which cast Lin as a martyr and Mao as the villain who had murdered him. Neutralizing the pro–Lin Biao forces became top priority for Mao and his coterie.

The first attempt to defame Lin Biao took the form of a drive against "ultraleftism" after Mao had decided that painting Lin Biao as "the root of ultraleftist thinking" could conveniently explain his rebellion. One problem: Mao and the Red Guard elite were the most ultraleft of all, so any blanket campaign against leftist radicals might backfire on the Chairman. Mao needed a way of maligning Lin Biao without jeopardizing the regime's revolutionary credentials. As a compromise formula, he elevated the operation to stamp out sympathy for Lin Biao into a broad offensive against Confucius—the cornerstone of China's orthodox philosophical tradition. By linking Lin Biao and Confucius, Mao hoped to maintain the thrust of the Cultural Revolution while discrediting Lin Biao as a feudal and reactionary creature who had schemed to overthrow the proletarian Mao. Newspapers and magazines carried page after page of stories exposing Confucius and Lin as archetypal revisionists. But the pain and suffering caused by the Cultural Revolution had drained the zeal of the people for mass campaigns, and the criticism of Lin and Confucius had little effect.

Kang had proved a master at manipulating such sensitive issues in the past, but the cancer eating away at his body deprived him of the

---

* The first news report of Lin Biao's death appeared in the West when *The Washington Post* ran the story "Lin Biao Believed to Be Dead" on November 27, 1971.

energy and mental concentration he needed to obtain personal advantage from the precarious stalemate in Peking. Kang did keep in touch by entertaining friends and associates at his home in Small Stone Bridge Lane, when he would still speak with animation and show off some of the rarer pieces in his art collection. Kang's most frequent guest was Jiang Qing, who brought get-well gifts—Pekinese terriers, potted plants, and albums of her photography—but quickly brought politics into the conversation; her visits had the main purpose of plotting with Kang on how to advance her cause.

Kang was not confined entirely to his house. He got out long enough to conduct one last raid on the Cultural Relics Bureau warehouse in 1972 to add to his hoard of stolen treasures. Kang also kept his name appearing in *The People's Daily* by sending wreaths in memory of deceased comrades—a sign to cadres throughout the nation that he himself had not yet passed from the scene. Kang was so eager to use funerals to keep himself in the spotlight that he even sent wreaths for men like Chen Yi and Wang Jiaxiang, whom he had hounded from office and done his best to kill.

Kang's fear that he might not outlive Mao sharpened his focus on his place in history. Jiang Qing, he decided, was the key. If she emerged on Mao's death as a modern empress dowager, Kang himself might be able to spend a few glorious months on the Chairman's throne. And if he did not live that long, Kang could at least die knowing he would be remembered as an honored figure in the annals of Chinese communism—again, assuming Jiang Qing inherited Mao's mantle. For three years, Kang operated and conspired on that premise.

Steering China in the direction Kang favored had not been easy. He had used every trick in the book to establish himself as one of the highest mandarins in the land, but his victories had come only after countless sessions of all-night planning and meticulous searches for incriminating documents. By the early 1970s, he lacked the energy for "Stalin hours" scheming.

Moreover, at the very time when Kang needed good fortune to compensate for his failing health, Mao upset Kang's calculations by naming Zhou Enlai the day-to-day head of the Party and the government. Zhou had done his best to maintain some stability throughout the Cultural Revolution, but never without having to share power and make compromises. For the last few years, though, his star had been on the rise. Opening China to the United States was just one of Zhou's initiatives that helped bring an element of rationality into

Chinese politics in the early 1970s. Now, with Mao's endorsement, Zhou had ascended to a new level of authority.

Kang was too sick to have taken on Zhou's new responsibilities himself, but he deeply resented the Chairman's decision to give Zhou so much power. As Kang knew, the irrational and nihilistic atmosphere so conducive to his manipulative politics would give way to more stable conditions under Zhou's moderating hand.

Kang and Zhou had worked closely together when Zhou placed Kang in command of the Communist secret service in Shanghai during the 1920s. But Kang's abuse of power in Yan'an and his brutal persecution of leaders like Liu Shaoqi had cooled their friendship; Zhou had at times criticized Kang's excesses. Mindful of each other's power, Kang and Zhou had maintained a surface harmony—at times even working together, as they did against Lin Biao at Lushan. Still, distrust deepened beneath their cordiality: from behind the scenes, Kang had his allies attack Zhou with subtle accusations of collaboration during the war with the pro-Japanese Wang Jingwei, of suffering from "professionalism," and of "only grasping production and not ideology." Zhou had weathered Kang's efforts to bring him down, but they reinforced his perception of Kang as a ruthless and dangerous man who needed to be watched.

For Kang to go to Mao and directly criticize Zhou would be futile if not dangerous, since it would openly challenge Mao's judgment. Kang's only hope was to poison Mao's trust in Zhou—no simple matter. During the mid-1960s, Kang had convinced Mao that the play *The Dismissal of Hai Rui* was part of a conspiracy, using innuendo and leaving it for Mao to draw the intended conclusions. That, Kang decided, was again the best way to handle Mao.

By mid-1973, convening a new Party congress had become a matter of extreme urgency. True, only four years had elapsed since the Ninth Party Congress, and CCP leaders had allowed longer periods to pass between the Seventh, Eighth, and Ninth congresses; but Lin Biao's stunning insurrection had made an early Party congress essential.

Kang took his place on the podium next to Zhou Enlai when the Tenth Congress opened on August 24, 1973. But Kang bore little resemblance to the dynamic individual of just a few years before: now he had the hunched posture, pale skin, and sunken eyes of a dying old man. Still in charge of the Organization Department, however, he had a major say in the personnel matters settled at the congress and the

Central Committee plenum that followed it. He was the moving force behind a resolution adopted to brand Chen Boda—Kang's former colleague, fallen from office at the Lushan plenum in 1970—"a Kuomintang anti-communist, a Trotskyite renegade, and a revisionist secret agent." By Kang's standards of proof, the charges against Chen were unexceptional: he had been in contact with Soviet Trotskyites while studying in Moscow and was arrested by the KMT while working as an underground Communist in China.

The congress endorsed yet another Party constitution—the third since 1958—and deleted the embarrassing references to Lin Biao as Mao's heir. In other respects, though, the latest constitution was a compromise, naming no successor to Mao and assembling a shaky leadership structure that combined radicals and pragmatists. Mao remained Chairman, and the congress appointed five vice chairmen: Zhou Enlai; Kang Sheng; Wang Hongwen, a leftist from Shanghai; Marshal Ye Jianying; and Li Desheng, the PLA commander in the northeast.

Never before had Kang held the rank of vice chairman. In spite of his illness, the promotion restored his appetite for politics and encouraged him to think he could undermine Zhou by turning the debate over Confucius against him. Using historical allusion to attack one's enemies—"pointing at the mulberry to curse the locust," as a Chinese idiom puts it—was such an ancient tradition in court intrigues, and so deeply ingrained in the popular consciousness, that Kang believed it would still work in the 1970s.

Kang put his plot against Zhou into motion by ordering his agents at the Party School to prepare an article on "The Problem of Confucius Killing Shao Zheng Mao," an age-old tale of how the sage had put to death a rival who had challenged his authority. Kang suggested that they enlist the services of Professor Zhao Jibin, a sixty-eight-year-old expert on Chinese philosophy who had once headed the literature department at Shandong University, transferred to the Party School in 1963, and become one of Kang's writers. Zhao was well qualified to draft the polemics that Kang now ordered. The story had no historical basis, but Kang used it to draw parallels between Confucius and Zhou Enlai, who shared upper-class origins, and Shao Zheng Mao and Mao Zedong, two men with humble backgrounds. Anyone familiar with Chinese politics would grasp the underlying message that Zhou was potentially Mao's deadly enemy.

Jiang Qing, overjoyed by Kang's renewed level of activity and his attacks on Zhou Enlai, joined in and staged an "Anti-Lin, Anti-Confucius Mobilization Meeting" actually aimed at Zhou Enlai. At the rally, attended by over ten thousand people in late January 1974, Jiang Qing acknowledged Kang's contribution without disclosing his masterminding of the criticism of Zhou.

Too weak to bear the brunt of the work himself, Kang directed others in what would be his last major operation. He telephoned one of his lieutenants at the Party School two days after Jiang Qing's rally and inquired about Professor Zhao's health. Commenting favorably on Zhao's contribution to the article about Confucius killing Shao Zheng Mao, Kang suggested that he now draft an essay in praise of Liu Xiazhi, who had led a slave revolt in ancient China and rejected Confucius and his philosophy. Like the other ancient tales Kang resurrected for contemporary purposes, the story of this Chinese Spartacus emphasized the gap between the patrician Zhou Enlai and the proletarian Mao.

Once he had activated the next phase of his scheme, Kang had his secretary write to Jiang Qing that "the Venerable Kang has mentioned that it is possible to find some material criticizing Confucius in ancient books. . . . [Kang] thought of the leader of the slave uprising in 'The Chapter of the Brigand Zhi' in [the philosophical classic] *Zhuangzi* criticizing Confucius and rebuking him very severely. He ordered me to tell the Party School to invite Professor Zhao Jibin to add footnotes and to translate it [from classical Chinese] into modern Chinese, under the title 'Liu Xiazhi Severely Criticizes the Younger Confucius.' When it is completed, it can be printed and circulated to central comrades for reference."

At Kang's direction, "Tang Xiaowen," his personal group of propagandists since the mid-1960s, wrote a paper outlining the attack by the proletarian Liu Xiazhi on the patriarchal Confucius. As more and more anti-Confucian pieces appeared in newspapers and magazines, the connection between ancient history and current events in the debate became obvious.

Kang next instructed researchers at the Party School to compile a series of essays about criticism of Confucius from the 1920s and 1930s, the period of intellectual ferment when Chinese writers and scholars challenged the stale orthodoxies that had guided Chinese life for two millennia. One article produced by Kang's men reviewed how Lu Xun, a famous satirical writer and a dominant intellectual force in modern China, had seen Confucianism as the source of all the diseased elements of Chinese culture. By invoking Lu Xun and linking him with the anti-Confucian writers who had surfaced during the Cultural Revolution, Kang created an ideological framework that portrayed Zhou Enlai, the unnamed but obvious representative of Confucianism, as a dangerous reactionary completely out of step with twentieth-century Chinese thought.

Kang also used the precedents of female rulers in Chinese history to prepare the masses to accept Jiang Qing, rather than Zhou Enlai, as Mao's successor. Under Kang's guidance, Tang Xiaowen wrote articles celebrating the consorts, concubines, and female warriors who had wielded maximum influence in the past—women like the empress Wu Zetian and the empress dowager Ci Xi. Wu Zetian was a lascivious palace maiden who usurped the throne in the eighth century, ruling China in her own right; Ci Xi seized control of the court and left a male figurehead on the throne near the end of the nineteenth century, much as Jiang Qing might do with Kang's backing.

Kang gave a revolutionary flavor to his reexamination of Chinese history by appearing to overturn the judgments of generations of conservative scholars. For more than two thousand years, orthodox Confucian philosophers and officials had opposed the idea of women's involvement in affairs of state, and so had reviled most of the empresses and concubines celebrated in Kang's propaganda campaign. Therefore, his glorification of female rulers previously seen as villains seemed completely in keeping with communism's antifeudal character; the prospect that Jiang Qing might rise to supreme power was articulated as a natural consequence of Marxist dogma.

Kang's efforts to promote Jiang Qing were limited by his deteriorating health. In May 1974, one of Kang's secretaries informed his group of writers that "the Venerable Kang" was too weak to read, and directed them to submit their articles directly to Jiang Qing. Jiang Qing, already in control of a writing team known as "Liang Xiao" ("Two Schools," being based at Peking and Qinghua universities), was delighted to inherit Tang Xiaowen, with its access to the invaluable archives at the Party School.

The crusade against Confucius and his so-called "modern representatives" generated much sound and fury but hardly affected the balance of power. This time around, Mao seemed to disregard the subtle messages planted in Kang's endless stream of allegorical essays. Moreover, the public, who had responded so overwhelmingly in 1966 to Mao's summons "to bombard the Party headquarters," ignored calls to overthrow "the modern Confucius." The forces grouped around Zhou Enlai—led by his newly rehabilitated lieutenant, Deng Xiaoping, who was promoted to vice chairman upon Zhou's hospitalization in 1974—gained strength as they reinstated an increasing number of the cadres purged in the late 1960s, built relations with the United States and the West, and revived the nation's economy. In spite of Kang's best efforts, Zhou, through his deputy Deng Xiaoping, remained in control.

Increasingly conscious of his advancing years, Mao began to find the company of people his own age depressing. He surrounded himself with members of the younger generation, among them his nephew Mao Yuanxin and his lover, Zhang Yufeng, as well as two women, Wang Hairong and Tang Wensheng, who worked as interpreters for the Foreign Ministry. Wang Hairong, better known as "Little Rat Wang," was rumored to be Mao's niece but was actually his second cousin; being a member of the Chairman's family had helped establish her as a political insider. Tang Wensheng (known as Nancy Tang in the West) was an American-educated Chinese who served as one of Mao's main interpreters in the last years of his life. These two women functioned as a team; Wang Hairong translated Mao's heavy Hunan accent into Mandarin Chinese, and Nancy Tang rendered Wang's Mandarin into English.

Even without Kang's guidance, Jiang Qing and her three main confederates—Zhang Chunqiao; Yao Wenyuan, the Shanghai Party boss who wrote the 1965 article criticizing *The Dismissal of Hai Rui*; and Wang Hongwen, a protégé of Zhang Chunqiao who had become a key member of the radical clique—redoubled their efforts to destroy Deng Xiaoping and usurp power. The four of them attempted unsuccessfully to undermine Deng by challenging his nationalistic credentials at a Politburo meeting on October 16, 1974. Jiang Qing, recognizing the clash with Deng as the decisive moment in her quest for power, plotted into the early hours of the next morning with her three radical allies. They desperately needed Mao's support but were uncertain how to win it. Jiang Qing's contact with Mao had diminished over the last two or three years; they had remained political allies after Zhang Yufeng appeared on the scene, but their relationship had dwindled to a series of long-distance written communications.

Eventually, the radicals decided to send Wang Hongwen as their emissary to Mao. Wang, as the youngest of their group, had the best chance of putting Mao in a receptive mood. Wang flew to Changsha in Hunan Province, where Mao was vacationing with Mao Yuanxin and Zhang Yufeng. Arriving after a chancy flight made without permission from anyone in the Zhou–Deng ruling camp, Wang Hongwen reported to the Chairman that "the atmosphere in Peking at present is like the Lushan plenum"—the meeting that had revealed Lin Biao's ambitions. "The four of us met all night and decided that I should come to report to you. I left when Premier Zhou was resting. I took a great risk coming. Premier Zhou is ill, but he spends all night calling people, talking to them, forming alliances. Among those who often go to the Premier's place are Deng Xiaoping, Ye Jianying, Li Xiannian, and other comrades."

Wang's message rang clear: Zhou was plotting to follow in Lin Biao's footsteps and overthrow Mao. For almost a year, radical propagandists had been writing articles intended to persuade Mao that history made inevitable a coup attempt by a Confucian chief minister against a peasant emperor. Mao listened to Wang's warning but, contrary to the radicals' hopes, continued to support Zhou Enlai and Deng Xiaoping. To emphasize his position, he returned a letter from Jiang Qing dated November 12, 1974, after writing a note in the margins directing her "not to make many public appearances, not to approve documents, and not to organize a cabinet or act like a backstage boss. The Premier is still the Premier."

The news of Wang Hongwen's failed mission to Mao forced Kang to admit to himself that Jiang Qing would never be in a position to install him as China's regent. He made a revealing comment during a long talk with one of his lieutenants at the Party School on December 26, 1974 (Mao's eighty-first birthday): "I have a tumor down below. I'm losing blood. I'm finished."

Jiang Qing's star began to fade more noticeably when Mao openly rebuked her at a May 1975 meeting of the Politburo. Kang was too ill to attend the session, but he quickly learned that Mao had warned the Politburo members that Jiang Qing respected nobody except herself and would try to seize power after his death. Mao again ordered her not to conspire with her three radical colleagues—Zhang Chunqiao, Wang Hongwen, and Yao Wenyuan—and behave with them like "a Gang of Four."

When Kang heard of Mao's rebuke, he set out to determine

exactly how far the relationship between Mao and Jiang Qing had deteriorated. He summoned to his residence the interpreters Wang Hairong and Nancy Tang, knowing that they regularly visited Mao's residence. Kang listened in silence as the two women outlined the situation. Too weak to speak at length, he merely nodded in acknowledgment when they had finished.

Before Kang could decide how to respond to this report, he slipped into a semicomatose state that lasted for several weeks, making him confused, disoriented, and at times delirious. In his hours of semiconsciousness, he rambled on, prodded by the fears that had haunted him since his stay in Shanghai a half-century earlier: "In 1920, 1921, 1922, I never defected; in 1923, I never defected; in 1924, I never defected; in 1925, I never defected; in 1926, I never defected; in 1927, I never. . . ."

In late June, Kang regained full consciousness and resumed grappling with the problems from the storm raging around Jiang Qing. After careful deliberation, Kang concluded that the time had come to jettison his protégé of nearly forty years. Cast aside by Mao, Jiang Qing could be of no further use to Kang, except as the ante for other high stakes. To Kang, ideology, art, friends, truth—anything could be sacrificed to realize his own grandiose dreams.

So Kang tried to turn Jiang Qing's impending downfall to his own advantage. He contacted Deng Xiaoping, in charge of the day-to-day operation of government ever since Zhou Enlai's hospitalization, and asked him to arrange another visit from Wang Hairong and Tang Wensheng. Upon their arrival, Kang began by assuring them—as he had assured so many others so often—that he had never been a traitor to the Party. He then asked them to convey an extremely sensitive message to Chairman Mao.

The first part of Kang's communication to Mao was that Jiang Qing had betrayed the Communists to the KMT during the mid-1930s, when she was a young actress in Shanghai. Details of her KMT connection had been reported at the time in southern Chinese and Hong Kong newspapers, Kang told the two women, suggesting that they seek corroboration from Wang Guanlan, a former Communist official in Shanghai and Yan'an who had married one of Jiang Qing's friends. Kang's disclosures entirely contradicted his position in Yan'an thirty-seven years earlier, when he had defended Jiang Qing against the same charges he was now making and so enabled her to marry

Mao. By denying those allegations in 1938, he had tied himself to Mao; by affirming them now, he was gambling that he would stay on the winning side.

Kang also asked the two women to tell Mao that Zhang Chun-qiao, one of Jiang Qing's "Gang of Four," had once been a special agent in the Blue Shirts Society, a KMT intelligence organization, in Jinan during the 1930s; Wu Zhongchao, the director of the Palace Museum in Peking,* could verify his charges against Zhang Chun-qiao, Kang added. According to Kang, Wu Zhongchao was an agent of Kang's who had infiltrated the KMT intelligence services in the late 1930s and early 1940s, working alongside Zhang Chunqiao (then a KMT operative) during his undercover days.†

Kang's accusations against Jiang Qing and Zhang Chunqiao had stronger factual support than many of the other charges of treachery he had made throughout his long career, but they failed to have the expected impact. "Little Rat Wang" and Nancy Tang, frightened by

---

* It was Wu who escorted President Nixon through the museum during his 1972 visit to Peking.

† Wu's version was slightly different. He had been one of Kang's deputies in Shanghai, and had become suspicious of Zhang Chunqiao. Although Wu met Zhang by acci-dent, Zhang had asked Wu at their first meeting whether he was a Communist. For a stranger to ask such a question during the White Terror was highly unusual. Wu's instinctive reaction was that Zhang might be a KMT agent. Exactly when Wu told Kang of his doubts about Zhang is unclear, but Wu and Kang crossed paths in Peking in the 1950s; Wu was one of Kang's neighbors on Small Stone Bridge Lane. Wu's appointment as head of the Palace Museum in 1958 also brought him into contact with Kang, who at times borrowed antiques through Wu and also imposed on Wu to have special pieces of calligraphy mounted by the experts at the museum.

Shen Zui, a former top official in the KMT Military Statistics Bureau, also provided proof that Zhang Chunqiao was once a KMT operative. In Shanghai before the outbreak of the Pacific war, Shen was close to another KMT intelligence agent, Cui Wanqiu, a prominent journalist who specialized in countering Communist influence in the city's cultural circles. At social occasions hosted by Cui, Shen Zui met both Jiang Qing and a journalist who used the pen name "Di Ke"—a Chinese transliteration of the English name "Dick." Shen knew that "Di Ke" worked for Cui Wanqiu, but only after the arrest of Zhang Chunqiao and the rest of the Gang of Four in October 1976 did Shen learn that "Di Ke" was, in fact, Zhang Chunqiao.

Shen Zui, himself a victim of the Cultural Revolution, was interrogated and im-prisoned from 1967 until 1972. It is entirely possible that Kang saw reports on Shen's questioning; put two and two together; realized what Shen had not figured out, that Zhang had been in the KMT, and guarded the information until "the perfect moment"—instead of blowing the whistle on Zhang at the time, as he should have done.

the explosive implications of Kang's message, hesitated to give it to the Chairman. Unsure of the safest course, they approached Foreign Minister Qiao Guanhua and his wife, Zhang Hanzhi, who was Mao's English tutor, a friend of Jiang Qing's, and a notetaker at Politburo meetings. Qiao told Wang and Tang that he knew nothing of Zhang Chunqiao's personal history, and that although the Shanghai newspapers had devoted their gossip columns to Jiang Qing's private life in the 1930s, he had never seen any articles accusing her of betraying the Communist Party.

Qiao and his wife advised the interpreters to keep Kang's message to themselves. After all, Qiao pointed out, Kang could have his own secretary write a memorandum on the subject and send it directly to the Chairman. The two women concluded that with Kang in such frail health, they could ignore his directions; if they were ever challenged, they could blame Qiao Guanhua for their silence.*

After his second visit from the two interpreters, illness immobilized Kang until October 1975, when he mustered the strength for what would be his last meeting with Chairman Mao. In a final attempt to secure his place in history, Kang turned his venom on Deng Xiaoping. Kang had worked closely with Deng in years past on the Sino–Soviet dispute and as a member of the Party Secretariat, controlled by Deng during the early 1960s; he had recently pretended to be Deng's friend and ally. But Kang knew that his persecution of Deng and many of his colleagues during the Cultural Revolution had eradicated every trace of Deng's trust in him. Taking advantage of Deng's absence (he was representing China at the United Nations General Assembly), Kang tried to persuade Mao that Deng should be purged again—and permanently. Kang played on Mao's deepest fears,

* The details of Kang's conversation with Wang and Tang were recorded in a letter Zhang Hanzhi wrote to Mao. Kang's message to the two women later surfaced as evidence to justify the second purge of Deng Xiaoping. Mao agreed in April 1976 to purge Deng again and stripped him of all his offices. But for the protection of General Xu Shiyou and other military leaders, Deng might have suffered a much worse fate. The pretext for Deng's removal was that he had allegedly incited the bloody riots that broke out when crowds gathered in Tiananmen Square on the traditional tomb-sweeping festival to honor the memory of Zhou Enlai, who had died on January 8, 1976. On April 25, 1976, following Deng's ouster, Qiao Guanhua and his wife wrote to Mao that Kang had "slandered" both Jiang Qing and Zhang Chunqiao. Qiao suggested that Kang had acted in concert with Deng, offering as proof that Deng had passed the message to Wang and Tang that Kang wanted to see them. Mao's response, if any, to these extraordinary accusations is unknown.

warning him that Deng secretly opposed the Cultural Revolution and wanted it to go down in history as a mistake. For the time being, however, Mao ignored Kang's advice.

Kang was correct about Deng Xiaoping: after he returned once again to power in 1978, Deng did reverse everything the Cultural Revolution had stood for. By then, though, both Mao and Kang were dead.

Could Kang have made at least one desperate attempt to betray Mao? According to Hu Yaobang, Kang went to great lengths to monitor the activities of Mao and Zhou, even wiretapping Mao's private study and the office of Zhou Enlai. By Hu's account, Mao rebuked Kang in September 1972 for trying to eavesdrop on him, but Kang strenuously denied the accusation. Three months later, a number of listening devices turned up in Mao's study. Kang once again insisted that he was not responsible—and then, Hu declared, arranged the murders of the three technicians who had installed them on his orders.

When Zhou Enlai, suffering from cancer like Kang, was admitted to Peking Hospital in April 1974, he expressed relief, according to Hu, that now he could speak freely without fear of being overheard by Kang or his agents. "I couldn't stay any longer at my place," Hu quoted Zhou as telling an ally, Marshal Ye Jianying. "All I could do was to hide in the hospital. At least here I can say whatever I want to say."*

It is difficult to know how much stock to put in Hu Yaobang's allegations. By the time Zhou was hospitalized, Kang was too ill to participate regularly in anything but the most limited political activity. He made only a single public appearance in 1971 and was not seen again until the Tenth Party Congress in August 1973. But while Hu's charges against Kang may have grown out of the rumors of the day, the ethos of terror that Hu evoked was real enough in the early to mid-1970s. Even Deng Xiaoping, a much more phlegmatic man than the excitable Hu Yaobang, was afraid to discuss sensitive political matters in his own home. A minor incident that occurred during his exile in Jiangxi Province showed Deng's fear of being spied on. Back home from a meeting on November 5, 1971, at which he and his

---

* A sense of the extreme phobia about eavesdropping that gripped the Peking elite is conveyed by Hu Yaobang's charge that between 1969 and 1975, Kang spent 230 million yuan (about 115 million U.S. dollars) on espionage equipment from abroad.

wife, Zhuo Lin, had first heard of Lin Biao's abortive coup, Deng was too worried by the presence of a Party watchdog to tell his daughter, Maomao, the news. So his wife took Maomao into the kitchen and, with a finger, traced four characters in the palm of her hand: "Lin Biao is dead."

Too weak to concern himself any longer with matters of state, Kang—an avowed atheist, like all Marxists—devoted his remaining energies to religion. In the last months of his life, he met often with Zhao Puchu, a Buddhist patriarch who had served since 1949 as a symbol of the regime's religious tolerance. Kang had ridiculed Zhao in front of Mao in 1964,* but as death loomed ever closer, he turned to the elderly scholar and sought solace in the Buddhist doctrine of reincarnation.

At five minutes past six on the morning of December 16, 1975, just as another bitter Peking winter was beginning, Kang Sheng's life ended. He was struck down at last not by any of his myriad enemies but by a terrible disease. Two days after Kang's death, his Politburo colleagues gathered to pay their last respects. His remains lay in state in the Qing dynasty pavilion that had been converted into the People's Cultural Palace. Fifteen thousand workers, peasants, cadres, students, People's Liberation Army officers, and foreign dignitaries attended the memorial service held three days later. Every member of the Politburo was present except Mao, who no longer attended funerals; the elderly and frail Marshal Zhu De; and Zhou Enlai, who was still hospitalized. Wang Hongwen presided over the ceremony, and Marshal Ye Jianying, who had survived several attacks instigated by Kang, eulogized him as "a proletarian revolutionary, a Marxist theoretician, and a glorious fighter against revisionism." Afterward, Kang's body was cremated and his ashes interred in the memorial for revolutionary martyrs and heroes at Babaoshan Cemetery in western Peking.

The Chinese handling of foreign involvement in the mourning of Kang's death essentially confirmed his distance from U.S. relations. The State Department, in a message sent over Secretary of State Kissinger's signature, authorized the United States Liaison Office in Pe-

---

* Zhao Puchu wrote a poem criticizing revisionism, "The Three Laments of a Certain Gentleman," during the early 1960s. After Kang came across it in December 1964 he sent a copy to Mao, angrily declaring that religious figures should not be allowed to oppose revisionism and suggesting that the poem be used as an example of the insidious dangers that the Party had to guard against.

king to sign a book of condolences if the Foreign Ministry observed the normal custom and invited all missions to do so. Nevertheless, the Foreign Ministry omitted to inform the Liaison Office, although it sent written notification to all other embassies. The logic that had led to this was obscure, but the message was clear enough: Kang had not been a sponsor of Sino-American relations. Less conversant with the subtleties of policy, the Chinese mission to the United Nations in New York took a broader view and invited all diplomatic representatives to sign a condolence register. The Americans signed at "working level." A telegram sent later by Ambassador Daniel Patrick Moynihan reported that a "photograph of Kang Sheng hung on a broad red curtain flanked on either side by a motionless, head-bowed member of China's mission and a number of wreaths with ribbons inscribed in Chinese."

Kang Sheng's life had ended after seventy-seven years. But his impact on China and its people was far from over.

Chapter XXII

THE LEGACY
OF
KANG SHENG

THE DEATH of Kang Sheng signaled the passing of Mao's last courtiers. The final phase of a period of change at the top had begun.

On January 8, 1976, less than a month after Kang's death, Zhou Enlai died of cancer of the bladder. Zhou had attempted to position Deng Xiaoping to take over the government, but no sooner had Zhou's memorial services concluded than a fight broke out within the Party. With Zhou, their archenemy, out of the way, the radicals led by Jiang Qing and Zhang Chunqiao launched an all-fronts crusade to curb the influence of Deng, and Zhou's pragmatic lieutenants. The battle was indecisive; Hua Guofeng, the former Hunan Party chief who had become public-security minister after Li Zhen's mysterious death in 1973, emerged in February 1976 as acting Premier.

At the time of the annual tomb-sweeping festival in early April 1976, when Chinese offer homage to their deceased ancestors, the people of Peking spontaneously gathered in Tiananmen Square to pay their respects to the late Premier, whom they had viewed as a guardian against anarchy. Zhou's mourners began assembling on April 1. Over the next three days, the crowd grew to several hundred thousand demonstrators who displayed posters, delivered emotional speeches, read poetry, and laid wreaths at the foot of the Monument to the Heroes of the Revolution, the stone obelisk in the middle of the square. By the time everyone had paid respects to Zhou Enlai, there was a hill of wreaths fifty feet high.

The authorities had been taken by surprise. They made no attempt to halt the tributes until the predawn hours of April 5, when the municipal administration sent two hundred trucks filled with workers to clear away the mound of flowers. People on their way to work later that morning saw the empty square and became infuriated. Thousands started to gather and protest the disappearance of the wreaths. The younger members of the crowd soon raged out of control—they hurled insults at authorities, burned down a small police station, set several cars afire, and tried to storm the Great Hall of the People.

A standoff between the authorities and the people lasted throughout the day. Wu De, the mayor of Peking and a onetime student at Kang's Shaanbei Academy in Yan'an, and acting Premier Hua Guofeng, with the backing of the radicals, decided to use force to disperse the rioters. After nightfall, columns of militiamen marched out of the Forbidden City, stormed the square, and waded through the crowd with electric shock sticks, killing about one hundred, injuring many more, and arresting several thousand. Scores of young protesters were seized by police and force-marched into one of the parks adjacent to the Forbidden City. There, according to rumors that circulated at the time, they were shot.

The radical leaders took advantage of the Tiananmen riots to accuse Deng Xiaoping of promoting counterrevolution. Chairman Mao had ordered Jiang Qing and her radical colleagues to defer to Zhou Enlai and Deng Xiaoping one year earlier, but this time Mao made no attempt to shield Deng. Mao, forewarned by Kang Sheng that Deng would seek to overturn the accomplishments of the Cultural Revolution, agreed that he should be removed from power. Deng was stripped of all posts and placed under house arrest in April 1976—his second purge in a decade.

Over the next few months, China lived with a palpable sense of impending catastrophe. All the signs suggested the dynasty was melting away. Zhu De, the ninety-year-old general who had seemed like an eternal pillar of the Maoist state, died on July 6, 1976. The radicals grew ever cockier, using their control of the press to make allegorical attacks on Hua Guofeng, portraying him as a "rightist." Government was paralyzed by uncertainty, factional fighting, and outright fear. Many ministers and high officials pretended to be ill and checked into hospitals; others stayed at home instead of going to work.

Even nature added to the sense that events had spun out of control. On July 27, 1976, fish in the ponds of the Diaoyutai State Guesthouse began jumping out of the water, as if agitated by some mysterious, invisible force. The following day, a gigantic earthquake thundered through northern China. The city of Tangshan, one hundred miles east of Peking, was flattened, and the surrounding area, including the port of Tianjin—where Red Guard contingents had helped Kang search for evidence against Liu Shaoqi during the Cultural Revolution—was heavily damaged. The worst disaster of its kind in the history of mankind, the earthquake took upward of 500,000 lives in the first five minutes; the total number of deaths is said to have exceeded 800,000.*

The awesome cataclysm confirmed the Chinese superstition that earthquakes portend the end of emperors, even dynasties. Less than two months later, on September 9—the ninth day of the ninth month, an omen to many Chinese—the glue that had held the fragile structure of the Chinese state together since 1949 was dissolved: Mao Zedong, after ten years of suffering from Parkinson's disease, died at eighty-three.

Although the pendulum of Mao's favor had swung toward the radicals in April when he agreed to purge Deng Xiaoping, Mao did not pass the mantle to Jiang Qing and her colleagues. Instead, he placed power in the hands of Hua Guofeng, acting Premier and first vice chairman. Hua conferred privately with Mao after the Chairman met with New Zealand Prime Minister Robert Muldoon on April 30; he now produced a sheet of paper on which Mao had written in a shaky scrawl, "With you in charge I am at ease." In the absence of any clearer arrangement, this document satisfied the Chinese elite that Mao had designated Hua as his successor.

Kang would have approved of Mao's choice, which in many ways fulfilled Kang's final objectives. He had betrayed Jiang Qing and Zhang Chunqiao and warned Mao against Deng, leaving the impression that he favored a compromise candidate like Hua Guofeng. Hua's appointment as public-security minister had required Kang's blessing, and Kang would have viewed Hua as a member of his network. Indeed, the rumors of the late 1970s that Hua was Kang's illegitimate son, though unfounded, showed how closely Kang and Hua were linked by observers of the political scene.

With Mao alive, the pretenders to his throne had merely been

---

* The Chinese government claimed that there were 240,000 dead and 160,000 missing or injured. Unofficial but seemingly well-based figures placed the number of deaths in the vicinity of 800,000.

shadow-boxing; now the infighting started in earnest. Various groups could strike against their rivals without worrying about how the Chairman might react. In the absence of the man who had been their key patron, the radicals became extremely vulnerable. Although they controlled the propaganda apparatus—the press, radio, TV, theater, and cinema—they had no claim on the police or the military. Zhang Chunqiao attempted to build up the militia (an urban-based, part-time reserve force) to counter the army, but the militia remained weak and ineffective.

Almost immediately after Mao's death, a clique of veteran leaders—including Ye Jianying, Wang Zhen, Nie Rongzhen, Li Xiannian, and Xu Shiyou—began secret negotiations with Hua Guofeng to free China from the influence of the small knot of men and women identified with Jiang Qing. On October 6, 1976, the troops of Unit 8341, acting on orders issued by Wang Dongxing after consulting with the Party elders, arrested Jiang Qing, Zhang Chunqiao, Yao Wenyuan, and Wang Hongwen—who quickly became known throughout China and beyond as "the Gang of Four." At last, the veterans who had tried to stop the Cultural Revolution in February 1967, the members of the so-called February Adverse Current, had won the day. The Gang of Four was "smashed at one blow," in the jargon of the times.

Hua Guofeng may have been China's supreme leader, but his authority scarcely compared to what Mao had acquired over the course of his career. A relative novice in the ways of the capital and a latecomer to power, Hua had to rely on cadres in the security services, the Party, and the army as a base to augment Mao's handwritten mandate. Deng Xiaoping, released from house arrest in October 1976, immediately after the Gang of Four fell, perceived at once how weak Hua was. Led by Deng, the Party stalwarts who had made the Long March and occupied important posts during the 1950s and early 1960s now campaigned to return to office. Their first step was to rehabilitate the victims of the Cultural Revolution—a process that gave the moderates a chance to recruit allies from among the purged cadres and to expose many of the men on Hua Guofeng's side as accomplices in the radicals' persecution of countless Party members.

Deng steadily gained support. He was formally restored to power in mid-1978, when the Central Committee named him vice chairman. Hua Guofeng remained chairman for nearly three years but in name only; since 1978, Deng has called all the shots. Deng continued to consolidate his power, and in December 1980 his faction on the Politburo mustered a majority to vote for Hua's removal from office. Hua stepped down several months later. Now in his early seventies, he still lives in Peking, an invisible man who briefly ruled the nation.

It did not take long for Kang's crimes to come under scrutiny. As Deng struggled to regain authority and the victims of the Cultural Revolution were redeemed, more and more evidence of Kang's malevolent influence came to light. By 1978, Kang's record had sparked an acrimonious debate within the Party. The Gang of Four could be attacked with impunity—apart from Jiang Qing's controversial marriage to Mao, none of the others had much claim to status or prestige—but Kang was a difficult target. For one thing, he had sponsored many cadres, including Hua Guofeng. And narrow-minded, nationalistic officials equated Kang with China's security and police system: to challenge Comrade Kang Sheng risked undermining the entire Communist structure.

At first, Kang's critics discreetly referred to him as "that adviser." But in November 1978 one of Deng Xiaoping's protégés, Hu Yaobang, censured Kang by name in a speech to a select group of cadres at the Party School. Hu's long harangue against Kang in itself revealed that Kang's techniques had penetrated to the very marrow of Chinese politics. Hu exaggerated some of the charges against Kang, at times making nonsensical accusations. In the heat of his attack, Hu accused Kang of being a Trotskyite—a charge that Kang had used against so many in the past.

While Hu might have borrowed some of Kang's tactics and fantasized about his crimes, the core of his case could not be denied. Hu opened the way for a detailed investigation of Kang's life. The Party established a special-case group—another of Kang's legacies —to investigate and collect material on his career, his political record, and his victims. As Kang had feared, his place in history was being threatened.

Kang's family realized the futility of defending his reputation. Hoping to preempt an embarrassing showdown with Kang's detractors, they removed his ashes from Babaoshan Cemetery in 1979. Nevertheless, the campaign against him continued. Even Kang's hoard of art and antiques was used as evidence against him. In the summer of 1980, the cream of his collection—including 12,080 rare books and 1,102 antiques and artifacts—was put on display for a restricted group of Chinese viewers in a courtyard at the rear of the Forbidden City. No visitors to the exhibition could doubt that Kang had used the destruction of China during the Cultural Revolution to enrich himself, although some of them marveled at his refined and eclectic taste.

This display coincided with the first public condemnation of Kang. On July 12, 1980, at a memorial ceremony for An Ziwen, one of Kang's Cultural Revolution victims, Hu Yaobang openly uttered some of the accusations he had first made against Kang two years earlier in his secret speech to the Party School. It was Kang, Hu charged, who had engineered An Ziwen's persecution during the Cultural Revolution.

China's cartoonists also had a field day at Kang's expense. An exhibit of the works of over seventy cartoonists that opened on October 15, 1980, in Peking's Beihai Park included several caricatures of Kang depicting him as the brains behind the Gang of Four. Other cartoons referred to Kang's ambidextrous calligraphy to make him out as both "rightist" and "leftist." Caricatures of Kang have continued to appear in China's press, illustrating stories that expose the dark side of his career. Taking advantage of his unusually long face and rather sunken features, the sketches show him with a cold sneer and, literally, a lean and hungry look.

The Chinese theatrical world also joined in the attack on Kang Sheng. *The Spirit of the Yellow River,* a play that exposed the abuses of the land reform program Kang had conducted in Shanxi Province in 1947, was performed to packed houses in Peking during the winter of 1979–1980. Although Kang was only identified as "That Adviser," the audiences, steeped as they were in a political culture of allusion and innuendo, had no trouble recognizing Kang as the villain who had plagued Shanxi until the Cultural Revolution.

By late summer 1980, Kang's critics had mustered enough evidence to take up the issue with the Central Committee. The findings of the special-case group were presented that October; at month's end, a resolution posthumously expelled Kang from the Party and rescinded the memorial speech delivered by Ye Jianying after Kang's death in 1975.

The special-case group's evidence on Kang did not go to waste. The assembled documents and statements were handed over to Ma Zhongyang and Li Kan—that is, "Zhongkan"—who used the material to write *A Critical Biography of Kang Sheng,* the text that inspired this book. "Zhongkan's" account was published in 1982; even from beyond the grave, however, Kang's clout got the book withdrawn after less than a week from the shelves of the "internal bookshops" that sell to Chinese only. Powerful men continued to believe that debunking Kang Sheng could jeopardize the regime.

The furor over Kang Sheng extended to his family. Cao Yi'ou lost her post on the Central Committee in 1978. She continued as a member of the National People's Congress, but was removed from that position, too, in February 1981. Still, Cao fared better than many of her victims, remaining at liberty and enjoying the privileges of Party membership. She was allowed to live in Building Number 22 on Chang'an Avenue in an exclusive apartment complex, where her neighbors included Wang Guangmei, the widow of Liu Shaoqi, whose family had suffered so terribly at the hands of Kang Sheng and Cao Yi'ou.

Although she escaped harassment, Cao Yi'ou was trapped in her own world of nightmares. After a lifetime of combining with Kang to hurl false accusations against their enemies, she started to suffer from delusions of persecution. By the mid-1980s, she was venturing outdoors only rarely. She insisted that her nephew and niece, Su Han and Ren Neiya, visit her once a week; anytime they failed to appear as planned, Cao was overcome by fears that they had been arrested and that before long she herself would be taken away.

Cao Yi'ou continued her fear-ridden existence until May 15, 1989, when she died in her sleep. She was in her early eighties. A few old friends, such as Shu Tong, who had worked in the Social Affairs Department and succeeded Kang as Party boss in Shandong in 1955, gathered in her apartment to pay their last respects. There was no public announcement of her death.

Zhang Zishi also fell into disgrace. He had left Shandong in the early 1970s and been appointed Party chief in Hangzhou, thanks to his father's backing. In 1978, during the debate over Kang's crimes, Zhang was removed from his post; he has since vanished from public view.

Of Kang's close relatives, only his daughter, Zhang Yuying, who was retired from a job in a tobacco factory and living in Qingdao as late as 1982, and his nephew and niece, Su Han and Ren Neiya, seem to have escaped reprisals aimed at the family patriarch.

Jiang Qing and her allies in the Gang of Four were put on trial, along with Chen Boda, in November 1980 for the various atrocities, conspiracies, and acts of destruction they had engaged in. Much of the trial was conducted in secret, but the public sessions afforded China's new regime a propaganda bonanza—especially the televised proceedings. The Chinese people were spellbound by the revelations about the unscrupulous and bloodthirsty individuals who had ruled their nation during the Cultural Revolution. The indictment accused Jiang Qing and her associates of having "persecuted to death" thirty-four thousand people. When the verdicts came down in January 1981, Jiang Qing and Zhang Chunqiao were handed death sentences (later commuted to life imprisonment), Wang Hongwen was given a life term, and Yao Wenyuan and Chen Boda were each sentenced to eighteen years in prison.

Although the authorities succeeded in destroying the reputations of Jiang Qing and her three henchmen, the prosecutors went to great lengths to shield Mao Zedong from criticism. When a defiant Jiang Qing (according to rumors, she tried to strip off her clothes to protest the conduct of the trial) told the prosecutors that she had simply been acting on Mao's orders, she was ejected from the courtroom. Mao was still the founding emperor of the dynasty; discrediting him would have threatened the entire Communist system.

The new regime had no such need to protect Kang Sheng, whose name cropped up in court time and again. He figured prominently in testimony about the persecution of Liu Shaoqi, He Long, Luo Ruiqing, and Wang Kunlun, a pro-Communist member of the Kuomintang who had elected to remain on the mainland after 1949, only to have Kang charge him with being "a special agent."

The trial of the Gang of Four implicated Kang in some of the most shocking acts of cruelty, including the case of Zhang Zhongyi, a professor of foreign languages at Furen University in Shanghai. Professor Zhang was arrested in October 1967 and brutally questioned about another professor, Yang Chengzuo, allegedly a friend of Liu Shaoqi and Wang Guangmei. At the time, Zhang Zhongyi was sixty-seven years old and suffering from terminal cancer of the liver. A tape recording of Zhang's interrogation was played in court. Amid the gasps and moans of the dying man, his interrogators' voices could be heard, alternately browbeating him to incriminate his innocent colleague and promising to take him to a hospital as soon as he cooperated. Zhang spent the last twenty-seven days of his life in detention, during which he was interrogated twenty-one times. His final grilling ran from nine o'clock on the morning of October 31,

1967, until midnight. Zhang died two hours later. By then, he had signed a confession, which Kang added to his pile of evidence that Liu Shaoqi and Wang Guangmei were special agents.

There is no reason why Kang should not have been cited time and again as one of the Gang of Four's most hardened and callous co-conspirators. The charges against him were true. But if alive, would he have been in the dock with them? Would his mask of "adviser" have kept him out of a "Gang of Five"?

Many observers of the events in Peking assumed that Kang would have been put on trial. But with Kang alive, things might well have had a wholly different complexion. Hu Yaobang speculated that if Kang had outlived Mao, the Gang of Four would not have been arrested. Maybe Hu was indulging in a rhetorical flourish in his portrayal of Kang as an all-powerful force of evil, but his assessment reflected Kang's direct links to the security apparatus and cannot be dismissed out of hand. The troops who carried out the arrests were led by Wang Dongxing, head of the General Office and commander of the palace guard, Unit 8341. Wang's ties to Kang dated back to the 1940s, when Wang, then in his twenties, headed the Pistol Company, an elite detachment in Yan'an that took orders from the Social Affairs Department. Such relationships carry great weight in Chinese politics. Wang might not have done Kang's bidding after Jiang Qing and her cohorts had been disgraced, but he almost certainly would have taken Kang's views into account.

Indeed, Ye Jianying and the other moderates who masterminded the operation against the Gang of Four took special pains to secure the unanimous endorsement of the Party leadership. Speaking cryptically in case his phone was tapped, Ye Jianying called several Politburo members who were away from Peking at the time to ask for their approval. If Kang had been alive and mentally competent, Ye and his circle of veterans would probably have approached him. Ye's main deputy in the operation was Wang Zhen, who also had ties to Kang dating from the early 1940s—Wang had commanded the Yan'an garrison troops when Kang was responsible for security. Besides, if Kang had survived Zhou and Mao, he would have been the highest ranking Party leader.

How would Kang have reacted? The only clue to Kang's views on Jiang Qing was his 1975 attempt to use Nancy Tang and Wang Hairong to betray Jiang Qing and Zhang Chunqiao as former Kuo-

mintang agents. Having recognized Mao's growing disenchantment
with Jiang Qing and her fellow radicals, Kang most likely would have
agreed to their arrest—and presented himself as one of their main
accusers. After all, Kang had made his career out of picking winners
and abandoning losers.

If he had approved the plan to strike at the radicals, Kang might
very well have emerged as a prosecutor at the trial, not a defendant.
His role in countless cases of persecution might have surfaced in
court, but the authorities would have silenced any attempt by Jiang
Qing and her codefendants to shift the blame to Kang. The handling
of Wang Dongxing is a telling example of how Kang would no doubt
have been treated. Wang had conducted the arrest of most of the
leaders who fell during the Cultural Revolution, including Peng Zhen,
Liu Shaoqi, Deng Xiaoping, and Luo Ruiqing. Yet Wang was saved
from disgrace by also arresting Jiang Qing. Given Kang's age and
seniority, and assuming he had turned thumbs down on the Gang of
Four, he probably could have distanced himself from them.

Some of the Red Guard leaders who had acted as Kang's agents were
brought to justice as well. Nie Yuanzi, the ambitious woman philosophy lecturer and author of the first big-character poster of the Cultural Revolution, was tried in March 1983 and sentenced to seventeen
years in jail. Kuai Dafu, the Qinghua University student leader who
helped Kang weed out his rivals in the Party School, received the same
penalty. Han Aijing, the student at the Peking Aeronautical Institute
who had beaten Peng Dehuai on Kang's orders, was given a fifteen-
year prison term.

Kang's protégés in the security-and-espionage community also
came under fire. Hu Yaobang's 1978 speech to the Party School
criticized Kang's use of the security services for personal ends. Deng
Xiaoping and his colleagues made a concerted effort to purge the
opportunistic and often incompetent cadres whom Kang had promoted within the Public Security Ministry and the Investigation Department. The process reached a climax in 1983, when the ministry
was divided in two, the department abolished, and a new Ministry of
State Security established.

Kang's most prominent supporters were rooted out, but many
security operatives with links to him retained influential posts. Ling
Yun, the first minister in charge of the newly created State Security
Ministry, had started his intelligence career forty years earlier as a

Social Affairs Department interrogator in Zaoyuan. Kang had supervised Ling Yun's purge during the Cultural Revolution, which made Ling his enemy but did not erase his years of experience at using the secret police to protect the Party from its enemies. The entire security-and-intelligence apparatus came under the supervision of Peng Zhen, who had both suffered and learned at Kang's hands: Peng, betrayed by Kang in 1966, had also served as his deputy in the Yan'an Rectification Movement during the early 1940s.

Although Kang Sheng's name has been blackened in Party propaganda, his legacy and its influence endure, as was demonstrated most dramatically during the crisis China underwent in 1989.

Hu Yaobang, the Chinese Communist Party chief whose advocacy of liberal values had cost him his post in January 1986, died on April 15, 1989. In the following weeks, the students and intellectuals of China, supported by workers and common people, led China to the threshold of becoming an open society. At the end of May, after martial law had been declared, the people of Peking halted a military drive into the city. Ordinary citizens pleaded with the soldiers being trucked into the capital, arguing that the people's army should never fire upon the people. Enormous crowds of citizens blocked columns of army vehicles, and the troops sat for hours in their trucks, weary, hot, and humiliated. For more than a week, the world watched mesmerized by the spectacle of an authoritarian regime unable to keep its people under control.

Then, on June 4, troops of the People's Liberation Army, clad in battle dress and wielding AK-47s and bayonets, used tanks and armored personnel carriers to smash through the barricades of buses and traffic barriers that protected the last group of student protesters camped in Tiananmen Square. By the middle of the following day, the soldiers had killed an estimated two thousand unarmed students and workers. Public savagery on a scale like this had not been seen in China since the Communist victory forty years earlier.*

The regime's sudden recourse to such excessive, bloody force in the very heart of Peking stunned and outraged a world that had come

---

* No accurate statistics have been produced to document how many died on June 4 and 5. But well-informed Chinese journalists in Peking told the authors in a 1990 interview that people who visited hospitals in the days after the massacre in search of missing relatives counted about two thousand dead.

to expect that reform-minded Communists would no longer maintain control with bayonets, rifles, and machine guns. Observers were at a loss to explain how a state that had made so many strides toward economic and social reform could inflict such brutal penalties upon its own young people for expressing discontent with the government.

In fact, this violent suppression of the democracy movement was a logical extension of Kang's methods. Against the background of twentieth-century Chinese history, the sudden and unprovoked use of force against the common people is no anomaly. Indeed, it seems inevitable under the despotic system established by Mao's triumphant forces. From the moment the CCP was formed in 1921, its leaders assumed a fundamental division between themselves and the rest of the country and so could not accept the results of the reforms they themselves had initiated. Men who had joined the CCP in the 1920s could not tolerate the notion that the Party should allow intellectuals and scientists to share power with generals, bureaucrats, commissars, and security officials.

Knowing Kang's story, we understand what was occurring in the inner chambers of Chinese politics during the period leading up to the emergency of 1989. After all, the sponsors of the crackdown had been colleagues of Kang's for half a lifetime. They included:

- Deng Xiaoping, who had worked closely with Kang Sheng on the Sino–Soviet dispute and sponsored his appointment to the Secretariat in 1962;
- Yang Shangkun, who had studied with Kang at Shanghai University, had been one of the Twenty-eight Bolsheviks who helped Kang boost Wang Ming in the 1930s, and had run the General Office in Yan'an, a unit with close ties to the Social Affairs Department;
- Chen Yun, the veteran economist whose protégés gained the most in the aftermath of the Tiananmen massacre, who had been a partner of Kang's in security work in Shanghai in the 1930s, his companion in Moscow, and his colleague in Yan'an in the 1940s;
- Peng Zhen, the overseer of the security services, who had been Kang's deputy during the Rectification Movement in Yan'an and his companion on several official trips abroad during the 1960s;
- Wang Zhen, an elderly general instrumental in the decision to suppress the students, who had been one of Kang's lieutenants during the Rectification Movement and who had been Yan'an garrison commander, a role that placed him under Kang's supervision;

- Yuan Mu, the chief spokesman for the hard-line regime that has ruled China since Tiananmen, who had studied at Kang's Shaanbei Academy and worked on his personal staff.

A look at Kang's association with the leaders behind the Tiananmen slaughter reveals that all of them were intimates of his and products of an age that regarded bloodshed as a legitimate means of protecting the state against its citizens. Many outsiders had come to view Deng and his cohorts as the human face of Chinese communism, but their use of Kang's methods suggests otherwise. These men may lack Kang's overwhelming capacity for deceit and cruelty, but beneath their façade as reformers bent on bringing China into the 1990s and beyond, there lurks fanaticism, paranoia, selfishness, and ultimately an inability to distinguish between their personal interests and the needs of the nation.

Even the way the Tiananmen massacre emerged out of the convoluted and faction-ridden Communist system reflects a pattern Kang himself had followed for years. Two and a half decades earlier, Kang had adroitly manipulated Mao's vanity to launch the first stage of the Cultural Revolution; in 1989, a number of ambitious and authoritarian functionaries like Li Peng and Yuan Mu preyed on the fears of Deng and his aged cronies to instigate a savage crackdown that allowed them to emerge as powerful men who could deprive their rivals of all standing and credibility.

The continuity in political mentality between the deceased and disgraced Kang Sheng and the men behind the Tiananmen carnage is underscored by the fact that the students who were shot had begun their protests by grieving the death of Hu Yaobang, the first Communist leader courageous enough to list and condemn the crimes of Kang Sheng. By silencing Hu Yaobang's mourners, China's new leaders were, in effect, turning their backs on a man who had sought to humanize Chinese politics and excise the arbitrary and personalized politics that Kang had represented. They would strenuously deny it, but when Deng and his henchmen cut down the flower of China's youth, they did so in pursuit of absolute power: a hallmark of Kang's life. Even their methods—murdering civilians, arresting people by the thousands, and breeding an atmosphere of endemic fear and terror—followed the precedents Kang had set as he clawed his way almost to the pinnacle of the Chinese Communist Party.

*   *   *

The events at Tiananmen show that Kang's spirit continues to haunt Peking, but what does his story mean for China as it prepares to enter the twenty-first century?

Driven by a craving for power, Kang cared for nothing but his own ambitions. That such a man should have risen so high reflected the character of his times: Kang flourished in an era of wars, revolutions, coups, poverty, and natural disasters. But the image he has etched on the historical record portrays more than a bestial, amoral man who won high office by chance in troubled times. On the contrary, Kang's story attributes his success to something much more predictable than luck—he knew how to channel the dark forces of Chinese society.

Kang had some exposure to Western education, but he never came to grips with the values that propel social and economic modernization; in the end, he rejected everything that was constructive, enlightened, and progressive. He loudly (if erratically) proclaimed his support for science yet undermined policies that were pragmatic and rational. He discounted economic expertise as ideologically suspect, but his true motive was the unspoken realization that his world of conspiracies and dreams of power was incompatible with the mentality of economic planners and administrators.

Out of place and ill at ease in the modern world, Kang was beguiled by the magic of the past. At times, he escaped into the aesthetic diversions of ancient China, using his painting and calligraphy and antiquarian interests to retreat from the realities of socialist China. But Kang was no sentimental dreamer pining for the glories and beauties of a mythical golden age; instinctively, he turned to ancient expedients as solutions to contemporary problems.

Indeed, Kang re-created the past, giving so much substance to select elements of tradition that they came to dominate the present and stifle progress. Although he masqueraded as an apostle of revolutionary change, his power derived from appeals to customs and thought patterns that dated back thousands of years. He played on the traditional sensibilities of his friends and associates, invoking an age-old mentality that turned common sense on its head, unleashed the terrible destructive forces represented by the messianic ethic of the secret societies, and threatened to overwhelm the nation in a wave of wild iconoclasm. Just as the pigs who led the revolution in *Animal Farm* assumed the appearance of the humans they had dispossessed, so Kang conjured up the elitism, authoritarianism, and emperor worship of the system he supposedly was trying to overturn.

Many of the differences between Kang and China's present leaders are simply a matter of degree. Deng and his cronies are more moderate than Kang in their appetite for privilege and more constructive in their policies. They have done much to curb the impulse toward brutality and treachery that Kang exemplified. But in the end, like Kang, they are Marxist rulers trapped in the ways of ancient China. Their socialist rhetoric represents an ersatz modernity that has failed to emancipate them from an imperial lust for centralized and unchallenged power. They indulge a taste for "the good life" behind a curtain of propaganda and within a labyrinth of exclusive shops, limousines with darkened windows, and luxurious homes hidden by high walls. Obsessed like Kang by threats to their status, they recoil at sharing power with a modern elite trained in science and high technology. (It may be no accident that Fang Lizhi, China's most prominent dissident long before he was allowed to leave his sanctuary in the U.S. embassy for the West in 1990, is an astrophysicist.)

By exposing Kang's crimes, China's current leaders have set limits on their own elitist tendencies. They have repudiated Kang personally, but they failed to dispel the dangers inherent in a revolutionary movement that amounts to nothing more than a new imperial system centered on a small, personalized elite. Mao Zedong was a peasant leader who established a fourteenth-century regime in the twentieth century; even his mausoleum, the contemporary version of an imperial tomb, recalls the dynasties of old. As long as Mao retains his place in the Chinese pantheon, the spirit of Kang Sheng, Mao's evil genius and hatchet man, will not likely be exorcised. Although the vocabulary of the Confucian bureaucrat has given way to the jargon of the Party cadre, the values of the old China remain intact.

Despite almost two centuries of exposure to the West, China has not lost its distinctive attitudes toward society, government, culture, and the forces that drive the universe. That "socialism with Chinese characteristics" should be Deng Xiaoping's prescription for China's future testifies to the existence—at least, in Deng's eyes—of values, sometimes hard to define, that are unique to China. Many of these are incontestably virtues, part of the wellspring from which the Chinese nation derives its resilience and creativity. But that culture still has a dark side; even with Kang now in disgrace, the Chinese political system has been remolded in only the most superficial manner. China's elitism, her seeming preference for paramount leaders with their retinues of courtiers willing to sacrifice the interests of the population to private visions and desires, and the tendency of democratic forms to degenerate into sly exploitation of the masses—all of these remain unchanged. The seeds of both tyranny and chaos lie just beneath the ground of China's culture.

Not that the danger of succumbing to the ghosts of the past is peculiar to China. Every society is haunted by demons from its collective memory—the graveyard of history. Men and women everywhere have to guard against the temptation to fall back upon the primitive, the barbaric, the demonic. In times of peace and prosperity, it is easy to resist the allure of totalitarianism. But setbacks and disasters can sweeten the siren song of nihilism that is found in all cultures.

Viewed against this background, Kang Sheng stands as a universal image of our perpetual struggle to expunge—or, at least, come to terms with—the nightmares in our own memories.

KANG SHENG'S CHRONOLOGY

1898 Born into a landed family in the Shandong Province village of Dataizhuang and named Zhang Zongke by his parents.

1906 Studied in school run by family tutor.

1911 Fall of the Manchu regime disrupted Kang's studies, and he began associating with village hoodlums.

1914 Sent by his father to the German middle school in Qingdao run by missionary-scholar Richard Wilhelm.

1915 Kang's father arranged his marriage to Chen Yi, daughter of Chen Yuzhen, a local landlord.

1917 Returned to his native village after finishing school. After bandits stormed their home, Kang's family moved to the walled town of Zhucheng. Changed his name to Zhang Yuxian.

1918 Adopting yet another name, Zhang Shuping, Kang taught at a local primary school and later met Jiang Qing, a future wife of Mao Zedong.

1919 The May Fourth Movement set off a wave of nationalism among China's youth, including Kang.

1921 CCP founded in Shanghai by Mao Zedong and twelve other radicals.

1924 Went to study at Shanghai University under the name Zhang Yun.

1925 Joined the CCP. Visited his family in Zhucheng in June for the last time. Became an organizer in the General Labor Union.

1926 Named secretary of the CCP committee at Shanghai University.

1927 Became secretary of the CCP's East Shanghai Committee. Fought in the March uprising and survived Chiang Kai-shek's massacre of Communists on April 12. Appointed to the CCP's

Jiangsu Committee; secretary of the Chapei District Committee. Married Cao Yi'ou, a fellow-Communist and former student at Shanghai University. Qu Qiubai replaced Chen Duxiu as Party leader.

1928 Appointed secretary, West Shanghai CCP Committee; secretary, Central Shanghai CCP Committee; director, Jiangsu provincial Organization Department. Renamed himself Zhao Rong. Xiang Zhongfa replaced Qu Qiubai as general secretary, but Li Lisan set Party strategy.

1929 Kang became Li Lisan's Party whip.

1930 Named secretary-general, Central Organization Department.

1931 Switched to Wang Ming's side. Elected to the Central Committee and made director of Central Organization Department in January. Betrayed He Mengxiong and others to the KMT. CCP master spy Gu Shunzhang was arrested in April; Kang succeeded him as security chief.

1933 Went to Moscow in July as Wang Ming's deputy on the Chinese delegation to the Comintern. Chose a new name: Kang Sheng.

1934 Elected in absentia to the CCP Central Committee and the Politburo.

1935 Mao became the dominant leader of the CCP during the Long March.

1936 Copying Stalin's Great Terror, Kang purged Chinese "counterrevolutionaries" in Moscow. Visited Paris in October to aid the Comintern effort in the Spanish Civil War.

1937 Japan invaded China. Kang returned to China after four years in Russia and moved to the Communist headquarters at Yan'an. Launched a Soviet-style attack on Trotskyites in China. Named head of the Party School.

1938 Abandoned Wang Ming for Mao and smoothed the way for Mao to marry Jiang Qing. Rewarded in August with command of the secret service, consisting of the Social Affairs Department and the Military Intelligence Department.

1939 Whipped up spy phobia by arresting a number of innocent Yan'an residents as enemy agents.

1941 Appointed chairman, Commission for the Investigation of Party and Non-Party Cadres, a powerful security organ.

1942 Named by Mao as his deputy on the General Study Commission, which ran the Rectification Movement—a thought reform campaign that exalted Mao.

1943 Served as chairman, Commission for Work Behind Enemy Lines, which controlled covert action in KMT and Japanese-occupied China. Helped turn the Rectification Movement into a witch-hunt.

1945 Reelected to the Central Committee and Politburo at the Seventh Congress but deposed as security and intelligence czar.

1947 Reviewed land reform in Shanxi and later Shandong. Advocated killing all landlords and rich peasants.

1948 Became second secretary, East China Bureau; promoted to first secretary of Shandong CCP Committee in September. Kang named Cao Yi'ou head of provincial Organization Department.

1949 CCP captured the mainland and exiled the KMT to Taiwan. Kang named first secretary, Shandong Sub-bureau, East China Bureau; military commissar, Shandong Military District; and chairman, Shandong Government, but missed out on a high post in Peking and claimed he was ill.

1950 Went to Hangzhou in May to convalesce. His sexual relationship with his sister-in-law, Su Mei, became a semipublic scandal, and she attempted suicide. Kang took up residence in Peking Hospital in July.

1955 Left Peking Hospital and moved into a large house behind the Forbidden City.

1956 Reappeared in public at the Chinese People's Political Consultative Conference on January 30. Appointed vice chairman, Committee for Popularizing the Common Language; observed the Socialist Unity Party Congress in East Berlin and visited the USSR. Attended the first session of the Eighth Congress in September. Reelected to the Central Committee but demoted to alternate member of the Politburo. Supervised the writing of "More on the Historical Experience of the Proletariat"— China's defense of Stalinism.

1957 Named deputy head of the Culture and Education Group.

1958 Attended the second session of the Eighth Congress in May and pushed the Great Leap Forward. Called for radical reforms in education.

1959 Observer at the Twenty-first Congress of the Communist Party of the Soviet Union (CPSU) in Moscow from January 27 until February 5. Deputy head, Editorial Committee for Mao Zedong's Selected Works; head, the Theoretical Small Group, a subsidiary of the Culture and Education Group; vice chairman, Chinese People's Political Consultative Conference. Vilified Marshal Peng Dehuai for criticizing Mao's economic ideas at the Lushan meeting.

1960 Delivered a landmark attack on Soviet policy at the Warsaw Pact Consultative Conference in Moscow in February. Attended the World Congress of Socialist and Workers Parties and the Romanian Workers Party Congress in Bucharest.

1961 Occupied himself by attending operas in Yunnan and Sichuan. Went to North Korea with Deng Xiaoping in September. Encouraged his friend Meng Chao to write *Li Huiniang*, a play about ghosts. Observer at the Twenty-second Congress of the CPSU. Edited Liu Shaoqi's selected works.

1962 Spent a month with Jiang Qing watching erotic drama in Hangzhou. Assumed a stern ideological posture after Mao declared that "class struggle is the key link." Promoted to the CCP Secretariat. Condemned the novel *Liu Zhidan* as a plot to exonerate Mao's rival Gao Gang. Supervised the drafting of anti-Soviet polemics.

1963 Participated in the Sino–Soviet talks in Moscow.

1964 Ensnared Yang Xianzhen, vice president of the Party School, in the "synthesis of two into one" debate.

1965 Vice chairman, Standing Committee of the National People's

Congress. Told Mao in May that the play *The Dismissal of Hai Rui* was connected with the case of Marshal Peng Dehuai.

1966 One of Peng Zhen's "Five Man Group" that investigated Wu Han's play. Kang discussed Peng Zhen's report with Mao in March; attacked Peng Zhen and Yang Shangkun at a Politburo meeting in mid-May; incited philosophy lecturer Nie Yuanzi to lambast Peking's municipal leaders in late May, igniting the Cultural Revolution; accompanied Mao to the Red Guard rallies in Peking from August through November. Gained control of security matters and relations with foreign Communist parties.

1967 Took over the Organization Department. Encouraged his son, Zhang Zishi, to seize power in Shandong. Purged thousands of cadres as enemy agents. Su Mei committed suicide in April. After the Wuhan mutiny in July, Kang tried to purge "capitalist roaders in the army," but when the generals resisted, he arrested his aides Wang Li and Guan Feng to cover his tracks.

1968 Continued his purge of high cadres, including many security officials. Ordered troops to search the public-security archives for material compromising himself or his allies. Took part in the October Central Committee meeting that officially purged Liu Shaoqi.

1969 Elected to the Politburo Standing Committee at the Ninth Congress in April. Executed Wang Yuncheng and Lu Futan, two Communist defectors who knew of Kang's treachery in Shanghai in the 1930s.

1970 Opposed Lin Biao at the Central Committee meeting in August at Lushan. Replaced the discredited Chen Boda as propaganda boss. Stricken with cancer in October.

1971 Too sick to attend the May Day parade but drafted papers for Jiang Qing. Told his men at the Party School to destroy copies of Lin Biao's selected works. On hearing of Lin Biao's ill-fated attempt to overthrow Mao, Kang had Cao Yi'ou assure his lieutenants that "Kang Sheng hated Lin Biao."

1972 Incapacitated by disease.

1973 Attended the Tenth Congress in August and elected CCP vice chairman, but worried by Deng Xiaoping's return to office.

1974 Tried to use the anti-Confucius campaign to oust Zhou Enlai.

1975 Told two Foreign Ministry cadres in August that Jiang Qing and Zhang Chunqiao had been KMT agents. Warned Mao in October that Deng Xiaoping would seek to reverse the Cultural Revolution. Died on December 16.

BIOGRAPHICAL NOTES

Ai Siqi (1910–1966) Ai studied in Japan, joined the Chinese Communist Party in 1935, and later taught at the Shaanbei Academy in Yan'an. An expert on Marxist philosophy, Ai helped Mao write his theoretical essays. Appointed deputy president of the Party School in 1959, Ai sided with Kang during the dispute over "the synthesis of two into one."

An Ziwen (1910–1980) A member of Liu Shaoqi's network of urban Communists, An was arrested four times by the KMT during the 1930s. Worked in the Party School in Yan'an, where he helped administer the Rectification Movement. A senior Organization Department cadre from 1945 until the Cultural Revolution, An was persecuted by Kang for refusing to incriminate his colleagues.

Bao Junfu (c. 1900–1970) A KMT secret-service agent, Bao was recruited by the Communists as a spy in 1928 and became an invaluable source of information for the CCP. Exposed by Gu Shunzhang in 1931 and arrested by the KMT, but later appointed deputy head of a reformatory for political prisoners. Falling on hard times, Bao had become a street peddler by the time the Communists captured Nanking in 1949. Arrested as a former KMT element in 1951, he was released after Zhou Enlai and Chen Geng intervened in his case. Savagely persecuted during the Cultural Revolution.

Blyukher, Vasili (1892–1938) Soviet general who, under the name Galen, supervised military instruction at the Whampoa Academy from 1923 until 1927. Arrested on Stalin's orders in 1938 and charged with spying for Japan; died under interrogation.

Bo Gu (1907–1946) After attending Shanghai University, Bo Gu (real name Qin Bangxian) spent four years in Moscow, returning to China as one of the Twenty-eight Bolsheviks. Worked with Kang in Shanghai and succeeded Wang Ming as CCP general secretary in September 1931. Bo was Mao's main rival during the early stages of the Long March but lost power after the Zunyi meeting in 1935. He headed the

New China News Agency and *The Liberation Daily* in Yan'an but died in the crash of a U.S. Army Air Force plane flying him and several other leaders from Chongqing to Yan'an on April 8, 1946.

Borodin, Mikhail (1884–1952) Comintern agent sent to China by the Soviets in 1924 to guide the fledgling Chinese Communist movement. He became Sun Yat-sen's political counselor in 1923 and spent the next four years at the KMT base in Canton. Wielded tremendous influence within the left wing of the KMT and groomed several young Communists, including Zhou Enlai and Lin Biao, who went on to be early leaders of the CCP. After Chiang Kai-shek's anti-Communist coup in 1927, Borodin returned to the Soviet Union, where he edited the English-language *Moscow Daily News*. Arrested during the Stalinist purges and died in a prison camp.

Braun, Otto (1901–1974) German soldier sent to China in 1932 by the Comintern as the military adviser to the CCP. Known to the Chinese as Li De, Braun supported the Wang Ming group and worked closely with Bo Gu during the Long March. Discredited at the Zunyi meeting, he left China in 1939 and fought with the Soviet army in World War II. Lived in Germany from 1949 until his death.

Cao Yi'ou (c. 1908–1989) Graduate of a prestigious girls' school in Jinan, she attended Shanghai University and became Kang's second wife in 1927. A senior cadre in the Yan'an municipal administration, she headed the Shandong branch of the Organization Department in the late 1940s and 1950s. After moving to Peking, she was assigned to the Party School. Elected to the Central Committee in 1966.

Chen Boda (1904–1989) Philosophy lecturer and propagandist who was Mao Zedong's ghostwriter in Yan'an. A close associate of Kang's, Chen was elected an alternate member of the Politburo in 1956 and later named editor of *Red Flag*. Headed the Cultural Revolution Group until 1970, when he was purged for having sided with Lin Biao.

Chen Qiren (1924–c. 1951) An intelligence officer who worked for Kang's Social Affairs Department, first in Yan'an and then in northeast China. Disillusioned with the Party after Communist troops killed his two children, Chen gave the U.S. vice consul in Dalian, Culver Gleysteen, extensive briefings on the inner workings of the Communist security system.

Chen Duxiu (1879–1942) An early advocate of revolutionary change and a founding father of the CCP, Chen served as its first general secretary. He turned to Trotskyism after the 1927 Shanghai massacre of the Communists, in which two of his sons—Chen Yannian and Chen Qiaonian—were executed. Expelled from the CCP in 1929. Mao, Zhou Enlai, and others tried to persuade him to rejoin the Party in 1937, but Kang Sheng and Wang Ming vetoed his reentry because of his Trotskyite record.

Chen Geng (1903–1961) Communist secret-service leader in Shanghai during the late 1920s and early 1930s. Chen moved to central China when Kang took over the Special Work Committee, but he stayed at Kang's house after returning to Shanghai. Detained by the KMT in 1933, Chen, a graduate of the Whampoa Academy, was saved by his link with Chiang Kai-shek. Fought with the Red Army against Japan and the KMT; later served as deputy commander of the Chinese forces in Korea and as vice minister of defense.

Chen Lifu (1900–   ) American-educated engineer who supervised the Investigation Section, the first KMT secret service. Together with his brother, Chen Guofu, Chen led the Central Club ("CC") faction of the KMT and competed with Dai Li for control over the security apparatus. Retired from politics in 1950; moved first to America and later to Taipei, where he still lives.

Chen Yi (c. 1900–??) A landord's daughter who married Kang in 1914 and bore him a son, Zhang Zishi, and a daughter, Zhang Yuying. She saw little of Kang after he went to Shanghai in 1924, but they never divorced and she lived in Zhucheng with Kang's parents until the Japanese invasion in 1937, and later in Qingdao with Zhang Zishi. Her fate is unclear.

Chen Yi (1901–1972) After joining the CCP in France, Chen became a guerrilla leader in southern China during the Long March. He commanded the New Fourth Army during the Sino–Japanese War and created a Communist enclave in the Yangtze Valley. Mayor of Shanghai after 1949, Chen was promoted to marshal in 1955 and named vice premier and foreign minister in 1958. During the Cultural Revolution, he defended the Foreign Ministry against the Red Guards but was banished to the countryside in 1969.

Chen Yun (1905–   ) A union organizer, Chen worked closely with Kang in Shanghai, served as Wang Ming's personal aide, and along with Kang was appointed to the group supervising the secret service in

1931. Joined the Red Army and participated in the first stages of the Long March but was sent to Moscow after the Zunyi meeting in January 1935. Returned to China on the same aircraft as Kang in 1937. Chen headed the Organization Department in Yan'an, a job that involved close contact with Kang. China's chief economist after 1949, Chen was purged during the Cultural Revolution. Restored to power along with Deng Xiaoping in 1978, he remains influential to date.

Chiang Kai-shek (1887–1975) The KMT's strongman from 1927 until his death on Taiwan almost fifty years later. Chiang was trained in military academies in China and Japan, supported the revolutionary forces in the 1910s, and in 1922 was appointed director of the Whampoa Military Academy established by Sun Yat-sen. Although a key KMT commander on the Northern Expedition of 1926 and 1927, Chiang broke with the leftists and massacred hundreds of Communists in Shanghai in April 1927. Warlords dissatisfied with his refusal to more firmly oppose Japan's aggression kidnapped him at Xian in 1936; his negotiated release led to a CCP–KMT alliance against Japan. Remained China's leader during World War II but presided over an increasingly corrupt regime. With his armies buckling under the Communist advance during the late 1940s, he fled to Taiwan. With American backing, he established a system that eventually emerged as one of "the Four Dragons," the newly industrialized countries of East Asia.

Dai Li (1895–1946) Kang's counterpart in the KMT, Dai Li was a confidant of Chiang Kai-shek and head of the Military Statistics Bureau, as the KMT secret police was known. Almost invisible to the public, he wielded immense influence behind the scenes, doing the dirty work necessary to keep Chiang in power. Killed in an aircraft crash in March 1946. Often identified as Tai Li.

Deng Fa (1906–1946) Labor agitator, chief of the CCP's Hong Kong branch, and later director of the Political Security Bureau, the internal-security unit of the Communist forces that made the Long March. Deng represented the CCP in Xinjiang in 1937–1938 and later became head of both the Party School and the Labor Department in Yan'an. Died in the same aircraft accident that killed Bo Gu.

Deng Tuo (1912–1966) A Communist journalist, Deng worked in the northern China underground during the late 1930s and 1940s. Editor-in-chief and publisher of *The People's Daily* from 1950 to 1958 and secretary of the Peking municipal CCP committee from 1958 to 1966. Satirical essays he wrote during the early 1960s were attacked by Jiang Qing, and Deng was persecuted to death in May 1966. After he died, his collection of antiques and rare books was looted by Kang.

Deng Xiaoping (1904–) After joining the CCP in France, Deng returned to China to be a military commissar and Party organizer; survived the Long March and became one of the top Red Army political officers. Appointed general secretary in 1956, Deng worked with Kang on the Sino–Soviet dispute. Purged in 1966, rehabilitated in 1973, only to be purged again in 1976. He regained power in 1978 and has been China's supreme leader ever since, although he officially retired in 1987.

Deng Zhongxia (1894–1933) Communist labor leader and influential teacher at Shanghai University. Arrested and shot by the KMT.

Ding Jishi (c. 1905–??) Radical activist arrested with Kang Sheng in Shanghai in 1930. Both Ding and Kang were released through the intervention of Ding's uncle, a Kuomintang veteran named Ding Weifen. After studying in Germany for several years, Ding Jishi became a KMT official. Stayed on the mainland after 1949 but disappeared from public view years ago.

Ding Mocun (1903–1947) A member of Kang's Red Squads in Shanghai, Ding was arrested by the KMT in 1933 and switched sides. Spent several years as a KMT secret agent, then jumped again, joining "Number 76," the pro-Japanese secret service. Shot as a traitor by the KMT.

Feng Jiping (1911–1983) An intelligence expert who headed the Public Security Bureau in the capital and became vice mayor of Peking responsible for security matters. Persecuted on Kang's orders during the Cultural Revolution but rehabilitated by Deng Xiaoping.

Gao Gang (1905–1954) CCP cadre who helped establish the liberated zone in northern Shaanxi, where the Long March ended. During the early 1950s, Gao, the Party boss in Manchuria, challenged Mao for leadership of the CCP. Accused of conspiring with Rao Shushi to stage a coup, Gao committed suicide. Because Gao had been a lieutenant of Liu Zhidan's during the 1930s, Kang used the relationship between the two men as "proof" that a biographical novel about Liu Zhidan was intended to rehabilitate Gao.

Gu Shunzhang (1902?–1935) A worker and gangster who joined the Communists and was trained as an assassin and security operative in the Soviet Union, Gu served as Borodin's bodyguard. As one of Zhou Enlai's chief secret-service operatives in Shanghai, Gu organized most of the assassinations carried out by Red Squads. Arrested by the KMT on April 25, 1931, he betrayed the Party—an act that eventually led to Kang's appointment as CCP security chief. Worked for the KMT until he was caught passing secrets to his former comrades and executed.

Gu Zhenghong (1905–1925) Kang's fellow-student at Shanghai University whose shooting by a foreman in a Japanese-owned factory in Shanghai triggered the May Thirtieth Movement in 1925.

Guan Feng (c. 1925–   ) Member of Kang's network in Shandong in the late 1940s; wrote on Marxist theory during the 1950s. Guan headed the Anti-Revisionist Writing Group and was named a member of the Cultural Revolution Group in 1966. Arrested on Kang's orders in 1967, scapegoated in the aftermath of the Wuhan mutiny, imprisoned until the late 1980s. Now retired.

Guo Bohe (c. 1900–1927) Shanghai University graduate who, like Kang, led a unit of armed workers during the March 1927 uprising. Arrested and shot by the KMT.

Guo Moruo (1892–1978) Japanese-educated scholar and writer who became the unofficial poet laureate of the Communist regime. He held a number of important posts, among them chairman of the Academy of Sciences. A friend of Kang Sheng's, Guo prominently displayed a work of Kang's calligraphy in his home.

Guo Yufeng (c. 1920–??) Military officer who managed the Organization Department on Kang's behalf during the Cultural Revolution and helped Kang forge evidence against many CCP officials. Disappeared from public sight after Deng Xiaoping's return to power in 1978.

He Long (1896–1969) A bandit in early life, He Long joined the KMT and then the Communists, made the Long March, and performed brilliantly as a field commander during the wars with Japan and the KMT. Purged by Kang Sheng and Lin Biao during the Cultural Revolution.

He Mengxiong (1898–1931) Communist labor organizer who opposed Li Lisan's reckless policies but later fell out with Wang Ming. Betrayed to the KMT by Kang Sheng, shot in February 1931.

He Zizhen (1909–1984) Mao's third wife and one of the few women who made the Long March. After Jiang Qing won Mao's affections, He Zizhen went to the Soviet Union, where she was confined in a mental hospital. She returned to China in 1947 and worked in the provincial women's movement after the establishment of the People's Republic.

Hu Yaobang (1915–1989) One of "the Little Red Devils"—the youngsters who made the Long March—Hu Yaobang spent much of his career in the Communist youth movement. Purged during the Cultural Revolution but rehabilitated after Deng Xiaoping returned to office in 1973; fell once again after Deng was removed in 1976. One of Deng's "stalking horses" after the death of Mao, Hu fired the first salvo against Kang Sheng in a secret speech at the Party School in November 1978. Appointed CCP chairman in 1981 and, when the chairmanship was abolished in 1983, general secretary. His advocacy of liberal values led to his ouster in January 1987. Hu's death in April 1989 inspired the demonstrations that culminated in the Tiananmen massacre on June 4.

Hu Yepin (1903–1931) A short-story writer, Hu was one of "the Five Martyrs" arrested and executed by the KMT after Kang Sheng betrayed their whereabouts in the course of consolidating Wang Ming's control of the Party.

Hua Guofeng (1921–   ) A provincial leader who had a spectacular rise in the early 1970s while Kang still supervised personnel matters: transferred to Peking in 1971, Hua took over the public security ministry in 1973 and became vice premier in 1975. Apparently getting special backing from Kang, Hua was rumored to be Kang's illegitimate son; although belied by Hua's birth in Shanxi, far from Kang's home, this suspicion seemed plausible given the twenty-three-year difference in their ages. Hua succeeded Mao as Chairman but lost power to Deng Xiaoping and retired in 1981.

Huang Huoqing (1900–   ) Party cadre, briefly married to Su Mei, Kang's sister-in-law, in the mid-1940s; fathered Su Han, Kang's nephew. Worked as a labor organizer in Shanghai in the 1920s, then went to Moscow; made the Long March with Zhang Guotao's troops; fought against the Japanese and the KMT in northern China. He was a high official in Tianjin after 1949 but moved to the northeast in 1958. Procurator general from 1978 to 1983.

Isaacs, Harold (1910–1986) American journalist who worked in Shanghai during the early 1930s and knew many left-wing Chinese, including local Trotskyites. Branded "a Trotskyite agent" in 1938 by Kang but also blacklisted by the KMT for alleged bias against their cause. Later returned to the United States and became prominent as a *Newsweek* correspondent and as a scholar based at the Massachusetts Institute of Technology.

Jiang Qing (c. 1912–1991) Actress from Zhucheng, Kang's hometown; married Mao Zedong in 1938. Intimate with Kang since her teens, she served for many years as his main channel to Mao. But shortly before his death, Kang betrayed Jiang Qing, asserting that she had been a KMT agent in Shanghai during the 1930s. Convicted with her fellow Gang of Four members of numerous crimes committed during the Cultural Revolution, she was imprisoned in Qincheng Prison near Peking until she died—reportedly by her own hand—in May 1991.

Ke Qingshi (1902–1965) Underground Communist worker who became the Party boss in Shanghai in the late 1950s and helped Kang and Jiang Qing initiate criticism of the play about Hai Rui.

Li Dazhao (1889–1927) Professor of economics at Peking University; greatly impressed by the Russian Revolution, he helped found Chinese communism. Seized from the Soviet legation in Peking by troops under the command of Zhang Zuolin and executed in 1927.

Li Jiantong (1920–   ) Writer whose novel about her brother-in-law Liu Zhidan was used by Kang Sheng as evidence of an anti-Maoist conspiracy to rehabilitate Gao Gang. Believed to be a writer in Peking today.

Li Kenong (1898–1962) Security expert, Kang's deputy in the Social Affairs Department from 1942 to 1945. Famous for his practical jokes.* In the early stages of the war against Japan, Li served as a liaison officer linking the Communists' Eighth Route Army and the KMT. Succeeded Kang as chief of the Social Affairs Department in

---

* Li's peculiar sense of humor was in evidence during the Communist retreat from Yan'an in 1947, when he sent Yang Shangkun, one of his closest friends, an envelope to be opened "by addressee only." When Yang opened the envelope, two scorpions crawled out.

1945 and also headed its successor organization, the Investigation Department. His public cover was as vice foreign minister and deputy chief of the General Staff.

Li Lisan (1903–1967) Brilliant but erratic leader who joined the CCP in France; his oratory evoked comparison with Trotsky's. Discredited by the failure of his policies, Li was recalled to Moscow in 1930 and ordered to study and do propaganda work. After crossing Wang Ming and Kang Sheng in Moscow, jailed for eighteen months during 1938 and 1939. Returned to China in 1945, worked in northeastern China during the civil war, became labor minister after 1949. Tried unsuccessfully to expose the crimes Kang had committed in Moscow. Harassed by Red Guards during the Cultural Revolution, he took his own life.

Li Shiqun (1905–1943) Soviet-trained member of the Red Squads who defected first to the KMT, then to Wang Jingwei's pro-Japanese puppet regime. Managed the Japanese puppet regime's "Number 76," the special-service organ established by Zhou Fohai. Poisoned to death by the Japanese.

Li Yuchao (c. 1900–??) Kang Sheng's cousin from Zhucheng, fellow-student at Shanghai University, and, according to Kang, the man who sponsored his entry into the CCP. Became a literary and propaganda worker and an official of the Central Research Academy in Yan'an. Faded into obscurity in later years.

Li Zhen (c. 1916–1973) General and deputy political commissar of the Shenyang Military Region who became public-security minister when Xie Fuzhi fell ill in 1971. Died mysteriously in 1973.

Li Zongren (1892–1969) KMT general and longtime rival of Chiang Kai-shek, he returned to China amid much fanfare in 1965. Hu Yaobang insinuated that Kang had poisoned Li to prevent him from divulging the names of KMT agents in the CCP. But Li did not die until three years after the time Hu indicated, so the validity of Hu's charges remains in doubt.

Lin Biao (1907–1971) A graduate of Whampoa Academy, Lin joined the CCP in 1925 and became the outstanding Communist military strategist. After several years in the Soviet Union during the late 1930s and early 1940s, Lin commanded the Red Army in northeastern China. Led the Chinese forces in Korea but fell sick and had a checkered career during the 1950s. Named defense minister in 1959, Lin made a comeback and rose to be Mao's successor. Died in an aircraft crash on September 13, 1971, while fleeing to the USSR after a botched attempt to overthrow Mao.

Lin Feng (1906–1977) Party organizer and military commissar who lost an arm during the war against Japan and became a Communist administrator in northeastern China, where he allegedly had a pretty Soviet mistress. Held a series of administrative posts after 1949; appointed president of the Party School in the early 1960s but purged by Kang in 1966.

Liu Ren (??–1973) Underground Party organizer and leading figure in the Urban Work Department, which operated as a front organization for the Social Affairs Department. Became Peng Zhen's deputy in the Peking municipal Party machine in the 1950s. Persecuted by Kang during the Cultural Revolution.

Liu Shaoqi (1898–1969) Onetime union leader who became the overlord of the urban wing of the CCP, running Communist activities in the cities while Mao and the Red Army were on the Long March. Supervised land reform work during the late 1940s and emerged as the supreme Communist administrator after 1949, supervising the intense organizational work necessary to give substance to Mao's utopian visions. Elected vice chairman of the Party in 1956, named state president in 1958. Eventually incurred Mao's resentment; purged in 1966. Kang helped orchestrate Liu's fatal persecution.

Liu Xiao (1908–1988) A student at Shanghai University, Liu was one of Kang's colleagues in the CCP underground. Arrested in Shanghai but later released; took part in the Long March, then returned to lead the Communist organization in Shanghai. Served as ambassador to Moscow from 1955 to 1963, accompanying Kang on several delegations; later named vice foreign minister. Appointed ambassador to Albania in 1967 but arrested later that year on Kang's orders. Rehabilitated after Deng returned to power in 1978 but was too feeble by then to be influential.

Liu Zhidan (1902–1936) Peasant-rebel-turned-Communist who established a liberated zone around Yan'an in northern Shanxi during the mid-1930s. Died fighting the Japanese. Kang used a novel based on his life to instigate a minipurge in the mid-1960s.

Long Yun (1887–1962) KMT general who ruled Yunnan as a semi-independent territory from 1927 until 1945. Abandoning the KMT,

Long went to Peking in 1950, spending his remaining years there. His art collection was rifled by Kang Sheng, who also had Long's characters "shi lin" removed from the Stone Forest outside Kunming and replaced with his own.

Luo Fu (1900–1976) A well-educated Shanghainese, Luo Fu (real name Zhang Wentian) was one of Wang Ming's Twenty-eight Bolsheviks. After the Zunyi meeting, however, he compromised with the Maoists and was appointed general secretary. During the 1950s, served as ambassador to Moscow and first vice foreign minister. Sacked for criticizing Mao at the Lushan plenum in 1959, persecuted by Kang Sheng during the Cultural Revolution.

Luo Ruiqing (1906–1978) One of the Whampoa alumni, Luo joined the Red Army in Jiangxi and was a commander of the Political Security Bureau during the Long March. A Red Army commissar in the 1940s, appointed public-security minister after 1949. Became chief of General Staff in 1959 but was purged by Lin Biao on conspiracy charges in 1965. Luo's death was at least hastened, perhaps caused, by the harsh treatment he received during the Cultural Revolution.

Mao Yuanxin (c. 1941–   ) Mao Zedong's nephew, he became political commissar of the Shenyang Military Region during the Cultural Revolution. A staunch ally of Jiang Qing and the Gang of Four, Mao Yuanxin was arrested in 1976. Present whereabouts unknown.

Mao Zedong (1893–1976) Involved in revolutionary politics from his early twenties, Mao was a founder of the CCP and among the earliest leaders of the Communist peasant movement. Led rural Communist forces during the late 1920s and 1930s, elected chairman of the Military Commission at Zunyi in January 1935. Consolidated his grip on the Party in Yan'an and emerged as the undisputed CCP leader by the early 1940s. Chairman of the CCP Central Committee and Politburo from 1943 until his death, and Chairman or President of the People's Republic from 1954 to 1959.

Meng Chao (1902–1976) Writer from Zhucheng who helped arouse Kang's interest in radical causes and accompanied him to Shanghai University. Wrote the historical play *Li Huiniang* with Kang's encouragement in the early 1960s but died at Kang's hands during the Cultural Revolution.

Mif, Pavel Aleksandrovich (1899–1938) Soviet official, Wang Ming's mentor at Sun Yat-sen University. Visiting China in late 1930, Mif engineered Wang Ming's promotion to control of the CCP the following January. Back in the Soviet Union, acted as the patron of Wang Ming, and of Kang Sheng after Kang reached Moscow in 1933. Arrested by Stalin in 1938, died in prison.

Nie Yuanzi (1921–   ) Lecturer in philosophy at Peking University who became involved in campus politics during the early 1960s. At the instigation of Kang, who allegedly knew her through her second husband (a member of the Discipline Inspection Commission), wrote a wall poster in late May 1966 that ignited the Cultural Revolution. A prominent radical leader during the late 1960s, Nie fell from power when order was restored in the early 1970s. Sentenced to seventeen years' imprisonment in 1983.

Pan Hannian (1906–1977) CCP literary activist and editor, and an agent of influence in the Shanghai cultural scene during the late 1920s. Along with Kang, Pan was appointed to the committee that supervised security work in 1931. Involved in secret-service work until he moved to the CCP base in Jiangxi in 1933. A propaganda cadre during the Long March, Pan served on the CCP delegation that negotiated the united front with the KMT. After 1949, he was vice mayor of Shanghai and head of the Social Affairs Department office in Shanghai. Arrested on trumped-up espionage charges in 1955; died in prison twenty-two years later but cleared posthumously in 1982.

Pan Jingyin (??–1971) Deputy political commissar of the elite air force unit that transported China's leaders. Piloted the plane in which Lin Biao tried to flee to the Soviet Union, killed with the rest of Lin's party when the plane crashed.

Peng Dehuai (1898–1974) A Long March veteran, Zhu De's deputy in the Eighth Route Army, and an outstanding general during the civil war. Replaced Lin Biao as commander of the Chinese forces in Korea, later appointed minister of defense. Purged in 1959 for criticizing Mao's Great Leap Forward policies. Brutally persecuted during the Cultural Revolution on Kang's orders.

Peng Zhen (1902–   ) Party organizer in northern China, deputized by Kang for the Rectification Movement in Yan'an. Managed the Organization Department and the Urban Work Department, a subsidiary of the Social Affairs Department, during the late 1940s. As director of "legal affairs," oversaw the campaigns against landlords, KMT agents, and other undesirables in the early 1950s. He was the

Peking municipal Party boss from 1949 until his purge in 1966, instigated by Kang. Rehabilitated in 1979 and returned to the Politburo. His age severely limits his current activities.

Qian Zhuangfei (1895–1935) Communist master spy who hid his revolutionary activities behind a busy social life. Penetrated the headquarters of the KMT secret service; after the 1931 defection of the CCP security chief, Gu Shunzhang, Qian's timely warning to Communists in Shanghai helped avert serious damage. Escaped to Mao's base in Jiangxi and took part in the Long March but was killed in a firefight with anti-Communist forces while crossing the Wu River on March 29, 1935.

Qu Qiubai (1899–1935) Communist author and educator. After visiting the Soviet Union in 1920, Qu promoted the idea of a Bolshevik revolution, writing articles and teaching at Shanghai University. Replaced Chen Duxiu as general secretary after the 1927 massacre but was ousted when his policies led to a series of disastrous defeats. Later joined the rural Communists but was captured and executed by the KMT.

Rao Shushi (1903–1975) A CCP member since 1925, Rao worked in Moscow under Kang during the 1930s. Back in China, became political commissar to the New Fourth Army and later headed the CCP's East China Bureau. By 1949, he was Kang's boss; Rao's elevated status so frustrated Kang that it contributed to Kang's long period of hospitalization in the early 1950s. Named chief of the Organization Department in 1953. Allegedly conspired with Gao Gang to challenge Mao and was arrested in 1954; died in prison twenty-one years later.

Ren Bishi (1904–1950) A Long March veteran and specialist in organization and political work; one of Mao's closest advisers. An outspoken critic of Kang's management of the Rectification Movement. Undoubtedly would have become a powerful PRC figure but for a fatal heart attack in October 1950.

Rou Shi (1902–1931) Short-story writer, magazine editor, CCP member; one of "the Five Martyrs" arrested and executed as a result of Kang Sheng's tip to the KMT in January 1931.

Shao Lizi (1881–1967) Well-educated radical who joined the CCP in 1921 and served as acting head of Shanghai University. After quitting the Party in 1926, Shao worked under Chiang Kai-shek at Whampoa

Military Academy. Held a number of KMT posts but stayed on the mainland after the Communist victory.

Shen Zhiyue (1918–   ) KMT agent who penetrated Mao's Secretariat in Yan'an. Escaped from the Communist region before he was exposed; later became a top intelligence official on Taiwan.

Smedley, Agnes (1890–1950) A progressive writer from a small mining town in Colorado, Smedley devoted her life to chronicling the international Communist movement. First went to China in 1928 and spent the mid-1930s in Moscow, where she had contact with Kang Sheng and Wang Ming before returning to China. Her best-known work was a biography of Zhu De. She died in London, but her ashes were interred in a place of honor in Babaoshan Cemetery in Peking.

Snow, Edgar (1905–1972) American journalist who went to China in 1928. Visited Yan'an in 1936; was the first foreign writer to interview the CCP leaders in Yan'an, writing the classic *Red Star over China*.

Su Mei (c. 1910–1967) Kang's longtime mistress and younger sister of Cao Yi'ou, Kang's second wife. A Party member, Su Mei apparently abandoned her original surname as a security measure. Lived with Kang and Cao in Shanghai, Moscow, Yan'an, Shandong, and Peking. Starting in the late 1940s or earlier, involved in educational activities, first in the Party School and later the Political and Legal Academy. Neither of her two marriages—first to Huang Huoqing, later to Zhang Dingcheng—lasted, most likely because of her sexual relationship with Kang Sheng.

Sun Chuanfang (1885–1935) Warlord general from Shangdong who ruled Greater Shanghai before the workers' uprising in 1927. Crushed on the battlefield, Sun retired to become a Buddhist scholar. Assassinated in 1935 by Shi Jianjiao, the daughter of Shi Chongbin, a military officer executed on Sun's orders.

Sun Yat-sen (1866–1925) Physician who was the driving force behind the first generation of Chinese revolutionaries and the founder of the Kuomintang. Frustrated by the failure of his plans for China's modernization, Sun drew inspiration from the Bolshevik victory in Russia and established a revolutionary government in Canton, which became the center for Soviet advisers like Borodin and Blyukher. Took as his second wife Song Qingling, whose younger sister, Song Meiling, later married Sun's military adviser, Chiang Kai-shek.

Vladimirov, Peter (1905–1953) Soviet journalist and diplomat who was a Tass correspondent and Moscow's envoy in Yan'an from May 1942 until September 1945. He served as consul general in Shanghai from 1948 until 1951 and ambassador to Burma in 1952; died of illness in Moscow. His impressions of Kang, whom he disliked intensely, and other Chinese leaders are recorded in his "diaries," which were published in 1973 (see Bibliography).

Wang Dongxing (1916–   ) Mao's chief bodyguard during the mid-1940s, when Kang supervised all security work. Vice minister of public security during the 1950s and head of the elite palace guard, Unit 8341. Assumed control over the General Office after the purge of Yang Shangkun in 1966. Handled the detention of the veteran leaders purged during the Cultural Revolution and helped conduct the arrest of the Gang of Four. Subsequently accused of corruption and embezzling official funds; never formally prosecuted, but removed from office. Today lives in retirement in Peking.

Wang Hongwen (1933–   ) Youngest member of the Gang of Four. A security official in a Shanghai factory at the outset of the Cultural Revolution, he served as one of China's rulers for almost a decade. Elected Party vice chairman in 1973 and presided over Kang's memorial service but was arrested in October 1976. Remains in jail.

Wang Jiaxiang (1906–1974) One of Kang's associates and, in later years, one of his main rivals. Wang combined experience in the Shanghai underground with expertise in Soviet affairs. Joined the CCP at Shanghai University and later studied in Moscow. Returning to China as one of the Twenty-eight Bolsheviks in March 1930, did propaganda work in Shanghai before joining the rural Communist forces. Badly injured during the Long March, Wang went to the USSR for medical treatment in June 1937, later replacing Wang Ming as representative to the Comintern. Back in Yan'an, together with Chen Yun, supervised the implementation of the Rectification Movement in organs that came under the Military Commission. Held several important posts during the late 1940s, including head of the security-related Urban Work Department. Served as Chinese ambassador to Moscow from 1949 until 1951, when he returned to Peking to establish the International Liaison Department; ran it until a clash with Kang got him eased out of office in the mid-1960s. Died as a result of persecution during the Cultural Revolution.

Wang Jingwei (1883–1944) Launching his career as an activist by plotting to blow up the Manchu regent, Wang avoided execution when his handsome features caught the fancy of a powerful figure at court. Went on to lead the left wing of the KMT but, ousted by Chiang Kai-shek in 1928, shifted to the right wing of Chinese politics. In 1939, started to work with Japan to establish the puppet regime in Nanking that ran the secret-service organ "Number 76." Survived several assassination attempts but died of an illness in Nagoya.

Wang Jinmei (1898–1925) Radical who helped organize the May Fourth uprising in Shandong in 1919; one of the founders of the CCP in July 1921.

Wang Li (1918–) A local cadre in Shandong when he met Kang, Wang worked in the Propaganda Department after the Communist victory. Allied himself with Kang in the 1960s, named to the Cultural Revolution Group in 1966. Arrested on Kang's orders in August 1967 and imprisoned until the late 1980s.

Wang Ming (1904–1974) Born Chen Shaoyu, Wang Ming studied in the USSR and returned to China as leader of the Twenty-eight Bolsheviks. Installed as the dominant CCP leader by Pavel Mif and became general secretary in 1931. Unable to withstand the dangers that went with his position, Wang abandoned it and fled to Moscow six weeks later. Led the Chinese delegation to the Comintern from 1931 until 1937, then flew to China with Kang to lead the united front against Japan. Competed with Mao for control of the CCP during the 1930s but lost all influence in the 1940s. Returned to Moscow in 1956; although remaining a CCP Central Committee member, spent the rest of his life in the USSR, where he published a number of critiques of Maoism.

Wang Xiaoyu (c. 1920–??) Kang's aide during the late 1940s, Wang combined with Kang's son, Zhang Zishi, to rule Shandong in the late 1960s. Has since disappeared from public view.

Wang Zhen (1908–) Communist general of peasant origins who commanded the Yan'an garrison in the 1940s, a position that involved cooperating with Kang on security matters. One of the Party elders who organized the arrest of the Gang of Four, Wang has remained a powerful backroom political force; helped sponsor the violent antidemocratic crackdown in 1989.

Wilhelm, Richard (1873–1930) German missionary-scholar who founded the Qingdao German School, where Kang studied from 1914 until 1917. Wilhelm translated the *I Ching* into German, introducing European Intellectuals like C. G. Jung to Chinese thought. An avid defender of the old China, he sheltered some of the high officials displaced by the 1911 revolution at his school; Kang later boasted that as a student he had been friendly with courtiers of the last dynasty. Wilhelm served as cultural attaché at the German legation in Peking in 1922 before returning to Germany and establishing the academic review *Sinica*.

Wu Han (1909–1966) Historian, author of *The Dismissal of Hai Rui*, the play that Kang and Mao used to trigger the Cultural Revolution. In name a member of the China Democratic League, Wu Han had good relations with the Communists and became a vice mayor of Peking.

Wu Xiuquan (1900–   ) Military-intelligence expert and Soviet-trained Communist who made the Long March and held a series of top army assignments. Vice foreign minister for Eastern Europe in the 1950s but also, more significantly, deputy head of the ILD. Purged when he tried to resist Kang's influence in 1967 but headed military-intelligence work after the Cultural Revolution. Now retired in Peking.

Xiang Zhongfa (1880–1931) Boatman and miner who, with Soviet support, became the CCP's general secretary in 1928. Captured and shot by the KMT.

Xie Fuzhi (1909–1972) Public-security minister during the Cultural Revolution, after succeeding Luo Ruiqing in 1959. Provided the secret police who conducted arrests on Kang's behalf. Fell ill in 1971, died in March 1972. His wife, Liu Xiangping, was minister of health during the Cultural Revolution.

Xu Jianguo (1904–1977) Army security expert, bodyguard to Mao Zedong in the later stages of the Long March and to Zhou Enlai during the Xian Incident in December 1936. Worked under Kang in Yan'an as head of the security division of the Social Affairs Department, subsequently transferred to the Social Affairs Bureau in northern China. After 1949, Xu was chief of the Public Security Bureau in Tianjin and Shanghai and then vice minister of public security. Also served as ambassador to Romania and Albania. Persecuted by Kang during the Cultural Revolution.

Xu Shiyou (1905–1985) Commander of the Nanking Military Region who resisted Lin Biao's efforts to dominate the army.

Xu Zirong (1907–1969) Underground Communist agitator who worked on security matters and attained the rank of vice minister of public security after 1949. Purged on Kang's orders in 1967 and died in prison on June 20, 1969.

Yang Shangkun (1907–   ) A colleague of Kang's at Shanghai University; after studying in Moscow, he returned to China as one of the Twenty-eight Bolsheviks. Was Kang's subordinate in the Shanghai labor movement during the early 1930s and part of the Wang Ming faction until he switched to Mao's side during the Long March. In Yan'an, became head of the General Office, a post with security responsibilities that put him in regular contact with Kang and Kang's deputy Li Kenong. Headed the General Office through the 1950s and early 1960s but was purged in 1966, accused of bugging Mao's study. Returned to office in 1978 as part of the Deng Xiaoping camp, holding a series of provincial and military posts that led to his appointment as president and his emergence as a strongman of the regime. Helped instigate the violent crackdown against the student demonstrators in June 1989.

Yang Zhihua (1900–1973) Kang's fellow-student at Shanghai University who married Party leader Qu Qiubai. Helped organize the Communist women's movement but went to Moscow in 1935 to join the CCP delegation to the Comintern. Returning to China in 1941, was imprisoned by the Xinjiang warlord Sheng Shicai until 1945. After 1949, headed the international side of the National League of Women's Organizations and was also active in the Chinese labor movement.

Yao Wenyuan (1925–   ) Son of a Shanghai writer who had spied for both the CCP and the KMT. A journalist by training, Yao wrote the criticism of Wu Han's play that set off the Cultural Revolution. One of the Gang of Four, Yao was arrested in 1976 and remains in prison.

Ye Jianying (1898–1986) Strategist and staff officer who graduated from the Yunnan Military Academy with Zhu De and helped plan the campaigns against Japan and the KMT. Resisted the radicals during the Cultural Revolution and attacked by Kang a number of times but always managed to cling to office. It was Ye who gave the eulogy at Kang's memorial service. Ye was the main figure behind the arrest of the Gang of Four and strongly supported Deng Xiaoping's comeback.

Ye Qun (c. 1920–1971) Lin Biao's second wife. Joined the Communists in Yan'an during the war against Japan; active during the Cultural Revolution; appointed to the Politburo in 1969, partly with Kang's help, but always suspicious of Kang. Died in the crash of Lin Biao's plane.

Yu Xiusong (1899–1938) A CCP activist from the early 1920s on, Yu studied and worked in the Soviet Union from 1925 to 1935. Opposed Wang Ming and Kang Sheng but went to Xinjiang before Kang could purge him. As a result of orders Kang gave the Xinjiang Communists in 1937, Yu was arrested by Sheng Shicai and handed over to Soviet officials. Died in the Soviet gulag.

Yuan Mu (c. 1925–   ) Journalist who studied at the Shaanbei Academy in Yan'an and later worked for the New China News Agency. Yuan served on Kang's staff during the Cultural Revolution. Since the Tiananmen massacre, he has been the State Council spokesman and a leading apologist for the violent suppression of the democracy movement.

Zeng Shan (1899–1972) Organizer and political commissar who spent two years in Moscow with Kang. On the eve of the Communist victory, known as "the Commissar of Curios," responsible for collecting high-quality antiques for display in state museums. Worked under ILD direction in the 1950s and 1960s and attended many international Communist events.

Zhang Chunqiao (1917–   ) Dour, unsociable opportunist from Kang's home province. Worked as a journalist in Shanghai, writing under the pseudonym "Dick," and joined the KMT intelligence service. After defecting to the CCP in the 1940s, Zhang prospered under the patronage of the Shanghai Party boss, Ke Qingshi. A sponsor of the attack on the play *The Dismissal of Hai Rui*, Zhang was the brightest member of the Gang of Four. Worked closely with Kang during the Cultural Revolution but was finally betrayed by Kang as a KMT agent and arrested in 1976. Widely reported to have died of cancer in prison, but Chinese Foreign Ministry officials insist he is still alive.

Zhang Dingcheng (1898–1981) Communist general who was Su Mei's second husband for several years during the late 1950s. Joined the CCP in 1927 and spent the early part of his career organizing guerrilla operations in his native Fujian Province. Was a leading official at the Party School in Yan'an during the Rectification Movement, when he had contact with Kang. After serving as the CCP military commander in central China during the civil war, Zhang was procurator general from 1954 until the Cultural Revolution. In that post, he clashed with Wang Xiaoyu, Kang's protégé in Shandong. Zhang was also a deputy director of the Organization Department and was persecuted during the Cultural Revolution, when Kang purged all the previous deputy directors of the department. However, Zhang survived to die of old age.

Zhang Guotao (1897–1973) Influential Communist organizer and military leader in the 1920s and 1930s; founding member of the CCP. Feuded with Mao during the Long March and at one point attempted to seize power by force. Defected to the KMT in 1938 and worked for Dai Li, concocting anti-Communist propaganda. After the Communist victory, moved to Hong Kong and later migrated to Canada. Provided much information about Chinese communism for U.S. officials in Hong Kong during the early 1950s, gave many interviews to Western journalists and scholars, and wrote a two-volume autobiography.

Zhang Yufeng (1944–   ) Young female railway attendant who caught Mao's eye in the mid-1960s and became the Chairman's de facto wife. Moved into Zhongnanhai in place of Jiang Qing and bore two daughters. Along with Wang Dongxing, controlled access to Mao in his final years. She has published several accounts of her days as Mao's "secretary" and lives today in a compound for elite cadres in the western suburbs of Peking.

Zhang Zishi (c. 1915–??) Kang's son by his first wife, Chen Yi. Worked for a KMT relief organization in Qingdao during the late 1940s, introduced into the CCP by his father. Became a Red Guard leader in Shandong, named Party boss in Hangzhou in 1975. Removed from office in 1978, has since faded from public view.

Zhao Jibin (1905–1982) Expert on Chinese literature and philosophy who joined the CCP in 1926. Appointed adviser to the Party School in 1963. Prepared scholarly essays during the anti-Confucius campaign that Kang used as indirect attacks on Zhou Enlai.

Zhou Enlai (1898–1976) A top CCP leader from the 1920s until his death. After joining the CCP in France, he returned to China as deputy head of the political department of the Whampoa Academy. Supervised Communist security work in Shanghai during the late 1920s, had Kang appointed secret-service chief in 1931. Took part in the Long March, represented the CCP in negotiations over Chiang Kai-shek's fate after Chiang was kidnapped by the warlord Zhang Xueliang in 1936, and later was the chief Communist envoy in the KMT capital during the war against Japan. Served as Premier from 1949 until his death. Kang crossed swords with Zhou during the Cultural Revolution (according to Soviet sinologist Mikhail Titarenko, Zhou described Kang as "the executioner of the Chinese revolution"), but Kang and Zhou combined forces against Lin Biao at the 1970 Lushan plenum.

Zhou Fohai (1897–1948) A compulsive schemer, Zhou belonged to every major political organization in China at one time or another. Though a founder of the CCP, he shifted his loyalties, first to the KMT and then, in 1938, to the pro-Japanese puppet government of Wang Jingwei. During the Sino-Japanese War, supervised "Number 76," the pro-Japanese special-service organ. Redefected to the KMT toward the end of the war but was arrested by the KMT and died of illness in prison.

Zhou Xiaozhou (1912–1966) Student leader and underground Party organizer; served as Mao's secretary during the 1950s before being appointed Party boss of Hunan Province. Purged after criticizing Mao and the Great Leap Forward at Lushan in 1959; persecuted to death during the Cultural Revolution.

Zhu De (1886–1976) One of Mao's most famous generals, his career an endless adventure story. An opium-smoking officer in a warlord army, Zhu later took part in almost every early Communist armed uprising, was often wounded and several times (in the Western press) reported killed. Popular with his troops. Even his years of studying military science in Germany and the Soviet Union failed to dilute his earthy Chinese qualities or turn him into an original thinker. Promoted to marshal in 1956 but never developed political skills to match his reputation as a soldier.

CHAPTER NOTES

Introduction: The Unseen Hand

page

15   Population when Mao came to power: China's 1953 census put the population at 602 million, 12 million of whom lived overseas. *Nagel's China* (Geneva: Nagel Publishers, 1980), p. 54.

16   Chen Qiren on Mao: Report no. 10 from U.S. Consulate General, Dairen, October 15, 1948, *Notes on the Chinese Communist Movement Based on Information Provided by a Disillusioned Party Member*, p. 39. This report is cited hereafter as "Chen Qiren."

17   Hu Yaobang's speech: Hu Yaobang delivered his speech—"Problems Concerning the Purge of Kang Sheng"—at the Central Party School in Peking on November 9, 1978. Hu's speech is reported in *Chinese Monthly*, vol. II, no. 4 (Hong Kong: May 1980), pp. 15–25. Hu's speech is cited hereafter as "Hu Yaobang, Secret Speech on Kang Sheng." Hu attributed the comparison between Kang on the one hand and Dzerzhinski and Beria on the other to the discredited Marshal Lin Biao, quoting Lin as saying, "Lenin needed Dzerzhinski; Stalin needed Beria . . . So we also needed such a man as Kang Sheng to use the sword in his hand to behead others." This quotation appears on p. 24.

17   Kang's comparing himself with Dzerzhinski: Lin Qingshan, *Persecution Mania* (Tianjin: Hundred Flowers Cultural Publishing Company, 1989), p. 26.

17   Kang's relationship with Mao: Eric Chou, *Mao Tse-Tung: The Man and the Myth* (New York: Stein and Day, 1982), p. 149.

18   "Right deviations": *Selected Works of Mao Tse-tung* (Peking: Foreign Languages Press, 1969), vol. IV, p. 231.

18   Mao's trust in Kang: September 1989 interview in Moscow with Mikhail L. Titarenko, director of the Institute of Far Eastern Studies, Academy of Social Sciences of the Soviet Union.

18   Kang's relationship with Jiang Qing: "Zhongkan," *A Critical Biography of Kang Sheng* (Peking: Red Flag Publishing Company, 1982), pp. 15–16 (cited hereafter as "Zhongkan"); Ross Terrill, *The White-Boned Demon: A Biography of Madame Mao Zedong* (New York: William Morrow and Company, 1984), p. 136.

18   Description of Kang's system and torturers: Chen Qiren, pp. 21–24.

19   Tortures: Chen Qiren, pp. 21–24, 38.

19   Treatment of prisoners: "Zhongkan," pp. 100–101.

19   Kang's exploitation of Mao's insecurities: Interview with Titarenko.

20   Hu's quote: Hu Yaobang, Secret Speech on Kang Sheng, p. 19.

20   Jiang Qing's circumstances in prison: A high cadre responsible for the housing and logistical requirements of the Chinese elite.

20   Jiang Qing's suicide: *The Washington Post*, June 5, 1991, pp. A27 and D4.

20   Rumors attributing Jiang Qing's death to Deng Xiaoping: *Zheng Ming*, July 1991, pp. 6–8.

20   If Kang had survived: Ibid.

21   Kang's relationship with Su Mei: "Zhongkan," pp. 5, 106, 110. Personal acquaintances of Kang's have confirmed his relationship with his sister-in-law.

21   Kang's opium smoking: U.S. intelligence reports from the 1940s, which identify him as an opium "addict"; a Hong Kong–based journalist, Ye Hongsheng; and Kang's female acquaintance mentioned here. For a full discussion of Kang's opium smoking and sources of this information see Chapter Ten.

21   Bourgeois wastefulness: U.S. State Department Intelligence Report no. 5838, March 12, 1952, *The Campaign Against Corruption in Communist China*, p. 6. The offender in question was Minister of Justice Shi Liang.

21   Pekinese terriers: "Zhongkan," p. 309.

21   Eating of dogs: Testimony of Chao Fu, a defector from Communist China, U.S. Congress, Senate, Committee on the Judiciary, *Hearings Before the Subcommittee to Investigate the Administration of the Internal Security Act and Other Internal Security Laws*, 87th Cong., 2d sess., November 29, 1962, p. 6.

21   Kang's cook: Peter Vladimirov, *The Vladimirov Diaries* (New York: Doubleday and Company, 1975), p. 99. Kang may have enjoyed elaborate meals, but Mao preferred much simpler cuisine—primarily, green vegetables, salted vegetables and peppers, and shredded meat, according to his chef. Li K'ai-wen, "I Was Chairman Mao's Cook" (Shanghai: Ertong Shidai, December 16, 1958), republished by U.S. Joint Publications Research Service (New York: April 6, 1959), p. 6.

22   Kang and the nuclear bomb: Richard Deacon, *The Chinese Secret Service* (New York: Ballantine Books, 1976), pp. 340–358, and Roger Faligot and Remi Kauffer, *The Chinese Secret Service* (London: Headline Book Publishing, 1989), pp. 243–258. In fact, as late as 1961, six years after Kang resurfaced as an expert on culture and ideology, the Chinese were still trying to develop their own nuclear capability. See Boris Meissner, "The Ideological Conflict Between Moscow and Peking," first published in *Politics and Contemporary History* (Bonn: March 1961) and republished by U.S. Joint Publications Research Service (Washington: June 1961), p. 9. The Chinese did not explode an atomic bomb until 1964. If Kang was responsible for kindling fire in the dragon, he took his own sweet time.

22   Dai Li's death: The plane crash that killed Dai Li apparently was caused by bad weather. Shen Zui and Wen Qiang, *Dai Li: The Man* (Peking: Cultural and Historical Materials Publishing Company, 1984), pp. 163–166. But U.S. Naval Intelligence records show that Dai Li's own people had reason to do away with him. One month before Dai Li's death, his rivals within the KMT secret service were plotting to kill him by means of "the usual accident, either in a plane or a car." Intelligence Division, U.S. Office of Naval Operations, Intelligence Report no. 35-S-46 dated November 6, 1946, from New Delhi.

22   Crash of American military aircraft: The U.S. War Department report on this crash reveals that the plane exploded when it flew into the side of a mountain after bad weather prevented it from landing at Yan'an. (U.S. Army Air Forces Report of Major Accidents, Norton Air Force Base, California.) Among the dead was Deng Fa, who headed the Political Security Bureau, a forerunner of the CCP secret police, during the early 1930s.

22   Kang's hypothesized involvement in Kennedy assassination: Robert Edward Eckels, "The K'ang Sheng Memorandum," reproduced in Eleanor Sullivan and

Chris Dorbandt, eds., *Tales of Espionage* (Secaucus, N.J.: Castle Books, 1989), pp. 67–76.

23   Bugging of Mao's office: Hu Yaobang, Secret Speech on Kang Sheng, p. 19.

27   Comparison with Jekyll and Hyde: Lin Qingshan, *Persecution Mania*, p. 12.

28   Communist pastimes: Chen Qiren, part II, pp. 7–8.

28   Kang's smoking preferences: Shanghai Municipal Police interrogation of Wang Yuncheng, February 15, 1933. Shanghai Municipal Police Dossier, D4454.

PART I: CAUGHT BETWEEN TWO WORLDS

Chapter I: From the Province of Confucius

page

35   Kang's place of birth: "Zhongkan," p. 2.

35   Village life in Shandong's Jiao County: Martin C. Yang, *A Chinese Village* (New York: Columbia University Press, 1945).

36   Kang's maternal family name: Chen Suimin, *Mao Zedong and Jiang Qing* (Taipei: New Asia Publishing Company, 1976), states at p. 110 that Kang's maternal grandfather was Li Zhaoming. "Zhongkan," p. 25, reports that Kang's maternal cousin was named Li Yuchao, thereby providing further evidence that his mother's family name was Li.

36   Kang's father's concubine: "Zhongkan," p. 21.

36   Kang's household: Ibid., p. 3.

38   Troubled life: Ibid., p. 5.

39   Kang's womanizing: Ibid.

39   Kang's blood brothers: Ibid.

40   Kang and martial arts: Dennis Bloodworth and Ching Ping, *Heirs Apparent* (London: Secker and Warburg, 1973), p. 55; "Zhongkan," p. 5.

40   Locked up by father: Lin Qingshan, *A Casual History of Kang Sheng* (Hong Kong: Constellation Publishing Company, 1987), p. 5.

40   Fate of Kang's sworn brother: "Zhongkan," p. 5.

41   Kang's marriage: Ibid.

42   War in Qingdao: Kyi Zuh-tsing, *Tsingtao: A Historical, Political, and Economic Survey* (Qingdao: The Catholic Mission Press, 1930), pp. 13–16.

43   Wilhelm's *I Ching*: Richard Wilhelm, *The I Ching* (Princeton, N.J.: Princeton University Press, 1987), is Wilhelm's classic work, rendered into English by Cary F. Baynes.

44   Kang and former officials: "Zhongkan," p. 12.

44   "seasoned wisdom": Wilhelm, *The I Ching*, p. xlvii.

44   The *I Ching* as source for strategy: Deacon, *The Chinese Secret Service*, pp. 261, 511. Deacon's source was a Chinese defector.

45   Killing of Kang's brother: "Zhongkan," pp. 14, 334.

45   House in Zhucheng: Ibid., p. 15.

47   Meeting with Wilcox: Ibid., pp. 18–19.

48   Jiang Qing's route along South Street: Ibid., pp. 15–16.

48   "primary school run by the county": Roxane Witke, *Comrade Chiang Ch'ing* (Boston: Little, Brown, 1977), p. 49.

48   Jiang Qing born in 1912: Edgar Snow, *Red Star Over China* (Middlesex: Penguin Books, 1972), p. 521.

48   Jiang Qing living in Kang's home: Zhu Shan (pen name of Zhu Zhongli), *The Secret Story of Jiang Qing* (Hong Kong: Xingchen Publishing Company, 1987), p. 1.

49   Jiang Qing as a concubine: Sima Buping, *Wang Hongwen and the Shanghai Gang* (Hong Kong: Wenyi Book Shop, 1978), p. 113.

49   Kang's sexual contact with Jiang Qing: Several informants in Peking who of necessity must remain anonymous have told the authors that during the late 1970s members of the Politburo believed that Kang Sheng had once had a sexual relationship with Jiang Qing.

49   Jiang Qing on sex and power: Witke, *Comrade Chiang Ch'ing*, p. 449.

49   Hu Yaobang on Kang's relationship with Jiang Qing: Secret Speech on Kang Sheng, pp. 22–23.

50   Gambling debts and father's concubine: "Zhongkan" reports both rumors but says that they cannot be confirmed. Still, given "Zhongkan's" circumspect approach, it is unlikely that such stories would have been raised without at least some corroborating evidence. At the very least, these rumors represent the sort of tales that Chinese told about their leaders. "Zhongkan," p. 21.

Chapter II: Shanghai, Haven for Revolutionaries

page

51   Descriptions of Shanghai: Ernest O. Hauser, *Shanghai: City for Sale* (New York: Harcourt, Brace, 1940); Samuel Merwin, *Drugging a Nation* (New York: Fleming H. Revell Company, 1908), p. 102; and U.S. Office of Strategic Services Report no. 68638, dated April 22, 1944, *The City of Shanghai*, pp. 15, 6. This document, based on a translation of book III, chapter 4, of a book titled *Modern Geographical Record of China*, which apparently was published in the early 1930s, is cited hereafter as OSS Report, *The City of Shanghai*.

52   Vehicles in Shanghai: OSS Report, *The City of Shanghai*, p. 12.

55   Accommodations at Shanghai University: Cheng Yongyan, "Remembering Shanghai University," *Party Historical Material*, no. 2 (Shanghai: People's Publishing Company, 1980), pp. 86–87.

55   Qu Qiubai's private life: Li Ang, *The Red Stage* (Chongqing: Masses Book Shop, 1942), p. 13.

55   Kang's notes: Yang Zhihua, "In Memory of Qu Qiubai," in *Red Flags Waving*, no. viii, Peking, 1958, p. 25.

55   Mao on Kang as a college graduate: Quoted in Tracy B. Strong and Helene Keyssar, "Anna Louise Strong: Three Interviews with Mao Zedong," in *China Quarterly*, no. 103, September 1985, p. 501.

56   Kang joins CCP: "Zhongkan," p. 25.

56   Party membership figures: Pamphlet entitled "The Chinese Communist Party and the Soviet Russian Activities in Mongolia," p. 7, sent from the U.S. Legation in Peking to the State Department on July 28, 1932.

57   Whampoa Academy: Jonathan Spence, *To Change China: Western Advisers in China 1620–1960* (New York: Penguin Books, 1980), pp. 190–192.

57   Kang's admission to the CCP: "Zhongkan," p. 25.

57   Kang's removal of papers on personnel file: Yu Yaobang, Secret Speech, on Kang Sheng, p. 23.

58   Kang's pledge: Ibid., p. 26.

59   Kang at Shanghai University: Quoted by Yang Zhihua, "In Memory of Qu Qiubai," p. 25.

59   Kang's contemporaries at Shanghai University: Huang Meizhen, Zhang Yun, and Shi Yuanhua, "Shanghai University: A New Revolutionary School," in *Party Historical Material*, no. 2 (Shanghai: People's Publishing Company, 1980), pp. 152–173.

61   Zhou Enlai: Howard L. Boorman, ed., *Biographical Dictionary of Republican China* (New York: Columbia University Press, 1967), vol. I, pp. 391–405.

61   Zhou's "high contralto voice": *The Statesman*, November 8, 1954 ("With Mr. Nehru in China—IV: Close-ups of Top Leaders and Lamas").

62   Kang on uprising: Kang Sheng, "Recollections of the Third Workers Uprising in Shanghai," *The Salvation Times*, March 21, 1937, p. 3.

62   Kang and uprising: Ibid.

64   Stalin on Chiang Kai-shek: Victor Serge, *Memoirs of a Revolutionary 1901–1941* (London: Oxford University Press, 1963), p. 217.

65   Chiang's fears of the Communists: Boorman, *Biographical Dictionary of Republican China*, vol. I, pp. 319–326.

66   Borodin: Spence, *To Change China*, pp. 184–185.

67-68 Communist casualties in April Massacre: Shanghai Municipal Police Dossier no. D4825; Harold R. Isaacs, *The Tragedy of the Chinese Revolution* (New York: Atheneum, 1966), pp. 177, 179–180.

68   Zhou Enlai's escape: Xu Meikun, "Recalling Some of the Circumstances of the Third Workers Armed Uprising," in *Party Historical Material*, no. 3 (Shanghai: People's Publishing Company, 1981), p. 94. Xu Meikun was one of the men who left the Commercial Press building with Zhou Enlai; his account should end speculation about whether Zhou was arrested at the time and, if so, how he escaped.

Chapter III: Living Dangerously

page

70   Kang's knowledge of Shanghai's lanes and alleys: "Zhongkan," p. 306.

70-71 Leftist writer on Kang's knowledge of Shanghai brothel life: Zhou Yurui, *Personalities of the Red Dynasty* (New York: The World Journal, 1976), pp. 119–120.

71   Wang Xiuzhen: SMP Dossier no. D4238, 1933.

71-72 Kang's family: "Zhongkan," p. 5.

72   "Glass-of-water" theory: Eric Chou, *The Dragon and the Phoenix* (London: Corgi Books, 1973), p. 281.

72   Mao's marriage to He Zizhen: U.S. Foreign Service Despatch no. 941 from the Consul General, Hong Kong, to the Department of State, *Biographic Information on Kung Ch'u*, dated November 16, 1953, pp. 8–9.

73   Du Yuesheng's "kidnapping" of Song Meiling: Ilona Ralf Sues, *Shark's Fins and Millet* (Boston: Little, Brown, 1944), pp. 71–72.

73   Background of Cao Yi'ou: Yueh Sheng, *Sun Yat-sen University in Moscow and the Chinese Revolution* (n.p.: University of Kansas, Center for East Asian Studies, 1971), p. 250.

74   Changes name to Zhao Rong: "Zhongkan," pp. 29, 337.

74   Personal assistant to Yu Qiaqing: Chen Suimin, *Mao Zedong and Jiang Qing*, pp. 109–110.

74   Popular view of compradors: Quoted in Pan Ling, *In Search of Old Shanghai* (Hong Kong: Joint Publishing Co., 1982), pp. 67–68.

77   Zhang Guotao on Li Lisan: Chang Kuo-t'ao, *The Rise of the Chinese Communist Party*, vol. 2 (Lawrence, Kansas: University of Kansas Press, 1972), p. 152.

77   Party membership: James P. Harrison, *The Long March to Power* (New York: Frederick A. Praeger, 1972), p. 202.

77   Kang's promotion: "Zhongkan," p. 30.

78   Wang Ming's arrest: Zhou Guojin and Guo Dehong, "A Simple Chronology of Wang Ming," in Chinese Academy of Sciences, Institute of Contemporary History, ed., *Contemporary Chinese Personalities* (Chongqing: Chongqing Publishing Company, 1986), vol. 3, pp. 471–503 at 474–475.

78   Kang's disciplining Wang Ming: "Zhongkan," pp. 32–33.

79   Kang's arrest: U.S. Foreign Service Despatch no. 588, *Biographic Information Furnished by Chang Kuo-t'ao [i.e., Zhang Guotao] on Leading Chinese Communist Figures (Part 7)*, dated September 15, 1953, from U.S. Consul General, Hong Kong, to State Department (cited hereafter as U.S. State Department Report, *Biographic Information Furnished by Zhang Guotao, 1953*), p. 1 of Enclosure no. 4.

79   Release of Kang and Ding Jishi: Ibid., p. 1.

79   Lu Futan's background: Yueh Sheng, *Sun Yat-sen University in Moscow*, p. 247.

79   Kang "arrested and betrayed the party": "Zhongkan," p. 300.

79   Kang's comment on his alleged arrest: Kang's arrest was reported in an anti-Communist magazine published in Taiwan, *Research into Bandit Circumstances*. See "Zhongkan," pp. 306–307. The Kuomintang authorities' publication of news of Kang's arrest suggests that he was never a KMT agent; otherwise, the Nationalists would not have placed such a valuable ally in jeopardy by drawing attention to his past.

80   SMP arrested ten people: SMP Dossier no. D4056, 1932.

80   SMP's use of informants: SMP Dossier no. D4111, 1932.

80   Communists' "uniform": SMP Dossier no. D627, 1929.

81   On KMT prisons: A Trotskyite named Wang Fanxi presented a firsthand explanation of how the KMT prison authorities often failed to establish the true identities or significance of prisoners. See Wang Fan-Hsi, *Chinese Revolutionary* (Oxford: Oxford University Press, 1980), pp. 164–165.

82   Medhurst Road meeting: Hong Yangsheng, "The Working Conditions of the Number One Cell of the Central Special Section," in *Party Historical Material*, no. 2, 1981, p. 20.

82   Kang's support of Wang Ming: "Zhongkan," p. 36.

83   Wang Ming's writings: Zhou Guojin and Guo Dehong, "A Simple Chronology of Wang Ming," p. 477.

83   Appearance of Wang Ming and Meng Qingshu: see photograph in this book's photo insert.

83   Meng Qingshu's arrest and release: Huang Liwen, "Some of the Circumstances of the Jiangsu Party Committee and the Zhabei District Committee in 1930," *Party Historical Material*, no. 3, 1981, p. 27.

84   Mif's return to China: Yu Jundao, "Concerning Mif," *Party Historical Research Material*, no. 3 (Sichuan: People's Publishing Company, 1981), pp. 554–555.

84   Circumstances of January 13 meeting: Mu Xin, *Comrade Chen Geng in Shanghai* (Peking: Cultural and Historical Materials Publishing Company, 1982), p. 12.

84   Communist gunmen: *Sin Wan Bao*, a Shanghai newspaper, on January 13, 1933.

86   Meeting at Eastern Hotel: Wu Guifang, "The Eastern Hotel and the Twenty-three Martyrs," *Party Historical Material*, no. 1, 1979, pp. 159–160.

86   "Secret report" to SMP: You Liang and Zhang Xiangen, "Some Historical Material Concerning the Twenty-four Martyrs," *Party Historical Material*, no. 2, 1980, p. 176.

86-87   Execution of Communist detainees: Ibid., pp. 176–179. A somewhat different account was provided by *The Daily Worker* (November 23, 1931) in a story entitled "Tell of Writers Kidnapped, Shot, Beheaded": five young writers were tortured by Chinese authorities for three weeks and then buried alive; the other nineteen Communists arrested with them were then shot atop their graves.

87   Protests by American writers: *The Daily Worker*, November 23, 1931.

87   Kang's role in betrayal of He Mengxiong: "Zhongkan," p. 300.

88   Wang Yuncheng's connection with Wang Ming: Wang Fan-Hsi, *Chinese Revolutionary*, p. 90.

88   Kang's reaction to He Mengxiong's arrest: Chang Kuo-t'ao, *The Rise of the Chinese Communist Party*, vol. 2, p. 144.

89   Admiration of Wang Ming: Wang Fan-Hsi, *Chinese Revolutionary*, p. 166.

Chapter IV: Secret Dangers, Secret Service

page

92   Communist security rules: See SMP Dossier no. D4723, which includes material gathered up to 1933.

92-93   Xu Enceng's background: U. T. Hsu, *The Invisible Conflict* (Hong Kong: China Viewpoints, 1958), pp. i–iii.

93   General Affairs Cell: Hong Yangsheng, "The Working Conditions of the Number One Cell of the Central Special Section," *Party Historical Material*, no. 2, 1981, pp. 17–23.

94   Red Squad operations: Warren Kuo, *Analytical History of the Chinese Communist Party* (Taipei: Institute of International Relations, 1968), vol. 2, pp. 290–293.

94   Communist assassinations: SMP document, "Political Assassinations or Attempted Assassinations in the Settlement Since July 1, 1927, for Which the Communist Party Is Believed to Have Been Responsible." Undated, no dossier number.

95   Management of Special Section: Hong Yangsheng, "The Working Conditions of the Number One Cell of the Central Special Section," p. 18.

95   Gu Shunzhang's background: Mu Xin, *General Chen Geng* (Peking: New China Publishing Company, 1985), pp. 55–56.

95   Gu as Borodin's bodyguard: U. T. Hsu, *The Invisible Conflict*, p. 61.

95   Gu Shunzhang in 1927 uprising: Harold R. Isaacs, *The Tragedy of the Chinese Revolution*, p. 176.

95   "playboy": Chang Kuo-t'ao, *The Rise of the Chinese Communist Party*, vol. 2, p. 175.

95   Zhou's attitude to Gu: Yueh Sheng, *Sun Yat-sen University in Moscow and the Chinese Revolution*, p. 244.

95-96   Chen Geng's background: Mu Xin, *General Chen Geng*, pp. 53–83.

96   Chen staying at Kang's house: Donald W. Klein and Anne B. Clark, *Biographic Dictionary of Chinese Communism, 1921–1965* (Cambridge, Mass.: Harvard University Press, 1971), vol. I, p. 425.

96   Case of He Zhihua: Chang Kuo-t'ao, *The Rise of the Chinese Communist Party*, vol. 2, pp. 61–62; Chen Yangshan, "Concerning the Central Special Section," *Party Historical Material*, no. 2, 1981, p. 13; Mu Xin, *General Chen Geng*, pp. 109–113.

96-97   Execution of Zhu De's grandson: 1985 interview with a Chinese with direct access to high police officials.

97   Ross spied on by Communist agent: Mu Xin, *General Chen Geng*, p. 110.

97   Connection with SMP officers: Chen Yangshan, "Concerning the Central Special Section," p. 8.

97   CCP agent's contact with Chinese detective: Mu Xin, *Comrade Chen Geng in Shanghai*, p. 29.

98   Role of Song Zaisheng: Mu Xin, *General Chen Geng*, p. 100.

98   Arrest of Communists: SMP Dossier no. D4825. This report gives an account of communism in Shanghai from 1927 until 1932.

98   Arrests in 1929: SMP Dossier no. D4825.

99   The Ruegg case: T'ang Leang-li, *Suppressing Communist Banditry in China* (Shanghai: China United Press, 1934), pp. 59–69.

100   On Li Kenong: Yang Shangkun, "In Memory of Comrade Li Kenong's Ninetieth Birthday," *The People's Daily*, September 14, 1989, p. 6.

101   Failure of KMT raids in Shanghai: Mu Xin, *General Chen Geng*, pp. 119–128; U. T. Hsu, *The Invisible Conflict*, pp. 56–64.

101   Defection of Xiang Zhongfa: Chen Yangshan, "Concerning the Central Special Section," p. 17.

101-2   Results of Gu's defection: Ibid., p. 11.

102   Arrest and imprisonment of Pan Hannian: Chen Xiuliang, "Pan Hannian," *Biographies from Chinese Communist Party History*, vol. 25, pp. 47–50.

103   Organization of secret service: SMP Dossier no. D4238; Chen Yangshan, "Concerning the Central Special Section," pp. 5–6.

103   Guang Huian, Pan Hannian, and Kang: Chen Xiuliang, "Pan Hannian," *Biographies from Chinese Communist Party History*, vol. 25, pp. 31–32.

104   Corruption in secret service: Chang Kuo-t'ao, *The Rise of the Chinese Communist Party*, vol. 2, p. 61.

104   Ding's and Li's private lives: Huang Meizhen, Jiang Yihua, Shi Yuanhua, *Number 76: The Special Service Headquarters of the Puppet Wang Regime* (Shanghai: People's Publishing House, 1984), pp. 4–6.

104   Execution of Gu Shunzhang: U. T. Hsu, *The Invisible Conflict*, p. 63.

105   Claims of Kang's failure: Otto Braun, *A Comintern Agent in China, 1932–1939* (Stanford, Calif.: Stanford University Press, 1982), p. 218. Braun's book, written at the height of the Sino–Soviet split, may reflect Soviet hatred of Kang, who was instrumental in driving a wedge between the two Communist giants.

105   Gu's contribution to the KMT: U. T. Hsu, *The Invisible Conflict*, p. 62.

106   KMT tortures: Shen Zui, *Inside the Military Statistics Bureau* (Hong Kong: Zhongyuan Publishing Company, 1985), pp. 96–99.

106   Red Squad activity: SMP Dossier no. D3549; U. T. Hsu, *The Invisible Conflict*, p. 81.

107   Kang in charge of Labor Department: "Zhongkan," p. 38.

107   Kang's propaganda writing: "Zhongkan," pp. 338–342.

107-8   Kang's propaganda line: "Zhongkan," pp. 40–41.

109   Description of Kang: SMP Dossier no. D4454. The SMP frequently referred to the Communist security service as "the Special Party" or "G.P.U." "Special Party" was a rough rendition of "Special Work Committee," while "G.P.U." was derived from the name of the Soviet secret police during the 1920s.

109   Arrest of Chen Geng: Mu Xin, *General Chen Geng*, pp. 157–158.

109   Chen Geng's comments to Snow: Edgar Snow, *Random Notes on Red China* (Cambridge, Mass.: Harvard University Press, 1957), p. 93.

109   Names used by Shi Jimei: Investigation Section, KMT Organization Department, ed., *Insight into the Chinese Communist Party* (Taipei: Wen Xing Book Shop, 1962), p. 426. This descriptive report on the history of the Chinese Communist Party shows that Ma Shaowu, the name known to the Shanghai Municipal Police, was in fact Shi Jimei.

110   Description of Shi's men: Quoted in SMP Dossier no. D4993. Salversan, an arsenic compound, was a popular treatment for syphilis in the 1930s.

110   "Sing-song house known as Sweet Heart": *Evening Post and Mercury*, Shanghai, June 15, 1933.

110   Ding's arrest: See SMP Dossier no. D4993; Huang Meizhen, Jiang Yihua, and Shi Yuanhua, *Number 76*, pp. 5–7.

110   Blue Gown death list: See SMP Dossier no. D4685, 1933.

110   Kang's transfer to Moscow: See Yueh Sheng, *Sun Yat-sen University in Moscow*, p. 250. Sheng Yue (who wrote his memoirs under the name Yueh Sheng) worked with Kang in Shanghai at the time of his departure. Sheng provided a firsthand account of the circumstances of Kang's move to Moscow.

Chapter V: Moscow, Finishing School for Sadists

page

112   Beria's whereabouts while Kang was in Moscow: Boris Levytsky, *The Uses of Terror: The Soviet Secret Service, 1917–1970* (London: Sidgwick and Jackson, 1971), p. 136.

112   Kang on studying in USSR: Vladimirov, *The Vladimirov Diaries*, p. 95.

112   "Holy City of Socialism": Eudocio Ravines, *The Yenan Way* (New York: Charles Scribner's Sons, 1951), p. 142.

113   Conditions in Moscow: Ibid.

113-14   Hotel Lux: Ma Yuansheng, *A Chronicle of My Soviet Travels* (Peking: Masses Publishing Company, 1987), p. 162.

114   Kang's Russian: Vladimirov, *The Vladimirov Diaries*, p. 9; Klein and Clark, *Biographic Dictionary of Chinese Communism, 1921–1965*, vol. 1, p. 425.

115   Wang Ming stays in Moscow: Yueh Sheng, *Sun Yat-sen University in Moscow*, p. 250.

115   Wang Ming's relations with Mif: U.S. Foreign Service Despatch no. 588 *Biographic Information Furnished by Chang Kuo-t'ao on Leading Chinese Communist Figures (Part 7)*, from the American Consulate General, Hong Kong, to the State Department, dated September 15, 1953, p. 2.

117   Kang's speeches in Moscow: "Zhongkan," p. 343.

117-18   Quotes from Kang's article: Kang Sheng, "The Development of the Revolutionary Movement in Non-Soviet China and the Work of the Communist Party," published in *China's Present Situation and the Mission of the Com-*

munist Party (Moscow: International Workers Press, 1934), pp. 100, 102, 109–110, 116.

119   Kang's membership in Politburo: "Zhongkan," p. 50; Chang Kuo-t'ao, *The Rise of the Chinese Communist Party*, vol. 2, p. 573.

119   Bo Gu's removal of Liu Bocheng: Zhou Erfu, "At the Crossroads of War and Peace," part 2, *Reportage*, no. 102 (Peking: Reportage Publishing Company, 1989), p. 56.

119   Long March: Harrison E. Salisbury, *The Long March: The Untold Story* (London: Macmillan London, 1985).

121   Kang's support for Wang Ming: "Zhongkan," p. 52.

121   "Long Live Comrade Wang Ming!": "Zhongkan," pp. 53, 345.

121   "Stalin! Stalin! Stalin!": Ravines, *The Yenan Way*, p. 145.

121   Wang Jiaxiang to Moscow: "Who Reported the Zunyi Situation to the Comintern?" in *Wenzhai Bao*, no. 138, May 25, 1984, p. 7.

122   Wang–Kang Directive: "Zhongkan," pp. 54–55.

122-23 Kang's Manchurian victims: Ibid pp. 58–59.

123   Wang–Kang Directive: Chong-Sik Lee, *Revolutionary Struggle in Manchuria: Chinese Communism and Soviet Interest, 1922–1945* (Berkeley: University of California Press, 1983), p. 267.

123   Kang's reaction to the controversy over the directive: "Zhongkan," p. 54.

123   Kang's volunteer military force: *Who's Who in Communist China* (Taipei: Institute of International Relations, 1983), pp. 184–185; *Compilation of Important Communist Bandit Personalities* (Taipei: Ministry of Internal Affairs, 1950), p. 77; "Kang Sheng, King of Hell—Mao Zedong's Counsellor," in *Chinese Communist Research*, vol. 16, no. 4, April 15, 1982, p. 53.

124   Reaction to Kirov murder: Ravines, *The Yenan Way*, p. 128.

124   Kirov assassination instigated by Stalin: Robert Conquest, *Stalin and the Kirov Murder* (Oxford: Oxford University Press, 1989), pp. 124–33.

124-25 Trials of Zinoviev and Bukharin and the Hotel Bristol: Lin Yutang, *The Secret Name* (New York: Farrar, Straus and Cudahy, 1958), pp. 84–87; Robert Conquest, *The Great Terror* (Middlesex: Pelican Books, 1971), pp. 163–164.

125   *Yezhovshchina*: Levytsky, *The Uses of Terror*, pp. 125–127.

125   Appearance of NKVD men: Ravines, *The Yenan Way*, pp. 134–135.

125   Kang and "Elimination Office": "Zhongkan," p. 57.

125   Kang's victims: Ibid., p. 60.

126   Hou Zhi's testimony: Ibid., p. 58.

126   Wang Runcheng and Korean Communists: Ibid., p. 59.

127-28 Extermination of foreign Communists: Conquest, *The Great Terror*, pp. 576, 579–581, 586–587.

128-29 Kang in Paris: "Zhongkan," p. 346.

129   Nanking massacre: Dick Wilson, *When Tigers Fight* (New York: Viking Press, 1982), p. 75; Hu Pu-yu, *A Brief History of the Sino–Japanese War (1937–1945)* (Taipei: Chung Wu Publishing Company, 1974), p. 98; Zhang Yijin, "Nanking Massacre: An Historical Fact That Brooks No Denial," *The People's Daily*, November 18, 1990, p. 6.

129-30 Kang's meeting with Stalin: Du Feng, "Kang Sheng and Mao Zedong," *Zheng Ming*, August 1980, p. 42; Wang Jiaxiang, "Recalling Comrade Mao Zedong's Struggle Against Wang Ming's Opportunist Line," *The People's Daily*, December 27, 1979, which was published posthumously after being revised by Wang Jiaxiang's wife, Zhu Zhongli; Zhou Guojin and Guo Dehong, "A Simple Chronology of Wang Ming," p. 487.

130-31 Cases of Li Lisan, Nosaka Sanzo, and Pavel Mif: Tang Liangchun, *A Biography of Li Lisan* (Harbin: Heilongjiang Publishing Company, 1984), p. 119.

131 Kang in Dihua: Zhou Guojin and Guo Dehong, "A Simple Chronology of Wang Ming," p. 488.

131 Yu Xiusong, Zhou Dawen, and Dong Yixiang: Zheng Xuejia, *The So-called Trotskyite Traitor Affair* (Taipei: Society for Research into Problems of International Communism, n.d.), p. 77.

131 Fate of Yu Xiusong: Qiu Zhizhuo, ed., *Biographical Dictionary of Chinese Communist History* (Chongqing: Chongqing Publishing Company, 1986), p. 340.

PART II: IN THE CAMP OF THE BANDITS

Chapter VI: Mao's Man

page

135-36 Conditions in Yan'an: David D. Barrett, *Dixie Mission: The United States Army Observer Group in Yenan, 1944* (Berkeley: University of California Center for Chinese Studies, 1970), pp. 39–40, 82; U.S. Office of Strategic Services Report no. 111, *Special Mission Notes*, dated January 13, 1945, pp. 2–4 (cited hereafter as OSS Report, *Special Mission Notes*, 1945); U.S. Office of Strategic Services, Research and Analysis no. 2793, *Routes to Yenan, Shensi, China*, dated December 22, 1944, pp. 2, 6 (cited hereafter as OSS Report, *Routes to Yenan*, 1944).

136 Kang's reception: Chang Kuo-t'ao, *The Rise of the Chinese Communist Party*, vol. 2, pp. 565–568.

136 Mao's corpulent figure and feminine appearance: G. Ward Price, "Mao May Wreck Fragile Structure of Peace: Ruthless Character of 'Far Eastern Bismark,' " *The Statesman* (Calcutta), November 10, 1950.

136 Primitive Communist equipment: OSS Report, *Special Mission Notes*, 1945, p. 5.

137 Peasants in CCP: U.S. State Department Intelligence Report no. 5777, *The Current Organization of the Chinese Communist Party*, dated February 5, 1952, p. 5. The figures on peasants in the Party were provided by Peng Zhen in 1948, but a roughly similar proportion of the Communist membership would have been from the peasant class ten years earlier in Yan'an.

137 Oath taken by soldiers of Eighth Route Army: *The Daily Worker*, March 22, 1938.

137 Kang's stubbornness in Yan'an: U.S. State Department Report, *Biographic Information Furnished by Zhang Guotao*, 1953, p. 1 of Enclosure 4.

137 Physical environment of Yan'an: Barrett, *Dixie Mission*, p. 36; OSS Report, *Routes to Yenan*, 1944, p. 2.

137 Yan'an pagoda: U.S. Foreign Service Despatch no. 804 from the embassy at Chongqing to the State Department, *Conditions at Yenan as Portrayed by a Foreign Observer*, dated March 6, 1941, p. 3 (cited hereafter as U.S. State Department Report, *Conditions at Yenan*, 1941). This summary, prepared by American diplomat Nelson Trusler Johnson, contained the observations of Professor S. Lautenschlager, an instructor at Jilu University in Chengdu who visited the Communist headquarters in late 1940.

137   Lighting in caves: Barrett, *Dixie Mission*, p. 29.

137   Temperature in caves: U.S. State Department Report, *Conditions at Yenan*, 1941, p. 3.

137   Northwest Hotel: U.S. Foreign Service Despatch no. 244, *Conditions in Shansi and Shensi*, from American diplomat Nelson Trusler Johnson in Chongqing to the State Department, dated June 20, 1939, p. 22 of Enclosure no. 1 (cited hereafter as U.S. State Department Despatch, *Conditions in Shansi and Shensi*, 1939). Johnson's message contained the observations of Andrew T. Roy, an American affiliated with the University of Nanking who traveled through the Communist-held areas of northern China in May 1939.

138   "Sameness of the sea": OSS Report, *Special Mission Notes*, 1945, p. 4.

138   "Mao's Platonic kingdom": Li Ang, *The Red Stage* (Chongqing: Minzhong Book Shop, 1942), p. 139.

138   Zhou kissing his wife: Barrett, *Dixie Mission*, p. 64.

138   Execution of jilted lover: U.S. State Department Despatch, *Conditions in Shansi and Shensi*, 1939, p. 30.

139   Work and pay scales at Yan'an: "I Was Chairman Mao's Cook," p. 7; U.S. State Department Report, *Conditions at Yenan*, 1941, p. 10; U.S. State Department Despatch, *Conditions in Shansi and Shensi*, 1939, p. 24; OSS Report, *Special Mission Notes*, 1945, p. 3.

139   CCP opium cultivation: Vladimirov, *The Vladimirov Diaries*, pp. 153–154; U.S. State Department Despatch no. 1541 from George Atcheson, Jr., U.S. Chargé d'Affaires, Chongqing, *Conditions in Communist-Controlled Areas in North China*, dated September 4, 1943.

139   Dress in Yan'an: OSS Report, *Special Mission Notes*, 1945, p. 3.

139   Kang's dress in Yan'an: Bloodworth and Ching Ping, *Heirs Apparent*, p. 56.

139   Photograph of Kang in Yan'an: "Kang Sheng and Zhou Enlai, Yan'an period," reproduced at p. 13 in *The Great Conspirator Kang Sheng* (Hong Kong: Mingren Congkan Company, 1979).

139   Kang's bodyguards: Bloodworth and Ching Ping, *Heirs Apparent*, p. 56.

139   Kang's chef: Vladimirov, *The Vladimirov Diaries*, p. 99.

140   Polish journalist on food in Yan'an: Sues, *Shark's Fins and Millet*, p. 258.

140   Musical instruments in Yan'an: U.S. State Department Despatch, *Conditions in Shansi and Shensi*, 1939, p. 27.

140   Kang's calligraphy in Yan'an: Jiang Qinfeng, *Around Chairman Mao* (Peking: China Youth Publishing Company, 1958), p. 12.

142   Stalin's portraits: Sues, *Shark's Fins and Millet*, p. 270. Stalin in newsreels: Memorandum, *Interviews with Chinese Communist Leaders*, from John K. Emmerson, Second Secretary, U.S. Embassy, Chongqing, dated December 24, 1944, p. 1.

142   Kang's support for Wang Ming: Yang Zhongmei, *The Zunyi Meeting and the Yan'an Rectification Movement* (Hong Kong: Benma Publishing Company, 1989) p. 80.

143   Kang's attack on Chen Duxiu: Kang Sheng, "Root Out the Japanese Spies and Public Enemies of the Nation, the Trotskyite Bandits," *Liberation*, nos. 29 and 30, 1938, reproduced in *The Trotskyite Party in China* (Jinhua, Zhejiang Province: New China Publishing Company, 1939), pp. 41–80.

143-44   Kang on American Trotskyites: Kang Sheng, "Root Out the Japanese Spies," p. 65.

144   Liu Renjing's contribution to *The Tragedy of the Chinese Revolution*: Wang Fan-Hsi revealed Liu's role in *Chinese Revolutionary*, p. 270. Isaacs himself, in the preface to the second revised edition of *The Tragedy of the Chinese Revolution*, simply refers to "my friend, J.C.L.," or Jen Ching Liu, the Wade-Giles transliteration of Liu Renjing with the family name placed, in the English manner, at the end.

144   Trotskyism "floated like a slow cloud": Dai Qing, "Wang Shiwei and 'The Wild Lily,' " in *Liang Shuming, Wang Shiwei, Chu Anping* (Nanking: Jiangsu Literary Publishing Company, 1989), p. 49.

144   Trotskyism remained a crime: Zheng Chaolin, "The New Edition of Mao's Works and the Unjust Case of the Trotskyite Faction," *Kaifang*, September, 1991, pp. 47–49. Zheng points out that in the new edition of Mao's complete works, which appeared on July 1, 1991, att references to Trotskyism as a crime have been removed.

144   Kang's praise of Wang Ming at Party School: "Zhongkan," pp. 346–347.

145   Date of Kang's appointment to head security and espionage work: Ibid., p. 75.

145-46 Jiang Qing's background: Terrill, *The White-Boned Demon*, pp. 57–109.

146   Jiang Qing's relationship with her jailer: Witke, *Comrade Chiang Ch'ing*, p. 92.

146   Jiang Qing's gift of a photograph: "Zhongkan," p. 76.

146   Cui Wanqiu's involvement in KMT intelligence: A number of mainland writers have reported Cui Wanqiu's connection with the KMT intelligence services. The collection of photographs reproduced at the front of Ye Yonglie's *The Rise and Fall of Zhang Chunqiao* (Hong Kong: South China Press, 1989) includes a copy of the personnel card that the Secrets Protection Agency, one of the KMT intelligence services, kept on Cui. Shen Zui, a former KMT intelligence official, also maintains that Cui was a KMT agent. See Shen Zui, *A KMT War Criminal in New China* (Peking: Foreign Languages Press, 1986), p. 304.

147   Jiang Qing's arrest as told to Witke: Witke, *Comrade Chiang Ch'ing*, pp. 91–94.

147   On feminine beauty in Yan'an and Jiang Qing: Barrett, *Dixie Mission*, pp. 54, 83.

147   Jiang Qing's attendance at the Party School: Witke, *Comrade Chiang Ch'ing*, p. 149.

148   Kang provides Jiang with musical accompaniment: "Zhongkan," p. 347.

148-49 Kang's handling of Jiang Qing's case: Terrill, *The White-Boned Demon*, p. 153.

149   Date of Kang's appointment to Social Affairs Department: "Zhongkan," p. 77.

149-50 Kang as Mao's escort and companion: Jiang Qinfeng, *Around Chairman Mao*, p. 19.

150   Dynamics of Kang's relationship with Mao: Eric Chou, *Mao Tse-tung: The Man and the Myth*, p. 149. Chou, who was a journalist in China until he fled abroad in 1961, quotes Dong Biwu, a CCP founder with close links to Mao, as the source of the comments he ascribes to Mao.

150   Kang's success at switching sides: "Zhongkan," p. 81.

150-51 Kang's denial of association with Wang Ming: Ibid., p. 79.

151   Kang's annotated copy of *The Two Lines*: Ibid., pp. 79–80.

152   Kang's prohibition on dealing with Soviets: Vladimirov, *The Vladimirov Diaries*, p. 46.

152   Kang's isolation of Soviets: Ibid., pp. 8, 12, 13, 35.

152   Description of Kang: Ibid., pp. 9–10. Vladimirov's description accords with that of others who met Kang. Sidney Rittenberg, for example, told the authors in a 1990 interview that Kang walked in a jerky fashion (Vladimirov's wooden puppet) and always seemed to be sucking the air through his nasal passages (in Vladimirov's words, hissing).

152   "Kang's ubiquitous men": Vladimirov, *The Vladimirov Diaries*, p. 47.

152   Kang's planting a female spy among Soviets: Ibid., p. 40.

152-53   George Hatem in Yan'an: See OSS Report, *Special Mission Notes*, 1945, p. 1; OSS Report no. YKX-YSX-65, *Information Concerning Ma Hai-Te, American at Yenan,* dated April 5, 1945.

153   Kang's criticism of Soviet war effort: Vladimirov, *The Vladimirov Diaries*, p. 52.

Chapter VII: Lord of the Snakes

page

154   Kang on secret agents: Kang Sheng, "Root Out the Japanese Spies," p. 75.

155   Establishment of Social Affairs Department: Warren Kuo, *Analytical History of the Chinese Communist Party*, book 3, p. 341.

157   Hu Yaobang on Kang's intelligence role: Hu Yaobang, Secret Speech on Kang Sheng, p. 17.

157   As powerful as Mao: Chen Qiren, p. 7. Chen also regarded Kang as a "possible successor to Mao, should the latter die or retire."

158   "Devious and crafty": Zhang Guotao, quoted in U.S. Foreign Service Despatch no. 1384, dated January 25, 1954, from the U.S. Consul General, Hong Kong, to the Department of State.

158   Li's role in 1940s: Yang Shangkun, "In Memory of Comrade Li Kenong's Ninetieth Birthday," *The People's Daily*, September 14, 1989, p. 6.

158   Privileges of Social Affairs operatives: Chen Qiren, pp. 23–24.

159   Forces around Yan'an: OSS Report, *Routes to Yenan*, 1944, p. 1.

159   Japanese bombing of Yan'an: U.S. State Department Despatch, *Conditions in Shansi and Shensi*, 1939, p. 23; OSS Report, *Special Mission Notes*, 1945, p. 4; U.S. State Department Report, *Conditions at Yenan*, 1941, p. 4.

159-60   Kang on Japanese intelligence methods: Kang Sheng, "Root Out the Japanese Spies," pp. 41–42.

162   Attribution of Dai Li's death to Kang: Deacon, *The Chinese Secret Service*, p. 299; Anthony Grey, *The Prime Minister Was a Spy* (London: Weidenfeld and Nicolson, 1983), p. 89; Faligot and Kauffer, *The Chinese Secret Service*, p. 193.

162   KMT plot to kill Dai Li: U.S. Naval Intelligence Report dated November 6, 1946, from New Delhi to Intelligence Division, Office of Naval Operations.

162   Dai's plane crashing into mountain: Shen Zui and Wen Qiang, *Dai Li: The Man* (Peking: Cultural and Historical Materials Publishing Company, 1984), p. 165.

163-64   Case of Qian Weiren: Lin Qingshan, *A Casual History of Kang Sheng* (Hong Kong: Constellation Publishing Company, 1987), p. 71.

164   Kang presiding over Qian's public interrogation: "Zhongkan," p. 77.

164   Kang's handling of Wang Zunji case: Ibid., p. 78.

165   Kang's treatment of Li Ning: Ibid., pp. 78–79.

166   "Department for Hoeing Traitors": Chen Qiren, p. 19.

166   Function of the Trial Office: Ibid., p. 21.

166   Mistreatment of inmates in Kang's prisons: Ibid., pp. 21–24, 38.

167   Communist agents in KMT: Shen Zui, *Inside the Military Statistics Bureau* (Hong Kong: Zhongyuan Publishing Company, 1985), pp. 266–267.

168   On Chen Lian: Wang Taidong, *A Casual History of Chen Bulei* (Peking: Chinese Cultural and Historical Publishing Company, 1987), pp. 187–201.

168   Shen Zhiyue: 1990 interview with Ku Chow, a former official at the embassy of the Republic of China in Washington and an authority on the history of CCP intelligence and security organizations who writes under the name Zhou Gu.

168-69   Kang and secret societies: Vladimirov, *The Vladimirov Diaries*, p. 100.

169   Kang's warning about German attack on USSR: Ibid., p. 30.

170   "Chinese Communist 'Gestapo' ": U.S. Foreign Service Despatch no. 2, *Conditions in Chinese Communist Occupied Areas of North Shensi*, from Everett F. Drumright, Second Secretary of U.S. Embassy on detail at Xian, to State Department, dated March 1, 1944, p. 2.

Chapter VIII: Connoisseur of Terror

page

172   "a problem of principle:" "Zhongkan," p. 348.

172   "the damage and dangers . . . of Wang Ming": Ibid., p. 83.

173   Western academic assessment: Mark Selden, *The Yenan Way in Revolutionary China* (Cambridge, Mass.: Harvard University Press, 1971), p. 194.

173   Selden on fate of Wang Shiwei: Ibid., p. 196.

173   Execution of Wang Shiwei: Dai Qing, "Wang Shiwei and 'The Wild Lily,' " pp. 41–107.

174   "claws and teeth": Vladimirov, *The Vladimirov Diaries*, p. 143.

174   Jin Maoyue's confession: Wang Ming, *Fifty Years of Chinese Communism* (Peking: Contemporary Historical Material Company, 1981), pp. 163–164. Originally published in Moscow, Wang's book was later translated into Chinese and published "internally"—i.e., for Chinese only—and distributed to a select group of top leaders.

174-75   Alleged attempt to poison Wang Ming: Vladimirov, *The Vladimirov Diaries*, pp. 110–113, 122, 135–136, 144, 163, 198.

175   "exquisite cruelty": interview with M. Titarenko.

175   Western skepticism about attempt to poison Wang Ming: Dick Wilson, *Mao: The People's Emperor* (London: Futura Publications, 1980), p. 214.

175   Investigation of Jin Maoyue: Wang Ming, *Fifty Years of Chinese Communism*, pp. 163–164.

176   "so many spies": "Zhongkan," p. 89.

176   "salvation": Ibid., pp. 85–86.

177   Kang's response when challenged about number of spies: Ibid., p. 86.

177-78   Case of Wang Shiwei: Dai Qing, "Wang Shiwei and 'The Wild Lily,' " pp. 41–107. "Zhongkan's" claim that Kang Sheng ordered Wang's execution (pp. 95 and 354) has been accepted wisdom for many years, but because Dai Qing's work is both more recent and based on detailed research that included "Zhongkan," it seems reasonable to accept her analysis. Although her outspoken criticism of the CCP led to her arrest after the Tiananmen Massacre in 1989, it is relevant that her former association with the public-security system enabled her to interview a number of the Social Affairs Department veterans directly involved in Wang Shiwei's case.

178   Identity and fate of Wang's executioner: 1991 interview with Geremie Barmé, an Australian sinologist who discussed the Wang Shiwei case at length with Dai Qing; Barmé's discussions with Dai Qing form the basis of an article entitled "Using the Past to Save the Present: Dai Qing's Historiographical Dissent," which is due to be published in *East Asian History* No. 1 in late 1991.

178   Wang Shiwei cleared of Trotskyism: Zheng Chaolin, "The New Edition of Mao's Works and the Unjust Case of the Trotskyite Faction," p. 49.

179-80   Kang's speech: "Zhongkan," pp. 86–89.

180   Kang's claims about number of secret agents in Yan'an: Ibid., p. 90.

180   Number of arrests in Yan'an: Ibid.

181   Kang's tactics in the Rectification Campaign: Ibid., p. 351; Dai Qing, "Wang Shiwei and 'The Wild Lily,'" p. 90.

181   Account of public meetings: Wang Ming, *Fifty Years of Chinese Communism*, p. 132.

181   Attitude toward false evidence: "Zhongkan," p. 92.

181   "New line" of dealing with the enemy: Ibid.

181   Kang's directions to interrogators: Ibid.

182   Thought reform over the decades: Robert Jay Lifton, *Thought Reform and the Psychology of Totalism* (New York: W. W. Norton, 1963), pp. 394–396, contains a brief discussion of the evolution of thought reform techniques in China.

182   Number of expulsions: Jacques Guillermaz, *A History of the Chinese Communist Party 1921–1949* (New York: Random House, 1972), p. 367.

182   Number of executions in Yan'an: Ibid., pp. 93, 351. Wang Ming, *Fifty Years of Chinese Communism*, p. 163, claimed that fifty thousand to sixty thousand people were executed during the Rectification Movement. Although this figure supposedly included deaths throughout the Communist-controlled areas and not just in Yan'an, it seems high. No accurate statistics exist, but the death toll was probably somewhere in the low thousands.

182   Kang orders secret execution: "Zhongkan," pp. 95, 354.

182-83   Rehabilitations at Seventh Party Congress: "Zhongkan," p. 93.

183   Zhou's ridicule of Kang's claims: Ibid., p. 93.

183   Number of confessed spies in Yan'an: *Liberation* (Yan'an), September 22, 1943.

183   "Firmly suppress the confirmed traitors": *Selected Works of Mao Tse-tung*, vol. II, p. 446.

183   Mao's dictum: Quoted in "Zhongkan," p. 94.

184   Kang's advice to Mao on Soviet war effort: Vladimirov, *The Vladimirov Diaries*, p. 42.

185   U.S. assessment of Chinese Communists: U.S. Office of Strategic Services Research and Analysis Memorandum no. 27795, *Leadership and Program of the Chinese Communists*, December 22, 1944, pp. 1–2.

185   Communist program: Ibid., p. 2.

185-86   Isolation of Barrett's group: Chen Qiren, p. 49.

186   U.S. knowledge of Kang's security-and-intelligence function: U.S. Military Intelligence Report, *China—Political—Activities of Chinese Communists*, from China–Burma–India Branch, Joint Intelligence Collection Agency, Chongqing, to Military Intelligence Department, Washington, April 22, 1944.

186-88   Conversation between Kang and Emmerson: U.S. State Department Report no. 63, *Interviews with Chinese Communist Leaders*, prepared by Emmerson, December 24, 1944, pp. 1–3.

188   Decline in Kang's power: "Zhongkan," pp. 94–95.

188   Kang's reaction: Vladimirov, *The Vladimirov Diaries*, p. 468.

188   Kang and "the Mao Zedong line": "Zhongkan," p. 353.

189   Kang replaced by Li Kenong: Yang Shangkun, "In Memory of Comrade Li Kenong's Ninetieth Birthday," p. 6.

189   Mao's "shadow, his will, his desire": Vladimirov, *The Vladimirov Diaries*, p. 122.

189   Ling Yun's role as an interrogator: Dai Qing, "Wang Shiwei and 'The Wild Lily,' " pp. 89–90.

189-90   Conditions in modern Chinese prisons: "Yao Yongzhan: A Year in a Chinese Jail," *News from Asia Watch*, September 1, 1990, pp. 1–9.

190   Imprisonment statistics: New China News Agency broadcast, English-language program, November 2, 1984.

Chapter IX: Partial Eclipse

page

192   Early CCP–KMT disagreement over land reform: U.S. Department of State Research and Analysis Memorandum no. 3024.1, *Economy of Communist North China, 1937–1945*, November 23, 1945, p. 4.

192   Mao's views on peasant uprising: *Selected Works of Mao Tse-tung*, vol. 1, pp. 23–24.

192   Kang's mission to Longdong: "Zhongkan," p. 354.

193   Kang on arousing the masses: "Zhongkan," p. 98.

193   Mao's comment on extermination of landlord classes: *Selected Works of Mao Tse-tung*, vol. 4, p. 181.

193   Kang's sadism in Haojiabo: "Zhongkan," p. 101.

194   Kang's treatment of Niu Youlan and Liu Shaobai: Ibid., pp. 100–101.

195   Kang accuses Liu of "moving stones": Ibid., p. 100.

195   Casualties of land reform in Chaijiaya: Ibid.

195   Mao's praise of Kang: *Selected Works of Mao Tse-tung*, vol. 4, p. 231.

195-96   Killings during land reform: Chow Ching-wen, *Ten Years of Storm* (New York: Holt, Rinehart and Winston, 1960), pp. 98–106.

196   Methods of killing landlords: Chen Qiren, p. 38; U.S. Foreign Service Despatch no. 314, *Communist Policy in One Village in Honan Province*, from U.S. Consul General, Hong Kong, to the Secretary of State, Washington, November 11, 1949, p. 12 of Enclosure.

196   Kang advocates completely equal land distribution: "Zhongkan," p. 355.

197   Kang's removal of Bohai district chief: Ibid., p. 104.

198   Deaths resulting from Kang's land reform methods: Ibid., p. 105.

198-99   Rao Shushi's background: Qiu Zhizhuo, *Biographical Dictionary of Chinese Communist Party History*, p. 356; Boorman, *Biographical Dictionary of Republican China*, vol. 2, p. 215.

199   Career of Li Yu: Klein and Clark, *Biographic Dictionary of Chinese Communism, 1921–1965*, vol. 1, pp. 540–542.

199   Rao's transfer to Shanghai: "Zhongkan," p. 108.

200   Cao Yi'ou as head of Shandong organization department: Ibid., p. 356.

200   Kang's alleged sexual misbehavior in Shandong: Hu Yaobang, Secret Speech on Kang Sheng, p. 23.

200   Kang and his children: "Zhongkan," p. 356.
200-201 Kang neglected in Shandong: Ibid., pp. 107–108.
201   Kang's investigation into votes against him: Ibid., p. 356.

PART III: AT THE COURT OF THE EMPEROR

Chapter X: A Family Affair

page
205   Western accounts of Kang in early 1950s: Boorman's *Biographical Dictionary of Republican China*, p. 227, gives nothing more than an inventory of Kang's formal positions during this period. Klein and Clark, *Biographic Dictionary of Chinese Communism, 1921–1965*, pp. 426–427, detail Kang's posts between 1949 and 1954, observing that he did not appear in public during these years and ascribing his "absence from the limelight" to either "illness or further involvement in security work."

205-6 Kang's alleged connection with China's atom bomb: Deacon, *The Chinese Secret Service*, pp. 340–358; Faligot and Kauffer, *The Chinese Secret Service*, pp. 243–258. U.S. consulate's view to the contrary: U.S. Foreign Service Despatch no. 1532, *K'ang Sheng*, from U.S. Consul General, Hong Kong, to Department of State, January 25, 1952.

206   Villa at Number 4 Rongcheng Road: Lin Qingshan, *A Casual History of Kang Sheng*, p. 102.

206-7 Kang as an invalid: "Zhongkan," pp. 106–111, 357; Lin Qingshan, *A Casual History of Kang Sheng*, pp. 101–121.

207   Kang's fear of being under suspicion: "Zhongkan," pp. 110–111.

208   Rao Shushi's telegram to Mao: Ibid., p. 109.

208   Kang's fear of ghosts: Lin Qingshan, *A Casual History of Kang Sheng*, pp. 107–108.

209-10 Symptoms of TLE: Eve La Plante, "The Riddle of TLE," *The Atlantic*, November 1988, pp. 30–35.

210   Opium use in China: Merwin, *Drugging a Nation*, p. 10; Report from U.S. Military Attaché, China, *The Narcotic Situation [in China]*, April 27, 1936, pp. 1–2; U.S. Foreign Service Despatch no. 187, *Extent of Opium Production, and Use and Enforcement of Opium Laws in China*, prepared by W. Walton Butterworth, Minister-Counselor, U.S. Embassy, Nanking, September 20, 1946, pp. 3–4.

210   Li Mingfang on Kang as "opium addict": Strategic Services Unit, U.S. War Department, Report no. A-68381, *A "Who's Who" of Chinese Communist Personalities*, April 22, 1946, pp. 19–20.

210   "big smoke color": Report from U.S. Military Attaché, China, *The Narcotic Situation [in China]*, April 27, 1936, p. 2.

210-11 Kang smoking in hospital in Peking: 1990 interview with a former CCP official who had known Kang personally for many decades.

211   Communists executing opium smokers: Anthony Billingham, "In China a Red Army Plays a Shrewd Political Game," *The New York Times Magazine*, June 6, 1937, p. 11.

211   "Old Opium Pipe": Ye Hongsheng, *Kang Sheng; Jiang Qing: The Thief and the Prostitute* (Hong Kong: Straits Cultural Publishing Company, n.d.), p. 25. The only other top CCP official known to have had a drug problem was

General Zhu De, a reformed opium addict. See Agnes Smedley, *The Great Road: The Life and Times of Chu Teh* (New York: Modern Reader, 1956), p. 130, and F. Tillman Durdin, "Red Hornets of China Sting the Nipponese," *The New York Times Magazine*, April 17, 1938, p. 17.

212   Background on Ren Neiya: 1990 interview with a Chinese who knew both Su Mei and Ren Neiya.

212   Huang Huoqing: Klein and Clark, *Biographic Dictionary of Chinese Communism, 1921–1965*, vol. 1, pp. 395–396.

212   Su Mei–Huang Huoqing marriage: 1990 interviews with two acquaintances of Su Han's.

212   Kang's relationship with Su Mei: "Zhongkan," pp. 106, 109–110.

213   Su Mei's attempted suicide: Ibid., p. 110.

213   Kang's persecution of Sha Tao: Ibid., pp. 110–111, and Lin Qingshan, *A Casual History of Kang Sheng*, pp. 108–111.

214   Liu Shaoqi on Kang as abnormal: Lin Qingshan, *A Casual History of Kang Sheng*, p. 111. The son of another top CCP official who worked closely with Kang for many years adds that in his opinion Kang was suspicious to the point of being "abnormal"—in a word, paranoid.

214   Sha Tao's continued persecution: "Zhongkan," p. 111.

214   Background of Zhang Dingcheng: Qiu Zhizhuo, *Biographical Dictionary of Chinese Communist Party History*, pp. 227–228.

214   Su Mei's marriage to Zhang: 1990 interview with acquaintance of Su Han.

214   Death of Su Mei: "Zhongkan," p. 289; Lin Qingshan, *A Casual History of Kang Sheng*, pp. 263–266; 1990 interview with a friend of Su Mei's.

215   Su Mei's sensitivities: Gao Gezhi, ed., *Records of History's Inside Stories* (Lanzhou: People's Publishing Company, 1988), p. 158.

215   Fate of those accused of involvement in Su Mei's death: "Zhongkan," p. 289; Lin Qingshan, *A Casual History of Kang Sheng*, pp. 263–266.

215   Chinese academic's suspicions of Kang: 1990 interview with a friend of Su Mei's.

217   Mao Zedong and Luo Ruiqing on executions: Roderick MacFarquhar, Timothy Cheek, and Eugene Wu, eds., *The Secret Speeches of Chairman Mao* (Cambridge, Mass.: Harvard University Press, 1989), p. 142; State Department estimates: U.S. Foreign Service Despatch no. 231, *Chinese Murdered in Chinese Communist Mass Purge*, from U.S. Embassy, Taipei, to the State Department, April 25, 1951, pp. 1–2; U.S. State Department Intelligence Report no. 5987, *The Chinese Communist Police System*, August 13, 1952, pp. 1–2.

218   Rao Shushi's death in prison: Qiu Zhizhuo, *Biographical Dictionary of Chinese Communist Party History*, p. 356.

218   "the root of my disease": "Zhongkan," p. 109.

Chapter XI: Comeback of a Courtier

page
219   "Patients of the Socialist Age": Feng Jianwei, "A Record of Comrades Lu Dingyi and Kang Sheng Inspecting Taiyuan's Schools of Higher Education," *China Youth*, no. 20, 1958, p. 10.

219   Kang's return to public life: Klein and Clark in *Biographic Dictionary of Chinese Communism, 1921–1965*, vol. 1, pp. 424–428, say that Kang "participated" in the Party's national conference at which Gao Gang and Rao

Shushi were formally purged in March 1955, giving an "important but un-published" speech. Kang may have participated in the meeting, but he did not make any public appearances until January 1956. He probably moved out of Peking Hospital near the end of 1955.

219-20   Reason for Kang's return: "Zhongkan," p. 112.

220   Kang assigned house in Small Stone Bridge Lane: Lin Qingshan, *A Casual History of Kang Sheng*, p. 113.

220   Kang's aesthetic pastimes: Ibid.

221-22   Changes in Kang's protocol standing: Roderick MacFarquhar, *The Origins of the Cultural Revolution, vol. 1: Contradictions Among the People 1956–1957* (London: Oxford University Press, 1974), pp. 145–146.

222   "Enigmatic and ambivalent" demeanor: 1987 interview with a member of a Chinese research organization.

222   Kang's replacement as Party boss in Shandong: Klein and Clark, *Biographic Dictionary of Chinese Communism, 1921–1965*, vol. 2, pp. 768–770.

223   East German Socialist Unity Party congress: Witold S. Sworakowski, *World Communism: A Handbook 1918–1965* (Stanford, Calif.: Hoover Institution Press, 1973), pp. 160–161.

223   Kang's Moscow stopover: "Zhongkan," p. 358.

224   "Consigned to limbo": U.S. Foreign Service Despatch no. 795, *The New Central Organizations of the Communist Party of China*, from U.S. Consul General, Hong Kong, to Department of State, March 20, 1957, p. 14.

225   Kang's office near to Mao's office: Lin Qingshan, *A Casual History of Kang Sheng*, p. 116.

225   Kang on tape recordings: "Zhongkan," p. 374.

226   Kang present at "contradictions" speech: Ibid., p. 359.

226   Absence of Liu Shaoqi and others: MacFarquhar, *The Origins of the Cultural Revolution, vol. 1*, p. 191.

226   Cadres walking out: Ibid., pp. 250–251.

226   Kang's interjections: MacFarquhar, Cheek, and Wu, eds., *The Secret Speeches of Chairman Mao*, pp. 196, 210, 218–219, 223, 246, 261, 264–265.

226   Kang's summing up at propaganda conference: "Zhongkan," pp. 359–360.

226   Kang's promotion: Ibid., pp. 114, 360.

227   Kang with Mao in Shanghai: Dai Qing, "Chu Anping and 'The Party's World,'" pp. 196–197.

227   "Things are just beginning to change": Ibid., p. 209.

228   Li Weihan: Ibid., pp. 210–211.

228   Kang's involvement at every step: Ibid., p. 130.

229   550,000 victims of the antirightist campaign: Ibid., p. 113.

229   Kang attacking Party School cadres: "Zhongkan," p. 360.

230   Mao's relations with Jiang Qing: Terrill, *The White-Boned Demon*, pp. 182–236.

231   "Education needs a great leap": "Zhongkan," pp. 121–124.

231   Kang on Ministry of Education: Ibid., pp. 123–124.

231   Kang on standard school instruction: Ibid., pp. 123–125.

232   Prose poem about Kang: *China Youth*, no. 2, June 1958, p. 14.

233   Readjusting accommodations: *The People's Daily*, October 22, 1958, p. 3.

233   "Cultivating the new socialist man": Ibid., p. 1.

233   Kang on "cultural revolution": "Zhongkan," pp. 123–124.

234   Kang on rockets: Ibid., pp. 130–131.

234   "Licensed to talk nonsense": Ibid., p. 130.

236 Kang as editor of Mao's works: Ibid., p. 114.

236 Mao on Peng Dehuai: Nikita Khrushchev, *Khrushchev Remembers* (Boston: Little, Brown, 1970), p. 372.

237 Kang's play on Peng's name: 1990 interview with Lu Keng, a Chinese journalist who publishes the Hong Kong magazine *Baixing*.

238 Kang's accusations against Peng Dehuai: "Zhongkan," p. 134.

238 Deaths during the Great Leap Forward: Roderick MacFarquhar, *The Origins of the Cultural Revolution, vol. 2: The Great Leap Forward 1958–1960* (New York: Columbia University Press, 1983), p. 330.

Chapter XII: Playing the Russian Card

page

240 Mao's admission to Snow: quoted in Wilson, *Mao: The People's Emperor*, p. 360.

241 Zhang Guotao on Deng Xiaoping: U.S. State Department Report, *Biographic Information Furnished by Zhang Guotao*, 1953, p. 1 of Enclosure 6.

241 Mao on Deng: Quoted in Uli Franz, *Deng Xiaoping* (New York: Harcourt Brace Jovanovich, 1988), p. 165.

242 Soviet attitude toward Social Affairs Department: Chen Qiren, p. 11.

242 Tass representatives suspected as agents: Telegram from U.S. Embassy, Taipei, to Department of State, February 23, 1950, reporting comments by Chu Kang, a defector "formerly connected with the Chinese secret police," p. 1.

242-43 Russian behavior in Manchuria: Ibid., pp. 13–14.

245 Dong Biwu's view of Mao–Kang relationship: Chou, *Mao Tse-Tung: The Man and the Myth*, p. 149.

245 Kang's trip to East Berlin: "Zhongkan," p. 358.

245 Kang editing "More on the Historical Experience . . .": Ibid., p. 359.

245-46 Text of article edited by Kang : *The People's Daily*, December 29, 1956.

246-47 Kang's attack on Tito: *The People's Daily*, June 14, 1958, p. 5.

247 Russian affiliations of Liu Shaoqi's family: MacFarquhar, *The Origins of the Cultural Revolution, vol. 2*, p. 285.

248 Kang's charges against Li Lisan: Tang Chunliang, *A Biography of Li Lisan* (Harbin: Heilongjiang Publishing Company, 1984), p. 160.

249 "Mayakovsky and Pushkin": "Zhongkan," p. 377.

249 Kang's discussion of "personality cult": Ibid., pp. 375–377.

249 Kang's attendance at the Warsaw Pact meeting: G. F. Hudson, Richard Lowenthal, and Roderick MacFarquhar, *The Sino–Soviet Dispute* (New York: Frederick A. Praeger, 1961), pp. 58–59.

250 Details on Liu Xiao: Edgar Snow, *Random Notes on Red China*, pp. 64–68.

250-51 Text of Kang's speech: Hudson, Lowenthal, and MacFarquhar, *The Sino–Soviet Dispute*, pp. 72–77.

251-52 Exchange with Khrushchev: *The Great Conspirator: Kang Sheng* (Hong Kong: Mingren Congkan Company, 1979), p. 6. The book does not describe when or where this exchange took place.

252 Misreporting Khrushchev's remarks: 1989 Titarenko interview.

252 "Old Baldy": Testimony of Chao Fu, a defector from Communist China, before the U.S. Senate Committee on the Judiciary, November 29, 1962, p. 8.

252-53 Titarenko's comments on Kang's mission and character: 1989 Titarenko interview.

253 Mao describes Kang as his Minister for Empty Talk: 1990 interview with Sidney Rittenberg.

254 Kang "sat there and spoke nothing": Burlatsky, editor of *Literaturnaya Gazeta*, was interviewed by telephone in Moscow in September 1989. Burlatsky was a speech writer to Nikita Krushchev.

254 Kang's involvement with "Long Live Leninism!": *The Great Conspirator: Kang Sheng*, p. 6.

255 Kang in Moscow: "Zhongkan," p. 378.

255–56 Kang's visit to North Korea: Ibid., p. 379.

256 Kang in Moscow in October 1961: Ibid., p. 380.

256 Removal of Stalin's corpse: Harry Schwartz, *Tsars, Mandarins and Commissars* (New York: Anchor Books, 1973), p. 203.

256 "Brainiest" CCP leader: U.S. Office of Strategic Services document no. XL 7138, *Sidelights on Chungking Personalities*, February 5, 1945, p. 3.

256 Khrushchev and Zhou argue over Albania: Schwartz, *Tsars, Mandarins and Commissars*, pp. 204–205.

257 Location of Kang's office: "Zhongkan," pp. 381–382.

257 Hu on Kang and "the Nine Criticisms": Hu Yaobang, Secret Speech on Kang Sheng, p. 21.

257–58 Final trip to Moscow: "Zhongkan," p. 386.

258 Kang misreporting Malinovsky: 1989 Titarenko interview.

Chapter XIII: Opera Lover

page

259 Kang on holidays: "Zhongkan," p. 123.

261 "Next-room plays": *The Great Conspirator: Kang Sheng*, pp. 6–7.

262–63 Kang studying erotica: Lin Qingshan, *A Casual History of Kang Sheng*, p. 314.

262 Kang's promotion of erotic novels: 1988 interview with Wang Yiling, a former employee of the Shanghai Classical Literature Publishing House.

262 Kang's attack on "the two Ma's": "Zhongkan," p. 149.

263 "Consider it mine": Ibid., p. 144.

264 "Don't play around with modern drama": Ibid., p. 150.

264 Removal of Long Yun's characters: 1987 interview with Long Shengwen. A son of General Long Yun, he had learned of Kang's vandalism of his father's calligraphy from officials of the Overseas Chinese Affairs Bureau in Kunming. Known in the United States as Van S. Lung, Long Shengwen was the proprietor of the Yenching Palace Restaurant in Washington, D.C. He died in 1991.

265 Kang's lyrics: From Xi Ersi, *Jiang Qing and the Mainland Artistic World* (Hong Kong: Ming Bao Monthly Press, 1981), p. 34.

266 Jiang Qing's favorite plays: "Zhongkan," pp. 146–147.

267 Kang's response to criticism of his playgoing: Ibid., pp. 150–152.

267 Kang on opera performance in Yan'an: Ibid., p. 148.

268 Plays "fit for . . . Khrushchev": Ibid., p. 382.

268 Kang on playwrights' thinking: Ibid., p. 151.

268 Kang distances himself from Meng Chao: Ibid., p. 150. Meng Jian, "The Literary Hell of *Li Huiniang*," in *The Great Conspirator: Kang Sheng*, p. 29, also recounts Kang's involvement with the production and suppression of *Li Huiniang*. Meng Jian was Meng Chao's son.

269 Meng Chao's fate: Lin Qingshan, *A Casual History of Kang Sheng*, pp. 152–153.

Chapter XIV: Dress Rehearsal for Destruction

page

272 Kang's response to *Liu Zhidan*: "Zhongkan," p. 380.

272 Kang's message to the General Office: Ibid., p. 156.

273 Using a novel for anti-Party activity: Ibid.

273 Victims of the *Liu Zhidan* case: *The Liberation Army Daily*, February 1, 1979.

273–74 Restaurateurs and other suspects implicated in the *Liu Zhidan* case: Ibid.

276 On the Party School: Lin Qingshan, *A Casual History of Kang Sheng*, pp. 170–203.

276 Background on Ai Siqi: Su Qiying, "Ai Siqi," *Biographies from Chinese Communist Party History* (Xian: People's Publishing Company, 1985), no. 21, p. 235.

276 Yang in 1962 and 1963: Merle Goldman, *China's Intellectuals: Advise and Dissent* (Cambridge, Mass.: Harvard University Press, 1981), pp. 96–97.

276 Handling of draft by Ai and Lin: "Zhongkan," pp. 162–163.

278 Mao's response to article on "synthesis": Lin Qingshan, *A Casual History of Kang Sheng*, p. 173.

278 Kang inspects layout of *Guangming*: "Zhongkan," p. 164.

279 Kang selects byline: Ibid., pp. 165–166.

280 Party School resistance to Kang: Lin Qingshan, *A Casual History of Kang Sheng*, pp. 181–186.

280 Fate of Yang: "Zhongkan," p. 167.

280 Fate of Ai Hengwu: Lin Qingshan, *A Casual History of Kang Sheng*, p. 195.

281 Suicide of Sun Dingguo: Ibid., p. 193.

281 Numbers of victims at Party School: "Zhongkan," pp. 167–168.

281 Death of Chen Bo: Ibid., p. 167.

PART IV: GODFATHER OF THE CULTURAL REVOLUTION

Chapter XV: The Play's the Thing

page

285 Kang and the Luo Ruiqing affair: *A Great Trial in Chinese History* (Peking: New World Press, 1981), p. 167. The book is a collection of documents about the trial of the Gang of Four; author or editor unknown.

286 Fate of Luo Ruiqing: David Bonavia, *Verdict in Peking: The Trial of the Gang of Four* (London: Burnett Books, 1984), pp. 191–196. Chen Kewei, ed., *The Tragedy of High-Level Chinese Communist Cadres* (Taipei: Liming Cultural Enterprise Company, 1980), pp. 32–35. Luo, who was imprisoned until 1973, was treated especially cruelly. In 1966, he broke a leg jumping from a building in an unsuccessful suicide attempt. The special-case group investigating him denied Luo proper medical care; Luo's injured leg went untreated, leaving him a cripple. He died in 1978 while undergoing corrective surgery in France.

286 Mao's endorsement of the play on Hai Rui: Ye Yonglie, *Yao Pengzi and Yao Wenyuan* (Hong Kong: Joint Publishing Company, 1989), pp. 262–263.

287 Communist infiltration of the China Democratic League: U.S. Foreign Service Despatch from the Consulate-General, Hong Kong, to the State Depart-

ment, dated August 20, 1951, *Chang Kuo-t'ao on the Organizational Structure of the Chinese Communist Party, p. 5.*

287 Mao and Hu Qiaomu as inspirations for *The Dismissal of Hai Rui*: "Zhongkan," p. 175.

287 Cai Xitao suggests new title: Ibid.

287 Kang's interpretation of "dismissal": Ibid., pp. 176, 387.

287–88 Mao's meeting with Zhang Yufeng and Wang Dongxing's role in their relationship: 1989 interview with a staff member of the Chinese State Council. Mao's relationship with Zhang Yufeng is the central focus of Jing Fuzi's *Mao Zedong and His Women* (Taibei: Lianjing Publishing Company, 1990). While written by a Peking insider (or perhaps several insiders), this exposé of Mao's private life unfortunately cites few sources and contains some passages that must be read with caution.

288 Zhang Yufeng's husband: *Zheng Ming*, July 1988, p. 14.

289 Likely first American references to Zhang Yufeng: Fox Butterfield, *China: Alive in a Bitter Sea* (London: Hodder and Stoughton, 1982), pp. 223, 485.

289 Wang Dongxing: Bloodworth and Ching Ping, *Heirs Apparent*, pp. 58–60.

290 Zhang Chunqiao's silence at trial: Bonavia, *Verdict in Peking*, p. 75.

290 Background on Zhang Chunqiao: Ye Yonglie, *The Rise and Fall of Zhang Chunqiao*, pp. 28–123.

291 Jiang Qing speaks to Ke and Zhang about Wu Han's play: Ye Yonglie, *Yao Pengzi and Yao Wenyuan*, p. 218.

291 Yao Pengzi works for KMT: Ye Yonglie, *The Rise and Fall of Zhang Chunqiao*, pp. 114–115.

292 Political role of Professor Zhu: Ye Yonglie, *Yao Pengzi and Yao Wenyuan*, p. 221.

292 Yao's use of his father as adviser: Ibid., p. 222.

292 Death of Ke Qingshi: Ibid.

294 On Group of Five: Goldman, *China's Intellectuals: Advise and Dissent*, p. 94.

294 Words of a sinologist: Simon Leys, *The Chairman's New Clothes* (New York: St. Martin's Press, 1977), p. 47.

295–96 Mao, Peng Zhen, Kang conversation: "Zhongkan," p. 176.

296–97 Kang's first overt move against Peng Zhen: Ibid., p. 388.

297 Kang's two-and-a-half-day speech: Ibid., pp. 223–224.

297 Kang's charges against Peng Zhen: Ibid., p. 389.

297 Kang's allegations about Peng's handling of the outline: Ibid., p. 180.

297 Kang's ally, "XX": Ibid., p. 180.

298 Kang to Ho Chi Minh: Ibid., pp. 180–181.

Chapter XVI: "Don't Fear Chaos!"

page

301 Details of Wu Gaizhi: Provided by a Chinese journalist with a detailed knowledge of the careers of the Communist elite.

301 Nie Yuanzi's political use of her marriage: Yue Daiyun and Carolyn Wakeman, *To the Storm* (Berkeley: University of California Press, 1985), p. 148.

301–2 "Even if Nie is a tortoise . . .": "Zhongkan," pp. 181–182.

302 Kang and Nie's poster: Ibid., pp. 182–183; Ren Jian, *The Death of the Head of State of the Republic* (Hong Kong: Haiming Cultural Enterprise Company, n.d.), pp. 21–22.

303   Wang Li's background: *Who's Who in Communist China* (Hong Kong: Union Research Institute, 1969–1970), p. 685.

304–5 Kang's response to violence at Peking University: *The Great Conspirator: Kang Sheng*, pp. 30–31.

305   Kang's speech: Cited in U.S. Joint Publications Research Service, no. 398, June 8, 1967, p. 5.

305   Kang's comments on campus violence: "Zhongkan," p. 200.

305   Diaoyutai under Gang of Four: Xu Yichun and Yu Jiafu, "News Feature: Diaoyutai State Guesthouse as Mirror of Diplomacy," New China News Agency, English-language radio broadcast, September 8, 1989.

306–7 Kang's role in Party School politics: Lin Qingshan, *A Casual History of Kang Sheng*, pp. 255–258.

308   Photograph of white-clad Kang Sheng: see photo insert in this book.

310   Kang's opium habit: Ye Hongsheng, *Kang Sheng; Jiang Qing: The Thief and the Prostitute*, p. 24.

310   Kang's role as Mao's court philosopher: "Zhongkan," pp. 223–226.

314   Kang's use of the term "productivism": Ibid., pp. 231–244.

314   Kang on Party School factions: Lin Qingshan, *A Casual History of Kang Sheng*, p. 239.

315   Committee to Investigate Kang Sheng: Neale Hunter, *Shanghai Journal* (Boston: Beacon Press, 1971), p. 231.

315   Kang is "a cruel official": Lin Qingshan, *A Casual History of Kang Sheng*, p. 240.

315   "Kang Sheng is not an able minister": Lin Qingshan, "Fear and Trembling When Kang Sheng Was at the Peak of His Power," in *The New Observer* (Peking, August 10, 1986), p. 30.

315   Anti-Kang posters: Lin Qingshan, *A Casual History of Kang Sheng*, pp. 241–242.

315   Chen Boda's telephone call to Kuai Dafu: Neale Hunter, *Shanghai Journal*, p. 231.

315–16 Attack on Kang's opponents at Party School: Lin Qingshan, *A Casual History of Kang Sheng*, p. 243.

Chapter XVII: The Spider Weaves His Web

page

318   Kang's meeting with Zhang Zishi: "Zhongkan," pp. 198, 400.

319   Exchange with Tan Zhenlin: Ibid., pp. 209–210.

319   Marshal Ye's broken fingers: Wilson, *Mao: The People's Emperor*, pp. 411–412.

320   Kang's presentation to Mao: "Zhongkan," pp. 208–213.

320   Kang and Mao drive around Peking: Ibid., pp. 401–406.

322–23 Kang's purging of the Organization Department: Ibid., , pp. 276, 406.

323   Use of Organization Department files to purge other cadres: Ibid., p. 415.

323   Three anti-elements: Yu Ruxin, *Dictionary of Chinese Communist Current Affairs Usage* (Hong Kong: Keenwitted Publications, 1989), p. 35.

323   Purging of National People's Congress: "Zhongkan," p. 285.

324   A "very black" organization: 1990 interview with a Chinese journalist who knew the daughter of the Malaysian Communist.

325   Wang Jiaxiang's knowledge of Kang: Dai Huizhen, "Wang Jiaxiang," *Biographies from Chinese Communist Party History* (Xian: People's Publishing Company, 1987), vol. 33, pp. 1–30.

325   Jiang Qing's resentment of He Zizhen: Chen Kewei, ed., *The Tragedy of High-Level Chinese Communist Cadres*, p. 54.

325   Wang Jiaxiang's letter of protest to Zhou, Deng, and Chen Yi: Dai Huizhen, "Wang Jiaxiang," pp. 49–50.

326   Kang's "time bomb" speech: "Zhongkan," p. 390.

326   Foreigner who struck Wang Jiaxiang: Salisbury, *The Long March*, p. 329.

326   Mao's solicitude for Wang Jiaxiang: Dai Huizhen, "Wang Jiaxiang," p. 51.

327   Wang Jiaxiang's imprisonment, exile, and death: Ibid., pp. 51–52.

327   Fate of Wang Jiaxiang's family: Chen Kewei, ed., *The Tragedy of High-Level Chinese Communist Cadres*, pp. 52–55.

328   Kang's defense of the American expert: "Zhongkan," p. 206.

328   Kang's appearance and manner: 1990 interview with Sidney Rittenberg.

329   Kang's address to the foreign experts: "Zhongkan," p. 405.

329   Kang's meeting with Han Suyin: "Zhongkan," at page 431, states that Kang "explained to the famous writer Han Suyin the differences between the Marxist theory of continuing revolution, Trotsky's theory of continuing revolution, and Comrade Mao Zedong's theory of continuing revolution" on November 7 and 8, 1969.

329   Han Suyin's assessment of Kang: Han Suyin, *Wind in the Tower: Mao Tsetung and the Chinese Revolution 1949–1975* (Boston: Little, Brown, 1976), p. 53.

330–31 Summary of Soviet views of the Cultural Revolution: Booklet by B. Zanegin, A. Mironov, and Ya. Mikhaylov, *On Events in China* (USSR: Publishing House of Political Literature, 1967), translated into English as *China and Its Cultural Revolution—A Soviet Analysis,* U.S. Joint Publications Research Service no. 48239, June 16, 1969.

331   Membership of Political and Legal Group: Parris H. Chang, "The Rise of Wang Tung-hsing: Head of China's Security Apparatus," *The China Quarterly*, no. 73, March 1978, p. 131.

332   Kang's ties to Yang Shangkun: Kang Sheng, "Root Out the Japanese Bandits," at page 61, refers to Yang Shangkun in favorable terms as the leader of striking workers in Shanghai in January 1932. Kang was then head of the Communist Labor Department, which would have made him Yang's boss. Kang's mention of Yang also includes the interesting revelation that Yang was kidnapped in 1932 by a group of police detectives working with what Kang alleged were "Chinese Trotskyites."

332   Kang's charges against Yang Shangkun: "Zhongkan," p. 227.

333   Yang Shangkun known as "Big Ears": Chinese journalist who knows Yang personally.

333   Background on Wang Dongxing: Bloodworth and Ching Ping, *Heirs Apparent*, p. 59.

333   Kang's control over the Investigation Department: "Zhongkan," p. 407.

334   Arrest of Peking Public Security Ministry officals: Ibid., pp. 295, 419–420.

334   Liu Ren's role in visit of Lieutenant Mackay's delegation: "Zhongkan," at page 295, identifies the American officer as Lieutenant "Meike," presumably a Chinese rendition of "Mackay." "Zhongkan" does not give the American lieutenant's first name.

335   Kang's directions on cases of Public Security Bureau officials: Ibid., pp. 295, 416–419.

335   Account of Xu Jianguo's circumstances written by his children: *The People's Daily*, February 27, 1981, p. 5.

335–36 Fates of Xu Zirong, Feng Jiping, and Ling Yun: Chen Kewei, ed., *The Tragedy of High-Level Chinese Communist Cadres*, p. 142.

336 Military clerks examine Public Security archives: "Zhongkan," p. 302.

336–37 Statistics on documents examined in Shanghai: Ibid., pp. 301–303.

337 Letter on incriminating material addressed to Zhang Chunqiao: Quoted in "Zhongkan," p. 303.

337 Security services run by Kang and Zhang Chunqiao: Hu Yaobang, Secret Speech on Kang Sheng, p. 19; Ye Yonglie, *The Rise and Fall of Zhang Chunqiao*, pp. 211–268.

338 Case of Larry Wu Tai Chin: 1986 interview with a journalist working in a Hong Kong–based Chinese news agency; Susan Katz, "Enigmatic Espionage by Old Pros," *Insight*, March 14, 1988, pp. 30–31; Luo Bote, "Yu Zhensan's Special Status," *Zheng Ming*, October 1986, pp. 86–87. These two articles attribute Chin's arrest to information provided by Yu Zhensan, a public-security official who defected to the United States in 1985. *Zheng Ming* reported that Yu "regarded Kang as his foster father," but sources close to Kang's family have told the authors that they are not aware of Kang's adopting any children.

338 The court eunuch Wei Zhongxian: Dennis Bloodworth and Ching Ping, *The Chinese Machiavelli* (New York: Dell Publishing Company, 1976), pp. 256–259.

339 Popular rhyme: Hu Yaobang, Secret Speech on Kang Sheng, p. 19.

Chapter XVIII: The King of Hell

page

342 Kang explains his criticism of Liu Shaoqi's policies: "Zhongkan," p. 271.

342 Liu's "pliable disposition": From a 1956 Zhang Guotao interview with a political analyst in the office of the American consul general in Hong Kong. U.S. Foreign Service Despatch no. 339 from Hong Kong, October 26, 1956.

342 Liu Shaoqi "not of the category of Stalin": Conversation between Zhang Guotao and *New York Times* correspondent Henry Lieberman, relayed to U.S. Department of State in Despatch no. 1057 from Hong Kong, January 31, 1951, p. 16.

342 Kang prepared to use document against Liu Shaoqi: Ren Jian, *The Death of the Head of State of the Republic*, p. 32.

343 English text of Mao's poster: See David Milton, Nancy Milton, and Franz Schurman, eds., *People's China* (New York: Vintage Books, 1974), p. 271.

343 "Bombard the Headquarters" as evidence of Mao's attitude toward Liu: Ren Jian, *The Death of the Head of State of the Republic*, pp. 35–38.

343–44 Kang's meeting with Tianjian Red Guards: Lin Qingshan, *A Casual History of Kang Sheng*, pp. 268–270.

344 Kang's note to Red Guards: Ren Jian, *The Death of the Head of State of the Republic*, p. 84.

345 Kang's praise of "the Sixty-one Renegades": Lin Qingshan, *A Casual History of Kang Sheng*, p. 273.

345 Kang congratulates Red Guards: Ibid., p. 270.

345 Kang's letter to Mao and others: Ibid., p. 274.

345 Establishment and activities of special-case group: "Resolution on the Rehabilitation of Comrade Liu Shaoqi Passed by the Fifth Plenum of the Eleventh Central Committee," *Ming Bao*, no. 175, July 1980, p. 19.

346   Treatment of An Ziwen: Lin Qingshan, *A Casual History of Kang Sheng*, p. 275.

346–47 Ding Juequn's and Meng Yongqian's testimony against Liu: "Resolution on the Rehabilitation of Comrade Liu Shaoqi," pp. 21–24.

347   Directive Number One: Marlowe Hood, "Deng's Days of Darkness," *South China Morning Post*, March 26, 1988, p. 1.

347   Banquet celebrating Liu's death: Bonavia, *Verdict in Peking*, pp. 180–189.

348   Kang's persecution of Xiao Ming: *A Great Trial in Chinese History*, p. 40.

348   Statistics on high officials purged by Kang: "Zhongkan," pp. 228, 284.

349   Kang's criticisms of Deng: Zhou Xun, "Deng Xiaoping Before and After 'the Criticism of Deng,' " in *Deng Xiaoping* (Hong Kong: Wide Angle Publishing Company, 1983), p. 74; *A Great Trial in Chinese History*, p. 161.

349   Deng's "revisionist" works: Zhou Xun, "Deng Xiaoping Before and After 'the Criticism of Deng,' " p. 74.

349   Kang criticizes Deng's attitude toward Twentieth Congress of CPSU: "Zhongkan," p. 221.

350   Deng's alleged desertion: Han Shanbi, *A Critical Biography of Deng Xiaoping*, 5th ed. (Hong Kong: East West Culture Publishing Company, 1986), pp. 153–154.

350   Deng's 1969 transfer to Jiangxi: Maomao, "Our Days in Jiangxi," *The People's Daily*, August 20, 1984.

351   Kang behind assault on Peng Dehuai: "Zhongkan," p. 409.

351–52 Kang's execution of Wang Yuncheng and Lu Futan: Ibid., pp. 300–301, 427–428, 431.

352   Fate of Wu Han and his family: Su Shuangbi and Wang Hongzhi, "Wu Han," in *Biographies from Communist Chinese Party History*, vol. 7, p. 293; Lin Qingshan, *A Casual History of Kang Sheng*, p. 283.

353–54 Kang's entrapment and arrest of Liu Xiao: Hu Yaobang, Secret Speech on Kang Sheng, p. 20.

354–55 Persecutions in Inner Mongolia: Lin Qingshan, *A Casual History of Kang Sheng*, pp. 281–282; *A Great Trial in Chinese History*, p. 21.

355–56 Persecution of Zhao Jianmin and casualties in Yunnan: *A Great Trial in Chinese History*, p. 175.

356   Kang's patronage of Pol Pot: Interview with a Chinese who was closely connected to the ILD.

357   Madame Deng Yingchao's remarks: From an interview with Japanese journalist and social worker Yukihisa Fujita, who was briefed by members of the Thai delegation.

357–58 Hu's description of Kang's victims: Hu Yaobang, Secret Speech on Kang Sheng, p. 19.

358   "Yan Wang": Ibid.; Hua Yang, "Kang Sheng, King of Hell—Mao Zedong's Counselor," *Research into Chinese Communism*, no. 4, April 15, 1982, p. 50.

Chapter XIX: The Kang Sheng Collection

page

359   Kang's aesthetic activities while claiming to be sick: Lin Qingshan, *A Casual History of Kang Sheng*, p. 102; "Zhongkan," pp. 106–107.

360   Kang's calligraphy in Guo Moruo's house: Details provided by a close friend of one of Guo Moruo's daughters.

360 Kang's calligraphy used for magazine logos: Hua Yang, "Kang Sheng, King of Hell—Mao Zedong's Counselor," p. 51.

360 Kang's calligraphy used for book title: *Ming Bao Monthly*, no. 70, October 1971, p. 82.

360 Inscriptions for "friends, associates, and public institutions": "Zhongkan," p. 262.

360 Kang's sharing aesthetic pleasures with friends: Ibid., p. 309.

361 Foreigners making late-night visits to Kang: 1990 interview with Sidney Rittenberg.

361 "Stalin hours": Chen Qiren, part II, p. 3, defined these as going to sleep at 3 A.M. and rising about noon.

361 "Lu Chishui": Meaning of the name confirmed by a leading Chinese artist in a 1984 interview.

362 Calligraphy telling story of tiger and donkey: Shown to the authors in Peking by a former official once close to Kang.

362 Arthur Waley on Mao's poetry: I. Morris, ed., *Madly Singing in the Mountains* (New York: Walker and Company, 1970), p. 82.

363 Mao's woodblocks: Associated Press report from Peking datelined September 7, 1986. AP cited an article in *The People's Daily* as its source.

363 Inkstones and unearthed artifacts: "Zhongkan," p. 262.

364 Kang's comment on Chen Banding: Ibid., p. 417.

364–65 Kang's methods of acquiring art: Ibid., pp. 264–265.

365 Kang's justification for seizing antiques: Lin Qingshan, *A Casual History of Kang Sheng*, pp. 313–314.

366 Kang specifying artifacts he wanted stolen: Ibid., p. 314.

367 Kang's order to confiscate Deng Tuo's art collection: Ibid., pp. 314–315.

367 Famous figures raided by Kang: "Zhongkan," p. 263.

367 Artistic pretensions of Ye Qun and Cao Yi'ou: Zhang Yunsheng, *The Memoirs of Lin Biao's Secretary* (Hong Kong: Cunzhen Publishing Company, 1988), pp. 290–292, 149–150.

368 Kang's plundering of Cultural Relics Bureau: "Zhongkan," p. 432.

368 "Lack of proletariat sentiment": Ibid., pp. 262–267.

Chapter XX: The Lin Biao Conspiracy

page

371 Photograph of Kang and Swedish Communist: *The Peking Review*, October 3, 1969, p. 22.

371 Helen Foster Snow on Lin Biao: Helen Foster Snow, *Inside Red China* (New York: Doubleday, 1939), p. lii. (Helen Foster Snow was the first wife of Edgar Snow, an American who was one of Mao's favorite Western writers; he was granted a number of exclusive interviews by the Chairman.)

371 Lin Biao in Soviet Union: Chen Qiren, Enclosure to Report, p. 10.

372 Lin Biao's reading habits: Nan Zhi, *An Informal History of Ye Qun* (Hong Kong: Mirror Post Cultural Enterprises, 1985), pp. 65–66, 143; Zhang Yunsheng, *The Memoirs of Lin Biao's Secretary*, pp. 10–11.

373 Speech on military coups: "Zhongkan," p. 189.

374 He Long's background: Snow, *Red Star over China*, p. 532.

374–75 Ye Qun in Yan'an: Dai Qing, "Wang Shiwei and 'The Wild Lily,'" p. 50.

375 Kang's treatment of He Long in hospital: "Zhongkan," pp. 185–192.

375 Lu Dingyi and Yan Weibing's accusations about Ye Qun: Nan Zhi, *An*

Informal History of Ye Qun, pp. 4–11. A similar account of Yan Weibing's persecution appears in Li Qiade, "Material Factors and Mental Illness," in *The Perspective*, January 16, 1988, pp. 32–33.

375   Ye Qun and Wang Shiwei worked in same institution: Dai Qing, "Wang Shiwei and 'The Wild Lily,' " p. 50.

375   Lin's and Ye's distrust of Kang: Zhang Yunsheng, *The Memoirs of Lin Biao's Secretary*, p. 149.

376   "Maojiawan": Zhang Yunsheng, *The Memoirs of Lin Biao's Secretary*, p. 16.

377   Kang orders assault on Chen Zaidao: "Zhongkan," p. 408.

377   Chen Zaidao rescued from Jingxi Guesthouse: 1987 interview with a Chinese journalist who worked for a military news service at the time.

377   Kang supervises articles attacking army: "Zhongkan," p. 409.

378   Kang's and Jiang's instructions to Kuai Dafu: Lin Qingshan, *A Casual History of Kang Sheng*, pp. 246–247.

378   Mao's response to campaign against army: Ibid., pp. 247–248.

379   Kang proposes scapegoating May 16 group: Ibid., p. 250.

379   Kang's denunciation of Wang Li and others: Ibid., p. 251.

379   Imprisonment of Wang Li and Guan Feng: Ye Yonglie, *Yao Pengzi and Yao Wenyuan*, p. 266.

380   Arrest of Lin Jie and Mu Xin: "Zhongkan," p. 413.

380   Li Guangwen beaten on Kang's orders after opposing Kang: Lin Qingshan, *A Casual History of Kang Sheng*, p. 253.

381   Kang's outburst at Jiang Zichen: Ibid., pp. 260–261.

382   Kang's role at the Ninth Congress: Zhang Yunsheng, *The Memoirs of Lin Biao's Secretary*, pp. 165–170, 196–198; "Zhongkan," pp. 247, 250; D. W. Fokkema, *Report from Peking* (Sydney and Melbourne: Angus and Robertson, 1971), p. 172.

382   Kang's praise of Lin Biao: "Zhongkan," p. 246.

384   Lin Biao's photo opportunity with Albanian defense minister: Zhang Yunsheng, *The Memoirs of Lin Biao's Secretary*, p. 262.

384–85 Lin's garbled speech: Ibid., pp. 263–264.

385   Lushan plenum: Ye Yonglie, "The Recently Deceased Chen Boda," in *The New Garden*, no. 2, 1990, pp. 23–58.

386   Kang's opposition to Lin's support for state presidency: Zhang Yunsheng, *The Memoirs of Lin Biao's Secretary*, p. 305.

387   Chen's head "a total disaster": 1990 interview with Sidney Rittenberg.

388   Kang's control of propaganda machine: "Zhongkan," p. 433.

389   Kang's illness: Ibid., p. 434.

389   Lin Biao's erratic behavior at Tiananmen: Nan Zhi, *An Informal History of Ye Qun*, p. 148.

389–90 Kang's instructions to Cao Yi'ou: "Zhongkan," p. 434.

390   Claim that Kang worked with Zhou Enlai against Lin Biao: Yao Ming-le, *The Conspiracy and Death of Lin Biao* (New York: Alfred A. Knopf, 1983), pp. 131–134.

390   Lin Biao's plot: Bonavia, *Verdict in Peking*, pp. 161–162.

391   Account of Lin Biao's coup attempt: "The True Account of Lin Biao's Coup d'Etat," in Li Guoqiang, ed., *Contemporary Chinese Personalities,* no. 8 (Hong Kong: Wide Angle Press, 1988), pp. 80–111.

392   Circumstances of Lin Biao's flight from Beidaihe: 1985 interview with a former Chinese military journalist briefed by witnesses to Lin Biao's departure;

Clare Hollingworth, *Mao and the Men Against Him* (London: Jonathan Cape, 1985), p. 249.

392   Description of the crash of Lin Biao's aircraft: Xu Wenyi, the Chinese ambassador to Mongolia, inspected the wreckage and the corpses several days after the accident. Xu's account was serialized in the pro-Communist Hong Kong newspaper *Wen Wei Po* on January 12–14 and 23–26, 1988.

392   "A marvelous ending": Fu Hao, "Addenda to the Handling of the Lin Biao Affair," *Wen Wei Po*, February 14, 1988, p. 3.

392   "Kang Sheng hated Lin Biao": "Zhongkan," p. 434.

392   Hu Yaobang suggests that Kang met Lin Biao before his flight: Hu Yaobang, Secret Speech on Kang Sheng, p. 24.

Chapter XXI: The Last Double Cross

page

395   Kang's alleged takeover of Lin Biao's secret service: Hu Yaobang, Secret Speech on Kang Sheng, pp. 19–20. Hu Yaobang recounted several examples of the sinister activities attributed to Kang in the years following Lin Biao's coup attempt.

395   Circumstances of Li Zhen's death: 1985 interview in Peking with a close friend of Li's family.

396   Hu Yaobang on date of Li Zongren's death: Hu Yaobang, Secret Speech on Kang Sheng, p. 17.

396   Details of compromising photograph: *Zheng Ming*, June 1986, p. 77.

396   Li Zhen's death and Lin Biao: *Zheng Ming*, January 1986, p. 20.

396   Lin Biao's criticisms of Mao correct: 1985 interview with a schoolteacher who left China in 1979.

397   Foreign Ministry's instructions to diplomats: Hollingworth, *Mao and the Men Against Him*, p. 251.

398   Kang's pastimes while he was ill: "Zhongkan," p. 309.

398   Kang's last raid on Cultural Relics Bureau: Ibid., p. 262.

399   Kang's criticism of Zhou Enlai: Ibid., p. 310.

399   Kang still head of Organization Department: Ibid., p. 316.

400   Resolution on Chen Boda: Jacques Guillermaz, *The Chinese Communist Party in Power, 1949–1976* (Boulder, Colo.: Westview Press, 1976), p. 461.

400   Composition of new leadership: Ibid., pp. 470–471.

400   Zhao Jibin: Qiu Zhizhuo, *Biographies of Chinese Communist Party History*, p. 330.

400   Kang's supervision of articles about Confucius: "Zhongkan," pp. 309–313, 435–436.

402   Kang oversees articles on former empresses: Ibid., p. 315.

402   Kang hands "Tang Xiaowen" to Jiang Qing: Ibid., p. 416.

403–4   Gang of Four's approach to Mao in October 1974: Ibid., p. 316–317.

404   Kang's remark to Party School lieutenant: Ibid., p. 317.

404   Mao rebukes Jiang Qing: Ibid., p. 318.

405   Kang's meeting with Wang and Tang: Ibid., p. 437.

405   Kang's semiconscious remarks: Ibid., p. 307.

405–6   Kang's disclosure of Jiang Qing's KMT associations: Ibid., pp. 319, 437; Sima Buping, *Wang Hongwen and the Shanghai Gang* (Hong Kong: Culture Book Shop, 1978), p. 88.

406   Zhang Chunqiao as a KMT agent: Sima Buping, *Wang Hongwen and the Shanghai Gang*, p. 88; "Zhongkan," pp. 319, 437; Shen Zui, *A KMT War*

Criminal in New China (Peking: Foreign Languages Press, 1986), pp. 257–261.

406   Wu Zhongchao's suspicions of Zhang Chunqiao and dealings with Kang: 1991 interview with a Chinese intellectual who had close contact with Wu.

407   Zhang Hanzhi's letter to Mao: *Issues and Studies*, vol. XIII, no. 10, October 1977, pp. 93–94.

408   Hu Yaobang on purchase of eavesdropping equipment: Hu Yaobang, Secret Speech on Kang Sheng, p. 19.

409   "Lin Biao is dead": Maomao, "Our Days in Jiangxi," *The People's Daily*, August 20, 1984.

409   Kang's criticism of Zhao Puchu: "Zhongkan," p. 386.

409   Reincarnation: 1990 interview with Lu Keng, publisher of *Bai Xing*.

409   Kang's death and interment of his ashes: *The People's Daily*, December 22, 1975, p. 1.

410   The arrangements for foreigners to sign book of condolences: Telegram from U.S. Liaison Office, Peking, to State Department, "Death of Kang Sheng," dated December 17, 1975; telegram from State Department to U.S. Liaison Office, Peking, "Death of Kang Sheng," dated December 18, 1975; telegram from U.S. Liaison Office, Peking, to State Department, "Death of Kang Sheng," dated December 19, 1975; telegram from U.S. Mission to the United Nations in New York to State Department, "Condolence Register for Deceased Communist Party of China Official Kang Sheng," dated December 23, 1975.

Chapter XXII: The Legacy of Kang Sheng

page
411   Tiananmen incident: Bonavia, *Verdict in Peking*, pp. 62–63, Roger Garside, *Coming Alive: China After Mao* (New York: New American Library, 1981), pp. 101–123.

412   Deng's second fall from office: Fan Shuo, "The Tempestuous October—A Chronicle of the Complete Collapse of the 'Gang of Four,' " *Yangcheng Evening News*, February 10, 1989, p. 6. Fan Shuo is an investigative journalist and the author of *Ye Shuai Geming Shi* (*The Revolutionary History of Marshal Ye*) (Macao: Macao Daily Publishing Company, 1989), a biography of Ye Jianying.

412   Peking in mid-1976: Garside, *Coming Alive: China After Mao*, p. 129.

413   Earthquake casualty figures: Millicent Anne Gates and E. Bruce Geelhoed, *The Dragon and the Snake* (Philadelphia: University of Pennsylvania Press, 1986), pp. 71–76.

413   Hua's meeting with Mao on April 30: Garside, *Coming Alive: China After Mao*, p. 127.

413   Rumors that Hua was Kang's illegitimate son: 1987 interview with a Chinese source active in the Democracy Wall movement in the late 1970s.

415   Removal of Kang's ashes: Agence France-Press news report, May 16, 1980, datelined Peking.

415–16 Exhibition of Kang's art collection: Lin Qingshan, *A Casual History of Kang Sheng*, p. 332.

416   First open criticism of Kang: Reuters news report on Kang, July 12, 1980, datelined Peking.

416   Cartoon of Kang as brains behind Gang of Four: New China News Agency report from Peking headlined "Cartoons on Exhibition in Peking," October 15, 1980.

416   Cartoon of Kang as rightist and leftist: *Wide Angle*, December 16, 1980, p. 42.

416   Kang with a lean and hungry look: Cartoons by Ding Cong in *The New Observer*, July 25, 1986, p. 29; August 10, 1986, p. 30; August 25, 1986, p. 30.

416   Play attacking Kang's land reform: Telegram from the U.S. Embassy, Peking, to the State Department, "Good Riddance, Kang Sheng, Wherever You Are," February 5, 1980.

416   Kang's expulsion from the CCP: New China News Agency report headlined "Expulsion from the CCP of Kang Sheng and Xie Fuzhi," October 31, 1980.

417   Fate of "Zhongkan's" book: 1990 interview with a cadre attached to the Party School and 1985 interview with a young intellectual who knew one of the authors.

417   Removal of Cao Yi'ou from NPC: New China News Agency report from Peking headlined "Kang Sheng's Widow Dismissed from Public Office," February 28, 1981.

417   Cao Yi'ou in Building Number 22: *Zheng Ming*, December 1980, pp. 19–20. Several cadres who live in the same compound have confirmed this information.

417   Cao Yi'ou's mental state: 1990 interview with a former staff member of the Party School who knew Kang and his family.

417   Cao Yi'ou's death: 1991 interview with an acquaintance of one of Cao's relatives.

417   Zhang Yuying: "Zhongkan," p. 5.

418   Indictment of Jiang Qing: Fox Butterfield, "Peking Indictment Accuses Radicals of Killing 34,000," *The New York Times*, November 17, 1980.

418   Sentences imposed on Jiang Qing, Zhang Chunqiao, Yao Wenyuan, Wang Hongwen, and Chen Boda: *A Great Trial in Chinese History*, pp. 232–233.

418   Jiang Qing's courtroom antics: Bonavia, *Verdict in Peking*, pp. 21–22.

418   References to Kang during trial of Gang of Four: Ibid., pp. 21, 31–35, 181, 186, 188, 191, 194.

418–19 Interrogation of Zhang Zhongyi: New China News Agency report headlined "Last Days of Professor Zhang Zhongyi," December 5, 1980.

419   Hu Yaobang's speculation that Gang of Four could have survived: Hu Yaobang, Secret Speech on Kang Sheng, p. 20.

419   Kang's ties to Unit 8341 and Wang Dongxing: Parris Chang, "The Rise of Wang Tung-hsing: Head of China's Security Apparatus," pp. 123–124, and Jiang Qinfeng, "Around Chairman Mao," p. 11. Jiang, who was one of Mao's guards, states explicitly that "Comrade Kang Sheng" directly led (*zhijie lingdao*) the security unit that protected Chairman Mao in Yan'an.

419   Wang Zhen as Ye's deputy in the operation against the Gang of Four: Fan Shuo, "The Tempestuous October—A Chronicle of the Complete Collapse of the 'Gang of Four,' " p. 6.

420   Wang Dongxing's arrest of Jiang Qing: Parris Chang, "The Rise of Wang Tung-hsing: Head of China's Security Apparatus," p. 132.

420   Imprisonment of Han Aijing: New China News Agency report headlined "Former Red Guards Sentenced," March 17, 1983.

422   Wang Zhen as Kang's deputy during the Rectification Movement and Yan'an garrison commander: Dai Qing, "Wang Shiwei and 'The Wild Lily,' " p. 77.

423   Yuan Mu's connection with Kang: 1990 interview with a former official, a colleague of Yuan's at the New China News Agency.

Biographical Notes

page
433   Bao Junfu became a street peddler: Chen Yangshan, "Concerning the Central Special Section," p. 8.
440   Li Kenong's joke on Yang Shangkun: 1990 interview with Sidney Rittenberg.
442   Lin Feng lost an arm during the war: 1990 interview with Sidney Rittenberg.
442   Lin Feng's pretty Soviet mistress: Chen Qiren, p. 10 of Enclosure.
451   "Commissar of Curios": Ibid., p. 16 of Enclosure.

Bibliography

page
489   "Zhongkan" cited as a source: MacFarquhar, Cheek, and Wu, *The Secret Speeches of Chairman Mao*, p. 515; Frederick C. Teiwes, "Mao and His Lieutenants," *The Australian Journal of Chinese Affairs*, nos. 19 and 20, January and July 1988.

BIBLIOGRAPHY

Note on "Zhongkan"

The most important source used in this book is *A Critical Biography of Kang Sheng* by "Zhongkan." *A Critical Biography* is a unique document: the only book ever written for an internal Chinese audience of Party cadres and intellectuals that exposes the crimes of a top Communist.

A Critical Biography of Kang Sheng, cited throughout the text as "Zhongkan," relies on information uncovered by the official investigation, undertaken from 1978 to 1980, into Kang's life. Rich in primary source material, it contains extracts from official documents not otherwise available, as well as statements by people who had direct dealings with Kang.

In recounting the details of Kang's life, "Zhongkan" takes care to distinguish between truth and rumor. At various points, the authors warn that particular items of information are uncertain. Their scrupulousness extends to material that makes Kang's character seem even blacker, which underscores their concern to be accurate and not simply to paint a sensational portrait of a disgraced leader.

While the integrity of "Zhongkan" is beyond question, the book suffers from two shortcomings. First, it skirts the controversial episodes in Kang's life that reflect poorly on other senior leaders and the Party at large. "Zhongkan" avoids exploring Kang's relationship with Mao, describing Kang's work as secret-service chief, or listing the members of his circle of friends. Second, "Zhongkan" is written from a Marxist viewpoint and thus seeks to explain Kang's misdeeds in terms of his failure to become a true member of the proletariat. But the authors' ideological explanations never seem to compromise the honesty with which they relate facts.

A Critical Biography comprises 436 pages of text. The first 332 pages are the biography proper, which is thirty-one chapters long. A chronology of Kang's life takes up the remaining 104 pages; this section summarizes the main text but also provides additional material, including the dates of meetings and journeys, quotations from Kang's conversations, and vignettes that fill out the portrait.

Although the copy of *A Critical Biography of Kang Sheng* that John Byron obtained in 1983 was probably the only one in non-Chinese hands at the time, the work is now available in a number of university libraries in the United States. Indeed, it has been cited as a source by Roderick Mac-

Farquhar, Timothy Cheek, and Eugene Wu in *The Secret Speeches of Chairman Mao* and by Frederick C. Teiwes in "Mao and His Lieutenants." "Zhongkan" was also used extensively by a postgraduate student, Catherine E. Johnston, in a Master of Arts thesis submitted to the University of Michigan at Ann Arbor in 1989.

Note on Chen Qiren

Another important source was an official of Kang Sheng's organization who met often with an American diplomat in 1948. Chen Qiren, who identified himself as assistant chief of the International Intelligence Section in Kang's secret police, visited the Dalian residence of Culver Gleysteen, U.S. Vice Consul there, on the evening of July 4, 1948. Gleysteen, who was entertaining friends in the hours after an Independence Day celebration at the consulate, met briefly with Chen that night and asked him to visit him in his office in the next day or two. Chen, then twenty-four, had previously called at the consulate, only to be informed that no Americans there spoke Chinese; Chen considered his information too sensitive to communicate through a translator. Upon hearing that the consular staff had added a member fluent in Chinese (Gleysteen), Chen called a second time. Gleysteen, now living in retirement in East Boothbay, Maine, remembers that Chen was "very nervous" when he burst in on that long-ago Fourth of July party. When a more composed Chen did call at Gleysteen's office, he disclosed what had led up to his desire to help the Americans, in hopes that he could defect, receive asylum, and "struggle against the Communists":

Chen joined the Communists' Eighth Route Army in 1937 to fight the Japanese after his two sisters were raped by Japanese soldiers. He was fourteen at the time. Seriously wounded in the groin during combat, he was sent to undertake military studies in Yan'an and then assigned to Kang's Social Affairs Department. By 1945, he had achieved the rank of lieutenant colonel and became a delegate to the Seventh Congress of the CCP. In the meantime, in 1941, Chen had married a fellow–Party worker, who bore him twin sons the following year. In 1947, while working in the Communist movement in the town of Yantai, she was captured by KMT forces and beheaded. Chen's parents took on the duty of raising his sons. Communist troops soon recaptured Yantai. Because Chen's parents had once belonged to the landlord class (but had given up their land during Yantai's previous Communist occupation), they were put to death by the troops—thrown down a well—along with the twins. Not until some months later, in the spring of 1948, did Chen learn of this. Immediately, he wrote to senior CCP leaders, acknowledging that his parents might be considered "enemies of the people" but protesting the slaying of his sons, who, he pointed out, were "children of a Communist father away on Party work and a Communist mother killed in the line of duty." From then on, Chen plotted to escape from communism. At the time he approached Gleysteen, Chen had received orders to go to South Korea as a CCP agent. Once in South Korea, Chen told Gleysteen, he hoped to defect to the American side.

Over the next few months, in a series of about fifteen meetings averaging ninety minutes to two hours, Chen uncovered to Gleysteen a wealth of information about the Chinese Communists in general and the security organization Kang had set up in particular. Gleysteen arranged a South Korean contact for Chen, but the Communists kept delaying Chen's departure. Finally, in mid-November 1948, Gleysteen received word of Chen's sudden reassignment to a post within China. Another American consular official reported to Washington, "Thus his arrival Seoul indefinitely postponed. Consulate told him it unable help him escape Communist system other than providing contact in Korea. Relations with subject thus seem ended."

The main record of Chen's account of the Chinese Communist organization was a sixty-page document, typed in single space, plus nineteen pages of biographical notes on important CCP personalities. Chen provided much detail about the Communists in Yan'an, his base for five years, and in Manchuria, where he was transferred in late 1945. He also described many aspects of his own unit, the Social Affairs Department. The authors have no reason to doubt the accuracy of Chen's information based on direct experience of Communist activities. For other matters, Chen had to rely on second-hand accounts, and his age limited his knowledge of Party history; even so, his conversations with Gleysteen reveal many important insights into CCP politics and organization.

The State Department handled Chen and his information in curiously careless fashion. Reports about him were initially transmitted in telegrams subject to wide distribution within the bureaucracy. Not until February 1949—three months after Chen's abrupt and somewhat ominous reassignment to China instead of South Korea—did the State Department upgrade communications about Chen from "Confidential" to "Secret," calling his material "excellent and vital." At the same time, the department instructed consular officials in Dalian to "protect source by not referring thus specifically to him in body material passed. When using source as sensitive as this, identity should be given only in separate message strictly classified and limited in circulation, and despatch should characterize source only enough for reader evaluation, not enough for dangerous identification."

Nevertheless, all of the information about Chen—including his name and many of his personal characteristics—was placed in open State Department files at the National Archives in 1980, where it was discovered by the authors 1990. Anyone going through the records on China could have found the data—including personnel from the Chinese embassy. Chen's betrayal of the Communist cause could instantly have become a death warrant. Almost certainly unknown to anyone within the State Department, Chen was beyond

Communist vengeance when the papers on him were declassified. According to well-placed sources within the People's Republic, Chen died in the early 1950s—reportedly of natural causes. Yet he was in robust health when he met Gleysteen, only two or three years before his death in his late twenties. (Gleysteen, the only U.S. official to have had direct contact with him, learned of his fate from the authors.)

Other Major Chinese Sources

The authors have drawn heavily on two other Chinese documents.

Lin Qingshan's *A Casual History of Kang Sheng* includes extensive detail about the later years of Kang's life. Although he borrows liberally from "Zhongkan" to describe Kang's early life, Lin uses fresh material for his account of Kang's activities during the 1960s. Lin, a worker at the Party School, was purged by Kang during the debate over the so-called synthesis of two into one. Clearly, his version of Kang's activities at the Party School comes from interviews with colleagues. Though written in a more popular style than "Zhongkan," Lin Qingshan's book is not a sensationalistic and semifictionalized work on modern Chinese history such as have appeared in Hong Kong, Taiwan, and China in recent years.

Hu Yaobang's secret speech to the Party School in 1978 (since translated into English) also contains much information about Kang. The statement of a politician locked in a battle for power rather than a detached analysis of the evidence against Kang, Hu's address has its share of exaggeration and speculation. Hu Yaobang was a highly volatile man; a Party School official who attended the presentation told the authors in a 1990 interview that Hu got carried away when he made it. Even so, Hu has made a major contribution to the available knowledge about Kang and deserves credit for being the first Chinese leader to dare criticize Kang Sheng by name.

Key Sources in English

We have drawn heavily on the Shanghai Municipal Police files stored in the U.S. National Archives and only recently made available to researchers. The National Archives is also the primary storehouse for the records of the U.S. Office of Strategic Services, the Central Intelligence Agency, the State Department, and American military intelligence. We have reviewed tens of thousands of documents from these arms of government that pertain to China, the Chinese Communists, Kang Sheng, Mao Zedong and the rest of the CCP leadership, Chiang Kai-shek and the Kuomintang, and other relevant topics. Most of these files were designated "Top Secret" or "Secret" or otherwise restricted. Some had been declassified previously, but by far most were classified until we discovered them, and are only now being made public.

BOOKS IN ENGLISH

Barrett, David D. *Dixie Mission: The United States Army Observer Group in Yenan, 1944.* Berkeley: University of California Center for Chinese Studies, 1970.

Bloodworth, Dennis, and Ching Ping. *Heirs Apparent.* London: Secker and Warburg, 1973. An underrated book that contains extensive detail about the background and personal proclivities of many Communist leaders.

————. *The Chinese Machiavelli.* New York: Dell Publishing Company, 1976.

Bonavia, David. *Verdict in Peking: The Trial of the Gang of Four.* London: Burnett Books, 1984.

Boorman, Howard L., ed. *Biographical Dictionary of Republican China.* New York: Columbia University Press, 1967.

Braun, Otto. *A Comintern Agent in China, 1932–1939.* London: C. Hurst and Company, 1982.

Butterfield, Fox. *China: Alive in a Bitter Sea.* London: Hodder and Stoughton, 1982.

Chang Kuo-t'ao (Zhang Guotao). *The Rise of the Chinese Communist Party.* Lawrence, Kansas: University of Kansas Press, 1972. One of the early Communist leaders, Zhang provides much information about the CCP up to 1938. Writing in exile from China, Zhang could not use notes or diaries and occasionally makes errors.

Chang, Parris H. *Power and Policy in China.* University Park, Pa.: Pennsylvania State University Press, 1978.

Chou, Eric. *The Dragon and the Phoenix.* London: Corgi Books, 1973.

————. *Mao Tse-tung: The Man and the Myth.* New York: Stein and Day, 1982.

Chow Ching-wen. *Ten Years of Storm.* New York: Holt, Rinehart and Winston, 1960.

Conquest, Robert. *The Great Terror.* Middlesex: Pelican Books, 1971.

————. *Stalin and the Kirov Murder.* Oxford: Oxford University Press, 1989.

Deacon, Richard. *The Chinese Secret Service*. New York: Ballatine Books, 1976.

Faligot, Roger, and Remi Kauffer. *The Chinese Secret Service*. London: Headline Book Publishing, 1989. Originally published in France as *Kang Sheng et les services secrets chinois* (Paris: Robert Lafont, 1987). Faligot and Kauffer use Kang Sheng as the focus of an account of China's secret service.

Fokkema, D. W. *Report from Peking*. Sydney and Melbourne: Angus and Robertson, 1971.

Franz, Uli. *Deng Xiaoping*. New York: Harcourt Brace Jovanovich, 1988.

Garside, Roger. *Coming Alive: China After Mao*. New York: New American Library, 1981.

Gates, Millicent Anne, and E. Bruce Geelhoed. *The Dragon and the Snake*. Philadelphia: University of Pennsylvania Press, 1986.

Goldman, Merle. *China's Intellectuals: Advise and Dissent*. Cambridge, Mass.: Harvard University Press, 1981.

A Great Trial in Chinese History. Peking: New World Press, 1981.

Grey, Anthony. *The Prime Minister Was a Spy*. London: Weidenfeld and Nicolson, 1983.

Guillermaz, Jacques. *A History of the Chinese Communist Party 1921–1949*. New York: Random House, 1972.

———. *The Chinese Communist Party in Power, 1949–1976*. Boulder, Colo.: Westview Press, 1976.

Han Suyin. *Wind in the Tower: Mao Tsetung and the Chinese Revolution 1949–1975*. Boston: Little, Brown, 1976.

Harrison, James P. *The Long March to Power*. New York: Frederick A. Praeger, 1972.

Hauser, Ernest O. *Shanghai: City for Sale*. New York: Harcourt, Brace and Company, 1940.

Hollingworth, Clare. *Mao and the Men Against Him*. London: Jonathan Cape, 1985.

Hsiao, Tso-liang. *Power Relations Within the Chinese Communist Movement, 1930–1934*. Seattle: University of Washington Press, 1961.

Hsu, Kai-Yu. *Chou En-lai: China's Gray Eminence*. New York: Anchor Books, 1969.

Hsu, U. T. *The Invisible Conflict.* Hong Kong: China Viewpoints, 1958.

Hu Pu-yu. *A Brief History of the Sino–Japanese War (1937–1945).* Taipei: Chung Wu Publishing Company, 1974.

Hudson, G. F., Richard Lowenthal, and Roderick MacFarquhar. *The Sino–Soviet Dispute.* New York: Frederick A. Praeger, 1961.

Hunter, Neale. *Shanghai Journal.* Boston: Beacon Press, 1971.

Isaacs, Harold R. *The Tragedy of the Chinese Revolution.* New York: Atheneum, 1966.

Karnow, Stanley. *Mao and China: From Revolution to Revolution.* London: Macmillan, 1973.

Ken Ling. *The Revenge of Heaven.* New York: Ballantine Books, 1972.

Khrushchev, Nikita. *Khrushchev Remembers.* Boston: Little, Brown, 1970.

Klein, Donald W., and Anne B. Clark. *Biographic Dictionary of Chinese Communism, 1921–1965.* Cambridge, Mass.: Harvard University Press, 1971.

Kuo, Warren. *Analytical History of the Chinese Communist Party.* Taipei: Institute of International Relations, 1968. Kuo was an upper-level Communist cadre who defected to the Kuomintang, bringing with him a detailed knowledge of the inner history of the Party. Although in some respects superseded by later works, Kuo's book stands as a landmark study in CCP history.

Kyi Zuh-Tsing. *Tsingtao: A Historical, Political and Economic Survey.* Qingdao, China: The Catholic Mission Press, 1930.

Lee Chong-Sik. *Revolutionary Struggle in Manchuria: Chinese Communism and Soviet Interest, 1922–1945.* Berkeley: University of California Press, 1983.

Levytsky, Boris. *The Uses of Terror: The Soviet Secret Service 1917–1970.* London: Sidgwick and Jackson, 1971.

Leys, Simon. *The Chairman's New Clothes.* London: Allison and Busby, 1977.

Lifton, Robert Jay. *Thought Reform and the Psychology of Totalism.* New York: W. W. Norton, 1963.

Lin Yutang. *The Secret Name.* New York: Farrar, Straus and Cudahy, 1958.

MacFarquhar, Roderick. *The Origins of the Cultural Revolution* [vol.] *1: Contradictions Among the People 1956–1957.* London: Oxford University Press, 1974.

———. *The Origins of the Cultural Revolution* [vol.] *2: The Great Leap Forward 1958–1960.* New York: Columbia University Press, 1983.

MacFarquhar, Roderick, Timothy Cheek, and Eugene Wu. *The Secret Speeches of Chairman Mao.* Cambridge, Mass.: Harvard University Press, 1989.

Mao Tse-tung (Mao Zedong). *Selected Works of Mao Tse-tung.* Peking: Foreign Languages Press, 1969.

Merwin, Samuel. *Drugging a Nation.* New York: Fleming H. Revell Company, 1908.

Milton, David, Nancy Milton, and Franz Schurman. *People's China.* New York: Vintage Books, 1974.

Milton, David, and Nancy Dall Milton. *The Wind Will Not Subside: Years in Revolutionary China, 1964–69.* New York: Pantheon Books, 1976.

Pal, John. *Shanghai Saga.* London: Jarrolds Publishers, 1963.

Pan Ling. *In Search of Old Shanghai.* Hong Kong: Joint Publishing Co., 1982.

———. *Old Shanghai: Gangsters in Paradise.* Hong Kong: Heinemann Educational Books, 1984.

Pasqualini, Jean, and Rudolph Chelminski. *Prisoner of Mao.* Middlesex: Penguin Books, 1976.

Petrov, Vladimir, and Evdokia Petrov. *Empire of Fear.* New York: Frederick A. Praeger, 1956.

Powell, John B. *My Twenty-five Years in China.* New York: Macmillan, 1945.

Ravines, Eudocio. *The Yenan Way.* New York: Charles Scribner's Sons, 1951.

Salisbury, Harrison E. *The Long March: The Untold Story.* London: Macmillan London Limited, 1985.

Schram, Stuart, ed. *Chairman Mao Talks to the People.* New York: Pantheon Books, 1974.

Schram, Stuart. *Mao Tse-tung.* Middlesex: Penguin Books, 1967.

Schwartz, Harry. *Tsars, Mandarins and Commissars*. New York: Anchor Books, 1973.

Selden, Mark. *The Yenan Way in Revolutionary China*. Cambridge, Mass.: Harvard University Press, 1971.

Serge, Victor. *Memoirs of a Revolutionary 1901–1941*. London: Oxford University Press, 1963.

Shen Zui. *A KMT War Criminal in New China*. Peking: Foreign Languages Press, 1986.

Sheng, Yueh. *Sun Yat-sen University in Moscow and the Chinese Revolution*. N.p.: University of Kansas, 1971.

Smedley, Agnes. *The Great Road: The Life and Times of Chu Teh*. New York: Modern Reader, 1956.

Snow, Edgar. *Red Star over China*. Middlesex: Penguin Books, 1972. Snow's portrait of Mao, the seminal source for almost every study of Mao's early years, also contains interesting biographical notes about other important CCP leaders.

————. *Random Notes on Red China (1936–1945)*. Cambridge, Mass.: Harvard University Press, 1957.

Snow, Helen Foster. *Inside Red China*. New York: Doubleday, 1939.

Spence, Jonathan. *To Change China: Western Advisers in China 1620–1960*. New York: Penguin Books, 1980.

Sues, Ilona Ralf. *Shark's Fins and Millet*. Boston: Little, Brown, 1944.

Sworakowski, Witold S. *World Communism: A Handbook 1918–1965*. Stanford, Calif.: Hoover Institution Press, 1973.

T'ang Leang-li, ed. *Suppressing Communist Banditry in China*. Shanghai: China United Press, 1934. This book contains a detailed description, from the Kuomintang perspective, of Communist espionage and subversion in Shanghai.

Teiwes, Frederick C. *Politics and Purges in China*. White Plains, N.Y.: M. E. Sharpe, 1979.

Terrill, Ross. *Mao*. New York: Harper & Row, 1980.

————. *The White-Boned Demon: A Biography of Madame Mao Zedong*. New York: William Morrow and Company, 1984.

Thornton, Richard C. *The Comintern and the Chinese Communists, 1928–1931*. Seattle: University of Washington Press, 1969.

Vladimirov, Peter. *The Vladimirov Diaries*. New York: Doubleday and Company, 1975. Originally published in Moscow in 1973. Released at the height of the Sino–Soviet split, Vladimirov's *Diaries* still provoke controversy, and commentators have questioned their authenticity. Some passages, including his rather simplistic analysis of the factions in Yan'an, seem exaggerated, but his comments on Kang Sheng are largely supported by other evidence and can be taken at face value. Vladimirov's outspoken criticism of Kang reflects the Soviets' general hostility toward him at the time the *Diaries* were published, and presumably long before. According to a February 28, 1990, letter to the authors from a senior Soviet specialist on China, Dr. Lev P. Delyusin of the Institute of Oriental Studies, Vladimirov's *Diaries* were compiled by his son using notes Vladimirov left behind at his death and the comments of other Soviet citizens who were in Yan'an in the mid-1940s.

Wang Fan-Hsi. *Chinese Revolutionary*. Oxford: Oxford University Press, 1980.

Who's Who in Communist China. Hong Kong: Union Research Institute, 1969–70.

Wilhelm, Richard (1873–1930) German missionary-scholar who founded the Qingdao School, where Kang studies from 1914 until 1917. Wilhelm translated the *I Ching* into German, introducing European intellectuals like C. G. Jung to Chinese thought. An avid defender of the old China, he sheltered some of the high officials displaced by the 1911 revolution at his school; Kang later boasted that as a student he had been friendly with courtiers of the last dynasty. Wilhelm served as cultural attaché at the German legation in Peking in 1922 before returning to Germany and establishing the academic review *Sinica*.

Willoughby, Charles A. *Shanghai Conspiracy: The Sorge Spy Ring*. New York: E. P. Dutton & Company, 1952.

Wilson, Dick. *Mao: The People's Emperor*. London: Futura Publications, 1980.

———. *When Tigers Fight*. New York: Viking Press, 1982.

Wise, David, and Thomas B. Ross. *The Espionage Establishment*. New York: Random House, 1967.

Witke, Roxane. *Comrade Chiang Ch'ing*. Boston: Little, Brown, 1977.

Yang, Martin C. *A Chinese Village*. New York: Columbia University Press, 1945.

Yao Ming-le. *The Conspiracy and Death of Lin Biao*. New York: Alfred A. Knopf, 1983. Purporting to be written by a Chinese official investigating the

Lin Biao affair, this book contains much accurate detail about the personalities and elite organizations of PRC politics. Its account of Lin Biao's death, however, contradicts completely the official Chinese version of those events. It also conflicts with information given to the authors by Chinese who had direct knowledge of the Lin Biao case.

Yue Daiyun and Carolyn Wakeman. *To the Storm.* Berkeley: University of California Press, 1985.

Zagoria, Donald S. *The Sino–Soviet Conflict.* Princeton, N.J.: Princeton University Press, 1962.

MAGAZINE AND NEWSPAPER
ARTICLES IN ENGLISH*

Bhatia, Prem. "With Mr. Nehru in China—IV: Close-ups of Top Leaders and Lamas." *The Statesman* (Calcutta), November 8, 1954.

Billingham, Anthony. "In China a Red Army Plays a Shrewd Political Game." *The New York Times Magazine,* June 6, 1937.

Butterfield, Fox. "Kang Sheng Dies in Peking at 76." *The New York Times,* December 17, 1975, p. 48.

———. "Peking Indictment Accuses Radicals of Killing 34,000." *The New York Times,* November 17, 1980.

Chang, Parris H. "The Rise of Wang Tung-hsing: Head of China's Security Apparatus." *The China Quarterly,* no. 73, March 1978, pp. 122–137.

"Chiang Kai-Shek's Son Writes About His 'Cur of a Father.'" *The Daily Worker,* July 17, 1936.

"Chiang's Shanghai Aide: World Racketeer No. 1." *The Daily Worker,* December 9, 1945.

"China Red Leader Purged by Party; Commits Suicide." *The New York Times,* April 5, 1955.

"Chinese Defector Reportedly Named Spy." The *Los Angeles Times,* September 5, 1986.

"Chinese Reds Firm for a Revolution." *The New York Times,* January 23, 1938.

* The authors found some of the articles cited here as clippings in collections at the U.S. National Archives. Page numbers are not given in those cases.

"Chinese Reds Give Special Attention to India; Snub Tito." *The New York Times*, June 12, 1950.

"Communist Cave-Dwellers." *The Illustrated Weekly of India*, September 21, 1947.

Deng Xiaoping. "Speech on Rehabilitation of Liu Shaoqi." *Issues and Studies*, Taipei, October 1980, pp. 79–82.

Durdin, F. Tillman. "Red Hornets of China Sting the Nipponese." *The New York Times Magazine*, April 17, 1938.

"From Jail to Minister of Justice." *The Daily Worker*, January 20, 1953.

Goldman, Merle. "China's Anti-Confucian Campaign 1973–74." *The China Quarterly*, no. 62, September 1975, pp. 435–462.

Hailey, Foster. "With the Chinese Communists." *The New York Times Magazine*, December 22, 1946.

Hood, Marlowe. "Deng's Days of Darkness." *South China Morning Post*, March 26, 1988, p. 1.

Kang Sheng. "The Development of the Revolutionary Movement in Non-Soviet China and the Work of the Communist Party." *China's Present Situation and the Mission of the Communist Party.* Moscow: International Workers Press, 1934, pp. 93–127.

La Plante, Eve. "The Riddle of TLE." *The Atlantic*, November 1988, pp. 30–35.

"Li [Lisan], China's Top 'Quisling.'" *The National Republic*, February 1951.

Li Ying. "Kang Sheng Is a Demon Not a Human Being." *Issues and Studies*, Taipei, October 1980, pp. 83–89.

"Loyalty Oath Taken by 8th Route Army." *The Daily Worker*, March 22, 1938.

"Mao May Wreck Fragile Structure of Peace." *The Statesman* (Calcutta), November 10, 1950.

"Marriage Law [of the People's Republic of China]." *The Daily Worker*, June 11, 1950.

"Real Rulers of Red China Hold Powers of War or Peace." *The Washington Star* (Associated Press), December 3, 1950.

"Shark's Fins and Millet." *The Daily Worker*, February 13, 1944.

"Son Repudiates Chiang Kai-Shek." *The New York Times*, February 12, 1936.

Strong, Tracy B., and Helene Keyssar. "Anna Louise Strong: Three Interviews with Mao Zedong." *The China Quarterly*, no. 103, September 1985, pp. 489–509.

Sullivan, Lawrence R. "Reconstruction and Rectification of the Communist Party in the Shanghai Underground: 1931–34." *The China Quarterly*, no. 101, March 1985, pp. 78–97.

Teiwes, Frederick C. "Mao and His Lieutenants." *The Australian Journal of Chinese Affairs*, nos. 19 and 20, January and July 1988, pp. 1–80.

"Tell of Writers Kidnapped, Shot, Beheaded." *The Daily Worker*, November 23, 1931.

"This Is Mao Tse-Tung, China Communist Chief," *PM*, September 2, 1945.

Wakeman, Frederick J. "Policing Modern Shanghai." *The China Quarterly*, no. 115, September 1988, pp. 408–440.

Wang, Shih-Hsiang. "Two Heroes of Fighting China." *The Daily Worker*, January 9, 1938.

Yang, Benjamin. "Complexity and Reasonability: Reassessment of the Li Lisan Adventure." *The Australian Journal of Chinese Affairs*, no. 21, January 1989, pp. 111–141.

———. "The Zunyi Conference as one step in Mao's rise to power: a survey of historical studies of the Chinese Communist Party." *The China Quarterly*, no. 106, June 1986, pp. 235–271.

"Yao Yongzhan: A Year in a Chinese Jail." *News from Asia Watch*, September 1, 1990, pp. 1–9.

"Yenan, China: New Concept in Living." *The Washington Post*, September 30, 1945.

"You'll Hear More About Red China's Big Six." *The Washington Daily News*, March 13, 1947.

Yurkevich, A. "The Huangpu Military School and the Chinese Revolution." *Far Eastern Affairs*, no. 4, 1985, pp. 99–107.

Zhelokhovtsev, A. "Deng Tuo's Posthumous Fate." *Far Eastern Affairs*, no. 4, 1985, pp. 83–91.

BOOKS IN CHINESE

Chen Kewei, ed. *The Tragedy of High-Level Chinese Communist Cadres* (Zhonggong Gaoji Ganbude Beiju). Taipei: Liming Cultural Enterprise Company, 1980.

Chen Suimin. *Mao Zedong and Jiang Qing* (Mao Zedong yu Jiang Qing). Taipei: New Asia Publishing Company, 1976.

Chinese Academy of Social Sciences, Institute of Contemporary History. *Biographical Dictionary of Foreigners in Contemporary China* (Jindai Laihua Waiguo Renming Cidian). Peking: Chinese Social Sciences Publishing Company, 1981.

Chinese Academy of Social Sciences, Institute of Contemporary History. *Contemporary Chinese Personalities*, vol. 3. (Jindai Zhongguo Renwu, Disanji). Chongqing: Chongqing Publishing Company, 1986.

Compilation of Important Communist Bandit Personalities (Gongfei Zhongyao Renwu Huibian). Taipei: Ministry of Internal Affairs, 1950.

Gao Gezhi, ed. *Records of History's Inside Stories* (Lishi Neimu Jishi). Lanzhou: Gansu People's Publishing Company, 1988.

The Great Conspirator: Kang Sheng (Da Yinmoujia Kang Sheng). Hong Kong: Mingren Congkan Company, 1979.

Han Shanbi. *A Critical Biography of Deng Xiaoping* (Deng Xiaoping Pingzhuan), 5th ed. Hong Kong: East West Culture Publishing Company, 1986.

Huang Meizhen, Jiang Yihua, and Shi Yuanhua. *Number 76: The Special Service Headquarters of the Puppet Wang Regime* (Wang Wei 'Qishiliu Hao' Tegong Zongbu). Shanghai: People's Publishing Company, 1984.

Investigation Section, KMT Organization Department, ed. *Insight into the Chinese Communist Party* (Zhongguo Gongchandang Zhi Toushi). Taipei: Wen Xing Book Shop, 1962.

Jiang Qinfeng. *Around Chairman Mao* (Zai Maozhuxi Zhouwei). Peking: China Youth Publishing Company, 1958.

Jing Fuzi, *Mao Zedong and His Women* (Mao Zedong he Tade Nürenmen). Taibei: Lianjing Publishing Company, 1990.

Li Ang. *The Red Stage* (Hongse Wutai). Chongqing: Minzhong Book Shop, 1942. Li Ang was the pseudonym of Zhu Qihua.

Li Gucheng. *The Highest Level of Chinese Communist Leaders* (Zhonggong Zuigao Lingdaoceng). Hong Kong: Ming Bao Publishing Company, 1988.

Liao Gailong, ed. *The Enlarged Dictionary of Chinese Communist Party History—Personalities*, vol. 1 (Zhongguo Gongchandang Lishi Dacidian—Renwu Fence, Diyijuan). Peking: Central Party School Publishing Company, 1988.

Lin Qingshan. *A Casual History of Kang Sheng* (Kang Sheng Waizhuan). Hong Kong: Xingchen Publishing Company, 1987; Peking: China Youth Publishing Company, 1988.

————. *Persecution Mania* (Pohai Kuang). Tianjin: Hundred Flowers Cultural Publishing Company, 1989.

Ma Yuansheng. *A Chronicle of My Soviet Travels* (Lu Su Jishi). Peking: The Masses Publishing Company, 1987.

Mu Xin. *Comrade Chen Geng in Shanghai* (Chen Geng Tongzhi Zai Shanghai). Peking: Cultural and Historical Materials Publishing Company, 1982.

————. *General Chen Geng* (Chen Geng Dajiang). Peking: New China Publishing Company, 1985.

Nan Zhi. *An Informal History of Ye Qun* (Ye Qun Yeshi). Hong Kong: Mirror Post Cultural Enterprises, 1985.

Qiu Zhizhuo. *Biographical Dictionary of Chinese Communist Party History* (Zhonggong Dangshi Renming Lu). Chongqing: Chongqing Publishing Company, 1986.

Ren Jian. *The Death of the Head of State of the Republic* (Gongheguo Yuanshou Zhi Si). Hong Kong: Haiming Cultural Enterprise Company, n.d.

Shen Zui. *Inside the Military Statistics Bureau* (Wo Suo Zhidaode Juntong Neimu). Hong Kong: Zhongyuan Publishing Company, 1985.

Shen Zui and Wen Qiang. *Dai Li: The Man* (Dai Li Qiren). Peking: Cultural and Historical Materials, Publishing Company, 1984.

Sima Buping. *Wang Hongwen and the Shanghai Gang* (Wang Hongwen yu Shanghai Bang). Hong Kong: Wenyi Book Shop, 1978.

Tang Liangchun. *A Biography of Li Lisan* (Li Lisan Zhuan). Harbin: Heilongjiang Publishing Company, 1984.

Wang Ming. *Fifty Years of Chinese Communism* (Zhonggong Wushi Nian). Peking: Contemporary Historical Material Company, 1981. Wang Ming's book was originally translated from Russian and published in China as a *neibu* ("internal document") that foreigners were not permitted to see. According to the foreword, it was published in China "to serve as a reference for senior leaders and relevant departments." Many of Wang's claims are grossly exaggerated, but his book remains an authentic statement of the views of one of Mao's most important rivals for supremacy within the CCP. As a source of historical fact, Wang's writings are perhaps only slightly less reliable than Mao's, many of which have undergone major modifications.

Wang Taidong. *A Casual History of Chen Bulei* (Chen Bulei Waishi). Peking: Chinese Cultural and Historical Publishing Company, 1987.

Wei Wei and Qian Xiaohui. *A Biography of Deng Zhongxia* (Deng Zhongxia Zhuan). Peking: People's Publishing Company, 1981.

Who's Who in Communist China (Zhonggong Renming Lu). Taipei: Institute of International Relations, 1983.

Xi Ersi. *Jiang Qing and the Mainland Artistic World* (Jiang Qing yu Dalu Wenyijie). Hong Kong: Ming Bao Monthly Press, 1981.

Yang Zhongmei. *The Zunyi Meeting and the Yan'an Rectification Movement* (Zunyi Huiyi Yu Yan'an Zhengfeng). Hong Kong: Benma Publishing Company, 1989.

Ye Hongsheng. *Kang Sheng; Jiang Qing: The Thief and the Prostitute* (Kang Sheng; Jiang Qing: Nandao Nuchang). Hong Kong: Straits Cultural Publishing Company, n.d.

Ye Yonglie. *The Rise and Fall of Zhang Chunqiao* (Zhang Chunqiao Fuchen Lu). Hong Kong: South China Press, 1989. Ye Yonglie, a Shanghai-based investigative journalist and writer, has written extensively about the inner politics of the Cultural Revolution. His writing is distinguished by first-hand research, including interviews with Chen Boda, Wang Li, and other Cultural Revolution leaders released from jail.

———. *Yao Pengzi and Yao Wenyuan* (Yao Pengzi yu Yao Wenyuan). Hong Kong: Joint Publishing Company, 1989.

Yu Ruxin. *Dictionary of Chinese Communist Current Affairs Usage* (Zhonggong Shishi Ciyu). Hong Kong: Keenwitted Publications, 1989.

Zhang Yunsheng. *The Memoirs of Lin Biao's Secretary* (Lin Biao Mishu Huiyilu). Hong Kong: Cunzhen Publishing Company, 1988.

Zheng Xuejia. *The So-called Trotskyite Traitor Affair* (Suowei 'Tuopai Hanjian' Shijian). Taipei: Society for Research into Problems of International Communism, n.d.

"Zhongkan." *A Critical Biography of Kang Sheng* (Kang Sheng Pingzhuan). Peking: Red Flag Publishing Company, 1982.

Zhou Yurui. *Personalities of the Red Dynasty* (Hong Chao Renwu Zhi). New York: The World Journal, 1976.

Zhu Shan. *The Secret Story of Jiang Qing* (Jiang Qing Mizhuan). Hong Kong: Constellation Publishing Company, 1987. An account of the dark side of Jiang Qing's life by Zhu Zhongli, the widow of Wang Jiaxiang. Zhu Zhangli used the pseudonym Zhu Shan.

MAGAZINE AND NEWSPAPER
ARTICLES IN CHINESE

Chen Qizhang and Jin Shi. "The Seemingly Loyal Traitor" (Da Jian Si Zhong). *Secret History of Cultural Revolution* (Wenge Mishi), no. 1. Hong Kong: Institute of International Political Research, 1986, pp. 185–196.

Chen Xiuliang. "Pan Hannian" (Pan Hannian). *Biographies from Chinese Communist Party History* (Zhonggong Dangshi Renwu Zhuan), vol. 25. Xian: People's Publishing Company, 1985, pp. 24–51.

Chen Yangshan. "Concerning the Central Special Section" (Guanyu Zhong-yang Teke). *Party Historical Material* (Dangshi Ziliao Congkan), no. 2. Shanghai: People's Publishing Company, 1981, pp. 4–17.

Cheng Yongyan. "Remembering Shanghai University" (Huiyi Shanghai Daxue). *Party Historical Material* (Dangshi Ziliao Congkan), no. 2, Shang-hai: People's Publishing Company, 1980, pp. 80–88.

Dai Huizhen. "Wang Jiaxiang" (Wang Jiaxiang). *Biographies from Chinese Communist Party History* (Zhonggong Dangshi Renwu Zhuan), vol. 33, Xian: People's Publishing Company, 1987, pp. 1–55.

Dai Qing. "Wang Shiwei and 'The Wild Lily' " (Wang Shiwei yu Ye Baihe-hua). *Liang Shuming, Wang Shiwei, Chu Anping*, Nanking: Jiangsu Literary Publishing Company, 1989, pp. 41–110.

———. "Chu Anping and 'The Party's World,' " (Chu Anping yu Dang Tianxia). *Liang Shuming, Wang Shiwei, Chu Anping*, Nanking: Jiangesu Literary Publishing Company, 1989, pp. 113–238.

Du Feng. "Kang Sheng and Mao Zedong" (Kang Sheng yu Mao Zedong). *Zheng Ming*, August 1, 1980, pp. 42–47.

Fang Jing. "Concerning the Purge of Kang Sheng and 'De-Maoization' " (Dui Kang Sheng de Qingsuan yu 'FeiMaohua'). *Research into Chinese Communism* (Zhonggong Yanjiu), vol. 14, no. 9, September 15, 1980, pp. 41–50.

Feng Jianwei. "A Record of Comrades Lu Dingyi and Kang Sheng Inspecting Taiyuan's Schools of Higher Education" (Lu Dingyi, Kang Sheng Tongzhi Canguan Taiyuan Gaodeng Xuexiao Ji). *China Youth* (Zhongguo Qingnian), no. 20, 1958, pp. 10–11.

Hong Yangsheng. "The Working Conditions of the Number One Cell of the Central Special Section" (Zhongyang Teke Yike de Gongzuo Qingkuang). *Party Historical Material* (Dangshi Ziliao Congkan), no. 2, Shanghai: People's Publishing Company, 1981, pp. 18–23.

Hu Ruquan. "Criticizing Kang Sheng's 'New Philosophy' " (Ping Kang Sheng de 'Xin Zhexue'). *Guangming Daily*, December 18, 1980, p. 4.

Hu Yaobang. "Problems Concerning the Purge of Kang Sheng" (Guanyu Qingsuan Kang Sheng Wenti). *Chinese Monthly* (Zhongguoren Yuekan), vol. II, no. 4, Hong Kong, May 1980, pp. 15–25.

Hua Yang. "Kang Sheng, King of Hell—Mao Zedong's Counselor" (Yan Wang Kang Sheng—Mao Zedong de Junshi). *Research into Chinese Communism* (Zhonggong Yanjiu), vol. 16, no. 4, April 15, 1982, pp. 50–60; vol. 16, no. 5, May 15, 1982, pp. 53–61.

Huang Liwen. "Some of the Circumstances of the Jiangsu Party Committee and the Zhabei District Committee in 1930." *Party Historical Material* (Dangshi Ziliao Congkan), no. 3, Shanghai: People's Publishing Company, 1981, pp. 18–28.

Huang Meizhen, Zhang Yun, and Shi Yuanhua. "Shanghai University: A New Revolutionary School" (Shanghai Daxue—Yisuo Xinying de Geming Xuexiao). *Party Historical Material* (Dangshi Ziliao Congkan), no. 2, Shanghai: People's Publishing Company, 1980, pp. 152–167.

"The Internal Resolution of the Chinese Communist Party Rehabilitating Liu Shaoqi" (Zhonggong Dangnei Wei Liu Shaoqi Pingfan de Jueyi). *Ming Bao*, no. 175, Hong Kong, July 1980, pp. 18–25.

Kang Sheng. "Recollections of the Third Workers Uprising in Shanghai" (Shanghai Gongren Sanci Qiyide Huiyi). *The Salvation Times* (Jiuguo Shibao), Paris, March 21, 1937, p. 3.

———. "Root Out the Japanese Spies and Public Enemies of the Nation, the Trotskyite Bandits" (Chanchu Rikou Zhentan Minzu Gongdide Tuolociji Feitu). Originally published in *Liberation* (Jiefang), nos. 29, 30, 1938, and reproduced in *The Trotskyite Party in China* (Tuopai Zai Zhongguo), n.p.: New China Publishing Company, 1939, pp. 41–80.

———. "Yugoslav Revisionism Just Fits the Needs of the American Imperialists" (Nansilafu de Xiuzhengzhuyi Qiaqia Shihe Meidiguozhuyizhe de Xuyao). *The People's Daily*, June 14, 1958, p. 5.

———. "Communist Party Members Should Be Marxist–Leninists, Not Party Fellow-Travelers" (Gongchandangyuan Yingdang Shi Makesi Lieningzhuyizhe, Bu Yingdang Shi Dang de Tongluren). *Red Flag*, no. 19, 1959, pp. 51–55.

Li Hong. "The Death of the Former Public Security Minister Li Zhen" (Qian Gonganbuzhang Li Zhen zhi Si). *Zheng Ming*, June 1986, p. 77.

Li Qiade. "Material Factors and Mental Illness" (Wuli Yinsu yu Jingshenbing). *The Perspective* (Nanbeiji), January 16, 1988, pp. 32–33.

Lin Qingshan. "Fear and Trembling When Kang Sheng Was at the Peak of His Power" (Kang Sheng Dingsheng Shiqi de Zhanli). *The New Observer* (Xin Guancha), no. 382, July 25, 1986, pp. 29–32; no. 383, August 10, 1986, pp. 30–32; no. 384, August 25, 1986, pp. 30–32; no. 385, September 10, 1986, pp. 30–32.

Liu Ying. "Kang Sheng's Wife and the Others Outside the Court, Wang Li, Guan Feng, and Qi Benyu" (Fatingwai de Kang Sheng Laopo yu Wang Guan Qi). *Zheng Ming*, December 1980, pp. 19–20.

Ma Zhongyang. "Kang Sheng's Theory of 'Development' and Modern Superstition" (Kang Sheng de 'Fazhan' yu Xiandai Mixin). *Red Flag*, no. 18, 1980, pp. 23–27, 48.

Maomao. "Our Days in Jiangxi" (Zai Jiangxi de Rizili). *The People's Daily*, August 20, 1984, p. 4. "Maomao" is the nickname of Deng Xiaoping's youngest daughter.

Mu Fu. "Another Zhou Enlai" (Ling Yige Zhou Enlai). *Zheng Ming*, January 1986, pp. 17–21.

Qi Zhenhai and Xu Hongwu. "Theorist or Political Fraud?" (Shi Lilunjia Haishi Zhengzhi Pianzi?). *Red Flag*, no. 16, 1980, pp. 28–32, 39.

"Resolution on the Rehabilitation of Comrade Lin Shaoqi Passed by the Fifth Plenum of the Eleventh Central Committee" (Zhongguo Gongchandang Dishiyijie Zhongyang Weiyuanhui Diwuci Quantihuiyi Guanyu Wei Liu Shaoqi Tongzhi Pingfan de Jueyi). *Ming Bao*, no. 175, July 1980, pp. 18–25.

Su Qiying. "Ai Siqi" (Ai Siqi). *Biographies from Chinese Communist Party History* (Zhonggong Dangshi Renwu Zhuan), no. 21, Xian: People's Publishing Company, 1985, pp. 225–247.

Su Shuangbi and Wang Hongzhi. "Wu Han" (Wu Han). *Biographies from Chinese Communist Party History* (Zhonggong Dangshi Renwu Zhuan), vol. 7, Xian: People's Publishing Company, 1983, pp. 244–295.

"The True Account of Lin Biao's Coup d'Etat" (Lin Biao Zhengbian Shilu). Li Guoqiang, ed., *Contemporary Chinese Personalities* (Zhongguo Dangdai Mingren Lu), no. 8, Hong Kong: Wide Angle Press, 1988, pp. 80–111.

Wu Guifang. "The Eastern Hotel and the Twenty-three Martyrs" (Dongfang Lushe yu Ershisan Lieshi). *Party Historical Material* (Dangshi Ziliao Congkan), no. 1, Shanghai: People's Publishing Company, 1979, pp. 159–161.

Xin Wen. "The Exposure of Mao Zedong's Lover, Zhang Yufeng" (Mao Zedong Qingren Zhang Yufeng Puguang). *Zheng Ming*, July 1988, pp. 14–15.

Xu Meikun. "Recalling Some of the Circumstances of the Third Workers Armed Uprising" (Huiyi Shanghai Gongren Sanci Wuzhuang Qiyi de Yixie Qingkuang). *Party Historical Material* (Dangshi Ziliao Congkan), no. 3, Shanghai: People's Publishing Company, 1981, pp. 91–94.

Yang Shangkun. "In Memory of Comrade Li Kenong's Ninetieth Birthday" (Jinian Li Kenong Tongzhi Danchen Jiushi Zhounian). *The People's Daily*, September 14, 1989, p. 6.

Yang Shilan, Lu Yongdi, and Li Huzi. "Deng Fa" (Deng Fa). *Biographies from Chinese Communist Party History* (Zhonggong Dangshi Renwu Zhuan), vol. 1, Xian: People's Publishing Company, 1980, pp. 347–381.

Yang Zhihua. "In Memory of Qu Qiubai" (Yi Qiubai). *Red Flags Waving* (Hongqi Piaopiao), no. viii, Peking, 1958, pp. 24–56.

Ye Bingnan. "Qian Zhuangfei" (Qian Zhuangfei). *Biographies from Chinese Communist Party History* (Zhonggong Dangshi Renwu Zhuan), vol. 34, Xian: People's Publishing Company, 1987, pp. 103–126.

Ye Yonglie. "The Recently Deceased Chen Boda" (Zuijin Bingside Chen Boda). *The New Garden* (Xin Yuan), no. 2, 1990, pp. 22–58. This article is based on extensive interviews with Chen Boda after his release from prison. It contains new material about Chen's role in the Cultural Revolution.

You Liang and Zhang Xiangen. "Some Historical Material Concerning the Twenty-four Martyrs" (Guanyu Longhua Ershisi Lieshide Yixie Shiliao). *Party Historical Material* (Dangshi Ziliao Congkan), no. 2, Shanghai: People's Publishing Company, 1980, pp. 175–179.

Yu Chengsi. "Kang Sheng's Slander Against Chen Duxiu" (Kang Sheng Dui Chen Duxiu de Wuxian). *Zheng Ming*, August 1980, pp. 48–49.

Yu Jundao. "Concerning Mif" (Guanyu Mif). *Party Historical Research Material* (Dangshi Yanjiu Ziliao), no. 3, Shanghai: People's Publishing Company, 1981, pp. 554–561.

Yu Ming. "Kang Sheng and Jiang Qing" (Kang Sheng yu Jiang Qing). *The New Observer* (Xin Guancha), no. 249, January 10, 1981, pp. 34–36; no. 250, January 25, 1981, pp. 34–36; no. 251, February 10, 1981, pp. 35–36.

Zhang Yijin. "Nanking Massacre: An Historical Fact That Brooks No Denial." *The People's Daily*, November 18, 1990.

Zheng Chaolin. "The New Edition of Mao's Works and the Unjust Case of the Trotskyite Faction" (Xinban Maoxuan Yu Tuopai Yuanàn). *Kaifang*, September 1991, pp. 47–49.

Zhou Binli. "Exonerating Liu Shaoqi and Exposing Kang Sheng" (Zhaoxue Liu Shaoqi yu Jiefa Kang Sheng). *Zheng Ming*, January 1980, p. 21.

Zhou Gu. "The Communist Agents Who Penetrated the Heart of the Kuomintang Sixty Years Ago" (Liushi Nian Qian Qianfu Zai Guomindang Xinzangzhong de Gongdie). *Biographical Literature* (Zhuanji Wenxue), vol. 65, no. 1, Taipei, January 1990, pp. 94–102; vol. 65, no. 2, January 1990, pp. 91–96.

Zhou Guojin and Guo Dehong. "A Simple chronology of Wang Ming" (Wang Ming Nianpu Jianbian). Chinese Academy of Sciences, Institute of Contempory History, ed., *Contemporary Chinese Personalities* (Jindai Zhongguo Renwu), vol. 3, Chongqing: Chongqing Publishing Company, 1986, pp. 471–503.

Zhou Xun. "Deng Xiaoping Before and After 'the Criticism of Deng' " ('Pideng' Qianhoude Deng Xiaoping). *Deng Xiaoping* (Deng Xiaoping), Hong Kong: Wide Angle Publishing Company, 1983, pp. 69–115.

U.S. GOVERNMENT RECORDS

CENTRAL INTELLIGENCE AGENCY

Jan. 13, 1948, *The Succession of Power in the USSR.*
Undated, mid-1948, *The Current Situation in China.*
Nov. 3, 1948, *Possible Developments in China.*

DEPARTMENT OF STATE

China Since the Revolution of 1911, February 1926.
Despatch no. 4062 from G. C. Hanson, American Consul, Harbin, February 16, 1927, *Biography of Jacob Borodin, Adviser to Cantonese Regime.*
Despatch no. 4514 from F. W. B. Coleman, U.S. Legation, Riga, Latvia, May 19, 1927, *Pravda Report on the Congress of the Chinese Communist Party at Hankow.*

Despatch no. 1220 from Richard M. Tobin, U.S. Legation, The Hague, Netherlands, July 21, 1927, *Jacob Borodin Hiding in Shanghai*.

Despatch no. 4623 from F. W. B. Coleman, U.S. Legation, Riga, Latvia, July 26, 1927, *Recent Changes in the Chinese Situation*.

Despatch no. 4955 from Edwin S. Cunningham, U.S. Consul General, Shanghai, September 9, 1927, *Nationalist Success over Sun Ch'uan-Fang. Communism and Communists*.

Despatch no. 4996 from Edwin S. Cunningham, U.S. Consul General, Shanghai, October 1, 1927, *Soviet Agents*.

Despatch no. 1223 from C. E. Gauss, U.S. Consul General, Tianjin, February 16, 1928, *A History of Communism in China*.

Telegram from J. V. A. MacMurray, U.S. Legation, Peking, May 3, 1928, *The Soviets Have Sent Jacob Borodin Back to China*.

Report from Edwin S. Cunningham, U.S. Consul General, Shanghai, May 15, 1928, *Labor, Student and Agitator Movements at Shanghai During April 1928*.

Despatch no. 1730 from J. V. A. MacMurray, U.S. Legation, Peking, October 31, 1928, *Account of a Pro-Communist Uprising in Shanghai*.

Despatch no. 5871 from Edwin S. Cunningham, U.S. Consul General, Shanghai, December 21, 1928, *The Communist Party in China*.

Telegram from Edwin S. Cunningham, U.S. Consul General, Shanghai, May 31, 1929; May 30th passed in Shanghai without serious disturbances.

Telegram from J. V. A. MacMurray, U.S. Legation, Peking, July 27, 1929; Chinese Communists attempted to stage a demonstration in front of the Soviet consulate.

Despatch from Louis Sussdorff, Jr., Chargé d'Affaires, U.S. Legation, Riga, Latvia, August 19, 1929, *Report on the Tenth Session of the Full Executive Committee of the Communist International at Moscow in July*.

Telegram from Gray, U.S. diplomat, Peking, December 14, 1929; Shanghai power company requests an American destroyer to protect it from extensive Communist agitation in Shanghai.

Despatch no. 491 from Coert du Bois, U.S. Consul General, Batavia, Java, December 24, 1929, *Confidential Report on Communist Activities in the Orient*.

Despatch no. 6760 from Edwin S. Cunningham, U.S. Consul General, Shanghai, February 19, 1930, *Communistic Organizations in Shanghai*.

Despatch no. 6799 from Edwin S. Cunningham, U.S. Consul General, Shanghai, March 13, 1930, *Political Conditions in the Shanghai Consular District During the Month of February 1930*.

Despatch no. 6870 from Edwin S. Cunningham, U.S. Consul General, Shanghai, April 17, 1930, *Growth of Communism*.

Despatch no. 6908 from Edwin S. Cunningham, U.S. Consul General, Shanghai, May 5, 1930, *Political Conditions in the Shanghai Consular District During the Month of April 1930.*

Despatch from Coert du Bois, U.S. Consul General, Batavia, Java, May 6, 1930, *Communistic Activities in the Orient.*

Despatch no. 6919 from Edwin S. Cunningham, U.S. Consul General, Shanghai, May 12, 1930, *Activities of Communists on May 1st—Measures Taken by Police to Prevent.*

Despatch no. 7002 from F. W. B. Coleman, U.S. Legation, Riga, Latvia, May 28, 1930, *Enclosure of Article from Leningrad Pravda, "A New Rise of the Chinese Revolution," by Pavel Mif.*

Telegram no. 433 from Mahlon F. Perkins, U.S. Counselor, Peking, June 11, 1930, *Communism in Shanghai Consular District.*

Despatch no. 6979 from Edwin S. Cunningham, U.S. Consul General, Shanghai, June 11, 1930, *Communist or Red Forces in China.*

Despatch no. 323 from Myers, U.S. diplomat, Mukden, June 11, 1930, *Communist Activities in Mukden District, May 1930 (Arrest of Li Lisan).*

Despatch no. 7072 from Edwin S. Cunningham, U.S. Consul General, Shanghai, August 5, 1930, *Political Conditions in the Shanghai Consular District During the Month of July 1930.*

Despatch from Coert du Bois, U.S. Consul General, Batavia, Java, September 2, 1930, *List of Persons Engaged in Subversive Activities in Shanghai Furnished Confidentially by the Head of the Secret Police in Batavia.*

Letter from Robert Morse Lovett, editor of *The New Republic*, to Joseph P. Cotton, Assistant Secretary of State, September 22, 1930; vouching for Agnes Smedley.

Despatch no. 1015 from Great Britain, February 10, 1931; Communist activities of Edgar Snow, who has associated with Agnes Smedley, an Indian [*sic*] extremist.

Despatch from K. S. Patton, U.S. Consul General, Batavia, Java, February 24, 1931, *Confidential Report on Communist Activities in the Orient.*

Despatch no. 847 from Mahlon F. Perkins, U.S. Counselor, Peking, March 10, 1931, *The Chinese Communist Party. A Sketch of the Present Situation.*

Despatch no. 7667 from Edwin S. Cunningham, U.S. Consul General, Shanghai, June 5, 1931, *Political Report for May 1931.*

Despatch no. 7789 from Edwin S. Cunningham, U.S. Consul General, Shanghai, August 4, 1931, *Monthly Political Report for July 1931.*

Despatch from F. W. B. Coleman, U.S. Legation, Riga, Latvia, August 28, 1931, *Forwarding Article Entitled "The Errors of the Chinese Communist Party, 1925–1927" by Comrade G. Voitinsky.*

Despatch from J. C. Huston, U.S. Consul, Shanghai, November 15, 1931,

Will Western Capitalism Be Willing to Save China from Chaos and Communism?

Despatch from Felix Cole, Chargé d'Affaires, Riga, Latvia, November 27, 1931, *Biographic Data on Comrade Grigory Voitinsky.*

Despatch no. 8047 from Edwin S. Cunningham, U.S. Consul General, Shanghai, December 30, 1931, *Information Regarding Alleged Communists.*

Despatch no. 8072 from Edwin S. Cunningham, U.S. Consul General, Shanghai, January 11, 1932, *Communist Activities in Shanghai During 1931.*

Despatch no. 147 from Walter A. Adams, U.S. Consul General, Hankow, May 5, 1932, *A Study of Communism in China.*

Despatch no. 8294 from Edwin S. Cunningham, U.S. Consul General, Shanghai, May 27, 1932, *China Forum,* a publication of the Searchlight Publishing Company, edited by Harold R. Isaacs. Described by Cunningham as pro-Communist and in favor of the Soviets.

Despatch from K. S. Patton, U.S. Consul General, Batavia, Java, May 31, 1932, *Transmitting Report of Communist Activities in Shanghai.*

Report from Robert F. Kelley, State Department Division of Eastern European Affairs, July 12, 1932, *The Financing of Communist Activities in the Far East.*

Despatch no. 1652 from Nelson Trusler Johnson, U.S. Legation, Peking, July 28, 1932, *Transmitting Pamphlet Entitled: "The Chinese Communist Party and the Soviet Russian Activities in Mongolia."*

Telegram no. 404 from Edwin S. Cunningham, U.S. Consul General, Shanghai, October 21, 1932, *Communistic Activities of Harold Isaacs and Agnes Smedley.*

Despatch no. D-431 from Willys R. Peck, U.S. Consul General, Nanking, January 28, 1933, *Communism: The Case of Ch'en Tu-siu.*

Despatch no. 441 from Walter A. Adams, U.S. Consul General, Hankow, April 17, 1934, *Policy of the Chinese Soviets.*

Despatch no. 9881 from Edwin S. Cunningham, U.S. Consul General, Shanghai, February 15, 1935, *Kiangsi Province: Investigation of Former Communist-Occupied Areas.*

Despatch no. 249 from F. P. Lockhart, U.S. Counselor, Peking, February 1936, *Capt. Henry S. Jernigan's Report on Chinese Communism.*

Despatch no. 144 from C. E. Gauss, U.S. Consul General, Shanghai, April 17, 1936, *Release of the Rev. R. A. Bosshardt: Communist Activities: Alleged Pact Between China and Soviet Russia.*

Despatch no. 632 from Nelson Trusler Johnson, U.S. Ambassador, Peking, August 7, 1936, *Communist Situation in Northwest China.*

Despatch no. 459 from C. E. Gauss, U.S. Consul General, Shanghai, November 3, 1936, *Anti-Japanese Policy of Chinese Communist Party.*

Memorandum from Edgar Snow, Peking, November 5, 1936; plus attached transcript of Snow's interview with Mao Tse-tung in Paoan, July 16, 1936.

Report from (unnamed) American chargé d'affaires, Moscow, December 14, 1936; on statement to him by Tsiang Ting-fu, Chinese ambassador to Moscow, *Groups into Which Chinese Communists Are Divided.*

Telegram no. 10 from C. E. Gauss, U.S. Consul General, Shanghai, January 7, 1937; situation at Xian worse than at any time during the detention of Chiang Kai-shek, according to American informant Edward Wingertee; prominent in pro-Communist radio broadcasts is an American, Agnes Smedley.

Telegram no. 12 from F. P. Lockhart, U.S. Counselor, Peking, January 8, 1937; British Embassy states that Agnes Smedley entered Mission Hospital complaining of nervous disorder several days prior to the coup but left hospital immediately following the coup and has been conducting the English (Communist) broadcasts over the Xian Radio.

Despatch no. 559 from C. E. Gauss, U.S. Consul General, Shanghai, January 11, 1937, *Movements and Activities of Agnes Smedley.*

Despatch no. 621 from C. E. Gauss, U.S. Consul General, Shanghai, January 30, 1937, *Activities of Miss Agnes Smedley.*

Despatch no. 458 from Willys R. Peck, Counselor, U.S. Embassy, Nanking, May 8, 1937, *The "Blue Shirts" Organization.*

Despatch no. 284 from Loy W. Henderson, U.S. Chargé d'Affaires ad interim, Moscow, May 12, 1937, *Moscow's Attitude Toward the Negotiations Between the Chinese Communists and Nanking.*

Despatch no. 244 from Nelson Trusler Johnson, U.S. Legation, Chongqing, June 20, 1939, *Conditions in Shansi and Shensi.*

Despatch no. 281 from Nelson Trusler Johnson, U.S. Ambassador, Nanking, July 19, 1939, *Chinese Communist Leaders Meet at Yenan.*

Despatch no. 804 from Nelson Trusler Johnson, U.S. Embassy, Chongqing, March 6, 1941, *Conditions at Yenan as Portrayed by a Foreign Observer.*

Despatch no. 3110 from Robert L. Smyth, First Secretary, U.S. Embassy, Peking, May 10, 1941, *Political Report for April 1941.*

R&A (Research & Analysis) no. 336, August 24, 1942, *General Chou En-lai's Views on the Chinese Situation.*

Despatch no. 1541 from George Atcheson Jr., U.S. Chargé d'Affaires ad interim, Chongqing, September 4, 1943, *Conditions in Communist-Controlled Areas in North China.*

Despatch no. 1591 from George Atcheson Jr., U.S. Chargé d'Affaires ad interim, Chongqing, September 18, 1943, *General Conditions in China.*

Despatch no. 2161 from John S. Service, U.S. Embassy, Chongqing, February 15, 1944, *Plot of Young Chinese Army Officers.*

Despatch no. 2171 from C. E. Gauss, U.S. Embassy, Chongqing, February 16, 1944, *Kuomintang Documents Attacking the Chinese Communist Party.*

Despatch no. 2 from Everett F. Drumright, Second Secretary on detail at Xian, March 1, 1944, *Conditions in Chinese Communist Occupied Areas of North Shensi.*

Despatch no. 2467 from C. E. Gauss, U.S. Embassy, Chongqing, April 21, 1944, *Chiang Ching-kuo: His Background and His Future.*

Enclosure to Despatch no. 2905 from Col. David D. Barrett, U.S. Army Observer Section, Yan'an, July 27, 1944, *General Report on U.S. Army Observer Section in Yenan.*

Memorandum from John S. Service, Second Secretary, U.S. Embassy, assigned to U.S. Army Observer Section at Yan'an, July 27, 1944, *Conversation with General Lin Piao.*

Report no. 2 from John S. Service, Yan'an, July 28, 1944, *Desire of Chairman of Communist Central Committee for Continued American Representation of Diplomatic Character at Yenan.*

Enclosure to Despatch no. 2813 from Robert S. Ward, U.S. Embassy, Chongqing, July 29, 1944, *The Communist Party in China.*

Enclosure no. 1 to Despatch no. 2923 from John S. Service, Yan'an, July 30, 1944, *Views of Communist Political and Military Leaders.*

Report no. 21 from John S. Service, Yan'an, September 4, 1944, *General Impression of the Chinese Communist Leaders.*

Report no. 29 from John S. Service, Yan'an, September 18, 1944, *Decision of the Chinese Communist Leaders to Use Chinese Name in Foreign Publicity.*

Memorandum no. 63 from John K. Emmerson, Second Secretary, U.S. Embassy, Chongqing, December 24, 1944, *Interviews with Chinese Communist Leaders.*

Memorandum from John Davies, U.S. Embassy, Chongqing, December 27, 1944, *Impressions of Chinese Communist Leaders.*

Memorandum apparently to General Albert C. Wedemeyer, Commanding General, U.S. forces, China theater, from Major Ray Cromley, U.S. Army Air Corps, with Dixie Mission, January 9, 1945; Mao Zedong and Zhou Enlai wish to secretly notify President Roosevelt that they are willing to meet with him at the White House if he will receive them as "leaders of a primary Chinese political party."

Memorandum apparently to General Albert C. Wedemeyer, Chongqing, from Major Ray Cromley, U.S. Army Air Corps, with Dixie Mission, January 10, 1945, *Details of Meeting with Chou Enlai.*

Letter from Chu Teh, Commander of the Chinese Communist 18th Group Army, to General Albert C. Wedemeyer, January 23, 1945; requesting

$20 million in U.S. currency to make it possible for the CCP to "destroy the puppet forces and obtain victory over the enemy."

Telegram from Patrick J. Hurley, President Roosevelt's personal representative to China, February 17, 1945, KMT–Communist Negotiations.

Report from John Davies, Jr., Second Secretary, U.S. Embassy, Tehran, February 28, 1945, *CCP Split into Two Factions*.

Memorandum from John S. Service, March 25, 1945, *Contact Between the Chinese Communists and Moscow*.

Memorandum from John S. Service, April 1, 1945, *Conversation with Mao Tsetung and Other Communist Leaders*.

Memorandum no. 168 from Edward E. Rice, Second Secretary assigned to Xian, April 7, 1945, *Methods of Disseminating Propaganda Employed by the Chinese Communists*.

Memorandum no. 209 from Edward E. Rice, Second Secretary assigned to Xian, June 5, 1945, *Allegations That High Officers in Shensi Are Engaged in Espionage for the Japanese*.

Telegram from Patrick J. Hurley, July 21, 1945; expressing surprise at arrest of John S. Service.

Telegram from W. Averell Harriman, U.S. Ambassador, Moscow, August 30, 1945; Stalin predicts KMT and CCP will reach accord; Soviet leader declares, "How stupid it would be to have two governments in China."

Memorandum no. 277 from Harry E. Stevens, Second Secretary detailed to Xian, September 10, 1945, *Alleged Differences of Opinion Among Communist Leaders*.

Memorandum from Patrick J. Hurley, September 11, 1945; observations on Chinese situation.

Letter from Walter S. Robertson, U.S. Chargé d'Affaires ad interim, Chongqing, October 17, 1945, *U.S. Intelligence Services in China*.

R&A no. 3024.1, November 23, 1945, *Economy of Communist North China, 1937–1945: Areas of Economic Control*.

Office of Research and Intelligence, Report no. 3024.5, June 15, 1946, *Economy of Communist North China, 1937–1945: Standards of Living*.

Memorandum no. 96 from John S. Service, U.S. Embassy, Nanking, September 4, 1946, *Reported Contemplated Disaffection of General Chen Yi, Commander of Communist New Fourth Army*.

Despatch no. 187 from W. Walton Butterworth, Minister-Counselor, U.S. Embassy, Nanking, September 20, 1946, *Extent of Opium Production, and Use and Enforcement of Opium Laws in China*.

Memorandum no. 455 from Moscow, October 4, 1946, *Return to China of Li Lisan*.

Memorandum no. 192 from W. Walton Butterworth, Minister-Counselor,

U.S. Embassy, Nanking, October 16, 1946, *Return of Li Lisan to Manchuria.*

Memorandum no. 231 from W. Walton Butterworth, Minister-Counselor, U.S. Embassy, Nanking, October 31, 1946, *Reported Schism in Chinese Communist Party and Connection of Li Lisan Therewith.*

Despatch no. 147 from Robert L. Smyth, U.S. Consul General, Tianjin, October 31, 1947, *Transmission of "A Study on the Chinese Communist Party by the Japanese United Research Bureau."*

Telegram from Cabot, U.S. diplomat, Shanghai, April 21, 1948; local press reports that CCP leader Lin Biao was murdered in Harbin on April 3.

Confidential Information Circular Airgram for Chief of Mission to Certain American Missions, May 4, 1948, U.S. Embassy, Tehran; reports USSR is buying entire opium production of Yugoslavia after failing to buy all the Iranian government opium stocks; USSR rumored to want the opium for political purposes in China.

Despatch no. 267 from Lewis Clark, Minister-Counselor, U.S. Embassy, Nanking, June 9, 1948, *Pronouncements by Prominent Leaders of the Chinese Communist Party Indicating a Change in Tactics.*

Office of Intelligence Research (OIR) Report no. 4729, August 20, 1948, *Biographic Data on Members of the Politburo and the Central Executive Committee of the Chinese Communist Party.*

Telegram no. 141 from U.S. Consulate General, Dalian, September 6, 1948; Chen Qiren says Kang Sheng goes over head of Mao and deals directly with Moscow.

Report from Culver Gleysteen, U.S. Vice Consul, Dalian, October 15, 1948, *Notes on the Chinese Communist Movement Based on Information Provided by a Disillusioned Party Member.*

Report no. 10 with October 15, 1948, report from Dalian, *Biographic Notes.*

Telegram from Paul Paddock, U.S. Consul, Dalian, October 27, 1948; Chen Qiren will delay departure from Dalian for ten days.

Telegram from Paul Paddock, U.S. Consul, Dalian, November 9, 1948; Chen Qiren's trip delayed again.

Telegram from Paul Paddock, U.S. Consul, Dalian, November 15, 1948; Chen Qiren unable to leave China; Chen has been told United States cannot help him unless he does leave China; "relations with subject thus seem ended."

Memorandum no. 3 from O. Edmund Clubb, U.S. Consul General, Peking, March 10, 1949, *Biographical Sketches of Nieh Jung-Chen and Lin Piao.*

Memorandum no. 38 from U.S. Consulate General, Shanghai, March 15, 1949, *Chart of Chinese Communists' Current Party, Political and Military Organization.*

OIR Report no. 4910 (PV), March 22, 1949, *New Light on Chinese Communism from a Disillusioned Party Member.*

Memorandum no. 58 from U.S. Consulate General, Shanghai, April 6, 1949, *Article Describing Chou En-lai's Present Standing in the Chinese Communist Party.*

Memorandum no. 62 from U.S. Consulate General, Shanghai, April 12, 1949, *Transmission of Article Entitled "A Roster of Chinese Communist Figures."*

Telegram no. 379 from Tianjin, June 3, 1949; Chinese Communists smuggling as much as one thousand pounds of opium at a time to the United States.

Telegram no. 996 from O. Edmund Clubb, U.S. Consul General, Peking, June 11, 1949; CCP leadership tilting away from USSR and toward the United States and Great Britain because USSR unable to supply all CCP economic needs.

Memorandum from U.S. Consulate General, Shanghai, July 1, 1949, *Transmission of Article Entitled "Liu Shao-chi, Heir Apparent to Mao Tsetung."*

From Culver Gleysteen, U.S. Vice Consul, Dalian, July 1, 1949, *Translation of "The Chinese Revolution and the Chinese Communist Party," by Mao Tse-tung.*

Report from Lewis Clark, U.S. Minister-Counselor, Canton, July 7, 1949, *Biographic Data on 21 Members of the Standing Committee of the Communist New Political Consultative Conference.*

Telegram no. 1168 from O. Edmund Clubb, U.S. Consul General, Peking, July 14, 1949; Mao rumored dead from stroke, but he has since appeared in public.

Telegram no. 2824 from Walter P. McConaughy, U.S. diplomat, Shanghai, July 18, 1949; widespread rumors in Shanghai that Mao died after stroke, and that Lin Piao was killed in battle.

OIR Report no. 5012 (PV), August 18, 1949, *The Long-Term Prospects of Chinese Communism.*

Telegram no. 1994 from Jones, U.S. diplomat, Nanking, September 3, 1949; CCP is "incomparably stronger than Bolsheviks at time they seized power," thanks in part to secret-police system.

Telegram no. 3790 from Shanghai, September 12, 1949; Communists, "motivated by urgent need [for] money," reviving opium production.

Memorandum from George F. Kennan to Dean Rusk, November 7, 1949, forwarding suggestions for "both overt and covert propaganda activities as they might be applied in China by this Government."

Despatch no. 314 from K. L. Rankin, U.S. Consul General, Hong Kong, November 11, 1949, *Communist Policy in One Village in Honan Province.*

OIR Report no. 5101, December 22, 1949, *The Status of Mao Tse-tung as Theoretician and Leader.*

From Mr. Merchant, State Department official, to Dean Acheson, Secretary of State, January 16, 1950; comments on January 16, 1950, letter from J. Edgar Hoover reporting approach to H. D. Long of Los Angeles by two unidentified CCP representatives suggesting that Long act as courier from President Truman to Mao Zedong, who is reportedly considering shift in allegiance from USSR to United States.

Telegram no. 315 from Walter P. McConaughy, U.S. diplomat, Shanghai, January 19, 1950; listing complete membership of CCP Central Committee.

Telegram no. 371 from Walter P. McConaughy, U.S. diplomat, Shanghai, January 23, 1950; Zhou Enlai considered most pro-Western of high CCP officials.

From James E. Webb, Undersecretary of State, to J. Edgar Hoover, January 24, 1950; expressing skepticism over credibility of H. D. Long's offer.

Telegram no. 430 from Walter P. McConaughy, U.S. diplomat, Shanghai, January 26, 1950; 30 percent of CCP leaders are actively pro-Moscow; 30 percent actively anti-Moscow; 40 percent unprepared to accept control from Moscow; Chinese public inherently hostile toward USSR.

Despatch no. 31 from Peking, February 11, 1950, *The Central Committee, Chinese Communist Party.*

Telegram no. 159 from Gross, U.S. diplomat, United Nations, New York, February 14, 1950; Mao steers course independent of USSR, would not hesitate to challenge any move by Stalin to exert control over China.

Telegram from Strong, U.S. diplomat, Taipei, February 23, 1950; recent defector from CCP secret police says Soviets exercise control in Red China primarily through visiting Tass reporters.

Telegram no. 820 from Walter P. McConaughy, U.S. diplomat, Shanghai, February 24, 1950; reports rumors that CCP leaders work long hours, mainly at night, and that many have TB or stomach ailments, including Mao, who has advanced case of TB and stomach ulcers.

Telegram no. 545 from Clubb, U.S. diplomat, Peking, March 18, 1950; Liu Shao-chi, as opposed to Mao, is "rabid[ly] pro-Soviet," may have been grooming himself to succeed Mao while Mao was in Moscow negotiating with Soviets.

Telegram no. 560 from Clubb, U.S. diplomat, Peking, March 21, 1950; Mao reportedly "extremely disconsolate" since recent return from Moscow.

Telegram no. 618 from Rankin, U.S. diplomat, Hong Kong, March 24, 1950; reliable Chinese source says Lin Biao and Chen Yi may attempt to overthrow Mao.

Despatch no. 429 from Alfred le S. Jenkins, U.S. Vice Consul, Hong Kong, May 11, 1950, *Organization of the Central Committee, Chinese Communist Party.*

External Research Staff, Department of State (Russian Research Center, Harvard University), series 3, no. 22, June 1, 1950, *The Communist Movement in China—A Chronology of Major Developments, 1918–1950.*

Letter to Livingston T. Merchant, Assistant Secretary for Far Eastern Affairs, from John B. Nason, Director, China Program, Economic Cooperation Administration (ECA), June 6, 1950; enclosing observations on Communist China by George St. Louis, former ECA Regional Director, Shanghai.

Despatch from Cloyce K. Huston, Counselor of Mission, Tokyo, June 16, 1950, *Organization of Chinese Communist Party Central Committee.*

Despatch from Alfred le S. Jenkins, U.S. Vice Consul, Hong Kong, June 21, 1950, *Chinese Communist Secret Service.*

Despatch from Alfred le S. Jenkins, U.S. Vice Consul, Hong Kong, July 3, 1950, *Organization of the Central Committee, Chinese Communist Party.*

Despatch from Donald R. Heath, U.S. diplomat, Saigon, July 13, 1950, *Chinese Newspaper Article Regarding Dissatisfaction of Chinese Communist Leaders with Ch'en Yi.*

From Dean Acheson, Secretary of State, to U.S. Consul, Hong Kong, July 14, 1950; requesting information about *New York Times* story that a disaffected Chinese Communist woman named Hsiao Ying has written a book entitled *I Was Mao Tse-tung's Secretary.*

Telegram no. 115 from Rankin, U.S. diplomat, Hong Kong, July 15, 1950; Mao has an "aversion [to] flying."

Airgram from Dean Acheson, Secretary of State, to U.S. Consulate, Hong Kong, August 4, 1950; providing background information on Zhang Guotao and list of questions to be asked during interrogation of Zhang.

OIR Report no. 5126, August 4, 1950, *Leaders of Communist China.*

Despatch from Charles N. Spinks, First Secretary of Mission, Tokyo, September 11, 1950, *Alleged Conference Between High Chinese [Mao and Kang Sheng] and Soviet Officials [Stalin].*

Despatch from Donald R. Heath, U.S. diplomat, Saigon, September 15, 1950, *French Intelligence Report of Molotov Meeting with Asiatic Communist Authorities.*

Despatch no. 671 from James R. Wilkinson, U.S. Consul General, Hong Kong, November 15, 1950, *Interview of Chang Kuo-t'ao by Mr. Robert C. North [of the Hoover Library, Stanford University].*

Despatch no. 704 from James R. Wilkinson, U.S. Consul General, Hong Kong, November 21, 1950, *Reported Program by Chinese Communists to Export Opium Through Hong Kong.*

Airgram from Dean Acheson, Secretary of State, to U.S. Consul, Hong Kong, January 27, 1951; requesting assessment of article in January 3, 1951, edition of *San Francisco Chinese World* stating that Chinese Communists support opium traffic.

Despatch no. 1057 from Walter P. McConaughy, U.S. Consul General, Hong Kong, January 31, 1951, *Statements by Chang Kuo-t'ao Concerning History of Chinese Communist Party.*

Despatch no. 1157 from Walter P. McConaughy, U.S. Consul General, Hong Kong, February 19, 1951, *Political Activities of Chang Kuo-t'ao.*

Airgram from Dean Acheson, Secretary of State, to U.S. Consul, Hong Kong, April 2, 1951; providing additional questions for further interrogation of Zhang Guotao.

Telegram no. 3031 from Walter P. McConaughy, U.S. Consul General, Hong Kong, April 16, 1951; Mao rumored to have died March 26, 1951, from "(1) too much drink and women, (2) Korean defeat and failure of Stalin to fulfill promises and (3) high blood pressure which had caused partial paralysis"; Stalin has forbidden release of the news, but it is leaking out anyway and "will soon be published."

Despatch no. 231 from Robert W. Rinden, Second Secretary, U.S. Embassy, Taipei, April 25, 1951, *[More than 2 million] Chinese Murdered in Chinese Communist Mass Purge.*

Despatch no. 1628 from Walter P. McConaughy, U.S. Consul General, Hong Kong, April 25, 1951, *Analysis of Situation Within Chinese Communist Government by Chu Kao-jung.*

Telegram no. 3234 from Walter P. McConaughy, U.S. Consul General, Hong Kong, May 1, 1951; April 27 letter from "reform committee of Chi Commie Party" reports that Mao died March 26, 1951, from "debility, coronary thrombosis and hypertension." Word of his death "has been kept strictly secret in fear of both internal and outside disturbances."

OIR Report no. 5528, May 4, 1951, *The Current Situation in Communist China.*

Despatch from Robert W. Rinden, Second Secretary, U.S. Embassy, Taipei, May 17, 1951, *Chinese Communist Mass Purge.*

Despatch from Walter P. McConaughy, U.S. Consul General, Hong Kong, July 6, 1951, *Members of the Central Committee, Chinese Communist Party, 1939.*

Memorandum from John Emmerson to Dean Rusk, July 10, 1951, *Hints of Dissension Within the Chinese Communist Party.*

Telegram no. 169 from Walter P. McConaughy, U.S. Consul General, Hong Kong, July 13, 1951; special branch of Hong Kong police has recently "shown increased interest in anti-Commie group here"; several people, including Zhang Guotao, were "subjected to polite but exhaustive interrogations."

Despatch no. 317 from Walter P. McConaughy, U.S. Consul General, Hong Kong, July 25, 1951, *Opinions of Chang Kuo-t'ao on Possible Development of a Young Communist Faction.*

Despatch no. 319 from Walter P. McConaughy, U.S. Consul General, Hong

Kong, August 20, 1951, *Chang Kuo-t'ao on the Organizational Structure of the Chinese Communist Party.*

Despatch no. 364 from Walter P. McConaughy, U.S. Consul General, Hong Kong, August 27, 1951, *The "Twenty-Eight Bolsheviks."*

Intelligence Report no. 5672, December 28, 1951, *Internal Conditions in Communist China.*

Intelligence Report no. 5681-S, January 11, 1952, *Communist China: Satellite or Junior Partner of the USSR?*

Despatch no. 1532 from Walter P. McConaughy, U.S. Consul General, Hong Kong, January 25, 1952, *K'ang Sheng.*

Intelligence Report no. 5777, February 5, 1952, *The Current Organization of the Chinese Communist Army.*

Despatch no. 1671 from Walter P. McConaughy, U.S. Consul General, Hong Kong, February 13, 1952, *Interview of Yugoslav Editor with Chang Kuo-t'ao in Hong Kong.*

Intelligence Report no. 5838, March 12, 1952, *The Campaign Against Corruption in Communist China.*

Despatch from H. L. T. Koren, Second Secretary, U.S. Legation, Bern, March 14, 1952, *Rumored Internal Dissensions in China.*

Intelligence Report no. 5987, August 13, 1952, *The Chinese Communist Police System.*

Despatch no. 496 from Julian F. Harrington, U.S. Consul General, Hong Kong, September 4, 1952, *Comments on the Central Organization of the Chinese Communist Party.*

Intelligence Report no. 6116, December 5, 1952, *Reorganization of the Chinese Communist Governmental Structure.*

Despatch no. 1166 from John M. Steeves, First Secretary, U.S. Embassy, Tokyo, December 18, 1952, *Communist [Chinese] Trade in Narcotics.*

Intelligence Report no. 6156, January 15, 1953, *The Hate America Campaign in Communist China.*

Telegram no. 1817 from Julian F. Harrington, U.S. Consul General, Hong Kong, January 17, 1953; list of CCP leadership.

Intelligence Report no. 6198, February 19, 1953, *Chinese Communist Methods of Extracting Confessions for Political Ends.*

Despatch no. 2183 from Julian F. Harrington, U.S. Consul General, Hong Kong, April 30, 1953, *P'eng Chen and the Politburo of the Chinese Communist Party.*

Despatch no. 2434 from Julian F. Harrington, U.S. Consul General, Hong Kong, May 28, 1953, *Comments on Leadership of the Communist Party in China, 1945–1953.*

Despatch no. 2765 from Douglas Dillon, U.S. Embassy, Paris, June 8, 1953, *Publication Alleged Views French Consul on Chinese Communist Government.*

Airgram from John Foster Dulles, Secretary of State, to U.S. Consul, Hong Kong, June 12, 1953; requesting that defector from Communist China's Foreign Ministry cited in Despatch no. 1446 of January 22, 1953, be questioned about CCP leaders, with focus on determining allegiances of individual military commanders to Mao or to Zhou or to other Party leaders.

Airgram from John Foster Dulles, Secretary of State, to U.S. Consul, Hong Kong, June 12, 1953; requesting that Zhang Guotao and other likely sources be questioned about the personal relationships of individual CCP leaders to Mao.

Intelligence Report no. 5714.3 (undated, mid-1953), *Analysis of Communist Propaganda in China.*

Despatch no. 45 from Julian F. Harrington, U.S. Consul General, Hong Kong, July 7, 1953, *Biographic Information on Kao Kang.*

Despatches from U.S. Consul General, Hong Kong, dated July 23, 1953, through April 9, 1954, *Biographic Information Furnished by Chang Kuo-t'ao on Leading Chinese Communist Figures,* parts 1–9, 11, 13–18. A seminal study of CCP leaders.

Despatch no. 300 from David H. McKillop, U.S. Consul, Hong Kong, August 5, 1953, *Biographic Information on Chinese Communist Officials in the Ministry of Foreign Affairs, Peiping.*

Despatch no. 343 from David H. McKillop, U.S. Consul, Hong Kong, August 10, 1953, *Biographic Information on Jao Shu-shih, Ch'en Yi and T'an Chen-lin.*

Despatch no. 588 from U.S. Consul General, Hong Kong, to Department of State, Washington, September 15, 1953, *Biographic Information Furnished by Chang Kuo-t'ao on Leading Communist Figures (Part 7).*

Memorandum from John Foster Dulles, Secretary of State, to U.S. Consulate, Hong Kong, October 1, 1953; commending Ralph N. Clough and Howard Boorman for work on Hong Kong's Despatch no. 45, July 7, 1953, *Biographic Information on Kao Kang.*

Despatch no. 1338 from Robert W. Zimmerman, Second Secretary, U.S. Embassy, London, October 7, 1953, *Transmittal of British List of Important Chinese Communist Office Holders.*

Despatch no. 687 from Samuel D. Berger, Counselor, U.S. Embassy, Tokyo, October 21, 1953, *Article on Chinese Communist Leaders by Japanese Authority on Chinese Communist Movement.*

Despatch no. 250 from K. L. Rankin, U.S. Embassy, Taipei, November 2, 1953, *Biographic Information on Chinese Communist Leaders Furnished by Jen Che-hsuan.*

Despatch no. 941 from Julian F. Harrington, U.S. Consul General, Hong Kong, November 16, 1953, *Biographic Information on Kung Ch'u.*

Despatch no. 1274 from Julian F. Harrington, U.S. Consul General, Hong

Kong, January 18, 1954, *Comments by Chang Kuo-t'ao on Mao Tse-tung and Decision-Making in the Chinese Communist Party.*

Despatch no. 1335 from Julian F. Harrington, U.S. Consul General, Hong Kong, January 26, 1954, *Comments on the Preparation of a Reference Book on Communist China.*

Telegram no. 3686 from Aldrich, U.S. Embassy, London, February 26, 1954; British diplomats in Peking expect shake-up in top ranks of CCP and report that Mao has not appeared at any function in two months, perhaps ill or ordered to rest.

Despatch no. 1567 from U.S. Consul General, Hong Kong, March 2, 1954, *Central and Regional Leadership of the Chinese Communist Party: February 1954.*

Despatch no. 1891 from Julian F. Harrington, U.S. Consul General, Hong Kong, April 15, 1954, *Chang Kuo-t'ao's Comments on Recent Developments in the Chinese Communist Party.*

Despatch no. 704 from John M. Steeves, Counselor, U.S. Embassy, Djakarta, May 17, 1954, *Biographies of the Chinese Delegation at Geneva.*

Telegram no. 1751 from Butterworth, U.S. Embassy, London, October 6, 1954; Mao reportedly "present but said nothing . . . looked older and not very healthy" at September 30, 1954, affair in Peking.

Despatch no. 693 from T. Eliot Weil, Counselor for Political Affairs, U.S. Embassy, New Delhi, December 31, 1954, *Articles on Communist China by Prem Bhatia of "The Statesman."*

Intelligence Report no. 6870.1, August 1955, *Chinese Communist World Outlook: Views on Relations with the Soviet Union and the Soviet Bloc.*

Intelligence Report no. 7416, January 15, 1956, *Eighth Party Congress of the Chinese Communist Party—Its Implications for Party Leadership and Organization.*

Despatch no. 1215 from Everett F. Drumright, U.S. Consul General, Hong Kong, March 6, 1956, *Chinese Communist Security Work.*

Intelligence Report no. 7208, March 22, 1956, *Nuclear Research and Atomic Energy Developments in Communist China.*

Despatch no. 607 from William O. Anderson, U.S. Consul, Singapore, June 29, 1956, *Development in Communist China: Transmittal of a Memorandum Summarizing Remarks of a Recent Resident of Canton.*

Intelligence Report no. 6870.2, September 1956, *Chinese Communist World Outlook: Views Regarding the United States.*

Despatch no. 339 from Everett F. Drumright, U.S. Consul General, Hong Kong, October 23, 1956, *Chang Kuo-t'ao's Comments on CCP Congress.*

Intelligence Report no. 7290, November 5, 1956, *The Chinese Communists Reevaluate the Intellectuals.*

Despatch no. 452 from Everett F. Drumright, U.S. Consul General, Hong

Kong, December 5, 1956, *8th General Committee of the Communist Party of China.*

Despatch no. 454 from Everett F. Drumright, U.S. Consul General, Hong Kong, December 5, 1956, *Publication of New History of Chinese Communist Party.*

Despatch no. 474 from Everett F. Drumright, U.S. Consul General, Hong Kong, December 11, 1956, *Chinese Communist Party Membership— Official Totals with Breakdown by Class and Occupational Groupings.*

Despatch no. 795 from Everett F. Drumright, U.S. Consul General, Hong Kong, March 20, 1957, *The New Central Organizations of the Communist Party of China.*

Despatch no. 1003 from Thomas P. Dillon, U.S. Consul, Hong Kong, May 28, 1957, *Peiping Personalities.*

Intelligence Report no. 7532, July 1, 1957, *Mao Tse-Tung's "Secret" Speech.*

Memorandum from Walter S. Robertson, U.S. diplomat, Washington, July 22, 1957, *Chinese Communists Publish Figures on 1955–1956 Purge.*

Despatch no. 953 from Harald W. Jacobson, U.S. Consul, Hong Kong, May 22, 1958, *Chinese Communist Party Conferences.*

Despatch no. 1007 from Harald W. Jacobson, U.S. Consul, Hong Kong, June 18, 1958, *Photograph of CCP Leaders at Closing of CCP Congress.*

Intelligence Report no. 8307, August 3, 1960, *Sino–Soviet Dispute Reaches Peak: Partial Accommodation Reached.*

Bureau of Intelligence and Research, External Research Staff, John Wilson Lewis, Department of Government, Cornell University, January 1964, *Chinese Communist Party Leadership and the Succession to Mao Tse-Tung: An Appraisal of Tensions.*

DEPARTMENT OF WAR

Army Air Forces Report (undated), *Major Accident, Involving a C-47B Aircraft That Flew into the Side of Hei Cha Mountain in Shansi, 290 Miles West South West of Peiping, on April 8, 1946.*

U.S. INFORMATION AGENCY

USIA CA-995, October 18, 1956, *Chinese Communist Leadership.*

U.S. JOINT PUBLICATIONS RESEARCH SERVICE

JPRS no. 1449-N, *I Was Chairman Mao's Cook.* April 6, 1959.

JPRS no. 4005, *Several Stories on Mao Tse-tung When He Was Young.* August 18, 1960.

JPRS no. 8375, *The Ideological Conflict Between Moscow and Peking,* by Boris Meissner. June 2, 1961.

JPRS no. 23578, *New Book Condemning Chinese Communist Leaders Published by Pravda.* March 9, 1964.

JPRS no. 41735, *USSR's Literary Gazette Reviews Mao's "Cultural Revolution."* July 7, 1967.

JPRS no. 48239, *China and Its Cultural Revolution—A Soviet Analysis.* June 16, 1969.

U.S. MILITARY INTELLIGENCE

File no. 108-300 from Shanghai (Navy), February 25, 1929, *Communist Activities in China and Other Countries.*

Special Intelligence Report no. 3 from Shanghai (Marine Corps Expeditionary Forces), June 26, 1933, *Survey of Communism in China.*

Report no. 9010 from China, February 7, 1935, *Secret Societies.*

File no. 935 from Peking (Navy), September 20, 1935, *Blue Shirt Society.*

Report no. 9283 from Colonel Joseph W. Stilwell, Military Attaché, China, January 29, 1936, *Present Trends of the Chinese Communist Party.*

Report from Military Attaché, China, April 27, 1936, *The Narcotic Situation [in China].*

Report no. 9490 from Colonel Joseph W. Stilwell, Military Attaché, China, November 30, 1936, *Recent Developments in the Communist Situation in China.*

Report no. 9504 from Colonel Joseph W. Stilwell, Military Attaché, China, January 14, 1937, *Chinese Communist Organization.*

Report no. 59222 from Colonel M. B. DePass, Jr., China–Burma–India Theater, October 28, 1943, *Biographies of Chinese Military Personnel.*

Report no. C-2833 from Chongqing (Army), February 14, 1944, *CHINA—Internal Political Situation.*

Memorandum, March 4, 1944, *Cliques Within the Chinese Communist Party.*

Report no. 1295 from Military Attaché, China, March 28, 1944, *Political Situation in China.*

Report no. C-3125 from Chongqing (Army), April 22, 1944, *China—Political—Political Activities of Chinese Communists.*

Report no. 104-200 from Chongqing (Navy), June 26, 1944, *Biographies of Important Communists.*

Report no. 1677 from China (Women's Air Corps), July 27, 1944, *Chinese Communism: Its Real Nature.*

Report no. 5704 from Chongqing (Army), August 8, 1944, *Narcotics.*

Report no. 5798 from Colonel David D. Barrett, Chongqing, August 14, 1944, *Communist Intelligence in North China.*

Report no. 10,128 from Chongqing (Air Force), September 30, 1944, *Morale in Communist Areas of Shensi.*

Report no. 1155 from China (Army), October 31, 1944, *Who's Who (Chinese Communists)*.

Report no. R 47-45 from China, January 20, 1945, *Secret Organizations in China*.

Report no. YH/CK 134/45 from China, May 30, 1945, *Chinese Secret Societies*.

The Chinese Communist Movement, vols. I, II, July 1945.

Report no. R 292-45 from China, July 10, 1945, *Who's Who (Chinese Communists)*.

Report from Lieutenant Colonel John J. McDonough, Ceylon, to Lieutenant Colonel Edward W. Harding, July 20, 1945, *Chinese Secret Intelligence and Special Service Operations*.

Report no. R 319-45 from China, August 7, 1945, *Chinese Communist Party During Past Ten Years*.

Report no. R 445-45 from China (Army), November 26, 1945, *Chinese Communist–Soviet Agreement on Exchange of Intelligence*.

Report from China (Navy), November 29, 1945, *Transportation Assistance Afforded Chinese Communists by United States Information Service*.

Report no. R 53-46 from China, January 31, 1946, *Who's Who (Chinese Communists)*.

Report no. 35-S-46 from New Delhi (Navy), November 6, 1946, *General Tai Li—Death Of*.

Report no. 1-S-47 from Nanking (Navy), January 7, 1947, *CHINA: Bureau of Investigation and Statistics*.

Report no. R-182-47 from Nanking (Army), April 10, 1947, *Yenan Under National Government Occupation*.

Report from General Headquarters, Far East Command, November 5, 1947, *Factional History of the Chinese Communist Party*.

Intelligence Report no. SR/65 from Hong Kong, May 10, 1951, *Mao Tse-Tung's Decision on the Offensive and Reinforcement on the Korean Front and Other Policies After His Return Home from Moscow*.

Interrogation Report of Dr. Torii, Ryuzo, archeologist, returnee from Peking, December 1951, *Chinese Personalities*.

Report from Headquarters, 500th Military Intelligence Service Group, March 12, 1954, *Most Likely to Succeed Mao*.

OFFICE OF STRATEGIC SERVICES

Report no. 9291, from J. Edgar Hoover, Director, FBI, to Colonel William J. Donovan, Coordinator of Information, January 10, 1942; transmitting copy of political report from Swedish Minister in Shanghai.

Memorandum from Pearl S. Buck to Colonel William J. Donovan, January 19, 1942; urging that President Roosevelt state clearly that "we are fully aware of the importance of the Axis war in the Orient and that there is no danger of our giving it secondary attention."

Report no. 32977, from John Davies, Jr., Second Secretary, U.S. Embassy, Chongqing, to General Joseph W. Stilwell, March 16, 1943, *Conversation with Chou En-lai*.

Report no. 41797, from Everett F. Drumright, Second Secretary, U.S. Embassy, Chongqing; memorandum of May 25, 1943, interview with General Zhang Chun, chairman of the Sichuan Provincial Government, re Chinese Communists' cultivation of opium.

R&A no. 1985, March 18, 1944, *List of Selected Materials on the Chinese Communists*.

Report no. 68638, April 22, 1944, *The City of Shanghai*.

Report no. 97143, from "An official of the Chinese Ministry of Information," Chongqing, August 28, 1944, *Interview with Mao Tze-tung*.

Report no. 94582, from "Well informed, reliable observer," Kunming, September 4, 1944, *Military and Political Trends in China*.

Report no. 95913, from "Chinese source," October 2, 1944, *Interview with Chu Teh*.

Report no. XL 2185, October 23, 1944, *Capabilities and Intentions of the Chinese Communists*.

Report from Guiyang, November 20, 1944, *Communists' Impression of OSS*.

R&A no. 2779S, December 22, 1944, *Leadership and Program of the Chinese Communists*.

R&A no. 2793, December 22, 1944, *Routes to Yenan, Shensi, China*.

Field Memorandum no. 116, January 8, 1945, *Notes on the Chinese Communists*.

Report no. XL 5198, January 8, 1945 (summary card only, not entire document), *The City of Yenan*.

Report from Headquarters, China, January 13, 1945, *Special Mission Notes*.

Report no. XL 7138, February 5, 1945, *Sidelights on Chungking Personalities*.

Report no. YKX-YSX-65 from Kunming, April 5, 1945, *Information Concerning Ma Hai-te, American at Yenan*.

Report no. A-53836, April 10, 1945, *Conditions in Communist China*.

R&A no. 3154, June 30, 1945, *Implications of Recent Policy Statements of the Chinese Communists*.

R&A no. 2254, July 1, 1945, *Political Implications of Chinese Secret Societies*.

R&A no. 3311S, July 27, 1945, *Chinese Communist Preparations for Civil Crisis in China*.

Report no. 143465, from "Chinese Major," September 4, 1945; loyalist troops in Shaanxi Province captured Mao's brother in the mountains, but he escaped.

STRATEGIC SERVICES UNIT, WAR DEPARTMENT

Report no. A-61639 from "Team Jackal," Kunming, September 17, 1945, *Communist Organization Including Names of Leaders.*

Report no. XL 22188 from Xian Field Team, October 5, 1945, *Communist Area of 8th Route Army.*

Report no. XL 27544 from Dr. Ina Telberg to Lieutenant Colonel Herbert S. Little, October 31, 1945, *Interim Report on Subversive Propaganda Pressures in China.*

Report no. A-64198 from "Chinese Military," November 24, 1945, *Shanghai: Communist Political Organizations.*

Report no. XL 42981 from Major Kijima, Japanese Liaison Office, December 17, 1945, *Chinese Communist Political Activities.*

Report no. XL 34583 from Shanghai, December 29, 1945, *Communist Political, Military and Party Structure.*

X-2 Branch, March 1946, *Summary Report on Chinese Intelligence Services.*

Report no. A-65869 from Shanghai, March 2, 1946; Dai Li would install Marshal Zhang Xueliang in power if anything happened to Chiang Kai-shek.

Document Translation no. 229 from Shanghai, March 4, 1946, *Names of Important Chinese Communist Leaders.*

Report no. XL 46938 from Shanghai, March 13, 1946, *Interview with Former Members of 8th Route Army.*

Report no. XL 46942 from Shanghai, March 13, 1946, *Shanghai—Reorganization in Soviet Consulate.*

Report no. A-66121 from Shanghai, March 13, 1946; Dai Li to visit Qingdao, ostensibly to arrange housing for the U.S. Seventh Fleet but actually to attempt to obtain control of the Chinese navy.

Report no. A-66737 from Shanghai, March 29, 1946; one source reports that Dai Li's body, mangled beyond recognition, was identified by his teeth, his personal seal, and his pistol; a Chinese air force officer asserts, "The released story of the plane accident which resulted in the death of General Tai Li is untrue. The plane was attacked and downed by three Chinese Communist planes."

Report no. A-66884, April 1, 1946; it is rumored that Zheng Jiemin, Nationalist Commissioner, will succeed Dai Li.

Report no. A-68381 from Shanghai, April 22, 1946, *A "Who's Who" of Chinese Communist Personalities.*

Report no. YKB-3111 from Shanghai, May 2, 1946, *Glossary of Communist Terms and Briefs of Leading Communists.*

U.S. CONGRESSIONAL PROCEEDINGS

U.S. Congress, Senate, Committee on the Judiciary, Hearings Before the Subcommittee to Investigate the Administration of the Internal Security Act and Other Internal Security Laws, *Testimony of a Defector from Communist China*, 87th Cong., 2d sess., November 29, 1962.

MISCELLANEOUS RECORDS

Memorandum to Dr. James T. Shotwell, Director of the Program of Research in International Relations of the Social Science Research Council, from Grover Clark (New York, June 1, 1932), *Research Needs and Opportunities in China*; includes chapter on "Secret Societies and Other Political Organizations."

Center for International Studies, Massachusetts Institute of Technology, August 1954, W. W. Rostow, in collaboration with Richard W. Hatch, Frank A. Kierman, Jr., and Alexander Eckstein, *The Prospects for Chinese Communist Society*.

CCP Research Newsletter no. 3 (summer 1989), *The Shanghai Municipal Police Files (Special Branch)*, by A. Tom Grunfeld, SUNY/Empire State College.

PHOTO CREDITS

INDEX

A

A-B Group (Anti-Bolshevik Group), 144
Ah Ying (Qian Xingcun), 367
Ai Hengwu, 276–77, 280
Ai Siqi, 276
air crashes, 22, 392
Albania, 256, 384
An Ziwen, 323, 345, 346, 416
ancestor worship, 35, 36
Angleton, James J., 22
Animal Farm (Orwell), 424
Anti-Bolshevik Group (A-B Group), 144
Anti-Revisionist Philosophy Writing Group, 275, 277, 278, 279
April 12 Massacre, 51, 67–69, 70, 91, 93, 98, 115, 116
archives, Kang's search of, 336–37
Army Illustrated, 390
Artillery Faction, 355
artists, persecution of, 22, 87
Assassination Corps, *see* Red Squads
atomic bomb, 205n

B

Ba Jin, 54
Bai Chongxi, 68, 350
Bai Jian, 273
Balluku, Beqir, 384
Bamboo Garden Hotel, 220n
Bao Junfu, 97–98, 102
Baowei Chu (Guard Unit), 156
Barrett, David D., 135n, 138n, 147n, 184–85
Beria, Lavrenti P., 17, 112n, 253

big-character posters, 300, 301, 302–4, 306, 394–95, 420
    anti-Kang, 315, 380–81
    Mao's writing of, 307, 343
"black gangs," 309
Black Shirts, 105
Blood on Wolf Mountain, 146
Blue Shirts Society (Blue Gowns; Special Agent Section of the Rejuvenation Society), 105–6, 110, 155, 161, 165, 180n, 406
Blyukher, Vasili (Galen), 57
Bo Gu (Qin Bangxian), 59, 79n, 82n, 85, 90, 119n, 120, 121, 141, 147
Bo Yibo, 345
"Bombard the Party Headquarters—My Big-Character Poster," 307, 343, 402
Boorman, Howard, 205n–6n
Borgia family, 360
Borodin, Mikhail, 66, 95, 128, 178, 242, 322
bound feet, 41
bourgeois mentality, 173, 309
Boxers (Society of Righteous Harmony), 29, 34, 35, 40, 321–22
Braun, Otto (Li De), 105, 119n, 120, 250
British, 59
    protests against, 51, 58, 74
Brocade Gown Guard, 338
brothels, 71
Brown Shirts, 105
Broz, Josip, *see* Tito
Buddhism, 409
Bukharin, Nikolai, 124
Burlatsky, Fyodor M., 254
Burma, 330

Q

R